HEROIC EPIC

AND

SAGA

HEROIC EPIC

AND

SAGA

*An Introduction to the
World's Great Folk Epics*

EDITED BY FELIX J. OINAS

Indiana University Press / *Bloomington & London*

This book was brought to publication with the assistance of a grant from the Andrew W. Mellon Foundation.

Manufactured in the United States of America

Library of Congress Cataloging in Publication Data
Main entry under title:
Heroic epic and saga.
    Includes bibliographies and index.
    1. Epic literature—History and criticism.
2.   Folk literature—History and criticism.   I.   Oinas,
Felix J.
PN56.E65H4   809.1'3   77-9637
ISBN 0-253-32738-5 1 2 3 4 5 82 81 80 79 78

CONTENTS

Preface   vii

Introduction / *Richard M. Dorson*   1

1. The Homeric Epics and Oral Poetry / *Wm. F. Hansen*   7
2. Mesopotamian Epic Literature / *Johannes M. Renger*   27
3. The Sanskrit Epics / *Barend A. van Nooten*   49
4. The Iranian Epics / *William L. Hanaway, Jr.*   76
5. *Beowulf:* A Contextual Introduction to Its Contents and Techniques / *Alain Renoir*   99
6. The *Nibelungenlied* as Heroic Epic / *Stephen L. Wailes*   120
7. The Icelandic Sagas / *Theodore M. Andersson*   144
8. Irish Saga Literature / *Seán Ó Coileáin*   172
9. The French Chansons de Geste / *Gerard J. Brault*   193
10. The Spanish Epic / *Merle E. Simmons*   216
11. Russian Byliny / *Felix J. Oinas*   236
12. Serbocroatian Heroic Songs / *Mary P. Coote*   257
13. The Balto-Finnic Epics / *Felix J. Oinas*   286
14. The Epic Tradition among Turkic Peoples / *Ilhan Başgöz*   310
15. The African Heroic Epic / *Daniel P. Biebuyck*   336

Index   369

Preface

This collection grew out of a series of lectures given within the framework of a course at Indiana University in 1972 and 1975. Several of us (Professors Ilhan Başgöz, William F. Hansen, W. Edson Richmond, Merle E. Simmons, Stephen L. Wailes, and myself), who had done research in heroic epics, pooled our efforts for a survey of epics around the world. The lecturers wrote up their lectures, expanded them, and included footnotes and bibliography for further study. The collection thus obtained was supplemented with surveys of other significant epics by experts outside the University: Professors Theodore M. Andersson of Stanford University; Daniel P. Biebuyck of the University of Delaware; Gerard J. Brault of Pennsylvania State University; Seán Ó Coileáin of the University College Cork (Ireland); Mary P. Coote of the University of California, Berkeley; William L. Hanaway, Jr., of the University of Pennsylvania; Johannes M. Renger of Freie Universität, Berlin (Germany); Alain Renoir of the University of California, Berkeley; and Barend A. van Nooten of the University of California, Berkeley.

Procuring and editing the surveys from individual contributors and obtaining opinions from outside readers have taken several years. Now in sending the manuscript to press, I would like to express my sincere thanks to Dr. Richard M. Dorson, Director and Distinguished Professor of Indiana University's Folklore Institute, whose encouragement, advice, and help have been paramount in the completion of this project; to Professor William F. Hansen, my next-door neighbor at Indiana University, who was ever ready to help evaluate the manuscripts and suggest improvements; to Professor Sidney Johnson, who during Professor Wailes's sabbatical leave abroad helped with editing his survey; to Professor Joseph J. Duggan of the University of California, Berkeley, for his help in planning this volume; to H. Michael Simmons, Greta E. Swenson, and Maria M. Carlson, our efficient editorial assistants (Miss Swenson also served as the manuscript editor); to the numerous scholars whose surveys of individual epic traditions have made this volume possible; and, finally, to the outside readers whose suggestions helped shape the surveys into a unified work.

Bloomington, Indiana   Felix J. Oinas
March 1977

HEROIC EPIC
AND
SAGA

Introduction

Richard M. Dorson

Heroic epics and sagas have enthralled two entirely separate audiences, one of listeners at the time of their oral performance and, much later, one of readers in modern European languages. The appeal in the first instance is tribalistic, or nationalistic, as the listeners identify with a hero of their blood, cast in their mold, and in the second is universalistic, as Western readers respond to the adventures of a champion. So the heroic epic and saga have passed from spoken, sung, and recited renditions into the pages of literature, and in so doing have created a tangle of problems for oral-literary scholars.

Some of these problems are suggested in the following fifteen essays written by authorities familiar with a particular epic or saga tradition. The field of epic studies has expanded to the point where no one student can speak with assurance of its status. In his highly regarded appraisal of *Heroic Poetry*, published in 1961, C. M. Bowra denied that African tribes possessed "songs of heroic action," and Ruth Finnegan in 1970 similarly denied the existence of African epic poetry in her impressive overview of *Oral Literature in Africa*. But we can see in Daniel Biebuyck's chapter on "The African Heroic Epic" in the present volume the vitality and variety of oral epic presentations in Africa. There was a time, as older handbooks show, when the folk epic signified fixed texts of the *Iliad* and the *Odyssey, Beowulf,* the *Niebelungen-lied,* the *Chanson de Roland,* the *Cid,* and the *Rāmāyana* and *Mahābhārata*—the great canon of Indo-European epic poems. While literary scholars recognized the distinction between these folk epics and the literary epics composed by the individual poet, such as Virgil's *Aeneid,* Dante's *Inferno,* and Milton's *Paradise Lost,* to all intents and purposes they treated them in the same manner: as written masterpieces to be read.

Two feats of scholarship revolutionized epic studies. Hector and Nora Chadwick in *The Growth of Literature* (1924–26) looked at the heroic epic as a cultural rather than a literary phenomenon. Epic poems grew out of appropriate cultural conditions, the so-called Heroic Age bridging nomadic and sedentary stages of civilization, a preliterate era when bards celebrated the

1

deeds of great warriors. In their broad net the Chadwicks captured a host of epic cycles around the world. The next step was taken by Milman Parry and his student Albert Lord, who in *The Singer of Tales* (1960) recorded the living epics of South Slavic bards and applied the theory of oral-formulaic composition to the Homeric epics. Captivated by the theory, a generation of oral-literature scholars tested the theory on romances, ballads, blues, sermons, and some ventured from the library stacks into the field. Yet the old notion of the fixed poetic text is not easily dislodged. At a conference on "Oral Literature and the Formula" held at the University of Michigan in November 1974, a Japanese classicist, who had translated Herodotus into Japanese, told me that he had gone to Hokkaido to record the Ainu epic, but kept obtaining different versions, varying in length and differing in content from village to village. He feared that somehow his field techniques were faulty. Why did not a fluent, consistent, Homeric-like epic fall into his tape recorder? By the end of the meeting he had ceased to question his field methods. At this conference one heard an Anglo-Saxon specialist recite *Beowulf* in the imagined style of the original bard, and another play tapes of the Xhosa oral poems he had recorded and to which he would thenceforth devote his career.

A major problem in the new field of oral literature studies concerns the relation of the oral performance to the written text, and those writers in this volume dealing with older epics and sagas all address this problem. The question is not so much whether or not oral poets once sang epic lays or oral narrators recited heroic saga, but how closely the oral basis lies behind the received text. Because the *Kalevala* was stitched together only in the past century, Felix Oinas can describe with certainty the process whereby Finland's national poet Elias Lönnrot created an epic cycle from a mass of scattered folk verses. In the case of the Sanskrit epics, Barend van Nooten notes that their existence for a thousand years in manuscript and printed versions has not produced a unified text, but an expansive one ingorging local folktales and saints legends. For Irish saga, Seán Ó Coileáin declares that no student would question the relevance of an oral tradition, still extant, although critics disagree as to the exact relationship between spoken legends and manuscript texts. Scholars of the Icelandic sagas have debated the issue of literary or bookprose versus oral or freeprose origins into the ground, so that Theodore Andersson in his summation settles for a compromise position, that the saga transmitters were men "making the transition from oral narrative to literary composition." Andersson recognizes that the issue of orality is crucial to determining the direction of further research, whether into the milieux of authors or into the sources of oral traditions. In the context of *Beowulf,* Alain Renoir agrees that the oral and the written modes produce quite different results, even though both may make use of oral-formulaic features. The scribe-composer may rely on formulaic phrases, as well as the performing bard, but unlike the scribe, the bard cannot revise his text while facing his audience. Writing on the Spanish epic, Merle Simmons sides with the traditionalist theory that assigns a gestation period of several centuries to oral traditions, culminating in the *Song of My Cid* as it is known today. Thanks to the influence of the Parry–Lord theory, Homeric scholarship has reached the point where William Hansen can say confidently that Homer belonged to a class of ancient Greek oral poets, although nothing is known about the origins of their art.

For the South Slavic epics Mary Coote reports the coexistence and interaction of oral and literate forms since the ninth and tenth centuries, when Christianity brought literacy to the South Slavs. The literary viewpoint injected a respect for fixed facts and words into the oral epics, in a reversal of the usual sequence. Then in the mid-eighteenth century the monk Andrija Kačić-Miošić wrote a poetic history of the South Slavs that descended into peasant folk tradition, inspired the collecting of folksongs, and stimulated the notion that heroic poetry transmits the people's history.

The medieval French *chansons de geste,* of which the most famous is the *Song of Roland,* were originally sung by *jongleurs* and then written down by clerks. In the case of the *Song of Roland* the events reported dealt with a campaign of Charlemagne's army in the eighth century, but did not reach manuscript form until the eleventh century. Scholars debate the relative contributions of the jongleurs and the clerks, and the extent to which they depended on oral and literary traditions. According to Gerald Brault, Turoldus, composer of the *Song of Roland,* fused the oral-formulaic poetry of the jongleurs and the literary techniques of the scribes. The Iranian epic *Shāhnāma* (Book of Kings) was arranged in its present form by Ferdowsi in the tenth century but drew from an earlier chronicle of the seventh century which included a number of oral heroic legends. William Hanaway tells us that Ferdowsi himself presumably used in addition books in Middle Iranian prose and verse and oral stories to which he had direct access. Ferdowsi often writes, "I heard this story from an old *dehgān.*" Covering the whole history of the Iranians from the creation of the world to their defeat by the Arabs in the seventh century A.D., the epic soars to epical grandeur in the earlier legendary periods that rely on oral accounts and falls to a prosaic level in the well-documented later period.

Meanwhile, other contributors can describe the techniques and repertoires of oral bards performing epics today. Ilhan Başgöz and Felix Oinas indicate that the day of the great bards has passed its apogee in Turkey and Russia, but Daniel Biebuyck reports that these singers still flourish in nations of Africa. We are thus able in this volume to obtain a panoramic view of epic traditions in every stage of their evolutionary development, from the finished literary fruition to the dynamic oral and histrionic staging.

To the folklorist, who deals in oral genres, the traditional epic offers much nutriment. He notices its interrelationship with other folklore forms: the heroic ballad, the medieval romance, the heroic legend, the rune, the folk drama, even the Märchen and riddle, as we see in the Mesopotamian epic in the tasks set in riddle form. He ponders the question of what constitutes the form of the epic itself. Bowra and Finnegan associate the epic with heroic poetry, but there is no good reason to exclude the prose of heroic saga from our conception of the folk epic, if we identify epic as a stirring traditional narrative of perilous adventure, daring, and manhood honoring the heroes of a people. The narrative may be sung, chanted, recited, acted out, danced, or presented in a combination of these ways. One of the questions now tantalizing oral literature scholars is the degree of improvisation employed by the performing bard. In his studies of Xhosa performers Jeff Opland has distinguished four ranges: the spontaneous poet who composes impromptu; the memorizer who commits to heart a traditional tribal poem; the improviser, who develops anew his composition at each rendering but relies on stock passages and epithets; and the literate poet who writes out his muse. Opland relates an incident in which an improvising bard effectively delivered a poem honoring his host, but a rival poet from another village attempted to contribute an *ad hoc* salutation and broke down completely, because he was a memorizer and could not compose. Within the following pages Seán Ó Coileáin challenges the founder of the Irish Folklore Commission, Séamus Ó Duilearga, who perceived the ideal storyteller as a kind of tape-recorder reproducing precisely the tale as it came to his ears, a concept that permitted no creative latitude for the bard. Rather, Ó Coileáin would side with the view of the oral process described for the Spanish epic in Simmons' chapter, in which the singer reshapes his text according to his own esthetic while remaining within the boundaries of folk norms. To what extent such reshaping, or improvisation, follows the reliance on formula and theme of the Yugoslav epic poets, as uncovered by Parry and Lord, remains an open question in each culture where folk epics have arisen.

Other questions besides oral theory engage the attention of epic enthusiasts. What kind of hero does a heroic epic portray? Bowra considered him to embody essentially human qualities, as distinct from the shamanistic hero who relied on magic rather than strength and bravery to register his triumphs. But we may query the meaningfulness of this distinction when we see heroes like Gilgamesh, Achilles, and Arjuna aided by gods and goddesses against their enemies. Rostam (Rustam) in *Shāhnāma* is the true epic hero superior in strength and daring to other men but not master of natural forces, as are the later heroes of Iranian romance, who wed magical princesses and slay not one lion but ten. Roland is the chivalric hero of the Christian era combining the superior physical qualities of the pagan epic heroes with the wisdom and valor of the knight and the humility and pure-mindedness of the believer. In his essay on the medieval chansons de geste, Brault compares the hero's suffering and death to the life of Christ and sees the hero as martyr rather than champion. The character of the epic hero may thus be altered by the bards and scribes of a later age, but in its earlier depiction the epic and saga hero is marked above all by physical might. *Óláfs saga* portrays its hero as "quicker and more skillful than any other man and bolder and more valiant in battle and even if one should search over the whole earth, no such man would be found in all the north to equal his prowess and courage.'' This is the classic mold, and yet there is another aspect, for the hero may employ guile as well as force. If Achilles is valorous, Odysseus is crafty. Gilgamesh is both; he lures the wild man of the steppe to town through the entrapment of a harlot, and then outwrestles him. Marko too tricks and deceives his enemies. In terms of status, Gilgamesh is a king, Marko is a prince, and others, like Beowulf, Roland, and the Vikings of Icelandic legend-sagas serve the king or lord. None of the heroes are commoners. Some are adventuresome, all are martial. There are no philosopher-heroes in epic and saga.

What are the underlying story patterns of heroic epics? To what extent are they historical or fictional? The Chadwicks and other critics, such as Lord Raglan, Otto Rank, and Joseph Campbell, have developed separate outlines of the hero's legendary biography extracted from the world's epics, agreeing on certain points, such as the hero's valor, conquests, and travels, but in basic disagreement on others, for example the Chadwicks' assertion and Raglan's denial of the historicity of the hero. Evidence of common epic-heroic features embodying folklore does appear in these essays, as, to take one instance, the precocious strength of the hero. Thus Manas, in the Turkish epic of the Kirghiz, is born with an erection and a clot of blood in his hand, thanks to his mother's having eaten a tiger's heart when she was pregnant; at the age of nine he attacks and defeats the Kalmuks. The hero Mubila of the Balega in Zaïre speaks from the womb, and is born holding a spear and other weapons, including a shoulderbag which conceals all his followers. One section of the Irish saga known as the ''Cattle Raid of Cooley'' deals with the boyhood deeds of the hero Cú Chulainn, who killed the hound of Culann, smith to the king of Ulster, and had to fill the services performed by the hound until its young grew up. Rostam in the Iranian epic slew an elephant as a youth. Another folkloric element lies in the demonic creatures overcome by the heroes. Typically they slay monsters and dragons. Beowulf's grapple with Grendel most familiarly typifies the encounter between the youthful savior-champion of his people and the loathsome creature of darkness terrorizing the land. But the heroes also face armies of their fellowmen on the plane of historical reality. The contributors to the present volume tend to agree that legitimate history merges with folklore, mythology, supernaturalism, and romance. Beowulf, Grendel, and the dragon belong to folklore, but Heremod and Hrothgar belong to history, in the epic of *Beowulf.* My own view on the question of historicity inclines toward a middle ground: the hero of history attracts splendid legends into his vita, and the hero of fiction assumes a realistic and historical dimension, so that they tend to converge over the course of the epic and saga process.

The reader of these informative and stimulating essays, adroitly assembled by Felix Oinas, will be able to pursue for himself these and other questions.

1   The Homeric Epics and Oral Poetry

Wm. F. Hansen

Legend and History

Men became so numerous that Earth was oppressed by their weight, and Zeus resolved to lighten her burden by bringing about a great war. Accordingly, when the gods were celebrating the wedding feast of the mortal Peleus and the nymph Thetis, Eris "Strife" caused the goddesses Hera, Athena, and Aphrodite to quarrel about which of them was the most beautiful. To settle the dispute, Zeus bade Hermes lead the three contestants to Paris, a son of King Priam of Troy. Each goddess tried to bribe the young man, Hera offering him political success, Athena offering him martial success, and Aphrodite promising him erotic success. Paris chose Aphrodite, thereby incurring the wrath of the two losers who remained thereafter hostile to Troy and its people.

Paris sailed to the Peloponnese where he visited King Menelaus of Sparta and his beautiful wife Helen. In the absence of Menelaus, Aphrodite brought Paris and Helen together in love. The couple helped themselves amply to the treasures of the palace and sailed to Troy where they were wed. When Menelaus learned of his guest's treachery he called his powerful brother, King Agamemnon of Mycenae, to raise an army against Troy. Helen's former suitors and their men were now summoned to join in a combined expedition against Troy, and with them were Peleus' and Thetis' son Achilles and his men.

The Achaean ships gathered at Aulis where the seer Calchas interpreted an omen to signify that the army would fight for nine years and capture Troy in the tenth. As predicted the attackers gained little advantage in the first nine years of the war. In the course of the tenth year the greatest of the Achaean warriors, Achilles, quarreled with Agamemnon, leader of the combined forces, and as a result the angry Achilles and his followers withdrew from the fighting. But when the Trojan champion Hector slew Achilles' companion, Patroclus, Achilles rejoined the fighting and slew Hector. The Trojans were

7

subsequently reinforced by various exotic allies such as the Amazons and the Aethiopians, whose leaders Achilles also killed. Eventually he himself was slain by Paris.

Finally, the architect Epeios constructed a large wooden horse inside of which a number of the Achaeans concealed themselves. The rest of the forces pretended to give up the siege by embarking on their ships while in fact waiting offshore. The trick deceived the Trojans, who were persuaded that it would be to their advantage to drag the wooden horse into their city. That done, they gave themselves over to celebrating. The hidden Achaeans stole out of the horse, admitted the rest of the army into the city, and together they slew most of the unsuspecting inhabitants. Only Aeneas and a few other Trojans managed to escape slaughter or enslavement. The Achaeans destroyed the city and apportioned among themselves the booty and the Trojan women. Some of the Achaeans reached their cities quickly and safely, others perished at sea, and several, such as Odysseus, arrived only after many years. Nor did a safe return necessarily mean the end of suffering for the heroes, for trouble sometimes awaited them at home. Shortly after his arrival Agamemnon was murdered by his wife Clytemnestra and her lover Aegisthus. Odysseus had to rid his palace of a gang of arrogant suitors who daily pressed his wife Penelope to wed one of them.

The legend of Troy was not a fixed and unchanging entity that remained the same through space and time. It differed with the teller, his region, and his generation: there was and is no single correct version. What we now know of the cycle is the result of our piecing together many partial accounts and scattered allusions from ancient writers of different periods. We possess no absolutely complete account from antiquity, and in any event a truly complete account would be an artificial amalgam of inconsistent texts.[1] The cycle is one of the legends set in the Greek Heroic Age, a time of great wars, quests, and other exploits. It was preserved only in oral tradition until perhaps the eighth century B.C., when the alphabet was introduced into Greece, or even until the seventh century B.C., when the alphabet seems first to have been used for literary purposes. For many centuries thereafter the story of the great Achaean siege of Troy was preserved and refashioned both in oral and in literary tradition, with mutual influence.

It is not possible to know precisely in what form Homer and his audience knew the legend, for Homer does not, like a chronicler, tell the tale from beginning to end. Instead he selects a few days from the many years of activity associated with the campaign and sings of them in depth and at a leisurely pace while now and then relating or referring to some of the events that preceded or followed. He focuses in the *Iliad* on the story of the wrath of Achilles in the tenth year of the war and in the *Odyssey* on the story of the return of Odysseus in the tenth year of his travels. Obviously his listeners are already acquainted with the legend, for some episodes are merely alluded to or told very quickly.

In later times, at least, connection with the heroes who fought at Troy carried considerable prestige. Fine families claimed descent from this or that Achaean warrior, and many a coastal city boasted that it had been founded by one of the Achaeans on his way home from the famous campaign. In fact, several veterans of the war passed their last years doing little else but founding cities and begetting children. Some peoples saw their own ancestors in the mysterious Trojans who seemed otherwise to have disappeared from the face of the earth. In Roman tradition Aeneas and a small band of other Trojans fled Troy and sailed to Italy where they founded a New Troy, and Julius Caesar boasted descent from Aeneas' own son Julus. Virgil treats the story in his literary epic, the *Aeneid*. Antiquity did not put an end to the Trojans' wandering and founding. In his *History of the Kings of Britain*, Geoffrey of Monmouth (twelfth century A.D.) traces the Britons back to the homeless Trojans. According to him, Brutus, the great-grandson of Aeneas, gathered together a number of Trojans living in Greece and led them to a northern isle, inhabited at that time only by a few giants. Brutus changed its name from Albion to Britain, naming it after himself, and also renamed the Trojan language, British. Similarly the great Icelander, Snorri Sturluson (thirteenth century), in the prologue to his *Edda*, derives some of the Norse gods from one of Priam's daughters. The Aesir left Troy, which was located at the center of the world in Asia, and traveled to northern Europe. Again, the Norse language is said to be Trojan.

The Heroic Age of Greek tradition corresponds to the Late Bronze, or Mycenaean, Age of Greek history, a period of some 500 years (ca. 1600–ca. 1100 B.C.). A few centuries earlier, groups of Indo-European-speaking peoples had begun to enter the land they would later call Hellas. They were not the first to occupy the land and their entry was not altogether peaceful, as the occasional burnt towns of previous settlers testify. At about the same time another group of people entered northwestern Asia Minor, near the entrance of the Dardanelles, where now there is a small hill called Hissarlik. This was the site of Ilios, or Troy. The place had been occupied for over a thousand years and been host to five successive cities before the newcomers, the folk of Troy VI (as the archeologists call it) arrived. Since the proto-Greeks and the founders of Troy VI both arrived at their respective homes at about the same time and used a pottery technique which was almost wholly unknown elsewhere (the pottery is called Minyan Ware), the Greeks and the Trojans may actually have been different branches of the same movement of peoples.

The Greeks developed Mycenaean culture under the influence especially of the civilization of Crete. From the Cretans they learned, among much else, to make records on clay tablets with a syllabic script adapted to the Greek language. The Mycenaeans were prosperous traders and probably daring raiders. They sailed widely in the Aegean, and even Troy imported their goods. Mycenae, ruled in legend by Agamemnon, was their most impressive citadel and may have enjoyed a hegemony over the other mainland fortresses. The Trojans were also a prosperous folk, their economy perhaps being founded upon the export of horses and textiles. They seem not to have had a system of writing; in any event, they have left no direct evidence of their language. Troy, like Mycenae and the other mainland fortresses, was a fortified palace with some appendages, and not (as Homer thought) a fortified city: most of the population dwelt outside the walls. It was not very large, covering only about five acres.

Troy VI was destroyed by an earthquake and rebuilt in a more humble fashion. In the thirteenth century Troy VIIa was utterly destroyed in a violent fire that was probably set by human hands. Troy VIIa is commonly believed to be the Troy of legend. A long time passed before it was rebuilt, and never again was it more than a village. No more enviable, however, was the fate of the wealthy Mycenaean palaces in Greece. For soon after the destruction of Troy, they were burnt or abandoned. The palace system disappeared and with it, no doubt, the literacy it had fostered. The causes of the destruction are not known: there may have been internal warring, economic difficulties, or conflicts with the Dorians, another branch of Greek–speakers who were perhaps making their entry into Greece at about this time. Many Greeks immigrated to the coast of Asia Minor. Greece itself returned to being a land of small and relatively humble communities with little commercial or cultural contact with Eastern civilizations.

For Greeks of later times, the Mycenaean Age was something special and exceptional. Physical strength and beauty, nobility, courage, and a desire for honor and glory, especially in battle, marked the men of that age and led them to perform impressive feats. The drastic changes at the end of the Mycenaean Age—the collapse of stable and highly organized communities, the material impoverishment, perhaps the humiliation of conquest, in some cases the forsaking of the mother country for new homes—must have made it easy for subsequent generations to glorify the splendors of the past.[2]

The main events of the Trojan cycle may reflect historical fact: there may have been a Greek campaign against Troy; it may have been under the leadership of the ruler of Mycenae, the wealthiest and presumably the most powerful of the mainland kings (the lesser kings may have been his vassals); it is not impossible that his name was Agamemnon; it may have been a long and difficult siege; it may have been these men who destroyed Troy VIIa; and upon their return they may have found troubles at home. While none of this is inconsistent with the archeological record, however, none of it is necessarily true. For there may have been no campaign at all, or several ancient campaigns may have been conflated in story into a single great campaign. If there was a combined expedition against Troy, we may speculate that the attackers' motive was not the retrieval of a woman, however attractive she might have been; nor was it a business-like desire to control the entrance to the Dardanelles, since no victors stayed to occupy the site. Possibly they went to plunder.

The Homeric Problem

The *Iliad* and the *Odyssey* are the two outstanding heroic epics of ancient Greece. Both are long narrative songs, composed in a single meter throughout, and have for their settings the Heroic Age. The men who lived in that age, or at least the more prominent ones among them, the Greeks called *hērōes,* whence our term heroic epic (epic is the adjectival form of *epē,* an epic poem). The titles *Iliad* (Greek *Ilias,* genitive *Iliados*) and *Odyssey* (*Odysseia*) are feminine adjectives for which one must supply a word such as *poiesis* (poetry). Thus *Ilias* means "poetry about Ilios" and *Odysseia* means "poetry about Odysseus." Together the two poems contain about 27,000 verses, the *Iliad* being slightly longer than the *Odyssey.* The language of the poetry is of course Greek, but in a peculiar form. While the Ionic dialect predominates, many words from other dialects also appear, as well as a number of very old words whose meaning was obscure even in antiquity. The nature of this special language is not yet fully understood.[3]

The meter is dactylic hexameter. In all ancient Greek poetry, rhythm comes from patterns of long and short syllables. Since one long syllable was considered to be the temporal equivalent of two short syllables, a poet composing in hexameters might substitute for any dactyl ($-\cup\cup$) a spondee ($-\,-$), although he might not substitute an anapaest ($\cup\cup-$), which could have threatened the dactylic identity of the verse. The number of syllables in a verse, or line, is therefore not fixed but can vary from seventeen in a fully dactylic verse to twelve in a fully spondaic verse, although the temporal value is, at least theoretically, constant.

$$\overset{1}{-\underset{\smile\smile}{}}\Big|\overset{2}{-\underset{\smile\smile}{}}\Big|\overset{3}{-\underset{\smile\smile}{}}\Big|\overset{4}{-\underset{\smile\smile}{}}\Big|\overset{5}{-\underset{\smile\smile}{}}\Big|\overset{6}{-\underset{\smile}{}}$$

The sixth foot is always made up of two syllables of which the last may be either long or short.

In 1795 Friedrich August Wolf published his *Preface to Homer (Prolegomena ad Homerum),* perhaps the single most influential essay on the Homeric poems in modern scholarship, for from Wolf's essay have sprung many of the major debates since his time. Wolf argued that the Homeric poems were composed before the Greeks were acquainted with writing, at least for literary purposes. Homer therefore did not write, and his audience did not read him, so that he could not have composed such long poems and would have had no occasion to do so. The poems thus must have been composed orally and in the form of short lays; in the subsequent centuries they were transmitted by oral recitation, suffering some additions and other changes. Finally, they were edited to provide them with the unity they now have.

Wolf's ideas were not so much original as carefully argued. While he helped to give the Homeric Problem its modern form, various basic questions together with a variety of answers had already been put forth in antiquity. Closer attention to the text and to details which were less important or unperceived in oral presentation had come about in the Classical period (ca. 500–ca. 300 B.C.) when the book trade became highly developed and private reading became more widespread, but the greatest and most systematic of ancient Homeric scholarship took place in the Hellenistic period (ca. 300–ca. 100 B.C.) at the famous library in Alexandria. Scholars compared Homeric manuscripts from different parts of Greece, trying to establish, amid conflicting witnesses, which verses were genuine and which spurious, and why. They developed elementary principles of textual criticism in their attempts to bring order into the chaotic state of the disagreeing papyri. Although their learned commentaries have not survived in their entirety, excerpts from them have been preserved in the form of *scholia,* notes written in the margins of manuscripts. Possibly one of these men first divided each epic into twenty–four books, one book for each letter of the Greek alphabet.

In the Middle Ages the Greek language was little known in Europe so that most educated people knew Homer only indirectly, through Latin sources. The poems first saw print in the fifteenth century, and then became more accessible through the translations into the vernaculars that followed the printed texts. In the next few centuries some praised Homer as the greatest poet who ever lived, while others rated him a poor inferior to Virgil because of his loose plots, repetition, questionable morality, and the like. Wolf's *Prolegomena* from the end of the eighteenth century directly or indirectly stimulated much of the Homeric criticism of the nineteenth century and some of that in our own century. In the last hundred years the new and significant knowledge relevant to the study of Homer has become voluminous and complex. In the 1870s–1890s Heinrich Schliemann excavated first Hissarlik, announcing to the world the discovery of the legendary city of Troy, or rather of many Troys, the one on top of the other, and then Mycenae, uncovering the wealthy palace of the legendary King Agamemnon. Homerists acquired an external world to which to relate their text. In the early years of our century, Sir Arthur Evans revealed the ancient civilization of Crete which had so much influenced Mycenaean Greece. Sometime later, Milman Parry was beginning to understand the nature of oral poetry, a discovery with such radical implications for the Homeric epics that his work had to wait years to be appreciated by all but a few scholars. In the 1950s the architect Michael Ventris began deciphering the mysterious syllabary Linear B, inscribed on clay tablets found both on Crete and on the mainland, and discovered that the language of the tablets was a very old form of Greek.

Opinion, modern and ancient, inclines to place the composition of the poems in Ionia, that is, in an area where many Greeks settled after the collapse of the Mycenaean socio-political system. The epic dialect is primarily Ionic. Of the numerous places which of old claimed to be the birthplace of Homer, the leading contender was the island of Chios. There was on Chios a guild or family of singers or reciters who called themselves the *Homeridai* (descendants of Homer), and claimed to perform his songs by the right of succession. But little is known of them. Chios' boast was also supported by some verses in the *Homeric Hymn to Apollo* (vv. 169–173), one of a number of short hexameter poems once attributed to Homer. The singer concludes the hymn in this way:

> Remember me when any man on this earth, any much-suffering stranger, comes here and asks you, "Girls, who do you believe is the sweetest of the singers who come here? Who delights you most?" All of you must then answer in a single voice, "He is a blind man and dwells on rocky Chios. His songs will always be the finest."

When were the epics composed? The Greeks believed that Homer was one of their oldest poets, although not the oldest of all, and that he lived considerably later than the events he sang about. Homer has been conjecturally located in nearly every available century between the fall of Troy and the Classical period. What evidence we have makes the eighth century B.C. a reasonable guess as the date of composition, but neither the ninth century nor the seventh may be excluded. Many critics believe that the *Iliad* is slightly older than the *Odyssey*.

Who composed the Homeric epics? The ancients attributed to Homer a number of otherwise anonymous hexameter poems, for example, the *Homeric Hymns* and the mock epic *Battle of the Frogs and the Mice (Batrachomyomachia)*, both still extant. In the course of time many ancient scholars decided that only the best of the lot, the *Iliad* and the *Odyssey*, were his. Some went even further, asserting that he was responsible only for the best of the best, the *Iliad;* these critics were called *Chorizontes* (Separators). The question is still argued. No one has yet hit upon a way to prove decisively whether there was one monumental poet or two of them. Despite these long-standing differences of opinion, it is convenient and customary to retain the name Homer and to call both epics Homeric.

The judgment that the *Iliad* is the superior poem is both an old and a persistent one: the *Iliad* is a tragic poem whereas the *Odyssey* is only a *Märchenepos* (a folktale-epic). More than one scholar has held that the *Odyssey* is a work of Homer's old age and declining powers. Sometimes the *Iliad* is not only better, it is also more manly: Richard Bently decided that Homer wrote the *Iliad* for men and the *Odyssey* for women, and more recently Samuel Butler in *The Authoress of the Odyssey* ingeniously argued that the *Odyssey* was actually written by a Sicilian lady and that Princess Nausicaa was the authoress' self–portrayal.

The question of who composed the epics is more complicated than whether it was one man (or woman) or two, whatever his or their names, generations, and birthplaces. Our answer will probably depend in some measure on how we think the poems were composed. It will be recalled that Wolf argued that Homer and his audience preceded the use of writing for literary purposes in Greece, that Homer therefore composed short lays that were transmitted by recitation for a number of centuries until they were edited to give them unity, and that before the editorial work the poems had been enlarged by other poets. Scholarly reaction tended to take the form of two great camps, with many a tent pitched here and there at points in between. While the one side defended the *unity* of composition of the poems, the other side denied historical unity and attempted to *analyze* the epics into the original lays. But if there were many lays, there could as well be many poets. And if that were the case, one could place Homer at either end of the process, as the poet either of the earliest lays or of the most recent, or at any point in between, and decide that he was the best or the worst of the lot.

To distinguish the older from the newer, analysts employed various criteria such as the appearance of relatively newer or older words in different passages, esthetic quality (they usually judged the best to be the oldest), and the mention of datable material objects or cultural practices. Narrative inconsistencies, already noticed and discussed in antiquity, were seen as the contradictions between songs of different poets or as traces inadvertently left by a clumsy editor when he joined alien songs together. Analysts assumed that since the Homeric epics were great poetry, there must naturally have been a great poet at work, that great poets do not produce poems with flaws, and that as the poems contained significant flaws, lesser poets must also have had a hand in the poems. Their own job was to distinguish and assign relative dates to the components of the poems, in other words, to write a history of the development of each epic. Their opponents heartily embraced the poems as great poetry and as having a great poet behind them. But while they might concede that there were to be found later and inferior accretions to the text, they tried to account for most of the alleged inconsistencies in other ways than as the byproducts of multiple authorship or multiple lays. Complaining that some scholars expected poets to compose like logicians, they pointed out that even literature known to be the work of a single author might contain occasional inconsistencies and that some of the alleged inconsistencies and awkwardnesses disappeared if the passages were understood properly.

The *Iliad* received the greater attention. Two major analytic models for its historical development were employed. According to the *compilation* model, essentially Wolf's view, a number of smaller songs had been compiled by a later editor into a single long poem. Others adhered to the *nucleus* model, arguing that an original song on the wrath of Achilles had grown to its present size by additions from the poetry of later, and usually inferior, men. Scholars continue to draw from both models. Since the *Odyssey* readily suggests a tripartite structure, it has often been analyzed into three main songs: the *Telemachy,* that is, those parts of the poem that deal primarily with Telemachus; Odysseus' travels, the middle part of the epic; and Odysseus' revenge, the conclusion of the poem. These three songs were supposedly joined together at different times or compiled on one occasion by an editor whose doubtful skill accounts for the awkward passages of the epic.

In our days fewer scholars adopt an extreme position, and many a writer now introduces his thoughts on the problem with the claim that he is a partisan of neither camp, but stands quite sensibly somewhere in the middle where he can judge the matter without prejudice. At any rate, the analysts have failed to reach a consensus as to just how many songs there were to be found, where they began and left off, and how many poets lurked behind the uniform text; and the unitarians have had to grant that the epics do pose some difficult problems which are not so easily explained as they once thought. Both sides were limited by an old assumption about Homer, an assumption so basic and simple that they did not realize the extent to which it underlay their thinking and their work. For over two millennia students of Homer imagined that the poet composed in more or less the same way as most contemporary poets. We now know that was not true.

Homer as Oral Poet

Thanks primarily to the efforts of the American Classicist Milman Parry (1902–35) and of his student Albert Lord, we have come to understand that Homer composed in a manner quite unlike that of most contemporary poets.[4] Although scholars had often spoken vaguely of Homer's composing orally, few of them had tried to understand just what oral composition, in particular Homeric oral composition, really meant. Parry's accomplishment was to demonstrate by close analysis of the texts that Homeric diction in some sense had to be traditional. Subsequently realizing that it had to be the diction of an oral poetry, he observed and recorded living oral poets in the course of two field trips to Yugoslavia in the 1930s. He perceived that Homeric diction was typical of oral poetry and understood as well the relevance of studying a living tradition of heroic epic poetry.

Oral poetry is a form of oral narrative art, perhaps once widespread in the world, but now rare. The expression ''oral poetry'' is a technical term for this art form and does not mean simply any poetry that is orally delivered or composed. An oral poet does not memorize songs beforehand and then recite them to his audience; rather, he recomposes songs during performance with the help of certain dictional and narrative techniques that have come largely to be habits with him. His songs are as a rule traditional ones. Since he never recites, he never sings a song twice in precisely the same words, but composes anew each time he performs. The poet himself may proudly claim that he always reproduces each song just as he first heard it, but he is wrong, for recordings show that no performances of the same song are identical although there may be no greater difference between two performances of a song given a decade apart than two performances given a few days apart. It is important to understand that the art is an oral art, its medium an oral performance for a live audience, and not a literary art for a reading public. The preservation of a given song is therefore not naturally the printed page, which freezes part of a single performance inadequately onto paper—inadequately, because print preserves only the text of the performance and omits the music, the singer's voice, the visual and temporal context, and the immediate contact between performer and audience. The natural mechanism of song preservation is the accomplished singer who learns, remembers, and performs songs, and then passes his repertoire on to younger singers. In a thriving tradition songs can theoretically be preserved indefinitely, handed on from one generation to the next.

Let us consider some of the techniques that enable singers to compose—or, more accurately, recompose—their songs as they sing. Contemporary singers, who are usually neither educated nor literate, are unable to give a good account of how they compose songs, but we can learn much about their compositional techniques by analyzing the texts of their songs. Homerists have devoted much of their thinking to the singer's *formulaic diction.* Parry was particularly interested in Homer's use of certain poetic formulas, the noun–epithet combinations, which occur very frequently and thus provided him with much comparative material. He demonstrated that Homer's use of these formulas was characterized by such economy and extensiveness that no single poet would have been able to have devised such a system. By economy he meant that the poet has not several, but only one way to express each idea in his poetry in any metrical position and that he regularly expresses it in just this one way. By extensiveness he meant that the poet has at his disposal a far–reaching system which he employs consistently throughout his composition. Parry concluded that the system could only have been developed by many poets over many years, that is, that it was traditional, and that its use could only have been for oral composition.

The diction of oral poetry is extremely thrifty in comparison with either literary diction or the diction of ordinary speech. The singer learns a special poetic language in which some of the varieties of expression are more limited; rapid composition is facilitated since he has less need to pause and choose between possible alternatives. A simple example will illustrate the kind of verbal skill that the poet has learned. On this level of analysis we may imagine that the poet's aim is to fashion a single line of metrical information, whether he chooses to continue the thought in the following verse or not. Let us say that he intends to introduce a speaker. He has standard and regular ways of verbalizing this notion, for introducing a character's speech is a common situation. Whenever he wishes to express the information, "And then— said," "And then—replied," "And then—laughed," etc., he does so in the same words, searching for no special or unique expression. Thus part of the line is readily versified. Although the clause would be complete if the singer should state the name of its subject, which will appear at the end of the Greek line, the verse itself would not then be complete because there would remain an unfilled metrical slot between the first part of the verse and the name of the speaker. Its length and metrical shape can vary, depending on the length of the introductory words and the length of the subject's name. How does the poet quickly fill this slot and so complete his line? For every major character in his story he has at his disposal an epithet or group of epithets that exactly fits the potentially vacant space. Once he has sung the first part of his verse, then, its conclusion is simple and in a sense predetermined. He need not search his mind at the moment of composition for metrically appropriate words to solve the immediate problem of finishing the verse he has begun. If, for example, the subject is to be Odysseus and if the initial words fill the first 2¾ metrical

feet, the poet will complete his verse with *polytlas dios Odysseus;* if they fill

the first 3½ metrical feet, he will sing instead *polymetis Odysseus,* which also exactly finishes his verse. Odysseus will be "much–suffering god–like Odysseus" in the former metrical situation and "clever Odysseus" in the latter, regardless of what he happens to be doing at the moment in the story. Notice that the specific epithet or epithets employed will depend not on the immediate story–context—with a few exceptions—but on the metrical context. Needless to say the adjectives in the noun–epithet combinations are appropriate to each of the characters in general, if not always the most relevant imaginable at the moment. Versification would be slower and more difficult if the singer each time had to come up with epithets both metrically and semantically specific. While this process sounds very consciously mechanical, rather like a bricklayer pausing to decide at each step which brick will best fit where, it is not so; if it were, it would hinder rapid composition, not help it. The poet does not pause to ransack a bag of formulas for an expression of just the right size to insert in a familiar metrical slot. Composing hexameters on familiar subjects is to speak a special language. An analysis of the language makes it seem laborious since we are made conscious of what for the speakers are mostly habits.

In sum, the oral poet has learned to use an extremely stylized language, one that would be neither necessary nor desirable for the literary poet, not even for the poet of the literary heroic epic. For the literary poet, who may compose at leisure and in private, there is a considerable delay from the time of composition to the time of performance; no audience is present and waiting for the next line while the poet is singing the present one. Nor is the stylized diction of the oral poet necessarily desirable, for the literary poet may exploit his leisure to vary his word–choice, choosing his epithets to suit precisely the immediate sense–context. In the *Aeneid* Virgil calls his hero *pius, bonus, pater* and *Tros,* that is, "dutiful," "good," "father," and "Trojan," all four of which are metrically equivalent, scanning either $\cup\cup\,|$ or —. The use of repeated epithets allows Virgil to give his epic some of the tone of the Greek oral epic, while as a literary poet he may select from among them the sense-context in mind. Homer ordinarily has only one such epithet for a character.

The oral poet also has techniques to facilitate the organization of his song on the narrative level as well as the verbal–metrical level. Since certain situations frequently recur in heroic song and in the singing of heroic song, he has learned also to handle them in stylized ways. Homeric heroes repeatedly feast, arm themselves, go to sleep, arrive at someone's palace, hold councils and assemblies, receive messages, engage in combat; Night falls, rosy-fingered Dawn shows herself, days pass; mortals and gods plead, rebuke, consult, complain, console, boast. Practiced in narrating such events, the accomplished poet can put his characters through the standard paces, either briefly or elaborately, according to the importance of the scene and to his and his audience's interest in it. These recurrent narrative elements are called *themes* or *typical scenes* (the terms "motif," "stock scene," and "topos" are sometimes used also). Whenever a singer describes a familiar scene, he tends to do so in a familiar way, the way he has learned and developed. The similarity between some themes, or rather multiforms of a theme, is often obvious as in the following examples in which a deity prepares to depart from Olympus in order to deliver a message.

> Thus she [Athena] spoke and bound under her feet beautiful sandals, ambrosial, golden, which carry her both over sea and over boundless earth with the speed of wind. And she took her mighty spear, tipped with sharp bronze, heavy, large, strong with which she overcomes ranks of men, heroes, at whom she is angry, daughter of a powerful father. And she went darting down from the peaks of Olympus (*Od.* 1.96–102).

> Thus he [Zeus] spoke, and the messenger Argiphontes [Hermes] did not disobey. Immediately he bound under his feet his beautiful sandals, ambrosial, golden, which carry him both over sea and over boundless earth with the speed of wind. And he took his staff with which he charms to sleep the eyes of men whom he will, or others again he awakens even from sleep. With this in his hands strong Argiphontes flew (*Od.* 5.43–49).

The forms of themes are usually not so fixed that the poet need only insert the appropriate names into the proper slots. It is frequently not possible to classify themes (or formulas) neatly, since the one gradates into the other, and a given passage is often a blend of materials elsewhere appearing independently. Like the verbal formula, the theme is an analytic convenience.

By their nature some types of scene require more variety than others. Meals, if they are not especially to be emphasized, can well be described in similar ways and, like arming, with a standard sequence of action. But it would hardly do, for the poet of the *Iliad* at least, to command only a single battle scene, however much he might be capable of varying it, or a single simile. Therefore he has a large repertoire of both stock encounters between Greeks and Trojans with which to vary the day–long fighting, and he knows many similes, both simple ones, as in "Apollo descends like night," and complex ones. The Homeric simile is usually content with only one or two points of comparison rather than several, as in much literary poetry. Regardless of how complex the simile is, there is not likely to be full parallelism to the narrative event. But the less situation–bound a simile is, the more freely and variously it can be applied. Minimal comparison is a feature of oral–poetic economy. As though to illustrate this, Homer uses several of the same complex similes more than once in the *Iliad*. For example, the simile of the lion who is driven back from the oxen is applied both to Ajax (*Il.* 11.544–557) and, six books later, to Menelaus (17.651–667).

Zeus father who sits on high roused fear in Ajax. He stood stunned, threw behind him his sevenfold oxhide shield, looking around anxiously at the crowd like a wild animal and turning always about, and retreated with slow steps. Just as when dogs and country men have driven a tawny lion away from the ox fold, and will not let him tear out the fat of the oxen, watching him throughout the night, and he in his desire for meat advances but gains nothing, for javelins rush at him, thickly from bold hands, and flaming torches, and he balks at them despite his eagerness, and at dawn he goes away disappointed in his desire; so Ajax then drew back from the Trojans disappointed in his heart, very unwillingly, for he feared for the ships of the Achaeans.

Ajax said to Menelaus of the great war cry: "Look now, god–nurtured Menelaus, if you can see Antilochus, great-hearted Nestor's son, still alive, and send him quickly to wise Achilles to say that his most beloved companion has perished." So he spoke and Menelaus of the great war cry obeyed him. He went like some lion from a fold who is worn out from harrying dogs and men, who do not let him tear out the fat of the oxen, watching him throughout the night, and he in his desire for meat advances but gains nothing, for javelins rush at him quickly from bold hands, and flaming torches, and he balks at them despite his eagerness, and at dawn he goes away disappointed in his desire; so Menelaus of the great war cry drew back from Patroclus, very unwillingly, for he feared that the Achaeans out of fear might leave him as spoil for the enemy.

For Ajax the main point of comparison is that, like the lion, he is being pressed back by his enemies, whereas in the second passage Menelaus is not really forced away at all, but leaves to look for Antilochus to tell him of Patroclus' death, so that here the main parallel lies rather in the combatant's deciding, for one reason or another, to depart, having been frustrated of his desire (ox/body of Patroclus).

Another level of compositional habit may be abstracted, one which in magnitude holds an intermediate position between the theme and the song itself: the narrative *sequence,* or economy in the composition of whole episodes.[5] The singer handles similar episodes in similar ways, and sometimes even dissimilar episodes in similar ways. One multiform of a sequence will be longer and more elaborate than another, and many contain themes absent from the other, but a succession of similar events will run through them both. Also, the narrative function of corresponding events in each episode may be quite different: a pattern is constant, but the meaning may vary. To illustrate a sequence, I append here two passages from the *Odyssey.* Only the parallels are shown, and they are much abbreviated; the rest is omitted.

Books 1–3	Book 15
Athena goes to Ithaca.	Athena goes to Sparta.
Telemachus sits, fantasying his father's return.	Telemachus lies awake, anxious for his father.
Athena bids him ask the suitors to go home, and go to Pylos and Sparta after news of Odysseus. She departs.	Athena bids him urge his host, Menelaus, to send him home. She departs.

So ends the first day. In both episodes the goddess starts the action by urging the young hero to journey somewhere. On the second day Telemachus acts on Athena's orders: he speaks to his guests or to his host.

Telemachus calls an assembly and bids the suitors return to their homes; if they do not, he will ask Zeus for just retribution.	Telemachus goes to Menelaus and bids him send him home; he wishes that Odysseus were home so that he might tell him of Menelaus' hospitality.
An omen (two eagles) appears. The assembly is amazed.	An omen (eagle and goose) appears. The onlookers rejoice.
An old man interprets: Odysseus may already be near, planning death for the suitors.	Helen interprets: Odysseus may already be home, planning death for the suitors.
Telemachus and his crew embark and sail all night.	Telemachus and his companion depart by chariot and pass the night in Pherai.

So ends the second day. On the third day the young hero reaches Pylos.

They reach Pylos and join Nestor and the other Pylians on the beach where they are sacrificing.	They reach Pylos, where Telemachus' companion drops him off at his ship.

Telemachus prays to Poseidon.	Telemachus prays to Athena.
Once they have eaten, Nestor asks who they are and what their mission is.	A stranger, Theoclymenus, approaches Telemachus and asks who he is.
Telemachus explains who he is and that he has come after news of Odysseus; he asks him to tell what he knows of Odysseus' fate.	Telemachus explains who he is and that he has come after news of Odysseus.
Nestor relates how he himself sailed from Troy to Pylos, escaping the wrath of Athena; but he knows little of Odysseus.	Theoclymenus explains that he himself has fled from Argos to Pylos to avoid his angry kinsmen; he asks to be taken aboard ship.

In the former account the conversation between Telemachus and Nestor continues. In the latter Telemachus, his crew, and Theoclymenus embark for Ithaca; while they sail, the poet temporarily shifts the scene to the hut of the swineherd Eumaeus on Ithaca where he has Odysseus and Eumaeus converse in the same manner as Telemachus and Nestor.

Telemachus asks Nestor to tell him of Agamemnon and Menelaus.	Odysseus asks Eumaeus to tell him of Anticlea and Laertes.
Nestor tells of Agamemnon's murder and of Menelaus' voyage.	Eumaeus tells of Anticlea's death and of Laertes' suffering.

In the second account the scene now shifts back to Telemachus, who has reached Ithaca.

Nestor invites them to stay with him in his palace.	Theoclymenus asks whether he should go on to Telemachus' palace.
Telemachus' companion (Athena in disguise) replies that he cannot but that Telemachus should do so.	Telemachus replies that he should rather go to the home of one of the suitors, although there may come a disaster before any wedding takes place.
Athena departs in the form of a sea-eagle.	An omen (hawk and dove) appears.
Nestor interprets: the gods are your escort, for that was Athena!	Theoclymenus interprets: that was an omen—there is no more kingly family in Ithaca than yours.

Here we witness one of the dangers of the poet's technique: the inappropriate persistence of a compositional habit. Theoclymenus' interpretation of the omen is not wholly satisfactory, for it is obvious that the function of the omen is to confirm Telemachus' remark about a possible catastrophe for the suitors.

The interpreter should have said something about Odysseus' revenge, as in the earlier omens. Possibly influenced by his memory of the earlier passage, the singer has Theoclymenus, like Nestor, give an honorific interpretation of the event, but in this context the theme is awkward.

Finally, we may say a few words about the highest level of narrative organization, the *song type,* the general plot or course of action in the song. This is a more difficult matter for us to learn about in the case of Homeric poetry since, unlike recurring word–groups, scenes, and sequences, recurring song types require for comparative study a number of similar, whole songs, and these we do not possess from antiquity. Sometimes we can partially make up for this lack in other ways. For example, the most abundant materials for comparison with the story of the *Odyssey* are traditional narratives from more recent times. The basic story, the hero's return in time to prevent the remarriage of his wife (AT 974), is known both in Slavic heroic epic and in European ballad and prose traditions. Insufficient study has been devoted to this subject.

The Parry–Lord theory of oral poetry wholly redefines the Homeric Problem with regard to composition. Wolf was almost certainly right in believing that Homer did not write, but illiteracy would not have restricted the bard to composing short songs, for we know that oral poets are capable of producing songs as long as the Homeric epics. It is not, however, easy to imagine occasions for which songs of such length were suitable. What the occasions may have been, and whether they were recurrent or extraordinary, we do not know. We do know that Homer was not an isolated poet, but rather part of a tradition of ancient Greek oral poets, from some of whom he first learned his diction and songs. The art form is at least as old as the destruction of Troy, that is, the thirteenth century B.C., for the poems preserve descriptions of artifacts such as a boar's tusk helmet (*Il.* 10.260–265) and body-shields (e.g., *Il.* 6.116–118 and 17.128) which went out of use in that century. There was, therefore, Achaean oral poetry in the Late Bronze Age, if not also earlier.

It is impossible to say with certainty whether the two poems were written down by scribes from an actual and special performance (if a singer can accustom himself to the slow pace of dictation, he can sometimes produce longer and better songs), or were first memorized by a gifted listener, a feat less improbable than it may sound or, least likely I think, were written down by the very composer(s). It was perhaps in the sixth century B.C. that the poems became the property of professional reciters (*rhapsodoi*) who performed at festivals and on the streets, knowing the epics by heart as apparently many an educated Greek did. A rhapsode stood and kept time with a staff while he declaimed. Plato describes a conversation between Socrates and a rhapsode in his dialogue *Ion,* giving us a brief portrait of one such performer. In contrast, the oral poet (*aoidos*) usually sat down while he sang, and played a lyre–like instrument called *phorminx* or *kitharis.*

When did the art of oral poetry die out in Greece? While it is often assumed that Homer marked the end or near end of the tradition, the truth of the matter is that there is no evidence on the point. That the ancient scholars and their successors were unaware of oral poetry as a special art form implies nothing at all regarding its presence or absence in their times. The non–systematic observer will find little or nothing in an oral–poetic performance to indicate that the poet is essentially different from other kinds of performing poets, especially in antiquity when it was not uncommon for poets to imitate features of the Homeric style. If one cannot compare different texts or recordings of a single poet's performances of the same song and see the variations, one has no reason to believe that he is not reproducing a memorized song in epic diction. Further, there is nothing at all unusual in urbanites' being wholly unaware of popular traditions among rural folk only a few miles away. The example of Yugoslavia shows that the tradition need not die out uniformly, for there can be costumed reciters in the city while there are still true oral poets in the villages. The appearance of rhapsodes in Greece, therefore, need not imply that oral poets were no longer to be found.

In the *Odyssey* we find an oral poet's portrait of two ancient oral poets, Demodocus and Phemius, and there are occasional references in both epics to singers and songs. Demodocus and Phemius are professionals who rely on their craft for their living, but a non–professional might also sing for his pleasure, as Achilles does in his tent at Troy (*Il.* 9.186–191). There is otherwise no mention of a bard at Troy who might preserve in song the valorous deeds of the illiterate Achaeans or stir them on with songs of earlier heroes. A bard could give historical permanence to deeds, good and bad, by recording them in song. Thus Achilles takes pleasure in singing the "famous deeds of men," and Helen imagines that in days to come Paris and she may be the subject of songs for those yet to be born (*Il.* 6.357–358).

Most of the songs mentioned in the *Odyssey* take their theme from some part of the Trojan affair—the wooden horse, the returns of the Achaeans and so on—but Demodocus also sings the ribald tale of Ares' affair with Aphrodite (*Od.* 8.266–369). A member of the audience could make a topical request (e.g., *Od.* 8.487–489). A singer might also accompany dancers (e.g., *Od.* 8.256–265). Singers are classified as public craftsmen (*demioergoi*) together with seers, doctors, carpenters, and heralds (*Od.* 17.382–385; 19.135); that is, they are useful and skilled men, not permanently attached to a house, but professionals at the service of the community. In the *Odyssey* their audiences are primarily leisured royalty and nobles, to whose houses they are summoned to entertain. Although Demodocus and Phemius sing only short lays, obviously there is no occasion for very long ones. Like Homer, these fictive singers start their tales where they wish, at the beginning or *in medias res*. If the singer is pleasing, one of his listeners might present him with a consumable gift, as when Odysseus gives Demodocus a rich cut of boar's meat from the feast (*Od.* 8.474–481), somewhat as one might give a cigarette, coffee or drink to a Yugoslav singer during his pause. Listening to an excellent singer at a feast was one of the true pleasures of life.

> It is really a fine thing to be listening to a singer such as this man here [Demodocus], whose voice is like the gods. For I do not think that there exists a fulfillment more delightful than when joy possesses a whole people, and banqueters sit listening to a singer, and beside them there are tables full of bread and meat, and a wine–pourer draws drink and carries it around and pours it into their cups. To my mind this seems to be the fairest thing there is (*Od.* 9.3–11).

Summary

About 4000 years ago the Greeks and the Trojans began to make their way into their historical homes in Greece and Asia Minor. In the Late Bronze Age (ca. 1600–ca. 1100 B.C.), also called the Mycenaean Age, coastal Greece was dotted with fortified citadels, each of which had a wealthy bureaucracy. Mycenae was the grandest of all, and its ruler may have led a combined expedition against Troy VIIa, perhaps for plunder, in the thirteenth century B.C.; in any event, Troy suffered a terrible destruction from which it never really recovered. Within a century or so of the fall of Troy the citadels on the Greek mainland were also destroyed, and in the period that followed (ca. 1100–ca. 900 B.C.), many Greeks moved across the Aegean to settle on the coast of Asia Minor. The emigrants carried with them traditions from the old country which both their storytellers and their oral poets kept alive. Sometime in the ninth to seventh centuries B.C., perhaps, the *Iliad* and the *Odyssey* were composed in Ionia and subsequently became well known over most of the Greek–speaking world. They were attributed to a bard named Homer. Professional reciters made their appearance by the sixth century B.C. and were common throughout the Classical period (ca. 500–ca. 300 B.C.). During these and the following centuries scholars busied themselves with the many problems of the Homeric epics, including the establishment of a reliable text of the poems. A second great period of European interest in Homer began in the Renaissance when the poems were printed for the first time, giving critics and translators easier access to them. From antiquity to the present day, students of Homer have asked how the epics were composed, who composed them, where and when they came into being and other very basic questions for which there have rarely been certain answers. Of the several recent advances in knowledge bearing upon Homer, our increasing understanding of the nature of oral poetry is no doubt the most important if not also the most exciting, while at the same time it has suggested many new problems. Most scholarly interest has hitherto been directed to the singer's diction, whereas the narrative phenomena—theme, sequence, and song type—have been less well explored. Other matters such as the nature of literary and oral poets, of written and oral narrative, of reading and listening audiences and of literary and oral esthetics,[6] remain to be investigated by philologists, linguists, folklorists, critics and psychologists of learning.

NOTES

1. However, a convenient synthetic account from late antiquity is found in the mythographer pseudo-Apollodorus, *Epitome*, 2.15–7.40. See *Apollodorus, The Library*, trans. James G. Frazer, II (Cambridge, Mass.: Harvard University Press, 1921), pp. 169–307. One may also consult the relevant fragments of the Epic Cycle, or ancient Greek epics relating events from the union of the Sky and Earth to the end of the Heroic Age. See *Hesiod, the Homeric Hymns, and Homerica*, trans. H. G. Evelyn-White (Cambridge, Mass.: Harvard University Press, 1936), pp. 488–533.

2. See further C. M. Bowra, "The Meaning of a Heroic Age," in *The Language and Background of Homer*, ed. G. S. Kirk (New York: Barnes and Noble, 1964), pp. 22–47.

3. For a recent discussion, see Fred W. Householder and Gregory Nagy, "Greek," in *Current Trends in Linguistics*, IX, ed. Thomas A. Sebeok (The Hague and Paris: Mouton, 1972), pp. 738–52.

4. See Milman Parry, *The Making of Homeric Verse: The Collected Papers of Milman Parry*, ed. Adam Parry (Oxford: Oxford University Press, 1971), and Albert B. Lord, *The Singer of Tales* (Cambridge, Mass.: Harvard University Press, 1960). Their works have attracted much interest and stirred considerable debate among literary scholars and folklorists. See, for example, Robert Scholes and Robert Kellogg, *The Nature of Narrative* (New York: Oxford University Press, 1966); Bruce Rosenberg, *The Art of the American Folk Preacher* (New York: Oxford University Press, 1970); and Alfred Heubeck, *Die homerische Frage: Ein Bericht über die Forschung der letzten Jahrzehnte* (Darmstadt: Wissenschaftliche Buchgesellschaft, 1974). See further Edward R. Haymes, *A Bibliography of Studies Relating to Parry's and Lord's Oral Theory* (Cambridge, Mass.: Harvard University Press, 1973); and David W. Packard and Tania Meyers, *A Bibliography of Homeric Scholarship: Preliminary Edition 1930–1970* (Malibu, Calif.: Undena Publications, 1974).

5. See my monograph, *The Conference Sequence: Patterned Narration and Narrative Inconsistency in the Odyssey*, University of California Publications in Classical Studies, 8 (Berkeley: University of California Press, 1972).

6. See James P. Holoka, "Homeric Originality: A Survey," *Classical World* 66 (1973): 257–93, and Michael N. Nagler, *Spontaneity and Tradition: A Study in the Oral Art of Homer* (Berkeley: University of California Press, 1974).

BIBLIOGRAPHY

Texts and Translations

Homeri Opera. 5 vols. Edited by David B. Monro and Thomas Allen. Oxford: Clarendon Press, 1902 (and later editions).
The Iliad of Homer. Translated and with an Introduction by Richmond Lattimore. Chicago: University of Chicago Press, 1951 (and later editions).
Homer, The Odyssey. Translated by Robert Fitzgerald. Garden City, N.Y.: Doubleday, 1961 (and later editions).

Studies

Chadwick, John. *The Mycenaean World*. Cambridge: Cambridge University Press,

1976. A very readable account of Mycenaean culture, including its relationship to the Homeric epics.

Hainsworth, J. B. *Homer*. Oxford: Clarendon Press, 1969. A brief survey of the present state of Homeric studies.

Hansen, Wm. F. *The Conference Sequence: Patterned Narration and Narrative Inconsistency in the Odyssey*. University of California Publications in Classical Studies, 8. Berkeley and Los Angeles, 1972. A study of stylized narration in the composition of episodes and of the etiology of some narrative inconsistencies.

Heubeck, Alfred. *Die homerische Frage: Ein Bericht über die Forschung der letzten Jahrzehnte*. Erträge der Forschung, 27. Darmstadt: Wissenschaftliche Buchgesellschaft, 1974. A detailed survey of Homeric scholarship, with an extensive bibliography.

Kirk, G. S. *The Songs of Homer*. Cambridge: Cambridge University Press, 1962. The standard work in English on the Homeric epics.

––––––, ed. *The Language and Background of Homer*. New York: Barnes & Noble, 1964. A collection of influential articles, mostly from scholarly journals.

Krischer, Tilman. *Formale Konventionen der homerischen Epik*. Zetemata, 56. Munich: C. H. Beck, 1971. A critical assessment of some features of Homeric epic such as simultaneous events, similes, and catalogues.

Lesky, Albin. *Homeros*. Stuttgart: A. Druckenmüller, 1967. A brief survey of Homeric studies.

Lord, Albert B. *The Singer of Tales*. Harvard Studies in Comparative Literature, 24. Cambridge, Mass., 1960. The standard introduction to the theory of oral poetry.

Myres, J. L. *Homer and His Critics*. Edited by D. Grey. London: Routledge & Paul, 1958. A selective study of Homeric scholarship through the ages, completed after the author's death by Miss Grey.

Nagler, Michael N. *Spontaneity and Tradition: A Study in the Oral Art of Homer*. Berkeley: University of California Press, 1974. A provocative study of Homeric art and esthetics in the light of oral poetry.

Owen, E. T. *The Story of the Iliad as Told in the Iliad*. Toronto: Clarke, Irwin & Co., 1946. A classic work of Homeric criticism.

Parry, Adam, ed. *The Making of Homeric Verse: The Collected Papers of Milman Parry*. Oxford: Clarendon Press, 1971. The complete writings of Milman Parry, edited and introduced by his late son. These brilliant essays are basic to the study of formulaic diction in oral poetry. Although the author generally assumes the reader to be acquainted with Greek, the Greekless reader will also find much of value here.

Vermeule, Emily. *Greece in the Bronze Age*. Chicago: University of Chicago Press, 1964. An account of bronze-age Greece for the scholar or the general reader.

Wace, Alan J. B., and Frank H. Stubbings, eds. *A Companion to Homer*. London: Macmillan, 1962. A collection of articles on many aspects of Homeric poetry and society.

Zielinski, Thaddaeus. "Die Behandlung gleichzeitiger Ereignisse im antiken Epos," *Philologus,* suppl. 8 (1899–1901): 407–49. An ingenious study of the possible ways a narrator can handle simultaneous events and of the peculiar conventions that Homer observes.

2 Mesopotamian Epic Literature

Johannes M. Renger

The epic tradition of Mesopotamia survived in several epic tales written either in Sumerian, a language of unknown affiliation spoken only until the end of the third millennium B.C. but used as a literary language as long as Mesopotamian civilization survived, or in Akkadian, sometimes also called Babylonian, a Semitic language which was spoken in Mesopotamia from the middle of the third millennium to the middle of the first millennium B.C.[1] This epic tradition is concerned with the early kings of Uruk (Biblical Erech) in lower Mesopotamia. The Sumerian King List, a pseudo-historical and propagandistic work created by Babylonian scribes, gives us the following account of the lineage:

> Kish [another Mesopotamian city] was smitten with weapons; the kingship [which it had exercised over Mesopotamia] was transferred to Eanna [the main temple of Uruk]. In Eanna Mes-kiag-gasher, son of the sun-god, became the "Lord" [or en-priest][2] and king and reigned for 324 years. Mes-kiag-gasher went into the sea and came out from it to the mountains. Enmerkar, son of Mes-kiag-gasher, King of Uruk, the one who built Uruk, became king and reigned for 420 years. Divine Lugalbanda, a shepherd, ruled for 1200 years. Divine Dumuzi, a fisherman, his city was Ku'ara, ruled for 100 years. Divine Gilgamesh, his father was a lillu-demon, an en-priest of Kullab; he ruled for 126 years. Urnungal, the son of the divine Gilgamesh, ruled for thirty years.[3]

Other sources of a pseudo-historical nature by and large confirm this traditional lineage. The heroic epics, however, concern themselves only with the kings Enmerkar, Lugalbanda, and Gilgamesh.

The epics in which Enmerkar and Lugalbanda are the protagonists reflect the relations between lower Mesopotamia and the Iranian plateau during the fourth and third millennia B.C. Archeological excavations on the Iranian plateau within the last decade have made available an ever increasing amount of data which corroborate the historical information given in these epics and enable us to better understand them from a cultural point of view. The epic tales in which Gilgamesh plays the central role do not share the historical background of the Enmerkar and Lugalbanda epics. The Gilgamesh cycle is less concerned with history and more concerned with the general themes of man's existence, specifically: the fear of death and the quest for eternal youth and eternal life. For this reason, *Gilgamesh* cannot be considered an heroic epic in the strictest sense of that term.

The Mesopotamian heroic epics of Enmerkar and Lugalbanda owe their continuing existence to the fact that a Sumerian dynasty, the Third Dynasty of Ur (ca. 2112–2004 B.C.), originated in Uruk, the city of these epic rulers. The rulers of the Third Dynasty of Ur even proclaimed that Lugalbanda was their father and Gilgamesh their brother. Since they represented a local tradition, the epic tales concerned with the heroic past of the city were cherished at court, written down, and thus passed on as a part of the curriculum in Sumerian schools. The earliest written copies of these tales, however, date only from the eighteenth and seventeenth centuries B.C. Whether this is due to the haphazard nature of archeological findings or to some other reason is still not known.

When Sumerian ceased to be a spoken language and Akkadian became the language in which written and oral communication took place in Mesopotamia, most of the Sumerian literary corpus (with a few exceptions) was no longer taught in the Mesopotamian schools. In exceptional cases the scribes simply added an interlinear Akkadian translation to the Sumerian text. This happened to a short episode of the Lugalbanda epic, but the bulk of the Enmerkar and Lugalbanda epics were never rendered into Akkadian. The various epic tales about Gilgamesh did not share this fate. They were not only translated into Akkadian, but were also completely reworked. The extent of the modification remains unknown at the present time, but on the basis of the different Akkadian versions of the Gilgamesh epic we can state that the several individual epic tales of the Sumerian Gilgamesh cycle were transformed into one comprehensive and unified story. Part of one of the Sumerian Gilgamesh tales was translated verbatim into Akkadian and now forms the twelfth tablet of the Ninevite version of the epic, to be discussed later.

The Enmerkar Epic: Enmerkar and the Lord of Aratta

The two protagonists of the Enmerkar epic are the King of Uruk, Enmerkar, and the "Lord of Aratta." The prologue describes two cities, Uruk in lower Mesopotamia and Aratta in eastern Iran. The Lord of Aratta has built a temple for Inanna, the goddess of Uruk, who is also worshipped in Aratta; this temple is adorned sumptuously with the precious stones for which Aratta is famous and on which its wealth is founded. Nevertheless, the goddess Inanna favors Enmerkar. Enmerkar is aware of Aratta's wealth in precious stones and metals and urges Inanna to subdue Aratta under Uruk's rule. The goddess agrees, but

suggests that he send a messenger to Aratta and describes the route in detail.
Enmerkar follows her advice and instructs his messenger. The message is
blunt and direct:

> I will make your people fall, lay waste your city and destroy it entirely unless you
> submit to my lord and send precious stones and metals to Uruk so that he can
> build a temple for Inanna.[4]

The messenger does as he is told. The Lord of Aratta at first finds a solution
to his dilemma. Rather than resorting to battle, he proposes a different kind of
contest: the accomplishment of tasks described in riddles will decide between
the two contestants. The Sumerian word for the contest is the same as that
used for a specific literary genre, the so-called disputations, or contest literature, in which antagonists or contestants, such as summer and winter or bird
and fish, dispute each other's value to civilization.[5]

The first task the Lord of Aratta asks Enmerkar to accomplish is to send
donkey-loads of barley to Aratta in nets, not sacks, saying that if Enmerkar is
successful he will gladly concede his superiority. The messenger returns to
Uruk. Enmerkar easily finds a solution with the aid of the grain goddess
Nisaba: he lets the barley sprout so that the sprouts keep the barley from
falling through the nets. Thus prepared, Enmerkar sends his caravan to Aratta,
but not without giving his messenger a task for the Lord of Aratta: he shall
have his craftsmen fashion a scepter which looks like Enmerkar's and send it
to Uruk.

In hunger-stricken Aratta there is great disappointment, since the barley
brought from Uruk cannot be used as seed-grain. The people of Aratta, feeling
deceived, want to respond in kind and suggest to the Lord of Aratta that the
scepter for Enmerkar be made not of carnelian and lapis lazuli, but of substi-
tutes. The elders of Aratta, however, consider this the wrong way to deal with
the situation. Nevertheless, the Lord of Aratta is unable to produce the scepter
and after painful searching for a solution, he answers with a new task for
Enmerkar to perform.

Enmerkar is asked to fashion a scepter which is made of materials hitherto
unknown to mankind. Enki, the trickster among the Sumerian gods, provides
the solution. Enmerkar plants a particular reed which is harvested after growing for ten years, and a scepter is made from it. It is then varnished to give the
appearance of an unknown material.

When the messenger of Enmerkar hands the scepter over to the Lord of
Aratta, the latter is again baffled, until he sees through the trickery. He
decides to respond with a new demand, suggesting they solve the contest with
a fight between two warriors. The warrior selected by Enmerkar must be
colorless—not black, not white, not brown, not [a word denoting some color,
not decipherable], not yellow, not dappled. Enmerkar, confronted with this
riddle, is unable to come up with a solution and in turn demands that a

comparable task be solved by the Lord of Aratta: he is to produce a colorless garment. But this time, unlike on earlier occasions, Enmerkar's messenger is not able to repeat the words of the message, so Enmerkar forms a clay tablet and writes the message down.[6] When the messenger delivers the tablet, the Lord of Aratta is clearly impressed, but obviously unable to understand the message.

At this juncture the whole contest between the two cities and their rulers moves in a different direction: divine intervention leads to a peaceful solution, and the contest between the two fighters is called off. Enmerkar's initial demand for precious stones and metals is satisfied, not through the submission of the Lord of Aratta, but through the establishment of peaceful trade relations.

The Lugalbanda Epic

The background of the Lugalbanda epic, like that of the Enmerkar epic, is the conflict between Uruk and Aratta. Again, the reason for the conflict is Uruk's need for access to the sources of precious stones and metals.

Enmerkar, the King of Uruk, marches toward Aratta with an impressive force. In addition to Enmerkar, the army has seven leaders called the brothers and friends of Lugalbanda, the hero of the epic who, according to the pseudo-historical tradition of the Sumerian King List, later succeeded Enmerkar to the throne of Uruk. Lugalbanda accompanies the army apparently with no specific commission. Soon he is stricken with a mysterious disease, and his brothers are convinced that he has died. They abandon his body where it lies, intending to retrieve it on their return journey; for the time being they place around him food and drink as for funeral rites.

After two days, with the army of Uruk on its way to Aratta, Lugalbanda awakens from his long period of unconsciousness. He is desperate and expresses his feelings in prayers directed to the sun-god, the moon-god, and Inanna, the goddess of Uruk. His prayers are heeded; the gods give him new strength, whereupon he tries to catch up with his brothers and the army of Uruk.

From this point on, the text is not completely preserved, which makes it difficult to determine exactly what happened. It seems, however, that Lugalbanda is unable to find his brothers alone and turns to the gods for help. Two attempts apparently fail. He then decides to go to the Anzu-bird, a mythological creature of divine status. Lugalbanda reaches the bird's nesting place while the bird is absent, feeds the bird's young, and decorates the young with black eye-paint and cedar twigs (both items are known from other sources to possess honorific and magical meaning). When the Anzu-bird returns and finds its young thus adorned, it is enchanted and promises the benefactor, if he be human, the fulfillment of a wish. When Lugalbanda steps into the open, the Anzu-bird makes three offers which Lugalbanda rejects: wealth, a strong weapon, and finally, a good life. Lugalbanda responds by asking instead for the ability to run fast and with endurance wherever he wants. Moreover, he offers the Anzu-bird worship in the temples of Uruk if he is allowed to return safely and with honors to Uruk. (This additional offer has the appearance of a later addition to the original plot. It could conceivably be an etiological interpretation of the worship of the Anzu-bird in Mesopotamian temples.)

After granting the wish, the Anzu-bird accompanies Lugalbanda on his way to the army of Uruk. Before leaving Lugalbanda, the Anzu-bird admonishes him not to reveal this encounter to his brothers. The bird departs, and Lugalbanda enters the camp. His brothers are perplexed, not to say frightened, because

> He who walks [alone] in the great mountains, where nobody dares to walk alone by himself,
> Never returns to the living. — How did you succeed?[7]

They try to make him reveal his adventures, but he gives them only evasive answers, telling them that he ate acorns and grass. It seems that they are not entirely satisfied with his answers.

The army proceeds toward Aratta and finally lays siege to the city. After a year of futile efforts to conquer the city, Enmerkar becomes desperate and seeks help and advice from the goddess Inanna. When nobody is willing to make the journey to Uruk in order to carry the message to the goddess, Lugalbanda steps forward, but requests that he go alone, in order to guard his secret. Having no other choice, Enmerkar agrees. He prepares a harsh and reproachful message to Inanna. Feeling that she has deserted him, he asks her permission to give up the siege and return to Uruk empty-handed.

When Lugalbanda emerges from the meeting with Enmerkar to begin his journey, his brothers try to hold him back and to force him to take a companion with him. Here the story strongly hints at a conflict between Lugalbanda and his brothers, since "They growl at him as if he were a strange dog who wants to join a pack of dogs."[8] They also threaten him with expulsion from their community, but Lugalbanda's brief reply puts them into a state of discomfort and anxiety.

Lugalbanda departs and, owing to his secret strength, quickly reaches Uruk, where he relates Enmerkar's message to Inanna. The goddess, however, does not accept Enmerkar's request. Instead she reveals to Lugalbanda a secret ploy for overcoming Aratta's strength: in the waters around Aratta lives a certain fish which has in it the strength of Aratta. Enmerkar is to cut down a particular tamarisk which grows apart from the other tamarisks on the bank of the river and to make a bucket from its wood. He must then catch the fish, prepare it elaborately, and place it before the *a'ankara*-weapon, Inanna's standard in the camp of the Uruk army. This magic ritual will place the victory in the hands of Enmerkar and his army. After the conquest, Enmerkar will bring not only Aratta's treasures, but also its craftsmen and their tools back to Uruk.

In the version that has come down to us, the epic does not give an account of Lugalbanda's return to the camp and the eventual victory of Enmerkar over Aratta. It ends abruptly here, taking for granted the successful outcome.

The Gilgamesh Epic

Gilgamesh is the most famous Mesopotamian literary epic. The form in which the story of Gilgamesh is known to modern man is the version which was found among the tablets of Ashurbanipal's library in Nineveh (668–27 B.C.). This version, called the Late, or Ninevite, Version, and another, slightly different rendition found in a few fragmentary tablets from Chaldean or Achaemenid times (seventh to fourth centuries B.C.), differ somewhat from the account of the epic given by the Greek writer Aelian (A.D. 170–235).

The version preserved on the tablets from Ashurbanipal's library was, according to its colophon, compiled in the second half of the second millennium B.C. by a man named Sinleqeunninni. It consisted of twelve tablets which, by and large, could be compared to the books of Homer's *Iliad*. Each tablet had 200 to 300 lines. However, only the texts of tablets 1, 6, and 10–12 are reasonably intact. Most of the others are so poorly preserved that sometimes not even a third of the original material is accessible. Parts of the lost passages, however, can be tentatively reconstructed from older versions of the epic. Caution is necessary with these reconstructions, since the older versions are only in part parallel to the more recent version. Nevertheless, the story of Gilgamesh and his quest for eternal life can be told in outline.

Some of the versions which served as forerunners to the Late or Ninevite version of the Gilgamesh epic are known to us. At the time Sinleqeunninni compiled his version, the epic was well-known outside Mesopotamia proper: fragmentary tablets of the Gilgamesh epic have been found in Megiddo in Palestine and in Hattusha, the capital of the Hittite empire, not far from present-day Ankara, Turkey. From Hattusha we also have fragments of the epic written in Hittite, an Indo-European language, and in Hurrian, a language of unknown affiliation. Several tablets from the Old Babylonian period (1894–1595 B.C.) containing parts of the Gilgamesh story have been discovered over the years. They parallel mainly those episodes which are contained in the second, third, and tenth tablets of the Ninevite version. The story of the Deluge, which is incorporated into the eleventh tablet of the Ninevite version, is also known from this period, but here it appears in the so-called Atrahasis myth.[9] A comparison of the Old Babylonian and Ninevite versions demonstrates the considerable transformation this story has undergone.

Another dimension is added when we consider the Sumerian predecessors of the story, of which five compositions are known. These all seem to be self-contained stories without direct relation to one another. The extant copies of these five compositions were written in the eighteenth century B.C., although the works are known to be older, presumably originating as early as the twenty-first century B.C. Their titles, as cited in modern scholarship, are: "Gilgamesh and Agga of Kish"; "Gilgamesh and the Land of the Living";

"Gilgamesh and the Bull of Heaven"; "Gilgamesh, Enkidu, and the Netherworld"; and "The Death of Gilgamesh."

THE SUMERIAN COMPOSITIONS

"Gilgamesh and Agga of Kish" centers around a historical event, a conflict between the city-states of Uruk and Kish, alluded to also in a hymn to King Shulgi (2094–47 B.C.). In the hymn, however, the event is connected with Agga's father Enmebaragesi, who was a historical personality, as a votive inscription of his which has survived affirms. This type of evidence reinforces the Mesopotamians' view of the protagonists of their epic tales as historical personalities.

The messengers of Agga demand Uruk's submission to the rule of Kish. Gilgamesh addresses the elders of Uruk, urging them to reject the demand. The elders, however, do not agree with this, so Gilgamesh turns to the young men of the city who, like himself, yearn for war. Agga lays siege to Uruk. To find a way out of the situation, Gilgamesh sends a man to Agga's camp. While the soldiers of the army of Kish are beating the man, the forces of Uruk behind the walls take advantage of this diversion and are thus able to defeat the army of Kish.[10] Agga is taken prisoner, but finds mercy at the hands of Gilgamesh, who sets him free out of gratitude for some good deeds done for him by Agga in the past. The story in its present form, although preserved in its entirety, lacks thrust and dramatic structure.

"Gilgamesh and the Land of the Living" contains the theme central to all of the Gilgamesh stories during their long histories of literary transformation: Gilgamesh's endeavor to make himself famous. This theme is reminiscent of the purpose of Mesopotamian royal inscriptions, which usually link fame to the building activities of a ruler. Only in the inscriptions of the kings of Akkad (2334–2154 B.C.), in a few earlier inscriptions, and in those from the last part of the second millennium B.C. are military achievements listed in order to establish fame.

In the context of epic tales, other elements, such as the protagonist's performance of outstanding deeds, like killing mythological monsters, become more prominent. In "Gilgamesh and the Land of the Living," the quest consists of a journey to the "Land of the Living," where Gilgamesh, with his friend Enkidu, cuts down fifty cedar trees and kills the guard, the mythical monster Humbaba. The motifs and the structure of this story are quite similar to those of fairy tales. Moreover, the Sumerian (as well as later versions) is filled with mythological allusions and topics which were added to the original story.

The third Sumerian Gilgamesh story, "Gilgamesh and the Bull of Heaven," is poorly preserved. It parallels the story related in the well-preserved sixth tablet of the Ninevite version.

"Gilgamesh, Enkidu, and the Netherworld" is the longest (some 330 lines) and best-preserved of the Sumerian Gilgamesh stories. Inanna, the goddess of

Uruk, plants a tree in her garden from which she wants to fashion a bed and a throne once the tree is grown. However, when the time comes to build, a snake is found nesting among the tree's roots, the Anzu-bird is perching in its branches, and a demon dwells in its trunk. Inanna asks her brother the sun-god for help, but he does not heed her plea. When she complains to Gilgamesh, he immediately consents to cut down the tree. As a sign of her appreciation, Inanna presents him with a ring and a staff (known from other sources to be a kind of plaything). With the help of these objects, Gilgamesh oppresses the people of Uruk (the meaning of this episode is not entirely clear). When the people complain about the oppression, the ring and the staff fall into the netherworld. Realizing that he cannot bring them back, Gilgamesh sits down at the gate to the netherworld and weeps.

Enkidu is moved by Gilgamesh's emotion and volunteers to go down to the netherworld to recover the ring and the staff. Gilgamesh gives him a detailed description of how to behave in the netherworld without arousing its inhabitants, but for reasons not clear to us, Enkidu does just the opposite of what Gilgamesh advises, and is consequently held back in the netherworld. Gilgamesh asks the gods for help. After two unsuccessful pleas, Enki, the trickster among the gods, comes to Gilgamesh's aid: he instructs the sun-god to dig a hole into the earth so Enkidu can escape. Enkidu reappears, but it is unclear to us whether he is still a living being or already a shade. Gilgamesh then asks about the fate of those inhabiting the netherworld:

> 'Did you see him who was cursed by his father and mother?'
> 'I saw him.' — 'How does he fare?' — 'He lacks an heir; his spirit roams
> about.'[11]

In some sixty questions patterned in this manner, Gilgamesh inquires after the fate in the netherworld of the deceased from all walks of life. His final question concerns his parents; here the story in its present form ends abruptly.

"The Death of Gilgamesh" is so poorly preserved that nothing definitive can be said about its plot. A few lines at the beginning of the composition employ the theme which is also an integral part of the other Gilgamesh stories: the quest for eternal life.

> Enlil, the great mountain, the father of the gods
> Has destined your fate, oh Gilgamesh, for kingship;
> For eternal life he has not destined it![12]

THE AKKADIAN VERSIONS

In the opening lines of the twelve-tablet Ninevite version of the Gilgamesh epic, Gilgamesh, the ruler of Uruk, is described as a man perfect in build, two-thirds god and one-third human, but restless and oppressive toward the people of Uruk. As the people beseech the gods in their desperation, the mother goddess decides to create Enkidu as a rival to divert Gilgamesh's energies.

Enkidu, the man of the steppe, lives among the wild animals. While roaming on the steppe, a hunter encounters him and later describes him in Uruk. Gilgamesh, who was forewarned of Enkidu's existence in two dreams, is fascinated. He orders the hunter to return to the steppe accompanied by a harlot who is to entice Enkidu so that the animals of the steppe will be estranged from him. The trick is successful: the animals flee, and Enkidu agrees to go with the harlot to Uruk. There the two men have an encounter culminating in a wrestling match, which apparently is won by Gilgamesh. Enkidu praises him and they become friends.

In the third tablet, Gilgamesh decides to journey to the forest of Lebanon to kill Humbaba and fell a certain cedar tree. The purpose of this adventure is not entirely clear, but Gilgamesh's motivation is made explicit:

If I am killed in battle my fame would remain:
"Gilgamesh has waged war against the frightful Humbaba,"
thus it will be said.[13]

A few lines later Gilgamesh phrases his intensions thus:

I want to see the one about whom people talk.
He, whose name they utter all over the country
I want to encounter in the middle of the cedar forest.
The country shall hear
that I who was born in Uruk am a mighty one.
I shall go forward, I shall cut down the cedar tree,
I will make my fame lasting.[14]

The fourth and fifth tablets of the Ninevite version, though preserved poorly, report the journey of Gilgamesh and Enkidu to the cedar forest where they eventually kill Humbaba.

After they return to Uruk with their fame established, Inanna desires Gilgamesh as her spouse. Gilgamesh, however, rejects her. His speech is reproachful, reminding her of her past lovers and husbands, all of whom she treated cruelly. Inanna, furious about the rejection, asks her father Anu to send the Bull of Heaven down to earth to kill Gilgamesh. She threatens that if he does not comply with her demand, she will open the gates of the netherworld for all the dead to emerge. So Anu sends the Bull of Heaven. The bull soon encounters Enkidu and Gilgamesh, who eventually kill him. Gilgamesh says:

Who is the most wonderful among the young warriors?
Who is the strongest among the valiant young men?
Gilgamesh is the most wonderful among the young warriors,
Gilgamesh is the strongest among the valiant young men.[15]

The beginning of the seventh tablet marks the turning point of the epic.

Enkidu is beset by alarming dreams which predict his death. At the end of the tablet he becomes sick and, facing death, tells Gilgamesh:

> Not as one fallen in battle shall I die.
> I feared the battle and shall die ingloriously.
> O my friend, he who falls in battle is blessed.[16]

Enkidu dies after nine days. Gilgamesh mourns his dead friend for seven days and, trying desperately to bring Enkidu back to life, he does not permit his burial. Finally, however, he realizes the inevitable.

With his search for fame and glory stopped so suddenly and so irrevocably by the basic human experience of the reality of death, Gilgamesh sets out on his quest for eternal life and youth. He decides to journey to his forefather, the mythical Utnapishtim, the Mesopotamian Noah who survived the flood.

The story told in the ninth to eleventh tablets of the Ninevite version is elaborately structured. On his way through desolate deserts and rugged mountains, Gilgamesh has several adverse encounters. First he drives away and kills the lions in the desert. Later he meets a pair of fear-inspiring mythical beings, half man and half scorpion, who turn out to be benevolent and give guidance to him for the next adventure—his journey through total darkness for twenty-four hours. From this adventure he emerges to find himself in a pleasure garden made entirely of precious stones.

In the second part of his journey, Gilgamesh encounters three benevolent persons: the woman Siduri, an innkeeper at the edge of the earth, Urshanabi, the ferryman who carries Gilgamesh across the "waters of death" to the goal of his journey, and his ancestor Utnapishtim. Crossing the waters of death is the final adventure. It is made dangerous by the fact that after his arrival at the edge of the earth, Gilgamesh, in a rage, had killed "those of stone," mythical beings which lie at the edge of the earth in order to guard those crossing over from touching the waters of death.

Gilgamesh's search for eternal life proceeds in three steps. When he meets the woman Siduri, she offers him little hope; in fact, she tells him to abandon his search and content himself with the joys of life as they are. Secondly, Utnapishtim reminds him of the futility of his quest, since the gods have already determined the destiny of every human being. Finally, as a third step, and only when Gilgamesh begs him desperately, Utnapishtim offers a magic means of gaining eternal life. Gilgamesh must stay awake for six days. When he fails, Utnapishtim offers him a second chance, letting him bathe in a well (this has been interpreted as the Fountain of Youth, but the text is not sufficiently clear to make this interpretation certain). Because he fails a second time, Utnapishtim finally tells Gilgamesh how to find the Plant of Life, whose name is "Man-becomes-young-when-he-is-old." Gilgamesh finds the plant, but on his way back to Uruk, a snake steals the plant while he is bathing. Gilgamesh thus misses his last chance in the quest for eternal life. Returning to Uruk, however, he proudly shows Urshanabi, the ferryman, his handiwork: the walls of the city of Uruk.

The poet's subtle approach in concluding the epic with praise of the magnificent walls of Uruk gains an added dimension when one considers the fact that when he compiled the epic (some time in the latter part of the second millennium B.C.), these walls, "the ancient work of the divine Gilgamesh,"[17] were still visible to proclaim his glory. This finale is set against the theme of the story, which leads Gilgamesh from a search for personal fame to a quest for eternal life.

The Function of the Epics

An attempt must be made to determine the function of the Mesopotamian epics. Were they written and recited for pure entertainment, or did they have other functions? The question of function is relevant to all genres of Mesopotamian literature. For instance, the creation story was regularly recited during the New Year's festival in Babylon and disputations were recited in the royal court for entertainment. It seems reasonable to suppose that the Sumerian epics were recited at the court for the same purpose. Such a *raison d'être* for these epics would not be surprising in view of the very nature of the tales, i.e., the glorification of great adventures. One might ask, however, whether this function also holds true for the Akkadian Gilgamesh versions. Despite all the artistry, elaborate structure, and wealth of narration in these versions, they have a tragic tone, a pessimistic note. The Akkadian Gilgamesh epic does not merely glorify adventure; it conveys a message. The emphasis lies not on entertainment, but on edification; the epic is didactic in intent.

A clue which helps us understand the purpose of the epic and determine its literary genre in terms of the Akkadians themselves is a line in the prologue to the Ninevite version:

He [Gilgamesh] has written upon a monument all his
burdensome adventures.[18]

The fiction that Gilgamesh himself inscribed his adventures on a monument and that the poet drew his information from this inscription when compiling the epic is not unique in Akkadian literature. There is a genre of didactic tales or legends which uses as its literary form the commemorative royal inscription or the tomb inscription. (Because of this convention, Assyriologists used to label this literary genre *narû* [monument]–literature.) In these tales of legends, a message to the audience follows the narration. This is a benediction or a reproach, depending upon the positive or negative nature of the narration.[19]

The Mesopotamian historical epics (*narû*–literature) can be divided into two groups according to their contents. The first is basically concerned with events that took place during the Dynasty of Akkade, the first Semitic dynasty in Mesopotamia, which for the first time brought large parts of the Fertile Crescent from the Persian Gulf to the shores of the Mediterranean Sea under Mesopotamian rule. The second group relates events which generally fall into the second half of the second millennium B.C. Our knowledge of both groups of texts is very limited since most of them have survived only in fragments. It is clear, however, that they are quite different in intent from the Sumerian epics̄about Enmerkar, Lugalbanda, and Gilgamesh. On the other hand, there are obvious connections between the *narû*–literature and the several Akkadian versions of the Gilgamesh epic. The fiction that they are commemorative royal inscriptions or purport to use such an inscription as a source is one parallel; the didactic intent of the message is another.

This adaptation of the Sumerian Gilgamesh stories and their transformation into a new literary genre by Akkadian-speaking scribes took place some time in the beginning of the second millennium B.C.

Literary and Stylistic Evaluation of the Mesopotamian Heroic Epic

The evaluation and appreciation from a literary point of view of the Mesopotamian heroic epic as well as of other works of Mesopotamian literature is still beset by many difficulties. In the first place, many of the epics are not preserved in their entirety. Secondly, most of them have been known to us for only thirty years or less. The standard edition of the Akkadian Gilgamesh epic by Thompson was published no earlier than 1930. For some of the epic tales concerning Gilgamesh and Lugalbanda we still must wait for a critical edition of the texts. In the meantime we must settle for preliminary outlines or translations, such as the first part of the Lugalbanda epic, or "Gilgamesh and the Bull of Heaven." It is understandable that under these circumstances scholars in the field of Assyriology are still heavily engaged in philological, text-critical, and editorial work concerning these epics. Although we are able to translate the epics to a large extent, numerous obstacles of a semantic or grammatical nature remain, which often make it impossible to gain a full understanding of crucial passages. Sometimes we do not even recognize the existence of difficulties which lie hidden beneath the surface of a seemingly problemless text.

It does not come as a surprise, therefore, that very little attention is being given to questions of a literary-critical nature, such as those of structure, style, and content. It seems most revealing in this context that in a volume of papers read during an international conference on Gilgamesh, only two papers dealt with questions of literary criticism in a wider sense. Th. Liagre-Böhl's paper is concerned with metrical problems.[20] The other paper is a German translation of B. Landsberger's introduction to a 1942 Turkish edition of the Gilgamesh epic.[21] He considers the Gilgamesh epic to be the national epic of the Babylonians. His evaluation is based on the fact that the epic addresses itself to every inhabitant of Babylonia, since the protagonist of the epic, Gilgamesh, represents in a unique way the ideal of a man as conceived by the Babylonians themselves. Furthermore, it deserves its status as the Babylonian national epic because it is deeply concerned with the question of human life.

There is, however, one major exception to the statement concerning this preoccupation with philological problems. Since the early days of Assyriology, many scholars have compared the Gilgamesh epic with Biblical narratives. There are a number of parallels; the story of the Flood as narrated in the eleventh tablet of *Gilgamesh* might serve as an example. One of the most recent illustrations of this approach is Alexander Heidel's book *The Gilgamesh Epic and Old Testament Parallels.*[22] The limitations of such an approach are obvious. Comparisons with epics and literary traditions of other cultures may, in general, be fruitful and lead to new insights. One should not, however, underestimate the danger that concepts and ideas alien to Mesopotamia could misdirect the evaluation and interpretation of the Mesopotamian epics. Therefore, the main emphasis in all future work on the Mesopotamian epic tradition should be placed on the uniqueness of the Mesopotamian elements in these epics.

A full and comprehensive view of the content and the message of these epics is dependent upon a full understanding of the formal aspects of the Mesopotamian epic texts. A short outline concerning these questions is, therefore, appropriate.

The basic unit of Akkadian poetry is the verse. It usually consists of four metric units, but shorter and longer ones are also found (it seems that semantic considerations are responsible for this). A metric unit in general consists of a word or a word combination, which is usually a noun followed by another noun in the genitive case or a preposition followed by a noun. The length of the words is of no importance. However, the question of meter in Akkadian poetry is still unresolved, and even successive verses often have different metric structures. The sort of rhythmic structure found in Greek metrics apparently does not exist, though many verses (but not all) have a trochaic ending. These lines from the Old Babylonian Gilgamesh epic serve as an illustration of verse structures:[23]

iṣṣabtuma kīma lē'îm ilūdu	(3)
sippam i' butu igārum irtud	(2+2)
Gilgāmeš u Enkidu iṣṣabtuma kīma lē'îm ilūdu	(3+2)
sippam i' butu igārum irtud	(2+2)

> They grappled with each other, they bent their knees like wrestlers;
> They shook the doorpost, the wall was trembling;
> Gilgamesh and Enkidu grappled with each other, they bent their knees like wrestlers;
> They shook the doorpost, the wall was trembling.

When considering the individual verse, we observe all those poetic features which transform an otherwise ordinary sentence into something poetic. Word order is different from normal prose syntax and, to a certain degree, is influ-

enced by metric considerations. Infrequent grammatical forms are used.
Words rare in occurrence or special in nuance are chosen carefully to bring a
particularly poetic note to the verse. This choice of words is realized on the
semantic level by the use of synonymous words, suggesting to the reader or
listener a wide range of allusions or word play. On the phonetic level, the
choice of words results in vowel and consonantal alliterations or rhyme patterns.[24] In addition to and complementing these features, comparisons,
similes,[25] proverbs and popular sayings are widely used in Akkadian and
Sumerian poetry to describe situations or actions delicately and to express
abstract notions which otherwise would be hard to render. Notice, for instance, a line from Lugalbanda's prayer to the sun-god. Deserted by his
companions, he lies sick in the mountains, facing almost certain death: "Like
a throwing stick I don't want to be thrown away in the steppe which I don't
know."[26] All the despair due to his loneliness and the awareness that his life
will end unfulfilled and senseless is put into this one verse.

In another example from the Old Babylonian Gilgamesh epic, a simple
comparison is combined with an allusion: "She [the harlot] clasped his [En-
kidu's] hand guiding him like a deity."[27] This verse is not immediately clear,
at least for modern readers. When one compares certain contemporary representations on cylinder seals, however, the intention of the poet becomes
apparent. The representations show a worshipper introduced to a deity by a
minor deity who extends its bent arm backwards to take the outstretched hand
of the worshipper. It seems that the author of this Old Babylonian Gilgamesh
version, by using the comparison "like a deity," wanted to specify a particular posture in which the harlot led Enkidu. The harlot and Enkidu are not
going side by side holding hands as a mother and child do, but she walks
ahead of him and he follows timidly. Moreover, the author's choice demonstrates a subtlety not shown in simple comparisons, such as "like a mother"
or "like a child."[28]

A stylistic feature that has not been sufficiently recognized as a poetic
device in Sumerian or Akkadian literature is the principle of ambiguity.[29] A
good example of this is provided in a line from the description of the wrestling
match between Gilgamesh and Enkidu found in the Old Babylonian version of
the Gilgamesh epic cited above. After stating that they grappled with each
other, the poet amplifies this statement with a second sentence, using a comparison. Scholars have translated this line in several ways:

> They held on to each other like bulls (Speiser);[30]
> They bent their knees like bulls (von Soden);[31]
> They bent their knees like wrestlers (Assyrian Dictionary).[32]

The ambiguity in this verse is based on the phonetic similarity of the comparison "like bulls" (*kīma lîm*) to "like wrestlers" (*kīma lē'îm*). The second
ambiguity in the verse concerns the verb. No distinction is made in the writing

of the verbal form: *i–lu–DU* can stand for *ilūṭu* (they kept [each other] in check) as well as for *iludu* (they bent their knees).

Individual verses are related to each other principally by formulating an idea or statement into two parallel syntactic units, including antithetic and supplementary statements. This device, which is generally evident in ancient Near Eastern literature and best known from the Biblical Psalms, is called *parallelismus membrorum*. In the simplest case, such as in the four lines from the Old Babylonian Gilgamesh epic quoted above, a statement is repeated, using a synonymous word to replace just one word within the verse. In another case half of a verse remains unchanged, whereas the other part adds a new statement:

> To face a battle he does not know,
> To travel a road he does not know.[33]

Simple examples of a supplementary parallelism are the following:

> Of ramparted Uruk the wall be built
> Of sacred Eanna the bright storehouse.[34]

Or, of Enkidu it is said that

> With gazelles he feeds on grass,
> With wild beasts he drinks at the watering place,
> With the creeping creatures his heart delights in water.[35]

The following lines illustrate an antithetic parallelism:

> The darkness is dense, there is no light;
> Unable is he to see what lies ahead of him or behind.[36]

Here the antithesis is expressed in two half-verses as plain statements of fact. The following verse, however, restates the antithetically expressed facts from the viewpoint of the protagonist, thus combining two types of parallelism within a pair of two verses. As these examples, and others in earlier passages, show, *parallelismus membrorum* as a poetic device has no limits to its possible variations.

Groups of verses united by their sense of meaning are the basic building blocks for the structure of a whole narrative. These units are not indicated by any graphic means such as spacing or dividing lines. Rather, the semantics and the flow of action provide structure, and many devices exist therein for giving shape to an epic poem. This is achieved, for instance, through dialogues between the characters. Another device is the sudden change of scene, which easily creates suspense. An especially typical device is repetition, a

good example of which can be found in the fourth tablet of the Ninevite
version of the Gilgamesh epic. In this tablet, Gilgamesh and his companion,
Enkidu, are on their way from Babylonia to the cedar mountains in distant
Lebanon in order to kill the monster Humbaba. Gilgamesh, obviously having
second thoughts about the adventure, seeks divine guidance and reassurance.
As the friends set up camp at the end of each day's journey, Gilgamesh lies
down, seeking a dream:

> After twenty double-hours they broke off a bite to eat;
> After thirty double-hours they stopped for the night;
> For fifty double-hours they traveled the whole day.
> A journey of a whole month and fifteen days they accomplished within three days
>   drawing closer to the Lebanon mountains.
> Before the sun-god, Shamash, they dug a well, set up . . .;
> Gilgamesh ascended to the mountain's summit.
> His toasted flour he poured out as offering to . . .:
> "Mountain, bring me a dream, grant me a propitious omen."
> Enkidu set up camp for him, . . .;
> As a protection against the storm-wind he fastened the tent-flaps;
> He made him lie down within the camp;
> . . . like grain of the mountains . . .;
> Gilgamesh rested his chin on his knees;
> Sleep which gushes forth upon men fell upon him;
> In the middle watch of the night he brought his sleep to an end;
> He rose and said to his companion:
> "My friend, did you not call me? Why am I awake?"
> "Did you not touch me? Why am I startled?"
> "Did not a god pass by? Why is my flesh paralyzed?"
> "My friend, I have seen a dream,"
> "And the dream I saw is very frightening."

After Gilgamesh has reported his dream the text continues:

> Enkidu opened his mouth and spoke;
> To Gilgamesh he said:
> "The dream, my friend, which you saw. . . ."

Now follows the explanation of the dream which, as it happens, does not
banish Gilgamesh's anxieties. Enkidu, however, concludes with a word of
consolation: "In the morning we will hear good news from the sun-god."[37]
Immediately afterwards the story begins again with the words: "After twenty
double-hours they broke off a bite to eat." Five dreams altogether are reported
in this manner.

In other cases of repetition, an idea or intent is given as an instruction and
subsequently repeated verbatim while it is being executed. The introduction of
intermediary characters, such as messengers, increases the number of repeti-

tions. The analysis of a few lines from the Old Babylonian Gilgamesh epic may demonstrate how repetition can be used in a less schematic way than that just shown. The text runs as follows:

šizba ša namaštê ītenneq
akalam iškunu maḫaršu
iptēqma inaṭṭal u ippallas
ul idi Enkidu akalam ana akālim
šikaram ana šatêm la lummud
ḫarimtum pīša īpušamma issaqaram ana Enkidu
akul aklam Enkidu simat balātim
šikaram šiti šīmti mātim
īkul aklam Enkidu adi šibêšu
šikaram ištiam sibit assammim
ittapšar kabtātum inangû
īliṣ libbašuma panūšu ittamru
ultappit gallābum šu'uram pagaršu
šamnam iptašašma awēliš iwwi
ilbaš libšam kīma mūti ibbašši.

He [Enkidu] used to suck the milk of the wild animals.
They placed bread in front of him;
He became tense, gazing and staring;
Not did Enkidu know how to eat bread;
To drink he had not been taught.
The harlot opened her mouth saying to Enkidu:
"Eat the bread, Enkidu, it is part of life";
"Drink the beer, as is the custom in the land."
Enkidu ate the bread until he was sated;
The beer he drank, seven goblets;
He became relaxed, his mood became jubilant,
His heart became enchanted, his face was beaming.
The barber went over his hairy body.
He [Enkidu] anointed himself with oil, thus becoming a human being;
He put on clothing thus becoming a man.[38]

The episode relates how Enkidu was transformed from a savage into a human being. This transformation removes him from the realm of creatures and places him into the realm of civilization. It is not expressed in abstract terms, but exemplified by focusing on his habits of subsistence. He ceases nourishing himself like a creature from the milk of wild animals; he accepts and likes the customs of civilization: eating bread, drinking beer, anointing himself with oil, and clothing himself with a garment. The author uses only two of these, eating and drinking, in the repetition, thus showing restraint and subtlety in choosing and applying his stylistic devices. The repetition itself is not schematic either, but first uses an infinitive construction as exposition and statement of the facts. This is followed by an order in the imperative which is introduced with the standard formula for introducing direct speech. The execution of the order is reported in the preterite.

In addition to featuring certain stylistic devices such as repetition, *parallelismus membrorum,* use of formulaic expressions, word play, and vowel alliterations, the episode also contains an allusion to the concept of the creation of the human race. According to mythological tradition and belief, man was created by the gods. Here, however, a distinction is made between the physical act of creation and that of becoming a human being, a member of the Mesopotamian civilization, without denying the mythological belief explicitly. This transformation is achieved by eating bread, drinking beer, anointing oneself, and clothing oneself. Here the author makes another allusion. Bread, beer, oil, and clothing are the staples which were distributed as daily rations by the central institutions, such as the temple or palace, to a large segment of the population; these rations were their only means of subsistence. Skillfully employed, as it is here, this device can enhance the poetic quality of an epic, although examples exist in which an unimaginative use of the device results in plain dullness.[39]

Another structuring device is contrast. This can be achieved in Sumerian and Akkadian poetry by putting elaborately and artfully devised features, such as those just described, in opposition to formulaic or stereotyped word pairs, epithets, or sentences which recur in all Sumerian and Akkadian epic and mythic texts.[40]

Dialogues, prayers, and dreams, with their interpretations, serve in the narrative as vehicles to express subtle reflections on matters of importance, or to convey to the listener the anxieties or other emotions of a character. The prayer of Lugalbanda to the sun-god illustrates this point:

O Utu, I want to greet you. I do not want to be ill any longer.
Hero, son of Ningal, I want to greet you. I do not want to be ill any longer.
O Utu, you made me take the road up into the mountains among my brethren—
In the most forbidden place inside the mountain region I do not want to be ill any
      longer.
At the place where the mother is not standing, the father is not standing,
Where an acquaintance is not standing, where a person I respect is not standing—
At that place my mother is not saying: "O my child."
At that place my brother is not saying: "O my brother."
Also, the neighbor's wife who has entered my mother's house, she does not
      lament me,
and—after the patron deities of my father and mother have stepped forward—
The patron deity of the neighborhood who used to pronounce (at childbirth): "A
      child is born," she does not lament me.
An unknown dog is bad, an unknown man is terrible.
But when one meets one on the unknown road at the edge of the mountain region,
O Utu, then an unknown man is even worse.
I do not want to rinse away at the . . . place;
Instead of barley I do not want to eat nitrous soil.

I do not want to be thrown away like a throwing stick in the unknown steppe.
Being known under a name which makes my brethren treat me with scorn—I do
    not want to be sick any longer;
Being mocked at by my brethren—I do not want to be sick any longer.
I do not want to find death in the mountains like a weakling.[41]

This short survey of the heroic epic in ancient Mesopotamia concludes with a note of caution. Works of Sumerian or Akkadian literature cannot yet be fully appreciated. We need more and better edited texts with good linguistic and lexicological analysis. Above all, however, literary-critical consideration of the texts based on their own merits, rather than in accordance with standards derived from other literatures, ancient or modern, is necessary.

NOTES

1. For a general introduction to Mesopotamian history and civilization, see A. Leo Oppenheim, *Ancient Mesopotamia: Portrait of a Dead Civilization* (Chicago: University of Chicago Press, 1964).

2. The en-priest or "high priest" represented the highest political and religious authority in Uruk during the first half of the third millennium B.C. Later the political power was vested in a king, and the functions of the en-priest were restricted to religious matters.

3. T. Jacobsen, *The Sumerian Kinglist,* Assyriological Studies, 11 (Chicago: University of Chicago Press, 1939), pp. 84 ff.

4. S. N. Kramer, *Enmerkar and the Lord of Aratta: A Sumerian Epic Tale of Iraq and Iran* (Philadelphia: The University Museum, 1952), pp. 13 ff., lines 115 ff., and pp. 18 ff., lines 188 ff.

5. For a general introduction to this literary genre, see J. J. A. van Dijk, *La sagesse suméro-accadienne* (Leiden: E. J. Brill, 1953), and C. Wilcke, "Sumerische Streitgedichte," in *Kindlers Literatur Lexikon,* VII (Zürich: Kindler Verlag, 1971), pp. 2151–54.

6. This episode has an etiological character, as it explains the invention of writing. Our archeological evidence shows that the first clay tablets with writing on them come from levels which date from the turn of the fourth to the third millennium B.C. They were found in Uruk, as well as at several sites on the Iranian plateau.

7. C. Wilcke, *Das Lugalbandaepos* (Wiesbaden: Otto Harrassowitz, 1969), pp. 112–13, lines 231–32.

8. Ibid., pp. 120–21, line 324.

9. W. G. Lambert and A. R. Millard, *Atra-Hasīs: The Babylonian Story of the Flood* (Oxford: The Clarendon Press, 1969).

10. This follows a suggestion made by my colleague W. Heimpel, who is at Berkeley.

11. A. Shaffer, *Sumerian Sources of Tablet XII of the Epic of Gilgamesh* (Ann Arbor, Michigan: University Microfilms, 1963), p. 120, lines 10–11.

12. S. N. Kramer, "The Death of Gilgamesh," in *Ancient Near Eastern Texts Relating to the Old Testament,* 3rd ed., ed. James B. Pritchard (Princeton: Princeton University Press, 1969), p. 50, lines 33–35.

13. R. C. Thompson, *The Epic of Gilgamesh* (Oxford: The Clarendon Press, 1930), p. 27, iv 13–15.

14. Ibid., p. 27, v 1–7.

15. Tablet VI, lines 182–85.

16. Tablet VII, vi 16–18.

17. F. Thureau-Dangin, *Die Sumerischen und Akkadischen Königsinschriften,* Vorderasiatische Bibliothek, I/1 (Leipzig: J. C. Hinrichs'sche Buchhandlung, 1907), p. 222, no. 2b.

18. Thompson, p. 11, line 8.

19. H. G. Güterbock, *Zeitschrift für Assyriologie* 42 (1934): 62 ff.; also a recent work by K. A. Grayson, *Babylonian Historical-Literary Texts* (Toronto and Buffalo: University of Toronto Press, 1975), pp. 7 ff., 42 ff.

20. F. M. Th. de Liagre-Böhl, "La métrique de l'épopée babylonienne," in *Gilgameš et sa légende,* ed. P. Garelli (Paris: Imprimerie Nationale/ Librairie C. Klincksieck, 1960), pp. 145–52.

21. B. Landsberger, "Einleitung in das Gilgameš-Epos (traduit du turc par F. R. Kraus)," ibid., pp. 1–30.

22. A. Heidel, *The Gilgamesh Epic and Old Testament Parallels* (Chicago: University of Chicago Press, 1964).

23. Thompson, p. 24, vi 15–23.

24. B. Groneberg, "Untersuchungen zum hymnisch-epischen Dialekt der altbabylonischen literarischen Texte" (Ph.D. diss., Münster, Westf., 1972), pp. 159 ff.

25. See W. Heimpel, *Tierbilder in der sumerischen Literatur* (Rome: Pontifical Biblical Institute, 1968); A. Schott, *Die Vergleiche in den akkadischen Königsinschriften* (Leipzig: J. C. Hinrichs'sche Buchhandlung, 1926).

26. Wilcke, pp. 79–81, line 163.

27. Thompson, p. 21, ii 31 ff.

28. J. Renger, in *Revue d'Assyriologie et d'Archéologie Orientale* 66 (1972): 190.

29. W. Empson, *Seven Types of Ambiguity* (London: Chatto and Windus/Oxford University Press, 1930); W. B. Stanford, *Ambiguity in Greek Literature: Studies in Theory and Practice* (Oxford: B. Blackwell, 1939).

30. E. A. Speiser in *Ancient Near Eastern Texts Relating to the Old Testament,* 3rd ed., ed. James B. Pritchard (Princeton: Princeton University Press, 1969), p. 78, line 21.

31. W. von Soden, *Das Gilgamesch-Epos* (Stuttgart: Reclam-Verlag, 1972), p. 29, line 224.

32. *The Chicago Assyrian Dictionary,* ed. A. L. Oppenheim et al., 50 (Chicago: The Oriental Institute, 1973), p. 36, s.v. "ladu."

33. Thompson, p. 31, ii 13 ff.

34. Ibid., p. 11, i 9 ff.

35. Ibid., p. 13, iv 3–5.

36. Ibid., p. 51, v 24 ff.

37. The reconstruction of this text follows the suggestions made by B. Landsberger, in *Revue d'Assyriologie et d'Archéologie Orientale* 62 (1968): 99.

38. Thompson, p. 21 ff., iii 1–17.

39. A good example is the Anzu-myth. For a translation see E. A. Speiser and A. K. Grayson, "The Myth of Zu," in *Ancient Near Eastern Texts Relating to the Old*

Testament, 3rd ed., ed. James B. Pritchard (Princeton: Princeton University Press, 1969), pp. 111–18, 514–17.

40. K. Hecker, *Untersuchungen zur akkadischen Epik* (Kevelaer/Neukirchen-Vluyn: Verlag Butzon und Berker/ Neukirchener Verlag, 1974), pp. 181 ff.

41. Wilcke, pp. 78 ff., lines 147–66.

BIBLIOGRAPHY

General

Groneberg, Brigitte, *Untersuchungen zum hymnisch-epischen Dialekt der altbabylonischen literarischen Texte.* Inaugural-Dissertation zur Erlangung des Doktorgrades der Philosophischen Fakultät der Westfälischen Wilhelms-Universität zu Münster (Westf.), 1972. This Ph.D. dissertation investigates a number of stylistic features of Akkadian poetry.

Hecker, Karl. *Untersuchungen zur akkadischen Epik.* Alter Orient und Altes Testament—Sonderreihe, Veröffentlichungen zur Kultur und Geschichte des Alten Orients, 8. Kevelaer/Neukirchen-Vluyn: Verlag Butzon und Berker/Neukirchener Verlag, 1974. A comprehensive study of all the known stylistic and poetic features of Akkadian literature.

Kramer, Samuel Noah. *The Sumerians: Their History, Culture, and Character.* Chicago: University of Chicago Press, 1963. A general introduction.

Oppenheim, A. Leo. *Ancient Mesopotamia: Portrait of a Dead Civilization.* Chicago: University of Chicago Press, 1964.

Roux, Georges. *Ancient Iraq.* London: Penguin Books, 1964.

Text Editions and Translations

Heidel, Alexander. *The Gilgamesh Epic and Old Testament Parallels.* Chicago: University of Chicago Press, 1964. Offers a translation of all the Akkadian Gilgamesh sources with a general discussion and interpretation of the epic. The main emphasis, however, is put on the parallels with the Old Testament. For a general audience.

Kramer, Samuel Noah. *Enmerkar and the Lord of Aratta: A Sumerian Epic Tale of Iraq and Iran.* Philadelphia: The University Museum, 1952. First edition of the text in transliteration and translation.

―――. "Gilgamesh and Agga." In *Ancient Near Eastern Texts Relating to the Old Testament.* 3rd ed., edited by James B. Pritchard, pp. 44–47. Princeton, N.J.: Princeton University Press, 1969. English translation with bibliography.

―――. "Gilgamesh and the Land of the Living." In *Ancient Near Eastern Texts Relating to the Old Testament.* 3rd ed., edited by James B. Pritchard, pp. 47–50. Princeton, N.J.: Princeton University Press, 1969. English translation with bibliography.

―――. "The Death of Gilgamesh." In *Ancient Near Eastern Texts Relating to the Old Testament.* 3rd ed., edited by James B. Pritchard, pp. 50–52. Princeton, N.J.: Princeton University Press, 1969. English translation with bibliography.

Labat, René. "Dieux et Heros: L'Épopée de Gilgamesh." In *Les religions du Proche-Orient asiatique, Textes babyloniens ougaritiques, hittites.* Edited by R. Labat et al., pp. 145–226. Paris: Fayard/Denoël, 1970. French translation with introduction and explanatory notes to the text.

Schott, Albert, and Wolfram von Soden. *Das Gilgamesch-Epos.* Neu übersetzt und mit Anmerkungen versehen von Albert Schott; ergänzt und teilweise neu gestaltet von Wolfram von Soden. Stuttgart: Reclam-Verlag, 1972. German translation of the Akkadian versions. Also containing short outlines of the Sumerian Gilgamesh stories.

Shaffer, Aron. *Sumerian Sources of Tablet XII of the Epic of Gilgamesh*. Ann Arbor, Michigan: University Microfilms, 1963 (no. 63–7085).

Speiser, Ephraim A., and A. Kirk Grayson. "The Epic of Gilgamesh." In *Ancient Near Eastern Texts Relating to the Old Testament*. 3rd ed., edited by James B. Pritchard, pp. 72–99, 503–07. Princeton, N.J.: Princeton University Press, 1969. Most up-to-date English translation with annotation and bibliography.

Thompson, R. Campbell. *The Epic of Gilgamesh: Text, Transliteration, and Notes*. Oxford: Clarendon Press, 1930. The only existing edition of the cuneiform text.

Wilcke, Claus. Lugalbandaepos. Wiesbaden: Otto Harrassowitz, 1969. Critical edition with introduction and extensive philological annotation.

Special Studies to Individual Epics

[Anonymous.] "Gilgameš-Epos." In *Kindlers Literatur Lexikon*, III. Zürich: Kindler Verlag, 1967. General discussion of the Akkadian, Sumerian, Hittite, and Hurrian versions of the epic.

de Vries, Jan. "The Epic Poetry of Non-Indo-European Nations." In his *Heroic Song and Heroic Legend*, pp. 138–43. New York: Oxford University Press, 1963.

Garelli, Paul, ed. *Gilgameš et sa légende*. Paris: Imprimerie Nationale/Librairie C. Klincksieck, 1960. Collection of papers read at the 7th Rencontre Assyriologique Internationale, Paris, 1958.

Landsberger, Benno. "Zur vierten und siebenten Tafel des Gilgamesch-Epos." *Revue d'Assyriologie et d'Archéologie Orientale* 62 (1968): 97–135.

Oppenheim, A. Leo. "The Creative Effort." In *Ancient Mesopotamia: Portrait of a Dead Civilization*, pp. 250–75. Chicago: University of Chicago Press, 1964. A very stimulating presentation of the problems of Mesopotamian literature. One of the most insightful discussions of the Gilgamesh epic.

von Soden, Wolfram. "Beiträge zum Verständnis des babylonischen Gilgameš-Epos." *Zeitschrift für Assyriologie* 53 (1959): 209–35. Text-critical notes to the author's revised edition of A. Schott, *Das Gilgamesch-Epos*.

3   The Sanskrit Epics

Barend A. van Nooten

The epics of ancient India are the *Mahābhārata* and the *Rāmāyaṇa*. Both are products of a long evolutionary history, the origins of which have been lost in antiquity. Both have come down to us in recensions that with certain reservations can be dated to a four-century span of time between the second century B.C. and the second century A.D. Both have a central heroic theme nested in a vast array of subordinate supporting stories. This is the case especially with the *Mahābhārata,* the longer of the two. The *Rāmāyaṇa* is a little more unified. Both epics, moreover, are attributed to authors whose historical reality cannot be verified. The author of the *Rāmāyaṇa* is said to be Vālmīki, a sage dwelling in a mountain range in Central India. But aside from this supposed authorship of the work, nothing is known about him except for a few late anecdotes invented to explain his name. In the case of the *Mahābhārata* we are on even less certain grounds. Its author is said to have been Vyāsa, a name meaning "Arranger" in Sanskrit and the name given also to the author of numerous other very ancient works. As will be shown later, there was no single author of the *Mahābhārata.* The epic itself admits of three redactors and there is clear evidence, as in the case of the *Rāmāyaṇa,* that some seemingly genuine parts were incorporated into the epic at a later date.[1]

The language in which the epics are composed, Sanskrit or Old-Indic, ceased to be a living language by the beginning of the Christian era. For a number of centuries it continued to be well understood among those segments of the Indian population that had studied Sanskrit, and presumably less completely understood by the people outside the original Sanskrit homeland, the area surrounding the confluence of the Ganges and the Yamunā Rivers. As the epic stories became popular and more widely distributed throughout India, in time a point must have been reached where they ceased to be intelligible to the majority of the audience, since the vernacular languages continued to develop, and Sanskrit found itself more and more an academic and sacerdotal language. It is a tribute to the excellence of the Indian epics that they were not merely forgotten or relegated to the archives of Indian culture. Instead, we find them translated into various Indo-Aryan languages from the fifteenth century onward, and they continue to be narrated and recited to this very day. But much earlier, from the early tenth century onwards, translations were made from the Sanskrit into the Dravidian languages of Southern India. Here the Indo-Aryan culture found an audience even less equipped to receive the epics in their original Sanskrit. Before too long the Tamil translation appeared, followed two centuries later by the translation into Telugu. In these South Indian regions some of the best poets exerted themselves to render into verse the stories of the *Rāmāyaṇa* and the *Mahābhārata*. At times the translations were literal, at other times the poet's own genius reformed the epics to conform to the tastes and predilections of the audiences he faced. Sometimes a vernacular language has both a literal translation and a poetic rendering of the same epic. In turn, these secondary versions spawned an ancillary literature of drama, poetry, ballads, folktales, fairy tales, and religious songs, and so the epics have left their imprint on India, from north to south and in practically every village. Many among the illiterate villagers have forgotten the Sanskrit source of their stories, and even fewer would be able to read the original. Fewer still will see anything but a religious story in the adventures of the epic characters. Priests sometimes hold recitations in the temples which the women and the older people attend. Here moral lessons are taught, and the ladies inspired by the haunting stories go home and tell them to their children. In this way, the continuity of the Indian tradition is secured, a continuity that has remained almost unbroken since the early years of the Christian era.

The great epics resemble one another in these general respects. In particulars, they differ. The *Mahābhārata* is a much longer work and much more involuted. Its structure is maintained consistently throughout as a set of narratives laid in the mouth of speakers introduced successively. As soon as the speaker has finished his account, the recital is resumed by the one that has introduced him until, in turn, the thread is taken up again by the one that has introduced him, and so on. It is the familiar structure of the *Rahmenerzählung* (frame story) and suggests that the original *Mahābhārata* was derived from a series of oral narratives. The structure also facilitates the incorporation of new materials. We have fairly good evidence that such insertions have taken place in the course of time. Almost unique in the Sanskrit literary history is the introduction of new speakers with a little phrase which is outside the versified context of the remaining narrative: "The gods spoke:" or "N.N. spoke:", after which the versified narrative continues. At other times the speaker is introduced within the verse preceding his speech, and occasionally the two methods are used together, thus reinforcing one another. The *Rāmāyaṇa* lacks these interstitial phrases. The verse narrative is continuous, and the whole work is more homogeneous in nature than the *Mahābhārata*. It contains fewer folktales, fewer digressions and fewer moralizing stories. In the following paragraphs we shall give a short account of the *Mahābhārata* and then of the *Rāmāyaṇa*.

Mahābhārata

To summarize the *Mahābhārata* is an unrewarding task. One is bound to leave out a great deal of interesting material and is apt to include a rather colorless account of events that follow one another chronologically. The epic pays little attention to formal plots and stories, and linear chronology is often avoided by the introduction of "flashbacks" that more often than not repeat events already told. At times, lengthy speeches are devoted to the elucidation of some trite point of morality, whereas an event crucial to the development of the plot, such as the death of a major figure, may be related in one line. It is perhaps best first to sketch the structure of the *Mahābhārata* and then give a brief outline of its contents.

SKETCH OF THE PLOTS

The *Mahābhārata* consists of eighteen Books (*parvans*) of varying lengths, subdivided into chapters. Some chapters are only a dozen or so lines long and others are longer than the shortest of the books. The total length is around 78,000 slokas, or two–line verses.

It is simplest to regard the six central books (Books 5–10), the so-called Battle Books, as the core of the epic. This core fits into a long narrative where events are related which lead up to the battle (Books 1–4) and the events that follow it (Books 10–11, 14–18). Books 12 and 13 consist wholly of sermons, salutary advice, theories of kingship, a few myths, and metaphysical and philosophical lectures.

The Battle Books. The battle books comprise approximately one third of the entire *Mahābhārata*. At stake is a fertile stretch of land, part of Kuru country, in north Central India, traditionally located near Delhi. Pitted against each other are the Pāṇḍavas, or Pāṇḍus, descendants of a mythical king Pāṇḍu, and the Kauravas, or Kurus, who were the original rulers of the land. The battle may have historical origins and, in fact, among many Hindus its historicity is not even a point of dispute. Traditionally, they date it to the year corresponding to 3102 B.C., but more conservative estimates assign the battle to a date within a thousand-year period after the Aryan invasion of India (around the sixteenth century B.C.) and before the composition of certain Buddhist and Hindu ritual works which contain references to its heroes. The account of the battle is placed in the mouth of Saṃjaya, an eyewitness with unique gifts. The gods had endowed him with a temporary ability to survey the battle scene with a special vision: he could observe all that was going on at any place in the battle at will. This ability colors his eyewitness account so that at times he "pans" the battlefield and describes the movements of the masses of troops, while at other times he "zeroes in" on smaller frays and individual duels and combats. Darkness does not impair his vision, and he is also able to report literally the speeches that the heroes are apt to deliver before attacking one another. All these talents are given to him by the gods so that his master, King Dhrtarāstra, the blind regent of the land, can see the battle through his eyes. The actual report of the battle takes place in Dhrtarāstra's camp after the entire battle is over and for that reason is narrated mainly in the preterit tense, with shifts to a historical present in lively scenes. The battle scenes are described in a fairly stereotyped manner. Usually, there is first a description of the massive armies approaching one another shouting and creating noises with the chariots, elephants, and by the warriors banging their weapons on their shields and slapping their armpits. The battle formations are often depicted; they have conventional names like "The Eagle" and "The Half-circle," and different flanks of the armies line themselves up in such formations. We get vivid descriptions of bloody massacres and carnage, and then a few heroic combats are singled out: the charioteers of the heroes steer close to one another while the warriors themselves shoot showers of arrows. The sun is frequently obscured by this cloud of missiles. As the combatants close, they go through the formality of neutralizing each other's arrows with their own. Next they may exchange insults, shoot each other's horses, disable the chariots, and shoot the charioteers before leaping to the ground and continuing hand-to-hand combat. Such combats often decide the battle of the day. At sunset the armies retire to their camps; the battlefield remains desolate in all its stark gruesomeness but is soon invaded by ghouls and ghosts who feast upon the remains of the bodies. The next day the combat begins afresh.

Two excerpts from combat scenes are given below. In another famous combat the hero Bhīsma is invincible until the opponents discover he has vowed not to fight one of their number. In a previous life he had known that person, Śikhandin, as a woman and although she was reborn as a woman, she had exchanged her sex with a wandering forest creature and had joined the battle to slay Bhīsma in retaliation for a pre-incarnate insult. Bhīsma is forbidden by his warrior code to shoot her and is felled by Arjuna who hides behind Śikhandin. Another combat opposes the old preceptor Drona to Dhrstadyumna, the general in command of the Pāndava army. Drona is told falsely that his son has been killed and he loses heart. Casting down his weapons he devotes himself to spiritual contemplation in the midst of the seething battle and so is killed. Another fateful combat is that between the Pāndava hero Bhīma and the vile Duhśāsana, who had violated his wife's honor. In one of the most awesome episodes of the epic, Bhīma, the famous wrestler and mace fighter, knocks Duhśāsana out of his car with his mace, jumps on him, then with his sword cuts open his chest and drinks his blood. The surrounding crowd reflects, very much like the Greek chorus, the various moods that can be expected: exultation, exhilaration, grief, disgust, fear, and so on.

After eighteen days of battle both armies have been all but annihilated. Three of the evil party escape, and we do not hear from them any more. Of the righteous faction, the Pāṇḍavas, only the five brothers, their wife, and Krishna survive. With their older relatives they continue ruling the land until they die.

Ante-Bellum History. In the first four books of the *Mahābhārata* we find a description of the events leading up to the battle, the genealogy of the heroes, and a number of related and unrelated incidents. This section is like a dense forest where it is easy to lose one's way. We shall first sketch the genealogy of the main heroes and then a few of their adventures in chronological succession.

The Pāṇḍavas who are to deliver combat are the five brothers: Yudhiṣṭhira, Bhīma, Arjuna, Nakula, and Sahadeva. The latter two are usually described as "the twins"; they are co-uterine twins from a mother Mādrī and the twin gods, the Aśvins. The other brothers are all born from Lady Kuntī and the gods Dharma (Righteousness), Vāyu (Wind), and Indra, the god of thunder and rain. These gods had impregnated the ladies on behalf of their common husband, Pāṇḍu, who through the curse of a brahman had become afraid to have intercourse, for his death was sure to follow. And so it did in time when in a weak moment he succumbed to Mādrī's charms. She followed him in death by burning herself on his funeral pyre. So the five Pāṇḍu brothers and Lady Kuntī survive and all are relevant to the later story.

The Kurus' immediate descent is more fabulous. They are one hundred brothers and one sister, all children of the blind king Dhṛtarāṣṭra and his faithful wife Gāndhārī. The children were born from a mass of flesh which had gestated for two years, then was doused with water and hatched in one hundred and one individual pots. Most of the brothers and the sister remain unimportant in the remaining story, and only Duryodhana and Duḥśāsana function as individual heroes.

Further family connections are also of interest. King Dhṛtarāṣṭra of Hāstinapura is King Pāṇḍu's brother and so the two opposing armies are related by blood. In name, the two kings are sons of a long-deceased King Vicitravīrya, but physically their father is the sage Vyāsa. They have different mothers. King Vicitravīrya's untimely death had made it necessary to appoint the sage Vyāsa, his half-brother, to beget Pāṇḍu and Dhṛtarāṣṭra upon his two wives. Moreover, Vicitravīrya's father Śantanu was also the father of the preceptor Bhīṣma. Bhīṣma in the *Mahābhārata* is a celibate, wise old warrior who tutors both Pāṇḍavas and Kurus. His mother was the River Ganges. Śantanu apparently was partial to rivers, for his other wife, the mother of Vicitravīrya, also has connections with rivers. She used to operate a ferry on the River Ganges. Unbeknownst to Śantanu, she had had a premarital affair with a charming, energetic sage, Parāśara. By his magic power her virginity was restored and Śantanu never knew. But her child was Kṛṣṇa Dvaipāyana

Vyāsa, to give him his full name, and, as was mentioned earlier, he became the real forefather of all Pāṇḍavas and Kurus. He is also credited with having composed the *Mahābhārata*.

There are two more epic figures to be described. One is the hero Karṇa, the other the charioteer Kṛṣṇa. Karṇa was the illegitimate son of Kuntī, born before her marriage to Pāṇḍu. His father was Sūrya, the sun god. As a baby he was floated down the river in a basket, like Moses, and was adopted by a charioteer. He later finds his way to the court and though he is the half-brother of Arjuna, Bhīma, and Yudhiṣṭhira, no one knows this except Kuntī herself. At one time, in the hope of averting the war, she finally tells him, but by then it is too late. Karṇa is the only truly tragic figure in the epic.

The princes, both Pāṇḍavas and Kurus, are raised at Dhṛtarāṣṭra's court in Hāstinapura. As tutors they have the aforementioned Bhīsma and a warrior, Droṇa. At the end of their training period they celebrate at a festival where they demonstrate their skill in weaponry. Bhīma is the foremost mace fighter, the twins are the best swordsmen, Yudhiṣṭhira the best charioteer, but Arjuna surpasses all others in every skill. As he is demonstrating his prowess, Karṇa stalks into the arena and imitates everything he does. The Kurus, who have been envious of their cousins for many years, view Karṇa as a welcome ally against the Pāṇḍavas. When Arjuna scornfully asks Karṇa for his lineage and country, Duryodhana immediately appoints him King of Aṅga. The onset of the night prevents a serious quarrel from erupting, but the Kuru brothers continue plotting the downfall of their cousins. They arrange for them to move into a combustible hut with their mother, intending to set it on fire. The brothers escape through a tunnel and wander through the forest for a long time with the powerful Bhīma often carrying his mother on his back. Bhīma also kills a demon and marries its sister. (Elsewhere he slays another demon who was terrorizing a village by demanding a human being for a meal every day.) Their journey ends when they hear of a marriage of self-choice (*svayaṃvara-*) of Princess Draupadī. Disguised as priests they attend the ceremony, and of all the suitors Arjuna alone is capable of passing the test: to string a bow and shoot down a clay pigeon. All five brothers agree to marry Draupadī, each taking turns sleeping with her.

At this svayaṃvara, Kṛṣṇa for the first time joins the brothers. He is a mysterious character from the west coast of India, a cousin of Kuntī's. The Pāṇḍavas subsequently receive half of Kuru country with a capital, Indraprastha, which they have to carve out of the jungle. They construct a magnificent palace with the help of a demon, Maya, and Kṛṣṇa visits them there. At his urging they invade the principality of Mithilā and murder its king, Jarāsandha, to settle an old feud that Kṛṣṇa had with him. They next make a formal conquest of the world, going as far west as Antioch and Alexandria. Upon their return Yudhiṣṭhira is solemnly consecrated as a Universal Monarch, at which time Kṛṣṇa disposes of another ancient enemy, Śiśupāla. A little later Yudhiṣṭhira is challenged to a dice game by Duryodhana. He accepts, but finds that he has to gamble against a professional gamester,

Śakuni, instead. He loses everything, including his wife and kingdom, to the Kurus. Draupadī is hauled into the dice hall and Duḥśāsana attempts to disrobe her in public. Through some miracle, however, a new robe appears every time he tears one off of her. In the end, the Pāṇḍu brothers and Draupadī agree to a voluntary exile of twelve years in the forest and another year unrecognized in the inhabited world.

The period of exile is described in the very long Forest Book of the *Mahābhārata,* the third volume. It abounds in stories and anecdotes of great interest in themselves but of little consequence to the main story. A few of them worth noting are Arjuna's struggle over a wild boar with God Śiva in the guise of a low-caste hunter; Arjuna's amorous adventures in various parts of India; the romance of Nala and Damayantī; the drying up of the ocean and the descent of the Ganges; the flood legend; the romance of Sāvitrī who persuaded Death to release her husband's soul; struggles with demons; the story of Rāma and Sitā; and numerous other stories. Suffice it to say that at the end of their forest exile the brothers return to the world and hire themselves out as servants at Virāta's court. They wrap their weapons in a bundle which they hang in a tree near the graveyard, pretending it is their mother who has died recently. Yudhiṣṭhira becomes the King's dice player, Bhīma a cook, Nakula a groom in the royal stables, and Sahadeva a counter of cattle. Arjuna takes on a female role as a transvestite and is appointed dancing master for the girls of the court. Draupadī becomes the Queen's hairdresser.

Wikander (1947) has made much of this episode, where a social distinction is drawn between the otherwise rather similar twins, Nakula and Sahadeva.[2] Whatever the merits of that distinction (there was very little status difference between the supervisor of the stables and the supervisor of the cattle in those days), the structural importance of the episode lies in the transitional nature of the phase the heroes have to go through in order to achieve full recognition as noblemen again. To an audience of courtiers, hairdressers, and cooks, as well as noblemen, this episode must have had special appeal. It is an instance of reversal of roles, reversal of polarity, of which the epic has many instances.

The Pāṇḍavas emerge triumphantly from their trial, and when they go to claim their share of the land, Kṛṣṇa joins them and acts as negotiator. The negotiations break down, since the Kurus feel strong enough to refuse any concessions to their cousins. War is inevitable.

Kṛṣṇa joins the Pāṇḍava faction as a non-combatant, acting as Arjuna's charioteer. It is in this capacity that he reveals himself to Arjuna as an incarnation of God Viṣṇu in the famous poem, the *Bhagavad-gītā* (Song of the Lord). It clearly is an interpolation, but one of very old standing, since not one *Mahābhārata* recension has come down to us without the *Bhagavad-gītā.* In the remainder of the epic Kṛṣṇa plays the role of the cunning adviser who is not beneath resorting to trickery to achieve Arjuna's victory.

After the War. When the battle is over, the victors derive little profit from their superiority. The Kurus have been defeated indeed, with all but a handful of their heroes killed. But these survivors at night stealthily invade the Pāṇḍava bivouac and in an orgy of rage massacre the entire army as it is lying asleep. The Pāṇḍu brothers had spent the night elsewhere and so escape. They bitterly assume the reign of the Kuru country from the capital, Hāstinapura. The war has left the country impoverished but Kṛṣṇa recovers a hidden treasure trove from the Himālayas which serves to support the economy. Soon thereafter Kṛṣṇa leaves for his home country of Vṛṣṇi, but after his people have destroyed themselves in a drunken brawl he wanders off into the forest and is finally shot in the heel by a roaming hunter, Jarā (Old Age) by name. He dies.

The Kṛṣṇa cycle of stories and their relation to the *Mahābhārata* has still not been interpreted convincingly. In the Harivaṃśa, an appendix to the *Mahābhārata,* the story of his divinity is related more coherently. It must be emphasized that for practically all Hindus writing from the ninth century onwards, the *Mahābhārata* represents no more than the Kṛṣṇa–avatāra in Viṣṇu's hagiology.

In Hāstinapura the Pāṇḍavas continue to rule jointly, looking after their aged relatives: Dhṛtarāṣṭra, his wife Gāndhārī, and a small retinue. The elderly people can never forgive their nephews for the genocide committed on their family, so soon they repair to the forest to lead an ascetic life until the end of their days. In time the Pāṇḍavas also feel old age encroaching. They take leave of the court and set out in a northerly direction until, one after another, Draupadī, Sahadeva, Nakula, Arjuna, and Bhīma fall down in their tracks. Yudhiṣṭhira continues alone accompanied by only a dog. Indra faces him and denies him admission to heaven unless he abandons the dog. Yudhiṣṭhira refuses and then the dog manifests itself as Dharma, the God of Righteousness. In recognition of his virtue, Yudhiṣṭhira is conveyed to heaven in a celestial chariot. After a brief ordeal in a make-believe hell he plunges into the sacred celestial River Ganges and emerges in a heavenly form to be united with his brothers and friends.

In Hāstinapura, Arjuna's grandson, Janamejaya, now rules Kuru country. It is at his instigation that a snake sacrifice is conducted during which the entire *Mahābhārata* is recited. Now the officiants go home, and the *Mahābhārata* ends with a few well chosen words describing the merits of people listening to its recitation.

Philosophy.   In the "philosophical" sections of the *Mahābhārata* there are discussions of the code of conduct of warriors. It has been pointed out long ago that there is an inconsistency in the depiction of the warriors' actions as opposed to the description of the moral code under which they are supposed to operate. The rules laid down for chivalry and fair fighting—for instance, that only a king should fight with a king, that a third man shall not interfere when two are fighting, that barbed or poisoned arrows should not be used, and so on—are repeatedly violated and, as often as not, by the warriors fighting on the side of moral justice. The insight we gain into the aspects of Sanskrit warfare that are not dominated by the ethical considerations of so-called Hindu theologians is rather revealing. If we study the "coarse, sensual, brutal, strife-loving, blood-hungry Hindu warrior," as one investigator puts it,[3] then the environment he lives in appears in a light distinctly different from the pious, meditative dissertations of the priests. Since the priests were entrusted with the educational system and usually with the transmission of the texts, their influence is felt in these parts of the epic where the battle is discussed and the warriors' behavior is analyzed.

Rāmāyaṇa

The *Rāmāyaṇa* is a more unified epic. The great battle here takes place between a group of semi-civilized demons living in a splendid city on the island of Laṅkā and a group of monkeys and bears, who have invaded the island at the bidding of their lord, Sugrīva. The demons are hideous, proteic monsters capable of assuming human form, even beautiful human form, but generally content to abide in a state of gross sensuality, violence, and self-indulgence. Their main criminality lies in the fact that they occasionally maraud human settlements, disturb the pious sacrificers, and try to tempt human beings to acts of sensuality. Rāma and his brother Lakṣmaṇa, like latter-day missionaries, carry on a lengthy battle against these transgressions.

The battle is described in the next but last of the seven books of the *Rāmāyaṇa*. In the six preceding books the events leading up to the battle are narrated from far back in the mythological past when the gods fought the demons. The birth of Rāma and his three brothers is surrounded by miraculous events. They are born through the intervention of a powerful royal priest, Vasiṣṭha, who cures Daśaratha's childlessness by feeding thin rice gruel to his three wives after performing a fire sacrifice. The queens conceive and Bharata is born to Kaikeyī, Rāma to Kausalyā, whereas Sumitrā gives birth to the twins Lakṣmaṇa and Śatrughna. In the subsequent story Rāma and Lakṣmaṇa become inseparable friends and the *Rāmāyaṇa* is mainly their story.

At puberty or thereabouts, Rāma and Lakṣmaṇa are taken by the sage Viśvāmitra to his forest hermitage to assist him in warding off the attacks of two marauding demons, Mārīca and Subāhu. Rāma does most of the fighting. As a reward for his assistance, Viśvāmitra gives Rāma magic weapons and formulas which he will use later in his combats against the demons. Some time later the sage takes them to Videha where King Janaka has announced the wedding of his daughter Sītā, who had not been born from a woman but had sprung from the earth itself, to any mortal who can string the mighty Śiva-bow. Rāma comes upon a rock which he kicks, only to see it change into a beautiful woman, Ahalyā. Gratefully she tells him that he has set her free from a curse which her husband had inflicted upon her as punishment for adultery with God Indra, long ago. She then leaves. Rāma not only effortlessly strings the bow but breaks it in the process. Rāma weds Sītā,

Lakṣmaṇa marries her younger sister Ūrmilā, and the other two brothers take two of Sītā's sisters for their wives. The princes return to Ayodhyā after Rāma has defeated an ancient warrior also named Rāma who was obstructing his path. When it is time for old King Daśaratha to retire, he appoints Rāma as his successor, but through the machinations of his wife, Kaikeyī, and her hunch-backed maid, he is forced to abdicate in favor of Bharata, and Rāma is exiled to the jungle for fourteen years. Sītā and Lakṣmaṇa accompany Rāma into the dangerous land of the Rākṣasas, or demons, who have occupied the formerly peaceful Daṇḍaka forest. Rāma lives with various hermits whom he protects from attacks of demons until one day a female demon, Śūrpaṇakhā, falls in love with him. He rejects her advances and suggests she go to his brother instead. Lakṣmaṇa cuts off her ears and nose, whereupon she seeks revenge by asking her two demonic brothers to attack with the full force of their army. Rāma defeats them. The female demon is the sister of the demon king Rāvaṇa of Laṅkā who is invulnerable to assaults from the gods and is living in great splendor, contemptuous of law and religion. When approached by his sister, he refuses to help until he is told of Sītā's beauty and virtue. With a confederate, Marīci, who had been defeated earlier by Rāma, he devises a ruse to win Sītā. Marīci disguises himself as a golden deer prancing about the hermitage where Rāma and Sītā are staying. Sītā desires to catch it and beseeches Rāma to go out and chase it. He does so, leaving Lakṣmaṇa in charge of the hermitage and urging him not to leave Sītā alone under any circumstances. Rāma is lured far into the forest and finally shoots the deer, who then momentarily regains his demonic shape and howls at the top of his lungs. The cry is heard in the hermitage. Sītā implores Lakṣmaṇa to go out to assist Rāma, but he refuses until she accuses him of having designs on her virtue. While he is searching for Rāma the demon Rāvaṇa in the disguise of an ascetic approaches the hermitage and slowly wins Sītā's confidence. When she finally lets him into the hut he seizes her and carries her off through the sky in his aerial chariot. After a brief fight with a heroic bird of prey, Jaṭāyu, he returns to Laṅkā and impounds her in a grove of Aśoka trees under the supervision of his other wives.

Meanwhile, Rāma and Lakṣmaṇa roam through the forest for a long period in search of Sītā. They finally meet two exiled monkeys, King Sugrīva and his aide-de-camp, Hanuman, who promise to help recover Sītā, provided Rāma will help Sugrīva to regain his kingdom. In the following rather strange episode Sugrīva challenges his brother Vālin, the usurper of his kingdom, to personal combat. Rāma stands by, ready with bow and arrow, but is unable to tell the two monkeys apart. During a pause in the fighting he hangs a garland around Sugrīva's neck and when the fight resumes shoots the fatal arrow into Sugrīva's back. This dishonorable deed is the price Rāma pays for armed support from the monkey army in the subsequent battle to recover Sītā. They all wait out the rainy season in the mountains, where Rāma longs for his abducted wife. In the spring they rouse the monkey army which had subsided into a blissful stupor, and they set out to conquer Laṅkā. First, however, the mighty Hanuman, son of the Wind God, is sent to Laṅkā to determine the whereabouts of Sītā. He takes a mighty leap from a South Indian mountain and soars across the strait separating it from Laṅkā. On the way he is confronted by a number of marine demons and in Laṅkā itself he conducts a battle against Rāvaṇa's palace guard, defeating them and then allowing himself to be captured. When dragged before Rāvaṇa he demands Sītā's return, but in reply Rāvaṇa has his underlings tie oily cloths around Hanuman's tail, then light them. With his tail ablaze, the monkey breaks loose and, jumping from roof to roof, sets the city on fire. Before returning to Rāma he visits Sītā in the Aśoka grove. Being fearful, at first she refuses to talk to him, but when he shows her a ring Rāma had given him as a token of his mission, she trusts him and asks to be remembered to Rāma. Hanuman in one mighty bound returns to the mainland and conveys her message. Rāma then decides to cross the ocean with his army by building a giant causeway across to Laṅkā. At first the Ocean is reluctant to grant permission, but Rāma with a blazing arrow stands before it threatening to dry it up. The god complies, and the monkeys and bears quickly build an enormous causeway, the remains of which are still visible, or so it is said. They cross and camp outside Laṅkā.

In the demon camp there are seeds of discord. Rāvaṇa has two brothers, Vibhīṣaṇa and Kumbhakarṇa. Vibhīṣaṇa questions Rāvaṇa's right to imprison Sītā; a dispute develops ending in Vibhīṣaṇa's desertion of the demon cause. Instead, he joins Rāma's army where he is accepted after he has allayed their suspicions. The other brother, Kumbhakarṇa, is a monstrous giant who sleeps six months of the year and has a voracious appetite. He, too, criticizes Rāvaṇa for his rash abduction of Sītā, but unlike Vibhīṣaṇa he remains faithful to his liege and promises to slay Rāma. The demons then attack the besiegers; they throw themselves upon the monkeys and drink their blood. Rāma and Lakṣmaṇa fight with bow and arrow, whereas the monkey heroes use rocks, tree trunks, their teeth, and fists to fight. Kumbhakarṇa alone swallows mouthfuls of monkeys. Then Rāvaṇa's son Indrajit applies black magic to harass the army. He wounds Rāma and Lakṣmaṇa, knocking them unconscious with magic arrows. Rāvaṇa takes advantage of the situation by conducting Sītā to the battlefield and exposing her to the cruel sight of the bodies of her loved ones. Needless to say, she does not yield to Rāvaṇa's cajolery. Rāma and Lakṣmaṇa recover when the giant bird Garuḍa approaches, and the battle continues. Rāma kills Kumbhakarṇa, but is again unable to withstand the black magic of Indrajit's arrows. He falls down, together with most of the monkeys. Hanuman, however, hears of a life-restoring herb that grows far away on a mountaintop. He flies there and, unable to find it, rips the top off the mountain and returns to the battlefield. Upon inhaling the fragrance of the herbs, the army rises again, and Hanuman returns the mountaintop to its place.

By means of a magic trick, Indrajit appears to bring Sītā to the battlefield and to behead her. The demon king's brother, Vibhīsana, sees through the ruse and restores Rāma's spirits. Laksmana kills Indrajit. Rāvana has gradually lost all his foremost warriors and brothers, and the time of the decisive battle against Rāma approaches. Omens announce the dreadful event: the sun becomes dark, birds shriek, jackals howl, a bloody rain falls, the earth shakes. Rāvana spots Vibhīsana and hurls a fatal weapon at him which Laks-mana intercepts by standing in front of his ally. Rāma believes his brother has perished and in anger approaches Rāvana's chariot on foot. To balance out this unequal combat God Indra sends his armed chariot and charioteer. Rāma ascends and immediately wards off a horde of fiery arrows which descend upon him as a mass of poisonous snakes. Rāma counters by shooting arrows which change into predatory birds and devour the snakes. The battle lasts one day and one night. Rāma repeatedly strikes off one of Rāvana's heads, but each time it grows back again. Finally, Rāma picks up the magic Brahman weapon given to him many years ago by the sage Agastya, and after pro-nouncing sacred formulas over it, he shoots it from his bow, striking Rāvana in the heart. The latter dies instantly.

Vibhīsana despondently helps cremate Rāvana's body and becomes regent of Lankā. Rāma charges Hanuman with finding Sītā. Everyone expects to witness a happy reunion of the long separated spouses, but instead Rāma rejects her and tells her to go to Laksmana, Bharata, Sugrīva, or Vibhīsana instead. The fact that she has remained in the power of the demon king for so long must have compromised her honor and even if she has been faithful, none of his subjects would ever believe it. How could Rāma become king under these circumstances? Sītā, deeply hurt, asks Laksmana to prepare a fire for her so she can immolate herself. Rāma watches somberly as she prepares to mount the pyre. Sītā first enounces an oath of truth: "As truly as my heart has never strayed from Rāma, so may the fire protect me wholly in the presence of the people." With these words she hurls herself into the fire. Rāma at the same time is visited by many gods of the Hindu pantheon who had suffered from Rāvana's tyranny. They inform him that he is an incarna-tion of God Visnu and has fulfilled his task of slaying the almost invincible demon. The God of Fire returns Sītā to Rāma with the assurance that she has remained pure, and Rāma accepts her back graciously. The fourteen years of Rāma's exile are almost over. In a large aerial chariot that had belonged to Rāvana, the happy couple with many monkeys as their retinue return to Ayodhyā. On the way they get an aerial view of all the places they have visited. In Ayodhyā, Rāma is consecrated King by the old priest Vasistha. The monkeys return home, and peace reigns in Rāma's kingdom.

The remaining book of the *Vālmīki-Rāmāyana* seems superfluous. The Rāma narrative is interrupted by stories describing the antecedents of Rāva-na's entry into the battle. About halfway through the book, the Rāma story resumes and we learn that Sītā has become pregnant, and that people gossip about her infidelity, so Rāma again rejects her. He sends her to the hermitage of the sage Vālmīki where two sons, Kuśa and Lava are born. Without telling them who their father is, he teaches them to recite the *Rāmāyaṇa* and when much later Rāma conducts a giant horse-sacrifice, the two boys recite the *Rāmāyaṇa* for the first time in public, to the accompaniment of a lute. Rāma learns who they are and has Sītā brought before the assembly to testify to her purity. Sītā with another act of truth begs her mother the Earth to open up for her. A chasm opens in the earth and a lion's throne appears. Sītā sits down and is carried into the earth never to be seen again. Rāma is later told in a private audience with Kāla, the God of Time, that he has to abandon his mortal coil, and so he proceeds to the River Sarāyu where he plunges into the waters to be united with his original glorious state of godhead.

There are many more legends in this last volume which seem to have been inserted into the Rāma story for no apparent reason. Some of them, such as Rāma's murder of the low-caste man Sambūka because he was practicing austerity, detract from Rāma's noble image, rather than reinforce it. The Rāvaṇa narrative seems to derive from another cycle altogether. In brief summary, it describes Rāvaṇa's demonic ancestors, their defeat at the hands of the gods, Rāvaṇa's birth, his penance to gain power, and his usurpation of Laṅkā. He abuses his power to torture gods, sages, and other benign creatures. Warned by the gods, he nevertheless persists, defeats the Guardians of the Quarters, battles and defeats Death and other gods. In an orgy of power he abducts women from all over the country, killing their male relatives if they object. He next defeats the King of Gods, Indra, but in turn suffers defeat at the hands of Śiva and a mighty warrior, Arjuna with the thousand arms (an Arjuna different from the one in the *Mahābhārata*). Nor does he measure up to Vālin's strength, the King of the Monkeys, who constrains him in his armpit. He returns to rule in Laṅkā; it is at this point in his life that his sister Śūrpaṇakhā reports to him that she has been mistreated by a human being. The human beings are to be his downfall, for Rāvaṇa, when he had forced the gods to give him power by means of his asceticism, had asked for permanent immunity against gods, animals, and other creatures, but had neglected to include human beings, whom he considered too weak to be a threat to his power.

PLOT STRUCTURE

The *Rāmāyaṇa* in terms of plot falls into five parts: (1) the mythical birth of Rāma and the stories surrounding his childhood; (2) Rāma's interaction with his father and brothers, his appointment as Daśaratha's successor, his fall from grace and his exile into the forest with his wife Sītā and his half-brother Lakṣmaṇa, and ending with Sītā's abduction; (3) Rāma's search for and recovery of Sītā with the aid of animal armies; (4) a description of the events and background of Rāvaṇa's involvement in the war; (5) Rāma's post-bellum reign, his progeny, and his death. Parts (1) and (5) are clearly later additions to the *Vālmīki-Rāmāyaṇa* and are perhaps created to expand the story. Part (4), Rāvaṇa's early history, is too complex to be an *ad hoc* invention and may well go back to an ancient Rāvaṇa cycle of which earlier traces survive only in

Rāvaṇa stories other than the Vālmīki. Parts (2) and (3) are connected but not interwoven to the extent that they are inseparable. Part (2), especially with its narrative of a court squabble resulting in the exile of the hero and his retinue, is reminiscent of the first few books of the *Mahābhārata*.

There are certain interesting features that distinguish the *Rāmāyaṇa* from other Sanskrit works. For one thing, it has beautiful poetic passages and contains many of the germs of the court poetry of later Sanskrit. It is often called the *Ādikāvya- (Ur-gedicht)* of Sanskrit literature. But at the same time, it is a warriors' poem. The king is in absolute command and has the power of life or death over his soldiers. The demons unquestioningly defend their Lord Rāvaṇa even though they do not stand to gain any benefit and are slaughtered by the thousands. Similarly, the monkeys are massacred in great numbers for the sake of their leader without anyone raising a voice of protest. Another feature worth noting is that the battle itself is conducted mainly between non-human opponents. The demons and the monkeys set the stage for the display of courage and virility of Rāma and Lakṣmaṇa. Gods do at times assist in the battle, but not by the wielding of weapons or the interception of lethal missiles. Magic tricks, illusions, and conjury play a much greater role here than in the *Mahābhārata*. Furthermore, the sections of the *Rāmāyaṇa* where a mood of strict martiality prevails are rather limited for a work that lays claim to the name of epic. Lengthy passages are taken up by descriptions of nature, scenery, and moods, often associated with outbursts of the passionate longing of Rāma for his wife and Sītā for her husband. Moreover, she bewails her fate in lengthy laments in the face of her distress at Rāvaṇa's advances. In this perspective, the work has overtones of a romance in the traditional medieval sense. This impression is reinforced by the aura of supernaturality that pervades some sections of the epic. Encounters in the forest with powerful semi-divine and demonic forces, talking beasts, magic weapons, flying chariots, and black magic used to destroy opponents—all of these add up to an atmosphere of wonder and unreality. Even the battle scenes, in spite of their graphic and unsentimental descriptions of injuries and mutilations, have an idealized quality about them. The heroes time and again sustain incredible injuries. They shoot clouds of arrows at each other and are capable of unbelievable acts of strength. The situation often arises that two irresistible magic weapons meet in mid-air. The poet has to extricate himself from this logical dilemma by invoking some *deus ex machina*.

The *Rāmāyaṇa*'s mythology has not been studied very well yet. The traditional Indian cultural complex views it as an allegory of the struggle between wicked and righteous forces and, as such, the Rāma story is still exceedingly popular. It appears in numerous translations in the vernacular languages of India and Southeast Asia, as well as in folktales, sculptures, festivals, dramas, and so forth. Traditional Indian culture looks for a moral paragon who, in spite of desertion by his peers, overcomes adversity by adherence to the Law, Dharma. Rāma fits this role quite well and in the Vālmīki version many of the less glorious sentiments and reactions that Rāma is likely to experience are credited to and expressed by Lakṣmaṇa. There are many other themes that recur in Indian mythology, for example, the conquest of gods by austerities, the rivalry of priest and king, the treachery of women, and its opposite: absolute virtue and wisdom of womankind, the benign potentate and the oppressive tyrant, rescue through trickery, rescue through violence, etc. There is very little humor in the *Rāmāyaṇa;* most of the work is deadly serious and melodramatic.

Studies and Editions of the Epics

Little work has been done on the systematic description of the tales, myths, and legends in the epics. Use of the epics in such generalized studies as those carried out by J. Fontenrose on the hero-slays-dragon myth[4] and by G. Dumézil on the recognition of a threefold social hierarchy in the epic, has demonstrated their relevance to the mythology of the ancient West. However, more fruitful work could be accomplished by applying such analyses as have been developed by Vladimir Propp (*Morphology of the Folktale,* 2nd ed., 1968), for we are likely to blind ourselves to some very important themes that are more specifically Indian and correspond more closely to the themes enumerated in Thompson and Roberts for the modern Indian folktales.[5] An awareness of the tripartite origin of the Indian social system becomes an academic curiosity when we ask ourselves why Rāma would ally himself with monkeys and bears in order to slay giants. But an awareness of the traditional Indian obsession with purity in social intercourse would make it a little more understandable that in order to root out something as vile as a horde of demons, one may have to take recourse to its opposite, a non-human creature, just as the Tantric aspirant in order to attain a position of supernatural power will engage in activities that are normally regarded as unlawful, such as eating forbidden foods and indulgence in sexual excesses.

At the time the British began to take an interest in the Indian epics, no printed editions existed. To vouchsafe the preservation of their literature, the Indians were relying instead on manuscripts and their copyists, as well as on a tradition of oral transmission. These manuscripts consist of bundles of sheets, usually not more than two inches by twelve inches in size, made of palm leaves, birch bark, or paper, and held together with a string. Such materials are perishable in the inclement climate of India, and the text has to be copied every two or three hundred years in order to survive. The copyists may or may not have been experts in Sanskrit, so the quality of the manuscript often depends on that. Since manuscript copying is a work of religious devotion, and old manuscripts are even worshipped in the houses of some devout people, there is usually no dearth of manuscripts of popular, orthodox works like the epics. Hundreds of them are in existence for both the *Rāmāyaṇa* and the *Mahābhārata.* Many of them were taken out of India to Germany, England, Russia, France, and the United States where they are preserved in museums and often outlast their Indian counterparts.

The first printed edition of the *Mahābhārata* was brought out in Calcutta between 1834 and 1839. It was followed in 1863 by the so-called Bombay edition. These two editions differed rather considerably from one another. Both were based on a number of manuscripts available to the editor, and although the outline of the story was rather much the same in both editions, there were variations in many details. The Bombay edition numbers the verses according to the books and the chapters of which they form a part; the Calcutta edition ignores the chapters, but numbers the verses in a book consecutively. Their extent differs, the Bombay edition being shorter by about 2000 verses. There are differences in episodes included in one text and omitted in another, etc. The first complete edition of the *Rāmāyaṇa* appeared in Paris between 1843 and 1850. The editor was an Italian scholar, Gaspare Gorresio. Two Indian pandits published the next edition, the so-called Bombay edition (1859) which was reprinted several times afterwards. It is on the basis of these printed publications of both *Mahābhārata* and *Rāmāyaṇa* that most of Western scholarship, at least until quite recently, became established.

The early printed editions were products of their time and were put together with the materials the editors had at hand. Gorresio, for instance, used only the six manuscripts (some incomplete at that) which he could find in the museums of Paris and London. The Indian editions were innocent of considerations of textual criticism.

Serious study of the epics began at the end of the last century. Scholars, mainly from Germany, Czechoslovakia, and America, attempted to analyze them according to the text-critical methods developed for the study of the Homeric epics and Western literature in general. Those attempts were not entirely fruitful. The enormous size of the *Mahābhārata,* equivalent to five *Iliads,* made it an unwieldy object of analysis. Also, many investigators approached it with preconceived ideas as to what an epic should be, and when the *Mahābhārata* failed to agree with their expectations, were apt to use Procrustean methods to make it conform.

The American scholar E. Washburn Hopkins operated with the notions of epic and pseudo-epic, and confined the last term to the contents of the twelfth and thirteenth books, the long disquisitions on morality in peace and war. He wrote:

> upon the original story... have been grafted many "secondary tales" (*up-ākhyāna*); and upon these, and apart from these, have been inserted whole poems of romantic, ethical and theological character, having nothing to do with the Epic itself. We must, however, remember that our Epic has been enlarged in two ways: first, by natural expansion of matter already extant; secondly, by unnatural addition of new material.[6]

But such disquisitions are found in other parts also, and some, like the *Bhagavad-gītā,* are so inextricably woven into the battle story that criteria for establishing original as opposed to secondary readings are arbitrary. They are arbitrary to the extent of making the task of higher criticism almost impossible. Faced with such problems, one often quoted critic, the Czechoslovakian Sanskritist Moritz Winternitz, has written:

> The *Mahābhārata* as a whole is a literary monster [*Ungeheuer*]. Never has the hand of an artist attempted the well-nigh impossible task of combining the conflicting elements into one unified poem. It is only unpoetical theologians and commentators and clumsy copyists who have succeeded in conglomerating into a heterogeneous mass parts which are actually incompatible, and which date from different centuries.[7]

The confused state of the printed editions did not improve with the appearance of two further editions of the *Mahābhārata* and the *Rāmāyaṇa*. The Kumbhakonam and Southern editions not only presented new readings and variants, but also completely new substories and incidents. Scholars realized that they were faced with a colossal problem of textual reconstruction, before they could realize their goal of establishing the "original" text of the epics. A proposal to carry out such an endeavor was voiced as early as 1897 by Winternitz, but it was not until 1929 that a group of Indian scholars, who had profited both from the indigenous system of education and from training in Western text-critical methodology, combined their efforts to produce just such an edition of the *Mahābhārata*.

It was a gigantic task. Hundreds of manuscripts from libraries all over the world were collected and sorted out. A staff of traditional pandits versed in Sanskrit and capable of reading the dozen or so scripts in which the manuscripts were written set out to collate them, and the chief editor, V. S. Sukthankar, established their *stemma*. The oldest manuscript is from Kashmir and not more than six hundred years old. The task took thirty-five years, and we have now an edition with variorum, some eighteen volumes in all. Yet we cannot make the claim that the text has been reconstructed definitively. The editors have, in general, been able to identify two recensions, a Southern and a Northern, which differ in many details, but above all, in extent. The Southern recension tends to be more inflated, to have incorporated more peripheral stories than the Northern. The Southern recension divides the *Mahābhārata* into twenty-four books, the Northern into eighteen. There are differences in the spelling of proper names; in the readings of words, phrases, lines, and verses; in the ordering of verses and groups of verses, the placement of whole chapters and blocks of chapters. Then there are omissions of episodes in both texts, not only of short fragments, but also of whole chapters and lengthy stories comprising several chapters. On the whole, the Southern story is richer in details and fills in gaps that in the Northern version would be left to the imagination of the reader or hearer. Among other things, it provides a detailed account of the age of the Pāṇḍu family and a time analysis of the story. These are obviously secondary insertions, since the remainder of the *Mahābhārata* has no demonstrable reference to this time analysis. The Southern recension also attempts to rectify apparent lapses in sexual propriety that appear from the Northern recension. For instance, when King Duḥṣanta marries the girl Śakuntalā without formal ceremony in the forest, the Southern recension is quick to add a few lines intimating that the royal domestic priest was called in to solemnize the wedding, lest their offspring, Bharata, be of illegitimate birth. Other free sexual liaisons in which the epic abounds are similarly made respectable, thus removing the stain of illegitimacy from their children and children's children, including the ancestors of some of the later royal families.[8]

The editors adopted as a principle of textual reconstruction the maxim that only those parts of the text that are common to all versions should be regarded as belonging to the original *Mahābhārata*. In a clear conflict between a Northern or Southern recension, however, the Northern was generally given preference.

When collecting the manuscripts for the two recensions, the editors discovered that, in turn, they could be subdivided into a number of versions. Some of these versions were represented by a great number of manuscripts so that a selection of the best one had to be made. Others consisted of only one manuscript, such as one of the oldest manuscripts, the Śārada, which originally came from Kashmir and which the editor has adopted as the archetype. It is curious to note that this archetype often upholds readings of the Southern recensions as opposed to the other versions of the Northern recension to which it belongs. There is contamination of versions and manuscripts throughout the *stemma,* mostly within one recension, but sometimes even manuscripts of versions of the two recensions will have readings in common against other manuscripts within the recension. More often than not they are rejected. Such contamination can occur as a result of the movement of the manuscript from one place to another. Neither the *Mahābhārata* nor the *Rāmāyaṇa* is a sacred text in the sense that its contents are regarded as inviolable and incapable of corruption. Rather, they were susceptible to emendation, correction, and interpolation. It was not uncommon for the possessor of a manuscript to travel to another part of the country and hear the recital of a local bard. If struck by a particularly appealing passage that was missing from his own account, he might then be induced to include it. This passage was usually written in a smaller hand in the margin of the original. A subsequent copyist would then include this passage within the text he was copying so that the reader of this latter version would be unaware of the location of the interpolation. The critical text has been useful in detecting such interpolations, but only back to a certain date. Since most of the manuscripts themselves do not go back further than about the fifteenth century, there is no objective method for determining by this procedure the corruptions and interpolations that have been introduced before that date. We may to some extent rely on external testimonies—early condensations of the epic, excerpts adapted to plays and poems, translations

recognized as a religious text by the Tamil Alvars, a Vaishnavite devotional sect. Through their concern the Southern recension has preserved the older form of the epic. Additional passages are easily identifiable by comparison with the Northern recension. Examples of such later interpolations in the Book of the Forest, for instance, are a seventeen–line expansion of a brief description of a forest, an account of the ancestry of one of the noble characters, the giant bird Jaṭāyu, and a lengthy expansion of a speech made by the demon Mārīca to dissuade his ruler Rāvaṇa from wreaking vengeance on Rāma. An interesting interpolation seems to give an answer to the question of what the faithful Sītā ate during her imprisonment in Rāvaṇa's palace. By accepting food from the demons she would transgress purity restrictions, and so this story exculpates her by having Lord Indra come to give her sacrificial food. At the same time he acts as a messenger to and from Rāma.

The lesson learned from the critical editions of the texts is in fact quite explicit: the epics have tended to expand in the course of the years, rather than to become condensed. The number of verses in the most inflated texts of the *Mahābhārata* amount to well over one hundred thousand; the number of verses in the reconstituted text dating back to perhaps A.D. 800 is seventy-eight thousand two hundred. If in the course of these past one thousand years the text has grown by fifty percent through the sheer process of incorporating new materials and retelling older materials in a different, more expansive manner, then it is reasonable to extrapolate this process and theorize that from its inception onwards the *Mahābhārata* has increased in size through the incorporation of local stories. It has, therefore, a rather sizable component of folktales from different provenance and different ages. Some are easily identifiable as stories belonging to certain holy places of pilgrimage; others are folktales of the simple narrative variety with an implied moral. There remain, however, a great number of episodes and passages that are doubtful. They could, on the one hand, have belonged to the original *Mahābhārata,* and thus function as part of the structure visualized by the original composer of the poem. But they may also be accretions of a later date. The matter cannot be decided on the basis of simple external criteria; to do so we enter into the field of higher criticism. Even the groundwork of higher criticism has not been laid, and since the variables are numerous, it is doubtful whether a satisfactory procedure will ever be established. In any case, the question of its usefulness may be raised. Indian scholars have been singularly disinterested in this problem, since for most of them the *Mahābhārata* is primarily a religious poem. Any quest for its origin may raise theological questions that are just as well left alone. In fact, even the purely textual criteria used for excising certain portions of the epic which were clear interpolations have often run into objections from traditional religious groups. Western scholars, on the other hand, are less well qualified to undertake reliable higher criticism, since in works such as these a vast knowledge of Indian *realia* of the past as well as the present and a kind of erudition that only comes from having received a lengthy traditional Indian education are involved. Even a poem as small as the *Bhagavad-gītā* has been tackled with singular lack of success by many different investigators. Each seems to come up with a different opinion as to what constitutes the original *Bhagavad-gītā* and what portions are interpolated.

Versification and Language

Most of the *Mahābhārata* and the *Rāmāyaṇa* are composed in a verse called *sloka,* a two-line stanza defined by both the number of syllables and, to a lesser extent, the succession of heavy and light syllables. The epic sloka consists of two verse lines, each of an independent metrical structure. Each is divisible into two quarter verses of eight syllables each. The preceding quarter verse is constructed according to a definite set of metrical rules and the following quarter verse similarly obeys another set of rules. The rules apply mainly to the succession of light and heavy syllables per quarter verse. A light syllable consists of a short vowel followed by at most one consonant; any other syllable is heavy. The constraints on the prior quarter verse are that the fifth, sixth, and seventh syllable must be light–heavy–heavy, respectively, and those on the following quarter sloka that the sixth and seventh must be light–heavy, respectively. There are other, more subtle constraints, but they often have exceptions. The caesura is variable, but usually falls after the fourth or fifth syllable in a quarter verse. Generalized, the patterns appear as follows:

	Prior quarter	*Following quarter*
Sloka:	˘ ˘ ˘ ˘ ˘ — — ˘	˘ ˘ ˘ ˘ ˘ — ˘ ˘
	˘ ˘ ˘ ˘ ˘ — — ˘	˘ ˘ ˘ ˘ ˘ — ˘ ˘

The meter lends itself effortlessly to composition and its freedom in using heavy and light syllables prevents it from becoming monotonous. A second common meter is the *triṣṭubh* which consists of four quarters of eleven syllables each:

˘ — ˘ — — ˘ ˘ — ˘ — ˘; repeated four times, with variations.

An example of a sloka is, for instance, *Mbhr.* I.30.9:

somasthānam idaṃ ceti darbhās te lilihus tadā
tato dvaidhākṛtā jihvā sarpāṇāṃ tena karmaṇā

> And [realizing] that the darbha grass had been the place where the soma had been, here, they licked it then,
> From then on the tongue of snakes has divided in two by that act.

An example of a triṣṭubh is the following verse from the *Mahābhārata:*

sa cā 'pi keśau harir udbabarha / śuklam ekam aparaṃ cā 'pi kṛṣṇam

tau cā 'pi keśau viśatāṃ Yadūnāṃ / kule striyau rohiṇīṃ devakīṃ ca

> And he, Hari, extricated two body hairs,
> a white one and another black one,
> and those two hairs entered into
> two women in the clan of the Yadus, Rohiṇī and Devakī.

In addition, a few rarer meters are found in both epics. Many chapters of the *Rāmāyaṇa* end in a verse of a different meter than the rest of the chapter. The meters are chanted in a lightly modulated melody which varies from region to region. The metrics on the whole pose few constraints upon the syntax of the language.

A word order determined by considerations of preference and custom, rather than by semantic requisites, gives the Sanskrit language a rather free syntax. Much of the syntactical information is conveyed by rules of agreement and concord rather than by word order, so that individual words can be shifted around rather arbitrarily within the verse. As a result, the transition between straight prose and versified prose is gradual and a moderately skilled *littérateur* can compose in verse as easily as in prose. Nevertheless, there is a characteristic epic style especially prevalent in the battle books. The vocabulary is rather restrained and sober, underplaying the awesome and gruesome events taking place on the battlefield. Take for instance this example from the Droṇaparvan, the Sixth Book of the *Mahābhārata:*

Saṃjaya spoke:
... During the progress, O king, of that battle in which the combatants fought without any regard for one another, Dhrishtadyumna caused his own steeds to be mixed up with those of Drona. Those steeds endued with the speed of the wind, that were white as pigeons and red as blood, thus mixed with one another in battle, looked exceedingly beautiful. Indeed, they looked resplendent like clouds charged with lightning. Then that slayer of hostile heroes, *viz.,* heroic Dhrishtadyumna, the son of Prishata, beholding Drona, O Bharata, arrived so near, cast off his bow and took up his sword and shield, for achieving a difficult feat. Seizing the shaft of Drona's car, he entered into it. And he stayed sometimes on the middle of the yoke, and sometimes on its joints and sometimes behind the steeds. And while he was moving, armed with swords, quickly upon the backs of those red steeds of Drona, the latter could not detect an opportunity for striking him. All this seemed wonderful to us. Indeed, like the sweep of a hawk in the woods from desire of food, seemed that sally of Dhrishtadyumna from his own car for the destruction of Drona. Then Drona cut off, with a

hundred arrows, the shield, decked with a hundred moons, of Drupada's son, and then his sword, with ten others. And mighty Drona then, with four and sixty arrows, slew the steeds of his antagonist. And with a couple of broad-headed shafts he cut off the latter's standard and umbrella also, and then slew both his *Parshni* charioteers. And then with great speed drawing his bow-string to his ear, he shot at him a fatal shaft, like the wielder of the thunder hurling the thunder (at a foe). But soon Satyaki, with four and ten sharp shafts, cut off that fatal arrow of Drona. And thus the Vrishni hero, O sire, rescued Dhrishtadyumna, who had been seized by that lion among men, the foremost of preceptors, like a deer seized by the king of the forests. Even thus did that bull amongst the Sinis, the prince of the Panchalas. Beholding Satyaki to rescue the prince of the Panchalas in the dreadful battle, Drona quickly shot at him six and twenty arrows. The grandson of Sini then, in return, pierced Drona in the centre of the chest with six and twenty arrows, while the latter was engaged in devouring the Srinjayas. Then all the Panchala car-warriors, desirous of victory upon the Satwata hero, proceeding against Drona, quickly withdrew Dhrishtadyumna from the battle.[10]

At times the poem becomes quite expressive, as images and similes, metaphors, and other figures of speech are used. The frequency of use, however, soon dulls their effectiveness, and in the end they are simply perceived as clichés marking a battle scene. Here is, for instance, a description of the slaughter of an elephant brigade by the warrior Sātvata:

Those elephants slaughtered with those shafts, whose touch resembled thunder sped by that foremost one among the Sinis began to fly away from the field, their tusks broken, bodies covered with blood, heads and frontal globes split open, ears and faces and trunks cut off, and themselves deprived of riders, and standards cut down, riders slain, and blankets loosened, ran away, O king, in all directions. Many amongst them, O monarch, mangled by Satwata with long shafts and calf-tooth-headed arrows and broad-headed arrows and *Anjalikas* and razor-faced arrows and crescent-shaped ones fled away, with blood flowing down their bodies, and themselves ejecting urine and excreta and uttering loud and diverse cries, deep as the roar of clouds. And some amongst the others wandered, and some limped, and some fell down, and some became pale and cheerless.[11]

For a folklorist the Indian epics are interesting from two different perspectives. On the one hand, their vast store of folktales, descriptions of holy places, and festivals makes them part of the folk tradition. India probably has a richer story literature than any other country in the world. There are several large collections of fables, tales, and merchant stories in Sanskrit literature, such as the *Pañcatantra*[12] and the *Kathāsaritsāgara,* the "Ocean of Stories."[13]

In the *Mahābhārata* and the *Rāmāyaṇa* we often find the earliest attestations of many of the stories that have become part of the later collections. Some of them, such as the story of the man in the well, have even become part of world literature. Others are variations on the theme of a hero killing a demon, too numerous to mention. Other stories again, such as the story of Sāvitrī, who by her persistence and conjugal devotion forced Death to return her husband's life to her, have become very popular within India and are still used to inculcate morality on the younger generation. In the comparison of these folktales and their literary provenance, much work has been done by Ludwik Sternbach in publications in the *Journal of the American Oriental Society,* the *Annals of the Bhandarkar Oriental Research Institute,* and elsewhere.

From another perspective, we can see that the epics themselves have become incorporated into the great tradition within India and outside of it in the countries that at one time fell within its cultural sphere. We find festivals celebrated in honor of Rāma and his brother Lakshmaṇa in many places in India.[14] Festivals such as the North-Indian *Dassara* act out Rāma's struggle against Rāvaṇa and his recapture of Sītā. This festival is accompanied by a recitation of the Rāma story in a modern vernacular. Into the same category fall the popular performances of dramas and shadow plays in Thailand, Malaysia, and Java which use themes derived from the epics. To this day most children in the small villages of Central Java are familiar with the stories of the Sanskrit epics and their heroes.

NOTES

1. See M. Winternitz, *History of Indian Literature,* 3 vols. (Calcutta: University of Calcutta, 1959–63), I, pp. 399 ff. for a summary of the chronological status of the epics.

2. S. Wikander, "Pândavasagan och Mahâbhâratas mytiska förutsättningar," in *Religion och Bibel* 6 (1947): 27–39.

3. See E. W. Hopkins, "The Social and Military Position of the Ruling Caste in Ancient India," *Journal of the American Oriental Society* 13 (1889): 182.

4. See J. E. Fontenrose, *Python* (Berkeley: University of California Press, 1959).

5. Stith Thompson, and Warren E. Roberts, *Types of Indic Oral Tales,* Folklore Fellows Communications, no. 180 (Helsinki, 1960).

6. Hopkins, p. 67.

7. Winternitz, p. 286.

8. V. S. Sukthankar, *Critical Studies in the Mahābhārata* (Poona: Karnatak Publishing House, 1944), pp. 44 ff.

9. Ibid., p. 129.

10. Translation by K. H. Ganguli in *The Mahabharata,* ed. P. C. Roy, V: *Dronaparva,* pp. 271–72.

11. Ibid., p. 676.

12. The *Pañcatantra* has been studied in great detail by Johannes Hertel in his four publications dealing with this text in the Harvard Oriental Series, vols. 11–14 (Cambridge: Harvard University Press, 1908–15). Also see F. Edgerton, *The Panchatantra Reconstructed,* 2 vols., American Oriental Series (New Haven, 1924).

13. The *Kathāsaritsāgara* was translated by C. H. Tawney and republished in 10 volumes with a wealth of notes and comments by N. M. Penzer (London, 1924–28); reprinted in Delhi: Motilal Banarsidass, 1968.

14. See Barend A. van Nooten, *The Mahābhārata* (New York: Twayne Publishers, 1971), p. 37, and notes. In the same work are references to the place of the *Mahābhārata* in Southeast Asia. A more complete summary of the epic narrative may also be found here.

BIBLIOGRAPHY

The Mahābhārata

Text Editions

Anonymous. *The Mahabharata: An epic poem.* Edited by the Pandits attached to the Education Committee. 5 vols. Calcutta, 1834–39. The *editio princeps,* also known as the "Calcutta Edition."

Atmarama Khadilkar. *Mahābhārata,* with Nilakaṇṭha's commentary. Bombay: Gaṇpat Kṛṣṇajī's Press, 1863. This is the "Bombay Edition" of Vulgate, printed in *pothi* form. Both the Bombay and Calcutta editions have been reprinted several times.

Krishnacharya, T. R., and T. R. Vyasacharya. *Srimanmahabharatam.* 23 vols. Kumbhakonam: Madhva Vilas Book Depot, 1906–14. This is the "Kumbhakonam Edition."

Sastri, P. S. S. *The Mahābhārata (Southern Recension).* 18 vols. Madras, 1931–36.

Sukthankar, Vishnu Sitaram. *Mahābhārata.* 19 vols. Poona: Bhandarkar Oriental Research Institute, 1933–66. Many different scholars edited the various volumes of this "critical edition." The text alone, without the critical apparatus, was published in 1973 by the same institute in two volumes.

Translations

Dutt, Manmatha Nath. *A Prose English Translation of the Mahabharata.* 6 vols. Calcutta: H. C. Dass, 1895–1905.

Roy, Protap Chandra, ed. *The Mahabharata.* 18 vols. Translated by Kisari Mohan Ganguli. Calcutta: Bharata Press, 1883–96. The translation is based on the Calcutta edition augmented by Bengali manuscripts. The translation is solemn and didactic in tone, its style Gothic and at times impressive. On the whole, because of errors in the translation and the inclusion of irrelevant materials, the work should be treated with caution; as a sourcebook for secondary studies it is untrustworthy. A second edition appeared in Calcutta, 1919–35, in 11 vols., and was recently republished in Delhi: Oriental Publishing House, n.d., 12 vols. Selections from the first and second volumes have been published. See S. C. Nott, ed., *The Mahabharata* (London: Janus Press, 1956).

Van Buitenen, J. A. B. *The Mahabharata, I: Beginning.* Chicago: University of Chicago Press, 1974. The first volume of a scheduled complete translation of the Critical Edition of the *Mahābhārata* into English.

Studies

Biardeau, Madeleine. "Bhakti et avatāra." Bulletin d'École française d'Hautes Études 63 (1974): 111–263. This article views the central Mahābhārata myth in relation to subordinate stories and Puranic accounts.

Dange, Dr. Sadashiv Ambadas. *Legends in the Mahabharata with a Brief Survey of Folk-tales.* Delhi: Motilal Banarsidass, 1969. This book of close to 400 pages deals with a few legends in detail and gives the outline of two dozen folktales. The legends dealt with are, among others, about the mythical giant bird Garuḍa and his battle against snakes, and the virtuous Kaca who was swallowed by his father and reborn from his right side.

Goldman, Robert P. *Gods, Priests, and Warriors*. New York: Columbia University Press, 1976. A close examination of the Bhṛgu clan in the *Mahābhārata*.

Hopkins, E. W. *Epic Mythology. Grundriss der Indo-Arischen Philologie*, I/4. Strassburg: Karl Trubner, 1915. An excellent, very thorough summary of the mythology of the *Mahābhārata* and the *Rāmāyaṇa*. It is based on the vulgate editions of the texts, but still quite useful. An Indian reprint appeared in Delhi in 1971.

————. ''The Social and Military Position of the Ruling Caste in Ancient India.'' *Journal of the American Oriental Society* 13 (1889): 57–376. By far the best source work for matters pertaining to warfare, battle orders, ethics of war, and conduct in peace.

————. ''Proverbs and Tales Common to the Two Sanskrit Epics.'' *American Journal of Philology* 19 (1898): 138–51.

————. ''On the Hindu Custom of Dying to Redress a Grievance.'' *Journal of the American Oriental Society* 21 (1901): 146–59.

————. ''Yoga Technique in the Great Epic.'' *Journal of the American Oriental Society* 22 (1901): 333 ff.

————. ''Epic Chronology.'' *Journal of the American Oriental Society* 24 (1903): 7–56.

————. ''The Sniff-kiss in Ancient India.'' *Journal of the American Oriental Society* 28 (1907): 120–34.

————. ''Magic Observances in the Hindu Epic.'' *Proceedings of the American Philosophical Society* 49 (1910): 29–40.

————. ''Mythological Aspects of Trees and Mountains.'' *Journal of the American Oriental Society* 30 (1910): 347–74.

————. ''Priestly Penance and Legal Penalty.'' *Journal of the American Oriental Society* 44 (1924): 243–57.

————. ''The Epic View of the Earth.'' *Journal of the International School of Vedic and Allied Research* 1 (1930): 65–87.

Hiltebeitel, Alf. *The Ritual of Battle*. Ithaca: Cornell University Press, 1976. The author views the epic within the framework of Dumézil's theories.

Jacobi, H. *Mahābhārata: Inhaltsangabe, Index und Corcordanz*. Bonn, 1903.

Sorensen, Soren. *An Index of the Names in the Mahābhārata*. London, 1904–25. Reprinted Delhi: Motilal Banarsidass, 1963. An excellent index of proper names in the Western alphabetical order, based on the Bombay and Calcutta editions.

Sukthankar, V. S. *Critical Studies in the Mahābhārata*. Poona: Karnatak Publishing House, 1944. A posthumous collection of Sukthankar's contributions to *Mahābhārata* text criticism.

————. *On the Meaning of the Mahābhārata*. Bombay: Asiatic Society, 1957. A criticism of Western appreciations of the *Mahābhārata* and an explanation of its metaphysical and philosophical significance.

van Nooten, Barend, A. *The Mahābhārata*. New York: Twayne Publishers, 1971. A brief survey of the *Mahābhārata* in relation to its history in India and Southeast Asia, with large bibliography.

The Rāmāyaṇa

Text Editions

Bhagvad-Datta, Pandit, Pandit Rama Labhaya, and Pandit Vishva-Bandhu Shastri.

Ramayana of Valmiki. Lahore: D.A.V. College Research Department, 1923–49. This is the Northwestern recension.

Dharmadhikari, Mahadev Shastri, and Tatya Shastri Khedkar. *Valmiki's Ramayana with Ramavarman's Commentary.* Bombay: Ganpat Krishnaji's Press, 1859. This is the so-called Bombay edition, reprinted several times. It is in *pothi* form.

Gorresio, Gaspare. *Ramayana, poema indico di Valmici.* 5 vols. Parigi: Stamperia Reale, 1843–50. This is the Bengal, or Eastern recension of the *Ramayana.* Prior to this edition, there were two partial editions, one by William Carey and Joshua Marshman (Serampore, 1806–10), and one by Augustus G. Schlegel (Bonn, 1829–38).

Krishnacharya, T. R., and T. R. Vyasacharya. *Srimad-Valmiki-Ramayana.* 3 vols. Kumbhakonam and Bombay: Nirnayasagar Press, 1911–13. The Kumbhakonam edition representing a text from Southern India.

Vaidya, P. L. *The Valmiki-Ramayana.* 9 vols. Baroda: Oriental Institute, 1960–74. The critical edition with important prefaces and a complete critical apparatus. Several different scholars edited the various volumes.

Translations

Dutt, M. N. *The Ramayana Translated into English Prose.* 7 vols. Calcutta, 1891–94. A complete translation of the Vulgate. In spite of its archaic phraseology and Victorian style it is still the most accurate rendering of the epic.

Griffith, Ralph T. H. *The Ramayan of Valmiki.* 5 vols. London: Trübner and Co., 1870–74. A translation into verse, not very literal, and very archaic in wording.

Hopkins, E. W. "The Original Rāmāyaṇa." *Journal of the American Oriental Society* 46 (1926): 202–19.

———. "Allusions to the Rama-story in the Mahabharata." *Journal of the American Oriental Society* 50 (1930): 85–103.

Sen, Makhan Lal. *The Ramayana.* 3 vols. Calcutta: Datta Bose and Co., 1939. It is a "modernised English version" and not a literal translation of the *Ramayana.*

Shastri, Hari Prasad. *The Ramayana of Valmiki.* 3 vols. London: Shanti Sadan, 1959. A relatively accurate rendition of the *Rāmāyaṇa*'s vulgate text.

Studies

Guruge, Ananda. *The Society of the Ramayana.* Maharagama: Saman Press, 1960. A comprehensive survey of the geographical, social, moral, and philosophical background of the *Ramayana.*

Jacobi, Hermann. *Das Ramayana.* Bonn, 1893. An often-quoted and valuable study of the text history of the *Ramayana.* It contains a concordance for the Bombay and Calcutta editions and a summary of contents. The first part of the work was (not very perfectly) translated into English by S. N. Ghosal (Baroda, 1961).

Pusalker, A. C. *Studies in the Epics and Puranas.* Bombay: Bhavan's Book University, 1955. A good survey of scholarly work done on the *Mahābhārata* and the *Rāmāyaṇa* between 1911 and 1954.

4

The Iranian Epics

William L. Hanaway, Jr.

The Iranian epic tradition has its roots in the general Indo-European epic tradition, and has been closely identified with the Iranian people as a whole from the earliest historical times until today. This tradition is expressed in literary form as extended narrative poetry, set in the distant past, which concentrates on the Iranian monarchs and a small number of heroes, and which embodies the history, the ideals, and the values of the Iranian nation. This poetry is written in the New Persian language, that is, the Persian language as it has come to us in literary works of the Islamic period, from the early ninth century onward. By comparison with English, Persian changed little between the ninth and the early twentieth centuries. Thus an educated Iranian of today can read the whole range of his epic poetry with about the same ease that the educated English-speaker reads Shakespeare.

This discussion of the Iranian epic will center on Ferdowsi's (Firdausi's) *Shāhnāma* (Book of Kings), the major epic poem in Persian, but will also cover some of the material from the national legend not found in *Shāhnāma,* and will touch on the romance tradition, which has many ties with the epic.

Shāhnāma

Sometime late in the Sasanian period (third–seventh centuries A.D.), a great chronicle was compiled by the Persian court and called *Khwadāy Nāmag* (Book of Kings). Although this chronicle does not survive as a whole, fragments of it are found in Arabic histories and, at a later time, in Ferdowsi's *Shāhnāma.* The Zoroastrian elements which one would expect to find in an official Sasanian chronicle were greatly reduced in the Islamic redactions, but the spirit of that older Iranian faith still breathes in Ferdowsi's epic. A number of strands were woven into this chronicle, the main ones being the religious and the national traditions, historical knowledge of past kings, Zoroastrian wisdom-literature, the *Alexander Romance,* and oral legends of local heroes and dynasties. The *Khwadāy Nāmag* was kept up to date until the Arab conquest of Iran and the death of the last Sasanian king in A.D. 651. This chronicle, through intermediate texts, was the basis for a great deal of the *Shāhnāma*.[1]

When Ferdowsi set himself to the task of "sowing the seeds of his words" (ca. A.D. 975), he had before him a prose text in Persian called *Shāhnāma*, which had been compiled in A.D. 951 by four experts at the order of the governor of Tus in eastern Iran. Based largely, though not entirely, on translations of Middle Iranian texts, this prose *Shāhnāma* undoubtedly contained much material deriving directly or indirectly from the *Khwadāy Nāmag*. This text has also perished, but the introduction to it is preserved, and this forms one of the links between the Sasanian chronicle and Ferdowsi's epic.[2] The sources of the other material in Ferdowsi's *Shāhnāma* are not known, but were most probably books that existed at that time (some titles of which we do know), and orally transmitted stories.

Abu al-Qāsem Manṣur, styled Ferdowsi (b. A.D. 932 or 936; d. 1020 or 1025), was a member of the landed gentry in Tus, a city in the eastern Iranian province of Khurasan. The *dehqān*s, the provincial landowners, were a class that had existed since Sasanian times and were the means whereby the older Iranian traditions, values, and ways of life were preserved after the Muslim conquest. The Arab governors had, by and large, kept the local administrative structures that they had found in eastern Iran, and it was in the petty courts of the dehqāns that not only local political power resided, but social status and cultural tradition as well. Among this class, the writing of *Shāhnāma*s after the Sasanian fashion was a strong tradition in Ferdowsi's time, and a poet ambitious to write the "history" of his people had not only texts in verse and prose to look to, but a tradition within which to work.

By the time that Ferdowsi wrote his *Shāhnāma*, which he completed in about 1010, the formal conventions of Persian poetry were firmly established. Little is known about pre-Islamic Iranian poetry, but it is thought that certain of the meters used in Islamic times derive, at least indirectly, from earlier Iranian meters.[3] By the tenth century, Persian prosody and rhyme had become systematized according to Arabic models, a fact which has led some scholars to believe that the meters themselves were derived from Arabic practice. The meters in use from the tenth century to modern times were quantitative, i.e., they were based on regularly recurring patterns of long and short syllables. Stress played an important but not clearly understood role. The form that Ferdowsi chose for his *Shāhnāma* was a line of eight feet in two hemistichs in the meter *motaqāreb:*

The hemistichs of each line have end-rhyme, but successive lines do not rhyme with each other. There is a regular caesura between hemistichs, but no regular one within each hemistich. There is almost no enjambment. An example of three lines follows:

1. Konun man ze Torkān–e jang āvarān

   Farāz āvaram lashkari bi kerān
2. Bar angizam az gāh Kāvus–rā
   Az Irān be-burram pey–e Ṭus–rā
3. Be Rostam daham takht–o gorz–o kolāh
   Neshānamsh bar gāh–e Kāvus shāh[4]

> Now I [Sohrāb] will raise a boundless army from among the war-like Turks. I will drive Kāvus [the Iranian king] from his palace, and I will obliterate from Iran all traces of Ṭus [a hero]. I will give to Rostam [Sohrāb's father] the throne and mace and crown; I will enthrone him in place of King Kāvus.

Until Ferdowsi's time this meter had been used for various kinds of narrative poetry, but after *Shāhnāma* its use became restricted almost entirely to epics, and poems written in the epic style.

Ferdowsi's *Shāhnāma* is a vast epic, both in terms of its size and of the time span and variety of material encompassed by it. The most recent critical edition (Moscow, 1966–71) runs to something over 45,000 lines, and this is a considerable reduction from earlier editions, some of which incorporated large blocks of other epics and grew to nearly 100,000 lines. It is a history of the Iranian people from the creation of the world until the fall of the Sasanian dynasty to the Arabs in the seventh century A.D. The established chronicle tradition provided Ferdowsi with a basic format for his epic, and through this grand tapestry of his nation's past, Ferdowsi wove the unifying thread of Iranian kingship and legitimate succession.

The narrative is a chronological account of four successive dynasties: the Pishdādian, the Keyānian, the Ashkānian (Parthian), and the Sasanian. Each of these dynasties is subdivided into the reigns of its kings, totalling fifty in all. The stories of these kings form the basic narrative units of the text. Cutting across this sequence of reigns, from the latter days of the Pishdādians through the Keyānians, is an extensive cycle of heroic tales centered on an eastern Iranian dynasty from Sistan, which forms a counterpoint to the succession of kings.

The Pishdādian dynasty is mythical, the Keyānian is probably legendary, and the Ashkānian (Parthian) (150 B.C.–A.D. 224) and Sasanian (A.D. 224–632) are historical. While the material appears to be divided evenly between the mythical/legendary and the historical, in fact the greater part of the narrative falls on the historical side. The Pishdādian kings descend from older

Indo-Iranian traditions, and some have their parallels in the Vedic texts. As evil and violence enter the idyllic Pishdādian times and the dynasty nears its end, the so-called Sistan Cycle of stories begins, and the mythical period gives way to the Keyānian dynasty and the heroic age.[5] The narrative moves ahead, gaining in color and excitement, especially with the entrance of the great hero Rostam. During the heroic age, the kings are mainly occupied with their wars against the Turanians. Rostam's career as the dynasty's mainstay against its enemies from across the Oxus River spans many generations, and the dynasty itself hardly outlives its greatest hero. The heroic age shades into the historical period with the arrival of Alexander the Great, and from this point on the narrative becomes much more of a historical chronicle.

The historical part of *Shāhnāma* deals very briefly with the Ashkānians, but treats the Sasanians at length. By no means is all of the material in this part "historical" in the strict sense, since Ferdowsi weaves legends and romances into the fabric of his narrative. It must be stressed that the historical part of *Shāhnāma* represents epic poetry only in a diluted sense. The epic spirit and excitement, and the sense of the hero being more gifted than his fellows as he fights in battle to gain honor and glory are lost. In the historical parts the king himself is often the hero, but being a king he has other concerns demanding his attention. He must rule, dispense justice, and plan his strategy against the enemy. Thus he has less time for the traditional pursuits of the hero and must temper his fierce individualism with a sense of corporate responsibility. These two impulses are basically at odds with each other, and the result is that kingship wins out over heroism and we are presented with a series of brave kings leading an orderly society. The focus of the narrative is on the king as ruler, and there is no Rostam to play the role of independent hero.

Some of the reasons for this change of spirit lie in the nature of the material with which Ferdowsi worked. The Sasanian chronicles and the texts derived from them were both fuller and of a different nature than works dealing with the mythical period and the heroic age. Works on the Sasanian period, when state records were kept, were without doubt relatively detailed. Information on the earlier periods would have been found largely in religious texts such as the Avesta and preserved in the oral tradition. Much written material on the Sasanians was available in the Islamic period to the historian (and the epic poet), whereas what was transmitted from the earlier periods, other than the religious texts, must have existed in many different versions and local variants, and at different lengths. Thus in working with the earlier periods the poet had more scope in which to exercise his imagination. Conversely, where much detailed material was available, the poet's scope was considerably more limited. Ferdowsi says that he tried to remain faithful to his sources, and the result is that in the historical part of *Shāhnāma* he becomes more of a historian than an epic poet. The present-day audiences for oral recitations of *Shāhnāma* (like the audiences of the past, as far as we can tell) prefer listening only to the mythical and legendary parts of the epic, and have no interest in the historical parts at all.[6] They rightly sense that with the death of Rostam and the appearance of Alexander, the epic spirit leaves the poem and all that remains is versified history.

If Ferdowsi's scope was narrowed by too much historical material, it was considerably broadened in the legendary parts of *Shāhnāma* by the cycle of tales from Sistan which centered on the heroes of one legendary dynasty. While the main narrative of *Shāhnāma* is a chronicle of kings, the Sistan Cycle is a chronicle of heroes, and derives from a different tradition. The great hero of Sistan, Rostam, and his father Zāl, were both Saka heroes, and tales about them were probably brought to Sistan (< Sakastan, "the land of the Sakas") when it was settled by invading Sakas in the second century B.C. Through a "nationalizing" process, probably during the Sasanian period, these Saka heroes were made to descend from King Jamshid and the hero Keresaspa, both of whom appear in the Avesta (the Zoroastrian sacred books). Although the national tradition recognizes Jamshid and Keresaspa as ancestors of Rostam, in actual fact, the Saka heroes have no connection with those of the Avesta. Down to the tenth century, more and more links were forged between this cycle and the national tradition, but it was Ferdowsi who effected the full-scale integration of the two. As the national tradition of legitimate kings marches on in the *Shāhnāma,* the Sistan Cycle moves at a different rhythm, sometimes in the foreground, sometimes in the background, but always maintaining its integrity although now fully a part of the main narrative.

It would seem useful to give here a brief synopsis of the *Shāhnāma*. In this summary the mythical and legendary parts of the text are stressed at the expense of the historical parts, and the focus is on certain characters and episodes which are both characteristic of the Iranian epic and which show thematic parallels with other epic traditions. A commentary on certain aspects of the narrative and a translation of one battle scene are included. Many interesting characters and events had to be omitted.

SYNOPSIS OF THE EPIC

The narrative of *Shāhnāma* begins with the origin of all things. After describing the creation of the world and man, Ferdowsi introduces Keyumars, the first king and founder of the Pishdādian dynasty. The kingship passes from father to son until it reaches the fifth in line, Jamshid. These first five rulers are the culture heroes who bring various elements of civilization to the world, among which are the concept of sovereignty, food and clothing, fire, the smelting of metals, agriculture, writing, and the organization of society into four classes: priests, warriors, agriculturalists, and craftsmen. Jamshid's rule lasted a thousand years, and for most of this time the world saw no hardship or death. Toward the end of his reign, vanity overcame him, and he claimed that he was supreme, forgetting his obligation to God. When he abandoned the fundamental principles of monarchy, the *farr* (the divinely bestowed legitimacy which an Iranian king had to have in order to rule) departed from him. The people lost confidence in him, the army deserted, and strife broke out in the land. Jamshid was deposed by the non-Iranian usurper Żaḥḥāk, who also ruled for a thousand years. Before conquering Iran, Żaḥḥāk had been corrupted by the Devil, who caused a large snake to grow from each of Żaḥḥāk's shoulders. This three-headed monster, who has counterparts in other Indo-European myths, caused evil to flourish in the world, and oppressed the people greatly by demanding the brains of two youths each day to feed his snakes.

A movement to overthrow Żaḥḥāk was led by Kāva the blacksmith, who had lost seventeen children to the tyrant's serpents and wanted to save his one remaining child. He rallied the people around Feridun, an Iranian hero who possessed the royal farr, and used his leather blacksmith's apron mounted on a spear as the standard for the Iranian forces opposing Żaḥḥāk. The population hated the tyrant, and Feridun had little trouble in capturing him and ending his rule.

Feridun married Jamshid's two sisters, and from them had three sons, Salm, Tur, and Iraj. When these sons had come of age, Feridun divided the world among them, and prepared to retire from the throne. To Salm he gave Byzantium and the West; on Tur he bestowed Central Asia (hence Turan) and China; Iran, Mesopotamia, and Yemen were given to the youngest son, Iraj. After a time, the older brothers grew jealous of Iraj and plotted war against him. Feridun warned Iraj of the impending trouble, but Iraj ignored the warning and met his brothers peaceably. They quarreled, and Tur murdered Iraj.

Iraj left a grandson named Manuchehr, whom Feridun brought up to be a warrior. Seeking to avenge the death of his grandfather, Manuchehr set out first to kill Tur, and then Salm. Soon after these acts of vengeance, Feridun died and Manuchehr succeeded to the throne of Iran.

At this point the Sistan Cycle enters the narrative. This cycle centers on a dynasty not related to the royal house of Iran. It consists of legends which originated outside of the national tradition, but which were integrated with it. Sām is the first member of the Sistan dynasty to figure prominently in the *Shāhnāma*. Out of a sense of pride and reputation, Sām rejects his son Zāl when he learns that he was born with snow-white hair, and he orders that the infant be exposed on a mountain. Zāl is found by the Simorgh, a giant bird, and is reared to manhood in the bird's eyrie. Later Sām, remorseful over the abandonment of his child, discovers him in the mountains and takes him back from the custody of the Simorgh. As they part, the Simorgh gives Zāl a feather which he is to use to summon the great bird in times of trouble.

Zāl, during a visit to the King of Kabul, falls in love with the King's daughter Rudāba. Their meeting and courtship are described in a long romantic episode which includes a famous scene where Rudāba lets down her long braids for Zāl to use as a rope to climb to her balcony. After many difficulties they marry, and from their union is born Rostam, the mightiest hero of the *Shāhnāma*.

Rostam is an extraordinary individual in all respects. His birth was by caesarean section, and it was necessary to call on the Simorgh to heal Rudāba's incision. As an infant, Rostam grew so rapidly that it took ten wet-nurses to feed him. When he was weaned he ate the food of five men, and rapidly grew to enormous stature. While still a youth, he slew the King's white elephant which had gone on a rampage.

As Rostam was growing up, relations between Iran and Turan began to worsen as a result of the death of Tur at the hands of Manuchehr. After Manuchehr's death, the King of Turan sent his son and army commander Afrāsiyāb to attack Iran, thus beginning a long series of wars which occupy the rest of the Pishdādians and all the rulers of the Keyānian dynasty. The line of Pishdādian kings ends, and Rostam begins to take a more active role in the wars against Turan.

The second of the Keyānian kings, Key Kāvus, was having difficulties in bringing to submission the region of Mazandaran, a wooded and mountainous area of northern Iran. The ruler there was the White Div, a demon, whom Kāvus attacked. The King was no match for the demon, however, and was captured. He sent a message to Rostam asking for help, and Rostam decided to take a dangerous short-cut to reach the King more quickly. On the way he was challenged seven times in a series of incidents referred to as the *Haft Khᵛān* (Seven Stages). Rostam confronts, among other opponents, a fierce lion, a dragon, and a sorceress in a series of triumphs reminiscent of the twelve labors of Hercules. The culminating battle is with the White Div, whom Rostam slays through his superior strength and valor. Mazandaran is eventually subdued and Rostam turns his attention again to Afrāsiyāb and the Turanians.

It is not unusual for Ferdowsi to interpolate in his narrative stories which seem to derive from the oral tradition, since no other references to them have appeared in Iranian texts. Rostam's romance with Tahmina, daughter of a local ruler, is an example of this. Their meeting quickly leads to marriage. Rostam spends one night with his bride and then departs, leaving her pregnant. From their marriage is born Sohrāb. The boy grows up not having seen his father, and in the best-known scene in the entire *Shāhnāma*, father and son meet in a tragic conflict which ends with Sohrāb's death.

The father-son battle is an archetypal conflict that echoes throughout Indo-European epic literature, appearing in German, Irish, and Russian heroic legends, and several times in the Iranian epic. In *Shāhnāma*, Ferdowsi builds up the story skillfully, using anticipation and suspense and carefully balancing the motivations of father and son against the force of destiny. The outcome is revealed to the listener in a prologue to the story in which Ferdowsi raises questions of justice and fate. This in no way diminishes the impact of the climax, when after a long struggle, father and son recognize each other while

Sohrāb lies dying from his father's dagger thrust. This episode was brought to the English reading public in 1853 with Matthew Arnold's "Sohrab and Rustum," which he wrote after reading Sainte-Beuve's long review of Jules Mohl's French translation of *Shāhnāma*.[7] The death of Sohrāb has always been a favorite of the storytellers and *Shāhnāma*–reciters in Iran, and in recent years an opera based on this story was written in Tajikistan.

The epic was an aristocratic art in Iran, produced in the courts with the courtly class as its original audience, and the epic heroes reflect this. Their activities are those of the nobility: hunting, feasting, and war, and they pursue these with equal vigor, alternating between excesses of violent action in the field and exuberance at the table. Epic conventions allow for little psychological development, except in the case of Rostam, whom we have a longer time to observe. In general, the heroes are born, not made. The hero is cast in the heroic mold from birth, and his life is only the working out of his predestined course. Thus the inner and outer worlds of the heroes are out of balance, since we know little of their motivations beyond a sense of honor and duty. Loyalty to the king, patriotism, and bravery in battle are the primary virtues.

Following the story of Sohrāb, Ferdowsi begins another long tale which, like the preceding one, has reflexes in other epics. A son, Siyāvush, is born to Key Kāvus and is entrusted to Rostam for training in the skills of the warrior. Siyāvush grows to be a handsome and modest youth who attracts the lustful eye of Kāvus' wife. In an incident which is an example of the "Potiphar's Wife" motif, she tries to seduce Siyāvush. He refuses her, and the rejected woman falsely accuses him to the King. Siyāvush's name is cleared in an ordeal by fire, but later, following a quarrel with his father, Siyāvush leaves the Iranian court and defects to the Turanian Afrāsiyāb. He marries Afrāsiyāb's daughter, but court jealousy leads to his murder. His wife and infant son are brought safely to Iran, where the son, Khosrow, grows up to be the greatest of the Keyānian kings.

Years pass and the war with Turan continues. Key Khosrow's vow to avenge the death of his father Siyāvush leads eventually to yet another full-scale confrontation between the Iranians and the Turanians, who now have powerful reinforcements from the Khāqān of China. In a battle scene organized in typical fashion, Ferdowsi begins with the preliminary skirmishes and leads up to the arrival on the field of the more important heroes:

A [Turanian] hero called Ashkabus roared like a drum and came out to seek battle with the Iranians, saying that he would lay his opponent's head in the dust. Rohhām [an Iranian] in mail and helmet, rode out quickly. The dust of battle rose to the clouds. Rohhām grappled with Ashkabus and drum rolls and trumpets sounded from both armies. [Ashkabus] rained arrows on Rohhām; his arrows were lying in wait for horsemen. Rohhām was protected by steel, and the arrows had no more effect than wind on his armor and helmet. This angered Ashkabus, who reached for his heavy mace; Rohhām also drew out his mace, and the

generals despaired of the outcome. Then Rohhām became afraid of the Koshāni
[i.e., Ashkabus] and headed for the mountains. Ṭus then jumped up in the center
of the [Iranian] army, and spurred on his horse to reach Ashkabus. Rostam also
leapt up, saying to Ṭus, "Rohhām's companion is a glass of wine. He flourishes
his sword and boasts among the warriors only when he is in his cups. Where is he
now with his red face? He was a lesser man than Ashkabus. You keep the center
of the army in order and I will go into battle on foot." He put his bow on his
shoulder by the string, placed several arrows in his belt, and roared out, "Your
opponent has come, fighter. Do not go away!"

The Koshāni laughed and looked at Rostam. Pulling in his reins, he said,
"What is your name? Who will weep over your headless body?"

"Why do you ask my name," said Rostam, "for you will not have any success
here. My mother named me 'your death,' and fate has made me the hammer for
your helmet."

"Without a horse you are giving yourself up to death right away," replied
Ashkabus.

"You silly brawler," said Rostam, "haven't you ever seen a man fight on foot
and put his opponent's head under a stone? Do lions and crocodiles and leopards
ride into battle in your country? Now, fierce rider, I will teach you how to fight
on foot. Ṭus sent me on foot just to take the horse from you. You should
dismount so that both sides can laugh at you. Today and right now, one man on
foot is worth 500 riders like you."

"Where are your weapons?" asked the Koshāni. "I see nothing except sighs
and chuckles."

"Look at this bow and arrow as your days now come to an end," replied
Rostam.

When Rostam saw him boastfully mounted on his horse, he strung his bow and
flexed it. He shot an arrow at the horse's chest, which brought the animal to the
ground. Rostam laughed and said, "Sit there beside your noble companion. You
had better hold its head and rest a bit from battle."

Ashkabus, trembling and red-faced, strung his bow and rained arrows on
Rostam.

"Don't tire your body, your arms, and your malevolent soul unnecessarily,"
said Rostam. He reached to his belt and drew out a poplar arrow, with a point
glittering like a diamond and four eagle feathers fixed to it. He rubbed his bow
and fitted the arrow. Bending his right arm and keeping his left straight, he made
the Chāchi bow creak. When the arrow's notch reached his ear, the stag-horn
bow groaned again. As his fingertip kissed the arrow, his arm drawn back past
his spine, heaven kissed his hand. The arrow struck the breast of Ashkabus, and
Fate said, "take," and Destiny said, "give"; the sky said "Bravo!" and the
moon said "Well done!" The Koshāni gave up his life; it was as if his mother
had never borne him.[8]

Rostam fought other such heroes, including the Turanian commander
Pulādvand, and finally the Iranians routed their foes. Sometime later Rostam
became involved in a strange adventure, as related in another story which
seems to have come from local oral tradition. A herdsman complained one

day to the King that an extraordinary wild ass was destroying the horses in his herd. Key Khosrow suspected that this was the demon Akvān and summoned Rostam from Sistan to fight it. Rostam sought out the beast, and when he found it, he decided to capture it alive and take it to the King. The demon appeared and disappeared repeatedly, always eluding the hero. Finally, Rostam lay down to sleep, exhausted from chasing it. Akvān turned himself into a windstorm, picked Rostam up, and cast him into the sea. With great difficulty he swam ashore, found his horse, and returned to pursue the demon. This time he caught it and killed it.

The romance of Bizhan and Manizha then follows. Bizhan, an Iranian hero, falls in love with Manizha, the daughter of Afrāsiyāb, and is discovered alone with her. Afrāsiyāb banishes her and imprisons Bizhan in a deep well. Rostam is sent by Key Khosrow to rescue Bizhan, and the lovers are taken safely to Iran. The war with the Turanians continues, but at last Afrāsiyāb is captured and slain by Key Khosrow. Khosrow later disappears mysteriously on a snowy mountain, and with his death, the character of the narrative changes. Demons and magic disappear, and the stories take on a more sober quality. The prophet Zoroaster appears and brings his religion to the Iranians, one of his first converts being King Goshtāsp. This change of ideology in the royal house sets the stage for Rostam's last great battle.

Esfandiyār is sent by his father, Goshtāsp, to bring Rostam to the royal court bound in fetters, because the King fears Rostam's power. In a long series of exchanges between Rostam and Esfandiyār, each reveals a distinct personality and outlook on the world. The two proud heroes, one old and the other young, cannot reconcile the demands made upon them by conscience and duty, and must resort to battle. Rostam has a difficult time of it on the first day, for Esfandiyār, as a result of a previous adventure with a Simorgh, has become invulnerable to injury except in the eyes. Wounded and tired at the end of the day, Rostam summons the Simorgh for help. The Simorgh heals Rostam's wounds and shows him how to make a magic double-pointed arrow which will pierce Esfandiyār's eyes and kill him. The next day, Rostam uses the arrow to dispatch his foe.

The Simorgh had warned Rostam that whoever used the magic arrow would suffer torment and decline for the rest of his life. This prediction comes true, as shortly afterward Rostam is treacherously killed by his jealous brother. The Keyānian dynasty soon ends, and Ferdowsi relates his version of the *Alexander Romance*. The Iranian *Alexander Romance* derives from the Pseudo–Callisthenes *Alexander Romance,* but has been changed to make Darius (II?) the father of Alexander the Great, and Darius III the Greek conqueror's half-brother. Thus, Alexander is incorporated into the Iranian royal genealogy, and his conquest of the Achaemenian empire is reduced to the dimensions of a family quarrel.

From this point on, the *Shāhnāma* increasingly resembles a historical chronicle, although it still includes legendary episodes. An example of these is the account of how Ardashir defeated Ardavān, the last of the Parthian (Ashkānian) kings, and founded the Sasanian Empire. The farr, the divine legitimacy of the king, leaves Ardavān and goes to Ardashir in the form of a ram, thus signaling the end of the Parthian's rule. The succession of Sasanian kings is described in detail, as are the appearance of the prophet Mani in the third century, the social reformer Mazdak in the fifth century, and the usurper Bahrām Chōbin in the late sixth century. As a counterpart to the earlier wars with the Turanians, the wars between Iran and the Hephthalites in the East and the Byzantines in the West occupy the attention of several kings.

There are also romantic episodes. The most famous of these, the story of Khosrow and Shirin, is part of a larger cycle of stories revolving around the Sasanian monarch Khosrow Parviz (A.D. 591–628) and the Armenian princess Shirin. This romance became extremely popular from the twelfth century on, when the courtly romances began to flourish. In all of the romantic episodes of the *Shāhnāma,* Ferdowsi was able to write in an appealing lyric style that brings out well the feelings of the lovers, their longings and delights. He has no difficulty in integrating these episodes into the stream of standard epic scenes of feasting, hunting, and war. The romantic sections are never over-done, and they provide a satisfying balance against the more martial epic scenes.

GENERAL CHARACTER AND THEMES

From pre-Islamic times until today, Persian literature has always had a strong didactic side, and *Shāhnāma* is squarely within the tradition. Didactic passages which point out morals, preach the virtues of wisdom, justice, and honesty, and stress the permanent human values of honor, manliness, free-dom, and patriotism, are scattered throughout the text. In the same category are the many lines which stress the transitory nature of earthly existence and the fickleness of fate. "This is the way of the harsh world," says Rostam to himself after his horse has been stolen, "sometimes you are in the saddle and sometimes the saddle is on you." This sense of fatalism and the vanity of human desires is strong in the legendary parts of *Shāhnāma,* but less so in the historical part, where there is a greater stress on ethical values.

Ferdowsi's didacticism is expressed by the characters' speeches and actions and by the poet himself who enters the narrative to comment on the action. In the historical part of the text, newly–crowned kings usually make a speech from the throne, stressing the need for justice and honesty in the world. Ferdowsi himself often steps in, as he does at the end of Rostam's adventure with the demon Akvān, where he tells the listener that the demon represents an evil man who displays ingratitude toward God, and that he who goes beyond the bounds of human decency should be considered a demon rather than a man. "If your reason does not accept these tales," he says, "it is probably because it has not properly grasped the essence of them." Many such observations, aphoristically expressed, have achieved the status of proverbs among the Iranians and are often quoted.

The world of *Shāhnāma* is centered in Iran and extends outward in all directions. The action flows in and out like the tide, and surges over much of the world as it was then known. The geographical scope of the action in the poem is vast. War and hunting expeditions carry the heroes far beyond the boundaries of Iran to encounter Arabs, Byzantines, Central Asians, Chinese, Indians, and other distant peoples. Lengthy journeys and marches are frequent, and prolonged absence from home is the rule for the heroes. With all this variety, however, local color plays almost no role. Other than descriptions of sunrise and sunset, nature is hardly noticed. Whether the action be in Arabia or China, the only variable is the enemy, and the terrain and climate might not exist.

Two ways to account for this outward-looking quality of the *Shāhnāma* are the varied sources of the national epic and the broad extent of the Iranian cultural area. As will be seen, these are related. The Iranians entered the plateau which is now the political state of Iran in the second millennium B.C., arriving from the north. They must have brought with them legends and tales pre-dating the time when they began to form a separate nation. It is probably in this era that the accounts of kings and heroes such as Hushang, Key Khosrow and other important figures in the *Shāhnāma* have their origin.

Long after the plateau was settled, the Iranian world remained geographically broad. Iranians were found from the Caucasus and the steppes north of the Black Sea to the borders of China and Tibet. As groups became isolated, variants of older legends must have developed, along with stories and tales peculiar to each group and locality. The fragments of the Rostam stories in Soghdian, a Middle Iranian language from Central Asia, are an example of this. These are parts of stories about Rostam which appear neither in *Shāhnāma* nor in the other epic poems from the Sistan Cycle.

As the Iranians made their way onto the plateau, over a period of time many of them became sedentary, shifting from a more nomadic to a more settled way of life. Conflicts undoubtedly developed between the pastoralists and the agriculturalists. From these transitional times and later, one of the major themes of Persian epic poetry began to emerge: the theme of Iran against Turan. Iranian religious and national traditions hold that the Iranians and Turanians were of one race, but that the Iranians became settled and developed urban life before the Turanians. This is reflected in the *Shāhnāma* where Afrāsiyāb, the ruler of Turan, is shown to be related to the Iranian royal house. The Oxus River traditionally formed the boundary between these hostile nations. Various traditions must have come together to make up Ferdowsi's version, however, for in the *Shāhnāma* the Turanians are identified as Central Asian Turks and sometimes as Chinese. To the basic conflict between settled peoples and nomads, Zoroastrianism added a moral dimension of good versus evil, so that in *Shāhnāma* we have the theme in its various dimensions objectified as an on-going war between Iran and Turan, beginning in the Pishdādian dynasty and continuing well into the Heroic Age of the Keyānians. In the entire national legend the Iranians have no more bitter an enemy than the Turanians.

LANGUAGE AND STYLE

The language of the *Shāhnāma* is consistent in being relatively simple and strong, and having no glaring stylistic discontinuities. It is considered simple largely because of the low number of Arabic loanwords in it. Other poetry of Ferdowsi's time contains a considerably higher percentage of Arabic words, but Ferdowsi deliberately adopted a less Arabicised style of Persian for his epic. The language is thought of as strong and supple because it displays relatively few of the many rhetorical devices available to the Persian poets of that time. These two aspects of the language are linked, since for technical reasons it is quite difficult to write highly figured poetry in Persian without resorting to an extensive use of Arabic borrowings. Why Ferdowsi chose this style is not entirely clear. The traditional explanation gives much credit to Ferdowsi as a nationalist but little credit to him as a poet. Great nationalists do not always make great poets (Ferdowsi is a striking exception), and one need not look far into the poetry of any culture to find evidence for this.

An explanation for this stylistic question could have two aspects. Tradition undoubtedly demanded a rather pure form of Persian. Ferdowsi uses a number of standard narrative devices, one of which is a conventional opening topos: "I have read this in an old book," or "I heard this story from a dehqān." In some cases the poet mentions the particular dehqān from whom he heard the story, and we have independent evidence for the existence of some of these persons.[9] In other cases the statement appears to be nothing more than a traditional device, used as conventional evidence for the truthfulness of the story to follow, since the *Shāhnāma* was presented as, and thought to be, a history of the Iranian people. Ferdowsi must have felt that stories claimed to have been read in old books or related by dehqāns would be in pure Persian and not be likely to contain many Arabic loanwords.

One could also argue that Ferdowsi was a good enough poet to recognize the tension which exists between the need to use rhetorical devices and figurative language to render vivid the action of the heroes, and the seductive dangers inherent in the use of such language—seductive because in poetry of heroic action, the listener's attention must remain fixed on that action. Much of the meaning of an event is the action of it. If the action is described in figurative and suggestive language, details and implications begin to crowd the listener's mind. Flights of associations are started up which will add dimensions and nuances to the action described. These will divert the mind to contemplation and interpretation and away from the speed, the give and take, the actions and reactions which are the stuff of this poetry. Ferdowsi struck the proper balance between hyperbole and metaphor, the former being a proper element of this poetry, while too much of the latter is a risk. His imagery is firmly rooted in the world of experience, and mythologizing has no place as far as the use of language is concerned. In this respect, Persian epic poetry is not autonomous, however. It demands the imaginative participation of the listener, as any Tehran storyteller will affirm. It will not bear the kind of imaginative extension which comes with lyric poetry. The lines of epic poetry should ring like a sword on a shield, not like a carillon in a bell tower.

In stylistic terms, there is no great discontinuity between the language of the narration and the language that the poet puts into the mouths of the characters. Nor is the social level of the characters differentiated by the use of language. Friends and enemies, kings, princes, and generals all speak the same language at the same stylistic level. This also applies to the language of the poet himself when he enters the narrative to comment on the action or draw a moral. This uniformity of language is characteristic of Persian epic poetry in general.

Post-Shāhnāma Epics

The example of *Shāhnāma* inspired others to write epic poems from the national legend, using the same meter and general level of language as *Shāhnāma*. In the three centuries following the completion of *Shāhnāma*, there were at least eight other important epic poems written. The first, the *Garshāsp Nāma* of Asadi Ṭusi, appeared about a half century after *Shāhnāma*, and the last, the *Sām Nāma*, possibly by Khvāju Kermāni, seems to have been written in the late thirteenth or early fourteenth century. They range in size from the *Bānu Gusasp Nāma* of about a thousand lines to the *Borzu Nāma* which exceeds the size of *Shāhnāma*. Of these eight epics, *Borzu Nāma* has not been published; *Sām Nāma, Bahman Nāma, Jahāngir Nāma, Bānu Gusasp Nāma,* and *Farāmarz Nāma* have come out in lithographed editions in India; *Shahryār Nāma* and *Garshāsp Nāma* have been critically edited; and only the last has been translated (see Bibliography). The lithographed editions are scarce and the manuscripts are scattered; consequently these epics have been little studied and it is difficult to form an accurate estimate of the whole epic tradition.

All the post-*Shāhnāma* epics are from the Sistan Cycle, and each is devoted to the adventures of one hero, for whom the poem is named. Some of these individuals play minor roles in *Shāhnāma,* while others were not mentioned at all by Ferdowsi. It is possible that the sheer magnitude of the Sistan Cycle as it must have been in Ferdowsi's time required that he concentrate on Rostam, his father, and grandfather, and omit other characters and adventures in the interest of completing his work. As it is, it took Ferdowsi some thirty years to complete his *Shāhnāma,* and if he had included the rest of the Sistan Cycle, even as we know it today, the *Shāhnāma* would have been more than twice as long as it is. Ferdowsi's choice of Rostam as the central character of the Sistan

Cycle appears to reflect the fame of this hero in the poet's own time and earlier, as the Soghdian fragments and references in Arabic and Armenian histories indicate.

Ferdowsi's *Shāhnāma* exerted a powerful influence on all epic writing that followed it. This influence can be seen in the meter, the language, the imagery, and the kind of adventures undertaken by the heroes. The later epics very often quote *Shāhnāma* directly and sometimes extensively.

Whereas in *Shāhnāma* the use of figurative language is restrained, beginning with the *Garshāsp Nāma* a gradual elaboration of the language becomes evident. The hyperbole becomes more frequent and more inflated. Most of the conventional similes and expressions that had become almost formulaic in *Shāhnāma* also appear in the later epics. The later poets, seeming to lack Ferdowsi's skill in balancing figurative and non-figurative language, increased their use of the former with the result that their language is less lively and direct than that of *Shāhnāma.*

Here, for example, is a typical battle description from the *Shāhnāma:*

> Rostam attacked, giving the reins over to his horse Rakhsh. He dripped blood on the moon's sphere, while the stars were watching the battlefield. Because of the dust that arose from the battlefield, the plain could not be seen. From the shouts of the riders and the clashing of the spearheads, one could not distinguish the stirrup from the bridle. The air became as black as Zanzibari's face, and they could not find their way on the battlefield for the bodies. The whole area was bodies and mail and helmets; the heads had bade farewell to their bodies. A cloud arose in the air from the dust of the horsemen, and the earth was filled with the ringing of steel. Many brave men in search of fame gave up their heads in vain.[10]

This may be compared with a battle description from *Garshāsp Nāma,* also typical:

> When heaven's brow took on the brightness of a mirror, and the sun showed its shining face, both armies hastened to prepare their ambushes and to form ranks. The violet sky was adorned with the various flags and finials. The rumble of the drums rose to the clouds, and from all sides was heard the clanking of steel. The dust raised by the armies obscured the sky, as the spear points and daggers obscured the plain. The packs, covered with blood, looked like tulips, while the lances resembled red pomegranate blooms. All around were rosebushes of proud fallen heroes, their flowers drops of blood from dripping daggers. From the many helmets scattered about, the plain glittered like a starry sky at night. Vultures from the clouds attacked the dead, and the fox hungered for the lion's brain.[11]

Parallel to the change in style were changes in the image of the hero and in the nature of the action. Rostam and the other heroes of *Shāhnāma* fall under Frye's definition of the epic hero, whom he states is an individual whose power of action is superior in degree to other men but not to the natural environment.[12] After Ferdowsi, the epic heroes gradually assimilate to the heroes of romance who are, in Frye's terms again, individuals whose powers of action are superior in degree to both other men and the natural environment.[13] These post-*Shāhnāma* heroes become almost supermen. They are daunted by no danger, and there is no enemy, human or supernatural, whom they can not defeat. Instead of killing one lion in the forest, they now kill ten, and whereas the older heroes would capture one opponent in battle, the new heroes capture forty. Romantic episodes sometimes take place between the hero and a fairy princess in these later epics, while in *Shāhnāma* the love scenes involved only humans. In these ways the post-*Shāhnāma* heroes begin to outgrow the generally human scale of their older counterparts.

Corresponding to the changes in the notion of the hero were comparable changes in the nature of the action. Almost immediately after *Shāhnāma,* the action starts to become more fantastic. The supernatural manifests itself more and more and in a variety of ways. *Div*s (demons) and *pari*s (fairies) become important as opponents or supporters of the hero. Dragons, serpents, and monsters of various kinds begin to appear, and it becomes almost obligatory for the hero to slay one of these during his travels. Evil wizards and the spells they cast complicate life for the characters. Divine intervention is more frequent, in the form of dreams or of inscribed tablets addressed to the hero alone. Hidden treasures are acquired, not by conquest as in the old days, but by breaking the spells protecting them. Human enemies tend to be dark-skinned "exotic" people such as Indians or blacks from Zanzibar. Even nature starts to play a role, as storms at sea scatter the hero's forces and cast him up on strange shores.

As the foregoing might suggest, the geographical scope of the action in the later epics is even broader than it was in *Shāhnāma.* With the increase in the Islamic world of geographical literature and travelers' tales, interest in the wonders of foreign climes grew. The post-*Shāhnāma* epics are less inward-looking, less focused on Iran proper and its enemies in Transoxiana. Most of the truly strange adventures of the later heroes take place outside of Iran, in India and the Maghreb. The lines between the Iranian and the non-Iranian world, while still implicit, can be more clearly sensed. There is a suggestion that the conflict is no longer the result of political and ethnic factors, but has become one of Iran versus the outer world, of civilization versus barbarianism.

All this reflects neither the degeneration of epic poetry, as Jules Mohl saw it, nor the imaginative creation of later poets, as Theodore Nöldeke maintained,[14] but the growing influence of the older Iranian romance tradition. Of the indigenous romance tradition we have evidence from before the third century, and we know that during the Sasanian period not only were several romance cycles current, but at some point the *Alexander Romance* was incorporated into the Iranian tradition. Thus from ancient times there was a romance tradition flourishing alongside the epic tradition. In *Shāhnāma* the two traditions were combined, although the weight is on the epic side. After *Shāhnāma* the weight began to shift to the romance side; this was influenced by changing social, religious, ideological, and other attitudes in society.

Ferdowsi began his *Shāhnāma* under the Samanids, an Iranian dynasty with ancient roots, and completed it under the Ghaznavids, a Turkish dynasty descended from slaves of the Samanids. It is generally agreed on the basis of internal and external evidence that *Shāhnāma* was not well received by Sultan Maḥmud of Ghazna when Ferdowsi presented it to him as patron. In the light of Maḥmud's generous patronage of poets, his indifference to such a masterpiece as *Shāhnāma* must be explained on ideological, not esthetic grounds. In his *Shāhnāma* Ferdowsi glorified Iranian kingship, Iranian ideals and values, and Iranian traditions. One must presume that these attitudes did not sit well with a Turkish monarch who in no manner shared this background.

The Ghaznavids and the succeeding Turkic and Mongol dynasties ruled the greater part of the Iranian cultural area from about the year 1000 until the twentieth century, with one Iranian interval in the eighteenth century. Although these dynasties were all sooner or later "Iranianized" culturally and linguistically, they were never fully a part of the ancient Iranian cultural tradition. The major patrons of literature may at times have been reluctant to preserve the Iranian heritage in epic form. Furthermore, as the political center of gravity in the Islamic world shifted to the east with the rise of the Turkish dynasties between the eleventh and the thirteenth centuries, the old Iranian *dehqān* class rapidly disappeared. It was this class above all that was the reservoir of Iranian oral and written tradition. During this same period the *ulama* or religious class gained greatly in influence at the expense of the secretarial and other classes of society. The development of the system of *madrasas* or Islamic religious schools affected the educational system throughout the eastern Islamic world, spreading Islamic learning and values in areas where previously Iranian tradition had been strong. All these factors and more produced profound changes in society in the Iranian cultural area, the upshot of which was a society in which the older Iranian heroic ideal was no longer compatible with the new Islamic values. Certain parallels to these changes can be seen in the European society of the Renaissance and the development of the Christian epic hero.

As those segments of society which patronized poetry became less receptive to the older Iranian values, at least as presented in *Shāhnāma,* the epic hero on the model of Rostam began to fade away, and his place was taken by the hero of romance. The model of *Shāhnāma* was so powerful that the form and language remained fixed, while the nature of the hero and the action evolved. It seems natural that elements of romance should infiltrate the epic at an ever increasing rate, until they became predominant and the romance replaced the epic entirely. The listener still could hear long and exciting stories of Iranian heroes, but the tales were now accommodated to society's new outlook. The rise to prominence of Persian romance literature began in the Ghaznavid period as the epic tradition went into eclipse.

As a model, *Shāhnāma* retained its power until the major changes in Iranian society in the twentieth century. Beginning in the twelfth century with Neẓāmi's *Eskandar Nāma* (a version of the Iranian *Alexander Romance*) and continuing until the nineteenth century, a series of at least forty historical and over fifty religious pseudo-epics were written. These, again, were in the same meter and language as *Shāhnāma*. Their contents, however, varied widely and can not be considered epic in the strict sense. The historical pseudo-epics were nothing more than versified history, often written ostensibly to bring *Shāhnāma* up to date, but actually to glorify the feats of a patron or dynasty.

The religious pseudo-epics were concerned, by and large, with the life and exploits of the Prophet Moḥammad, his cousin and son-in-law ᶜAli, and another figure named Mokhtār, or were about the martyrdom of the Prophet's grandson Ḥoseyn and his family at Karbala. The latter poems are interesting because they set the principal figures of Islam directly within the Iranian epic tradition by following *Shāhnāma* in form and language. A careful investigation of these little–known poems would reveal, among other things, how the "Islamic hero" was developed within the frame of the Iranian epic tradition.

The Study of the Iranian Epic

The study of the Iranian epic and Persian epic poetry in the West began only in the nineteenth century, and has not advanced as far as has the study of the Greek, French, German, and other European epics. The first to attempt a general analysis and appraisal of the Iranian epic was the French orientalist Jules Mohl. In a lengthy preface to his edition and prose translation of *Shāhnāma,* Mohl approached the text both as a work of literature and as a historical source.[15] Basing his discussion largely on evidence provided by *Shāhnāma* itself, he attempted to set *Shāhnāma* in a historical context by describing conditions in Khurasan up to the time of Ferdowsi, and by compiling a biography of the poet. He also discussed the epic poems that were written after *Shāhnāma,* which contained material from the national legend not included by Ferdowsi. Mohl felt that these other epic poems were written by poets who wanted to fill in the gaps left by Ferdowsi by putting into a form similar to that of *Shāhnāma* the abundant traditional epic material available in those times.

Mohl believed that the verse and prose romances which were written in the twelfth century and later were direct descendants of the earlier epic poems, and that they represented a decadence in epic writing. "It is the fate of epic traditions," he wrote, "to degenerate into romances and tales of wonder."[16] He went on to say that in Persia, "we see two new genres of literature born from the ruins of epic poetry: the historical romance and the epic tale."[17] Due to the state of scholarship on Persian literature during his time, many of

Mohl's conclusions are doubtful or wrong. His survey is important, however, because it is the first attempt to provide a comprehensive view and appraisal of Persian epic poetry. In this process, Mohl brought to light many previously unknown texts and drew together in a synthetic manner much scattered information.

After Mohl, scholarship on the Iranian epic made slow progress until the turn of the century when the massive *Grundriss der iranischen Philologie* was published.[18] In this comprehensive and scholarly survey, Theodore Nöldeke published the first edition of *Das iranische Nationalepos,* the second edition of which appeared two decades later.[19] Deeply learned in both Semitic and Iranian philology, Nöldeke produced in this essay a fundamental work of scholarship which in many respects has not been superseded. He began by investigating the classical Greek and Avestan sources to look for the roots of the Iranian epic in order to establish as fully as possible the historical antecedents of Ferdowsi's *Shāhnāma.* By surveying Middle Iranian, Arabic, and New Persian texts, he was able to make substantial progress toward identifying the immediate sources of Ferdowsi's epic poem. He then focused on the *Shāhnāma* itself and discussed its form, characters, historical content, contradictions and anachronisms, language, and other matters in a detailed and critical manner. With regard to the epic poems that followed *Shāhnāma,* Nöldeke took a position opposite from Mohl's and declared them all to be nothing more than fiction, entirely the creation of their authors and with no basis whatsoever in tradition.

Nöldeke restricted his scope to *Shāhnāma* and its historical antecedents. The weaknesses in his work are due largely to a lack of critically edited texts, to the problems inherent in a strictly philological approach to literature, and, again, to the general state of scholarship in matters Iranian. Nöldeke himself greatly advanced scholarship in this field with the combination of his erudition and his systematic approach to the texts. It is he who first put the study of the Iranian epic on a firm basis.

Iranian scholars have not been idle in the study of their national epic. Important contributions by Qazvini, Taqizāda, and others were published in the volume which was a product of the millennium of Ferdowsi celebrated in Tehran in 1934.[20] The major work of Persian scholarship to date is Ṣafā's comprehensive survey of the subject, based partly on European sources and partly on his own research.[21] Ṣafā takes some of Nöldeke's topics, such as the formation of the national epic, and expands them greatly. He defines the epic very broadly, and includes lengthy discussions, not only of epic poetry in the strict sense, but also of what he calls "historical" and "religious" epics.

Because of his familiarity with a large number of texts, Ṣafā has achieved a broader perspective on the Iranian epic than did Mohl or Nöldeke. While in essential agreement with Nöldeke on the question of the genesis of the Iranian epic and its development culminating in Ferdowsi's *Shāhnāma,* he differs with his German predecessor on the question of the post-*Shāhnāma* epic poems. These Ṣafā declares to be entirely within the tradition, although not of the intrinsic interest or literary quality of *Shāhnāma,* and suggests that esthetic concerns were an important factor governing Ferdowsi's choice of material. Ṣafā's work is the most broadly based and most inclusive of the three discussed. It is also the most interesting for the student of literature because it presents the judgments of a widely read Iranian scholar deeply immersed in his own tradition.

The scholars just discussed have studied the Iranian epic largely in terms of the Iranian and Indo-Iranian tradition. Georges Dumézil, on the other hand, has investigated the Iranian epic tradition within the larger context of Indo-European ideology, myth, and social structure. By examining in a comparative fashion a broad range of Indo–Iranian, Greek, Roman, Germanic, and Celtic texts, Dumézil has evolved a theory which holds that ancient Indo-European society was characterized by a tripartite ideology. Within this system, the "functions" of sovereignty, force, and nourishment gave rise to a tripartite social organization of a priestly/ruling class, a warrior class, and a herder/cultivator class. This social structure was reflected in turn in myth and epic by a tripartite set of gods and heroes representing the three abstract "functions." It is asserted that this tripartition is uniquely Indo-European, having no parallels in any other ancient civilization, and that it was carried by the Indo-European peoples across the far–flung area which was or is now inhabited by Indo-European–speakers. Dumézil, and others applying his theory, have discovered many examples of tripartition in various ancient Indo-European communities. Notable among these is the Indo–Iranian community, where a clearer picture emerges, due largely to the age and relative abundance of Indo-Iranian textual material.

In his study of the Iranians, Dumézil has focused mainly on their mythology and has discovered considerable evidence for tripartition on this level. The Avesta, the fourteenth-century B.C. treaty between the Hittites and the Mitanni, and the Vedic texts show remarkable parallels on the level of myth and social organization. Although Dumézil has not yet studied the *Shāhnāma* as thoroughly as he has the Indian epic, research in this area has been carried out by Stig Wikander following Dumézil's lead. In an article entitled "Sur le fonds commun indo-iranien des epopées de la Perse et de l'Inde," Wikander examines correspondences between the *Shāhnāma* and the *Mahābhārata* against the background of their common heritage.[22] Clear examples of tripartition can be pointed out in the *Shāhnāma,* such as Feridun's dividing the world among his three sons and the test he puts them to prior to this, and the foundation of the three sacred fires of the Zoroastrians. On the other hand, his argument that Rostam and Zāl are an almost undifferentiated pair and correspond to a second-function pair in the Indian epic will simply not stand up to the facts. Neither will his assertion that Goshtāsp and Lohrāsp are almost undifferentiated and correspond to the Aśvins of the *Mahābhārata,* who are third-function figures.

One problem with the investigations of Wikander and others is that the textual scope has always been too narrow. In the future, the large amount of post-*Shāhnāma* epic material must be taken into account, for Ferdowsi's work by no means represents the entire Iranian epic. In applying the tripartite theory to specific cases in the Iranian epic, other factors must also be considered such as variant versions and the relative age of the texts. Lohrāsp and Goshtāsp, for example, appear in the Avesta, while with the exception of the Soghdian fragments and a few minor mentions, the stories of Rostam are all in the *Shāhnāma* and later texts. With regard to the place of Iranian myth and ideology in the larger Indo-European context, however, one must accept a good deal of what Dumézil and his followers have said.[23]

Much remains to be learned about the Iranian epic. In addition to the Dumézilian approach, scholars are now beginning to explore the *Shāhnāma* in the manner in which the *Iliad* and the *Chanson de Roland,* for example, have been explored. Unfortunately the post-Ferdowsi epics, their sisters the romances, and their cousins the pseudo-epics still remain largely unknown. Critical editions of all these texts are badly needed. We can expect significant results for Iranian studies in particular and epic studies in general when modern literary scholarship is finally applied to this rich store of epic tradition.

NOTES

1. The above information is largely from Mary Boyce, "Middle Persian Literature," in *Handbuch der Orientalistik,* ed. B. Spuler, I. Abt., IV. Bd., 2. Abschn., 1. Lief., pp. 57–60.

2. For a translation and discussion of this introduction, see V. Minorsky, "The Older Preface to the *Shāh-Nāma,*" in his *Iranica* (Tehran: University of Tehran Press, 1964), pp. 260–73.

3. See L. P. Elwell-Sutton, "The Foundations of Persian Prosody and Metrics," *Iran* 13 (1975): 75–97; and his *The Persian Metres* (Cambridge: Cambridge University Press, 1976).

4. Ferdowsi, *Shāhnāma,* ed. E. Bertel's, 9 vols. (Moscow: Akademija nauk SSSR, 1966–71), I, p. 179.

5. The heroic age is a period in the history of a people when the heroic element is dominant in society. The concept and the term derive from Hesiod. For a full discussion of the idea of a heroic age, see H. M. Chadwick, *The Growth of Literature,* 3 vols. (Cambridge: University Press, 1932–40), I, and C. M. Bowra, "The Meaning of a Heroic Age," in his *In General and Particular* (London: Weidenfeld and Nicolson, 1964), pp. 63–84.

6. Considerable fieldwork conducted by the writer with Persian storytellers in Tehran and other cities supports this assertion.

7. Hasan Javadi, "Matthew Arnold's 'Sohrab and Rustum' and Its Persian Original," *Review of National Literatures* 2/1 (1971): 61–73.

8. *Shāhnāma*, IV, pp. 194–97.

9. Mojtabā Minovi, *Ferdowsi va Shećr-e U* (Tehran: Anjoman-e Āsār-e Melli, 1967), pp. 76–78.

10. *Shāhnāma*, IV, pp. 249–50.

11. Asadi Ṭusi, *Garshāsp Nāma*, ed. Ḥabib Yaghmāʿi (Tehran: Berukhim, 1938), pp. 372–73; French tr., II, p. 196.

12. Northrop Frye, *Anatomy of Criticism* (Princeton: Princeton University Press, 1957), p. 33.

13. Ibid.

14. See below for a discussion of these theories.

15. Ferdowsi, *Le Livre des rois,* trans. Jules Mohl, 7 vols. (Paris: Imprimerie Nationale, 1838–78; reprinted in 7 vols. without the Persian text, Paris: Imprimerie Nationale, 1876).

16. Ibid., 1876 ed., I, p. lxxxii.

17. Ibid.

18. W. Geiger and E. Kuhn, *Grundriss der iranischen Philologie,* 2 vols. (Strassburg: Trübner, 1895–1904), II, pp. 130–211.

19. Berlin: De Gruyter, 1920. English translation by L. Bogdanov (Bombay: K. R. Cama Oriental Institute, 1930).

20. *Hazāra-e Ferdowsi* (Tehran: Ministry of Education, 1944).

21. Zabiḥollāh Ṣafā, *Ḥamāsa Sarāʿi dar Irān,* 2nd ed. (Tehran: Amir Kabir, 1954).

22. *La Nouvelle Clio* 1 (1950): 310–29.

23. For a thorough discussion of Dumézil's theories and an extensive bibliography, see C. Scott Littleton, *The New Comparative Mythology,* rev. ed. (Berkeley: University of California Press, 1973).

BIBLIOGRAPHY

Ferdowsi's Shāhnāma

Shāhnāma. Edited by E. Bertel's et al. 9 vols. Moscow: Akademija nauk SSSR, 1966–71. The most recent full edition, critically edited by a team of Soviet scholars. Due to the discovery of new material during the course of the edition, the later volumes are better than the earlier ones.

Shāhnāma. Edited by Saʿid Nafisi. 10 vols. Tehran: Berukhim, 1934–36, and later printings. A reliable and still widely quoted text, based upon earlier European editions.

Dāstān-e Rostam o Sohrāb [The Story of Rostam and Sohrāb]. Edited by Mojtabā Minovi. Tehran: Bonyād-e Shāhnāma-e Ferdowsi, 1973. The first fascicle of a projected complete re-edition of the text by the late dean of Persian literary scholars.

Translations into English

The Sháh Námeh. Translated and abridged by James Atkinson. London: Oriental Translation Fund, 1832. A translation of mixed prose and verse. Atkinson ended his translation with the death of Alexander the Great.

Sháhnáma. Translated by A. J. and E. Warner. 9 vols. London: Kegan Paul, 1905–25. A verse translation of the full text, accompanied by useful notes.

The Epic of the Kings. Translated by Reuben Levy. Chicago: University of Chicago

Press, 1967. Persian Heritage Series, 2. An abridged prose translation of the whole text, with summaries of the omitted passages.

Bibliography

Afshār, Iraj. *Ketābshenāsi-e Ferdowsi* [Bibliography of Ferdowsi]. Tehran: Anjoman-e Āsār-e Melli, 1968. A comprehensive listing of material covering the life of Ferdowsi, with studies, translations, manuscripts, and printed editions of the *Shāhnāma*, in all languages.

Other Epics, and Prose Romances

Asadi Ṭusi. *Le Livre de Gerchāsp.* 2 vols. Paris: Geuthner, 1926–51. Volume I contains a critical edition and French prose translation by Clément Huart of approximately one fourth of the poem. Huart died before he could complete his work, and in 1939 a critical edition of the text by Ḥabib Yaghmāʻi was published in Tehran. The remainder of the French translation, based now on the Tehran text, was completed by Henri Massé and published as vol. II.

Bighami, Moḥammad ebn Aḥmad. *Love and War: Adventures from the Firuz Shāh Nāma.* Translated by William L. Hanaway, Jr. Delmar, N.Y.: Scholars' Facsimiles & Reprints, 1974. Persian Heritage Series, 19. An abridged translation of a major prose romance, with an introduction discussing the genre in general and the special characteristics of the *Firuz Shāh Nāma.*

Farāmarz ebn Khodādād. *Samak-e Ayyar.* Translated by Frédérique Razavi, I. Paris: Maisonneuve & Larose, 1972. Bibliothéque des oeuvres classiques persanes, 3. A French translation of the first part of the earliest and most extensive of the prose romances.

Studies

Barthold, W. "Zur Geschichte des persischen Epos." *Zeitschrift der Deutschen Morgenländischen Gesellschaft* 98 (1944): 121–57. The article, translated from Russian, concentrates on the epic in pre-Islamic and early Islamic times, leading up to *Shāhnāma,* and brings in more detail than most other studies. Barthold maintains that epics have been created and cast into literary form in eastern Iran from Achaemenian times or earlier.

Massé, Henri. *Les Epopées persanes.* Paris: Perrin, 1935. An excellent general survey. Massé breaks little new ground, but brings together much of what was known about the epic between Nöldeke and Ṣafā.

Molé, Marijan. "L'Epopée iranienne après Firdōsī." *La Nouvelle Clio* 5 (1953): 377–93. Molé reviews the post-*Shāhnāma* epics and the relationships among them, and indicates some of the main areas for future research.

5

Beowulf: A Contextual Introduction to Its Contents and Techniques

Alain Renoir

Assumptions are always risky when they concern a long-dead tradition of secular poetry whose preservation must perforce have depended upon the selective good will of the monastic scriptorium, and they are even riskier when the written records have been so thinned out by successive confrontations with the Scandinavians, the Normans, and the Reformation as to lead us into accepting views necessarily based upon a pitifully small number of surviving texts. Understandably, the bulk of Old English poetic materials which have come down to us is of a religious nature, but there are, nevertheless, grounds for assuming that a considerable body of secular epic poetry must have been composed in England before the Norman Conquest. Besides *Beowulf,* for instance, we have fragments of two heroic poems dealing respectively with the bloody conflict between the forces of the Danish King Hnaef and those of his Frisian brother-in-law, Finn, and with the adventures of Walter of Visigothic Aquitaine; and the availability of the Medieval Latin *Waltharii Poesis* enables us to conjecture about the form and contents of the latter. In addition, scholars have argued the probability of an Old English original for the German *Hildebrandslied* and have tried to connect certain Old English poems with hypothetical heroic cycles devoted to Odoacer and to Offa. Finally, we have no reason to doubt the facts cited by Alcuin in a famous letter dated A.D. 797, where he admonishes the Bishop of Lindisfarne to stop banqueting Christian priests from listening to poetry about the pagan king Ingeld.[1]

For the student of poetry, the wording of Alcuin's letter is as important as the contents. Not only does the text argue that the words of God are what ought to be read aloud whenever priests feast together, but it specifies that *someone who reads* ought to be heard instead of *someone who plays a string instrument,* as well as the sermons of the Church Fathers instead of local *songs* of presumably heathen origin ("Ibi decet *lectorem* audiri, non *citharistam;* sermones patrum, non *carmina* gentilium"). The contrast here is not only between the sacred and the profane but also between the written and the oral, as well as between what is actually read from a book and what is sung to the tune of a musical instrument. Assuming Alcuin to have been in control of both his vocabulary and his evidence, we may suppose that some Old English narrative poetry was sung by musical performers who seem to have dispensed with the use of written materials. This supposition finds corroboration in Bede's *Historia Ecclesiastica Gentis Anglorum,* where we read that an untutored lay brother named Caedmon was divinely inspired to compose poetry after long years of running out in the middle of beer parties for shame of exposing his ineptitude whenever his turn would come to play music and sing his own compositions. Students of literature will recall that Caedmon eventually became the first great English narrative poet still known by name today, and the fact that he performed orally may be inferred from the statement that his poems were taken down in writing by others. That the account refers to the actual performance of oral composition rather than to the mere recitation of set texts, and that it was construed accordingly by its intended audience, may likewise be inferred from the wording of the assertion that he was inspired to *make* poetry (*poemata facere*), which the Old English translation of the *Historia* renders with an exact equivalent (leoð *wyrcan*).[2] These observations necessarily raise a question about the means whereby an oral poet may be able to compose a sustained and organized narrative of some length, be it at the request of a small group of scholars formally intent upon recording the performance or within the context of a less formal priestly feast or a totally informal beer party; and the scope of the question becomes obvious when we recall that at least one of the poems attributed in part to Caedmon, the Old English *Genesis,* counts nearly 3000 lines.

The most significant answer which the twentieth century has had to offer to the foregoing question is found in the theory of oral-formulaic composition, first set forth by Milman Parry in respect to Homer and subsequently elaborated into a full-scale demonstration by Albert B. Lord. The contributions of Parry and Lord, their revolutionary significance, and the way in which they have provided scholars with a methodology for the analysis of certain kinds of poetry on the basis of metrical formulas, themes and type scenes, and larger traditional topics will be discussed in Mary P. Coote's essay, "Serbocroatian Epic Songs" in this volume. We need only note here that the first application of the theory to the study of Old English poetry was a seminal essay entitled "The Oral-Formulaic Character of Anglo-Saxon Narrative Poetry," published in 1953 by Francis P. Magoun, Jr., and that Magoun's endorsement was vindicated as a working hypothesis when Robert P. Creed actually composed a poem in Old English according to the oral-formulaic method. In the intervening years, most Anglicists have accepted the general validity of the theory of oral-formulaic composition, but few are in agreement about the reliability of existing criteria for determining the actual mode of composition of specific poems. A case in point will be found in Larry D. Benson's essay,

"The Literary Character of Anglo-Saxon Formulaic Poetry," whose very title was presumably intended to suggest a rebuff of Magoun's position and which cogently argues that certain Old English poems which exhibit marked oral-formulaic features must nevertheless be considered the product of written composition. An account of the many positions taken by Anglicists is of necessity beyond the scope of the present discussion, but the situation at the outset of the third quarter of the twentieth century has been summed up by Donald K. Fry, according to whom "a consensus seems to be emerging that written Old English poetry used oral forms, but no reliable test can differentiate written from oral poems."[3] In other words, it seems that an Old English poetic text devoid of oral-formulaic features ought initially to be considered written composition but that a text with a high density of oral-formulaic features need not necessarily be considered oral composition, since oral-formulaic features are necessary but not sufficient to demonstrate orality within a formulaic tradition. As a result, scholars can usually do no better than surmise about those aspects of Old English poetry whose interpretation would require certain basic assumptions about the conditions under which composition was carried out. The relevance of these considerations to the subject at hand lies in the fact that several investigations, including Magoun's aforementioned essay, have shown the diction of *Beowulf* to be marked by an extremely high density of oral-formulaic and traditional features.

In the light of the materials covered thus far, we may look upon *Beowulf* as the sole relatively intact survivor of what seems to have been a rich tradition of secular heroic poetry which included stories apparently composed orally in connection with various social activities. Despite its highly oral-formulaic diction, the specialists have reached no agreement as to the mode of composition of the poem, which could be either a written work or an oral performance recorded in a manner similar to that described in Bede's account of Caedmon. It occupies a special place in the history of literature, not only because it is generally recognized as the earliest substantial masterpiece of English secular poetry, but also because it is likewise the earliest full-length heroic epic to have survived in any Germanic language and its contents make it almost mandatory to the historical study of several otherwise separate literatures. The only known version is in the West-Saxon dialect but is usually considered a copy of a lost eighth-century Anglian or Mercian original, and it has come down to us in a tenth-century section of Manuscript Cotton Vitellius A.XV, at the British Museum, and in two copies of that text made in 1786–87, at a time when the process of deterioration started by a fire in 1731 was less serious than it has since become. The manuscript text is divided into forty-three sections irregularly numbered in Roman numerals; it prints 3182 lines of verse in a modern edition, but, in keeping with Old English practice, it is recorded like prose without regard for individual metrical units. The following outline arbitrarily stresses those elements which will prove relevant to the subsequent discussion. To facilitate reference to standard editions and translations, line numbers corresponding to key words and passages are listed between parentheses.

Outline of Contents

The action of *Beowulf* takes place in Scandinavia. After an initial account of the founding of Denmark's Scylding Dynasty by the mythological Scyld Scefing (1–52), the narrative traces the royal succession down to King Hrothgar, who decides to advertise the might of his realm by erecting near the modern town of Lejre a magnificent hall which he names Heorot (78). Here, king and warriors spend much time feasting at night until a troll-like and cannibalistic creature of darkness named Grendel (102), descended from Cain (107), takes such vehement exception to the constant uproar of revelry that he submits the hall to a series of murderous attacks which end all nightly occupancy by human beings for the next twelve years (146). Apparently nonplused by the monster's irresistible savagery, Hrothgar finds no better solution than to bear his grief (147) and hold apparently fruitless meetings with his advisors (171–74).

Somewhere in the land of the Geats—presumably the modern Östergötland—a physically powerful young man identified as a retainer of King Hygelac (194–98), whose name we shall later learn to be Beowulf (343), hears of this situation and immediately sets sail for Denmark with fourteen companions (215) to free the world of Grendel's depredations. The Geats make land the next day, and, with the boarlike crests on their helmets shining in the sun (303–04), they march to Heorot, where Beowulf announces the purpose of his visit and his determination to fight Grendel alone and without weapons (435–37), though he will wear a corslet made by Weland himself (455). Hrothgar invites the Geats to sit at a banquet during which Beowulf is in turn taunted by a retainer named Unferth (506–28) and honored by Queen Wealhtheow's gracious attention (620–27). The Geats are then left alone to wait for Grendel, who soon breaks into the hall and succeeds in devouring one of them before grappling for life with Beowulf, from whom he escapes mortally wounded, leaving an arm behind (815–20).

The next day is devoted to celebrations during which a poet entertains the company by singing a song about Beowulf's exploit (871–74), which he likens by implication to the marvelous deeds of the Germanic heroes Sigemund and Fitela (874–900) and contrasts to the crimes of a wicked king of old named Heremod (901–15). During the sumptuous banquet which follows, Hrothgar bestows priceless gifts upon Beowulf (1020–53), and the poet sings once again to tell of the death of Finn and Hnaef (1063–1159) before Wealhtheow presents Beowulf with a necklace as valuable as the one which Hama once stole from Eormanric (1197–1201). That night, a contingent of Danes remains in Heorot, but Grendel's mother attacks them to avenge her son and carries off a warrior named Aeshere, who is Hrothgar's dearest companion (1296).

Early the next morning, Beowulf is asked to help with the new peril (1376–77) and is taken to a pond where Grendel and his mother presumably have their lair and on whose shore he receives a valuable and tried sword from Unferth (1455–56), who has now forgotten his earlier antagonism. He dives into the pond and enters an underwater cave where he kills Grendel's mother beside the body of her dead son, although Unferth's weapon fails him (1522–25) and he must use an ancient sword which seems to have been waiting for him there (1557–68). Back in Heorot, his accomplishments are praised by Hrothgar, who again contrasts him to Heremod (1709) and seizes upon the occasion to deliver a little sermon on the sins of pride, sloth, and covetousness (1724–48). On the fourth day, the Geats sail back to their homeland, where Hygelac expresses some surprise at the success of the expedition (1992–97). Beowulf tells a slightly different version of his adventures, mentions that Hrothgar has promised his daughter Freawaru in marriage to Ingeld (2024–25), and gives Hygelac and his queen some of the gifts which he previously received in Heorot (2000–176).

We now learn that he was considered somewhat worthless in his youth (2183–88), and the narrative jumps over half a century to a time when Beowulf has been king of the Geats for fifty years (2209). When a dragon, enraged at the theft of part of a treasure which he has been guarding (2214–31), begins spewing fire at the Geats and their dwellings (2302–27), Beowulf decides to fight him single-handed (2345–47). The narrative flashes back to Hygelac's death on a battlefield in the Rhineland (2355), his son Heardred's death at the hands of the Swedish usurper Onela (2379–88), and Beowulf's subsequent accession to the throne (2389), then back again to the occasion when Beowulf hugged a Frankish warrior to death during Hygelac's last battle (2506–08).

In front of the dragon's lair, the aged Beowulf now addresses the eleven retainers who have accompanied him and orders them to keep away from a fight which he describes as nobody's responsibility but his own (2532–35). As the fight begins and Beowulf's sword once again fails him (2577), his retainers run for cover to a nearby grove, with the exception of his nephew Wiglaf, who gives them a brief lecture on the nature of duty toward one's lord and comes to his uncle's rescue in time to help him slay the monster (2694–708). Beowulf, however, has been mortally wounded (2711–15), and he dies thanking God that he has been able to win the dragon's treasure for his people, asking that a barrow be erected for his ashes, and bidding Wiglaf to continue acting in a manner befitting the last of his family (2794–820). Wiglaf has the event announced to the Geatish nation by a messenger who predicts forthcoming trouble with the Franks and Frisians (2910–13), takes us back once again to the Geatish raid in the Rhineland (2915) and to the Swedish King Ongentheow's killing of Hygelac's brother Haethcyn at the battle of Ravenswood (2923–27) before falling at the hands of one of Hygelac's retainers (2977–81), and finally warns us that the Swedes will set out against the Geats as soon as they hear of Beowulf's death (2999–3003). The poem comes to an end by the sea, on a promontory where a woman sings a song of sorrow (3150–51) by Beowulf's barrow, around which twelve mounted retainers mournfully ride while chanting a lament for their dead lord, whom they praise as the mildest, the gentlest, the kindest to his people, and the most eager for fame of all the kings in the world (3169–82).

Organization

Sketchy though it be, this outline illustrates some important points about the organization of *Beowulf* and the manner in which it handles time and history. We note, for instance, that three major principles of organization operate in the poem: from the point of view of emotional intensity, *Beowulf* divides into three sections centering in turn upon each of the hero's mortal fights against Grendel, Grendel's mother, and the dragon respectively; from the point of view of chronology, it divides into two sections centering in turn upon the hero's daring adventures as a young man and his exemplary deeds as an old king; from the point of view of narrative sequence, it again divides into three parts centering in turn upon the hero's adventures in Denmark, his own account of these adventures, and his deeds as King of the Geats. We also note that, with the exception of a few reminiscences and allusions by various members of the cast, the section concluding with Beowulf's return to his homeland handles time in a basically linear manner, so that we need never question the chronology of the events which unroll before us. In contrast, the remainder of the poem repeatedly plays upon our sense of time by intermingling past, future, and present, as when both Beowulf's past exploits and the future catastrophes resultant from his death are brought to bear upon his present sacrifice to impress us with the tragic dignity of the event.

Finally, we note the functional interweaving of legitimate history with what we are wont to dismiss as folklore or mythology. On the one hand, the eponymous founder of the Scylding Dynasty belongs to the latter category because we have no accredited record of his existence, as does Beowulf for the same reason; Grendel, his mother, and the dragon join them there because we do not believe in monsters. On the other hand, Heremod gets credit as a probable member of a royal line preceding that of the Scyldings, and Hrothgar clearly belongs in the former category because historical sources have led us to believe in his existence and to locate his death about A.D. 525. The same thing holds true of Ingeld, who married Freawaru about A.D. 518, of Hygelac, who triumphed at the same battle of Ravenswood where Ongentheow and Haethcyn lost their lives about A.D. 510, and of the raid in the Rhineland where Hygelac was killed a year later. We also have evidence for the existence of Heorot, which was burned to the ground about A.D. 520, and for Onela's invasion of Geatish territory and killing of Heardred about A.D. 533, as well as for other characters and events in the poem which have been left out of our outline. The evidence, like much early medieval history, is open both to question and to interpretation, but it is solid enough to suggest a degree of historicity behind a fair portion of the materials in *Beowulf* and to help us locate the action within the context of the sixth century.

Oral-Formulaic Features

The outline also illustrates some salient traditional and oral-formulaic features of the narrative. Just as one of the heroic fragments mentioned earlier gives us tangible evidence of the fact that the bloody conflict between Finn and Hnaef was not our poet's exclusive property, so Alcuin's admonitory letter makes it probable that the deeds of Ingeld were in favor as topics for poetic performance in England at a time not far removed from that during which scholars believe *Beowulf* to have been composed. The extent to which the poem draws upon Old English literary tradition may be inferred both from these and from other names listed in the outline. Eormanric, for example, figures prominently in two poems, entitled respectively *Widsith* and *Deor,* which are generally considered highly representative of the heroic repertory of Old English literature. In addition, Weland—the same whose picture on the Franks Casket may be seen by every visitor to the British Museum—plays an important part in the latter, while Hama, Finn, Hnaef, and Ongentheow are included in the former, where we also find Hrothgar's political situation described in a manner consonant with the account in *Beowulf.*

The most cursory and random glance at medieval German and Scandinavian traditional literature will show that the same kind of observation may be made in respect to the broader Germanic context. The Eormanric of the Old English poem is central to the German epic cycle of Dietrich von Bern and the Old Norse *Thidrek's saga*—both of which include Hama—and the sixteenth-century Low German *Koninc Ermenrikes Dot* makes it clear that the impetus of his fame was strong enough to carry beyond the Middle Ages. Weland also appears in the *Thidrek's saga* and rates an entire poem in the *Edda.* Sigemund and Fitela are probably best known as the central figures of the Old Norse *Volsunga Saga,* and the latter's death is commemorated in a special prose link in the *Edda,* while the former is remembered as Siegfried's father in the Middle High German *Nibelungenlied.* The extent of their reputation is illustrated in the Old Norse *Eriksmál,* probably composed at Queen Gunnhild's request to glorify her husband, Eric Bloodaxe, who was killed soon after being driven out of Northumbria in A.D. 954: as the slain king enters Valhalla, the God Odin finds no more suitable means of proclaiming the magnitude of his heroic deeds on earth than to have him escorted by Sigemund and Fitela themselves. Sigemund, Ongentheow, Heremod, and Eormanric likewise appear in an Eddic poem, known in English as ''The Lay of Hyndla,'' which also mentions the Scyldings.

In addition to these and other characters, important elements of the action in *Beowulf* find obvious echoes within the Germanic context, with close analogues to the first half of the poem occurring in the Old Norse *Grettis Saga* and *Hrólfs Saga Kraka* as well as in less widely known texts, and with a fair analogue to the dragon fight occurring in Saxo Grammaticus' *Gesta Danorum*. We may therefore say that the contents of *Beowulf* are highly traditional and that the density of surviving attestations leads one to suppose that the tradition was alive and familiar at the time the poem was composed.[4]

The oral-formulaic aspect of the poem is as obvious as its traditional aspect, though we must momentarily turn away from the outline for an example of metrical formula. To illustrate the oral-formulaic nature of the metrical units in *Beowulf,* Lord has provided a simple analytic chart of fifteen consecutive lines, thus demonstrating graphically that only one-half of one of them fails to conform to an oral-formulaic paradigm. In other words, his chart yields a ratio of over ninety-six percent in favor of conformity with the principles of oral-formulaic versification. The quickest glance at one of these lines will suffice to illustrate a fundamental aspect of the principle in question: "Beowulf spoke, the son of Ecgtheow" (1473: *"Beowulf maðelode, bern Ecgþeowes"*)[5] occurs in precisely the same form—except for irrelevant spelling differences—eight additional times throughout the poem, and it obviously follows a pattern similar to that of "Hrothgar spoke, the protector of the Scyldings" (371: *"Hroðgar maþelode, helm Scyldinga"*), which occurs three times. We may thus conclude that we have here a verse formula whose grammar includes: (a) a subject proper name (Beowulf/Hrothgar), followed by (b) a verb conveying the utterance of speech (spoke/spoke), followed by (c) a noun appositive (son/protector), and (d) a possessive noun (of Ecgtheow/of the Scyldings), and which may be schematized as follows: *Y spoke + appositive noun + X possessive*. As long as the two halves of the line conform to a traditional alliterative pattern (as do "Beowulf/bearn" and "Hrothgar/helm" in the Old English lines), we have a verse regardless of the actual words with which we fill out the schema. The flexibility of the system is evident from the variant "Wiglaf spoke, Weohstan's son" (2862: *"Wiglaf maðelode, Weohstanes sunu"*), which occurs twice in the poem and which switches appositive and possessive around in answer to the requirements of rhythm and alliterative pattern.[6]

An equally strong point may be made with respect to individual narrative units, which Lord discusses along with the verse formulas. One example recorded in our outline is illustrated in David K. Crowne's demonstration that the scene where Beowulf and his Geats have just crossed the sea and begin marching toward Heorot conforms precisely to the paradigm of an oral-formulaic theme which often occurs before a reference to a mortal combat or the actual performance thereof. In this theme, a hero in the presence of his retainers, at the outset or conclusion of a journey, which is usually near a beach or an equivalent thereof, finds himself within proximity of something shiny (in this case, the boarlike crests noted in the outline, of which the poem specifically says, *"Eoforlic scionon / ofer hleorberan,"* 303–04). Crowne has pointed out four additional occurrences of this theme in *Beowulf* and many more in other Old English poems, while yet others have been discovered elsewhere, so that we are dealing here with a frequent and carefully studied oral-formulaic element which also happens to be one of many similar devices in the poem. When applied with the proper caution, these and similar considerations may provide us tentatively with theoretical explanations for otherwise puzzling similarities between the Old English poem and some apparently unrelated works. Nobody reading such a close analogue to *Beowulf* as the *Hrólfs Saga Kraka* is likely to experience much surprise at finding therein a counterpart of Unferth's taunting of Beowulf, but the reaction must surely be quite different when another counterpart turns up in the *Odyssey,* along with a counterpart to the scene in Heorot where Beowulf hears his own exploits turned into song by a poet. Here, the oral-formulaic theory suggests the possibility that both the Archaic Greek and the Old English poets may have used a common Indo-European theme extant in both the Hellenic and the Germanic poetic traditions.

The story of *Beowulf* as a whole likewise conforms to the paradigm of a traditional tale known by students of folklore as the "Bear's Son," which is abundantly documented in European and other languages. It tells the story of a young man of superior physical strength who kills a monster in a strange place, though he tends to shy from the use of weapons, as is the case with Beowulf when he wrestles Grendel and later a Frankish warrior. The poet emphasizes this with the assertion that "it was not granted him that edges of iron could help him in battle" (2682–84: *"Him þæt gifeðe ne wæs / þæt him irenna ecge mihton / helpan æt hilde"*). We may therefore say that the mechanics and contents of the poem conform to the principles of oral-formulaic composition, but it must be repeated that the experts are by no means in agreement about the actual mode of composition of the text as we know it.[7]

Pagan and Christian Elements

Another central matter about which the experts have been at odds for a long time is the juxtaposition of pagan and Christian elements. The temptation for disagreement on this point is hard to resist when considering a poem which draws on pagan mythology in order to offer Scyld Scefing, Fitela, and Sigemund as models of conduct, but turns around to trace the monster Grendel's family line back to Cain (107 and 1258–63) and threaten the warriors in Heorot with damnation for their failure to subscribe to Christianity (175–88). The ambiguity is compounded when the very same warriors who are threatened with damnation are seen listening to a song about the Creation (92–98) which sounds in nearly every respect like the first Christian poem attributed to Caedmon, and when their leader warns Beowulf against three of the Seven Deadly Sins (1724–78). It is further compounded by the contrast between Beowulf's code of honor and the nature of his funeral: just as the former, with the hero's insistence upon fighting his mortal battles alone, cannot fail to remind us of Tacitus' observation in *Germania* that the leaders of the ancient Germans were under constant obligation to demonstrate their superior courage and thought it utterly disgraceful to be surpassed in battle by anyone of their followers, so the latter, with twelve retainers and a woman mourning by their dead lord's barrow, cannot fail to remind us of the death of Jesus, especially if we happen to be reasonably familiar with the Old English *Dream of the Rood* and the Medieval Latin *Stabat Mater*.

Because of these and other similar discrepancies, scholars have argued both the Christian coloring and the pagan coloring of the poem, in which they have both detected and rejected Christian interpolations into a pagan story and found everything between so-called essential paganism at one extreme and the story of Christian salvation at the other. Robert E. Kaske has pointed out that the poet's pervasive concern for the union of wisdom and action may well be a key to this apparent ambiguity of allegiance, since the ideal of *sapientia et fortitudo*—to use the Latin formulation under which it has been generally known since the Renaissance—was shared by pagans and Christians alike and is found, for example, in the *Edda* as well as in Isidore of Seville's *Etymologiae*. Notwithstanding the logic of Kaske's argument, there is no reason to expect an end to what has thus far proved a lively, fruitful, and occasionally entertaining controversy. Students approaching *Beowulf* for the first time might do well to heed Michael D. Cherniss' sensible advice when he points out in his *Ingeld and Christ* that we "have no evidence that the *Beowulf*-poet intended that his poem be read as allegory, Christian, pagan or otherwise . . ., especially when the various symbols may depend upon fortuitous similarities not intended by the author himself."[8]

The Characters

However debatable the intended lesson and possible allegory, the subject matter of the poem is clear enough when considered from the point of view of an eighth-century English audience which was certainly not composed exclusively of literary critics and which may have been willing to accept poetic utterances at face value. *Beowulf* quite simply tells the story of a young man who becomes an old king, and it lets us see something of the process whereby he learns to conform to the ideal union of wisdom and action which is a necessary component of leadership. Early in the poem, the aging Hrothgar is introduced as a wise and good (279: *"frod ond god"*) king whose devotion to wisdom may be inferred from his holding apparently interminable meetings with his advisors to consider appropriate solutions to the problems presented by Grendel's nightly forays (170–174), but whose ability to act has so declined that he can only sit and wait (see lines 130, 171, 356, 1313) in deliberation or meditation when immediate action is obviously called for. Both Kaske, in the course of the argument already mentioned, and Beowulf himself, in the course of his altercation with Unferth (590–97), have cogently argued that this inability to act has in effect proved an encouragement to

Grendel, who is basically all action. From the same point of view, however, Beowulf is almost as clear-cut a foil to Hrothgar as is Grendel. Whereas after seventy lines (100–69) of Grendel's murderous onslaughts the wise old king is still attending committee meetings and debating what would be best to do, the young warrior needs only five lines (194–98) to hear of the situation and immediately begin doing something about it by procuring a boat with which to sail to the rescue—without giving a thought to the possible implications of his undertaking. We may thus say that, as the story begins, the former is long on wisdom but short on action, while the latter is long on action but short on wisdom: neither conforms to the ideal union of wisdom and action.

Like most unthinking men of action, Beowulf in the first half of the poem appears unnecessarily brash and self-satisfied. Within the context of a society where good manners are so highly esteemed that an outstanding retainer is praised especially for his observance of the proper social behavior (359), we can hardly fail to question the young warrior's fitness for leadership when we hear him declaring publicly his intention to teach old Hrothgar how to deal with monsters (277–79), trying to impress the assembled Danes with boasts of a martial reputation (415–18) which has yet to be earned (1990–97, 2183–88), or failing to realize his own arrogance when, in the presence of the experienced warriors who have thus far proved no match for Grendel's superhuman strength, he confidently proclaims his intention to overpower the monster alone and unarmed (424–32). These youthful shortcomings become even more obvious by contrast with Hrothgar's meticulously urbane answer, which credits Beowulf for his honorable intentions (457–58), acknowledges his own warriors' helplessness before Grendel (473–77 and 480–88), and suggests that God will easily solve the problem as He sees fit (478–79). It is noteworthy that Beowulf may not be accused of wasting time on any sort of reflection until the middle of the poem and his victory over Grendel's mother: up to that point, his view of the world is simplified by the convenient belief that "fate always goes as it must" (455: "*Gæð a wyrd swa hio scel*"). His faith in his own "physical strength, the hand-grip of might" (1533–34: "*strenge . . . , mundgripe mægenes*") as a solution to everything is so total that, when it seems possible that divine will may have had a hand in Grendel's temporary escape from their original encounter, he must qualify the possibility with the assertion that he did not "cling to him so earnestly" (968: "*no ic him þæs georne ætfealh*") as to prevent his going. His single-minded concern for the glory of his own name is so obsessive that his last request before going after Grendel's mother is that his own king be given tangible proof of his having acted "with manly excellence" (1486: "*gumcystum*"), and he dives into the pond with the assertion that he "will either earn fame or be taken by death" (1490–91: "*ic me . . . / dom gewyrce, oþðe mec deað nimeð*").

When Beowulf returns to Heorot after his victory, however, his tone shows signs of change: not only does he admit having survived the experience only "with difficulty" (1655: "*unsofte*"), but his further admission that he would have perished "if God had not protected" him (1658: *"nymðe God mec scylde"*) suggests both his having given the matter some thought and his having learned to share with divine power the glory which is now his by right. In view of the number of mutually contradictory interpretations to which *Beowulf* has been subjected, one should exercise the greatest caution when assigning individual statements a place into a scheme which may or may not have been intended by the poet; the admittedly artless reading presented here is by no means intended to invalidate more sophisticated analyses of the meaning of the poem. Its main point of interest, in addition to affording us an easy key to the action, is that it receives Hrothgar's own sanction within the narrative. We have already noted how Hrothgar's polite answer to Beowulf's boasting implies faith in God rather than in any young upstart in search of renown, and it is relevant in this respect that his immediate reaction to the latter's victory over Grendel is to offer "thanks to the Almighty" (928: *"alwealdan þanc"*) rather than to the victor, whom he initially credits only with having acted "through the might of God" (940: *'þurh drihtnes miht''*), before finally expressing the proper admiration for his fighting prowess by recalling how he has bestowed rewards upon many a warrior "weaker in fighting" (953: *"sæmran æt sæcce"*).

Now that Beowulf's account of his encounter with Grendel's mother hints at a newly-acquired willingness to reflect upon a world where divine will may be more important than blind fate and where physical strength alone may not prove a solution to all problems, not only does Hrothgar give him full credit for the deed, but he pays him the supreme compliment of praising him precisely for possessing the ideal combination of "might with wisdom of mind" (1706: *"mægen mid modes snyttrum"*) and of predicting that he will become the support of his people (1707–09). In other words, Beowulf has now achieved much more than the purely martial fame which he claimed upon his arrival at Heorot, and Hrothgar is telling us that the brash young man has suddenly matured into a thoughtful warrior worthy of assuming the leadership of his people if need be.

Hrothgar's judgment is amply vindicated by the remainder of the narrative, during which Beowulf becomes both a "wise king" and a "defender of the homeland" (2209–10: *"frod cyning, / . . . eþelweard"*) after having shown enough self-control to turn down an earlier offer of kingship (2373–76) and having wisely served his own young lord with "friendly counsel" (2377: *"freondlarum"*). Nowhere in the poem is this union of wisdom and action more obvious than in Beowulf's speech to his retainers as he readies for the dragon fight that will cost him his life. Here, we find none of the thoughtless bravado that marked his tone when he first announced to Hrothgar his intention to confront Grendel. Instead, we find reflection leading to a quiet determination to act in a manner befitting his position. As he refers to himself as an "old guardian of the people" (2513: *"frod folces weard"*), he makes clear his full awareness of both his royal duty and the difficulties which age has put in the way of his discharging it; he accordingly determines to stand his ground and do battle if (2514: "*gif*") the dragon comes out of his lair to seek him. Contrary to his earlier practice (2521), he now carries a sword and feels the need to explain that he would not do so if (2519: "*gif*") he knew how else to deal with a dragon. Long ago in Heorot, he had already used the conjunction *if,* but he had done so in a boastful manner to suggest that Grendel might not dare (684: "*gif he . . . dear*") meet him in combat. Now, on the contrary, the repetition of the same conjunction drives home the fact that he has weighed at least some of the alternatives before choosing the solutions on which he finally settles, and it lends the passage a reflective tone which is totally absent from his utterances in the first half of the poem.

Nor does he decide to fight alone in a reckless attempt to prove his martial valor before the world, as he did years ago with Grendel: he will fight alone quite simply because he knows that, as king and formal protector of his people, he alone bears the responsibility of meeting the unequal challenge. He thoughtfully sets matters straight when he tells his retainers, "this is not your venture or the measure of any man, except mine alone . . ." (2532–33: "*Nis þæt eower siþ / ne gemet mannes, nefne min anes*"). In view of his awareness of the odds against him, his decision not to retreat by a single foot (2525) fully deserves the poet's admiring litotes: "such is not a coward's undertaking!" (2541: "*Ne bið swilc eages sið!*"). In effect, Beowulf has bridged the gap between foolhardiness and true courage in the Aristotelian sense. In so doing, he has raised his claim to fame above that of Hrothgar himself: like the old king in Heorot, he has learned to reflect and listen to the voice of wisdom before making decisions. Unlike him, however, he has retained the will to act, so that he has become an embodiment of the ideal union of wisdom and action, and we have witnessed the process whereby the brash young man who enters near the beginning of the poem turns into the wise and formidable old warrior whom the conclusion praises as the best of all earthly kings.

The foregoing observations, incidentally, are in keeping with J.R.R. Tolkien's view of the structure of the poem as "essentially a balance, an opposition of ends and beginnings . . . . an elaboration of the ancient and intensely moving contrast between youth and age, first achievement and final death," as well as with Stanley B. Greenfield's illuminating perception that this balance "is emphasized further in the contrast between the *tones* of the two halves of the poem. The heroic dominates the first part. . . . The elegiac dominates the second. . . ."[9]

Although there is no room here for a detailed discussion of secondary characters, a few words about Queen Wealhtheow are in order, since she is the only woman with a lasting part in this overwhelmingly masculine poem. With her entering the narrative at line 612, leaving it at line 2174, and making numerous appearances in between, she participates in more of the action than anyone else except the principal actors, and her name is mentioned more often than any but six others, including Grendel's. As we see her hosting a great banquet in Heorot and strolling through rows of rejoicing warriors (611) to bring greetings and mead to Beowulf and others (624), her outward appearance shows all the grace, cheerfulness, and poise befitting a great lady and the wife of a powerful king. Her behavior both illustrates the function of a queen in Germanic society and conforms to the expectations of the audience as we find them stated in the Old English *Maxims*. There is another and more subtle side to Wealhtheow, however, which reveals itself in her repeated and seemingly unwarranted quest for reassurance concerning the future of her two sons (see lines 1180–87 and 1219–27).

Especially for those who happen to recall that, in actual history, her sons never acceded to the throne and may have met with untimely and violent death, Wealhtheow's concern adds to the feeling of insecurity which pervades the poem as a result of strategically located reminders of the transitory nature of human glory and happiness. No sooner has Heorot been erected, for example, than we are forewarned of its eventual destruction by fire (82); no sooner has Beowulf's youthful vigor received full recognition for its triumph over Grendel's mother and her son than we are reminded of the ravages which old age holds in store for all of us before the unavoidable moment of death (1766–79); or no sooner have we learned of Princess Freawaru's betrothal to Ingeld than we hear a prediction of the disastrous and bloody outcome of that union (2029–69). In thus alerting us to the elusive signs of an unstated but impending catastrophe, Wealhtheow not only contributes to the tone of the entire poem but illustrates something of the justified anxiety which mars the lives of nearly all the women in Germanic secular poetry.[10]

Narrative Technique

The emphasis on the transitory nature of human achievements necessarily yields an element of suspense, since we are constantly reminded that all the glory of the world, and by implication all the good things toward which human beings tend to aspire, must come to an ineluctable end whose time may not be predicted. This element of suspense is intensified by the poet's masterful control of his technique, which finds ready illustration in his accounts of physical motion at key points in the action. As the makers of horror films discovered long ago, the monster's slow approach is likely to prove far more suspenseful and terrifying than his sudden appearance on the screen, since it allows the audience to anticipate and share emotionally the fate of the intended victims. Consciously or otherwise, the *Beowulf* poet has composed in accordance with this principle, as we can see in his handling of Grendel's last raid upon Heorot (703–21). With the opening words of the passage, we are made to sense vividly the evil presence of some mysterious and destructive force of the night silently moving toward us, as well as toward the Geats in Heorot, but we can only scan the darkness for the direction and distance whence it will reveal itself: "There came the walker in the shadows gliding through the dark night" (702–03: *"Com on wanre niht / scriðan sceadugenga''*). Only eight lines later is the approaching danger specifically identified as Grendel and its general location established with the statement that "then from the moors came Grendel advancing under the mist-covered slopes" (710–11: *"Ða com of more under misthleoþum / Grendel gongan''*); the inexorable process goes on until the monster finally reaches his goal. The mechanics of the passage have been submitted to an especially fine and revealing analysis by Arthur G. Brodeur in *The Art of Beowulf.* He says:

> . . . it is a hair-raising depiction of death on the march. . . . Three several, *distinct* stages of the action are here set forth. This is not the familiar static trick of poetic conventions; it is dynamic and progressive. Each successive statement of Grendel's oncoming represents an advance in time, in forward movement, in emotional force; each shows an increase over the preceding in the use of horrific detail; each imposes increased strain upon the audience.[11]

The strain is here for all but the most insensitive reader, and we need not have delved very deeply into the mysteries of literary psychology to realize that it must have been even stronger with an audience for whom lurking monsters were altogether as real and difficult to control as air pollution and the dangers of radiation in the fourth quarter of the twentieth century.

The converse of this technique is used with equal mastery in the account of the march to the pond where Grendel and his mother have taken refuge. Whereas the passage discussed above forces us to endure the action from the point of view of the fixed target toward which the bloodthirsty monster is moving closer with every line, the march to the pond makes us participate in the action from the opposite point of view as it takes us in pursuit of Grendel's mother along the mountain path leading to the dark waters (1400–21) whose horror we have been made to anticipate through a previous account (1361–76). Like a traveling motion picture camera, we accompany Hrothgar as he follows the monster's foot tracks until we reach the edge of the pond and come to an abrupt stop at the chilling sight of Aeschere's severed head, before shifting our focus to the chilling sight of blood welling on the water (1422–23).[12]

The attention given to Aeschere's head and the blood on the water brings up another aspect of narrative technique worth noting here. Like Stendhal, whose *Charterhouse of Parma* has impressed the battle of Waterloo upon generations of readers by focusing on bits of soil sent flying by cannon balls, the *Beowulf* poet almost unfailingly comes up with the detail most likely to impress an entire scene upon our mind. When Beowulf leaves his homeland to seek Grendel, for instance, we are given no description of the ship which the Geats are boarding: instead, our attention is called to a single detail which sets our imagination working as we are told that "the sea-currents eddied, water against sand" (212–13: *"streamas wundon, / sund wið sande''*). Elsewhere, as Grendel enters Heorot, we are again made to concentrate upon a single detail which is far more suggestive than any description of the monster himself: the "ugly light" (727: "*leoht unfæger*") which shines from his eyes into the pitch darkness of the hall where Beowulf is waiting in silence.

Perhaps as typical as the techniques discussed above is the extent to which *Beowulf* seems to call upon its audience to take an active part in the composition of the narrative. The device, which is probably as old as literature itself, requires the listener or reader to manipulate information drawn either from the text itself or from his own store of knowledge and to apply it to a framework designed by the author. In the novel, the modern period has provided us with a plentiful source of clear instances of the first alternative. Nearly everyone recalls reading one or more novels in which an unexpected piece of information provided by the author suddenly forces the reader to reformulate everything which has preceded it and thus to participate retroactively in the creation of a literary artifact which is unlikely to be the same for any two readers. In the *Aeneid* and the *Nibelungenlied*, Classical Antiquity and the Middle Ages have provided us with equally clear instances of the second alternative. When, in the twelfth book of the *Aeneid*, we find a crucial section of a council patterned upon a similar event in the first book of the *Iliad*, we are in effect invited to interpret the action in the light of unstated similarities and differences between the two situations, and we are clued in by the fact that the Latin word by which King Latinus refers to the scepter (*sceptrum*) on which he swears to maintain peace happens to be precisely the same as the Greek word by which Achilles refers to the staff (*skēpteron*) on which he swears never to be reconciled to Agamemnon. The same principle operates in the concluding section of the *Nibelungenlied*, when we are reminded of the time when Hagen passively sat on his shield while Walter of Spain massacred his companions. The reference is to an episode recorded in the *Waltharii Poesis*, where we find Hagen so hopelessly torn between conflicting allegiances that he can only look on and brood over his own impending loss of knightly honor while warriors to whom he owes equal support try to kill each other. When brought to bear upon the action of the *Nibelungenlied*, the information which we are thus invited to draw from an outside source forces us to reformulate our own view of Hagen's character only a few lines before we see his head roll under the sword of a vengeful queen.

Both alternatives occur in *Beowulf*, with the first one illustrated in Hygelac's surprise at the news of the successful cleansing of Heorot (1992–97), which prompts us to reconsider Beowulf's earlier assertion that he undertook the adventure at everybody's instigation (415–18); or in the poet's belated allegations that Beowulf had a "wretched" (2183: "*Hean*") childhood, which prompts us both to reconsider our hero's earlier boasting about his glorious youth (408–09) and to perceive a kind of structural relationship between him and the mythological Scyld Scefing, whose early childhood was also "wretched" (7: "*feasceaft*") but who nevertheless rose to the full glory of an ideal king and protector of the people. We may thus say that, in the case of the novel, the *Beowulf* poet presents us with information which we are invited to manipulate in order to see certain key elements of the story not specifically mentioned in the text.

The second alternative is illustrated during the banquet in honor of Beowulf's victory over Grendel when, at the conclusion of a brief account of the exemplary social behavior shown by Hrothgar and his nephew Hrothulf, and of the atmosphere of warm friendship which fills Heorot (1011–18), we are suddenly told that the Scyldings have not yet performed "treason" (1018–19: *"facenstafas"*). The statement stands out because its tone clashes with that of the festivities that are going on, because the information seems irrelevant to the immediate action, and because we find no justification for it in the preceding narrative. Precisely because it is so clearly out of place, however, it sends us searching through our own store of information, where we find what the poet presumably assumed to be common knowledge in his audience: upon Hrothgar's death in A.D. 525, it seems that the historical Hrothulf—the Hrolf of the *Hrólfs Saga Kraka*—usurped the throne and presumably rid himself of the legitimate claimants. Once properly impressed upon our mind, this and other similar reminders of historical facts outside the scope of the narrative become powerfully relevant to the immediate context. By keeping us aware that the glory before us is doomed to nought, they lend a tangible reality to the sense of transiency which pervades the poem; by keeping us aware that Hrothgar's sons will never succeed their father, they add tragic intensity to the concern which their mother shows for their future, as was suggested earlier in this essay. We may thus say that, like Virgil and the anonymous author of the *Nibelungenlied,* the *Beowulf* poet clues us in to information which lies outside the text and which we are invited to manipulate in order to add a major emotional dimension to the narrative. These and the many other hints and allusions which invite us to join in the composition of the poem must have been especially effective with the original audience, at a time when much of what has since become recondite and uncertain history was presumably common lore, as obvious as a mention of George Washington's cherry tree is to most Americans.

The presence of the technique described above may possibly provide some explanation for the multiplicity of interpretations which have been noted earlier, and it certainly bears out Kenneth Sisam's view that "there is no one key to the appreciation of *Beowulf,* "[13] for the fact is that there are probably as many versions of the poem as there are readers of it. In addition, this technique tells us that, much more than a millennium after its composition, *Beowulf* remains a poem for active readers. Passive readers will find it a good story about a man who kills monsters, but those willing to follow the hints and allusions in order to participate actively in the composition of the story will find themselves sharing to the full in the joys and sorrows of human beings, while experiencing the growth, the victories, and the death of one who has learned to recognize his own place in the scheme of things.

In view of the place of eminence which *Beowulf* occupies in the history of English literature, we must agree with William Alfred when he writes that it is "a national monument as well as a poem,"[14] but one should add that it is a very special monument. On the one hand, it is a grand and monument-like celebration of the ideal of human excellence; on the other hand, the way in which it involves each one of us personally and intimately in the action is as unmonument-like as it is moving and effective.

NOTES

1. For the text of the Finn-Hnaef fragment, see Friedrich Klaeber, ed., *Beowulf and the Fight at Finnsburg* (Lexington: D. C. Heath, 1950), pp. 245–47; for the Walter fragment, see Frederick Norman, ed., *Waldere* (London: Methuen, 1933); for the *Waltharii Poesis,* see Karl Langosch, ed., *Waltharius, Ruodlieb. Märchenepen* (Basel: Benno Schwabe, 1956), with face-to-face German translation, and English translation in Francis P. Magoun, Jr., and Hamilton M. Smyser, *Walter of Aquitaine: Materials for the Study of His Legend* (New London: Connecticut College, 1950). For the possibility of a lost Old English *Hildebrandslied* and for discussions of hypothetical Odoacer and Offa cycles, see Moritz Trautmann, *Finn und Hildebrand* (Bonn: University of Bonn, 1903), Rudolf H. R. Imelmann, "Die altenglische Odoaker-dichtung," in his *Forschungen zur altenglischen Poesie* (Berlin: Weidmann, 1907), and Edith Rickert, "The Old English Offa Saga," *Modern Philology* 2 (1904–05): 28–48. For the text of Alcuin's admonition, see Letter no. 81 in *Monumenta Alcuiniana,* ed. Wilhelm Wattenbach and Ernst Duemmler (Berlin: Weidmann, 1873).

2. For accounts of the string instrument and its function in poetic performances, see Jess B. Bessinger, Jr., "The Sutton Hoo Harp Replica and Old English Musical Verse," in Robert P. Creed, ed., *Old English Poetry: Fifteen Essays* (Providence: Brown University Press, 1967), pp. 3–26, and John Nist, "Metrical Uses of the Harp in *Beowulf,*" ibid., pp. 27–43. The relevant sections of both the Latin and the Old English texts of Bede's *Historia* are conveniently printed in Frederic G. Cassidy and Richard N. Ringler, eds., *Bright's Old English Grammar and Reader* (New York: Holt, Rinehart and Winston, 1971), pp. 125–34.

3. Donald K. Fry, "Cædmon as a Formulaic Poet," in *Oral Literature: Seven Essays,* ed. Joseph J. Duggan (New York: Barnes and Noble, 1975), pp. 41–46. Magoun's "Oral-Formulaic Character" first appeared in *Speculum* 28 (1953): 446–67; Creed's formulaic poem in Old English was published as part of his "The Making of an Anglo-Saxon Poem," *English Literary History* 16 (1959): 445–54; Benson's "Literary Character" appeared in *PMLA* 81 (1966): 334–41. For additional relevant studies by these and other scholars, consult Edward R. Haymes, *The Haymes Bibliography of the Oral Theory* (Cambridge: Harvard University, 1973).

4. The historical background and the analogues of *Beowulf* are succinctly discussed in the introduction and appendices to Klaeber's *Beowulf and the Fight at Finnsburg;* detailed discussion will be found in Raymond W. Chambers, *Beowulf: An Introduction,* 3rd ed., with supplement by C. L. Wrenn (Cambridge, England: Cambridge University Press, 1963).

5. Old English quotations are from *Beowulf and Judith,* ed. Elliott Van Kirk Dobbie (New York: Columbia University Press, 1953).

6. Lord's chart appears on p. 199 of *The Singer of Tales* (Cambridge: Harvard University Press, 1960), with supporting evidence on pp. 297–301. For studies of Beowulfian rhythms and alliterative patterns, see John C. Pope, *The Rhythm of Beowulf: An Interpretation of the Normal and Hypermetric Verse-Forms in Old English Poetry,* rev. ed. (New Haven: Yale University Press, 1966), and Thomas Cable, *The Meters and Melody of Beowulf* (Urbana: University of Illinois Press, 1974).

7. Crowne's study of the formulaic theme in question was published as "The Hero on the Beach: an Example of Composition by Theme in Anglo-Saxon Poetry," *Neuphilologische Mitteilungen* 61 (1960); the *Haymes Bibliography* lists subsequent essays on the same theme by Donald K. Fry, Janet Thorman, Carol Jean Wolf, and Alain Renoir, and others have appeared since the publication of the *Bibliography;* another equally important formulaic theme in *Beowulf* was pointed out by Francis P. Magoun, Jr., in "The Theme of the Beasts of Battle in Anglo-Saxon Poetry," *Neuphilologische Mitteilungen* 56 (1955): 81–90, and discussed by Adrien Bonjour in *"Beowulf* and the Beasts of Battle," *PMLA* 72 (1957): 563–73. For the similarities noted between *Beowulf* and the *Odyssey,* see Albert B. Lord, "Beowulf and Odysseus," in *Franciplegius: Mediaeval and Linguistic Studies in Honor of Francis Peabody Magoun, Jr.,* ed. Jess B. Bessinger, Jr., and Robert P. Creed (New York, 1965), pp. 86–91, and Robert P. Creed, "The Singer Looks at His Sources," in *Studies in Old English Literature in Honor of Arthur G. Brodeur,* ed. Stanley B. Greenfield (Eugene, 1963), pp. 44–52. Nagler, *Spontaneity and Tradition,* p. 114, finds that the theme of the waking leader is shared by Beowulf (703–09) with "Odysseus, Achilles, Gilgamesh, Arjuna, and many others . . . ." Klaeber includes a discussion of the Bear's Son in the introduction and appendices to his *Beowulf and the Fight at Finnsburg;* the argument for this theory was developed by Friedrich Panzer in *Studien zur germanischen Sagengeschichte,* I: *Beowulf* (Munich, 1910).

8. Michael D. Cherniss, *Ingeld and Christ* (The Hague: Mouton, 1972), pp. 130–31. Kaske's argument is developed in *"Sapientia et Fortitudo* as the Controlling Theme in *Beowulf,"* *Studies in Philology* 55 (1958): 423–36; examples of the other views discussed above will be found in F. A. Blackburn, "The Christian Coloring of *Beowulf,"* *PMLA* 12 (1897): 205–25, where the theory of interpolations was first suggested, though it is now associated primarily with H. Monro Chadwick's *The Heroic Age* (Cambridge, England, 1912), pp. 47–56; Larry D. Benson, "The Pagan Coloring of *Beowulf,"* in Creed, *Old English Poetry,* pp. 193–213; Charles Moorman, "The Essential Paganism of *Beowulf,"* *Modern Language Quarterly* 28 (1967): 3–18; Maurice B. McNamee, S. J., *"Beowulf:* An Allegory of Salvation?" *Journal of English and Germanic Philology* 61 (1960): 190–207; Morton W. Bloomfield, *"Beowulf* and Christian Allegory: An Interpretation of Unferth," *Traditio* 7 (1949–51): 410–15.

9. J. R. R. Tolkien, *Beowulf: The Monsters and the Critics* (Oxford, 1958), p. 29; Stanley B. Greenfield, *A Critical History of Old English Literature* (New York, 1968), pp. 87–88; for a more detailed discussion of Beowulf's last speech, see Alain Renoir, "The Heroic Oath in *Beowulf,* the *Chanson de Roland,* and the *Nibelungenlied,"* in Greenfield, *Studies in Old English,* pp. 237–66.

10. For a more detailed discussion of Wealhtheow and Freawaru within the context of Germanic poetry, see Alain Renoir, "A Reading Context for *The Wife's Lament,"*

in *Anglo-Saxon Poetry: Essays in Appreciation,* ed. Dolores W. Frese and Lewis E. Nicholson (Notre Dame: University of Notre Dame, 1975), pp. 224–41.

11. Arthur G. Brodeur, *The Art of Beowulf* (Berkeley, 1960), pp. 90–91; for elaborations upon Brodeur's analysis, see Stanley B. Greenfield's illuminating essay, "Grendel's Approach to Heorot: Syntax and Poetry," in Creed, *Old English Poetry,* pp. 275–84, and Alain Renoir, "Point of View and Design for Terror in *Beowulf,*" *Neuphilologische Mitteilungen* 63 (1962): 154–67.

12. For an analysis of the technique underlying this account, see Alain Renoir, "The Terror of the Dark Waters: A Note on Virgilian and Beowulfian Techniques," *Harvard English Studies* 5 (1974): 147–60.

13. Kenneth Sisam, *The Structure of Beowulf* (Oxford, 1965), p. 1.

14. William Alfred, trans., "Beowulf," in W. Alfred et al., *Medieval Epics* (New York, 1963), p. 9.

BIBLIOGRAPHICAL SUGGESTIONS

Because the bulk of first-rate and immediately relevant *Beowulf* scholarship is staggering, and the poem has been edited and translated over and over again, a brief bibliography must perforce be both unrepresentative and misleading. The entries below are accordingly offered as mere suggestions picked almost at random. Readers wishing to pursue ideas outlined in the foregoing essay are accordingly directed to Donald K. Fry, *Beowulf and the Fight at Finnsburg: A Bibliography* (Charlottesville: Bibliographical Society of the University of Virginia, 1969) and to the annual account of *Beowulf* scholarship in the *Old English Newsletter.*

Editions

Chickering, Howell D., Jr., ed. and trans. *Beowulf: A Dual-Language Edition.* New York: Doubleday/Anchor Books, 1977. Provides the best available introduction to the original text for readers with little or no knowledge of Old English. The comprehensive introduction and notes are up to date, lucid, and invaluable to both the general reader and the student of Old English.

Klaeber, Friedrich, ed. *Beowulf and the Fight at Finnsburg.* 3rd ed. Lexington: D. C. Heath, 1950. This also includes the *Hildebrandslied,* Waldere, Deor, and sections of *Widsith.* The critical apparatus gives the gist of the analogues, discusses the archeological, historical, and philological evidence, and includes bibliographical commentaries to 1946.

Translations

Alfred, William, trans. "Beowulf." In *Medieval Epics.* New York: Random House, 1963. Includes translations of the *Song of Roland,* the *Nibelungenlied,* and the *Poem of the Cid,* thus providing materials for comparison.

Tuso, Joseph F., ed. *Beowulf.* New York: Norton, 1974. Includes E. Talbot Donaldson's translation, an up-to-date, generous, and representative bibliography, and judicious selections from essential studies by distinguished authorities. Donaldson's text is also available in Meyer H. Abrams, ed., *The Norton Anthology of English Literature,* rev. ed., I (New York: Norton, 1968).

Background and Criticism

Brodeur, Arthur G. *The Art of Beowulf.* Berkeley: University of California Press,

1959. Provides the most comprehensive scholarly appreciation and analysis of the poem.

Chambers, Raymond W. *Beowulf: An Introduction.* 3rd ed. With supplement by C. L. Wrenn. Cambridge, England: Cambridge University Press, 1963. Provides an enormous amount of indispensable lucid information about the poem and its background.

Fry, Donald K., ed. *The Beowulf Poet: A Collection of Critical Essays.* Englewood Cliffs: Prentice Hall, 1968. Includes essays by several scholars on various aspects of the poem.

Nicholson, Lewis E., ed. *An Anthology of Beowulf Criticism.* Notre Dame: University of Notre Dame Press, 1963. Includes essays by several scholars on various aspects of the poem.

Whitelock, Dorothy. *The Audience of Beowulf.* Oxford: Clarendon Press, 1951. Provides a context for the poem.

6   The *Nibelungenlied* as Heroic Epic

Stephen L. Wailes

The *Nibelungenlied,* a Middle High German epic poem of approximately 9,000 lines composed in four-line stanzas, was written down in the Austro-Bavarian region about the year 1200. It has been preserved in three main 13th-century manuscripts: A (now in Munich), B (the most trustworthy, now in St. Gall), and C (now in Donaueschingen). The title of the epic, *Nibelungenlied,* comes from the term *Nibelung,* which is used in two functions. In the first part of the epic, it is applied to Siegfried's lands, peoples, and his treasure, and in the second, to the Burgundian warriors.

Little is known, though much is conjectured, about the anonymous poet. He appears to have moved in the higher cultural circles of his day, and he probably had a sophisticated knowledge of literature. Whether he was a knight, a cleric, or possibly a professional storyteller cannot, however, be known, and of the particular cast of his mind, his philosophical orientation, his values, his view of human nature and final verities, only the most guarded statements can be made. These must be guarded in part because of the real difficulties and ambiguities of the poem, and in part because scholarly interest in the *Nibelungenlied* has only recently turned away from an almost antiquarian obsession with the earlier history of the stories told in the poem to an examination of the poem as an autonomous literary work.

Synopsis of the Nibelungenlied

The two major parts of the *Nibelungenlied* are linked by the figure of Kriemhild, sister of the Burgundian Kings Gunther, Gernot and Giselher. The first part recounts the wooing of Kriemhild by the hero Siegfried, their eventual marriage and his treacherous murder. The second part tells of a second wooing of Kriemhild, this time by the widowed Etzel (Attila) of Hungary, their marriage and Kriemhild's ultimate revenge on her Burgundian relatives for Siegfried's death. The two parts are of approximately equal length, and the entire work is divided formally into thirty-nine cantos (*aventiuren*) with a varying number of stanzas in each canto.

The first canto not only introduces Kriemhild but also sets the mood of the poem. Kriemhild had dreamed of having tamed a wild falcon which then flew away only to be killed by two eagles. Her mother Uote thinks the falcon foretells a noble knight, but Kriemhild rejects any thought of love since it also brings sorrow. Parallel to the introduction of Kriemhild in the first canto is the introduction of Siegfried in the second. He is shown as having grown up in the area of the lower Rhine in Xanten, the son of King Siegmund and Queen Sieglind, and receiving his investiture as a knight in a magnificent ceremony.

When Siegfried arrives in Worms in the third canto, determined to woo Kriemhild despite his parents' admonitions, he has already had several adventures in which his prowess has been tested. Hagen, a faithful vassal of King Gunther, tells the Burgundians how Siegfried had obtained the treasure of the Nibelungs by killing the Nibelung princes Schilbung and Nibelung and seven hundred of their men, how he got his sword Balmung and conquered the dwarf Alberich, from whom he had obtained a magic cape (*tarnkappe*) and whom he had left to guard the treasure. Hagen also reports how Siegfried had slain a dragon and bathed himself in its blood, thereby making himself invulnerable. Although Siegfried presents a challenge to King Gunther, they become friends and Siegfried agrees to help Gunther in battle against the threatening Saxon King Liudeger and his brother the Danish King Liudegast. Siegfried defeats the kings, captures them and returns them to Worms, where he finally gets to see Kriemhild.

However, before he can marry Kriemhild, Siegfried must first help Gunther win a bride. Gunther is intent on winning the hand of the beautiful, but physically extremely powerful Queen Brunhild of Isenstein. Brunhild will marry only the man who can defeat her in three contests: spear throwing, boulder hurling and leaping. Siegfried, Gunther, Hagen, and another vassal, Dancwart, set out alone on their mission to Isenstein. Eventually with the help of his magic cape, which renders him invisible, Siegfried defeats Brunhild for Gunther, although Brunhild believes that Gunther did it and that Siegfried is Gunther's vassal.

There is a great celebration when the men return to Worms with Brunhild. Siegfried and Kriemhild are formally engaged, but Brunhild is very unhappy to see Siegfried, whom she had thought to be of inferior rank, sitting next to Kriemhild. At night when Gunther seeks her love Brunhild ties him up with her girdle of silk cord and hangs him on a nail on the wall, determined not to lose her virginity until she has learned the truth about Siegfried. Again Gunther asks Siegfried for help. He subdues Brunhild for Gunther, allowing Gunther to deflower Brunhild himself, thereby depriving her of her great strength. On an impulse, however, Siegfried takes Brunhild's ring and girdle with him and gives them to Kriemhild.

Siegfried and Kriemhild are married and return to Siegfried's ancestral lands, where Siegfried takes over the rule from his father. Ten years pass, but Brunhild is still dissatisfied and angry. She persists in asking Gunther to order his vassal, Siegfried, to court. Eventually Gunther does invite Siegfried, and a great celebration is held when Siegfried and Kriemhild arrive. But the festival turns into a disaster. Brunhild and Kriemhild get into an argument concerning the relative rank and merit of their husbands. Angry words are exchanged at the entry to the minster. When Brunhild tries to precede Kriemhild, the latter puts her to shame by stating that Siegfried, not Gunther, had deflowered her. As proof she produces Brunhild's ring and girdle. When confronted by Gunther, Siegfried apologizes for his wife's behavior and swears that he had not robbed Brunhild of her virginity. This is of course technically correct, but Hagen, incensed at the disgrace of his queen, swears revenge and lays plans to have Siegfried killed.

Under the pretext of a campaign against the hostile Saxons, Hagen cleverly finds out from Kriemhild the one place where Siegfried can be wounded (a linden leaf had fallen between his shoulder blades so that the dragon's blood did not cover the skin at that spot). The war against the Saxons is then called off and turned into a great hunt. Despite Kriemhild's premonitions in two dreams, Siegfried takes part in the hunt, outracing everyone at one point to reach a spring first. Here Hagen murders him ruthlessly. Siegfried's body is dropped at Kriemhild's door. Kriemhild is distraught. When Hagen passes Siegfried's bier, blood oozes from the mortal wound. As the first part comes to a close after Siegfried's burial, Giselher and Gernot fetch the treasure from the Nibelungs for Kriemhild, but when she appears to be spending it too lavishly, Hagen seizes it and sinks it in the Rhine secretly. For thirteen long years Kriemhild stays in Worms ever mindful of Siegfried's murder.

The scene shifts in the second part of the *Nibelungenlied* first to Etzel's castle in Hungary. His wife Helche has died and on the advice of his men he sends Rüdiger von Pöchlarn to Worms to woo Kriemhild. Initially reluctant, she finally agrees, thinking always of an opportunity for vengeance. The return is described in considerable detail with stops in Passau and Pöchlarn, followed by the royal wedding with Etzel in Vienna and the trip on back to Hungary. Kriemhild bears Etzel a son, Ortlieb, but in her thirteen years with Etzel her yearning for revenge for Siegfried's death does not diminish. Eventually she asks Etzel to invite her relatives to a great festival, and messengers are sent to carry out her wish.

Hagen is suspicious and initially advises against accepting the invitation but is finally persuaded to go, provided the men are well armed. When they arrive at the Danube crossing, they find no ferryman at first. Hagen, however, meets two water nymphs, who warn him that everyone except the King's chaplain will perish in Hungary. After an argument Hagen kills the ferryman and ferries the company across the Danube himself, in the course of which he throws the chaplain in the river, only to see that he does not drown but rather gains the shore safely to return to Worms.

The Burgundians are received warmly by Bishop Pilgrim in Passau, and there is a splendid celebration at Pöchlarn, when Giselher is engaged to Rüdiger's daughter. However, the mood becomes ominous when Dietrich rides out to warn the men against Kriemhild, who still mourns for Siegfried. Kriemhild receives her relatives coolly. Upon her inquiry, Hagen relates that he has hidden the treasure in the Rhine. The tension in the atmosphere builds up when Kriemhild sees Hagen holding Siegfried's sword across his knees. She weeps and reminds him that he had killed Siegfried, a deed that he readily admits as repayment for Kriemhild's having insulted Brunhild.

Suspicions grow, insults are exchanged, and soon a full-scale fight breaks out, which eventually involves almost everyone. Dancwart kills Etzel's brother, whose death is then avenged by a Hunnish troop. Hagen kills Ortlieb, Etzel's son. Kriemhild, Etzel and Dietrich are allowed to leave the hall, and the fighting continues throughout the castle with the Burgundians trapped in the great hall. Many individual combats are depicted, but through it all Kriemhild is urging her men to capture Hagen, to no avail. Finally she has the hall put to the torch. She reminds Rüdiger of his obligation as a vassal, although he is also bound to the Burgundians by the engagement of his daughter. Rüdiger reluctantly fights for the Huns and dies in battle.

As the carnage increases fewer and fewer heroes are left until only Gunther, Hagen, and Dietrich and his vassal Hildebrand remain alive. Dietrich seizes Hagen, ties him up, and brings him to Kriemhild, who promises him his freedom if he will tell her where the treasure is. Hagen replies that he will not tell her so long as one of his liege lords still lives. Kriemhild has Gunther's head cut off and brings it to Hagen, who says that now only God and he know where the treasure is and again refuses to divulge its location. Incensed, Kriemhild seizes Siegfried's sword and cuts off the head of the defenseless Hagen, whereupon Hildebrand slays Kriemhild. At the end Dietrich and Etzel are left to lament the many dead heroes.

Concept of Heroism

Discussion of the *Nibelungenlied* as heroic epic must begin with a concept of heroism and with the admission that the composition of the poem is far removed in time and cultural context from the "Heroic Age" of the Germanic peoples. This discussion is organized around a definition of heroism which we believe accurately describes the behavior of the principal characters in Germanic heroic literature, and which permits us to evaluate the action of the poem that is particular to the feudal and chivalric culture for which it was created. The same definition is valid for the archaic patterns of story which underlie the epic. Heroism is defined as the exemplary behavior of prominent persons. It is important to understand that this is not limited to consideration of admirable or laudable actions, those viewed by the audience with favor, which are associated with the general usage of terms such as "hero" and "heroism." This definition lacks an ethical orientation, remaining true in this regard to the legends of the Germanic Heroic Age which are filled with characters who are not admirable. Indeed, one of the most familiar and memorable types in these legends is the great tyrant—for instance, Atli or

Jormunrekk—and we meet as well great villains (Hagen, murderer of Siegfried), calumniators (Unferth), hotheads (Hadubrand, Wolfhart), and, to be
sure, heroes admirable in all respects (Walther). The subject of Germanic
heroic poetry is character; the vision of the poetry includes character of all
qualities. Unless we wish to limit the term "heroism" to particular moments
of the poetry when nice people do good things, we shall find the proposed
definition true to the breadth and realism of the depiction of character in the
poems, which deal with many varieties of human motives and experiences,
provided these are not trivial. The poems set forth examples of human types
and human behavior, but not of trifling character traits or prosy experiences.
For the medieval audience, Siegfried and Hagen exemplified contrasting
human types, but the fact that they contrast does not lessen the reality or
importance of either. Both are deeply rooted in man's experience.

Another question is the distance in time of the *Nibelungenlied* from the
"Heroic Age"—a term we use to designate the Period of Migrations (*Völker-
wanderung*), roughly from the second through the eighth centuries of the
Christian era, when the Germanic tribes were moving south and west through
Europe from their earlier homes in Scandinavia and along the southern coasts
of the Baltic Sea. We apply the term "Heroic Age" to this epoch by analogy
to the Heroic Age of Greece, because the historic and quasi-historic events
and personalities of Germanic heroic poetry belong to that period of Germanic
history. It is broadly true that the Germanic Heroic Age was tribal and pagan.
But the development of feudal medieval society virtually eliminated the tribal
nature of Germanic civilization, and the dominance of Christianity in western
Europe left few vestiges of pagan religion in the time when the *Nibelungenlied*
was composed. This poem is filled with the culture of chivalric courts, including at least the forms of Christianity. Its socio-political foundation is feudal
monarchy. The author and his audience knew far less of the Germanic Heroic
Age than we know, nor can we assume that they had much greater exposure to
stories and tales reflecting this age than do diligent scholars of the present day.
Thus the poem we read is not a direct emanation from the pagan and tribal
culture of the fifth century; its connection to Germanic culture is more tenuous
than that of *Beowulf,* composed nearly five hundred years earlier. It must be
read first as it was understood by the feudal and chivalric audience for whom
it was written.

We will proceed by examining the heroism of three levels of story in the
Nibelungenlied: that of A.D. 1200, that of the Heroic Age, and that of the
archaic period of Germanic culture, by which is meant simply the period
before the Heroic Age, extending back thousands of years to the quite uncertain origins of the Germanic peoples. This approach is indeed similar to the
tradition of *Nibelungenlied* scholarship one might call archeological, which
has regarded the poem as a kind of literary midden to be probed and sifted for
traces of earlier life, but the excesses of that approach will hopefully be
avoided here. We shall not stop at particular lines and stanzas to suggest that

they, like little diamonds, have withstood the abrasion of time and reveal to us an earlier poem on the subject. (The distinguished scholar Helmut de Boor, in his edition of the poem, suggests that the first line of stanza 1717 may be "an archaic word of Kriemhild from the primal song.") Instead, the essential heroism of the story for each of the three cultures will be examined.

Nibelungenlied *as Feudal Epic*

Let us begin with the *Nibelungenlied* as a feudal epic and focus attention immediately on those episodes and that embroidery of the story which seem inconsistent with the heroic character of the tale, however it might be defined. The reference is to the sartorial stanzas, the long passages of pomp and ceremony, the long and digressive story of the Saxon War, Siegfried's point-less journey to the land of the Nibelungs, the extravagant hunting contest, and the rather "slow" chapters following the double wedding. Although there might seem to be a similarity between these retarding episodes and the fre-quent interpolated tales in heroic poems like the *Iliad* and *Beowulf,* the phenomena are quite different. *Beowulf* is particularly famous as a repository of legends not directly connected to the plot line of the story, and, although on the first reading these legends can irritate one by seeming to distract from the matter at hand, their thematic and tonal unity with the story of Beowulf soon becomes apparent. The theme of *Beowulf* is German heroism, refracted into the text in differing shades and intensities from sources more or less remote in Germanic culture. This is not the case in the *Nibelungenlied,* where the plot is unitary and remarkably controlled, where we have only one significant digres-sion into legends not integral to the plot (Hagen's summary of Siegfried's youthful exploits) and where a few allusions to other stories (references to Hagen's residence with Etzel, to Nuodung and Witege) exist. In the *Nibelungenlied,* episodes in the life of Siegfried himself seem to retard the movement of the story: why are the Saxon war and Siegfried's trip to the land of the Nibelungs for a host of warriors who are never needed described at such length? The story of Siegfried's love and death is little advanced by these chapters. And why does the author linger over banquets, journeys, and the glories of wardrobe? Must the critic apologize for these episodes and descrip-tions when presenting the poem as heroic epic?

One must realize the tremendous importance of externals for the estimation of internal worth in chivalric culture. Though the sartorial stanzas are too frequent, a compositional defect, they express an understanding of human dignity gained through the estimation of worldly stature which is basic in the epistemology of feudalism. For the poet and audience of the feudal epic, the great man could not be separated from the insignia of greatness, including the magnificence of dress. This way of seeing things is very foreign to the modern reader, but in the period of the *Nibelungenlied* there was no conception of honor and distinction based on the individual's own self-respect apart from the respect accorded him by members of society. This was rooted in wealth and class. By reminding the audience continually of the wealth and class of his principals—seen in dress, jewels, generosity, banquets, jousts, ceremonious journeys, and receptions—the poet emphasizes that these are prominent persons whose behavior is exemplary. One may object that the passages under discussion are too long or too frequent, but this is a criticism of the literary craft of the author, not a rejection of the character of the passages as inappropriate to heroic story.

The apparently digressive adventures of Siegfried require justification on different grounds. The only explanation of the Saxon war that is obvious is that it shows Siegfried ingratiating himself with the Burgundians in order to bring closer to reality his dream of marrying Kriemhild. This is an unsatisfactory explanation, because in terms of his marriage quest the Saxon war does him little good, and the bargain he presently strikes with Gunther, through which he obtains Kriemhild's hand, has nothing at all to do with the Saxons. A more interesting interpretive possibility is this: by leading the Burgundian forces against the Saxons and Danes, Siegfried redresses exactly the error of his own behavior when he first came to Burgundy. On that occasion he belied his careful education and training in princely conduct by challenging the king, Gunther, to single combat for possession of lands and wealth. This unprovoked aggression amazed the royal court, which responded by rejecting violence as a means of territorial expansion: "We do not aspire to gain any land by force at the price of the slaying of one warrior by another. . . ."[1] In the next chapter the Danes and Saxons announce an attack on Burgundy quite as unprovoked as Siegfried's, and at Hagen's suggestion Siegfried is made leader of the defensive forces. Thus there is balance and symmetry between the chapters. The Saxon war may depict a positive social example, a powerful man acting responsibly in defence of legitimate authority.

Another possibility, and one which complements without excluding the foregoing, is to understand the Saxon war as a way of studying the character of Siegfried in relation to the characters of Hagen and Gunther, both of whom shrewdly exploit Siegfried's capacity as a fighting man. Hagen even diminishes his own luster as first asset of the King by proposing that Siegfried be given the job of defeating the Saxons. The episode also reveals the calculating nature of Gunther, who can mask his face in sorrow to elicit Siegfried's inquiry, then pretend to doubt Siegfried's good faith ("One should complain of one's wrongs to proven friends"),[2] and finally seem to act graciously by accepting an offer of help which he had counted on from the start. The episode suggests contrasting characters: Siegfried the natural and spontaneous warrior, Hagen the chancellor and dynastic statesman, Gunther the subtle king. One thinks of Othello among the Venetians.

Following this interpretation, Siegfried's trip to the land of the Nibelungs may be understood as a further study of character. Once again it is Hagen who pushes Siegfried into action. Quite emphatically he expresses concern that Brunhild may go back on the agreement once she is surrounded by her kinsmen and vassals, whereupon Siegfried volunteers to sail off alone and fetch a thousand men. This is a curious moment, for surely Brunhild—still possessed of her fabulous strength, backed "by over seven hundred bold fighting-men that were seen there under arms,"[3] as well as by the kinsmen and vassals who had been arriving "day by day, morning and evening . . . by companies"[4] before Hagen commented on the possibility of danger—had power enough to overwhelm the three Burgundians and Siegfried. One may suspect Hagen of voicing a pretended fear (Brunhild never, in fact, threatens violence after the contest), knowing that Siegfried in his headstrong way will rush off to distant lands for help. Brunhild being won, perhaps Hagen is trying to get rid of a man whom the Burgundians no longer need.

Whatever Hagen's motive, Siegfried does rush off. Arriving in Nibelungenland, he does not go about raising forces in a direct and efficient manner, as the alleged urgency of his mission would demand, but makes a game of it instead. Disguising his voice and keeping his identity secret, he picks a fight with his own gatekeeper and then with his vassal Alberich. Both fights are so violent that Siegfried fears for his life. Here, as in his appearance before the Burgundians, Siegfried seems to be an enormously vital but immature young man, unable to restrain his craving for physical adventures, insensitive to the psychologies and interests of persons around him. It is as though the poet were studying naive and robust masculine character through the person of his hero.

The three episodes leading immediately to Siegfried's death—the pretended second Saxon war, the hunt, and the footrace to the spring—demonstrate again the manipulative control of Hagen over Siegfried and the enthusiasm with which Siegfried enters into any kind of physical contest. His behavior in the hunt lacks all temperance and moderation (cardinal virtues in chivalric society), and by accepting the handicap of a single dog rather than a pack, he seems to flaunt his prowess. Although Siegfried dominates the story here with his raw strength and vitality, the audience never forgets that the whole episode is part of Hagen's plot to kill him. Accepting Hagen's challenge to a footrace, Siegfried insists on the handicap of lying in the grass at the start and of carrying all his gear and weapons as he runs. Thus he literally carries the instrument of his murder to the place where he may be safely killed. He acts like an exhibitionist of strength, and his strength is harnessed for his own destruction. Hagen, who has harnessed it, strikes the final blow.

It seems possible that the story of Siegfried sketched out in the episodes considered above was intended by the author and viewed by his audience as a representation of a human type and a testing of that type under political circumstances around the year 1200. Siegfried's behavior is heroism in the sense defined earlier. His life exemplifies a particular aspect of human nature, a particular kind of masculine character; Siegfried is a standard of this potentiality in human life. His career is glorious and unsuccessful. This does not mean that the poet viewed him with distaste or meant him to seem stupid or fatuous; it means that the poet and his audience recognized the limits of exuberant masculine character in the real world, where the forces of pride, ambition, jealousy, greed, and political expedience manipulate and even destroy such personalities.

If portions of the feudal epic permit the audience to regard Siegfried as heroic, what of his killer? Hagen has already been referred to as a great villain, and in the sense that this term is generally applied to a doer of evil deeds, it is justified. But if a moral posture is discarded, Hagen becomes the great example of a blood-and-iron chancellor, a Bismarck to his king, whose behavior is governed by the political interests of the house of Burgundy as he understands them.

One can trace in the *Nibelungenlied* the ominously powerful and assertive figure of Siegfried as it impinges upon Burgundy, and thus upon Hagen, from the early days when "Fired by his courage, he tried the mettle of many kingdoms and rode through many lands to put his strength to the test,"[5] through his assault on Gunther (barely averted by statesmanship) and the remarks of Kriemhild to Brunhild, which no doubt reached Hagen's ears and seemed to show a threatening ambition in the Netherlandic king ("I have a husband of such merit that he might rule over all the kingdoms of this region. . . . He ranks above my noble brother Gunther . . .").[6] Finally, Hagen urges that Gunther extend his power by elimination of his rival ("Hagen kept putting it to Gunther that if Siegfried were no more, Gunther would be lord of many kingdoms . . .").[7] Hagen's reaction to Siegfried seems always to favor putting him in responsible—and dangerous—situations. That he should finally propose and contrive his murder is merely the last expression of the interests and attitudes that motivate Hagen throughout the epic. Conduct such as Hagen's, governed by the single-minded pursuit of power, is a familiar theme in literature, as in life; yet even as the murderer of Siegfried, Hagen lives in a pattern of heroism. He exemplifies with grandeur a fundamental part of human nature. For the feudal author and audience, Hagen was proof of the proposition made many years later in the *Leviathan* by the political philosopher Thomas Hobbes: "So that in the first place, I put for a general inclination of all mankind, a perpetual and restless desire of power after power, that ceaseth only in death."[8]

The scholar Johann Jacob Bodmer, who in 1757 first published part of the *Nibelungenlied,* gave it the title "Kriemhild's Revenge." He saw clearly that the figure of Kriemhild dominates the latter part of the poem through her ineluctable drive for vengeance, and one may say that the two main parts of the poem, the story of Siegfried and the story of the Burgundians' visit to Etzel, are united by Kriemhild. She motivates every critical event of the Siegfried story, and her power of will drives the poem on after Siegfried's death. But were her deeds heroic in the vision of the courtly audience of the year 1200? A version of the poem that considerably softens the portrait of Kriemhild (version C) and seems to have been made shortly after the version on which Hatto's translation is based (version B) suggests that the maniacal and bloody Kriemhild was too strong a concept for the general taste. It surely is no kin to the lovely and gentle conventional heroine of chivalric narrative, whom Kriemhild is made to resemble in the period of her courtship with Siegfried.

Yet the audiences of 1200 recognized in Kriemhild, no less than in Hagen, the heroic trait of will, that utter tenacity of purpose which will not be deflected from its object. Such power of will, which need not be exerted for a good cause, is the essence of heroic literature. Germanic poetry is concerned more with the deed than with the immediate cause, more with the character than with the deed; we need not admire the ends to which their wills are bent in order to stand in awe of Kriemhild and Hagen, who are locked in a struggle which death must resolve. One of the most exalted moments in the poem is Hagen's remark when he sees the head of Gunther carried in by the hair, just before he defies Kriemhild for the last time: "You have made an end as you desire, and things have run their course as I imagined."[9] One laconic phrase ("as you desire") summarizes the terrible power of will possessed by this woman who has brought thousands of knights and her three brothers to their deaths. Another phrase ("as I imagined") epitomizes the marvelous strength of will possessed by the man who has hastened events toward his own foreseen destruction. Such will is a quality of human character which European civilization has always held to be heroic.

The final aspect of heroism in the feudal epic is of quite a different stamp; it is found in the story of Rüdiger. Introduced at the beginning of the second part of the epic, Rüdiger, who is entrusted by Etzel with a most responsible and sensitive mission, is distinguished from the other warriors around Etzel by his gentility and grace. He shows a keen sense of the debt he owes Etzel, his liege lord, when he refuses to travel to Burgundy except at his own cost. Received in friendship by the Burgundians, he persuades Kriemhild to marry Etzel merely by taking oaths to act as her advocate and champion should her honor be threatened in the future. Thus, Rüdiger is bound to his king and queen by the sacred ties that bound vassal to lord in feudal society, as well as by the personal vows exacted by Kriemhild.

The ties which soon bind him to the Burgundians are no less earnest. He offers them hospitality while they are on their way to Etzel, thus incurring the traditional obligation of a host to his guests; his daughter is betrothed to Giselher, and as part of her dowry, Rüdiger makes his pledge to Giselher and his brothers: "I shall be your sincere and devoted friend always."[10] He and his wife bestow gifts upon their guests, an act which binds the givers no less than the recipients. In addition, Rüdiger personally escorts the Burgundians to Etzel, thus tacitly vouching for the safety of their journey.

Readers have long appreciated the artistry with which the poet achieves such a division of loyalties in Rüdiger. When called upon by Etzel and Kriemhild to enter battle against the Burgundians, Rüdiger tries to escape from the agonizing dilemma—"Whichever course I leave in order to follow the other, I shall have acted basely and infamously."[11] Ultimately, he cannot deny the justice of the claims pressed upon him by the King and Queen. It is the institutional obligations that Rüdiger respects when forced to make a choice, not those arising from customs or human feeling. Although the decision brings him to despair, he honors the claims of liege upon vassal, which he holds superior to those of friend upon friend. As Volker puts it when he sees Rüdiger advancing toward them, "Rüdiger means to earn his lands and castles from us."[12] This is a positive standard of behavior in feudal society, for Rüdiger represents the sacrifice of personal inclination for the sake of social laws, the subordination of individual feeling to the order of the whole. To the audience of A.D. 1200, this was exemplary.

But the story of Rüdiger has a further aspect in Hagen's request that Rüdiger surrender his shield to him. In this incident, the values of friendship and social role are juxtaposed once again, for Hagen gives Rüdiger the opportunity to affirm his love for the Burgundians at the very moment when his actions might seem to deny it. Hagen's request allows Rüdiger to make a gesture of affection, and to the medieval audience for whom gestures and symbolic actions spoke far more eloquently than words, Hagen's act bespeaks a deep humanity. Of course, Rüdiger is admired for agreeing to the gift, thus affirming the friendship and concern he expressed when first giving gifts to the Burgundians (and specifically a shield to Hagen), but many will find Hagen's request more remarkable. All will agree that Hagen's behavior after the gift is exceptional: the first vassal of the Burgundians steps aside from the assault of Rüdiger and says he will not fight him, even if he should kill the kings. Here we seem to have a preference for affection rather than institutional obligation, just the opposite of the situation in which Rüdiger acknowledged Etzel's claims. For the poet of the *Nibelungenlied*, fidelity seems to have been a virtue above all. The story of Rüdiger may be read as a study of fidelity, in which one man exemplifies loyalty to the high laws of society, and another man exemplifies loyalty to the heart's ties. As a whole, the story does not seem to be directed toward a judgment on the primacy of one kind of fidelity over the other on occasions when they conflict, though Rüdiger's decision conforms to the general values of the day.

Lay of Atli

We will now turn to the stories that comprise the *Nibelungenlied* as they were known during the Germanic Heroic Age. This is in large part a speculative enterprise, for the textual evidence of such stories is slender. The Old Norse "Lay of Atli," which is preserved in the *Edda* and may date from the ninth century, is the earliest literature on the story of the Burgundians, but the historical connections of the legends suggest that some form of heroic song preserved them during the Heroic Age. It will be useful at this point to review the historic content of the epic, for, like *Beowulf,* it reflects historical figures and events.

We know that the Burgundians, a Germanic tribe, crossed to the left bank of the Rhine and established themselves there in the first years of the fifth century. Around A.D. 435 they attempted to move further west, which led to fighting with troops under the command of the Roman soldier Aetius. Then in A.D. 437, the Burgundians suffered an annihilating defeat at the hands of "Huns," probably Hun troops under Roman leadership. In this battle, King Gundaharius was killed "along with his people and family." Clearly the name Gundaharius is the name we know as Gunther, and other members of the family mentioned by the sixth-century "Burgundian Law" (in Latin)—Gislaharius, Gundomaris, and Gibica—evidently correspond to the characters Giselher, Guthorm (in Old Norse sources), and Gibech. (In the main manuscript tradition of the *Nibelungenlied,* Gibech is reduced to a minor character, but in one fifteenth-century manuscript, "Gibich" is the name of the father of Gunther and his siblings.) Thus the second part of the *Nibelungenlied* deals with historic personalities, the Burgundian kings, and may reflect the decisive defeat inflicted upon them by Hun armies. These, however, were not commanded by Attila.

Of course, the character Etzel corresponds in some respects to the Attila of history. Phonetic differences between the names are easily explained by laws in the evolution of the Germanic languages. Both Etzel's geographic seat of power and the vast array of peoples and princes under his sway agree with history, and it is possible that his actual marriage in A.D. 453 to a Germanic princess whom the chronicles name "Ildico" is mirrored by his fictional marriage to Kriemhild, the element *-ild* or *-hild* being common to the names. The Gothic historian Jordanes tells us that Attila died during his wedding night with Ildico, apparently from a severe hemorrhage. By the early sixth century there were two versions of Attila's death current in Europe, as recorded by the chronicler Marcellinus Comes: "Attila was slain at night by a knife and the hand of a woman. Some maintain that he was killed by a hemorrhage."[13] The more sensational version is reflected in the work of the ninth-century Poeta Saxo, who declares that Attila was killed by his queen and goes on to supply a motive—revenge, specifically revenge for her father. (We are not told what happened to her father.) Thus the historic and quasi-historic accounts center on two events: the destruction of the Burgundians and the death of Attila. Of these events, the former is the base for the second part of the *Nibelungenlied,* but the latter plays no role in the epic. Some believe that Kriemhild's revenge on Hagen and the others is derived from the early accounts of the queen's revenge on her husband, and some early Old Norse poems, such as the "Lay of Atli," show Atli (= Attila) killed by Gudrun (= Kriemhild) in revenge for his destruction of her brothers. But the fact remains that continental European tradition as documented in the *Nibelungenlied* tells of the fall of the Burgundians, but not of the death of Attila.

A good way to appreciate the heroic content of the fall of the Burgundians in the Heroic Age is to analyze the "Lay of Atli" and note the correspondences between this early poem and the *Nibelungenlied*. The poem begins with the arrival of a messenger from Atli at the court of Gunnar (= Gunther). The invitation to visit Atli which he delivers is received with mistrust and foreboding. Gunnar says that none of the material inducements promised by Atli are of any interest to him. Hogni (= Hagen) speaks of the warning sent by their sister, Atli's wife. The people are silent; no one advises Gunnar to go. And then, in a passage difficult to understand in detail but eloquent in spirit, Gunnar accepts the fatal challenge and announces that he will travel to Atli. Here heroic character is in evidence: men embrace danger gladly because they can not seek to avoid it. Gunnar and Hogni, despite virtual foreknowledge of death, accept Atli's invitation because no brave man would do otherwise. For the cultures of the Heroic Age, discretion and prudence were not heroic qualities; the leader who weighed every hazard in a delicate balance did not enjoy the respect of his followers. This moment in the "Lay of Atli" is comparable to Hagen's role in the second part of the epic, for Hagen understands the sinister implications of the invitation, and once the decision to accept is made, he embraces his fate with a reckless courage like that of Hogni and Gunnar.

The fighting in the "Lay of Atli" is compressed into a few lines. With Gunnar and Hogni captive, Atli demands the treasure. Gunnar demands that the heart of Hogni be cut out and brought to him, but he does not say why. They first cut out the heart of a cowardly thrall, which Gunnar recognizes and scorns because of its unmanly quivering; only then do they kill Hogni and bring his heart. "Hogni laughed when they cut out his heart"—and in this instance one finds a heroic apotheosis. The man who walks bravely toward death is the man who laughs as they take his life, laughs because he is fearless and because the pain is nothing, laughs because the only defeat to be dreaded is the defeat of spirit and the spirit that exults in the final instant is unbroken. Perhaps Hogni understands the device Gunnar has invented to make sure Atli never obtains the treasure. Seeing Hogni's heart, Gunnar pays tribute to him and then defies Atli: now that only Gunnar knows of the treasure, it will be forever hidden. He meets his horrible death with high dignity, playing the harp as the vipers slither around him in the snake pit. Here again is the exemplary indifference that seems to have been dearly valued in Germanic culture of the Heroic Age, an age of turmoil and relentless warfare in which the warrior who could laugh at death must have been a model to his society. Readers of the *Nibelungenlied* will see how well the epic follows the "Lay of Atli" in the spirit of these final events, although the details of the action are rather different and the roles have been changed.

It will be interesting to digress briefly and to consider the correspondences in tone and attitude between the Germanic heroism of the "Lay of Atli" and the Germanic mythology of the life and death of the gods. Heroism is grace in death, for the certainty of death is always present, and in the last analysis the hero is the man who meets the inevitable with style. The Germanic universe presented by the poems in the *Edda* and by Snorri Sturluson in his *Prose Edda* is a precarious equilibrium of opposed forces, with the sense of imminent destruction hanging over the whole. The rule of Thor, Odin, and other gods known collectively as the Aesir is achieved by constraining great monsters: the wolf Fenrir, bound but certain to slip his bonds in the future; the hound Garm, tethered but sure to break the tether; the enormous World Serpent, thrown into the seas by Thor but alive and ominous; the diabolical giant Loki, bound and tormented by dripping poison but certain to get free. The entire universe tends toward the last days, the cosmic confrontation of powers of life and order with powers of death and chaos: Ragnarök. All the slain heroes in Valhalla train daily for it; their life after death is a continuing preparation for the final battle. In that battle the gods will be destroyed as they destroy the monsters; cosmic fire will envelop the world, and the waters will rise; the universe will revert to its primal elements; and then life will begin again, a new generation of gods will take power. In this cyclical conception of the universe we see the inevitability of death, the tendency of all things and all orders to move toward dissolution. The heroism of the gods—and this term is used advisedly, referring to the exemplary behavior which all gods exhibit to their believers—consists in their struggle against chaos despite the knowledge that chaos will prevail. Their victories are all the more poignant because they are doomed. No wonder the Heroic Age valued the man who acted with courage, gladly accepting the battles that would lead eventually to his death. It makes no difference whether the ethos exists prior to the cosmology or the cosmology is a pattern influential on the ethos; the simple agreement between them is eloquent.

The "Lay of Atli" concludes with the murder of Atli by Gudrun, a story which, as noted earlier, does not appear in the *Nibelungenlied*. This tale of a woman's revenge well illustrates the importance of blood feud in Germanic tradition and also the prominent role which the Heroic Age gave to women. It is comparable to a well-known story told by the eighth-century historian Paul the Deacon in his *History of the Langobards*. Rosemund was carried off by Alboin after a battle in which he killed her father. He married her and had the skull of her father made into a wine goblet. At a banquet, having had too much to drink, Alboin passed the goblet made of her father's skull to Rosemund "and . . . invited her to drink merrily with her father." Rosemund was deeply aggrieved, "and straightway she burned to revenge the death of her father by the murder of her husband." She did so very efficiently. Women of heroic will and uncompromising devotion to a principle of honor are frequent figures in Germanic literature. In the *Nibelungenlied,* this theme underlies both the story of Kriemhild and that of Brunhild.

Brunhild has hardly any active role in the epic once she has married Gunther. Although it is her complaint to Gunther that leads directly to the murder of Siegfried, the instigator of the murder remains Hagen. (The poet's remark, "the hero was to lose his life at the instigation of Brunhild . . .," is hard to reconcile with the story he tells.[14]) However, if the poems which survive in the *Edda* offer any evidence, Brunhild's role was far more important in the Heroic Age. A fragmentary poem about the death of Sigurd (= Siegfried) is a good source for studying the role of Brunhild, and the *Thidreks saga,* a thirteenth-century Norwegian prose saga based on continental traditions, is another. These and many other poems of varying age indicate that for the Heroic Age the betrayal of Brunhild by Siegfried, which always involves his refusal to take her as his wife, created an instance of a woman who has been dishonored and burns for vengeance. The "Fragment of a Sigurd Lay" in the *Edda* tells that Brunhild instigates the murder of Sigurd, greeting the news of his death with an awful laugh, then revealing that the accusations she made in order to have him killed were false. She is a character of the Rosemund and Kriemhild pattern: the strong, tormented, vengeful woman who drives events forward to the bloody righting of wrong. By comparisons with other tales that more directly express the ethos of the time, the *Nibelungenlied* can also be understood as illustrative of the Heroic Age and its ethos of conflict and violence. We recognize heroism, i.e., exemplary behavior of prominent persons, in the uncompromising correction of injury to family or person (Kriemhild and Brunhild) and in the splendid fatalism with which fighting men go to their death (Hagen). During the Heroic Age, stories were told about historic personalities, though the lack of agreement on historic backgrounds for Siegfried and Brunhild suggests that heroic poetry was not limited to inspiration from history, and the episodes of the *Nibelungenlied* apparently were autonomous tales which were linked together on some occasions.

The Enigma of the Nibelungenlied

The discussion of the epic thus far represents ideas familiar to most students of the poem and espoused by many. When the question of archaic patterns of story underlying the poem arises, the sense of movement in an accepted frame of reference is lost. Indeed, the very existence of such patterns is a matter of debate. It is one aspect of the important problem of history and myth as foundations of heroic epic.

For the better part of a century, this problem was argued by scholars of the *Nibelungenlied.* One group held that the stories of Siegfried were nature myths of the kind found among all primitive peoples. Another group believed that it was possible to identify the hero and his adventures with particular gods and divine acts of Germanic religion: Odin, Baldr, and Freyr were advanced as the model of the hero; Siegfried's death by a woman's betrayal was likened to Baldr's, and his fight with a dragon recalled the battle of Thor and the World Serpent. On the other side of the issue were those who saw not only the evident connections to history—the empire of the Huns, the destruction of the Burgundian dynasty—but also a host of other connections. Siegfried and Brunhild were derived from actors in Merovingian politics, Rüdiger was thought to represent a twelfth-century Spanish hero, the entire *Nibelungenlied* was taken as a satire on figures and events of the reign of the German emperor Henry V. The excesses of both points of view are obvious today, and they were a matter of concern long ago. In 1909 the German scholar Andreas Heusler, whose famous book on Nibelung saga and the *Nibelungenlied* was to appear twelve years later, reminded scholars that the historical and mythological approaches to heroic story stood like Scylla and Charybdis, wrecking many efforts to reach the truth.[15]

Heusler acknowledged four sources drawn upon by the *Heldendichter* responsible for heroic poetry: history, private life, personal invention, and narrative matter at hand (in which he included myth and folktale).[16] Of these sources he regarded personal invention as by far the most important, stressing that heroic poetry was *poetry* and that history and myth, whatever contribution they might make to the tale, were fundamentally changed by the process of artistic creation. Thus Heusler saw no need to search for archaic foundations of the Nibelungen story: elements and details might be archaic, but the foundations were the work of Frankish poets of the fifth and sixth centuries. In his classical analysis, he passed over in silence the question of historic or mythic bases for the tales of Siegfried and Brunhild, presenting instead the content of the first poems.[17] When discussing the earliest version of the fall of the Burgundians he acknowledged the role of historical event—"the subject matter may be understood as freely formed history"—but the trend of his discussion was to show that art, not history, accounted for the character of the tales:

> One sees that this saga is something quite different than distorted history garbled by the mouth of the people. What is bruited from house to house may finally have precious little resemblance to the real event, but all this does not produce a work which one must only cast in verse in order to have a Lay of the Burgundians. This Lay is, in structure and thought, a child of art, the creation of an anonymous poet.[18]

The position of the Chadwicks with regard to Germanic heroic poetry is comparable to, though not identical with, that of Heusler. In their monumental study of early literatures they represent the view that heroic poetry is inspired by real persons and events, although it admits a good deal of "fiction"—that kind of imaginative story attributed by Heusler to "personal invention"—and also draws frequently on the superhuman or supernatural. Rejecting the theory that Siegfried and Brunhild have their origins in mythic conceptions, the Chadwicks also regard as unlikely the view that they spring from the personal invention of a poet. The Chadwicks' knowledge of heroic literature suggests an origin in history: "Our belief is that primary heroic stories are contemporary, i.e., that the first stories which celebrate a hero's exploits are composed within living memory of the events.... We do not know any examples of heroic poetry or saga relating to recent events, in which the leading characters are fictitious.''[19] The supernatural elements so abundant in the Siegfried stories are to be explained as ''poetic conventions, which are themselves based upon real beliefs of the time or of former times . . . . The superhuman prowess attributed to heroes is another convention, but due to other causes—hero-worship, in the modern sense, and the tendency to exaggeration stimulated thereby.''[20]

Both Heusler and the Chadwicks would deny that there are underlying, archaic patterns of story which are vital to the understanding of the tales in the *Nibelungenlied* as they were known in Germanic culture. Following their approach to heroic poems, we would seek to go back no further in time than the fifth century, when the first poems were composed. There would be no justification in considering mythical models for the two main stories in the epic: the life and death of Siegfried and the fall of the Burgundians. But if it is true that Heusler and the Chadwicks speak for a majority of recent scholars on this problem, important objections to their views have been made. These concern the first part of the *Nibelungenlied,* the story of Siegfried and Brunhild.

Early in this century, Friedrich Panzer brought to light surprisingly close agreements between this story and several folktales. Of particular importance was his juxtaposition of the wooing of Brunhild with a Russian folktale of bridal quest, which led him to the conclusion that the heroic tale was derived from the folktale.[21] Although many criticisms of his theory have been made, and the folktale in question has been shown to be international rather than strictly Russian, Panzer's thesis that this tale underlies the wooing of Brunhild by Siegfried has by no means been disproved, and the relation of epic to broadly distributed popular stories remains puzzling. In recent years the idea that Siegfried is derived from a mythical archetype has been advocated by Franz Rolf Schröder and Otto Höfler, though with differing emphases.[22] Schröder connects Siegfried to the mythological pattern of the conquest of chaos by divine sons who themselves die, but are resurrected. Höfler breaks new ground by proposing that historical events were understood in Germanic culture as re-enactments of myth, and that the figure of Siegfried derives from the historical Arminius, leader of Germanic warriors in a successful battle against Roman troops in the first century. Arminius' exploit was then understood as the re-enactment of a cosmic victory, expressed in the story of Siegfried by his slaying of a dragon. Höfler's reasoning is bold and rests on a number of hypotheses; it remains to be seen whether his thesis will be accepted.

Thus it is clear that no unanimity exists regarding the origins of the tales told in the first part of the *Nibelungenlied.* The influence of history and myth is esteemed differently in different quarters, and the prudent scholar will probably admit a complex pluralism of sources and many unanswered questions.[23] It is also clear that the second part of the *Nibelungenlied* is thought to be based on history. Even Schröder, an advocate of mythic patterns behind heroic saga, holds the fall of the Burgundians to be completely non-mythical.[24] As our own contribution to the problem of myth and history in the *Nibelungenlied,* we would like to challenge this received opinion. A few preliminary remarks are necessary.

Mythologization of History

One must assume that the Germanic peoples had traditional stories long before any record of these stories was made, and that the foundation of their traditional lore was mythic in nature, serving to explain the universe and human existence. One assumes that this tradition did not come to an abrupt end with the Period of Migrations, nor did it end abruptly with the nominal Christianization of Germanic tribes, but continued to exist at least until the thirteenth century, when mythological poems were recorded in the *Edda* with the "Lay of Atli" and the "Fragment of a Sigurd Lay." No doubt there was a gradual attenuation of the religious content of the traditional stories, so that the tales of Thor which seem ludicrous to us may have seemed ludicrous to the educated Icelanders who caused them to be preserved in writing, although the narrative patterns of the stories, the sequence of incidents and clusters of motifs, remained visible if not fully intact.

Making these assumptions, one still requires a theory of the relationship of traditional narrative, mythic in origin, to the unique facts of history. Only such a theory can be a guide in an analysis of the fall of the Burgundians, a tale long in tradition but with historic detail so near the surface. This guiding theory is essentially that of Otto Höfler, who speaks of "the mythological transposition of historical events."[25] These are the formulations of the eminent scholar of comparative religion, Mircea Eliade:

> ... the historical character of the persons celebrated in epic poetry is not in question. But their historicity does not long resist the corrosive action of mythicization. The historical event in itself, however important, does not remain in the popular memory, nor does its recollection kindle the poetic imagination save insofar as the particular historic event closely approaches a mythical model.[26]

> ... the recollection of a historical event or a real personage survives in popular memory for two or three centuries at the utmost. This is because popular memory finds difficulty in retaining individual events and real figures. The structures by means of which it functions are different: categories instead of events, archetypes instead of historical personages. The historical personage is assimilated to his mythical model (hero, etc.), while the event is identified with the category of mythical actions (fight with a monster, enemy brothers, etc.).[27]

The task at hand, then, is to examine the account of the Burgundians' fall in the *Nibelungenlied* for evidence of the assimilation of history to mythical models.

Let us begin by noting the major differences between the account in the

Nibelungenlied and what we understand to be historic fact. Attila had nothing to do with the destruction of Gundaharius and his people, but Etzel presides over the death of Gunther and the others. The destruction of Gundaharius took place in west-central Europe, on the left bank of the Rhine, as the Burgundians tried to move further westward, but in all sources the Germanic heroes must undertake a long journey to their enemy's kingdom to the east, where they meet battle and death. In the poetic accounts, a legendary treasure plays a vital role: Attila craves it and the Germanic heroes take the secret of its whereabouts to their death. They die, and the treasure is lost. Historic records give no indication that the Burgundians had a vast treasure, much less that it had anything to do with the destruction of the tribe. These discrepancies are at least as striking and important as the agreements between poetry and history. They easily permit the theory that history provides no more than coloration and incidental detail to a traditional pattern of story.

The thesis is this: in the fall of the Burgundians we are dealing with the Journey to the Other World. Attila has been assimilated to the giant, ogre, or fiend who rules that world; the Burgundians have been assimilated to the god who makes the journey.

Many Germanic myths exist in which a god travels to a world of chaos or death, usually on the quest for some precious object necessary for the maintenance of order and continuation of life. The god Freyr sends his servant (or, perhaps, his alter-ego) to the frost ogres to woo for him a woman without whom he languishes miserably. Thor travels to the realm of the giant Hymir to obtain a huge cauldron in which ale for the banquet of the gods may be brewed. Odin travels to the old giant Vafthrudnir, ostensibly for a riddling contest, but in effect to destroy a rival for his position as master of arcane lore; Thor travels to the land of the giants to regain his hammer, the weapon on which the security of the Aesir rests, from the giant-king Thrym. All these journeys result in conflict, and most end with the god's destruction of his enemy: Thor smashes Hymir and Thrym with his hammer and kills them, Odin's triumph costs the life of Vafthrudnir, and Skirner, armed with Freyr's magic sword, compels the giantess to meet the god. One might also mention the journey of Thor and three others to Utgard, where his divine power seems ineffective until the deceptions involved are understood.

These myths, preserved in the *Edda* or in Snorri's *Prose Edda* in late and adulterated forms, tell of gods who travel to a hostile Other World where they triumph in replicated conflict with monsters, obtaining something precious—a bride, a cauldron (symbolizing the plenty of life), a divine weapon, unrivaled mastery of wisdom—something that could be considered great treasure. The contours of similarity with the story in the *Nibelungenlied* are clear, and if space permitted, it would be worthwhile to discuss similarities of detail such as the extraordinary journey which signals the transition from this world to the other, represented in myths by the passing of mountains and a ring of fire (the story of Skirnir) or by a river, a bridge, and a sentinel (Hermod's journey to

Hel), or other devices, and continued in the poems about the Burgundians with a crossing of the fabulous forest Myrkwood ("Lay of Atli") or the Danube crossing in the *Nibelungenlied*. The Danube crossing is rich in motifs suggesting a transit to the Other World: the river is raging and nearly impassable, mermaids with knowledge of the future are present, a single ferryman guards the crossing and must be slain by Hagen. The Danube functions here like the River of Death's Domain in Finnish tradition, the river bordering the kingdom of Gorre in Celtic tradition (see Chrétien's *Lancelot*), and the river Styx in Greco-Roman myth. Hatto's sarcastic comparison of the Danube and the Styx[28] holds more truth than he realizes.

But if the contours are clear, there are still some big differences. The fate of the heroes is not that of the gods, and the role of the treasure seems exactly the reverse—it is sought by the power of death, and lost.

In his influential book *The Singer of Tales,* Albert Lord suggests that patterns of story told about gods are eventually told about demigods and then about mortals. His point is very nearly that of Eliade's. However, he states the important point that patterns with heroes assimilated to gods must make adjustment for the mortality of men: "When gods became demigods, the possibility of a dying god who is not resurrected came into being . . . when a mortal took over the story of the dying god, it was inevitable that eventually in tradition his death without resurrection would have to be recorded."[29] With respect to this problem, though gods might travel to the kingdom of death and return from it victorious with a boon symbolizing life, human heroes traveling to that kingdom must succumb, for it is not given to men to carry away the victory from death. Thus the victory of the enemy in that distant kingdom to the east was an inevitable part of the pattern of story once this pattern accepted men in the archetypal role of the gods. The fall of the Burgundians has a meaning far older and far deeper than the destruction of a Germanic tribe in A.D. 437. It means no less than that all men must die.

Let us turn to the motif of the great treasure. The gods of Germanic myth characteristically possess treasures coveted by the powers of death. These treasures are often the goddesses themselves, especially Freyja, who we know was linked to love and fertility, but also the enigmatic goddess Idun, who guarded the apples of youth. Idun was once abducted by a giant, and the Aesir aged rapidly. The attempts of giants and dwarves to gain control of goddesses are symbols of the continuing threat to life itself. In two stories told of Freyja, the gods are placed in the impossible position of having to buy their own security by surrendering her to the giants: Thrym will return Thor's hammer only if given Freyja in exchange, and a clever giant bargains to build a fine defensive wall around Asgard provided that he be given Freyja, the sun, and the moon if he completes his work in one season. The gods face a choice in these situations, but no alternative. The loss of Freyja means the loss of fertility, or the triumph of death, a meaning made more clear by the associated loss of the sun and moon in the second story. But the gods, being gods, can solve these dilemmas, and in each case the divine power of Thor brings the final solution by destroying the enemy.

By the craft and power of death, the Burgundians are placed in the same predicament as the Aesir—they must surrender their treasure to save their lives. Understanding the symbolism of the treasure in Germanic tradition, we see that this is no choice at all, for the symbol of life cannot be abandoned and life itself retained. While gods might solve the dilemma with their own craft and power, men cannot. Men must die and their treasure must be lost. If one were to question the events of the Nibelung legend rationally, one might ask why the Germanic heroes always refuse to buy their lives at the cost of their gold. In fact, ransoms for political leaders were a common phenomenon. To explain their decision as heroic defiance is certainly true to one level of the story, but at a deeper level, that of the archaic pattern, there is simply no possibility of ransom. At the time when the old pattern was told of men, the treasure could not be retained by the heroes, as it had been obtained and retained by the gods.

It is interesting to consider the mythic history of the Nibelung treasure in this connection. It originated as the ransom paid by a group of gods for their very lives. Odin and two other gods travel to a weird place—possibly the Other World—where they kill an otter, which turns out to be the son of a powerful dwarf. That night the dwarf seizes the gods "and set(s) this as their ransom: they must fill the otterskin, and cover it outside too, with gold." One god obtains this gold from another dwarf who, in the shape of a fish, lives in a pool of water; with it he purchases the gods' freedom. Thus in the story of the treasure's origin we see just the situation in the story of the treasure's end: it must be produced by and surrendered to a malevolent power, or the heroes of the story will die. Because it did not belong to the gods, its loss to the dwarf does not symbolize the gods' death, but from this point on in its history there is an essential connection between its possession or surrender and the life or death of the owner. The dwarf's son, Fafnir, kills him to obtain it, Sigurd kills Fafnir and obtains it, the Burgundians kill Siegfried to obtain it. The treasure thus passes from a purely mythic level of story, through the history of a demigod (Sigurd), to final possession by men. (The alternate account sketched in the *Nibelungenlied,* whereby Siegfried's slaying of the dragon has nothing to do with his obtaining the treasure, runs counter to dominant tradition.) When the men die, the treasure passes into oblivion in the depths of the great river. Brought forth by the gods from obscure, watery-subterranean origins to ransom their lives, it is consigned by men to watery obscurity when demanded as ransom for their lives. The tradition is symmetrical and beautiful, the symbolism consistent.

It may seem that this discussion has wandered rather far from the notion of heroism which was to provide its theme. In fact, it has not. In archaic societies, where historical personages were assimilated to archetypes and historic events to categories, tales told of these persons and events could not but be exemplary because they expressed again the universal examples which myths embody. The archaic patterns of story which underlie the fall of the Burgundians show the exemplary behavior of prominent persons, that is, their heroism.

NOTES

1. The *Nibelungenlied*, trans. A. T. Hatto (Baltimore: Penguin Books, 1965), p. 29.

2. Ibid., p. 34.

3. Ibid., p. 64.

4. Ibid., p. 69.

5. Ibid., p. 20.

6. Ibid., pp. 111-12.

7. Ibid., p. 117.

8. Thomas Hobbes, *Leviathan* (Oxford: Blackwell, 1946), p. 64.

9. The *Nibelungenlied*, p. 290.

10. Ibid., p. 209.

11. Ibid., p. 267.

12. Ibid., p. 269.

13. Marcellinus Comes, "Chronicon," in *Chronica minora saec. IV.V.VI.VII*, ed. Theodor Mommsen, II (Berlin: Weidmann, 1894; reprint Berlin: Weidmann, 1961), p. 86.

14. The *Nibelungenlied*, p. 124.

15. The historical and mythological approaches are conveniently reviewed by Elizabeth Bohning, *The Concept "Saga" in Nibelungen Criticism* (Bethlehem, Pa.: Times Publishing Co., 1944), pp. 87-155, though with bias toward the position taken by Heusler. For his position regarding history and myth in Germanic heroic saga, see Heusler, "Geschichtliches und Mythisches in der germanischen Heldensage," *Sitzungsberichte der Königl. Preussischen Akademie der Wissenschaften* 23 (1909): 920-45.

16. Heusler, p. 943.

17. *Nibelungensage und Nibelungenlied*, 6th ed. (Dortmund: F. W. Ruhfus, 1965), pp. 6-7.

18. Ibid., p. 27.

19. H. Munro Chadwick and N. Kershaw Chadwick, *The Growth of Literature*, 3 vols. (Cambridge: The University Press, 1932-40), I, pp. 235-36.

20. Ibid., p. 215.

21. See the summaries of his early work in Bohning, *The Concept "Saga" in Nibelungen Criticism*, pp. 160-62, and his article "Das russische Brautwerbermärchen im Nibelungenlied," *Beiträge zur Geschichte der deutschen Sprache und Literatur* 72 (1950): 463-98; reprinted in *Zur germanisch-deutschen Heldensage*, ed. Karl Hauck (Bad Homburg vor der Höhe, 1961), pp. 138-69.

22. Franz Schröder, "Mythos und Heldensage," *Germanisch-romanische Monatsschrift* 36 (1955): 1-21.

23. See for example, the review in Bert Nagel, *Das Nibelungenlied: Stoff—Form—Ethos,* 2nd ed. (Frankfurt am Main: Hirschgraben, 1970), pp. 14–52.

24. *Zur germanisch-deutschen Heldensage,* pp. 287, 294.

25. Höfler, p. 9, contents of pp. 19–20.

26. Mircea Eliade, *Cosmos and History: The Myth of the Eternal Return,* trans. Willard R. Trask (New York: Harper, 1954), p. 42.

27. Ibid., p. 43.

28. The *Nibelungenlied,* p. 339, n.

29. Albert B. Lord, *The Singer of Tales* (New York: Atheneum, 1965), p. 201.

BIBLIOGRAPHY

Texts

Bartsch, Karl, and Helmut de Boor, eds. *Das Nibelungenlied.* 13th ed. Wiesbaden: F. A. Brockhaus, 1956. Bartsch's edition first appeared in 1866. It is the basis of de Boor's revised text, reprinted many times since the 13th edition. Introduction, notes, and glossary. The standard Middle High German text, though its authority is not accepted in all quarters.

Hatto, A. T., trans. *The Nibelungenlied.* Baltimore: Penguin Books, 1965. Prose translation with extensive background material and a long essay which is an excellent introduction to interpretative problems. Frequently reprinted.

Ryder, Frank G., trans. *The Song of the Nibelungs.* Detroit: Wayne State University Press, 1962. A verse translation in a form analogous to that of the original. Substantial introductory essay.

Studies

Bekker, Hugo. *The Nibelungenlied: A Literary Analysis.* Toronto: University of Toronto Press, 1971. Close study of the text which avoids psychological character delineation and stresses the role of Brunhild. With English translation of Middle High German quotations, an interpretation for non-specialists as well as scholars.

Hauck, Karl, ed. *Zur germanisch-deutschen Heldensage.* Bad Homburg vor der Höhe: Hermann Gentner Verlag, 1961. Reprint of sixteen important essays on Germanic and German heroic poetry. Of these, six deal extensively with the *Nibelungenlied,* and the poem is a subject of several others. See especially "Das Motiv der Macht bei Siegfrieds Tod" by Siegfried Beyschlag, stressing the theme of *Realpolitik* in the first part of the epic; and "Mythos und Heldensage" by Franz Rolf Schröder, largely a presentation of the "mythic-cultic level" in the story of Siegfried.

Heusler, Andreas. *Nibelungensage und Nibelungenlied: Die Stoffgeschichte des deutschen Heldenepos.* 5th ed. Dortmund: Ruhfus, 1955. First published in 1921, and reprinted regularly, Heusler's monograph remains the basic work on the history of the stories comprising the epic, although all agree that this history is far more complicated than Heusler believed.

Höfler, Otto. *Siegfried, Arminius und die Symbolik. Mit einem historischen Anhang über die Varusschlacht.* Heidelberg: Carl Winter, 1961. Höfler argues that the Siegfried-figure roots in the Germanic hero Arminius, with the dragon-slaying a symbolic account of Arminius' defeat of Roman legions. He believes that there was a Germanic cult-ritual of the killing of Siegfried by Hagen.

Krogmann, Willy, and Ulrich Pretzel. *Bibliographie zum Nibelungenlied und zur Klage.* 4th ed. Berlin: Erich Schmidt Verlag, 1966. Discussion of the manuscripts of the *Nibelungenlied* (and the associated *Klage*), followed by 554 entries under 11 headings. An essential tool for research.

Mowatt, D. G., and Hugh Sacker. *The Nibelungenlied: An Interpretive Commentary.* Toronto: University of Toronto Press, 1967. A commentary on selected points which represents *avant garde* interest in immanent properties of the epic. Provocative and controversial.

Nagel, Bert. *Das Nibelungenlied: Stoff—Form—Ethos.* 2nd ed. Frankfurt am Main: Hirschgraben-Verlag, 1970. A reliable monograph slightly to the left of the main tradition of *Nibelungenlied* scholarship. The contrastive discussion of heathen and Christian ethos is the most problematic of the three sections.

Panzer, Friedrich. *Das Nibelungenlied: Entstehung und Gestalt.* Stuttgart: Kohlhammer, 1955. The first long study to focus on the epic as part of the literary and social culture of Europe about the year 1200. Reveals a high level of sophistication in the poet.

Singer, Carl S. "The Hunting Contest: An Interpretation of the Sixteenth Aventiure in the *Nibelungenlied.*" *Germanic Review* 42 (1967): 163–83. An imaginative essay departing from Gottfried Weber's position (see below). The analysis is very suggestive for an understanding of Siegfried and Hagen.

Thorp, Mary. *The Study of the Nibelungenlied: Being the History of the Study of the Epic and Legend from 1755 to 1937.* Oxford: The Clarendon Press, 1940. An excellent history of scholarship, especially on the manuscript tradition and the evolution of stories comprised by the epic.

Wapnewski, Peter. "Rüdigers Schild. Zur 37. Aventiure des *Nibelungenliedes.*" *Euphorion* 54 (1960): 380–410. Basic study of the Rüdiger story, stressing the pertinence of feudal law and the positive role played by Hagen.

Weber, Gottfried. *Das Nibelungenlied: Problem und Idee.* Stuttgart: Metzler, 1963. An interpretation of the epic, without regard to problems of its origins and evolution, by a prominent scholar. Weber sees the main characters tangled in a web of demonic forces, their fates profoundly tragic.

———, and Werner Hoffmann. *Heldendichtung,* II: *Nibelungenlied.* 3rd ed. Stuttgart: Metzler, 1968. A compact but inclusive introduction to the epic and the status of scholarship. Bibliography. This is the best book to orient the serious student approaching the *Nibelungenlied.*

7 The Icelandic Sagas

Theodore M. Andersson

Saga (connected with *segja*, "to say") is an Icelandic word originally applied to any form of narration or report regardless of length or literary ambition, but in modern usage it has come to mean an extended, novel-like prose narrative dating from the medieval period. The sagas are of various kinds, most readily distinguishable by subject matter, but also to some extent by style and structure. There are lives of Icelandic bishops (*biskúpa sǫgur*), biographies of Norwegian kings (*konunga sǫgur*), stories of early Icelanders (*Íslendinga sǫgur*), stories of legendary heroes (*fornaldarsǫgur*), and a complex of sagas about twelfth- and thirteenth-century events known as *Sturlunga saga* after the leading Icelandic family of the period. In addition, there were translations of Continental and English works which were also styled sagas: *heilagra manna sǫgur* (saints' lives), *riddara sǫgur* (romances and related genres), *Karlamagnús saga* (a redaction of *chanson de geste* material), and *Þiðreks saga* (a compilation of twelfth-century north German heroic material centering upon the legendary figure of Theodoric). Of these various categories, the kings' sagas and family sagas stand out because of their historical orientation and their intrinsic literary merit. The bishops' sagas, legendary sagas, and *Sturlunga saga* are bland by comparison, and the translated sagas, like most translations, fall short of the originals. The following exposition will therefore concentrate on the more rewarding genres in the interest of emphasizing the special achievement of saga-writing.

Kings' Sagas

The oldest group (the kings' sagas) is devoted to the lives of Norwegian monarchs from the period ca. 900–1300, although the chief compilation (*Heimskringla*) reaches back into the quasi-mythical prehistory of the Swedish Yngling and names kings who may have lived as early as the fifth century. The genre is distinctly biographical, accounting for the birth, reign, and death of each king. The first such biographies, presumably in the form of brief notes, were composed in the early twelfth century by the learned Icelanders Sæmundr Sigfússon (ca. 1056–1133) and Ari Þorgilsson (ca. 1068–1148). Their kings' lives are no longer extant, but are referred to a number of times by later writers. The second stage in the writing of kings' sagas is represented by two Latin epitomes, Theodoricus monachus' *Historia de Antiquitate Regum Norvagiensium* and the anonymous *Historia Norwegiae,* and by one vernacular epitome of unknown authorship titled *Ágrip af Nóregs konunga sǫgum,* all written in Norway toward the end of the twelfth century. At about the same time, a group of Icelandic writers began to compose fuller biographies of individual kings, in particular Olaf Tryggvason (995–1000) and Saint Olaf (1015–30). The two Olafs attracted special attention because they were responsible for the final conversion of Norway and Iceland to Christianity. The writing of fuller individual kings' sagas led in turn to the composition of expanded epitomes around 1220 (*Morkinskinna* and *Fagrskinna*) and, around 1230, to the masterpiece of the genre, the compilation by Snorri Sturluson (1178/79–1241) known as *Heimskringla.* Later redactions combined and merged the writings of this earlier period.

The century between Ari Þorgilsson's only extant work, *Íslendingabók* (ca. 1130), and Snorri's *Heimskringla* (ca. 1230) constitutes a remarkable chapter in the growth of vernacular history writing. The most striking feature of the Icelandic historical school is the narrative vigor which it quickly developed. The turning point was around 1200. Early in the twelfth century Sæmundr Sigfússon, and at the end of the century Oddr Snorrason and Gunnlaugr Leifsson, still wrote in Latin. Oddr's *Óláfs saga Tryggvasonar* may serve to illustrate this stage in the development of the king's saga. Though we do not have his original, we are able to judge his tone from the known Icelandic translation (preserved in three differing redactions) and it is clear that he belongs to the European mainstream by virtue of his hagiographic and eulogistic emphases. The birth of his hero is modeled on the birth of Christ. Olaf is born "in a little shed," is "swaddled," and is soon forced into exile by the enmity of Norway's rulers. After wonderful adventures in Estonian thralldom (there is an explicit reference to the selling of Joseph into slavery), an equally wonderful rise to power as the favorite of "King" Vladimir of Russia (972–1014), and further adventures in Wendland, Olaf is instructed in the Christian faith in Greece (the so-called *prima signatio*) and returns to the north to participate in conversion activities in Russia and Denmark. Eventually he is himself officially converted by a clairvoyant hermit on the Scilly Islands (an incident borrowed from the *Life of Saint Benedict*) and embarks on his greatest adventure, the conversion of Norway and the North Atlantic islands, including Iceland. At the height of his success he is beset by a coalition of his enemies in Norway, Sweden, and Denmark and succumbs under mysterious circumstances in a naval battle at Svǫldr (in the Öresund)—mysterious because of persistent rumors that he survived by jumping overboard and swimming to a friendly ship, which carried him to safety. Oddr goes so far as to report the possibility that he ended his days as a monk in Greece or Syria.

When vernacular saga writing reaches its peak, particularly in *Heimskringla,* this devout tone gives way to the unadorned and matter-of-fact prose style which is the most salient feature of the Icelandic saga and which continues to this day to fascinate the modern reader with its single-minded concentration on the story for its own sake. While his contemporaries in Europe wrote with religious and political tendencies clearly exhibited for all to see, Snorri worked behind a mask of impartiality. He does not declare his intentions or directly express his views. Though he changes his sources extensively, he never engages in open discussion or controversy with his predecessors. Whatever we deduce about his methods must be gleaned from internal observations, from what he does, not what he states.

A comparison of Snorri's treatment of Olaf Tryggvason's career with the earlier version by Oddr Snorrason affords a clear idea of his objectivizing tendency. The Scriptural models are covered over: there is no little shed, no swaddling clothes, no reference to selling Joseph into slavery. The more improbable aspects of Olaf's Christianity are dropped: the report of his *prima signatio* in Greece, his participation in the conversion of Russia, and the tale of his *moniage* in Greece or Syria. We are given the impression, not so much that he is a divinely predestined missionary king, as that he was caught up in the advancing tide of Christianity from the south, and that he pursued the conversion of Norway as an extension of the earlier abortive mission undertaken, according to Oddr, by the German emperor Otto, but, according to Snorri's surmise, by the Danish king Harald Bluetooth. The Norwegian mission is therefore seen not altogether as an individual feat, but to some extent as a historical impulse. Accordingly, the bright focus on Olaf's religion is diffused; he is no longer credited with a procession of miracles and visions, and the eulogistic passages are pruned to a more credible compass.

Not only does Snorri consistently avoid miraculous and supernatural material along with occurrences which he judges to be intrinsically improbable, he also controls his prose sources with the use of contemporary skaldic stanzas, the value of which he explains in his "Prologue" to *Heimskringla.* Thus, when Oddr relates that Olaf sailed off to his fatal encounter at Svǫldr with only eleven ships and Snorri has access to a skaldic stanza by Halldórr ókristni specifying that Olaf in fact sailed with seventy-two ships, he chooses the latter authority.

Fundamental to Snorri's presentation is a pervasive sense of orderliness, which is most conspicuous in his treatment of Olaf Tryggvason's mission. Here Oddr provided a confused model, causing Olaf to skip from one part of the country to the next, prosecuting the conversion seemingly at random and with no apparent guiding principle. Snorri intervened in this chaos with a clear plan for the progress of the mission, according to which it began in the south (the province of Vík, where a previous German or Danish mission had already prepared the way) and moved gradually west and north along the coast to the provinces of Þrándheimr and Hálogaland and eventually to the outlying colonies of Iceland and Greenland. At the same time, Snorri consolidated what he found in his sources into logical units: whatever concerns the conversion of a given province is gathered together in one place and not left scattered about as in Oddr's saga.

There is no reason to believe that Snorri had more reliable sources than Oddr and no reason to believe that his account is more accurate or truthful. It is, however, more rational—Snorri has devised a scheme whereby Oddr's clutter makes sense. He has in fact formulated a hypothesis about the conversion of Norway, suggesting how it might reasonably have been expected to take place. The narrative reorganization is tantamount to a historical theory, although it is never enunciated as such.

Somewhat more analysis has been devoted to the stylistic upgrading in *Heimskringla* than to the historical qualities, notably by the Norwegian scholar Hallvard Lie.[1] Lie singled out what he found to be prevailing patterns in Snorri's reworking of his sources. He found that Snorri had an aptitude for scenic presentation in the sense of providing background indications in scenes left unclear and non-specific by his predecessors—indications of time, place, or natural scenery. In other words, Snorri progressed from an epic to a scenic presentation. There is at the same time an effort to relate scenes more explicitly to what has gone before, to see later experience on the basis of earlier experience and therefore to provide a sense of psychological continuity, what Lie calls "retrospection."

Finally, Snorri undertook revisions in the area of dialogue, simplifying and dramatizing what he found in his models. The changes are guided by an overriding sense of economy. There is no dwelling on the obvious and no rambling. The account of Olaf Tryggvason's reign is substantially briefer than Oddr Snorrason's version and correspondingly less tedious. Oddr requires patience, as do the later and longer kings' sagas, for example the biography of Hákon Hákonarson (1217–63) by Snorri's nephew Sturla Þórðarson, but it is no task to return to *Heimskringla,* which remains to this day an accessible book and a popular classic for Scandinavian readers.

The overall development of the kings' sagas reveals itself to the literary historian in a remarkably clear way when one considers the vicissitudes of incomplete information and partial transmission which beset most branches of medieval study. The genre originates in the form of brief lives in the early twelfth century, develops into full biographies in Iceland and historical synopses in Norway at the end of the twelfth century, experiences a merging of the biographical and synoptic trends in *Morkinskinna* and *Fagrskinna* at the beginning of the thirteenth century, culminates in *Heimskringla,* and declines in the form of interlarded compilations through the remaining thirteenth century. Snorri's accomplishment is the centerpiece and, aside from the mysteries which always attend literary masterpieces, it is historically comprehensible in terms of what preceded it. We know roughly what Snorri's sources were, are able to study his use of them and to analyze the techniques which constitute his distinction.

Family Sagas

Such a well-defined development is not what we find in the second great saga genre, the *Íslendinga sǫgur* (family sagas).[2] Despite three centuries of awareness and more than a century of intensive study, many of the fundamental questions remain unanswered. This group of some thirty stories about notable Icelanders during the so-called Saga Age (ca. 930–1050) emerges quite suddenly at the beginning of the thirteenth century and persists through that century only to cease almost as abruptly as it began without leaving any clear legacy. There is no organic growth similar to what we observe in the kings' sagas, no transition from the historical, biographical, panegyric, hagiographic, or romance genres familiar elsewhere in Europe. A somewhat more likely derivation is from the kings' sagas themselves since several of the family sagas considered to be early have affinities to the stories of Norwegian kings. One recent survey identified the earliest group (1200–30) as comprising *Heiðarvíga saga, Fóstbrœðra saga, Kormaks saga, Hallfreðar saga, Bjarnar saga hítdœlakappa,* and *Egils saga Skallagrímssonar.*[3] A glance at the list shows that five out of six are so-called skald sagas, that is, sagas dealing with the lives of prominent Icelandic skalds of the tenth and eleventh centuries either in the service of, or in touch with, a series of Norwegian monarchs. There are close connections between kings' sagas and skald sagas in the manuscript transmission, in the practice of citing skaldic verse, and to some extent in narrative overlap. This situation suggests that an interest in Norwegian kings and the Norwegian court may have provoked an independent interest in the Icelandic sources of information, notably the skalds in whose verse the information was imbedded. The interest in skalds may then have expanded to include early Icelandic affairs generally and thus have given rise to a whole school of *Íslendinga sǫgur*.

Unfortunately, this convenient solution may not be adequate. *Fóstbrœðra saga,* which has often been regarded as the oldest of all the family sagas and which appears to be the closest link to the kings' sagas, has recently been redated to the end of the thirteenth century.[4] At the same time, a saga generally assigned to the middle of the thirteenth century (*Reykdœla saga*) has been reassigned to the years 1207–20 and may turn out to replace *Fóstbrœðra saga* as the oldest known family saga.[5] *Reykdœla saga* has no affinities to the kings' sagas and appears to embody purely Icelandic family traditions handed down without the aid of skaldic verse. If this is the case, we must judge that the family sagas reflect a spontaneous interest in the codification of Icelandic history beginning in the early thirteenth century. Rather than being indebted in the first instance to the kings' sagas, the family sagas may be seen as a logical extension of the interest in family genealogies referred to already at the end of the twelfth century and blossoming in the thirteenth century in various redactions of *Landnámabók* (an account of Iceland's colonization), notably the redaction of Sturla Þórðarson (*Sturlubók*), who arrived at his version by combining genealogical sources with passages from those family sagas which were known to him.[6]

The various adaptations of *Landnámabók* demonstrate a widespread and systematic study of the settlement and early history of Iceland. They suggest that the family sagas were inspired by a similar interest, but a comparison of *Landnámabók* with the family sagas gives rise to a whole new complex of puzzles. It is possible that *Landnámabók* is an abstract of the same oral traditions that are recorded in fuller form in the family sagas, but it is also possible that *Landnámabók* represents a more or less total account of what was known and that the family sagas are inventive elaborations of the meager genealogical notices set down there. This is the point of view argued by a succession of Icelandic scholars in their introductions to the standard edition of the sagas in *Íslenzk fornrit* (1933–). It appears, however, that the discrepancies between *Landnámabók* and the sagas are substantial enough that one cannot simply derive one from the other. It is more likely that both derive from common traditions and that the discrepancies are due to the mutable nature of such traditions, which tend to be recorded at different times in slightly different forms.

The probability is therefore that the sagas do contain traditional material. The likelihood is confirmed by one of the few skaldic poems composed, not in the service of the Norwegian monarchy, but for the purpose of commemorating Icelandic events, Haukr Valdísarson's *Íslendingadrápa*. This poem refers to a number of occurrences narrated at length in the sagas. If it was composed late in the thirteenth century, one might assume that the references are to written Icelandic family sagas familiar to the Icelandic public. But if, as the most recent judgment holds,[7] it was composed around 1200, it must refer to stories which had not yet been set down in writing and which Icelanders could be expected to know in oral form. The written sagas of the thirteenth century should then be considered as the final versions of stories which had circulated orally for some time prior to their recording.

The question of whether there were such older traditions has produced an abundant scholarly literature.[8] In the nineteenth century it was customary to believe that the written sagas were tantamount to verbatim copies of oral sagas and that the writers acted largely in the capacity of scribes. This view was formulated in the early twentieth century by Andreas Heusler as the so-called freeprose theory and was reinforced by the Norwegian folklorist Knut Liestøl.[9] The evidence used to support it comprises the anonymity of the sagas (implying that the authors did not consider themselves to be individually responsible for the creation of their stories), the difficulty of explaining the transmission of stories from the Saga Age to the thirteenth century without the aid of oral traditions, the objectivity and homogeneity of saga style (suggesting a period of oral schooling and development), and the uniqueness of the family saga, which has no literary antecedents in Europe and must therefore be explained as a specifically Icelandic phenomenon with specifically Icelandic roots.

The opposing view, which Heusler called the bookprose theory, holds that the sagas were the work of a talented group of thirteenth-century authors who dealt freely with whatever oral traditions were known to them from the Saga Age and who composed their works more or less as a modern novelist would. This theory has been represented chiefly by an active group of Icelandic scholars, Björn M. Ólsen in Heusler's generation and more recently the editors of *Íslenzk fornrit,* notably Sigurður Nordal and Einar Ólafur Sveinsson.[10] In 1956 it was given an even more radical turn by the German scholar Walter Baetke.[11] The case for bookprose rests on the absence of any proof that there were oral sagas, the view that oral tradition is generally a legacy from Romantic literary doctrine, and the conviction that literary activity is always the work of gifted individual artists, who should not be dispossessed by special hypotheses in the case of the family sagas merely because they are not named.

To some extent this split in opinion is still with us, but the oppositions have worn smooth in recent years. No one is now prepared to argue the freeprose theory in its extreme form, and there seems to be a corresponding reluctance to argue for free invention. Many scholars now share the view that there were substantial traditions about the Saga Age current in Iceland and that these traditions were the most important source for the family sagas. At the same time, most or all scholars believe that the saga authors were by no means slaves of oral stories and that, despite their insistence on anonymity, they had and used an author's prerogatives: they criticized and formed the traditions known to them (just as Snorri did), they combined sources, and they formulated conjectures when the traditions were incomplete or contradictory.

It has been argued that the question of orality is of little moment, but it is clear that our understanding of the sagas depends to a large degree on how we think they developed. If we assume they are novels created by skilled writers, the emphasis in our study will rest on the identification of these writers, their relationships to one another, their literary culture, the circumstances under which they lived and worked, the relationship of their experiences and of contemporary events to the stories they wrote, and the implicit or explicit messages which they tried to convey, in short, all the emphases of traditional literary history. If, on the other hand, we judge that the stories were largely preformed and binding on the authors, we will focus our attention, not on the writer's circumstances, but on the conditions of oral transmission, the possibility of reconstructing the pre-literary form of the stories, and the relationship of the oral tradition to the actual events of early Iceland.

Both avenues are beset by difficulties. Traditional literary inquiry, which has been carried on intensively especially since 1930, has produced little. None of the saga authors has been revealed with anything approaching certainty. There are no hints as to their identities, their intentions, or their literary backgrounds. Few allusions to learned works or other sagas appear, and when sagas are referred to, it is not always clear whether an oral or a written version is meant. Sometimes it is evident that two sagas are interrelated, though no mention is made of the fact in either. In such cases, however, it requires a good deal of sleuthing to decide which saga is using the other. Nor are there explicit references to contemporary thirteenth-century occurrences; attempts at unraveling certain sagas as *romans à clef* have not been persuasive. Above all, it does not seem possible to isolate particular personal or political viewpoints or clearly enunciated attitudes such as we might expect from individual authors working on a deliberately constructed piece of literature. It has not even been possible to agree on the underlying ethical standard, whether it be, at one extreme, some belated form of the heroic ideal or, at the opposite extreme, the dictates of medieval Christianity. The limited success of this line of questioning might well convince us that we are asking the wrong questions and that conventional literary history is not the right approach.

On the other hand, the study of oral tradition is peculiarly unproductive. We have no certainty that such traditions really existed, and any generalization about oral form encounters the justified suspicion of oversimplification. Style is an equally indecisive guide. It is possible to argue that the sagas are both strikingly homogeneous in diction (an indication of oral standardization) and at the same time that each saga has an idiosyncratic manner which reflects the literary personality of a particular individual. At this stage in the debate it may be safest to take refuge in the vague formulation that the sagas are based on pre-existing stories and pre-existing narrative modes, but that the shape in which they have come down to us is the work of men making the transition from oral narrative to literary composition.

Another persistent problem has been the question of historicity. If the family sagas are based on older traditions, to what extent are they an accurate reflection of events in the Saga Age? At the height of the freeprose theory, when the sagas were held to be true copies of traditions which solidified shortly after the actual events related, they were believed to be substantially reliable. Knut Liestol went so far as to say that "where there is no reason to believe that something is unhistorical, there is reason to believe that it is historical."[12] This view has been reversed, and we are now inclined to consider historical only what is demonstrably so. More commonly, the problem is simply ignored in the absence of documents that might be used to resolve it. About all we can say is that the sagas claim to be historical and no doubt ultimately derive from historical situations. To what extent they describe events more or less as they occurred will never be known, but the larger-than-life dimensions of the action and the characters suggest that the sagas are more likely to be highly embellished versions of what actually happened rather than sober reality.

As inquiries into the orality and historicity of the sagas have declined in recent years in the face of a recognition that the arguments have been exhausted, more and more attention has been paid to artistic aspects. Particular efforts have been made to identify the dominant patterns which define saga structure. One of the shorter sagas from the later thirteenth century, *Hœnsa-Þóris saga*, may serve to exemplify the structure:

Hœnsa-Þórir is a generally disliked social upstart who acquires wealth by peddling chickens around the countryside. In order to secure his position, he offers to foster a certain Helgi, the son of the chieftain Arngrímr, in exchange for a promise of protection. Arngrímr, though doubtful about such a disreputable satellite, agrees to the bargain when Hœnsa-Þórir proposes to bestow half his wealth on Helgi.

Sometime later the Norwegian merchant Qrn brings his trading vessel to the district of another chieftain, Tungu-Oddr, but he rejects the chieftain's customary right to set prices on goods sold in his domain. In retaliation, Oddr places him under a ban. Hersteinn, the son of the respected farmer Blund-Ketill, converses with Qrn, learns of the situation, and reports it to his father, who recognizes in Qrn the son of an old acquaintance. Despite Tungu-Oddr's prohibition, Blund-Ketill offers him generous hospitality. Tungu-Oddr chooses not to react for the time being.

A dry summer results in a hay shortage, and Blund-Ketill issues instructions to his tenants designed to meet the crisis, but his orders are ignored and the shortage is not averted. In their distress, first one and then two other tenants appeal to him for relief. He provides for them at the expense of reducing his own needs and slaughtering some of his own animals, but he is unable to meet yet a third request and applies to Hœnsa-Þórir, who is known to have a surplus of hay. Despite increasingly generous offers, he is met with a series of surly refusals and eventually takes matters into his own hands by removing what hay can be spared and leaving proper payment in its place. Hœnsa-Þórir claims theft and brings his case first to Arngrímr and then to Tungu-Oddr. Both turn to his foster son Helgi for verification of the story, and when Helgi fails to corroborate Hœnsa-Þórir's version of theft, they decline to intercede.

Sometime later Tungu-Oddr's son Þorvaldr returns from abroad and Hœnsa-Þórir seeks him out to lodge yet a third appeal for help. He offers Þorvaldr half his wealth and once more his money proves to be irresistible. Accompanied by Þorvaldr and his followers, Hœnsa-Þórir now rides out to initiate legal action against Blund-Ketill. Despite repeated and generous efforts at conciliation, Þorvaldr, prompted by Hœnsa-Þórir, rejects all offers and delivers a sharply worded summons. To avenge this insult to his host, Qrn shoots an arrow into the crowd of summoners and has the ill fortune to kill the boy Helgi. Hœnsa-Þórir seizes the opportunity, puts his ear to the boy's mouth, and claims that his dying words were to burn Blund-Ketill in his house ("Brenni, brenni Blund-Ketill inni"). Swayed by this malicious fiction, Þorvaldr withdraws until the men who have come to Blund-Ketill's aid disperse, then returns to burn Blund-Ketill together with his whole household.

Blund-Ketill's son Hersteinn, advised of the burning in a dream, conspires with his foster father Þorbjǫrn to form, through a series of tricks and inducements, an alliance with Þorkell trefill, Gunnarr Hlífarson, and Þórðr gellir against his father's killers. The following spring they summon Arngrímr, Hœnsa-Þórir, and Þorvaldr, and both sides gather forces for the legal contest. At the local Thing Hersteinn is outnumbered and must defer proceedings to the Allthing. Here he has the advantage and, after surprising and killing Hœnsa-Þórir as he lies in ambush, he is able to outlaw or exile the arsonists.

The saga concludes with an epilogue recounting chiefly the reconciliation of Tungu-Oddr and Gunnarr Hlífarson through the marriage of Oddr's son Þóroddr to Gunnarr's daughter Jófríðr.

Hœnsa-Þóris saga is the only family saga that can be compared to a substantially older version of the same events with a better claim to historical authenticity. This version is provided by Ari Þorgilsson in his *Íslendingabók:*

There was a great legal contest between Þórðr gellir, the son of Óláfr feilan from Breiðafjǫrðr, and Oddr, who was called Tungu-Oddr. He was from Borgarfjǫrðr. His son Þorvaldr was at the burning of Þorkell, the son of Blund-Ketill, together with Hœnsa-Þórir in Ǫrnólfsdalr. And Þórðr gellir was in charge of the prosecution because Hersteinn, the son of Þorkell and grandson of Blund-Ketill, was married to his niece Þórunn. She was the daughter of Helga and Gunnarr and the sister of Jófríðr, who was married to Þorsteinn the son of Egill. And they were prosecuted at the Thing in Borgarfjǫrðr at the place since called Þingnes. It was then the law that murder cases should be tried at the Thing that was closest to the place of summons. But they fought there and the Thing could not be legally convened. Þórólfr refr, the brother of Álfr in Dalir, fell there from the ranks of Þórðr gellir. Then the litigants went to the Allthing and they fought again. There men fell in the ranks of Oddr and Hœnsa-Þórir was outlawed and later killed together with others who were at the burning.

Ari's oral informants, whom he names and for whose truthfulness he vouches, lived within fifty or seventy-five years of the burning (962) and his account may therefore be fairly close to the mark. More immediately prob-lematical is the relationship between Ari's version and the version told in *Hœnsa-Þóris saga.* It is apparent that there are a number of minor but real discrepancies: Ari tells us that it was not Blund-Ketill himself but his son Þorkell who was burned (the saga knows of no Þorkell Blund-Ketilsson), that the first encounter between Þórðr gellir and Tungu-Oddr was contested on the Thinggrounds (in the saga Þórðr is barred from entering the Thinggrounds), and, finally, that Hœnsa-Þórir was killed after the final verdict instead of before, as in the saga. How do we account for these discrepancies?

The problem is analogous to the interpretation of discrepancies between *Landnámabók* and the sagas; they are either the product of oral metamor-phosis or they are deliberate departures, changes made by the author of *Hœnsa-Þóris saga* perhaps to correct what he considered to be errors or to achieve certain literary effects.[13] Since no consistent principle can be adduced to explain them, it seems unlikely that the changes are deliberate and more likely that they are the product of spontaneous transformations which took place as the story was handed down from the beginning of the twelfth century to the middle of the thirteenth. The saga was surely written down without consulting Ari. We must therefore conclude that the story circulated in differing forms around 1130 and again something over a century later.

Although we cannot say much about the changes which took place between the original event of 962, the reference of 1130, and the full narrative of the later thirteenth century, we can study the form of the saga in order to judge the end result of the transmission. *Hœnsa-Þóris saga* is particularly rewarding because it illustrates many typical saga features. It begins with an introduction of the protagonists and their characterization, which is in itself an anticipation of the action insofar as it suggests the patterns of behavior which will come to dominate the story: Hœnsa-Þórir is an ambitious but deceitful ne'er-do-well, the kind of scoundrel frequently used by the sagas to sow dissension, while Blund-Ketill is a moderate, high-minded, universally admired leader of the community, who embodies the sort of exemplary goodwill sometimes associated with saga heroes destined to succumb to the baser instincts of the men who surround them, the type most fully represented by Njáll, the central figure in the longest and greatest of the family sagas. The contrast of troublemaker and noble victim (the saga writers in the wake of a long tradition of Germanic heroic poetry had a fascination with the steadfast victim analogous to the Christian preoccupation with martyrdom) foreshadows the development of the story. Hœnsa-Þórir provokes Blund-Ketill for no good cause and, having been put in his place firmly but patiently, he initiates a campaign of slander to bring down his blameless adversary. The sequence of episodes is designed to underscore Hœnsa-Þórir's malice and Blund-Ketill's restraint, but it is the pessimistic view of the sagas that in such a contest the nobler qualities are doomed to defeat.

The tragic dénouement is followed by a counterbalancing sequence in which the wrong is righted: Hersteinn prepares to retaliate, his allies affirm their support by swearing oaths , there are two inconclusive encounters, then the vengeance is accomplished through the killing of Hœnsa-Þórir and the outlawing of the arsonists. The result is legal equipoise, but the tension between the two warring factions persists. This tension is finally resolved through the marriage of Þóroddr and Jófríðr, the children of the opposing leaders, and the saga concludes with brief notes on the fortunes of the younger generation.

The structure of the story can be broken down into fairly distinct sections: the introduction of the characters, the conflict fomented between a group around Tungu-Oddr and Blund-Ketill, the climactic burning of Blund-Ketill, the revenge engineered by his son Hersteinn, a reconciliation between the factions, and an epilogue in the form of concluding notes. This structure is characteristic of the family sagas in general. Introduction and epilogue are almost universal; they bracket the action with a historical framework calculated to convey authenticity. At the same time, they contain a good deal of genealogical lore and are of more antiquarian than narrative interest. The drama is reserved for the conflict, climax, and vengeance sections and is effected through the gradual construction of a high point over a series of escalating encounters. Typically, the trouble begins with some minor matter (in *Hœnsa-Þóris saga* the forcible purchase of hay) and is then magnified by slander, legal harassment, oblique attacks, and finally direct confrontations. The hostile counterpoint most often culminates in an armed clash between the principal individuals or parties, ending usually in the death of one or the other and followed by the reprisals of the revenge section. The sagas are thus essentially feud stories, but there is a widespread instinct in them calling for peaceful settlement. The conflicts are seen as temporary aberrations which subside. It is this view that dictates a special reconciliation section in about a third of the sagas and allows for a relaxation of the tensions built up during the feud.

The sagas lend themselves to formal analysis because they are formal constructions. They work with themes and episodes that recur again and again from one saga to the next: thefts, insults, seductions, litigation, personal injury. We learn from experience that horse matches, ballgames, stranded whales, missing sheep, erotic verses, alleged sorcery, and compromising rumors are the stuff of conflicts. We also learn that the material is formed in symmetrical ways which suggest the influence of the oral storyteller working according to stylized patterns. This tendency is more evident in *Hœnsa-Þóris saga* than in most, particularly in the frequent use of the so-called epic triad. Blund-Ketill's charity is established in three successive appeals from his tenants, the last of which precipitates the difficulties with Hœnsa-Þórir. Hœnsa-Þórir seeks support from three powerful men and succeeds on the last occasion. Hersteinn organizes his revenge by enlisting the aid of three increasingly powerful allies. At Hersteinn's wedding two oaths are sworn, but the third defaults. The final execution of vengeance is preceded by two inconclusive encounters. Such structures are characteristic of oral literature.[14]

A recent study has shown that the same sort of stylization applies to the formation of individual scenes.[15] The scenic patterning persists even in sagas translated from other languages and would seem to involve underlying habits of mind. The form of the scene is tripartite: preface, dramatic encounter, and conclusion. The substance of the scene is the center, chiefly dialogue with minimum stage directions and indications of changes in speakers ("He said: . . ." "She replied: . . ."). All narrative matter is restricted to the preface and conclusion. There is thus a division of labor between narrative and scenic presentation. The former is used to frame the latter. The preface is likely to include information about the persons involved in the scene and about time, place, or circumstances. The conclusion marks the end of the scene by stating that the conversation was broken off, that one or more of the participants departed or rode home, that time passed, or that word got around about what had transpired. In such a scene there is the same sort of contrived symmetry and the same alternation of level narrative and dramatic peak that characterizes the saga as a whole.

To illustrate the typical saga scene we may single out Blund-Ketill's seizure of Hœnsa-Þórir's hay. The preface provides information on the time, weather conditions, and Hœnsa-Þórir's reaction: "They set out early in the morning. There was a stiff wind from the north, and a cold one at that. Farmer Þórir was standing outside at that moment. When he saw the men approaching the yard, he went in and closed the door and put the latch on. Then he sat down to breakfast." After some preliminaries between Blund-Ketill and Þórir's foster son Helgi, the episode culminates in a direct confrontation of the two principals consisting almost entirely of dialogue:

> "The fact of the matter," said Blund-Ketill, "is that we want to buy hay from you, Þórir." Þórir answered: "Your money is no better to me than my own." Ketill said: "That's neither here nor there." Þórir replied: "Why is a rich fellow like you out of hay?" Blund-Ketill said: "I'm not exactly out of hay and I am asking for my tenants, who seem to need a helping hand; I would like to get something for them if it is available." "You are at perfect liberty to give others what is yours, but not what is mine." Blund-Ketill answered: "We're not asking for a gift; let Oddr and Arngrímr decide a fair price on your behalf and in addition I will give you gifts." Þórir said he had no hay to sell—"and anyway I don't want to sell."

The conversation continues in this vein for some time and ends with the seizure. The conclusion is as terse as the preface: "Then Þórir became silent, and he was in an ominous state of mind. Blund-Ketill had ropes fetched to truss up the hay; then they loaded up the bundles and carried off the hay, but they made ample provision for the cattle." Through the concatenation of such scenes a saga becomes a sequence of dramatic moments.

The encounter between Blund-Ketill and Hœnsa-Þórir is described without authorial comment. This peculiarity of saga style has often been covered by the term "objective," but in recent years efforts have been made to define and limit the concept of saga objectivity.[16] It has been demonstrated that the saga authors are not so impartial as they appear and that they have a variety of techniques for controlling the reader's opinion. These techniques are sometimes explicit. When we are told from the very outset of *Hœnsa-Þóris saga* that Blund-Ketill "was the richest and most estimable of the men of the old faith . . . and was the most popular man in the district" while, despite his newly acquired wealth, Hœnsa-Þórir's "unpopularity remained unchanged because there was hardly a more despicable man than Hœnsa-Þórir," we are scarcely in a position to judge the encounter of these two men objectively. Such direct characterizations are not infrequent in the sagas, but they can also operate in a more oblique manner. It has been noted, for example, that blond, good-looking people in the sagas tend to be less problematic than their dark-haired, less well-favored counterparts, so that even the barest mention of physical characteristics may serve to predispose the reader. A character can be damaged by the information that he or she is given to sorcery or heathen practices, or a favorable view can be induced by mentioning some charitable deed or simply by depicting the character in a normal, comfortable domestic situation—villains are not given the benefit of a homey atmosphere. Frequently, the author's view is disguised as an expression of public opinion. If a man is described as "popular in the district," the reader is likely to concur without giving it much thought.

The technique can also be rhetorical or even syntactical. The author can locate opinions which are to be taken seriously and remembered in a well-turned speech or at some crucial juncture in the story, for example at the end of a chapter or section. A favored character can be given more "air time," or the "last word." Authors may speak to the reader through "reliable" or "unreliable" narrators or spokesmen; if a view has been expressed by someone who has been described as a "wise man," the reader will of course espouse his view. Another technique used to shape the reader's outlook is the citing of aphoristic or proverbial expressions which tend to be equated with general truths. "Most of the proverbs and aphorisms ... emphasize such social values as respect for the law, patience, restraint, peacefulness and correct procedure."[17] In sum, the saga, though remarkably impassive, is by no means objective in the full meaning of the word.

The question of objectivity leads to the broader question of whether the sagas are pure narrative or interpretable in some moral or exemplary sense. It has long been held that the sagas tell stories for their own sake without passing judgment on the events or characters and without suggesting general conclusions to be drawn from the action. This type of objectivity, however, is also questionable, and many sagas (among others *Gísla saga, Hrafnkels saga, Valla-Ljóts saga, Njáls saga*) clearly suggest moral themes. *Hœnsa-Þóris saga* is, once again, a good illustration. Hero and villain are clearly designated. Hœnsa-Þórir is a villain because he is mean and devious. Blund-Ketill is a hero because he is candid, socially responsible, conciliatory, and dignified. His story is tragic because the better man succumbs to the lesser man. This amounts to a moral framework and a message to the reader about what constitutes admirable and reprehensible behavior. Despite many gestures borrowed from the heroic tradition, the underlying outlook is not heroic, as has often been argued, but social. Whereas the heroic fable emphasizes individual feats without social considerations,[18] the saga emphasizes reconciliation. The heroic lay breaks off at the height of the disaster, the saga resolves the conflict and reconstructs the peace. The sagas are not blood-curdling tales of reckless heroes, but stories of temporary breakdowns in a normal society.

It is the fundamental concern with values as well as the well-wrought construction that makes the best of the kings' sagas and family sagas a classical literature, that is, a literature with a humane and harmonious outlook. Such sagas are a code as well as an art, a distillation in which the idea is more important than the realities. Though not explicitly didactic, they often conceive of their heroes as models to be emulated. Generations of readers have returned to these sagas not only because they are good stories, but because they represent a heightened vision of the human alternatives.

This is not true of the two saga genres which remain to be considered, the collection known as *Sturlunga saga* and the legendary sagas. The former turns to ordinariness, the latter to fancy.

Sturlunga Saga

Although *Sturlunga saga* was composed at the same time as the family sagas and although the chief contributor was Snorri Sturluson's nephew Sturla Þórðarson (died 1272), the reading experience is distinctly different from that of the classical saga.[19] *Íslendinga saga,* the core section composed by Sturla and covering the period 1183–1264, is a sober record of current events, not an imaginative recreation of the past. It deals with the same type of material found in the family sagas (feuds, litigation, attacks, counterattacks), but these matters are treated with less dramatic intensity than in the stories of the Saga Age. The episodes succeed one another in reportorial style; one has the feeling that the author is too close to the events to invest them with a literary perspective. There is a restricted use of the lapidary dialogue which heightens the effect of the kings' sagas and family sagas and a reduction of the patient detail used by the family saga authors to mark the high points in their narratives. As a consequence, *Íslendinga saga* is less clearly articulated and more difficult to follow.

The characters, like the action, are less fully developed. The leading figures are not so arresting as the great men of the Saga Age, Egill Skallagrímsson, Snorri goði, Njáll, or Grettir. Exceptionally full is the characterization of Gizurr Þorvaldsson: "Gizurr was of moderate height, a very accomplished man, with shapely limbs and keen-eyed—he had piercing eyes, intelligent in expression; he was better spoken than most men here in the land, affable, with a very low voice; not an impetuous man but one always considered of very substantial value in all counsels. And yet it often happened when he was in conflict with chieftains or with his kinsmen that he seemed rather indifferent about the issue, even uncertain whom he would support."[20] This portrait is quite analogous to what can be found in the classical sagas, but it is an aside to the reader; Gizurr's personality as it is here described is not woven into the story. The result of such under-exploitation is that there are no characters of such memorable dignity as Blund-Ketill and no knaves of such picturesque meanness as Hœnsa-Þórir. We are left with the impression that contemporary life provided Sturla with the raw material for a saga, but that he formed it as a chronicle instead.

The gap between *Íslendinga saga* and the old school is not only one of

artistic achievement, but also one of moral tone. Readers of *Íslendinga saga*
have traditionally been disturbed by the imperfect humanity they encounter
there. Unpleasant realities lie heavy on the text. There is killing without the
justification of the feud, for example the political assassination of Snorri
Sturluson in 1241.[21] There is a taste for beating, torture, and execution practically unknown in the family sagas. During the conflict between Bishop Guðmundr Arason and the chieftains, one of the bishop's men is captured: "He
was Eyjólfr hríðarefni, an unruly man. He was seized and beaten; they
dragged him to the house half-dead and then killed him."[22] Sturla Sighvatsson
has his cousin Órækja methodically tortured: "There they seized Órækja, and
Sturla ordered Þorsteinn langabein to torture him... Órækja called on Saint
Þorlákr to help him; during the tortures he also chanted prayers to the Virgin
Mary, the mother of Our Lord Jesus Christ."[23] There are new and more
atrocious forms of violence, most conspicuously castration and the severing of
hands and feet.[24] There are three great burnings, the last of which took place
at Flugumýri in 1253 and is described in more horrid detail than the reader is
accustomed to from a *Hœnsa-Þóris saga* or a *Njáls saga*.[25] Generally speaking, the fighting is reported with more explicitness than in the classical sagas
and without the saving grace of a moral framework or a moral posture.[26]
There is a particular fondness for registering the exact nature of wounds:
"Then Oddr struck Ásbjörn Ljótsson in the shoulder, cleaving right down the
side so that one could see into his body. He next struck Þorsteinn Óláfsson
and split his face; Þorsteinn fell dead there. Ásbjörn Finnsson thrust at Grímr
with his spear; Grímr did not fall down but bent toward the stroke so that the
point went through to his spine. He twisted himself so that the spear ran out
between the ribs;..."[27] Most foreign to the modern reader is the matter-of-
fact tone in which horrors and outrages are reported, what Einar Ól. Sveinsson
calls "the apparently cold indifference of the accounts of *Sturlunga saga*."[28]

Along with the violence of the Sturlung Age goes an apparent relaxation of
ethical standards. Writers have been struck by the changes in sexual mores
signaled, for example, by the occasions when men beget children with other
men's wives.[29] There is a new preoccupation with money, which strikes the
reader as more cynical than the disputes over property in the family sagas.
Quarrels over inheritances are not uncommon[30] and there is a pervasive covetousness and eagerness to amass wealth, not least of all on the part of Snorri
Sturluson.[31] This is part and parcel of the large-scale consolidations in the
thirteenth century. There are expanded military operations and troop
movements requiring unprecedented expenditures. We are told on one occasion that Gizurr and Kolbeinn marched south with thirteen hundred men and
that a short time later the southerners raised a similar number.[32] Such campaigns doubtlessly encouraged anonymity in numbers and a degree of reck-
lessness not documented in the older sagas, notably widespread looting and
pillaging.[33] There were massive confrontations between rival leaders, between secular claims and the claims of the Church put forward in an uncom-

promising form by Bishop Guðmundr Arason, and between the interests of
the Icelandic chieftains, weakened as they were by factionalism, and the
interests of the Norwegian king, who was eventually able to avail himself of
the crisis to absorb Iceland under the Norwegian Crown in 1262–64 and put an
end to the Icelandic Republic.

The signs of moral decay and political decline in *Sturlunga saga* have
tended to promote the view that it signals the loss of the "old values" in the
family sagas and opens the way for the popularity of the vapid tales in the
legendary sagas. The eminent Icelandic literary historian Sigurður Nordal
once offered a general theory of saga development spanning the three centuries from the twelfth to the fourteenth.[34] The theory traced an emerging
interest in history at Oddi, the homestead of Sæmundr Sigfússon in the early
twelfth century, and a coalescing of this learned trend with a new taste for
literary entertainment first evident in works connected with the northern
monastery at Þingeyrar in the late twelfth century. Some years later this
fusion produced the balance between historical setting and literary expression
found in the family sagas, a state of equipoise which persisted through the
thirteenth century and then succumbed to a split between scholarly and literary
pursuits. The split resulted in dry annals on the one hand and extravagant
stories on the other.

Nordal's theory describes the written record, but it may be misleading in
the picture it draws of a rising and declining literary culture. The legendary
sagas, which had been in oral circulation at least since the beginning of the
twelfth century, may well be older than the family sagas and are certainly
older than the historical writing of the twelfth century. The question is therefore not why they developed late, but why they were set down late, and the
answer may be simply that the excellent sagas had already been committed to
final written form during the thirteenth century, thus obliging the scribal
industry, which must have developed in step with the saga writing of the
classical period, to cast about for new materials and resort to the recording of
works with a less clear-cut claim to truthfulness and historical validity. Since
the classical sagas continued to be copied and read (the best manuscripts and
those on which our modern editions are based are from the fourteenth century), the admission of legendary sagas to the written canon does not necessarily mean a decline in taste, but perhaps only a growing literary enterprise and
expanded consumption. On the other hand, it is possible that the thirteenth
century produced, along with other mass phenomena, a sort of literary democ-
ratization, a larger and less discriminating readership in search of easier
effects. If so, the legendary sagas relate to the classical sagas more or less as
the popular reading of the twentieth century (mystery stories, science fiction,
Gothic novels) relates to the classical novel of the nineteenth century.

Before turning to the legendary sagas, we may focus our attention briefly
on a transition phenomenon in the form of *Grettis saga Ásmundarsonar*. It is
traditionally classed as a family saga, but it dates from the end of the classical

period (ca. 1300) and has a number of features in common with the post-classical sagas, folktale motifs, supernatural adventures, inflated heroism, and romantic intrusions. Grettir's childhood is cast in terms of the male Cinderella and the obstreperous pranks of the folktale wag. His adventures include such stock *fornaldarsaga* motifs as the subduing of the ghostly inhabitant of a burial mound, the killing of a ferocious bear, the elimination of twelve berserks, a wrestling match with the revenant Glámr (familiar to many readers from the analogue in *Beowulf*), and a second wrestling match with a giantess. After his death as a lonely outlaw on a desolate island off the northern coast of Iceland, he is avenged by his brother in Constantinople under romantic circumstances borrowed from the story of Tristan and Isolde.

It has been argued convincingly that the biographical, heroic, and frequently anti-social emphases of *Grettis saga* are a concession to the new taste for hero worship that developed in Icelandic literature around 1300.[35] The argument goes on to show, however, that the older moral and social concerns persist and that the saga constitutes a tacit critique of hero orientation at the same time that it betrays a longing for individual precedence over social restrictions. Grettir's sometimes monstrous behavior is rejected by society, but society also dwells admiringly on the feats of a freer spirit and a superior capacity not shackled by the customary rules. The tension between social and individual demands provides the special resonance of *Grettis saga*. This conflict is lost in the later sagas.

Legendary Sagas

In contrast to the family saga, the pre-literary stage of which is totally obscure, there is one ray of light to illuminate the oral precursors of the legendary sagas. *Sturlunga saga* contains the account of a wedding held at Reykjahólar in 1119, including a description of the entertainment provided for the guests:[36]

Something is told, though it is of small importance, of who the entertainers were and what their entertainment was. What is related is now contradicted by many, who maintain that they have never accepted it, for many are blind to the truth and think what is false to be true and what is true to be a lie. Hrólfr from Skálmarness told a story about Hrǫngviðr the viking and Óláfr liðmannakonungr and the mound-breaking of Þráinn the berserk and Hrómundr Gripsson, with many verses in it. This story was used to entertain King Sverrir and he declared that such "lying sagas" were most amusing; men can however trace their genealogies to Hrómundr Gripsson. Hrólfr himself had composed this saga. Ingimundr the prist told the story of Ormr Barreyjarskáld, including many verses and with a good *flokkr*, which Ingimundr had composed, at the end of the saga. Nevertheless, many learned men regard this story as true.

The nature of the saga told by Hrólfr of Skálmarness may be deduced partly from the cast of characters (a "viking" and a "berserk") and the one incident mentioned (a "mound-breaking") and partly from an extant *Hrómundar saga Gripssonar* transmitted in copies from the seventeenth century on and apparently based on a rimed version (one of the so-called Icelandic *rímur*), which in turn must have derived from a prose story akin to the one narrated at Reykjahólar.

In the saga Óláfr liðmannakonungr appears as ruler of Denmark and Hrómundr as one of nine sons of the wealthy farmer Gripr and his wife Gunnlǫð. During a raiding expedition in Norway the viking Hrǫngviðr kills two of Óláfr's men and Hrómundr avenges them. Óláfr and his men then sail on to the Hebrides where they are given directions to the treasure-filled mound of Þráinn six days' sail to the south in Valland. Hrómundr plunders the mound, overcomes and kills the ghostly barrow-dweller Þráinn, and distributes the treasure among his companions, retaining only three items—a ring, a necklace, and the sword Mistilteinn.

Once back in Denmark, he exhibits an interest in Óláfr's sister Svanhvít, but is slandered by the two villains Bíldr and Váli and compelled to leave the court. Two Swedish kings, both named Haddingr (they coalesce into one without explanation as the story progresses), together with Hrǫngviðr's brother Helgi, now organize an attack against Óláfr. Hrómundr at first refuses to come to his defense, but relents under the persuasion of Svanhvít. He and his eight brothers assemble on the ice of Lake Vænir, but Hrómundr, warned by a premonition, does not enter battle immediately. In the first encounter his brothers succumb to Helgi aided by his mistress Lára, who appears over the host as a swan. Then Hrómundr joins the combat, kills Lára, Helgi himself, and finally Váli (Bíldr has been slain in the previous action) after losing his sword Mistilteinn through the ice.

In order to elude Haddingr he takes refuge with the fisherman Hagall and Mistilteinn is recovered from the stomach of a pike which Hagall catches. The sorcerer Blindr the Bad is dispatched to find Hrómundr, but he is tricked by Hagall's wife and abandons the search. Subsequently Blindr has a series of monitory dreams, the last one depicting an iron ring around his neck and signifying death by hanging. The dream is borne out when Óláfr surprises his enemies, Hrómundr clubs Haddingr to death, and Blindr is hanged. Hrómundr and Svanhvít are married and beget a distinguished progeny.

This story illustrates as well as any other the characteristics of the *fornaldarsaga*.[37] The hero is a man of overwhelming prowess and physical strength attached to the service of royalty. He is presented to the reader as a full-fledged warrior engaged in a viking expedition, during which he travels widely and proves himself in a stereotyped barrow adventure. The sequel runs its course according to the romance convention whereby the hero woos a princess, is temporarily thwarted by scoundrels, but perseveres in winning her hand by dint of his superior abilities. The *fornaldarsaga* is to be defined by these typical and recurrent motifs rather than by persistent structural patterns as in the case of the family saga. It is constructed as a string of episodes (martial, erotic, supernatural) in which the protagonist or protagonists prevail and which can end happily with a marriage or unhappily with the death of the hero. Proposed distinctions within the genre have been based on the predominance of a particular type of episode in a given saga. Thus *Vǫlsunga saga* (a prose harmonization of the heroic lays preserved in the *Poetic Edda*), *Heiðreks saga*, and *Hrólfs saga kraka*, which draw their narrative stock exclu-(*rvar-Odds saga, Hrómundar saga*) are called viking sagas (*Wikingersagas*) sagas (*Heldensagas*). Those sagas which are set primarily in a viking milieu (*Qrvar-Odds saga, Hrómundar saga*) are called viking sagas (*Wikingersagas*) and those that depend more heavily on common folktale motifs (*Bósa saga, Gǫngu-Hrólfs saga*) are called adventure sagas (*Abenteuersagas*). On occasion the nucleus may be ultimately historical as in the case of *Gǫngu-Hrólfs saga*, in which the hero is probably to be equated with the Rollo who annexed Normandy in 911, or *Ragnars saga loðbrókar*, in which the hero may or may not be identical with the viking Ragnarr who plundered Paris in 845. Whatever historical nucleus may once have existed, however, has disappeared under an accumulation of folktale, mythological, supernatural, and romance motifs from the most varied and usually untraceable sources.

The situation is further complicated by the gradual encroachment of European romance (the Icelandic mutations of which are termed *riddarasögur*) on the native *fornaldarsaga*.[38] The appearance of these romances in Scandinavia began with the translation in 1226 of Thomas' *Tristan* into Norse by a certain Brother Robert working under the auspices of King Hákon Hákonarson in Norway. The same sponsorship produced translations or adaptations of Chrétien's romances under the titles *Erex saga*, *Ívents saga*, and *Percevals saga*.[39] *Chanson de geste* material was naturalized in a compendium known as *Karlamagnús saga*. Eventually motifs from these cycles merge with indigenous stories to produce sagas in which the romance world of tourneys and lovely ladies exists side by side with viking adventures. How such material reached Iceland is illustrated by the opening lines of *Clari saga:* "We begin this story (which the reverend bshop Jón Halldórsson [Bishop of Skálholt 1322–39] of blessed memory told, and he found it written in Latin in France in that form which they call *rithmos* and we call rime) at the point where Tiburtius, the Emperor of Saxony, governed his realm with great honor and glory."[40] Bishop Jón had been in Paris in his youth and brought back either manuscripts or the memory of tales he had read and heard there.

Whatever the derivation of the motifs, the legendary sagas may be considered in a broad sense as the romantic aftermath of Icelandic classicism, and the departures may be understood in the light of categories traditionally used to distinguish romantic from classic. Time has no binding force. Whereas a fairly exact chronology can be worked out for the kings' sagas, the family sagas, and *Sturlunga saga*, the legendary sagas are not chronologically fixed, but are vaguely placed in the period preceding the settlement of Iceland. In addition, they frequently distort our normal sense of time by telling of persons who live to be several hundred years old (Qrvar-Oddr, Starkaðr) or who are capable of periodic rejuvenation (Mágus in *Mágus saga jarls*). Freedom from historical and natural laws has its counterpart in freedom from social laws. Characters and events are not controlled by the rules that prescribe conduct in the older sagas. Impulse and a lack of clear psychological motivation are common. The conventions of feudal society, which give shape to the family sagas, and the conventions of court behavior, which provide the framework of the kings' sagas are more superficially applied in the legendary sagas. With the removal of social convention, fantasy is given freer rein. There is more latitude for monsters, dwarves, gods in human disguise, trolls, revenants, witches, dragons, and so forth. There are werewolves deriving perhaps ultimately from the Norse translation of Marie de France's *Bisclavret* and there are cyclops and cynocephali showing the infiltration of ancient and encyclopedic lore along with romance material.[41] The action is not restricted to familiar regions but circulates at will from Tartary to India to exotic realms of pure fancy, sometimes with the aid of such conveyances as automotive ships and magic carpets.

In this new world of altered reality, human qualities tend to become distorted in one direction or the other: there are giants and midgets, perfect gentlemen and utter villains, magicians and fools, women of unblemished beauty and repulsive ugliness (there are no ugly women in the older sagas and few paragons). Extreme appearance is matched by extreme behavior; there are incidents of wanton violence, crudity, and anti-social behavior. The peerless beauty Sedentiona in *Sigurðar saga þögla* seizes two brothers, who have had the temerity to sue for her hand, has their heads shaved and covered with pitch, orders them flogged, has hot coals placed on their stomachs (a motif borrowed from the unique conversion atrocities in *Óláfs saga Tryggvasonar*) and designs carved on their backs with a knife. But it is part of the unreal atmosphere in these sagas that such treatment is not to be taken seriously; victims recover rapidly, often with the aid of magic balms and salves.

Whereas the older sagas attempted to convey a sense of permanent institutions with a strong emphasis on the law and binding standards of conduct, the adventures of the legendary sagas are set outside an institutional or normative context. They are less problematical, less probing, less preoccupied with the delicate adjustments in human relationships. Friendships and enmities do not evolve, and virtue tends to be equated with faithful service rather than a negotiated understanding. Instead of the psychological interest in erotic problems such as we find in a *Gísla saga* or a *Laxdœla saga, fornaldarsaga* and romance exhibit a new fascination with sexual adventure, or even sexual bravado, as in an episode from *Bósa saga,* which documents the scatological fabliau for Iceland.[42] Perhaps the increased popularity of free fiction in late medieval Iceland indicates no more than a rise in literary production, but it will remain tempting to speculate that political factors were also involved and that the strong sense of individual and social responsibility cultivated in the classical sagas began to decline with the collapse of the Icelandic Republic and the loss of political independence at the end of the thirteenth century.

NOTES

1. Hallvard Lie, "Studier i Heimskringlas stil: Dialogene og talene," *Skrifter utgitt av Det Norske Videnskaps-Akademi i Oslo, hist.-filos. kl.* (1936), 5, pp. 1–136.

2. Chief among these are *Egils saga, Hœnsa-þóris saga, Gunnlaugs saga ormstungu, Bjarnar saga hítdœlakappa, Heiðarvíga saga, Eyrbyggja saga, Laxdœla saga, Gísla saga Súrssonar, Fóstbrœðra saga, Hávarðar saga ísfirðings, Grettis saga Ásmundarsonar, Bandamanna saga, Vatnsdœla saga, Hallfreðar saga, Kormaks saga, Víga-Glúms saga, Svarfdœla saga, Valla-Ljóts saga, Ljósvetninga saga, Reykdœla saga, Vápnfirðinga saga, Hrafnkels saga freysgoða, Droplaugarsona saga, Fljótsdæla saga, Njáls saga, Kjalnesinga saga, Þórðar saga hreðu, Finnboga saga, Harðar saga Grímkelssonar,* and *Flóamanna saga.*

3. Kurt Schier, *Sagaliteratur* (Stuttgart: Metzler, 1970), pp. 50–51.

4. Jónas Kristjánsson, *Um Fóstbrœðrasögu* (Reykjavik: Stofnun Árna Magnússonar, 1972).

5. Dietrich Hofmann, "Reykdœla saga und mündliche Überlieferung," *Skandinavistik* 2 (1972): 1–26.

6. *Landnámabók* has been edited most recently by Jakob Benediktsson in *Íslenzk fornrit,* I/1–2 (Reykjavik: Hið íslenzka fornritafélag, 1968), and is available in an English translation by Hermann Pálsson and Paul Edwards, *The Book of Settlements: Landnámabók,* University of Manitoba Icelandic Studies, 1 (Manitoba: The University of Manitoba Press, 1972).

7. Jónas Kristjánsson, "Íslendingadrápa and Oral Tradition," *Gripla* 1 (1975): 76–91.

8. The controversy is reviewed by Marco Scovazzi, *La saga di Hrafnkell e il problema delle saghe islandesi* (Arona: Paideia, 1960), and T. M. Andersson, *The Problem of Icelandic Saga Origins: A Historical Survey,* Yale Germanic Studies, 1 (New Haven: Yale University Press, 1964). Some of the pertinent contributions are included in Walter Baetke's critical anthology *Die Isländersaga,* Wege der Forschung, 151 (Darmstadt: Wissenschaftliche Buchgesellschaft, 1974). A new survey is promised by Kurt Schier as a sequel to his volume *Sagaliteratur* (1970) in the Sammlung Metzler.

9. Andreas Heusler, "Die Anfänge der isländischen Saga," *Abhandlungen der Königlich Preussischen Akademie der Wissenschaften, Phil.-hist. Kl.* (Berlin, 1913), pp. 1–87; reprinted in Heusler's *Kleine Schriften,* ed. Stefan Sonderegger, II (Berlin: de Gruyter, 1969), pp. 388–460; Knut Liestøl, *Upphavet til den islendske ættesaga* (Oslo: Aschehoug, 1929); trans. A. G. Jayne, *The Origin of the Icelandic Family Sagas* (Oslo: Aschehoug, 1930).

10. B. M. Ólsen, "Um íslendingasögur," *Safn til sögu Íslands* VI/5–7 (1937–39), and S. Nordal and E. Ól. Sveinsson in their introductions to the standard series of saga editions in *Íslenzk fornrit,* II (1933), III (1938), V (1934), VIII (1939), and XII (1954).

11. W. Baetke, "Über die Entstehung der Isländersagas," *Berichte über die Verhandlungen der Sächsischen Akademie der Wissenschaften zu Leipzig, Philol.-hist. Kl.* 102/5 (1956): 1–108. The fullest application of this view to a single saga is Rolf Heller, "Die Laxdœla saga: Die literarische Schöpfung eines Isländers des 13. Jahrhunderts," *Abhandlungen der Sächsischen Akademie der Wissenschaften zu Leipzig, Philol.-hist. Kl.* 65/1 (1976): 5–152.

12. Liestøl, *Upphavet,* p. 230 (trans., p. 247).

13. This is the view argued by S. Nordal in his introduction to *Hænsa-Þóris saga* in *Íslenzk fornrit*, III (Reykjavik: Hið íslenzka fornritafélag, 1938), pp. vii–xxi. See also T. M. Andersson, *The Problem of Icelandic Saga Origins*, pp. 104–08, and W. Baetke, "Die 'Hœnsa-Þórissaga' " in *Die Isländersaga*, ed. W. Baetke, pp. 293–314.

14. Alfred L. Bock, "Die epische Dreizahl in den Íslendinga sögur: Ein Beitrag zur Beschreibung der isländischen Saga," *Arkiv för nordisk filologi* 37 (1921): 263–313, and 38 (1922): 51–83.

15. Carol J. Clover, "Scene in Saga Composition," *Arkiv för nordisk filologi* 89 (1974): 57–83.

16. Lars Lönnroth, "Rhetorical Persuasion in the Sagas," *Scandinavian Studies* 42 (1970): 157–89, and Richard F. Allen, *Fire and Iron: Critical Approaches to Njáls saga* (Pittsburgh: University of Pittsburgh Press, 1971), pp. 95–116.

17. Lars Lönnroth, "Rhetorical Persuasion in the Sagas," p. 172.

18. Klaus von See, *Germanische Heldensage: Stoffe, Probleme, Methoden* (Frankfurt am Main: Athenäum, 1971), pp. 65–66.

19. The standard edition is that of Jón Jóhannesson, Magnús Finnbogason, and Kristján Eldjárn, *Sturlunga saga*, 2 vols. (Reykjavik: Sturlungaútgáfan, 1946). It includes *Geirmundar þáttr heljarskinns*, *Þorgils saga ok Hafliða*, *Haukdæla þáttr*, *Sturlu saga*, *Prestssaga Guðmundar góða*, *Guðmundar saga dýra*, *Hrafns saga Sveinbjarnarsonar*, *Íslendinga saga*, *Þórðar saga kakala*, *Svínfellinga saga*, *Þorgils saga skarða*, *Sturlu þáttr*, and *Arons saga*. The collection has been translated by Julia McGrew and R. George Thomas, *Sturlunga saga*, 2 vols. (New York: Twayne Publishers, Inc., and the American-Scandinavian Foundation, 1970–74). The following quotations are from this translation with minor orthographic adjustments for consistency.

20. *Sturlunga saga*, I, p. 402; trans., I, p. 306.

21. Ibid., p. 454; trans., p. 360.

22. Ibid., p. 276; trans., p. 170.

23. Ibid., p. 395; trans., p. 299.

24. Ibid., pp. 288, 292, 294, 311, 363, 395, 502. Einar Ól. Sveinsson, *The Age of the Sturlungs: Icelandic Civilization in the Thirteenth Century*, Islandica, 36, trans. Jóhann S. Hannesson (Ithaca: Cornell University Press, 1953), pp. 72–73.

25. *Sturlunga saga*, I, pp. 75, 322–23, 489–94.

26. Ibid., pp. 93, 233–34, 316, 436.

27. Ibid., pp. 85–86; trans., I, p. 83.

28. Sveinsson, *The Age of the Sturlungs*, p. 7.

29. E.g., *Sturlunga saga*, I, pp. 294, 338. Sveinsson, *The Age of the Sturlungs*, pp. 63–65.

30. *Sturlunga saga*, I, pp. 237, 303, 347, 452.

31. Ibid., pp. 106, 111, 235, 240, 241, 243, 303, 304. Sveinsson, *The Age of the Sturlungs*, pp. 45–48.

32. *Sturlunga saga*, I, pp. 417, 423.

33. Ibid., pp. 75, 91, 247, 253, 327–29, 365, 373, 376, 383, 407, 495.

34. S. Nordal, *Snorri Sturluson* (Reykjavik: B. Þorláksson, 1920), pp. 129–33; *Sagalitteraturen*, Nordisk kultur, VIII B (Copenhagen: Schultz, 1953), pp. 270–71; "Formáli" in *Íslenzk fornrit*, II (Reykjavik: Hið íslenzka fornritafélag, 1933), pp. lxiii–lxx. See also the reservations voiced by Bjarni Guðnason, *Um skjöldungasögu* (Reykjavik: Menningarsjóður, 1963), pp. 269–78.

35. Kathryn Hume, "The Thematic Design of *Grettis saga*," *Journal of English and Germanic Philology* 73 (1974): 469–86.

36. *Sturlunga saga*, I, p. 27. The translation is from Peter G. Foote, "Sagnaskemtan: Reykjahólar 1119," *Saga-Book of the Viking Society* 14 (1953–57): 226.

37. The *fornaldarsögur* are printed in *Fornaldar sögur norðurlanda*, ed. Guðni Jónsson, 4 vols. (Reykjavik: Íslendingasagnaútgáfan, 1954; reprinted, 1959). They include *Hrólfs saga kraka ok kappa hans*, *Völsunga saga*, *Ragnars saga loðbrókar*, *Þáttr af Ragnars sonum*, *Norna-Gests þáttr*, *Ásmundar saga kappabana*, *Hervarar saga ok Heiðreks*, *Hálfs saga ok Hálfsrekka*, *Ketils saga hængs*, *Gríms saga loðinkinna*, *Örvar-Odds saga*, *Áns saga bogsveigis*, *Hrómundar saga Gripssonar*, *Yngvars saga víðförla*, *Þorsteins saga Víkingssonar*, *Friþjófs saga ins frækna*, *Sturlaugs saga starfsama*, *Göngu-Hrólfs saga*, *Bósa saga ok Herrauðs*, *Egils saga einhenda ok Ásmundar berserkjabana*, *Sörla saga sterka*, *Illuga saga Gríðarfóstra*, *Gautreks saga*, *Hrólfs saga Gautrekssonar*, *Hjálmþés saga ok Ölvis*, *Hálfdanar saga Eysteinssonar*, *Hálfdanar saga Brönufóstra*, *Þorsteins þáttr bæjarmagns*, *Helga þáttr Þórissonar*.

38. A selection of romances has been edited by Bjarni Vilhjálmsson in *Riddarasögur*, 6 vols. (Reykjavik: Íslendingasagnaútgáfan, 1953–54; reprinted., 1961–62). This edition includes *Saga af Tristram og Ísönd*, *Möttuls saga*, *Bevers saga*, *Ívents saga*, *Partalópa saga*, *Mágus saga jarls*, *Mírmanns saga*, *Sigurðar saga þögla*, *Konráðs saga*, *Samsons saga fagra*, *Elis saga og Rósamundu*, *Flóres saga og Blankiflúr*, *Percevals saga*, *Valvers þáttur*, *Clari saga*, *Flóres saga konungs og sona hans*, *Ála flekks saga*, *Rémundar saga keisarasonar*, *Vilmundar saga viðutan*, *Sigurðar saga fóts*, *Tristrams saga og Ísoddar*, *Drauma-Jóns saga*, *Jarlmanns saga og Hermanns*, and *Sarpidons saga sterka*.

39. King Hákon's sponsorship is referred to in *Tristrams saga*, *Ívents saga*, *Möttuls saga*, and *Elis saga og Rósamundu* and is assumed for other sagas.

40. See Henry Goddard Leach, *Angevin Britain and Scandinavia* (Cambridge, Massachusetts: Harvard University Press, 1921), pp. 165–66; Margaret Schlauch, *Romance in Iceland* (Princeton: Princeton University Press, and New York: American Scandinavian Foundation, 1934), pp. 9–10; Einar Ól. Sveinsson, *Leit eg suður til landa: Ævintýri og helgisögur frá miðöldum* (Reykjavik: Heimskringla, 1944), pp. xv–xvi, and *Viktors saga ok Blávus*, ed. Jónas Kristjánsson (Reykjavik: Handritastofnun Íslands, 1964), p. cxii; Alfred Jokobsen, *Studier i Clarus saga: Til spørsmålet om sagaens norske proveniens*. Acta Universitatis Bergensis. Series Humaniorum Litterarum. Årbok for Universitetet i Bergen. Humanistisk serie. 1963, no. 2 (Bergen: Universitetsforlaget, 1964), pp. 16–33.

41. Leach, *Angevin Britain and Scandinavia*, pp. 201–202, and Schlauch, *Romance in Iceland*, pp. 44–45.

42. Birger Nerman, *Studier över Svärges hedna litteratur* (Uppsala: K. W. Appelberg, 1913), pp. 201–202 (pointed out to Nerman by Hans Sperber); Franz Rolf Schröder, "Motivwanderungen im Mittelalter," *Germanisch-romanische Monatsschrift* 16 (1928): 12; Hermann Pálsson and Paul Edwards, *Legendary Fiction in Medieval Iceland*, Studia Islandica Special Edition (Reykjavik: Prentsmiðjan Leiftur, 1970), pp. 79–84. Three versions of the French fabliau are printed by Jean Rychner in *Contribution à l'étude des fabliaux: Variantes, remaniements, dégradations*. Université de Neuchâtel. Recueil de travaux publiés par la Faculté des lettres, 28 (Neuchâtel and Geneva: Faculté des lettres, 1960), II, pp. 120–35, under the title "De la demoiselle qui ne pouvait ouir parler de foutre."

BIBLIOGRAPHY

The Icelandic Background

Foote, Peter G., and David M. Wilson. *The Viking Achievement: A Survey of the Society and Culture of Early Medieval Scandinavia.* New York: Praeger, 1970.
Kuhn, Hans. *Das alte Island.* Düsseldorf: Eugen Diedericch, 1971.
Turville-Petre, Gabriel. *Origins of Icelandic Literature.* Oxford: Clarendon, 1953.

General Surveys of the Sagas

Baetke, Walter, ed. *Die Isländersaga.* Wege der Forschung, 151. Darmstadt: Wissenschaftliche Buchgesellschaft, 1974. An anthology of some of the more important older articles on the sagas.
Bekker-Nielsen, Hans, Thorkil Damsgaard Olsen, and Ole Widding. *Norrøn fortællekunst: Kapitler af den norsk-islandske middelalderlitteraturs historie.* Copenhagen: Akademisk forlag, 1965. Individual essays introducing the various periods and categories of sagas.
Nordal, Sigurður. *Sagalitteraturen,* Nordisk kultur, 8B. Copenhagen: Schultz, 1953. Pp. 180–273.
Schier, Kurt. *Sagaliteratur.* Stuttgart: Metzler, 1970. The best concise introduction to all varieties of sagas.
Sveinsson, Einar Ól. *Dating the Icelandic Sagas: An Essay in Method.* London: Viking Society for Northern Research, 1958.

Bibliography

Bekker-Nielsen, Hans (and Thorkil Damsgaard Olsen from 1963 to 1967), eds. *Bibliography of Old Norse-Icelandic Studies.* Copenhagen: Munksgaard, 1963–. The essential annual bibliography.
———. *Old Norse-Icelandic Studies: A Select Bibliography.* Toronto: University of Toronto Press, 1967.
Hannesson, Jóhann S. *The Sagas of Icelanders (Íslendinga sögur): A Supplement to Islandica I and XXIV.* Islandica, 38. Ithaca: Cornell University Press, 1957.
Hermannsson, Halldór. *Bibliography of the Icelandic Sagas and Minor Tales.* Islandica, 1. Ithaca: Cornell University Press, 1908.
———. *Bibliography of the Sagas of the Kings of Norway and Related Sagas and Tales.* Islandica, 3. Ithaca: Cornell University Press, 1910.
———. *Bibliography of the Mythical-Heroic Sagas.* Islandica, 5. Ithaca: Cornell University Press, 1912.
———. *The Sagas of Icelanders (Íslendinga sögur): A Supplement to Bibliography of the Icelandic Sagas and Minor Tales.* Islandica, 24. Ithaca: Cornell University Press, 1935.
———. *The Sagas of the Kings (Konunga sögur) and the Mythical-Heroic Sagas (Fornaldar sögur).* Islandica, 26. Ithaca: Cornell University Press, 1937.

Kings' Sagas

There is no generally accessible introduction to the kings' sagas. The basic information may be found in Kurt Schier's *Sagaliteratur,* pp. 9–33, and Thorkil Damsgaard Olsen's chapter "Kongekrøniker og kongesagaer" in *Norrøn fortællekunst,* pp. 42–71. The following are the more important specialized treatises:

Aðalbjarnarson, Bjarni. *Om de norske kongers sagaer.* Skrifter utgitt av Det Norske

Videnskaps-Akademi i Oslo. II. Hist.-filos. kl., 4 (1936). Oslo: I kommisjon hos Jacob Dybwad, 1937. Pp. 1-236.

Beyschlag, Siegfried. *Konungasögur: Untersuchungen zur Königssaga bis Snorri. Die älteren Übersichtswerke samt Ynglingasaga.* Bibliotheca Arnamagnæana, 8. Copenhagen: Munksgaard, 1950.

Ellehøj, Svend. *Studier over den ældste norrone historieskrivning.* Copenhagen: Munksgaard, 1965.

Louis-Jensen, Jonna. *Kongesagastudier: Kompilationen Hulda-Hrokkinskinna.* Bibliotheca Arnamagnæana, 32. Copenhagen: Reitzel, 1977.

Nordal, Sigurður. *Om Olaf den helliges saga: En kritisk undersøgelse.* Copenhagen: Gad, 1914.

──────. *Snorri Sturluson.* Reykjavik: B. Þorláksson, 1920.

Storm, Gustav. *Snorre Sturlassöns historieskrivning: En kritisk undersögelse.* Copenhagen: Bianco Lunos Bogtrykkeri, 1873.

Family Sagas

Andersson, Theodore M. *The Icelandic Family Saga: An Analytic Reading.* Harvard Studies in Comparative Literature, 28. Cambridge, Mass.: Harvard University Press, 1967. An attempt to define the structure and rhetoric of the family sagas.

Einarsson, Bjarni. *Skáldasögur: Um uppruna og eðli ástaskáldasagnanna fornu.* Reykjavik: Bókaútgáfa Menningarsjóðs, 1961. Casts doubt on the authenticity of the skaldic verse in the "skald sagas" and emphasizes the artistic inventiveness of the authors.

Hallberg, Peter. *Den isländska sagan.* Stockholm: Svenska bokförlaget, 1956. English translation by Paul Schach. *The Icelandic Saga.* Lincoln: University of Nebraska Press, 1962. Conveniently available as a Bison paperback.

Ker, William Paton. *Epic and Romance: Essays on Medieval Literature.* London: Macmillan, 1896. Reprinted New York: Dover Paperback, 1957. Contains a classical essay on the sagas, pp. 179-284.

Steblin-Kamenskij, M. I. *The Saga Mind.* Translated by Kenneth H. Ober. Odense: Odense University Press, 1973. Concerned chiefly with the saga authors' view of historical truth.

Sturlunga saga

Sveinsson, Einar Ól. *The Age of the Sturlungs: Icelandic Civilization in the Thirteenth Century.* Islandica, 36. Translated by Jóhann S. Hannesson. Ithaca: Cornell University Press, 1953.

Legendary Sagas

Hume, Kathryn. "The Thematic Design of *Grettis saga.*" *Journal of English and Germanic Philology* 73 (1974): 469-86. Comments on differences in outlook between family saga and legendary saga.

Mundt, Marina. "Omkring dragekampen i Ragnars saga loðbrókar." *Arv* 27 (1971): 121-40. Studies some types of narrative degeneration in the legendary sagas.

Pálsson, Hermann, and Paul Edwards. *Legendary Fiction in Medieval Iceland.* Studia Islandica Special Edition. Reykjavik: Prentsmiðjan Leiftur, 1970.

Reuschel, Helga. *Untersuchungen über Stoff und Stil der Fornaldarsaga.* Bühl-Baden: Konkordia A. G., 1933.

Romantic Sagas

Halvorsen, Eyvind Fjeld. *The Norse Version of the Chanson de Roland.* Bibliotheca

Arnamagnæana, 19. Copenhagen: Munksgaard, 1959. Contains an introductory chapter on the romantic sagas in general.
Leach, Henry Goddard. *Angevin Britain and Scandinavia*. Harvard Studies in Comparative Literature, 6. Cambridge, Mass.: Harvard University Press, 1921.
Meissner, Rudolf. *Die Strengleikar: Ein Beitrag zur Geschichte der altnordischen Prosaliteratur*. Halle a. S.: Niemeyer, 1902.
Schlauch, Margaret. *Romance in Iceland*. Princeton: Princeton University Press, and New York: American Scandinavian Foundation, 1934.
Sveinsson, Einar Ólafur. "Viktors saga ok Blávus: Sources and Characteristics." In *Viktors saga ok Blávus*. Edited by Jónas Kristjánsson, pp. cix–ccix. Reykjavik: Handritastofnun Íslands, 1964. A model analysis of one romantic saga.

Saga Origins

Andersson, Theodore M. *The Problem of Icelandic Saga Origins: A Historical Survey*. Yale Germanic Studies, 1. New Haven: Yale University Press, 1964.
Baetke, Walter. "Über die Entstehung der Isländersagas." *Berichte über die Verhandlungen der Sächsischen Akademie der Wissenschaften zu Leipzig, Philol.-hist. Kl.*, 102/5 (1956): 1–108.
Heusler, Andreas. "Die Anfänge der isländischen Saga." *Abhandlungen der Königlich Preussischen Akademie der Wissenschaften, Phil.-hist. Kl.*, pp. 1–87. Berlin, 1913. Reprinted in Heusler's *Kleine Schriften*. Edited by Stefan Sonderegger, II, pp. 388–460. Berlin: de Gruyter, 1969.
Liestøl, Knut. *Upphavet til den islendske ættesaga*. Oslo: Aschehoug, 1929. English translation by A. G. Jayne. *The Origin of the Icelandic Family Sagas*. Oslo: Aschehoug, and Cambridge, Mass.: Harvard University Press, 1930.
Scovazzi, Marco. *La saga di Hrafnkell e il problema delle saghe islandesi*. Arona: Paideia, 1960.

Individual Sagas

Egils saga: Einarsson, Bjarni. *Litterære forudsætninger for Egils saga*. Reykjavik: Stofnun Árna Magnússonar, 1975.
Fóstbrœðra saga: Kristjánsson, Jónas. *Um Fóstbræðrasögu*. Reykjavik: Stofnun Árna Magnússonar, 1972.
Hrafnkels saga: Nordal, Sigurður. *Hrafnkels saga freysgoða*. Translated by R. George Thomas. Cardiff: University of Wales Press, 1958; Pálsson, Hermann. *Art and Ethics in Hrafnkel's Saga*. Copenhagen: Munksgaard, 1971; Heinemann, Fredrik J. "*Hrafnkels saga freysgoða* and Type-Scene Analysis." *Scandinavian Studies* 46 (1974): 102–19; Hofmann, Dietrich. "Hrafnkels und Hallfreðs Traum: Zur Verwendung mündlicher Tradition in der Hrafnkels saga Freysgoða." *Skandinavistik* 6 (1976): 19–36.
Laxdœla saga: Madelung, A. Margaret Arent. *The Laxdœla saga: Its Structural Patterns*. University of North Carolina Studies in the Germanic Languages and Literatures, 74. Chapel Hill: University of North Carolina Press, 1972; Heller, Rolf. "Die Laxdœla saga: Die literarische Schöpfung eines Isländers des 13. Jahrhunderts." *Abhandlungen der Sächsischen Akademie der Wissenschaften zu Leipzig, Philol.-hist. Kl.*, 65/1 (1976): 5–152.
Njáls saga: Allen, Richard F. *Fire and Iron: Critical Approaches to Njáls saga*. Pittsburgh: University of Pittsburgh Press, 1971; Lönnroth, Lars. *Njáls saga: A Critical Introduction*. Berkeley: University of California Press, 1976.

A Few Saga Translations

Edwards, Paul, and Hermann Pálsson, trans. *Arrow-Odd: A Medieval Novel*. New

York: New York University Press, and London: University of London Press Ltd, 1970.

Fell, Christine, trans. *Egils saga Skallagrímssonar*. London: Dent, 1975.

Fox, Denton, and Hermann Pálsson, trans. *Grettir's Saga*. Toronto: University of Toronto Press, 1974.

Hieatt, Constance, trans. *Karlamagnús saga: The Saga of Charlemagne and His Heroes*, I–II. Pontifical Institute of Mediaeval Studies: Mediaeval Sources in Translation, 13 and 17. Toronto: The Pontifical Institute of Mediaeval Studies, 1975.

Hollander, Lee M., trans. *Heimskringla: History of the Kings of Norway* by Snorri Sturluson. Austin: University of Texas Press for the American-Scandinavian Foundation, 1964.

Johnston, George, trans. *The Saga of Gisli the Outlaw*. Notes and an Introductory Essay by Peter Foote. Toronto: University of Toronto Press, 1963. Paperback reprint, 1973.

Jones, Gwyn, trans. *Eirik the Red and Other Icelandic Sagas*. London: Oxford University Press, 1961. Includes, among others, *Hœnsa-Þóris saga, Hrafnkels saga*, and *Hrólfs saga kraka*.

————. *Egil's saga*. Syracuse: Syracuse University Press, 1960.

Magnusson, Magnus, and Hermann Pálsson, trans. *Laxdæla saga*. Harmondsworth: Penguin Books, 1969.

————, trans. *Njal's Saga*. Harmondsworth: Penguin Books, 1960.

McGrew, Julia, and R. George Thomas, trans. *Sturlunga saga*. 2 vols. New York: Twayne Publishers, Inc., and the American-Scandinavian Foundation, 1970–74.

Pálsson, Hermann, and Paul Edwards. *Egil's saga*. Harmondsworth: Penguin Books, 1976.

Schach, Paul, trans. *The Saga of Tristram and Ísönd*. Lincoln: University of Nebraska Press, 1973.

8   Irish Saga Literature

Seán Ó Coileáin

The subject of this essay is Irish literature, particularly prose literature, prior to the twelfth century. The reason for a division at this point will become apparent in the course of the discussion. Occasional references will be made to the later period where considered relevant as, for instance, in connection with the argument concerning the orality or non-orality of the early literature. The fact that so little work has been done in the field means that we are often dependent on the individual judgments of one or two scholars rather than on an accepted consensus of opinion. It is, then, better to begin with the peculiar problems that confront the student, rather than to assume that Irish studies has reached the level of development which would allow us to make general statements of the same order as those made in other areas of epic scholarship.

Translation and Study of Sagas

The immediate problem which confronts the student of Irish saga literature is its inaccessibility. Although most of the relevant texts have been translated into English, these translations remain buried in learned journals, and the only comprehensive collection readily available is the recently reprinted *Ancient Irish Tales,* compiled from the journals and elsewhere by T. P. Cross and C. H. Slover. Even these translations are largely unreadable except by the dedicated student, as they are written in a strange kind of Germanic dialect which reflects a concern for grammatical accuracy rather than for literary expression, or even common sense. Frank O'Connor in the second volume of his autobiography, *My Father's Son,* which contains some very lively sketches of a number of Irish scholars, repeats the story of how Professor Osborn Bergin was once asked by a student who was exasperated with his literal translations of the later bardic poetry, "But what is it all about?"[1] Bergin's translations are by no means the worst, but the point was a valid one. The modern student who cannot read the texts in the original might well be forgiven for asking the

172

same question about the saga literature if he is not fortunate enough to stumble upon one of the few readable translations available. For instance, the twelfth-century version of the beginning of the most famous early Irish tales, *Táin Bó Cuailnge* (The Cattle Raid of Cooley), appears as follows in *Ancient Irish Tales:*

> Once on a time, when Ailill and Medb had spread their royal bed in Cruachan, the stronghold of Connacht, such was the pillow-talk betwixt them:
> Said Ailill, "True is the saying, O woman, 'She is a well-off woman that is a rich man's wife.'"
> "Aye, that she is," answered the wife, "but wherefore say'st thou so?"
> "For this," Ailill replied, "that thou art this day better off than the day that first I took thee."
> Then answered Medb, "As well-off was I before I ever saw thee."
> "It was a wealth, indeed, we never heard nor knew of," said Ailill, "but a woman's wealth was all that thou hadst, and foes from lands next thine were wont to carry off the spoil and booty that they took from thee."[2]

At this point one might well give up, in the belief that the early Irish carried on extremely boring conversations, and that their saga literature has been greatly overrated.

Concern for literature as such has not had an important place in the short tradition of Irish scholarship which has never quite recovered from its beginnings as a branch of the study of Indo-European linguistics. Editions of texts are still prefaced by a discussion of the various manuscript versions, with the inevitable attempt to trace the *Urtext* and varying degrees of linguistic analysis. Literary criticism is not yet quite respectable, and it has been largely left to the enthusiastic amateur. There have been some notable exceptions. Kuno Meyer, although a German and a linguist, has produced some very fine translations of early Irish poetry. Robin Flower, an Englishman whose spiritual home was the Irish-speaking Great Blasket island off the coast of Kerry, has left us *The Irish Tradition* in which sensitive and knowledgeable criticism is illustrated by his own translations. In our own day, James Carney has managed to combine scholarship with a mature literary sense. But the most successful translator of the early poetry has been Frank O'Connor, who received no formal academic training. He has also managed to write one of the major works on early Irish literature, *The Backward Look*. As critic he was a sort of Irish Boswell who attached himself to a number of Irish scholars and published opinions that they would not dare publish. His work is somewhat uneven: on occasion he seems wildly astray, but will then recover with an inspired guess. Seán O'Faoláin, who has himself translated some of the early Irish verse, comments on this unevenness in his autobiography, *Vive Moi:*

> I do not think he ever reasoned out anything. He was like a man who takes a

machine gun to a shooting gallery. Everybody falls flat on his face, the proprietor at once takes to the hills, and when it is all over you cautiously peep up and find that he has wrecked the place but got three perfect bull's eyes.[3]

Undoubtedly the major work of prose translation has been that of another amateur, Thomas Kinsella, whose *The Táin* not only is eminently readable in itself but also brings coherence to an entire cycle of tales to be discussed below. O'Connor and Kinsella are both creative writers of some distinction—although it may seem strange that O'Connor, the prose writer, should have translated the poetry, and Kinsella, the poet, the prose—and it is not surprising that their translations from the Irish were successful. They also had the advantage of beginning with a feeling for the work of literature, rather than a sense of admiration for the grammatical contortions of early Irish. Kinsella's translation of the beginning of "The Cattle Raid of Cooley" may be compared with Dunn's quoted above:

> Once when the royal bed was laid out for Ailill and Medb in Cruachan fort in Connacht, they had this talk on the pillows:
> "It is true what they say, love," Ailill said, "it is well for the wife of a wealthy man."
> "True enough," the woman said. "What put that in your mind?"
> "It struck me," Ailill said, "how much better off you are today than the day I married you."
> "I was well enough off without you," Medb said.
> "Then your wealth was something I didn't know or hear much about," Ailill said. "Except for your woman's things, and the neighbouring enemies making off with loot and plunder."[4]

Sagas and Oral Tradition

Considering the general lack of attention paid to it, it is not surprising that many fundamental questions regarding the nature of early Irish literature remain unanswered and even unasked. One question that has been asked and vigorously disputed is the relationship of the texts as we have them to oral tradition. No one would seriously question the fact that there *was* an oral tradition which, indeed, has persisted to our own time. Rudolf Thurneysen, who has written the major survey of early Irish hero tales, *Die irische Helden- und Königsage,* chose to ignore it altogether and concerned himself only with manuscript transmission. Gerard Murphy, on the other hand, regarded these tales, or at least some of them, as having been written down from oral narration and attributed their imperfections to difficulties of recording. He notes that:

> Several of the best manuscripts texts begin well, but tail off badly as the story proceeds. This strange procedure can be easily explained on the hypothesis of recording from oral recitation. Everyone who has tried to record Irish folktales

from peasant reciters before the introduction of recording machines has noticed the curtailment and imperfection which tend gradually to creep into the recorded narrative owing to the growing weariness of the reciter.[5]

He proceeds to suggest that the narrator begins the tale in his usual way, but then, frustrated by the restrictions imposed upon him by the scribe, gradually begins to summarize events which he would normally have described in much greater detail. He quotes Radloff's experience as a collector of Tatar epic poetry in support of this phenomenon, but it should be noted that the experience of Albert Lord was quite the reverse, at least regarding the better narrators:

> From the point of view of verse-making, dictation carries no great advantage to the singer, but from that of song-making it may be instrumental in producing the finest and longest of songs. For it extends almost indefinitely the time limit of performance.... The "ordinary" singer in a mediocre tradition will not have enough material at his command nor the imagination to avail himself of it. The extraordinary singer will enjoy the opportunity to the full.[6]

Myles Dillon proposes a solution closely related to Murphy's. He too notices the shortness of many of the early texts which, he deduces, cannot represent their oral form. (He does not explain why he thinks that an oral form must be postulated.) He continues: "I think it probable that the oldest texts are summaries of the story and that the form was given by the *fili* in actual performance and was his personal achievement."[7] It is not quite clear what he means by this, although I fear that he may have thought of the narrator as being rather like a modern orator speaking with the aid of notes. A similar statement is made by Séamus Ó Duilearga (Delargy): "The literary sagas in the form in which they have been preserved to us in the vellums of the twelfth to the fifteenth century are really tale summaries only, containing all the essential framework and detail, which the *sgélaige* [storyteller] expanded when reciting the tales to an audience."[8]

Either this is badly expressed—it is not correct to speak of a storyteller expanding written texts if he is not using these texts in his performance—or we have here a phenomenon which is completely at variance with the essence of oral tradition. He later states: "The story-teller of the eighth century as well as his successor, the Gaelic *sgéalaí* of to-day, depended upon mnemonics and memorized tale-synopses, which they expanded later when called upon, impressing on their narrative all the skill derived from long training and experience."[9]

Whatever of mnemonics, it is hardly true to say that the storyteller of today, at least a genuine one, depends on "memorized tale-synopses," unless we understand this to mean an unconscious appreciation of structure which is not the meaning that Ó Duilearga intends. Clearly the idea that the early texts were closely related to oral tradition has led to some unlikely theories in its defence.

This brings us to the crucial point in the discussion. In a sense, the position of the proponents of the oral theory of early Irish literature was unreal, as they never quite defined what they meant by it. Reading them now one finds no sense of the essential difference between written and oral composition. If this difference is not seen to exist, then there is little point in continuing the argument, and the question of whether a scribe wrote a tale from the dictation of an oral narrator or whether he composed and wrote it himself becomes mere quibbling. The leading Irish folklore scholar of the day, Ó Duilearga, seems to have regarded the ideal storyteller as a sort of tape-recorder, and he praises one of his informants for his fidelity to the text as he had heard it: "He never made the slightest change in a story, always telling it as it had been told to him, neither lengthening nor shortening it."[10]

He relents a little elsewhere, allowing the narrator a slight measure of freedom in expression, although one feels that preferably he should not make too much use of it: "The tale should be passed on as it has been received unaltered, not in regard to language, but in form and plot."[11]

Here memory is everything, and the highest form of artistry is the exact reproduction of the "original"; there is no suggestion that one might compose within the tradition and thereby continue and renew it. Instead of changing written tales to oral ones, the final effect of this concept is to change oral tales to written ones. Although a great deal of fieldwork was being carried out in Ireland at the time, I know of no experiment to test the degree to which a storyteller reproduced a tale as narrated to him or the variation which might occur in a tale as told by the same narrator on two or more occasions. It may have been thought unnecessary to do so, and in any case the system of analysis was directed outwards towards the international type and motif rather than inwards upon itself. The end result was that the living oral tradition was not in itself properly understood, and any attempt to explain an unknown past in terms of the partially-known present was ultimately doomed to failure. Unknown to Irish scholars, Milman Parry, in his analysis of Homeric and South Slavic traditions, had already shown how an oral theory of early literature could be buttressed by the actual practice of oral singers in his own day. It seems that any valid argument regarding the orality or otherwise of early Irish literature will ultimately have to proceed along the same lines, while not neglecting the problems of translating and redefining methodologies devised for other literatures. Only then will scientific proof take the place of preconceived notions and the arguments become internationally acceptable.

James Carney would admit a general oral background to early Irish literature, but would stop far short of conceding that the texts were actually recorded from oral narration:

Early Irish saga literature shows in its vocabulary that it was given its present form well within the Christian period. Without any doubt this literature was based in part upon an oral tradition going back to the remote pre-Christian past. But the traditional element is often a mere nucleus because the Christian authors, in presenting the pre-Christian past, drew not only on native material but upon their total literary experience....

The general theory put forward in this book [*Studies in Irish Literature and History*] is as simple as this: that early Irish written work has the character of written work. It is a literature based in part upon oral tradition, but the assumption that it is oral tradition in any very full sense cannot be made.[12]

If Carney's position now seems the more credible, this is at least partially due to the fact that his opponents knew of no exact discipline of oral scholarship which could be applied to the texts in question. The proponents of the oral theory were eventually forced back upon mere statements of opinion, and such "proof" as they were able to provide, such as Murphy's argument that tales which begin well and finish badly were probably written down from oral dictation, now seems very questionable. It is true that, as Murphy points out, " 'telling' and 'hearing' stories is commonly referred to" in the texts themselves, but we know from later tradition that stories were often read aloud to audiences, and while words such as 'telling' or 'hearing' might be applied to this process it certainly is not oral tradition in the true sense. (The degree to which literary stories might enter oral tradition by this means, and the subsequent changes they might undergo, is a separate and equally complicated question.)

We know also, however, that the later bardic poetry (ca. 1200–1650) was composed in darkened rooms. The most complete description of a bardic school is that contained in the *Memoirs of the Marquis of Clonrickarde*, first published in 1722, which, though it post-dates the events it describes, may be regarded as generally accurate. In any case, it is the only comprehensive account we have. The relevant section reads:

The Structure was a snug, low Hut, and Beds in it at convenient Distances, each within a small Apartment without much Furniture of any kind, save only a Table, some Seats, and a Conveniency for Cloaths to hang upon. No Windows to let in the Day, nor any Light at all us'd but that of Candles, and these brought in at a proper Season only. The Students upon thorough Examination being first divided into Classes, wherein a regard was had to every one's Age, Genius, and the Schooling had before, if any at all, or otherwise, the Professors (one or more as there was occasion) gave a Subject suitable to the Capacity of each Class, determining the number of Rhimes, and clearing what was to be chiefly observed therein as to Syllables, Quartans, Concord, Correspondence, Termination and Union, each of which were restrain'd by peculiar rules. The said Subject (either one or more as aforesaid) having been given over Night they work'd it apart each by himself upon his own Bed, the whole next Day in the Dark, till at a certain hour in the Night, Lights being brought in, they committed it to writing. Being afterwards dress'd and come together into a large room, where the Masters waited, each Scholar gave in his Performance, which being corrected or approv'd of (according as it requir'd) either the same or fresh subjects were given against the next Day.[13]

The practice of composing in the dark is confirmed by references in the poems themselves, and we even find one poet reproving another for disregarding the convention and composing poetry on horseback. He appeals to the authority of the great poets of the past, and defends his own preference for the traditional method of composition by stating that it keeps his mind from wandering and maintains the quality of his verse. The practice was no doubt an ancient one and relevant to the earlier period also, but it raises certain problems. For instance, we know that these poets were literate, and elsewhere the *Memoirs* state that "The Qualifications first requir'd were reading well, writing the Mother-tongue, and a strong Memory."[14] Is this then oral composition proper, or merely composition accompanied by memorization and a consequent fixed text? Composition without the aid of writing materials may still be literary in concept and structure, just as a literary text so remains even when memorized and recited. Certainly one does not find in different manuscript versions of bardic poems the degree of variation one would expect in true oral poetry, that is, poetry that was re-composed at each separate performance. It would be interesting to examine the chevilles in which bardic poetry abounds in order to determine whether they form a formulaic system corresponding to that which Milman Parry has shown to exist in Homeric verse. Initially it would seem that in this instance, composition in the dark is an example of the notorious conservatism of Irish tradition insisting on the appearance of oral composition long after it had ceased to be a necessity, or even a fact, at this level of society. True oral composition continued among the illiterate, but we can only guess at its content, for in Ireland as elsewhere, no attention was paid to it until the nineteenth century.

The methodology of formulaic analysis developed by Milman Parry, and extended by Albert Lord to include thematic analysis as well, might also be applied directly to the earlier literature. Of the two complementary methods, analysis by theme is the more relevant to the Irish material since all of the texts consist primarily of prose, and the concept of the formula, dependent as it is on a fixed metrical situation, can only be applied scientifically to verse. But many of the prose tales are interspersed with passages of verse, the most interesting of which are the "rhetorics," passages of archaic verse of which only a few have yet been satisfactorily reconstructed and explained. Similar verse passages form an early stratum in the law tracts which, we are told, were preserved "by the joint memory of the ancients, the transmission from one ear to another, the chanting of the poets,"[15] before being committed to writing. These tracts are as old as anything in Irish (with the exception of the *Ogam* inscriptions, mere names which cannot be classed as literature), and D. A. Binchy has suggested that they were first written down "in the seventh or perhaps even in the sixth century."[16]

The Nature of Saga Literature

Although the problem of whether early Irish literature is essentially literary or oral is an important one, even more important is the concept of what literature is in this context. Even if we succeed in divesting ourselves of the usual romantic notions of what literature should be, and of creations such as Gray's bard ("Loose his beard and hoary hair/Stream'd, like a meteor, to the troubled air") or phrases such as "the Celtic twilight"—the twilight being entirely in the minds of those who popularized the phrase—it still requires a great effort of the imagination to appreciate the nature of the tradition. This tradition is best summarized by Dubhaltach Mac Fir Bhisigh, one of the last and greatest of the old school of native learning which was rapidly disappearing as he wrote in the seventeenth century: "As to the historians of Ireland, indeed, scarcely any difference is found in ancient times between them and experts in law and the class called men of art [i.e., poets] today, for at that time the learned men of Ireland were often of one school."[17]

The Irish man of learning was not, then, simply a littérateur, and indeed literature as we understand it today forms a very small part of the great medieval manuscripts in which the early material has been preserved. The earliest of these manuscripts, *Lebor na hUidre* (The Book of the Dun Cow), was compiled about the year 1100, although at least one item of its contents dates from the end of the sixth century: this is the *Amra Choluim Chille* which was probably composed on the death of Colum Cille in Iona in 597 and which continues to be an embarrassment to modern scholars because of its difficulty. We are then in a position where tales, which in their written form may date from anywhere between the sixth to the eleventh century and which may have had a previous oral existence, are available to us only as copied into manuscripts, none of which is earlier than the year 1100. This causes a great many linguistic, literary, and historical problems, and often results in widely differing opinions as to the date of composition of the original. The question of whether the concept of an original is relevant at all depends on whether we suppose a given text to be essentially a written or an oral one.

The compilers of the early manuscripts, such as "The Book of the Dun Cow" or the so-called "Book of Leinster" (ca. 1150), or of such later tomes as the "Book of Lecan," the "Yellow Book of Lecan," the "Book of Uí Mhaine," the "Book of Ballymote," and the *Leabhar Breac* (Speckled Book), all of which date from the end of the fourteenth century or the beginning of the fifteenth century, were not concerned with the literature of entertainment, which is not to say that some of it at least is not entertaining. More important to them were such ponderous works as the *Dinnshenchas* (i.e., The Lore of Famous Places), which set out the traditions relating to the famous places of Ireland, historical or pseudo-historical works such as the *Lebor Gabála* (The Book of Invasions), genealogies, regnal lists, and even religious material such as *Saltair na Rann* (The Psalter of Quatrains).

In one respect it is unfortunate that the bulk of the literature, for such it was held to be, has been ignored in favor of the occasional lyric which figures prominently in the modern anthologies, although it may occur only in the margin of the original manuscript, a mere idle thought briefly interrupting the serious work of scholarship. The fact that we are grateful for this human relief does not justify us in distorting a tradition which was largely concerned with more serious matters. Even if we finally choose to ignore the mainstream of tradition, we should at least be aware of it. In the case of the sagas it would be difficult not to, for they intrude into what we might now like to regard as pure literature. For instance, one cannot read the most famous of the early Irish sagas, "The Cattle Raid of Cooley," referred to above, without being struck by the seemingly inordinate concern for place names, which reflects the author's training in the *Dinnshenchas*. Similarly it is not possible to deal adequately with the tales relating to the early Irish kings without a knowledge of the historical ramifications; while these tales are not strictly historical, they share a common framework with the historical sources.

Ideally, then, all the traditional materials form a unit and, while one finds a good deal of contradiction and variation in practice, this becomes meaningful only when viewed in the context of the whole tradition. Here the task of the student of literature is made still more difficult by the fact that this secondary material is, on the whole, even more inaccessible than the literature proper. Much work remains to be done in providing even proper diplomatic editions of primary sources such as annals and genealogies. The amount of commentary available is small, although generally of a high standard. Indeed, part of the problem is that the standard has been too high and scholars too intolerant of each other's errors. Celtic scholarship in general has been notorious for personal acrimony, and, as a consequence of this, much useful work has been suppressed by scholars fearful of making the slightest mistake. While many specialized articles have been written, the overall shape of early Irish civilization has yet to emerge. The student of literature, then, is in the impossible position of being advised to consult a context which is largely non-existent. It is with an awareness of the problem rather than the solution to it that we now turn to what is more usually regarded simply as literature.

It is usual now to divide the tales into cycles with such titles as the Mythological Cycle, the Heroic (or Ulster) Cycle, the Historical Cycles, the Fionn (or Fenian) Cycle. These categories are modern ones, for the traditional division was by subject, ignoring the time frame in which the action is set. Two lists of these early tales are extant, and Thurneysen has suggested that both derive from a list compiled in the tenth century. This provides us with a useful *terminus ante quem* when the title of a given tale occurs in both lists. The division here is, as already stated, by subject, and the tales are arranged under such titles as *Tána* (Cattle Raids), *Togla* (Destructions), *Echtrai* (Ad-

ventures), *Immrama* (Voyages), *Serca* (Love Tales), and *Catha* (Battles).
Many of these tales have been lost in the meantime, and we now know them
only by title or by secondary reference; many others have survived only in
mangled or fragmentary form. Considering the relative lateness of even the
earliest manuscripts and a turbulent history, we should feel grateful for what
we have. In a fascinating paper entitled "On the Colophons and Marginalia of
Irish Scribes," Charles Plummer brings the faithful custodians of the literature to life.[18] We find one scribe complaining of his poor circumstances:
"Twenty nights from to-day will Easter Monday, and I am cold and weary,
without fire or covering." Another rescues a single miserable evening from
the past with the note: "It is the Friday before Christmas to-day, and it is
pouring heavily now at the beginning of night." Others in less resigned mood
curse the poorness of their writing materials, and one later scribe chafes at the
unreasonable restrictions of his religion: "On my word it is great torment to
be keeping the Friday of the Passion on water, with the excellent wine which
there is in the house with us." Complaints about the hardships of their life are
commonplace, yet they continued confident of the value of what they were
doing, aware also, as they often note, that their work would outlive them and
that it was their duty to preserve the past for future generations. It is difficult
now to fully appreciate this wholly unselfish and traditional frame of mind.
The most famous of the colophons, however, was written by a man who was
not altogether sure of his place in tradition, or even of the tradition itself. This
is the man who on completing his transcription of the "Book of Leinster"
version of "The Cattle Raid of Cooley" writes:

> But I who have written this story, or rather this fable, give no credence to the
> various incidents related in it. For some things in it are the deceptions of demons,
> others poetic figments; some are probable, others improbable; while still others
> are intended for the delectation of foolish men.[19]

It is the first critical voice in Irish literature.

Fortunately for the survival of the literature, such crises of conscience were
rare even for clerics, and generally these scribes were considerably less
squeamish than some modern editors, who, if they give them at all, leave the
salacious passages untranslated or translate them into Latin, that most chaste
and sobering of languages.

Mythological Cycle

The principal text for the Irish Mythological Cycle is *Cath Maige Tuired*
(The Battle of Moytura) which describes the conflict between the Tuatha Dé
Danann (The People of the Goddess Danu) and the Fomorians, and in doing
so introduces virtually the entire Irish pantheon. Some idea of the mood of the
tale and the character of the Dagda (Good God) who appears on the side of the

Tuatha Dé Danann may be obtained from the following passage:

> So the Dagda went to the camp of the Fomorians and asked them for a truce of
> battle. This was granted to him as he asked. Porridge is then made for him by the
> Fomorians, and this was done to mock him, for great was his love of porridge.
> They fill for him the king's cauldron, five fists deep, into which went four score
> gallons of new milk and a like quantity of meal and fat. Goats and sheep and
> swine are put into it, and they are all boiled together with the porridge. They are
> spilt for him into a hole in the ground, and Indech told him that he would be put
> to death unless he consumed it all; he should eat his fill so that he might not
> reproach the Fomorians with inhospitality.
>
> Then the Dagda took up his ladle, and it was big enough for a man and a
> woman to lie in the middle of it. These are the bits that were in it, halves of salted
> swine and a quarter of lard.[20]

As the bloated Dagda staggers away from this revolting smorgasbord he
encounters the daughter of Indech. This meeting is described in a passage
omitted by the editor partly on account of its difficulty but also for reasons of
prudery. A central feature is an account of the difficulties occasioned by the
Dagda's protruding stomach.

This type of grotesque description is very much different from what we find
in another important tale in this cycle, *Tochmarc Étaíne* (The Wooing of
Étaín). Although less valuable for the information it provides on mythology, it
is a much more coherent tale whose haunting diaphanous beauty is heightened
by the otherworldly atmosphere. The following passage describes how Fuamnach, wife of Midir, who has just rejected her in favor of Étaín, takes her
revenge:

> When Étaín sat down on the chair in the middle of the house, Fuamnach struck
> her with a rod of scarlet quickentree, and she turned into a pool of water in the
> middle of the house . . . . After that Midir was without a wife.
>
> The heat of the fire and the air and the seething of the ground aided the water
> so that the pool that was in the middle of the house turned into a worm and after
> that the worm became a purple fly. It was as big as a man's head, the comeliest in
> the land. Sweeter than pipes and harps and horns was the sound of her voice and
> the hum of her wings. Her eyes would shine like precious stones in the dark. The
> fragrance and the bloom of her would turn away hunger and thirst from anyone
> around whom she would go. The spray of the drops she shed from her wings
> would cure all sickness and disease and plague in any one round whom she would
> go. She used to attend Midir and go round about his land with him, as he went.
> To listen to her and gaze upon her would nourish hosts in gatherings and as-
> semblies in camps. Midir knew that it was Étaín that was in that shape, and so
> long as that fly was attending upon him, he never took to himself a wife, and the
> sight of her would nourish him. He would fall asleep at her humming, and
> whenever any one approached who did not love him, she would awaken him.[21]

The study of Irish mythology is still in its incipient stages and native scholars, on the whole, have tended to avoid it. One important exception was T. F. O'Rahilly who had an encyclopedic knowledge of Irish tradition but no proper theoretical framework to which he might refer. Ultimately, the school to which he belonged was the discredited one of Max Müller, peopled with solar deities, although he avoided the worst absurdities of Müller and his disciples, and even made bold to criticize them on occasion. The impression one gets now in reading his *Early Irish History and Mythology* is of an immense wasted talent. More recent attempts to interpret Irish mythology according to the tripartite system of Georges Dumézil have not been altogether successful; here we often find the reverse of O'Rahilly's problem, too much system and too little acquaintance with the sources. The most successful studies along these lines are those of Jan de Vries, particularly his *Keltische Religion,* and of Alwyn and Brinley Rees whose *Celtic Heritage* generated a great deal of interest, if not altogether a revolution in Irish studies. It was and remains the only comprehensive work in English which attempts to relate Dumézil's Indo-European framework to Celtic, particularly Irish, materials. De Vries, for instance, would see the battle of Moytura, referred to above, as one between the forces of Dumézil's third function (i.e., fertility), represented by the Fomorians and those of the first and second function (i.e., sovereignty and force) represented by the Tuatha Dé Danann. In a recent work, entitled *Celtic Mythology,* Proinsias Mac Cana gives a balanced summary of the arguments to date, while at the same time making a significant personal contribution to the discussion.

Heroic Cycle

Of the early Irish literary cycles the heroic is probably the best known, and most readily appreciated in having clear parallels in other heroic literatures so well described by the Chadwicks. The central figure in this cycle is Cú Chulainn, The Hound of Culann. His name is explained in that section of the "Cattle Raid of Cooley" known as the *Mac-gnímrada* or Boyhood Deeds: he killed the hound of Culann, smith to Conchobar, King of the province of Ulster, and had to act as replacement for the dog until its young matured and relieved him of his task. The central tale in the cycle is the "Cattle Raid of Cooley," often referred to simply as the *Táin* from its Irish title *Táin Bó Cuailnge,* although it should be remembered that *Táin* is a generic term rather than the title of a specific tale, and there are several other *Tána* (pl.) extant. There are two principal versions of *Táin Bó Cuailnge;* the earlier is found in the "Book of the Dun Cow" and the "Yellow Book of Lecan," the later in the "Book of Leinster." The later version is much more coherent, and it is here that the reason for this particular cattle raid is explained.

I have given two different translations of part of this explanatory episode at the beginning of this article: Ailill and Medb, king and queen of Connaught, who reside at a place called Cruachu or Cruachain (now Croghan, Co. Roscommon), begin to compare their possessions, at first good-humoredly enough, and then with gathering resentment. It is discovered that their possessions are exactly equal with the exception of a bull, Finnbennach, the White Horned, which Ailill has. There is only one other bull in Ireland the equal of this, Donn Cuailnge, the Brown (Bull) of Cooley, but it is far away in the province of Ulster. Messengers are sent to acquire it, and at first no problem is encountered. A bargain is readily made, but then one of the Connaught messengers is heard to boast that they would have taken the bull by force if necessary. The owner of the bull is infuriated and promptly dismisses the messengers, and the forces of Connaught assemble to invade Ulster and take away the bull. Meanwhile the men of Ulster have been rendered powerless as the result of a debility incurred by giving offence to the goddess Macha, from whom Emain Macha (now Navan fort near Armagh), the site of Conchobar's court, is named. Cú Chulainn alone of the men of Ulster is unaffected by Macha's curse, and the *Táin* is chiefly an account of how he single-handedly defends the province against the Connaught invaders. The Connaught forces are finally routed, but the tale ends as it began with the bulls who battle their way throughout Ireland before the Donn Cuailnge vanquishes the Finnbennach. Kinsella translates:

> Then the bulls fought each other for a long time. Night fell upon the men of Ireland and they could only hear the uproar and fury in the darkness. That night the bulls circled the whole of Ireland. When morning came, the men of Ireland saw the Donn Cuailnge coming westwards past Cruachan with the mangled remains of Finnbennach hanging from his horns.[22]

There follows a section inspired by the *Dinnshenchas* in which the names of various places in Ireland are explained as deriving from the discarded sections of the Finnbennach which the victor tosses from his horns, before he himself collapses and dies.

The central position of the *Táin* was reinforced by the attachment to it of various *remscéla,* or prefatory tales. Some of these obviously had no original connection with the *Táin;* this is the case with *Aislinge Óengusso* (The Dream of Oengus), one of the most beautiful of the early Irish tales. Indeed, Professor Kelleher of Harvard has recently suggested that the prestige of the *Táin* was artificially created by a Louth family who brought the story with them to Clonmacnois and by their control of the scriptorium there gave what was originally a local tale a national significance.[23] The best known of the *remscéla,* and one that has a real function in the cycle, is *Longes mac nUislenn* (The Exile of the Sons of Uisliu), which explains why Fergus mac Roich, one of the greatest of the Ulster heroes, came to be aiding the Connaught forces in their attack on Ulster. Naoise, one of the sons of Uisliu, had eloped with

Deirdre whom Conchobar, King of Ulster, had intended for himself. Naoise flees to Scotland with Deirdre and his brothers, but returns on Conchobar's guarantee of safety. Fergus mac Roich acts as guarantor of Conchobar's good faith, but the king slays the sons of Uisliu on their return and takes Deirdre to himself. At this outrage to his honor, Fergus leaves Ulster and begins to harry the province from Connaught. But he never altogether overcomes his old loyalties, and his reluctant guidance of the Connaught forces in their advance on Ulster is one of the finest pieces of characterization in the *Táin*. *Longes mac nUislenn* itself has been retold many times in English, beginning in the eighteenth century with that endearing old forger, James Macpherson. The most successful re-enactment is undoubtedly Synge's *Deirdre of the Sorrows*, produced in a period of literary brilliance which in its own way rivals the flowering of the saga literature a thousand years earlier.

Apart from the *Táin* the two most important tales in the Heroic Cycle are *Fled Bricrend* (The Feast of Bricriu) and *Scéla Mucce Meic Da Thó* (The Story of Mac Da Thó's Pig). The first of these is a particularly irreverent portrait of the Ulster heroes as they strive for the champion's portion, the prime cut of meat, due to the best warrior among them. The contest is not confined to the men alone, for the rivalry is reinforced by a corresponding contest among their wives. In each case Bricriu is the instigator of the trouble. We are told that his mastery of incitement was such that he would cause the breasts of every woman in Ireland to strike against one another, and so wither away. Aroused by the elaborate praise which Bricriu has bestowed on them individually, each of the foremost warriors, Cú Chulainn, Conall Cernach, and Lóegaire Buadach, lays claim to the champion's portion, and uproar ensues. Peace is temporarily restored, but then the wives of the disputants leave the house and Bricriu tells each as she departs that the first to return will have precedence over the women of Ulster. They advance to a distance of three ridges from the house before returning. Each of them is unaware that the others have been given the same information. On the first ridge they walk with dainty mincing steps, hardly putting one foot before the other. On the next ridge their steps are shorter and quicker. At the final ridge all pretence of dignity is abandoned as they raise their clothes over their buttocks and rush towards the house. To those within it seems as though fifty chariots are approaching and the doors are barred against them, for, as Sencha the druid says, if this were not done "our dead would be more numerous than our living." Conchobar, who is also present, comments that "it will be a bad night," and Sencha advises that a war of words would be more suitable for women than a war of weapons. But this expedient only aggravates the situation, for the husbands are further inflamed by their wives' praise, and Cú Chulainn lifts up the side of the house allowing his wife, Emer, to enter. When he lets the house fall back to its original position Bricriu is thrown out among the dogs and is so besmirched with dung that none of the people of Ulster would have recognized him except for his speech.

The matter of supremacy among the men is not yet resolved and the warriors journey first to Cruachain to seek the verdict of Ailill and Medb, and thence to Cú Roí who dwelt at Cathair Chon Roí (now Cahirconry in West Kerry). In each case Cú Chulainn is judged to be the best warrior, but in each case also the verdict is disputed by the others. Finally, the matter is settled by means of *cennach ind ruanada* (the warrior's bargain), well-known to Arthurian students from its occurrence in *Sir Gawayne and the Grene Knight*. Cú Roí visits Emain Macha in disguise and contracts with each of the contending Ulster warriors in turn; each of them is to be allowed to behead the giant on condition that he allow the giant to behead him on the following night. They all accept the challenge, but each in turn fails to appear on the following night except for Cú Chulainn, who for his courage is proclaimed supreme among the warriors of Ulster in the presence of the assembly. Even at the climax, the heroic ideal is treated with ridicule as Cú Roí complains that Cú Chulainn's neck is too short and that he will have to stretch it if he is to behead him. Finally Cú Chulainn manages to extend his neck over the massive block that the giant has brought with him, but so great is the effort that a warrior's foot would have fitted between each two vertebrae. The execution, of course, is not carried out.

Cú Chulainn does not appear in *Scéla Mucce Meic Da Thó*, where Conall Cernach takes his place as the chief warrior of Ulster. The central episode in this tale concerns the division of a pig, but it begins and ends with a hound. Mac Da Thó, the wily King of Leinster, possesses a famous hound, Ailbe, and messengers arrive simultaneously from Ailill and Medb of Connaught, and Conchobar of Ulster to demand it. It is Mac Da Thó's wife who solves his predicament by suggesting that he promise it to both parties. He takes aside the Connaught messengers and informs them that after much deliberation he has decided to give the hound to Ailill and Medb. Likewise he tells the Ulster messenger that he has decided to give the hound to Conchobar. Both parties are to arrive to collect it on the same day. Again they arrive simultaneously, and Mac Da Thó feigns surprise, but welcomes them both and seats them opposite one another. We are told that "the faces that were in that house were not those of friends at a feast." The development of the situation so far resembles that of *Fled Bricrend*, as Mac Da Thó achieves under duress a confrontation similar to that which Bricriu contrived out of malice.

Bricriu, too, plays a part in this tale. Mac Da Thó has a pig killed for them; it had been fattened for seven years on the produce of sixty cows, and now sixty oxen are required to bring it in, and those are followed by nine men supporting its tail. Immediately a dispute arises as to how and by whom the pig should be divided among them. Bricriu, who is also present, suggests that the matter should be settled on the basis of previous victories. This, of course, closely parallels the episode in *Fled Bricrend* where the warriors contend for the "champion's portion." They set to taunting and discrediting one another until eventually Cet mac Mágach of Connaught puts down the opposition and holds the floor against all his Ulster challengers; he has defeated one in single combat, taken off another's cattle, emasculated a third, and so on. Then Conall Cernach of Ulster arrives and he and Cet greet one another respectfully. When the formalities have been observed the real business begins:

> "Get away from the pig," said Conall.
> "And what would bring you to it," said Cet.
> "Indeed," said Conall, "to obtain victory for myself. I will give you an example of victory, Cet," said Conall. "I swear by what my people swear that since I took a spear in my hand there has not been a day that I have not slain one of the Connaughtmen, or a night that I have not plundered them with fire, and that I have not slept without the head of a Connaughtman under my knee."
> "It is true," said Cet, "that you are a better warrior than I. If it were Ánluan who were here he would match you victory for victory. It is unfortunate that he is not present."
> "Indeed he is present," said Conall, taking the head of Ánluan from his belt, and hurling it at Cet's chest so that a gush of blood burst over his lips. He left the pig and Conall sat down to it.

The Connaughtmen are disappointed with the share of the pig given to them by Conall, and they set upon the Ulstermen. The tumult spreads into the surrounding countryside. Mac Da Thó looses his hound, letting it support whatever side it wishes. This is an ironic twist to the theme of the "champion's portion"; since the warriors cannot be trusted to divide the animal (pig), the animal (hound) is now to decide among the warriors.

The hound chooses to support the Ulstermen and begins to slaughter the Connaught forces. Eventually it is killed as it pursues the chariot of Ailill and Medb westwards; in this section, as at the conclusion of the *Táin*, various place names are said to derive from the events of the pursuit. The Ulstermen do not escape unscathed either, for Fer Loga, charioteer of Ailill and Medb, takes Conchobar unawares and compels him to take him with him to Emain Macha where the young women of Ulster must sing to him every evening for a year: "Fer Loga is my darling." When he returns home to Connaught at the end of the year, he does so with two of Conchobar's horses, complete with golden bridles.

Like *Fled Bricrend, Scéla Mucce Meic Da Thó* is finally an amused, detached and sceptical interpretation of the heroic milieu. If our sympathies lie anywhere they are with Mac Da Thó as he maneuvers the powerful enemies, just as in *Fled Bricrend* the real hero is the most unheroic Bricriu as the great warriors and their wives become increasingly incongruous and ridiculous figures. The tradition was by now sufficiently mature to permit itself to be laughed at.

The events of the Heroic Cycle are imagined as taking place about the time of Christ. Indeed, one tale has the news of Christ's passion relayed to Conchobar, who is so seized with fury that an enemy projectile (a petrified human brain in fact) which had been lodged in his head by a Connaught enemy bursts forth, and he dies. The legend was no doubt developed to save a favorite pagan hero from hell, although one could think of many candidates more worthy of this privilege than Conchobar.

A similar tale is told of Cormac mac Airt, who belongs to the Cycles of the Kings and who is traditionally placed in the third century A.D. (Historical records are not generally reliable before the second half of the sixth century and have to be treated with caution even then.) He thus belongs to the pre-Christian period, for St. Patrick did not arrive on his mission until the fifth century, but the storytellers arrange for a personal conversion. The only alternative to this method is to somehow preserve the hero until Patrick's arrival, and this device is used in the Fionn cycle where Fionn's son Oisín (or, according to other versions, Caílte mac Rónáin) is sent off to a land of eternal youth, returning only on the arrival of the saint. This option is much more fertile in terms of literary production, as the old warrior describes the former state of things and compares the feeble present with the glorious past. The dialogue between Patrick and Oisín/Caílte is the subject of *Acallam na Senórach* (The Conversation of the Ancients), which belongs to the twelfth century and is the last great creative work in Irish prose literature. Although generally classified as belonging to different cycles, Fionn and Cormac are closely associated in that Fionn is visualized as leader of a nomadic army which protects Ireland during Cormac's reign. The separate classification results from a change of mood; it is the difference between the world of epic and the world of romance, and the reasons for it will be discussed below.

Other Cycles

The king tales are set in many different periods, but a very significant body of them is assigned to the early seventh century. It is likely that the great plague which swept the country in the 660s made this period appear in later memory as a golden age. One of these tales is *Fingal Rónáin* (Rónán's slaying of his Kinsman) which describes how Rónán, King of Leinster, slew his own son. It is an Irish version of the story of Phaedra and Hippolytus, although the plot is so uncomplicated that it is not necessary to presume any borrowing from the Greek. Rónán's second wife, grown weary of her aging husband, attempts to seduce his son Máel Fhothartaig and when he rejects her, falsely accuses him to Rónán. Having had his son put to death, the old man discovers his error, and presides, a helpless Lear-like figure, over the denouement which sees the suicide of his wife, his son's killers slain, and his own death.

The Fionn cycle becomes prominent only in the twelfth century. No doubt it had long been popular among the peasantry, but only now became respectable in a rapidly changing society. Gerard Murphy, the foremost authority on this cycle, would attribute the change to the coming of the Normans. For my own part, I believe that the Normans had only a very marginal effect on developments which would have taken place in any event, and which had begun long before the invasion. These developments were extensive and profound, affecting ecclesiastical, political, artistic, and literary affairs. We have seen that our earliest Irish manuscripts date from the beginning of that century. It was also a great period of antiquarian activity in which works such as the *Dinnshenchas* were compiled, probably with an awareness of the changing times and a resolve to preserve the past. One finds the same sort of activity in the seventeenth century when Irish men of learning gathered together the fragments of tradition as the old Gaelic world collapsed about them. The twelfth-century change was less drastic, and, while we may question the reasons he proposes for it, Murphy's description of its effects is entirely accurate:

> There is less grandeur in the post-Norman tale than in the pre-Norman tale. Kings in it have, as it were, become lords, heroes have become adventure seekers, gods have become fairies. Pre-Norman fiction seems to have sprung from an insight which could endow heroic and even mythological fiction with the substantiality of what is real. Post-Norman fiction usually gives nothing more than the impression of pure fiction, which, however charming, is to the best examples of pre-Norman fiction what a stain-glass window is to an oil painting.[24]

With this quotation we pass out of our period. There is much else within it that we have not discussed, most notably the Vision and Voyage tales. Vision tales are usually designated by the titles *Fís* (from Lat. *Visio*), or *Aislinge,* which Cormac mac Cuillenáin fancifully explains ca. 900 as *lingid as,* (it leaps out). These terms are generally used without distinction of meaning, and the treatment also owes something to the *Baile,* or Frenzy tale. The best known example is *Fís Adamnáin* (The Vision of Adamnán) which may date from the tenth century. The genre was so well-known that a twelfth-century author could write *Aislinge Meic Conglinne* (The Vision of Mac Conglinne), which among other things parodies the Vision tales, confident in the knowledge that the nuances of his mockery would be readily appreciated.

A significant part of *Aislinge Meic Conglinne* is also devoted to the *Immrama* or Voyages. These are most noteworthy for their imaginative descriptions of what lies beyond in the unknown seas, and one of them, *Immram Máile Dúin* (The Voyage of Máel Dúin), is sometimes held to be the source of *Navigatio Brendani,* which became so popular in medieval Europe. In *Immram Máile Dúin* and *Immram Brain* (The Voyage of Bran) we have a blending of pagan and Christian motifs without any consciousness of conflict. This merging of traditions is the essence of early Irish literature and therefore a suitable note on which to conclude this survey.

NOTES

1. Frank O'Connor, *My Father's Son* (New York: Alfred A. Knopf, 1969), p. 108. The questioner was Kenneth Jackson, later to become one of the foremost Celtic scholars.

2. Tom Peete Cross and Clarke Harris Slover, *Ancient Irish Tales,* 2nd ed. (New York: Barnes and Noble, 1969), pp. 281–82.

3. Seán O'Faoláin, *Vive Moi* (London: Hart-Davies, 1965), p. 284.

4. Thomas Kinsella, *The Táin* (London: Oxford University Press, 1970), p. 52.

5. Eleanor Knott and Gerard Murphy, *Early Irish Literature* (London: Routledge and Kegan Paul, 1966), pp. 98–99.

6. Albert B. Lord, *The Singer of Tales* (Cambridge, Mass.: Harvard University Press, 1960), p. 128.

7. *Modern Philology* 43 (1945): 17. Cf. Myles Dillon, *The Cycles of the Kings* (London: Oxford University Press, 1946), pp. 2–3.

The word *fili* means "seer" etymologically, and is generally translated as "poet," but in fact there does not seem to have been a clear distinction between the various functions of the Irish literary man. It is used here as synonymous with *sgélaige* (mod. *sgéalaí*), "storyteller."

8. J. H. Delargy, *The Gaelic Story-teller* (Chicago: University of Chicago Press, 1969; reprinted from *PBA* 31, 1945), p. 32.

9. Ibid., p. 33.

10. Séamus Ó Duilearga, *Leabhar Sheáin Í Chonaill,* 2nd ed. (Dublin: Browne and Nolan, Ltd., 1964), pp. xviii–xix.

11. Delargy, *The Gaelic Story-teller,* p. 20.

12. James Carney, *Studies in Irish Literature and History* (Dublin: Institute for Advanced Studies, 1955), pp. 321–22.

13. Most readily available in Osborn Bergin, *Irish Bardic Poetry* (Dublin: Institute for Advanced Studies, 1970), p. 6.

14. Ibid.

15. D. A. Binchy, "The Linguistic and Historical Value of the Irish Law Tracts," *PBA* 29 (1943): 205.

16. Ibid.

17. T. Ó Raithbheartaigh, *Genealogical Tracts,* 1 (Dublin: Stationery Office, 1932), p. 12.

18. Charles Plummer, "On the Colophons and Marginalia of Irish Scribes," *PBA* 12 (1926): 11–42.

19. Cecile O'Rahilly, *Táin Bó Cúalnge* (Dublin: Institute for Advanced Studies, 1967), p. 272.

20. *Ancient Irish Tales,* p. 39 (reprinted from *Revue Celtique* 12, 1891).

21. Osborn Bergin and R. I. Best, *Tochmarc Étaíne* (Dublin: Royal Irish Academy, 1938), pp. 21–23.

22. Kinsella, *The Táin,* p. 252.

23. John V. Kelleher, "The Táin and the Annals," *Ériu* 22 (1971): 126–27.

24. Brian Ó Cúiv, ed., *Seven Centuries of Irish Learning* (Dublin: Stationery Office, 1961), p. 76.

BIBLIOGRAPHY

Anthologies

Prose (translations only)
Cross, T. P., and C. H. Slover. *Ancient Irish Tales*. 2nd ed. New York: Barnes and

Noble, 1969. The most representative selection of Irish tales available, containing material from the four principal cycles as well as a number of other items such as the "Voyage of Bran" and selections from the *Dinnshenchas*. This edition also contains a bibliography by Charles W. Dunn, which traces the origins of the translations.

Gregory, Lady Augusta. *Cuchulainn of Muirthemne*. New York: Oxford University Press, 1970. First published in 1902, this work which concerns itself with the tales of the Heroic or Ulster Cycle is still readable.

Joyce, P. W. *Old Celtic Romances*. London: David Nutt, 1879. Reprinted many times, this contains a good selection of tales from the Fionn cycle, as well as earlier material such as the "Voyage of Máel Dúin." Proper names tend to be disfigured in these translations.

Kinsella, Thomas. *The Táin*. London: Oxford University Press, 1970. A very readable translation based on the earliest version of the *Táin*. Gaps in the narrative have been filled from other sources, which are always noted. It also contains the prefatory tales such as the "Exile of the Sons of Uisliu."

Prose and Poetry (translations only)
Jackson, Kenneth H. *A Celtic Miscellany*. London: Routledge and Kegan Paul, 1951. Contains selections by a leading scholar from all the Celtic languages at all periods to illustrate such topics as hero tale and adventure, nature, love, Celtic magic, humor, and satire.

Poetry

Texts and Translations
Carney, James. *Medieval Irish Lyrics*. Dublin: Dolmen Press, 1967. Exceptional in that it contains Latin as well as Irish poems. Has a useful introduction.

Greene, David, and Frank O'Connor. *A Golden Treasury of Irish Poetry* A.D. *600 to 1200*. London: Macmillan, 1967. No account is given of the division of labor, although we may assume that Greene is primarily responsible for the textual readings and O'Connor for the translations. The introduction also seems to have been written by O'Connor as it repeats observations made by him in *The Backward Look* (see Commentary section of bibliography below).

Murphy, Gerard. *Early Irish Lyrics*. Oxford: Clarendon Press, 1956. From the scholarly point of view, by far the most satisfactory of the three anthologies in this section. Provided with an elaborate critical apparatus and extensive notes on the poems which the other two lack.

Translations Only
Meyer, Kuno. *Selections from Ancient Irish Poetry*. 2nd ed. London: Constable and Company, 1913. The earliest collection of its kind, and also one of the most successful. The introduction contains some classic comments on early Irish nature poetry.

O'Connor, Frank. *Kings, Lords, and Commons*. London: Macmillan, 1961. Contains vigorous translations of poems from all periods, including modern folksong.

Commentary

Carney, James. *Studies in Irish Literature and History*. Dublin: Institute for Advanced Studies, 1955. While this comprises a number of specialist essays rather than a general survey of the period, it also makes some very valuable general, but controversial, observations on the nature of early Irish tradition.

de Vries, Jan. *Keltische Religion*. Stuttgart: Kohlhammer Verlag, 1961. Although he disagrees with Dumézil on points of detail, this work is an attempt to show that the latter's tripartite system is valid for Celtic, including Irish, mythology.

Dillon, Myles. *Early Irish Literature*. Chicago: University of Chicago Press, 1948. A conventional introduction to the literature. Summaries of the tales are provided, and each item is preceded by a note on the manuscripts and its approximate date. Dull but useful.

————. *The Cycles of the Kings.* London: Oxford University Press, 1946. Arranged in the same way as the previous work. The only survey of the King tales available.

————, ed. *Irish Sagas.* Dublin: Stationery Office, 1959. Originally formed part of series of radio lectures in honor of Thomas Davis. Deals mainly with the Heroic Cycle, but there are also articles on tales from the other cycles. General but stimulating.

Dillon, Myles, and Nora Chadwick. *The Celtic Realms.* New York: The New American Library, 1967. A comprehensive work on different aspects of Celtic life and tradition, including a chapter on Irish literature.

Flower, Robin. *The Irish Tradition.* Oxford: Clarendon Press, 1947. Several of the essays which make up this work are now regarded as classics. It is arranged under such chapter headings as "The Founding of the Tradition," "Exiles and Hermits," "The Rise of the Bardic Order," "Ireland and Medieval Europe," "Love's Bitter-Sweet," and others. It is a sensitive and scholarly work.

Hughes, Kathleen. *Early Christian Ireland: Introduction to the Sources.* London: The Sources of History Ltd., in association with Hodder and Stoughton Ltd., 1972. Although primarily of interest to the historian, this work places the literature in its context as well as containing a chapter which deals with it directly. Has an excellent and up-to-date bibliography.

Jackson, Kenneth H. *The Oldest Irish Tradition: A Window on the Iron Age.* Cambridge: Cambridge University Press, 1964. Considers the degree to which the early Irish tales reflect on archaic, "heroic" society; discusses such matters as head-hunting and "the champion's portion."

Knott, Eleanor, and Gerard Murphy. *Early Irish Literature.* London: Routledge and Kegan Paul, 1966. A reprint of two booklets by Murphy entitled *Saga and Myth in Ancient Ireland* and *The Ossianic Lore and Romantic Tales of Medieval Ireland,* and Knott's booklet on bardic poetry entitled *Irish Classical Poetry.* The introduction is by James Carney.

Mac Cana, Proinsias. *Celtic Mythology.* London: Hamlyn, 1970. A beautifully illustrated and concise account of Celtic, and particularly Irish, mythology.

Mercier, Vivian. *The Irish Comic Tradition.* Oxford: Clarendon Press, 1962. A survey of Irish humor and satire at all periods, including Anglo-Irish literature.

O'Connor, Frank. *The Backward Look.* London: Macmillan, 1967. Almost equally divided between the early Irish and Anglo-Irish literatures. Original and stimulating. A very readable book.

O'Rahilly, T. F. *Early Irish History and Mythology.* Dublin: Institute for Advanced Studies, 1946. A formidable work. Although its interpretation of the mythology is outdated, this work would be indispensable if only for the footnotes.

Rees, Alwyn, and Brinley Rees. *Celtic Heritage.* London: Thames and Hudson, 1961. Scholars' reactions to the appearance of this book varied between delight and dismay. A most original work, it seeks to interpret Celtic traditions and literatures in the light of the theories developed by Georges Dumézil.

Thurneysen, Rudolf. *Die irische Helden- und Königsage.* Halle: Verlag von Max Niemeyer, 1921. The title is misleading since the book does not actually deal with the *Königsage.* Although it needs updating on some points, it remains the indispensable introduction to the heroic literature. Unfortunately it has never been translated into English.

9   The French Chansons de Geste

Gerard J. Brault

Chansons de geste, as their name implies, are songs recounting heroic deeds.[1] They were composed by singers of tales known as *jongleurs* who probably learned the plot or story line and, no doubt, certain key phrases from others but improvised the rest.[2] The jongleurs made use of stock themes, motifs, and formulas but varied these somewhat so that each performance was different.[3] However, neither the jongleur nor his audience paid much attention to these variations, and the overall impression, whether the same or a different singer was involved, was that the identical poem was being chanted. A large body of traditional stories concerning legendary figures circulated in this fashion during the Middle Ages.

We cannot be certain that any of these poems survived in the manner in which they were composed. About a hundred works also referred to as chansons de geste—twenty-four for the Cycle of William of Orange alone[4]—have come down to us in written form, but there is much controversy about how the latter came into being.[5] Some scholars believe that the French epics found in medieval manuscripts, often in several copies, were simply dictated by jongleurs. However, most specialists feel that the extant chansons de geste were based on oral tradition but reworked by the clerks who set them down in writing.[6] Clerks had received schooling and their compositions reflect this learning. The influence of the Bible, the Classics, and rhetorical treatises can sometimes be detected. The differences between one copy and another of the same chanson de geste do not reflect variations in the jongleur's improvisation, but scribal habits. Clerks routinely introduced many changes whenever copying except, of course, when transcribing sacred or canonical works. A few scholars have even argued that clerks drew almost exclusively on written tradition for both the content and the form of the chansons de geste. In short, there is a far greater tendency among students of the medieval French epic than among scholars of other heroic poems to see clerical influence.

Since the Middle Ages, it has been customary to divide the chansons de geste into three families or groups: (1) the Cycle of the King, that is, Char-lemagne; (2) the Cycle of William of Orange; and (3) the Epics of Revolt.[7] Most Old French epics fall into one of these groups, but this classification, like many other medieval categorizations, is limited in its usefulness. Some chansons de geste are attached only very superficially to any family, and cyclical considerations never put any restraint on their authors. It is true, however, that there was a natural tendency to trade on the popularity of an epic hero by inventing new adventures for him in song, notably *enfances,* that is, youthful escapades.

The earliest surviving chansons de geste were composed at the turn of the twelfth century and the genre flourished for many decades. In the second half of the twelfth century, romances came into favor and exerted an important influence on French epic poetry. Originally composed in assonance and in strophes of varying length called laisses, many chansons de geste were sub-sequently recast in rhyme. In the fourteenth and fifteenth centuries, a good number of the earlier epics were reworked into prose.[8] The genre persisted in drastically altered form well into the sixteenth century and later, but many characteristic traits had long since disappeared.[9]

The standard meter of the early chansons de geste is decasyllabic. The fourth and tenth syllable is always stressed. The cesura at the end of the first hemistich generally divides the verse into two sense groups:

Halt sunt li pui / e li val tenebrus.
(The mountains are high / and the valleys are shadowy.)
Song of Roland, v. 814.

As a rule, there is no running over (enjambement) at the cesura or from one verse into the next. When scanning verse, mute *e* at the cesura or after the tonic accent at the tenth syllable is not counted. Because of dialectal or orthographical peculiarities, it is not always easy to spot elisions. For exam-ple, in the following verse, *ki est = k'est:*

Fors Sarraguce, ki est en une muntaigne.
(Except Saragossa, which is on a mountaintop.)
Song of Roland, v. 6.

The rules governing hiatus and enclisis can at times be very complex. There are some early eight-syllable (*Gormont et Isembart*) and twelve-syllable (*Pèlerinage de Charlemagne*) chansons de geste; several of the latter were composed in the thirteenth century. Many of the later jongleurs tend to disre-gard the rules of epic versification.

It is often said that the chansons de geste were originally composed for the nobles, that is, the warrior class who enjoyed listening to accounts of deeds of valor and feats of arms. However, epics probably appealed to all classes of medieval society. Upper-class frolics were very popular with proletarian

American motion picture audiences during the Great Depression. It seems reasonable to suppose that heroic poetry provided a similar kind of escape for medieval serfs. Also, once written down by clerks, epics were read and doubtlessly much appreciated by other members of the same class.[10]

The chansons de geste are largely neglected today and few individuals other than graduate students have ever read an entire medieval French epic. There is, however, one notable exception. The *Song of Roland,* probably the earliest chanson de geste, is universally acknowledged and widely read as one of the greatest masterpieces of Western literature.[11]

Song of Roland

The *Song of Roland* survives in several manuscripts, but the twelfth-century copy preserved in the Bodleian Library at Oxford offers the oldest and best version.[12] The copy in question is believed to reflect rather closely the original poem which was probably composed about 1100.[13] Some time after the Oxford manuscript was copied, another scribe (the "revisor") endeavored to correct it by erasing letters and words and by adding others. Many of these changes show that the revisor lacked a firm grasp of his predecessor's language but others ring true. The systematic comparison of each word in this poem with the corresponding form found in the other versions has yielded many plausible emendations, especially in the 300-odd instances where a verse does not scan or assonate properly.

The poem, which is in Anglo-Norman dialect in the Oxford copy, tells how Charlemagne's nephew Roland died at Roncevaux in the Pyrenees as the Emperor and his men were making their way home after a military campaign in Spain. The event in question actually took place in the year 778, some three hundred years before the poem is believed to have been composed.[14] The best-known account of the historical event is in the Latin *Vita Karoli Magni* by Einhard, Charlemagne's biographer (died 840):

> While the war against the Saxons is being fought energetically and almost continuously, he [Charlemagne], having stationed troops at strategic places along the borders, attacks Spain with all the forces that he can muster. He crosses the Pyrenees, accepts the surrender of all the towns and fortified places that he encounters along the way, and returns without his army having sustained any losses except that, during the withdrawal, while traversing the Pyrenees, he happened to experience Gascon treachery. While his army was marching in a long column, because of a narrow pass, some Gascons lying in ambush at the top of the mountain—for the thick woods which are very plentiful in that area afford a great opportunity for sneak attacks—swoop down on the last elements of the baggage train and on the rear guard protecting the main body of the army. They drive them back into the valley, join battle, and massacre every last one of them. Then, having looted the baggage train, they disperse very rapidly in every direction under cover of night which was falling. On this occasion, the Gascons had the advantage of light armament and control of the terrain; the Franks were

greatly hindered by their heavy armament and lower position. In this battle were slain Eggihard, the royal seneschal; Anselm, count of the palace; and Roland, prefect of the Breton march, and many others. This reverse could not be avenged immediately because the enemy, having done this deed, dispersed in such a way that no one could even tell in which direction they might have been sought.[15]

Note that, according to the latter account, the defeat was occasioned by Gascon treachery.[16] The presence of Saracens at Roncevaux is open to debate.[17] The most significant aspect of Einhard's narrative is the amount of space devoted to the disaster, which suggests the impact of the defeat on the people of that time, the listing of illustrious victims, including *Hruodlandus Brittanici limitis praefectus,* the hero of the *Song of Roland,*[18] and the mention of treachery which will later motivate the action of the poem.

The myth of Charlemagne (742–814) began to grow during his lifetime; numerous anecdotes about him were circulated and his name was intimately associated with the idea of Empire.[19] There are scattered mentions of the incident in the Pyrenees in medieval annals, and it is safe to assume that, by the eleventh century, a fairly elaborate legend had developed, perhaps giving rise to more than one work in Latin or French, none of which, unfortunately, appear to have survived.[20]

Whether inspired by legend or poem, a man of genius—we shall refer to him as Turoldus, the name found in the Oxford manuscript[21]—composed the work known today as the *Song of Roland.* The precise manner and form in which Turoldus received his material and how much of the poem's style is due to his creativity and skill are much-debated questions.

Turoldus' masterpiece is superior to the kind of verse which singers of tales usually compose, but it has many features in common with this oral literature. The poet was obviously familiar with the formulaic diction used by the jongleurs and he skillfully fused this procedure with the techniques of written literature taught in the schools.

Most commentators consider that the *Song of Roland* has the following four parts.[22]

THE BETRAYAL OF GANELON

Charlemagne has conquered all of Spain except the city of Saragossa, which is still in Saracen hands. King Marsile, the pagan ruler, sends messengers to Charlemagne, offering to become his vassal and a convert to Christianity if the Emperor will lift the siege and return home. Roland urges Charlemagne to reject Marsile's proposal but is contradicted by his stepfather Ganelon. The Emperor decides to negotiate: he will accept the Saracen ruler's offer but only if the Caliph, Marsile's uncle, returns home with him. Several Franks, including Roland, volunteer to carry Charlemagne's reply to Saragossa but are turned down by the Emperor. Roland nominates Ganelon and this proposal meets with instant approval. Smarting from what he considers to be an insult, Ganelon hurls defiance at Roland and his friends and, at Saragossa, plots with Marsile to do away with his stepson. Back at Charlemagne's camp, the traitor makes a lying assertion: Marsile will keep his promises but cannot deliver up the Caliph, who has drowned. Charles believes him and immediately gives the order for the army to head for home.

THE DEATH OF ROLAND

Ganelon now nominates his stepson to lead the rear guard. Warned in a dream to beware of Ganelon, Charlemagne nevertheless gives his consent when Roland accepts this responsibility. Meanwhile, Marsile and his men lay an ambush and, when the main body of Charlemagne's army has crossed the Pyrenees, they attack the rear guard at Roncevaux. Oliver, Roland's companion-in-arms, pleads with his friend to sound the oliphant to call for help, but the hero steadfastly refuses to do so. At first the Franks overcome all their adversaries, but eventually they are reduced to a handful. Roland now sounds the oliphant. The Saracens overwhelm the Franks but suffer terrifying losses. After a last desperate onslaught, they flee the field, leaving Roland standing alone victorious. The hero has escaped without a scratch, but was mortally wounded sounding the oliphant. Having arranged the bodies of his slain companions before the dying Archbishop Turpin, a formidable warrior in his own right, Roland lies down facing the enemy, confesses his sins, and dies.

THE PUNISHMENT OF THE SARACENS

Charlemagne arrives at Roncevaux and, thanks to a miracle—the day lengthens—overtakes and destroys the fleeing Saracens. Grievously wounded, Marsile manages somehow to escape. The Emir Baligant now comes to his aid with a vast army. After a fearsome struggle, the pagan forces are routed and Charlemagne personally slays Baligant. The Emperor takes Saragossa by storm and removes all trace of paganism there. (Some scholars believe that the entire Baligant episode—roughly a thousand verses or about one-fourth of the poem in the Oxford version—was an interpolation by Turoldus.)[23]

THE PUNISHMENT OF GANELON

Charlemagne returns to his capital at Aix (Aachen in modern Germany) and summons his court. When informed of Roland's death, Alda, the hero's fiancée, succumbs at the Emperor's feet. Ganelon is formally accused of treason. Intimidated by Ganelon's relative Pinabel, the judges ask Charlemagne to drop the charge against Ganelon. Thierry of Anjou dissents and proposes a judicial combat. In the duel which ensues, Thierry slays Pinabel and the outcome is viewed as a judgment of God. Ganelon and thirty of his relatives are promptly executed. Bramimonde, Marsile's wife, receives baptism. The Archangel Gabriel appears to Charlemagne in a dream and summons him to undertake new campaigns against the Infidel.

This outline suggests that the *Song of Roland* has but one story line and that its various parts are well-defined. However, Turoldus' essential narrative procedure is parallelism.[24] For example, Roland and Oliver are plainly antithetical as are Charlemagne and Baligant. The nomination of Roland contrasts with the earlier nomination of Ganelon. The hero gives a number of reasons for not sounding the oliphant; Oliver turns the same arguments against his companion when Roland decides to blow the horn after all. It seems more in keeping with Turoldus' dual modes of expression, then, to view the poem as a two-fold narrative hinging on betrayal: Plot A (Charlemagne-Marsile-Baligant), the attempt by Marsile to deceive the Emperor, and Plot B (Roland-Ganelon), the villain's treachery.[25]

The Abraham archetype plays a key role in the *Song of Roland*. Like Abraham, Charles is a priest-king, he is associated with great age, is venerated as the Father of his people, and is personally summoned by God to accomplish certain acts, the most significant of which is the sacrifice of a close relative. For medieval exegetes, Abraham was the perfect example of Faith.

Anyone endeavoring to justify Roland's behavior has to contend with a number of ambivalent character traits, in particular his boasting and his apparent indifference to the fate of his men at Roncevaux. The hero's death is viewed by some as atonement for the sin of pride he committed in refusing to sound the oliphant.[26]

It was Joseph Bédier who put forth the theory that the Roland-Oliver debate was the key to Turoldus' poem. For the French scholar, the *Song of Roland* was born in that "sacred moment" when the contrast between the two comrades-in-arms was conceived and epitomized in verse 1093: *Rollant est proz e Oliver est sage.*[27] When taken out of context, this line does have an aphoristic quality, but it is simplistic and grossly misleading to suggest that it is the gist of Turoldus' poem. The word *proz* here does not mean "brave," but "worthy." Thus, rather than standing out in sharp contrast to *sage, proz* complements it. Turoldus' point is that Roland and Oliver are equal in chivalric virtue. On a purely human plane, the two knights are identical in worth, but Roland surpasses by far his companion by the nature of his aspiration.[28] Bédier's view has gained widespread acceptance, and much evidence has been collected in support of this interpretation. Curtius, for example, pointed out that the ideal hero of Antiquity possessed physical strength as well as wisdom (*fortitudo et sapientia*) but that, in literature, these qualities were often found in two opposing characters. The idea of a contrast between Roland and Oliver would thus be a classical topos.[29] The abundant *fortitudo et sapientia* scholarship all hangs together very nicely, but it does not come to the heart of the matter. The central meaning of the *Song of Roland* lies elsewhere.

There is, in addition to the literal sense conveyed by the story line, another dimension in Turoldus' poem. This deeper meaning has to do with its moral and spiritual significance. The essential statement made by Turoldus is that Christianity transcends all other faiths. The poet also stresses the fact that God has chosen Charlemagne and the Franks for a special task, that of establishing His rule throughout the world by means of armed conquest or conversion.[30] The notion that all worldly wisdom is vanity and that the Folly of the Cross is the only true Wisdom is much in evidence, too.[31] The hero's suffering and death are an imitation of Christ, and his sacrifice constitutes a new kind of martyrdom.[32]

The poem is compartmentalized to a certain degree, but the major themes (Good vs. Evil, Betrayal, Conversion, Victory) provide important links between its various parts and constitute a matter of far greater consequence than the precise number of sections. The Abraham archetype which dominates Plot A relates to a Christ figure, Roland, in Plot B.[33]

One of the least appreciated facets of the *Song of Roland* is the remarkable extension of its meaning and themes in the form of recurring images. The most important metaphors in this poem are: the Struggle, the Road, the Ascent, the Two Cities, and Roncevaux. The desperate fighting which makes up a good part of the narrative may be viewed as a reflection of the battle for man's soul.[34] In the gospels and the writings of the Fathers of the Church, earthly life was often compared to a road, a distant journey, a peregrination, a voyage home.[35] There is obvious metaphoric significance in the hero's arduous climb.[36] Saragossa is a symbol of Pride and a connection with ancient Babylon is inevitable; Aix, the place where justice is dispensed in an awesome Day of Retribution, represents the Heavenly Jerusalem.[37] Finally, Turoldus altered the toponym *Rozaballes* to *Rencesvals* (Modern French *Roncevaux, Vale of Thorns*) to suggest that the locale of his hero's agony was related to the Valley of Tears of Psalms 84:7 and the Crown of Thorns.[38]

Nowhere is the distance between modern practice and the art of the *Song of Roland* greater than in the depiction of characters. It has been said that Turoldus' personages lack depth and that they tend to conform to stock types: the Hero, the King, the Traitor.[39] Individuals in this epic often do look and think alike and use the same kind of language. However, characters each have a nature, good or bad, identified from the outset by an epithet or phrase, or by being Christian or Saracen. The more important the character, the more his goodness shines forth or his villainy looms large. This black or white constitution governs behavior and outlook to a remarkable degree, for, as a rule, characters do not change their essences. The only exception is the convert, epitomized by Bramimonde, whose complete transformation from evil to good is wrought through the miracle of grace.[40] Other personages simply do not change or develop in the modern understanding of these terms.

Turoldus' characters are motivated by a central virtue or vice, each of these traits being associated with or in conflict with corresponding qualities or faults.[41] Although this system of virtues and vices is firmly rooted in Biblical and Patristic sources, the mundane aspect of moral strengths and weaknesses is also depicted. Thus, while Largesse, the chief virtue of the king, is at times viewed as a reflection of divine Largitas, it can also refer to more familiar forms of liberality.

A character's virtues or vices are chiefly manifested through his actions and words. Physical appearance provides important clues to an individual's nature but looks can also be deceiving. Ganelon's attractive features have misled many scholars into believing that Turoldus stood in grudging admiration of the traitor or, for some reason or other, refrained from painting him completely black.[42] Nothing could be further from the truth. Conrad, the twelfth-century German translator of the *Song of Roland,* makes this abundantly clear when he compares the handsome villain to a tree which is green on the outside but is rotten to the core.[43] An individual's observations about another furnish us with information of another kind, for they must always be carefully weighed in light of the fact that the speaker represents a point of view which is not necessarily shared by the poet. For instance, the stories which Ganelon tells about Roland are intended to vilify his stepson.[44] Finally, a character may provide important insights into his own psychological make-up while boasting or talking about others, especially in tense moments.

Self-praise strikes the modern reader as being unseemly in the hero. However, the medieval audience drew a distinction between truthful claims and hollow assertions.[45] Thus Roland's detailing of his past and future accomplishments not only constitutes behavior which is quite acceptable, but also provides information which is essential to the narrative. On the other hand, the Saracens' boasting is repeatedly shown to be vain.

Charlemagne is the most complex figure in the *Song of Roland.* Biblical associations abound in Turoldus' depiction of this character; he is first and foremost a Messianic figure who incarnates Wisdom and plays the role of Abraham. The narrative of the Sacrifice of Isaac in Genesis mentions no emotion on Abraham's part. Charlemagne evinces the same blind and spontaneous obedience to the strange promptings of the Almighty, but Turoldus portrays him in a more human light, repeatedly showing the Emperor's great anguish as the dimensions of his role are gradually revealed to him. Charlemagne survives his nephew, and it is obvious that Turoldus attached a good deal of importance to his serving as a posthumous witness to Roland's edifying death.[46] The debate over whether the Emperor or his nephew is the chief hero of Turoldus' poem is pointless: one character is the extension and reflection of the other, and the author clearly had no intention of according one precedence over the other.[47]

Roland is the ideal knight, his prowess combining all chivalric virtues, the ability to impart sound advice (*consilium*) as well as the courage and the strength to be of assistance in combat (*auxilium*). The hero personifies Humilitas. In medieval thought, true humility consisted in recognizing one's lowly condition compared with God's greatness, one's need to surrender oneself completely to the dictates of the divine Will, and one's total dependence upon grace.[48] Having demonstrated his humility in his speech urging Charlemagne to carry on the struggle against Marsile and in his debate with Oliver maintaining that Folly is Wisdom, Roland begins his spiritual ascent.

The hero is also the incarnation of Virginitas, that is, purity of the heart, mind, and soul.[49] Virginity means intactness, integrity, and inviolability.[50] Roland dies but suffers not a single wound except that his temples burst from sounding the oliphant. Durendal, his sword, reflects the hero's shining virtues, but the fact that it cannot be destroyed implies that nothing can break its owner's spirit. Roland carries a white ensign lashed to the tip of his spear; at Roncevaux, his heart is placed in a white casket and, later, his body in a white coffin. Whiteness is associated with martyrdom but also, of course, with purity of heart and virginity.[51]

It is difficult for present-day readers to accept the fact that a character can be all bad and there is a tendency—especially since the Romantic period—to view villains as alienated, misunderstood, or, for one reason or another, not entirely to blame for the crimes they perpetrate. Many critics feel a decided sympathy for Ganelon and suggest that he is goaded into his fury and treason by a tactless Roland, that he shows courage in his dealings with Marsile, and has a strong case when he pleads justifiable homicide during the trial at Aix.[52] The plain fact is that Turoldus and his contemporaries considered Ganelon to be completely evil. Like the Saracens or Satan himself in the *Song of Roland*, Ganelon has no redeeming trait whatsoever.

Scholars have long puzzled over the answer to the following question: why does Ganelon hate Roland?[53] Turoldus makes it absolutely clear that greed is his motive.[54] Most critics, however, are inclined to believe that the real reason for Ganelon's betrayal is the slight he suffers from his stepson.[55] Others suggest that a feud between Ganelon and Roland has been smouldering for some time when the poem begins.[56] At any rate, the allegation of greed is generally viewed as a secondary motive at best, when it is not dismissed out of hand as totally irrelevant.[57]

Such an interpretation reflects modern values which regard avarice as a lesser vice and a certain amount of acquisitiveness as justifiable and even normal. In Turoldus' day, Pride and Avarice were considered to be the root of all evil, a view based on Scripture.[58] As a matter of fact, Lester K. Little has shown that Avarice begins supplanting Pride as the mother of vices precisely in the eleventh century.[59] Covetousness was Judas' sin and the mortal enemy of Caritas, the chief virtue counseled by the New Law.[60] Ganelon is essentially a Judas figure and it is Avarice that leads him to betray Roland and, by implication, Charlemagne and God.

The Latin *Pseudo-Turpin Chronicle* and the German *Rolandslied* are important witnesses to the process of medieval interpretation of the *Song of Roland*. The first of these works was strongly influenced by Turoldus' epic and the second is essentially a translation of the French poem.

Opinions vary as to the exact date of the prose work purported to be by Archbishop Turpin, but it would appear that the earliest surviving version was composed about 1130 by a Frenchman who knew Spain.[61] Considerable controversy also swirls around the date of Conrad's German adaptation of the *Song of Roland* which appears to have been composed about 1170.[62] Turoldus tends to narrate events and leave their interpretation to his audience, whereas the Latin chronicler and the German translator not infrequently explain them to us. Their glosses may at times seem bizarre or destructive of the obscurity or variety of possible interpretations that enhance the interest which the poem holds for us. On the other hand, Turoldus had no intention of mystifying his audience. His art is one of subtle suggestion, but he also wished his meaning to get through. Many renderings in the *Pseudo-Turpin* and the *Rolandslied* ring false and must obviously be ignored. This does not mean, however, that their novel interpretations and commentaries should all be summarily dismissed. There is, after all, a good chance that Conrad and the Latin chronicler were at times more attuned to Turoldus than modern readers can ever hope to be.

Other Epics

The *Song of Roland* is the only medieval French epic which is widely known today. However, several others are full of interest and make good reading.

The *Pèlerinage de Charlemagne* (Charlemagne's Pilgrimage) is one of the most interesting early chansons de geste in the Cycle of the King.[63] The poem, which is generally dated at the beginning of the twelfth century, survived in only one relatively late manuscript which has been lost since 1879. Fortunately, copies were made and the text is available in a number of modern editions.[64] The work is relatively short (870 verses) and seems to be a parody of the epic genre. It is in alexandrines rather than in the customary decasyllables.

Stung by his wife's observation that King Hugo, Emperor of Greece and Constantinople, is reputed to have a more majestic bearing, Charlemagne sets out for Jerusalem where he is given many relics by the Patriarch. Later, at Constantinople, Hugo entertains him royally in his enchanted palace. After a feast, Charlemagne and his men retire to a bed chamber. In a euphoric mood, each tries to outdo the other in vowing to accomplish incredible feats, some of them embarrassing to Hugo. A spy informs the latter, who forces them to keep their word. With the help of an angel, the Franks manage to execute their self-imposed tasks. When Hugo places a crown on Charlemagne's head, the Franks recognize that their sovereign wears it more fittingly than their host. The Emperor returns to France and rejoins his wife, who begs his forgiveness.

Other poems in this group include *Aspremont,* the *Chevalerie Ogier, Gui de Bourgogne, Huon de Bordeaux,* and *Mainet.*

The *Chanson de Guillaume,* the earliest epic in the Cycle of William of Orange, relates how Vivien, Count William's nephew, made a stand at Archamp—the exact location of this battle is problematic—against a marauding band of Saracens.[65] Count Tedbald and his knights are idling at Bourges when they hear the news of Saracen King Deramé's incursion. Tedbald decides not to send for William and waits until morning. When he sights the enemy, he and most of his men flee. However, Vivien stays with ten thousand men. Soon they are reduced to twenty. After his remaining companions are slain, Vivien sends Girart as a messenger to William at Barcelona and is left alone. Girart reaches Barcelona and beseeches William to come to the aid of the French knights. William has recently returned from battle. Encouraged by his wife Guibourc, William sets off with thirty thousand men. The Saracens have remained because of a foul wind. Soon all the French are slain, and the Count remains alone. Before he returns to his castle, Guibourc has raised another thirty thousand men. After resting until dusk, William leaves for the battlefield with his new army which includes Guiot, Vivien's fifteen-year-old brother. All are annihilated except William. Many scholars believe that the original poem ended at this point (verse 1980).

William finds his nephew and begins a lament over his body. Suddenly Vivien opens his eyes and receives communion from his uncle's hand. A new Saracen army appears, forcing the Count to abandon his nephew's body. William escapes and eventually rejoins Guibourc, who is now at Orange. Several French knights, including Guiot, have been captured by the Saracens. Encouraged by Guibourc, William travels to Laon to ask King Louis for help. They raise an army of thirty thousand men, including the giant kitchen boy Rainouart, who is armed with an enormous *tinel* (club). After a battle during which Rainouart frees the French prisoners and helps mightily to rout the Saracens, the Christians return to Orange. The spoils are divided, but Rainouart is forgotten. The kitchen boy sets out for Spain, vowing to raise an army to besiege Orange. William realizes his oversight, catches up with Rainouart, and manages to persuade him to return. After this reconciliation, Rainouart is baptized, and it is discovered that he is Guibourc's long-lost brother.

The only surviving version of this poem, which is preserved in British Museum, MS. Add. 38663, appears to be a composite. Many internal contradictions and stylistic variations suggest that two different epics (G^1 and G^2) were conflated at the point mentioned above (verse 1980). G^2 is probably a more recent work. In the latter part of the twelfth century, the same subject as that found in G^1 forms the basis for a new epic called the *Chevalerie* (or *Covenant*) *Vivien* while that of G^2 is echoed in the chanson de geste known as *Aliscans*. The poem has a great affinity to the *Song of Roland.* There are also comic effects as, for example, when the kitchen boy, Rainouart, sets out with his club to do battle against the pagans.

In the *Charroi de Nîmes,* an epic composed about the middle of the twelfth century, William, now in his 60s and having given away all his fiefs, asks his sovereign, King Louis, for "Spain," that is, all the lands currently occupied by the Saracens.[66] His request is granted, and in order to capture the city of Nîmes in the South of France, he resorts to a Trojan horse ruse. The Count's men hide inside barrels and are borne inside the city in a convoy of ox-drawn carts. Another chanson de geste in this cycle, the *Prise d'Orange,* tells how William later captured the nearby city of Orange.[67] The *Moniage Guillaume* relates how he became a monk after his wife's death.[68] The *Couronnement de Louis* straddles the Cycle of the King and that of William of Orange: Charlemagne and his weak son Louis are central characters, but the real hero is William, the latter's protector.[69]

The Epics of Revolt are sometimes referred to as the Cycle of Doon de Mayence after the ancestor of a large clan of traitors. *Girart de Roussillon, Raoul de Cambrai,* and *Renaud de Montauban* are poems belonging to this group.[70]

The hero of *Girart de Roussillon* rebels against his sovereign, Charles, King of France and rival for the hand of the daughter of the Emperor of Constantinople. A desperate struggle ensues for Girart's castle at Roussillon. The two adversaries war against each other for many years until finally Girart is forced to flee to the Ardennes Forest where, for twenty-two years, he does penance and ekes out a livelihood as a charcoal burner. Pardoned by Charles, he helps found the church at Vézelay. War breaks out anew between the King and his rebel vassal. In the end, Girart surrenders and turns once again to penance and charitable works. The origins of this legend and the identification of Charles, Girart, and Roussillon are much-debated questions.

Renaud de Cambrai deals with the hereditability of benefices in feudal society. Originally, a benefice was held for life. However, from the earliest times, lords often granted the son of a deceased vassal the benefices held by his father, and beginning with the end of the ninth century, hereditability became increasingly common. In this poem, Raoul is denied Cambrai, a fief his father had received in benefice from King Louis of France. The latter grants it temporarily to Gibouin le Mancel, but promises that Raoul will be eligible for the first fief which becomes vacant. A year later, Raoul learns that he has been granted the Vermandois but that he must conquer it without the King's help. Raoul's squire, Bernier, is torn between his loyalty to his lord and his relatives, who claim the Vermandois. Bernier eventually slays Raoul, but the rival families continue their feuding for many years afterward.

Les Quatre Fils Aymon (The Four Sons of Aymon) were folk heroes in various parts of Europe well into the present century, attesting to the extraordinary popularity of the legend. The earliest version of the story appears in the late-twelfth-century chanson de geste *Renaud de Montauban*. The brothers Alard, Guichard, Renaud, and Richard, knights at Charlemagne's court, are forced to flee to the Ardennes Forest, then to Gascony, and finally to Tremoigne (modern Dortmund in Germany) after Renaud slays the Emperor's nephew. They repeatedly elude Charlemagne's grasp with the aid of their resourceful cousin, Maugis, a sorcerer, and of the remarkable horse Bayard. In the end, Renaud is reconciled with his sovereign and does penance. After he is slain, his body, which was thrown into the Rhine, is miraculously recovered. The epic is associated with the legend of Saint Reginald of Dortmund.

Many chansons de geste cannot be relegated to any particular cycle. One of these poems has received considerable scholarly attention. *Gormont et Isembart*, preserved in a single 661-verse fragment, is contemporary with the *Song of Roland* and the *Chanson de Guillaume*.[71] The story, which has been reconstructed on the basis of later versions in French and German, culminates in a battle at Cayeux in Normandy. After rallying the English King Gormont's pagan army and struggling against his fellow countrymen for four days, the youthful French renegade Isembart is finally slain. Before dying, however, he repents and invokes the Virgin. An episode in which a knight unwittingly strikes a close relative or friend—in *Gormont et Isembart*, the French deserter attacks his own father—is a recurring motif in the chansons de geste.[72] This narrative device is familiar to readers of Matthew Arnold's *Sohrab and Rustum*.

Ami et Amile, another isolated French epic, offers a variation on the Abraham archetype encountered in the *Song of Roland*.[73] When Ami is stricken with leprosy, an angel informs him that he can only be restored to health by the blood of children. Ami's devoted friend, Amile, decapitates his own sons to effect the cure. The leper immediately heals and the children are miraculously resuscitated.

Not all chansons de geste are anonymous. One of the better-known French authors at the beginning of the twelfth century, Jean Bodel of Arras, composer inter alia of several fabliaux and the *Jeu de Saint Nicolas*, wrote the *Chanson des Saisnes*,[74] an epic poem about Charlemagne's military campaigns in Saxony. The incident takes place after the Battle of Roncevaux. Guiteclin, King of the Saxons, attacks Charlemagne. During this campaign, Sebile, Guiteclin's wife, falls in love with Baudouin, Roland's brother. After the Saxon ruler is slain by Charles, she becomes a convert to Christianity and marries Baudouin.

A century later, Bertrand de Bar-sur-Aube composed *Girart de Vienne*,[75] whose main character is the same as the hero of *Giraat de Roussillon*. Bertrand's poem includes an episode which recounts how Roland and Oliver first met. When Charlemagne is besieging the city of Vienne, Oliver, Girart's champion, is challenged by Roland. The two heroes duel but one cannot vanquish the other—this is the origin of the expression "to give someone a Roland for an Oliver"—and, mercifully, an angel intervenes. The two knights make a solemn friendship pact and Roland takes Alda, his companion's sister, as his fiancée.

In the second half of the thirteenth century, Adenet le Roi[76] reworked older French epics into the chansons de geste called *Buevon de Conmarchis* and the *Enfances Ogier.* His masterpiece, *Berte aus grans piés,* is one of the most delightful tales of the Middle Ages. After his first wife dies, Pepin (Charlemagne's father) takes Berte, daughter of the King of Hungary, as his bride. Informed of a plot against her life, Berte consents to have her double, a servant girl, take her place in the marriage bed. The next day, Berte flees to the Forest of Le Mans. The servant girl continues to deceive Pepin into believing that she is his true wife. Nine and a half years later, the impostor is unmasked: the real Berte is known to have abnormally large feet (*grans piés*)! Pepin's wife is found and their marriage is finally consummated.

Numerous relics and place-names throughout Europe attest to the popularity of the French chansons de geste.[77] The Holy Roman Emperors found it politically advantageous to associate themselves with the memory of Charlemagne. Frederick Barbarossa arranged to have his illustrious predecessor canonized at Aachen in 1165. On the other hand, a legend concerning a mysterious but terrible sin which Charlemagne was alleged to have committed has been traced to the year 858.[78] By the middle of the thirteenth century, the Emperor's sin was said to have been incest with his sister who, as a consequence, gave birth to Roland. Charlemagne, the story went, repented and received absolution from Saint Egidius. The legend probably stems from the Emperor's well-known indifference to the teachings of the Church concerning chastity.[79]

REWORKINGS AND PUBLICATION OF THE
CHANSONS DE GESTE

Heroic poetry is indigenous to many European countries. During the Middle Ages no tradition flourished or enjoyed as great an international vogue as did the French epics, especially the Cycle of the King. The chansons de geste were translated into English, German, Italian, and several Scandinavian languages.[80]

The fame of French epic heroes spread far and wide, and exercised an important influence in art at home and abroad.[81] Charlemagne and his Paladins are depicted in a late-twelfth-century stained glass window of the Cathedral of Strasbourg[82] and several episodes of the *Pseudo-Turpin Chronicle* were portrayed in the silver-gilt repoussé panels of the reliquary, dated 1215, of Saint Charlemagne at Aachen[83] and in the celebrated early-thirteenth-century Charlemagne window of the Cathedral of Chartres.[84] Many manuscripts of the chansons de geste are masterpieces of medieval illumination.[85] In the fourteenth and fifteenth centuries, numerous giant statues of Roland—

Lejeune and Stiennon list no fewer than twenty-seven[86]—were erected in city marketplaces throughout the Holy Roman Empire, notably in the Brandenburg region of Germany. A few, like the stone statue dated 1404 at Bremen,[87] are still standing. Several different theories have been advanced to explain these monuments which, in many cases, seem to have been symbols of imperial justice or of freedom from seignorial authority.

At the beginning of the thirteenth century, French writers began to turn earlier poems, in particular the Arthurian romances,[88] into prose. Many chansons de geste underwent a similar change, especially after the Hundred Years War. In the process of recasting and elaborating these works, the gap which separated epic from romance was often narrowed. Scholars now customarily refer to such products of the latter part of the Middle Ages as romances of chivalry.[89]

The great vogue for these works continued well into the modern period. The first printed romance of chivalry appears to have been *Pierre de Provence* published at Lyons in 1472. By the end of the fifteenth century, at least twenty-four titles had appeared in France, some of them several times.[90] In addition to many old favorites, thirty-nine new titles had been brought out by the time Francis I's reign came to a close (1547).[91] The most popular romance of chivalry of this period was *Les Quatre Fils Aymon.* No fewer than eighteen separate editions appeared before the latter date.[92] Other chansons de geste which survived in this form include *Ogier le Danois* and *Fierabras.*

The romances of chivalry continued to be popular among middle- and especially lower-class readers even after Cervantes satirized the genre in his *Don Quixote* (1604). In the early seventeenth century, Jean Oudot, a bookseller at Troyes and later at Paris, founded the famous *Bibliothèque bleue.* This series of chapbooks bore a distinctive blue cover—hence its name—and continued to appear until 1863. Similar collections were published elsewhere in France and Belgium.

A number of French epics of the Middle Ages are found in adulterated form in the Marquis de Paulmy d'Argenson's *Bibliothèque universelle des romans,* a vast collection begun in 1775.[93] In the following years, the Comte de Tressan contributed numerous adaptations of romances of chivalry, including a version of the *Song of Roland,* to this series. The Count is credited with having originated the *genre troubadour,* a kind of bogus medievalism which was destined to exert a major influence on the Romantic movement. His stylish reworkings were published separately in 1781 with the title *Corps d'extraits des romans de chevalerie* and again, from 1787 to 1791, as *Oeuvres choisies du comte de Tressan,* in twelve volumes.

Immanuel Bekker, a German philologist, is credited with having published the first scholarly edition of a chanson de geste, *Fierabras,* in Berlin in 1828. Three years later, Paulin Paris brought out an edition of *Berte aus grans piés* in Paris, the first in the series entitled *Romans des Douze Pairs.*[94] In 1835, Francisque Michel discovered the oldest and best copy of the *Song of Roland* in the Bodleian Library at Oxford. His edition of that poem appeared in Paris in 1837.[95]

The fame of French epic heroes spread far and wide. The farthest peregrination of the chansons de geste may be the dramatic representations of the Carolingian legends in Kerala in the South of India, which are performed to this day.[96] The Portuguese, who made contact with India as early as 1498, are known to have related stories about Charlemagne to local Christian converts in the sixteenth century as a means of encouraging the latter in their struggles against the Moslems. Operas known as *ĉavittunatakam* were composed in the Tamil language, lasted two weeks, and required forty-odd singers and dancers. In 1869, an opera based on *Fierabras* was written by Mahakavi Kattakayathil Cherian Mappila. A popular novel about Charlemagne in the related language, Malayanan, was first published in 1870. It follows very closely for the most part the Spanish *Historia de Carlomagno* by Nicolás de Piamonte.

An interesting survival of the chansons de geste can also be seen today at the marionette theatre of the Musée de la Vie Wallonne in Liège, Belgium. These shows, which captivate young and old alike, are revivals in Modern French of plays in the Walloon dialect performed in marionette theatres which flourished in worker districts of that city a century ago.[97]

Marionettes date back to antiquity and were popular throughout Europe in the Middle Ages. There is a fine pen-and-ink drawing of two marionettes portraying dismounted knights fighting with swords in the twelfth-century *Hortus Deliciarum*.[98] The Italian Alexander Conti, who arrived in Liège in 1854, is believed to have founded the first marionette theatre there before 1886 in association with an individual named Talbot. He may have learned his craft at Modena which had a marionette theatre as early as 1803.[99] However, the plays he and his successors produced in Liège were probably adapted from chapbooks published in the latter city.

NOTES

1. The most useful survey in English is Jessie Crosland, *The Old French Epic* (Oxford: Blackwell, 1951). For current bibliography, consult the *Bulletin Bibliographique de la Société Rencesvals (pour l'étude des épopées romanes)* (nine fascicules since 1958) and, especially, *Olifant,* a publication of the American-Canadian Branch of this international society (quarterly since 1973). The Société Rencesvals sponsors triennial international congresses and has published several volumes of proceedings.

2. The classic work on the jongleurs is Edmond Faral, *Les Jongleurs en France au Moyen Age,* 2nd ed., Bibliothèque de l'Ecole des Hautes Etudes, IVᵉ section, Sciences historiques et philologiques, 187 (1910; reprinted Paris: Champion, 1964).

3. Jean Rychner, *La Chanson de geste: Essai sur l'art épique des jongleurs,* Société de Publications Romanes et Françaises, 53 (Geneva: Droz, 1955).

4. Jean Frappier, *Les Chansons de geste du cycle de Guillaume d'Orange*, I (Paris: Société d'Edition d'Enseignement Supérieur, 1955), p. 15.

5. On the various theories concerning the origins of the chansons de geste, consult Joseph Bédier, *Les Légendes épiques*, 2nd ed., III (Paris: Champion, 1921), pp. 192–288; Italo Siciliano, *Les Origines des chansons de geste: Théories et discussions*, trans. P. Antonetti (Paris: Picard, 1951); Martín de Riquer, *Les Chansons de geste françaises*, 2nd ed., trans. Irénée-M. Cluzel (Paris: Nizet, 1957); Ramón Menéndez Pidal, *La Chanson de Roland et la tradition épique des Francs*, 2nd ed., trans. Irénée-M. Cluzel (Paris: Picard, 1960), pp. 3–50; Italo Siciliano, *Les Chansons de geste et l'épopée. Mythes. Histoire. Poèmes*, Biblioteca di Studi Francesi, 3 (Turin: Società Editrice Internazionale, 1968).

6. Robert Scholes and Robert Kellogg, *The Nature of Narrative* (New York: Oxford University Press, 1966), pp. 17–56, is a helpful introduction to this complex question.

7. The traditional classification is found in the early-thirteenth-century epic *Girart de Vienne* by Bertrand de Bar-sur-Aube. The passage in question is cited in full by Crosland, p. 18.

8. Georges Doutrepont, *Les Mises en prose des épopées et des romans chevaleresques du XIVᵉ au XVIᵉ siècles*, Académie royale de Belgique, Classe des Lettres et des Sciences morales et politiques, Mémoires, 40 (Brussels: Palais des Académies, 1939).

9. Arthur Tilley, *Studies in the French Renaissance* (Cambridge: University Press, 1922), pp. 12–25.

10. Faral, pp. 44–47.

11. The following discussion of Turoldus' epic is condensed from the introduction to my two-volume work, *The Song of Roland: An Analytical Edition* (University Park and London: The Pennsylvania State University Press, 1978).

12. *La Chanson de Roland: Reproduction phototypique du manuscrit Digby 23 de la Bodleian Library d'Oxford*, ed. Comte Alexandre de Laborde and Charles Samaran (Paris: Société des Anciens Textes Français, 1933).

13. On the date of the poem, see Pierre Le Gentil, *La Chanson de Roland*, Connaissance des lettres, 43 (Paris: Hatier-Boivin, 1955), pp. 23–32. There have been numerous attempts at tracing the evolution of the poem from its earliest form to that found in the Oxford copy. See, for example, Jules Horrent, *La Chanson de Roland dans les littératures française et espagnole au moyen âge*, Bibliothèque de la Faculté de philosophie et lettres de l'Université de Liège, 120 (Paris: Les Belles Lettres, 1951), pp. 287–304, 315–19, 330; Hans Erich Keller, "La conversion de Bramimonde," *Société Rencesvals pour l'étude des épopées romanes. VIᵉ Congrès international (Aix-en-Provence, 29 Août-4 Septembre 1973). Actes* (Aix-en-Provence: Université de Provence, 1974), pp. 173–203.

14. Menéndez Pidal, pp. 181–230; Jules Horrent, "La bataille des Pyrénées de 778," *Le Moyen Age* 78 (1972): 197–227; and Paul Aebischer, *Préhistoire et protohistoire du Roland d'Oxford*, Bibliotheca Romanica (Bern: Francke, 1972), pp. 37–92, provide detailed analyses of this event.

15. Eginhard, *Vie de Charlemagne*, ed. and trans. Louis Halphen, 3rd ed. (Paris: Les Belles Lettres, 1947), pp. 28–30. English translation mine.

16. "Wasconicam perfidiam." Horrent, pp. 202–03, suggests that the attackers were Pyrenean, not French, Gascons (often referred to as Basques). Cf. Aebischer, pp. 75–88.

17. Menéndez Pidal, 204–09, and Barton Sholod, *Charlemagne in Spain: The Cultural Legacy of Roncesvalles* (Geneva: Droz, 1966), p. 41, interpret certain statements by Arab chroniclers to mean that the Saracens were there. Horrent, p. 204, and Aebischer, loc. cit., express reservations about Saracen complicity in this respect.

18. In the poem, Roland is not a Breton but a *Franc de France.* Horrent, *La Chanson de Roland,* pp. 305 and 306, n. 2.

19. Gaston Paris, *Histoire poétique de Charlemagne* (1865; reprinted Paris: Bouillon, 1905); Robert Folz, *Le Souvenir et la légende de Charlemagne dans l'empire germanique médiéval* (Paris: Les Belles Lettres, 1950).

20. André Burger, "La légende de Roncevaux avant la *Chanson de Roland,*" *Romania* 70 (1948–49): 453–73; idem, "Sur les relations de la *Chanson de Roland* avec le *Récit du faux Turpin* et celui du *Guide du Pèlerin,*" *Romania* 72 (1952): 242–47. See, however, Jean Rychner, "A propos de l'article de M. André Burger 'La légende de Roncevaux avant la *Chanson de Roland*'," *Romania* 72 (1951): 239–46, and Burger's reply, *Romania* 73 (1952): 42 ff.

21. For bibliography relative to this personage, see Jean Dufournet, *Cours sur la Chanson de Roland,* Les cours de Sorbonne (Paris: Centre de documentation universitaire, 1972), pp. 16–17.

22. For a typical outline, see Rychner, *La Chanson de geste,* pp. 38–39.

23. For an extensive bibliography on this question, consult Marianne Cramer Vos, "Aspects of Biblical Typology in *La Chanson de Roland*" (Ph.D. diss., University of Rochester, 1970), pp. 165–66.

24. The most elaborate study is Herman Gräf, *Der Parallelismus im Rolandslied,* Inaugural-Dissertation (Wertheim-am-Main: Bechstein, 1931).

25. This section is based on my article, "Structure et sens de la *Chanson de Roland,*" *French Review* 45 (1971), Special Issue no. 3, pp. 1–12.

26. For bibliography and discussion, see William W. Kibler, "Roland's Pride," *Symposium* 26 (1972): 147–60; Larry S. Crist, "A propos de la desmesure dans la *Chanson de Roland:* Quelques propos (desmesurés?)," *Olifant* 1/4 (1974): 10–20.

27. Bédier, III, p. 448.

28. Gerard J. Brault, *"Sapientia* dans la *Chanson de Roland,"* *French Forum* 1 (1976): 99–118.

29. Ernst Robert Curtius, *European Literature and the Latin Middle Ages,* trans. Willard R. Trask, Bollingen Series, 36 (New York: Pantheon, 1953), p. 176.

30. Karl-Heinz Bender, "La genèse de l'image littéraire de Charlemagne élu de Dieu au XIe siècle," *Boletín de la Real Academia de Buenas Letras de Barcelona* 31 (1965–66): 35–39; Dufournet, pp. 183–85.

31. This idea is frequently expressed in the Epistles of St. Paul.

32. Gerard J. Brault, "Le Thème de la Mort dans la *Chanson de Roland,*" *Société Rencesvals. IVe Congrès international. Heidelberg, 28 août-2 septembre 1967. Actes et Mémoires,* Studia Romanica, 14 (Heidelberg: Winter, 1969), pp. 229–35.

33. In medieval typology, Abraham's sacrifice was considered to be a prefiguration of God the Father sacrificing his son Jesus. Marcel Viller, "Abraham," *Dictionnaire de spiritualité ascétique et mystique, doctrine et histoire,* ed. Marcel Viller, S. J., I (Paris: Beauchesne, 1937), p. 110.

34. Prudentius (d. 415) gave this combat its classic form in the Latin poem entitled *Psychomachia,* which made a profound mark on the art, literature, and thought of the Middle Ages. H. J. Thomson, ed. and trans., *Prudentius,* The Loeb Classical Library

(1949; reprinted Cambridge, Mass.: Harvard University Press, and London: Heinemann, 1962), I, pp. 274-343; Emanuel J. Mickel, Jr., "Parallels in Prudentius' *Psychomachia* and *La Chanson de Roland*," *Studies in Philology* 67 (1970): 439-52.

35. Albert Blaise, *Le Vocabulaire latin des principaux thèmes liturgiques* (Turnhout: Brepols, 1966), para. 254, 297, 402, 426-28.

36. Jenkins, note to v. 2397; Le Gentil, pp. 109, 116.

37. Gerard J. Brault, "Quelques nouvelles tendances de la critique et de l'interprétation des chansons de geste," *Société Rencesvals. VIe Congrès international,* pp. 19-20.

38. Ibid., p. 20.

39. William Wistar Comfort, "The Character Types in the Old French *Chansons de geste,*" *PMLA* 21 (1906): 279-434.

40. Gerard J. Brault, " 'Truvet li unt le num de Juliane': Sur le rôle de Bramimonde dans la *Chanson de Roland,*" *Mélanges de langue et de littérature médiévales offerts à Pierre Le Gentil par ses collègues, ses élèves et ses amis* (Paris: S.E.D.E.S. et C.D.U. Réunis, 1973), pp. 134-49.

41. W. J. Brandt, *The Shape of Medieval History: Studies in Modes of Perception* (New Haven: Yale University Press, 1966), pp. 130-31, 154-56, 160, 162.

42. Bibliography in Albert Gérard, "L'axe Roland-Ganelon: Valeurs en conflit dans la *Chanson de Roland,*" *Le Moyen Age* 76 (1969): 452, n. 10.

43. *Le Texte de Conrad,* trans. Jean Graff, in *Les Textes de la Chanson de Roland,* ed. Raoul Mortier, X (Paris: La Geste Francor, 1944), vv. 1962-75.

44. Gerard J. Brault, "Ganelon et Roland: Deux anecdotes du traître concernant le héros," *Romania* 92 (1971): 392-405.

45. C. M. Bowra, *Heroic Poetry* (London: Macmillan, 1952), p. 51; Charles A. Knudson, "Serments téméraires et gabs: Notes sur un thème littéraire," *Société Rencesvals. IVe Congrès international,* pp. 254-60.

46. The author of the *Pseudo-Turpin* felt a similar need to emphasize this aspect of Charlemagne's role, for he has Baudouin and Thierry transmit in person the manner of Roland's passing. On this Latin chronicle, see below.

47. Cf. Albert Pauphilet, *Le Legs du Moyen Age* (Melun: Librairie d'Argences, 1950), pp. 77-90; see also the discussion in *Olifant* 1/3 (1974): 8; 1/4 (1974): 75.

48. Blaise, para. 494.

49. Anna Granville Hatcher, "Eulalie, lines 15-17," *Romanic Review* 40 (1949): 241-49; F. J. Barnett, "Virginity in the Old French Sequence of Saint Eulalia," *French Studies* 13 (1959): 252-56. Cf. Matthew 5:8.

50. Blaise, pp. 63-65, s.v. "intactus," "integer," "inviolabilis," "inviolatus."

51. Blaise, para. 109, 492.

52. See above, n. 42.

53. T. Atkinson Jenkins, "Why Did Ganelon Hate Roland?" *PMLA* 36 (1921): 119-33.

54. *Roland,* vv. 1148, 1407, 3756.

55. Leslie C. Brook, "Le 'forfait' de Roland dans le procès de Ganelon: Encore sur un vers obscur de la *Chanson de Roland,*" *Société Rencesvals. IVe Congrès international,* pp. 120-28.

56. *La Chanson de Roland,* ed. Jenkins, note to v. 217; Bédier, III, p. 413.

57. For example, *La Chanson de Roland,* ed. and trans. Gérard Moignet, Bibliothèque Bordas (Paris: Bordas, 1969), pp. 45, 49, 262, note to v. 3758.

58. Brault, "Quelques nouvelles tendances," pp. 21–22.

59. Lester K. Little, "Pride Goes Before Avarice: Social Change and the Vices in Latin Christendom," *American Historical Review* 76 (1971): 16–49.

60. John 12: 6; *Psychomachia*, v. 530.

61. *Historia Karoli Magni et Rotholandi ou Chronique du Pseudo-Turpin*, ed. C. Meredith-Jones (1936; reprinted Geneva: Slatkine, 1972), pp. 71–75.

62. André de Mandach, "Encore du nouveau à propos de la date et de la structure de la *Chanson de Roland* allemande," *Société Rencesvals. IVᵉ Congrès international*, pp. 106–16.

63. Jules Horrent, *Le Pèlerinage de Charlemagne: Essai d'explication littéraire avec des notes de critique textuelle*, Bibliothèque de la Faculté de philosophie et lettres de l'Université de Liège 158 (Paris: Les Belles Lettres, 1961).

64. The most accessible edition is *Le Voyage de Charlemagne à Jérusalem et à Constantinople*, ed. Paul Aebischer, Textes Littéraires Français, 115 (Geneva: Droz, 1965).

65. *La Chanson de Guillaume*, ed. Duncan McMillan, Société des Anciens Textes Français (Paris: Picard, 1949–50), 2 vols. The most useful studies are by Frappier in *Les Chansons de geste du cycle de Guillaume d'Orange*, I, pp. 113–233, and Jeanne Wathelet-Willem, *Recherches sur la Chanson de Guillaume: Etudes accompagnées d'une édition*, Bibliothèque de la Faculté de Philosophie et Lettres de l'Université de Liège, 210 (Paris: Les Belles Lettres, 1975), 2 vols.

66. *Le Charroi de Nîmes: Chanson de geste du XIIᵉ siècle*, ed. Duncan McMillan, Bibliothèque Française et Romane, Série B, 12 (Paris: Klincksieck, 1972); Frappier, *Les Chansons de geste du cycle de Guillaume d'Orange*, II (Paris: Société d'Edition d'Enseignement Supérieur, 1965), pp. 179–253.

67. *Les Rédactions en vers de la "Prise d'Orange,"* ed. Claude Régnier (Paris: Klincksieck, 1966); Frappier, II, pp. 255–317.

68. *Les Deux Rédactions en vers du Moniage Guillaume*, ed. Wilhelm Cloetta, Société des Anciens Textes Français (Paris: Didot, 1906–11), 2 vols.; Crosland, pp. 40–41.

69. *Le Couronnement de Louis: Chanson de geste du XIIᵉ siècle*, ed. Ernest Langlois, Classiques Français du Moyen Age, 22, 2nd ed. (1925; reprinted Paris: Champion, 1938); Frappier, II, pp. 47–178.

70. William Calin, *The Old French Epic of Revolt: Raoul de Cambrai, Renaud de Montauban, Gormond et Isembard* (Geneva: Droz, 1962). For the first of the three epics mentioned in the text, see *Girart de Roussillon: Chanson de geste*, ed. W. Mary Hackett, Société des Anciens Textes Français (Paris: Picard, 1953–55), 3 vols. in 2.

71. *Gormont et Isembart: Fragment de chanson de geste du XIIᵉ siècle*, ed. Alphonse Bayot, Classiques Français du Moyen Age, 14, 3rd ed. (Paris: Champion, 1931). Recent studies include the work by Calin mentioned above in note 70 and Stephen G. Nichols, Jr., "Style and Structure in *Gormont et Isembart*," *Romania* 84 (1963): 500–35.

72. Murray A. Potter, *Sohrab and Rustem: The Epic Theme of a Combat Between Father and Son. A Study of its Genesis and Use in Literature and Popular Tradition* (London: Nutt, 1902).

73. *Ami et Amile: Chanson de geste*, ed. Peter F. Dembowski, Classiques Français du Moyen Age, 97 (Paris: Champion, 1969); William Calin, *The Epic Quest: Studies in Four Old French Chansons de geste* (Baltimore: Johns Hopkins Press, 1966), pp. 57–117 (mention of Abraham archetype in *Ami et Amile*, p. 115).

74. *Jean Bodels Saxenlied,* eds. Friedrich Menzel and Edmund Stengel, Ausgaben und Abhandlungen aus dem Gebiete der Romanischen Philologie, 99-100 (Marburg: Elwert, 1906 and 1909), 2 vols. See Charles Foulon, *L'Oeuvre de Jehan Bodel,* Travaux de la Faculté des Lettres de Rennes, 1ère série, 2 (Paris: Presses Universitaires de France, 1958).

75. *Girart de Vienne: Chanson de geste, edited according to MS. B XIX (Royal) of the British Museum,* ed. Frederic G. Yeandle (New York: Columbia University Press, 1930).

76. *Les Oeuvres d'Adenet le Roi,* ed. Albert Henry, Rijksuniversiteit te Gent, Werken uitgegeven door de Faculteit van de Wijsbegeerte en Letteren, 109, 115, 121; I, *Biographie d'Adenet. La tradition manuscrite* (Bruges: De Tempel, 1951); II, *Buevon de Conmarchis* (1953); III, *Les Enfances Ogier* (1956), Université Libre de Bruxelles, Travaux de la Faculté de Philosophie et Lettres 23; IV, *Berte aus grans piés* (Brussels: Presses Universitaires de Bruxelles, and Paris: Presses Universitaires de France, 1963).

77. Robert Folz, *Le souvenir et la légende de Charlemagne dans l'Empire germanique médiéval* (Paris: Les Belles Lettres, 1950).

78. Baudouin de Gaiffier, "Le péché de l'empereur et son pardon," *Recueil de travaux offerts à M. Clovis Brunel,* Ecole des Chartes, Mémoires et documents, 12 (Paris: Société de l'Ecole des Chartes, 1955), pp. 490-503; Rita Lejeune, "La péché de Charlemagne et la *Chanson de Roland,"* *Studia Philologica. Homenaje ofrecido a Dámaso Alonso por sus amigos y discípulos con ocasión de su 60.° aniversario,* II (Madrid: Gredos, 1961), pp. 339-71; Gerard J. Brault, "The Legend of Charlemagne's Sin in Girart d'Amiens," *Romance Notes* 4 (1962): 72-75.

79. De Gaiffier.

80. Crosland, pp. 230-70.

81. Rita Lejeune and Jacques Stiennon, *La Légende de Roland dans l'art du Moyen Age* (Brussels: Arcade, 1967), 2 vols.

82. Lejeune and Stiennon, I, ch. 15.

83. Ibid., ch. 19.

84. Ibid., II, ch. 1.

85. Ibid., II, ch. 2.

86. Ibid., pp. 354, 356.

87. Ibid., p. 360, p. lviii.

88. *Arthurian Literature in the Middle Ages: A Collaborative History,* ed. Roger Sherman Loomis (Oxford: Clarendon Press, 1959).

89. Arthur Tilley, "The Prose Romances of Chivalry," in *Studies in the French Renaissance* (Cambridge: University Press, 1922), pp. 12-25.

90. Ibid.

91. Ibid.

92. Ibid.

93. Henri Jacoubet, *Le genre troubadour et les origines françaises du Romantisme,* Etudes Romantiques, 6 (Paris: Les Belles Lettres, 1929).

94. Dorothy Doolittle, *The Relations Between Literature and Mediaeval Studies in France from 1820 to 1860* (Bryn Mawr, 1933).

95. Joseph Bédier, "De l'édition princeps de la *Chanson de Roland* aux éditions les plus récentes. Nouvelles remarques sur l'art d'établir les anciens textes," *Romania* 63 (1937): 433-69.

96. Zacharias P. Thundyil, "La tradition de Charlemagne chez les Chrétiens de

Kerala (Inde),'' *Société Rencesvals. VIe Congrès International (Aix-en-Provence, 29 Août-4 Septembre 1973). Actes* (Aix-en-Provence: Université de Provence, 1974), pp. 389–98.

97. Maurice Piron, *Tchantchès et son évolution dans la tradition liégeoise,* Académie royale de Belgique, Classe des lettres et des sciences morales et politiques, Mémoires, Collection in 8°, 2ème sér., 45/4 (Brussels: Palais des Académies, 1950).

98. Gérard Cames, *Allégories et symboles dans l'Hortus deliciarum* (Leiden: Brill, 1971), pl. 45, fig. 76.

99. Maurice Piron, ''L'origine italienne du théâtre liégeois des marionnettes,'' *Mélanges Elisée Legros,* Enquête du Musée de la Vie Wallonne, 12 (Liège Musée de la Vie Wallonne, 1973), pp. 327–63; Paul Aebischer, ''Contribution à la préhistoire italienne des marionnettes liégeoises,'' *Marche Romane* 24 (1974): 31–36.

BIBLIOGRAPHY

Texts and English Translations of the Chansons de Geste

Bédier, Joseph, ed. *La Chanson de Roland.* Paris: Piazza, 1921.

Brault, Gerard J., ed. *The Song of Roland: An Analytical Edition.* University Park and London: The Pennsylvania State University Press, 1978. 2 vols. Volume 1 contains introduction and laisse-by-laisse commentary; Volume 2, Oxford text and modern English translation. Full-dress study intended primarily for medievalists and serious students.

Jenkins, T. Atkinson, ed. *La Chanson de Roland, Oxford Version.* Revised edition. Heath's Modern Language Series. Boston: Heath, 1929. Reprinted in 1977 (with a bibliographical supplement by Gerard J. Brault) by the American Life Foundation, Box 349, Watkins Glen, N.Y. 14891. For many years, the standard American edition. Historical and textual notes still very useful.

Guillaume d'Orange: Four Twelfth-Century Epics. Translated by Joan M. Ferrante. New York: Columbia University Press, 1974. The chansons de geste are: the *Couronnement de Louis,* the *Prise d'Orange, Aliscans,* and the *Moniage Guillaume.* Excellent introduction situating each epic in its historical context.

The Song of Roland. Translated by D. D. R. Owen. Unwin Classics, 3. London: Unwin Books, 1972. One of the best available translations in English. Useful introduction. The Baligant episode is set in italics. Laisse 186 is moved to what the author believes was its original position.

The Song of Roland. Translated by Dorothy L. Sayers. The Penguin Classics, 175. Baltimore: Penguin Books, 1957. Introduction emphasizes the poem's feudal elements. The translation has many quaint archaisms.

The Song of Roland. Translated by Robert Harrison. Mentor Book, MQ 1023. New York: New American Library, 1970. Excellent introduction. Author is well-informed and has several original views concerning the poem. Translation is lively but at times a bit free.

Studies in English about the Chansons de Geste

Auerbach, Erich. *Mimesis: The Representation of Reality in Western Literature.* Translated by Willard R. Trask. Princeton: Princeton University Press, 1953. Chapter 5, ''Roland Against Ganelon'' (pp. 96–122) has an often-quoted view concerning Turoldus' paratactic style.

Calin, William. *The Epic Quest: Studies in Four Old French Chansons de Geste.*

Baltimore: Johns Hopkins Press, 1966. Author is successful in his attempt to apply the techniques of modern literary criticism to the four epics studied: *Aymeri de Narbonne* (The Quest for the Woman and the City), *Ami et Amile* (The Quest for the Absolute), *Gaydon* (The Quest for Comedy), and *Huon de Bordeaux* (The Quest for Adventure).

————. *The Old French Epic of Revolt: Raoul de Cambrai, Renaud de Montauban, Gormond et Isembard*. Geneva: Droz, 1962. Earlier effort to treat the poems in question as literature. Author is more concerned with traditional problems than in his *Epic Quest*.

Crosland, Jessie. *The Old French Epic*. Oxford: Blackwell, 1951. Good general introduction to the background of the French heroic poems and to the major cycles. Sound if conventional treatment of such topics as the heathen, the traitor and his punishment, and epic traditions (characters, episodes, sentiments).

Curtius, Ernst Robert. *European Literature and the Latin Middle Ages*. Translated by Willard R. Trask. Bollingen Series, 36. New York: Pantheon, 1953. Celebrated theory of traditional literary patterns (*topoi*). Important for views concerning the Classical learning (especially the rhetorical training) of the medieval clerks.

Dorfman, Eugene. *The Narreme in the Medieval Romance Epic: An Introduction to Narrative Structures*. University of Toronto Romance Series 13. Toronto: University of Toronto Press, 1969. Author endeavors to apply the methods of modern linguistics to literary analysis. The narreme is a minimal structural unit analogous to the phoneme and morpheme. Stimulating discussion of the *Roland* and the *Cid*.

Duggan, Joseph. *The Song of Roland: Formulaic Style and Poetic Craft*. Publications of the Center for Medieval and Renaissance Studies, U.C.L.A., 6. Berkeley and Los Angeles: University of California Press, 1973. Exhaustive analysis of the *Roland*'s formulaic repertoire. Author maintains that Turoldus' poem is as much a product of oral tradition as the other chansons de geste.

Hatzfeld, Helmut. *Literature Through Art*. New York: Oxford University Press, 1952. Pioneering study. The sections dealing with "The Majestic-Hieratic Approach to Divine and Human Mysteries" and "Static Presentation of Fantastic Concepts" analyze the *Roland* in terms of the tympana at Moissac and Vézelay.

Jones, George Fenwick. *The Ethos of the Song of Roland*. Baltimore: Johns Hopkins Press, 1963. Using a semantic approach, author argues that the poem's heroes reflect a "shame" rather than a "guilt" culture and are more concerned with their honor and reputations than with Christian ideals and values.

Le Gentil, Pierre. *The Song of Roland*. Translated by Frances F. Beer. Cambridge, Mass.: Harvard University Press, 1969. Concise but elegant analysis. Author's moderate views are often cited.

Sholod, Barton. *Charlemagne in Spain: The Cultural Legacy of Roncesvalles*. Geneva: Droz, 1966. Thoroughgoing review of the Spanish background of the *Song of Roland*. Work is intended to serve as an introduction to the Carolingian tradition in medieval Spanish literature.

Vance, Eugene. *Reading the Song of Roland*. Landmarks in Literature. Englewood Cliff, N.J.: Prentice-Hall, 1970. Interesting views concerning the hero's character, the narrative setting, and tragic perspective. Perceptive and stylish.

10   The Spanish Epic

Merle E. Simmons

The epic tradition in Spain is a strong one. For centuries it has been cultivated with great vigor, particularly by those Spaniards who inhabit the arid and starkly beautiful mountains and plains of that part of central Spain known as Castile (land of castles). Here some of the oldest of Spanish epic themes were born over a thousand years ago, and many of them are still alive in oral folklore. They have not been confined, however, solely to the region of their origin. Some have, in fact, penetrated practically all areas of the Iberian Peninsula including Portugal. Following the Spanish conquest of the New World in the sixteenth century, many also passed into the folklore, mostly ballad lore, cultivated in the hamlets of Mexico, Argentina, Chile, and the Philippines, or in the remote mountain villages of Peru and Ecuador.

Yet, strong as the epic tradition has been on the traditional folkloric level, the student of Spanish folklore and literature cannot fail to be intrigued by the degree to which epic legends and epic heroes have proved to be over many centuries a vital and seminal force, not only among the unlettered peasants and villagers living in isolated areas where folklore normally prospers, but also among the poets, prose writers, and dramatists—that is, writers of "artistic" literature—who have at various periods in the history of Spanish and Portuguese letters found ever fresh inspiration in their country's epic poems and ballads. This phenomenon, which appeared most vigorously in the sixteenth and seventeenth centuries during Spain's "Golden Age" of literature, has renewed itself with surprising energy in the nineteenth and twentieth centuries. Modern-day theater-goers in Madrid are no less familiar with the Cid, Spain's most famous epic-ballad hero, than were their medieval ancestors, and even world-wide movie audiences have within the past decade seen Charleton Heston sally forth to engage Moors in mortal combat in a cinemascope version of one cycle of Cid legends. It is, indeed, precisely the *Cantar de mío Cid (Song of My Cid),* a fourteenth-century manuscript copy of a twelfth-century poem, to which we must turn for the major part of what we know about Spain's epic tradition in its earliest form.

The Cantar de mío Cid

Copied in 1307 in a Castilian monastery by an unidentified monk known to literary history only as Per Abbat, the *Cantar* or *Poema de mío Cid* is an anonymous poem of nearly 4000 lines written in an irregular meter that has long given scholars no little pause. It was composed probably around 1140, less than a half a century after the death of the historical Cid in 1099.[1] Close to the events it narrates, the *Cantar* displays innumerable touches of historicity and a taste for realistic details which contrast strikingly with the tone of those epic poems of some other cultures that are based upon legendary or imaginative accounts of events so fantastic in their conception or so remote in time or space as to have taken on an aura of unreality. Not so in the case of the Cid who rides Spain's dusty plains and mountains in the *Cantar*. Here we witness the very birth of a legendary figure, and not the least interesting aspect of his rise in subsequent centuries as a folk and literary hero is the way in which his character evolves as folksingers, the Spanish people, and literary artists mold his acts and deeds to conform to their views of what a legendary epic hero should be.

One of the great misfortunes of Spanish epic studies is that the *Cantar de mío Cid* is the only substantially complete example of an old epic text that has survived in poetic form, though fortunately, as we shall show, it has been possible to learn a great deal about the Spanish epic tradition from lengthy passages of other similar poems that were rendered into prose and incorporated into numerous medieval chronicles. Even more gratifying to students of the Spanish epic is the fact that *Mío Cid* is a very good work indeed and, for reasons which will become clear, occupies a distinguished place among the epic poems of world literature.

Ramón Menéndez Pidal, Spain's most outstanding student of its epic tradition, divides the *Cantar* as we know it into three separate sections, or *cantares*. The events narrated therein are as follows:

CANTAR DEL DESTIERRO (SONG OF EXILE)

Rodrigo Díaz de Vivar, the Cid, having been exiled unjustly by King Alfonso VI of Castile because of false accusations made against him by his enemies, leaves the town of Vivar in order to bid farewell to his wife, Ximena, and his daughters, Doña Elvira and Doña Sol, who have taken refuge in the monastery of Cardeña. The Cid entreats the abbot of the monastery to take good care of his family during the period of his exile. With a small band of some three hundred faithful followers, he is obliged to depart in great haste lest he fail to exit from Castile within the time limit set by his sovereign. Entering Moorish territory, he initially enjoys few successes, but matters improve when he attacks and takes two Moorish towns, Castejón and Alcocer, thereby winning considerable booty, which he immediately shares with his king by sending him thirty horses as a token of his unshaken fealty. Upon receipt of this gift, the King, though not disposed to pardon the Cid, consents to permit other soldiers from Castile to join the doughty warrior's marauding band, and with these reinforcements the Cid takes the town of Huesa. Then joining forces with the Moorish king of Zaragoza, the Cid moves against other Moors at Lérida, which is under the protection of the Catalán Count of Barcelona. The Cid wins this town also and captures the Count, but he generously releases his prisoner after only three days of captivity.

CANTAR DE LAS BODAS DE LAS HIJAS DEL CID
(SONG OF THE NUPTIALS OF THE CID'S DAUGHTERS)

The Cid now attacks Moorish settlements on the Mediterranean coast, lays siege to Valencia, and conquers the city after defeating a relief army sent by the Moorish king of Seville. The Cid names a warrior-priest, Don Jerónimo, to be bishop of Valencia, thereby solidly establishing Christianity in the area, and he sends a munificent gift of one hundred horses to King Alfonso. At the same time he begs the latter to permit his family to join him in Valencia, and the request is granted. From a tower of the Alcázar of Valencia the Cid proudly shows Doña Ximena and his daughters the city he has conquered. The King of Morocco besieges Valencia, but the Cid defeats him, and as a result of his victory he is able to send another handsome gift to his king, this time two hundred fine horses. The Infantes of Carrión, high-born Castilian noblemen who are looking for wealthy wives in order to enrich themselves, convey to King Alfonso their wish to marry the Cid's daughters, and the King intervenes with the exiled leader in their behalf. At the same time the King lifts the Cid's exile and pardons him. The Cid, though unimpressed by the fatuous Infantes, is hesitant to refuse his king's request, so he consents with little enthusiasm to the marriage of his daughters. He returns to Valencia with his future sons-in-law and the weddings take place with celebrations befitting the occasion.

CANTAR DE LA AFRENTA DE CORPES
(SONG OF THE DISHONOR OF CORPES)

The Infantes soon prove to be cowards in battle. Also, on an occasion when a lion escapes in the Cid's palace, they hide in a most shameful manner. To escape from being the butt of palace jokes, the Infantes ask for permission to take their wives to Carrión, but on reaching an oak grove near Corpes, motivated by a desire to take revenge upon the Cid for the mockery they have suffered, they strip their wives naked, whip them cruelly, and abandon them. A nephew of the Cid happens to find the girls and returns them to their father. Now the Cid demands justice from the King, who shares his dishonor because of the role he played in arranging the marriages. The King convokes Cortes in

Toledo, and supporters of the two parties are summoned to argue their cases. The Cid peremptorily calls upon the Infantes to return to him Colada and Tizón, two favorite swords that he had given to them, he demands the return of his daughters' substantial dowries, and his men challenge the Infantes' supporters to a duel in order to restore their leader's honor. The Cid's material demands are met, and his soldiers vanquish the Infantes' band. At almost the same moment the princes of Navarra and of Aragon ask for the Cid's daughters in marriage. Thus at the end of the poem, through a manly display of a wide range of human and chivalric virtues (fortitude, bravery, enterprise, loyalty to his sovereign, love of wife and family, and the like), the Cid has gained great wealth and fame. His relationship with his king has been reestablished on a firm footing, his honor has been restored, and the new marriages of his daughters, who are destined to become queens, assure that the Cid and his descendants will be related through marriage with the royal lines of Spain.

THE CHARACTERS

Obviously the Cid was no ordinary man, and his heroic and soldierly qualities were uppermost in the minds of the singer of the *Cantar* and his audience. Yet, almost as striking as the larger-than-life image of the Cid that the singer creates is the measured restraint with which he depicts a hero whose feet remain planted firmly on the earth of Castilian reality, whose passage through the poem conforms in its major points to the history of the Cid as recorded in other sources, and whose qualities as vassal, soldier, husband, and father are kept within reasonable and believable bounds. Students of the epic have often noted that the Spanish hero offers a striking contrast to most other heroes of folk-epic tradition in that here is a man who is depicted *primarily as a human being* with intensely human and practical problems such as troubles with his king, the need to provide for his wife and daughters during his exile, heartrending goodbyes to his loved ones (the singer describes this leave-taking as being like tearing a fingernail away from the flesh), and the need to raise money quickly to pay his small army. He solves this latter problem by tricking some Jewish money-lenders. Furthermore, his feats of arms, though by no means those of an ordinary soldier, are not beyond the reach of an audience's sense of reality. For example, the Moors killed in battle with the Cid and his army number in the hundreds, not the many thousands slain personally by his French epic counterpart in the *Chanson de Roland*. And the Cid never falls into such extremes as condemning himself and 20,000 others to die in the name of a military code of honor as does Roland at Roncesvalles, where reinforcements could have saved the day had the French hero not been stubbornly unwilling to call for help. The Cid is always the consummate soldier and leader, but never the fool, and in his virtues and even his failings (for example, the trickery mentioned above) he always seems to display warmly human qualities. He is simply an exceptional man of his time writ large by popular tradition.

If the central events of the *Cantar* and the Cid's existence are based to a very considerable degree on historical events recorded in the written chronicles of his time, and if the singer's conception of his hero is characterized by remarkable realism, so also the secondary figures who surround the hero reinforce the aura of historical reality that pervades the entire poem. Ximena Díaz, daughter of the Count of Oviedo, was indeed the wife of the historical Cid, and they had two daughters as the poem records, though their names were not the ones used by the poet. The Count of Barcelona, prisoner of the Cid, was also a figure from history, as, in fact, were almost all of the important personages named in the *Cantar*. The singer does not hesitate on more than one occasion to take certain liberties with historical fact in the name of art or legend. History, for example, knows nothing of the marriage of the Cid's daughters to the Infantes de Carrión, though the latter are mentioned in chronicles as being enemies of the Cid. This, however, does not destroy the overriding fact that the *Cantar* is a most notable example of early realism in art. In fact, the *Cantar de mío Cid,* the first true monument of either oral or written literature in the Castilian language, points the way for an infinite number of examples in Spanish folklore, literature, and painting that from the twelfth to the twentieth centuries have attested to a strong Spanish tendency toward sober and earthy realism in practically all forms of art, from epic poetry and ballads to the novel, and from the paintings of Velázquez or Goya to the religious images that grace Spanish altars.

Let it be noted that the poetry of the *Cantar de mío Cid,* restrained by the singer's serious and factual approach to his subject, does not soar with the sublime flights of poetic fantasy that give epics such as the *Chanson de Roland* their inimitable power to fire the imagination and stir the spirit. Yet, the imaginative narrative techniques of the Castilian singer and his deft and subtle poetic touches as he skillfully orders events and portrays the characters both of his hero and the people around him have a sublimity of their own that touches the sensibilities and evokes deep emotions. Indeed, Edmund de Chasca, one of the ablest of modern Cid scholars, exalts its poetic excellence by stating: "the Castilian *Cantar* is ... [an] outstanding example of epic structuring if by poetic we understand the total effect of the narrative as a creative act and the felicitous arrangement of each and every one of its component elements toward achieving that end."[2] In support of his thesis, De Chasca calls attention to the poem's structural perfection and its author's skill in weaving all the elements of his work around a central theme, the honor of the Cid. He points also to many stylistic devices that are masterfully employed: the rapid enumeration of place names to suggest haste, dramatic movement evidenced by terse dialogue to express psychological reactions in moments of crisis, the passage of time poetically conveyed by reference to the rising or setting of the sun or such other phenomena as the crowing of the cock, the depiction of character by economical but very graphic selection of a few expressive descriptive details, the dramatic revelation of character through action (the Cid and his followers are, like most folk heroes, men of action, not Hamlets), and the subtle development of transcendental meanings for certain key words in the singer's poetic vocabulary (for example, the word *cabalgar,* conveying much more than its mere literal meaning of "to mount" or "to ride horseback," signifies instead the undertaking of almost any kind of important activity).[3] In fact, on a poetic level the singer of the *Cantar* compensates through such displays of undeniable poetic talent for the some-times recalciorant character of the Castilian language of his day, a mode of oral expression that was still crude and rough-hewn. Several centuries were to pass before the Spanish language achieved the flexibility and richness of expression that characterize it in the sixteenth century, but this did not deter the epic singer from achieving effects of great poetic merit through the use of what a modern scholar, Dámaso Alonso, has described as "creative style." Alonso holds that the singer of the *Cantar* relates his tale "with such variety, so profoundly and so richly, that here I see one of the notes that most justify our considering the *Poema del Cid* as a masterpiece of our art."[4] The com-poser's success stems, of course, from his masterly adaptation of the folk vernacular to poetic uses, though he was, as we shall see shortly, surely drawing upon an existing and long-standing oral tradition as he did this.

Concerning certain other aspects of the poem, there has been no little disagreement among the most knowledgeable of literary scholars, critics, and folklorists. Some, like Ferdinand Wolf in the nineteenth century, have stressed the poem's value as an expression of the Spanish "national charac-ter,"[5] and more recently, Menéndez Pidal has expressed substantial agree-ment, though he adds a few perceptive observations. Unlike the French *Chan-son de Roland,* which he praises for its broad synthesis of many contemporary values that taken together add up to a clear feeling for the unity of France, the *Cantar de mío Cid* does not, in Pidal's view, express a patriotic ideal so precisely understood. Forcefully expressed, to be sure, is a heartfelt longing for their native Castile which the Cid and his men experience as they go into exile, and the hero's unshakable veneration for his king, who personifies his native region, contains both tenderness and magnanimity; but this, Pidal notes, should not be equated with the tragic grandeur that the French singer achieves so dramatically in the *Chanson de Roland.* The *Poema del Cid* is not, Pidal observes, "national" because of any marked sense of patriotism dis-played in it, but rather in the more restricted sense that the Cid's character as therein depicted undeniably reflects the most noble qualities of the people among whom it was written, that is to say, the Castilians who made the Cid the most notable of their folk heroes. Pidal calls attention to some of the praiseworthy traits of character already treated above, with special additional stress on the democratic spirit personified by the Cid who, according to the singer of the *Cantar,* was that "good vassal who does not have a good lord."[6]

Other scholars have seen these problems in somewhat different lights. Karl Vossler considers the personal problem of the Cid—the defense and restoration of his honor—to be much more important than any regional, national, or religious sentiment, either incipient or well-developed.[7] De Chasca also considers the Cid's honor to be the theme that overshadows everything else.[8] Leo Spitzer, on the other hand, while stressing the importance of the many moral and spiritual values intertwined with the question of the Cid's personal honor, is of the opinion that these concerns stem from a general chivalric spirit that is probably more universally European than uniquely Castilian in its essence.[9] From such learned discussions it is fair to conclude only that the poem is multifaceted and rich in nuances, and that it lends itself to fruitful analysis from many divergent points of view.

The Origins of the Spanish Epic

That the *Cantar de mío Cid* does not represent the Spanish epic in its most primitive form should be obvious from the preceding discussion of its well-developed literary qualities. Though in some respects an unpolished gem lacking certain refinements to be found in the epic poems of some other regions, most notably France, it is clear that *Mío Cid* is masterfully executed in so many respects that it cannot conceivably be the trail-blazing work of an innovating literary artist groping his way toward the development of a new poetic genre. It represents instead—and this is obvious even in the absence of corroborating texts—an epic tradition that had been evolving for a long time before the author of this particular work was moved to celebrate the Cid's fairly recent exploits in song.

The origins of the Spanish epic and many ancillary problems have long occupied the attention of numerous distinguished scholars in many parts of the world, though the work of all of them is overshadowed by the monumental scholarship of Ramón Menéndez Pidal, who from the latter years of the nineteenth century until his death in 1969, only days short of reaching his one-hundredth birthday, dedicated himself with particular zeal, though by no means exclusively, to the study of the epic and ballad traditions of his native Spain. His theories and the masterly works he produced to support them revolutionized a whole field of study, and the works of others, whether written to support or to refute his hypotheses, always had as their focal point the massive body of scholarship which the great Spanish philologist-historian-folklorist offered to the world. This is still true today. Our discussion of epic problems in Spain must, perforce, revolve primarily around Menéndez Pidal's studies.

Before considering some general problems, it is desirable to set down a few basic and generally accepted facts about *cantares de gesta* and the oral tradition that produced them. A *cantar de gesta,* the term used in Spain to signify an epic composition, is a song (*cantar*) or recitation about outstanding or heroic deeds (*gesta*) sung or recited by a performer known as a *juglar*. The Spanish cantares, it should be noted, surely came into being as *oral,* not written, literature, and they were usually diffused by oral means, that is, by traveling *juglares* who moved from town to town or from castle to castle putting on shows for the entertainment of noblemen and the common people. Of juglares there were many types. Some were singers, and these were the individuals to whom epic scholars and folklorists are most indebted for the diffusion and preservation of Spain's vigorous epic tradition, but also called juglares were acrobats, sleight-of-hand artists, mimes—in short, a wide variety of public performers of almost any type. Medieval documents from many parts of Europe indicate that moralists everywhere looked with disfavor upon the juglares, who were frequently censured as an immoral lot. It is notable, however, that in the famous *Siete Partidas* of King Alfonso the Wise of Castile, wherein Spanish society of the thirteenth century is described in great detail, the singers of narrative songs about feats of arms and other heroic deeds are highly esteemed and characterized in much more favorable terms than are other types of juglares.

The narrative songs of the juglares seem to have served two main purposes: first, to entertain an audience and to satisfy its curiosity about exciting or stirring events, and second, to inform the community in general about those matters or happenings that were important to its destiny. Menéndez Pidal states that the cantar de gesta was born as a substitute for a nonexistent historiography at a time when word of important events was spread among people on all social levels by means of song. This phenomenon manifests itself, he observes, at those times in history when a people, swept up by a keen and fairly unanimous national interest, and possessing a warm and affective, rather than practical, political sentiment, has need of recurrent information about its own important events both present and past. Not having arrived in its cultural development at a point where it possesses a literature normally expressed in written form, much less a genre of historical prose writing expressed in the vulgar tongue, such a people uses meter, rhyme, and song—in some ways more powerful than writing—as means of publication in order to set down and diffuse narrative accounts of general interest. Such, in Menéndez Pidal's view, were the conditions that obtained in Spain during the medieval period when the Castilian epic made its appearance.[10]

Where the Spanish epic came from has been a source of much controversy. Many nineteenth-century investigators, under the influence of the great French scholar, Gaston Paris, subscribed for the most part to a theory of French origins for the Spanish epic.[11] That the earliest French texts we know today admittedly preceded the *Cantar de mío Cid* lent credence to this hypothesis, and certain obvious similarities between the Spanish and French songs seemed to support such a view. As in so many other areas, however, Menéndez Pidal's investigations led him to modify radically, though not reject totally, this widely accepted theory. Agreeing with almost all other scholars that the French epic stemmed primarily from Germanic origins, Pidal suggested that the Spanish epic likewise evolved from the same source, the French and Spanish epic traditions being simply two vigorous but separate branches of the same Germanic trunk. The carriers who brought to Spain the Teutonic tradition of celebrating important events in song were, of course, the Visigoths. In support of his conclusions the Spanish scholar marshals an impressive array of evidence that the epic tradition had taken root in Spain long before the later highly developed French epic came into being.[12] Among the most important of these proofs is a passage from San Isidoro's *Institutionum disciplinae,* written in the seventh century, wherein the Spanish bishop recommends that young nobles in the exercise of their voices choose songs about their ancestors (*carmina maiorum*) over love songs or other unworthy types, since the recounting of famous deeds is an uplifting influence for singers and listeners. This was a century and a half before Charlemagne ordered that the ancient barbaric songs of the Franks be learned by memory.[13]

The upshot of all this is, of course, that the oldest Spanish epics were, Menéndez Pidal believes, Germanic in character, though he does recognize in his own theory that the French epic began to exert very strong and significant influences on its Spanish counterpart around the beginning of the twelfth century. This phenomenon can be attributed principally to the pervasive influence of French culture on many aspects of Spanish life as political relations between the Spanish and the French courts were intensified, as the monks of Cluny became active in Spain in the eleventh century, and, most importantly for folk poetry, as thousands of pilgrims from all parts of Europe came into Spain while making their long trek to the shrine of Saint James in Galicia.[14] With the pilgrims came many French *jongleurs* (called *juglares* in Spanish) who were the main purveyors of the great French epic songs and whose mission it was to entertain the pilgrims on the way to Santiago de Compostela. Given the intrinsic merit of the French songs and their overwhelming popularity, they inevitably influenced the existing Spanish epic tradition in important ways, for example, by introducing new themes and new poetic techniques.

Besides the theories of French or Germanic origins for the Spanish epic, at one time a third hypothesis was espoused by a leading Spanish Arabist, Julián Ribera, who held that the Spanish epic grew out of early Andalusian tradition.[15] However, his theory of decisive Arabic influence on the genesis of the genre has not prospered in the face of Menéndez Pidal's brilliant defense of its Germanic origins.

Theories of the Epic in Spain and France

Basic to Menéndez Pidal's entire study of the Spanish epic and its development is a fundamental premise concerning the character of traditional (i.e., oral) poetry, a conception which in its essence is applicable to both the medieval epic *and* the later ballad tradition which we shall deal with shortly. Menéndez Pidal's hypotheses in this area challenge the theories of another well-defined school of epic scholars whose most able and energetic spokesman for many years around the turn of the present century was the eminent Frenchman, Joseph Bédier. For Bédier the great epic poems in French and

Spanish, such as the *Chanson de Roland* and the *Cantar de mío Cid*, were the works of erudite and gifted clerical poets who wrote them many centuries after the events narrated, taking their raw materials from written sources preserved in some monastery or abbey; that is to say, they were essentially the inspired personal creations of individual poets who as conscious literary artists drawing upon written history sought to create works of art that would give expression to their personal genius, their view of life and man, and the values in their own society that stirred them to write.[16] Epic scholars, then, should necessarily be concerned with determining the identity of the individual artist who wrote each epic creation, studying his personality, noting the peculiarities of his personal style, and when possible, ascertaining his source materials. In diametric opposition to this "individualist" approach, Menéndez Pidal proposed a "traditionalist" theory to explain the genesis of the Spanish epic. "Traditionalism believes," he wrote, "that the origins of the Romance literatures are much earlier than the surviving texts and that these cannot be explained without taking into account a long tradition of lost texts...."[17] To believe that the *Chanson de Roland* or the *Cantar de mío Cid* could have been the primitive first fruits of the epic muse in France or Spain or that they are in their essence the personal inventions of a pair of inspired poets, he declares, would be to believe the impossible, given the literary excellence of both works. These can be explained, he insists, only by hypothesizing many years of linguistic and literary refinement of an epic tradition that surely must have preceded the appearance of such highly developed poems. Furthermore, the formal and ideological characteristics of these compositions diverge so greatly from the old Latin and high-medieval texts, which some scholars have suggested as their putative literary ancestors, that these simply cannot be accepted as the immediate or sole inspiration of the poems in question. A long period of gestation must, therefore, be hypothesized to explain the development of the mature French and Spanish epic genre.[18]

Menéndez Pidal believes that the characteristic anonymity of heroic poetry must be considered along with the passage of time as a factor in the epic's evolution. The individualist theory indulges in a great anachronism, he avers, when it assumes the composer of an epic cantar to have the same sense of personal identity a modern poet feels with his work. Quite to the contrary, as the author of each primitive poem works, he has no idea of the permanency of an artistic composition, and he would be astonished if anyone were to tell him that his name should be associated with the fruits of his labors. He simply receives from his community an anonymous cultural legacy, expressed in verse or perhaps in some less precise form, and he sets this material to verse or reworks the poetry he has received, feeling himself to be just as anonymous as everybody else. Pidal goes so far as to hypothesize that this anonymity is a general law in all periods of literary origins and is to be observed almost universally in the first preserved texts; only at a later time do works begin to appear with the name of an author, and with these begins the period of personal art.[19] The authorship of an epic work cannot, then, in truth be assigned to any single individual. The reworking of the work of one author by another, he insists, is not a fortuitous accident but rather is performed recurrently and regularly; and if each reworking may have several authors and always presupposes successive authors, then the criticism that is content to say that the *Chanson de Roland* begins and ends with a single poet falls into a naive anachronism. The fact is, Pidal declares as he takes up and develops an idea originated by Gaston Paris, the authors of an epic poem are legion![20]

Support for this theory is, to be sure, hard to come by when, as has been noted earlier, epic texts are so scarce and none in Spain precedes the well-developed *Cantar de mío Cid*. Nevertheless, Menéndez Pidal and his followers, in an impressive display of painstaking and frequently ingenious research, have assembled a large body of documentary evidence of various kinds designed to prove that the Spanish epic, and the French epic too, during their primitive period existed in oral tradition for several centuries before the texts we know were committed to writing. While the details of this evidence are too numerous to deal with here, the most striking body of proof is based upon Menéndez Pidal's careful reconstruction of a substantial number of epic passages that in prose form were imbedded in several medieval chronicles. In some cases a chronicler, using traditional songs as source materials for the writing of serious history and apparently working in some instances with a manuscript of an epic poem before him (probably like the manuscript we have of the *Cantar de mío Cid*), rendered long poetic passages into prose that not infrequently still has lines that scan like poetry, retains unsuppressed rhymes, and in general preserves a lively and dramatic style that makes such passages stand out from the less sprightly narrative that surrounds them. Menéndez Pidal first dazzled the world of scholarship in 1896 when as a young man he published a study entitled *La leyenda de los Infantes de Lara*, wherein he was able to reconstruct long passages of not one but two old poems about a family feud.[21] These he had discovered in prose form in several fourteenth-century chronicles. Subsequently he and other scholars have been able to reconstruct substantial portions of several other epic poems. As a result of such studies we now know that in addition to the *Cantar de mío Cid* there were similar epics about at least thirteen other clearly defined themes dealing with particular heroes or notable episodes in history or legend, and it is clear, furthermore, that in some cases not one but many different poems dealt with a single subject. Unfortunately, except for *Mío Cid*, only one small fragment of about one hundred lines from a *Cantar de Roncesvalles* has been discovered in its poetic form, but brief though it is, this little manuscript fragment is of extreme importance. Not only does it show how Spanish singers imitated and adapted French themes (as the title indicates, the poem deals with the famous battle of Carolingian tradition), but it serves mightily to confirm many observations about such matters as metrics, style, and narrative techniques that scholars had formulated earlier on the basis of their study of only the *Cantar de mío Cid* and reconstructed poems.[22]

Another development of great import to Menéndez Pidal's defense of his "traditionalist" theory occurred in 1954 when a short text known as the *Nota Emilianense* was uncovered in the Spanish Monastery of San Millán and revealed to the world in a study by Dámaso Alonso.[23] The *Nota*, whose date as established by rigorous methods has been set between 1065 and 1076, or some thirty or forty years before the extant text of the *Chanson de Roland* was written, contains some most interesting folkloric material about the French defeat at Roncesvalles and anticipates details contained in the *Chanson*. Furthermore, it gives the names of some of the principal heroes of the *Chanson* and other French epic poems as well. Apparently, then, the essentials of the Roland theme had been widely diffused long before the poem as we know it was given written form. This graphic proof of a pre-existing poem, apparently in the guise that characterized it later in the *Chanson*, effectively undermines the "individualist" position of Bédier who, it will be recalled, studied the *Chanson de Roland* and the *Cantar de mío Cid* as the first fruits of their respective epic traditions and as the personal creations of two gifted literary artists. Correspondingly, the *Nota Emilianense* is corroborative support for the theory of "latent" epic traditions on an oral level which is so important to "traditionalist" scholars.

Periods in the Epic's Development in Spain

If Menéndez Pidal's traditionalist theory and his hypothesis of Germanic origins for the Spanish epic be accepted, then the character of whatever lost texts preceded the twelfth-century poems we now have becomes a question of considerable interest. There were, Menéndez Pidal believes, four periods in the development of the epic genre in Spain. During the first of these, a formative period beginning after the tenth century and lasting until the appearance of poems like *Mío Cid* around the beginning of the twelfth century, the stock-in-trade of early Spanish epic juglares seems to have been relatively short songs of from 400 to 600 lines. The themes treated in these primitive compositions were some of the old legends about such subjects as Don Rodrigo, the Visigoth king whom legendary history blames for the loss of Spain to the Moors, Count Fernán González, the heroic defender of Castile's independence, the Infantes de Lara, seven brothers who died as victims of one of the great blood feuds of Spanish history, and the siege of Zamora, a dramatic episode replete with elements of human greed and treachery. In support of his belief in the existence of relatively brief epic poems during the formative period, Menéndez Pidal cites evidence that has accrued from many sources, principally his study of the prose forms of traditional songs he discovered in various chronicles, but also including documented references to lost epic poems. Worthy of note also at the end of this first period is the introduction of French influences, most importantly Carolingian themes, into Spain's epic tradition.

A second period from about 1140 to 1236 marks the plenitude of the Spanish epic. Though only the *Cantar de mío Cid* and the fragmentary *Cantar de Roncesvalles* have survived in their traditional poetic form, the general literary quality of the poems sung at this time was apparently much enhanced over that of the primitive epics and they became much longer. *Mío Cid* is on both counts a worthy representative of the changes that had occurred. At this time also, the prestige of the epic as a literary genre and the esteem accorded to singers of epic poetry apparently reached new heights.

The year 1236 witnessed the appearance of the *Chronicon Mundi,* a Latin chronicle by one Lucas de Tuy, which is the first of a long line of historiographic works that draw upon cantares de gesta as sources of historical information about past events. Had this use of epic songs by historians not occurred, the fairly numerous texts that have been so brilliantly reconstructed by modern scholars would have been lost forever. Actually, the period when prose versions of traditional epic poems were systematically incorporated into important chronicles, now written in the vernacular, lasts until about the middle of the fourteenth century, and this period is the third epoch in the history of the Spanish epic.

The fourth and last period, which extends into the middle of the fifteenth century, marks the decadence of the old epic. It is characterized by the entry into epic tradition of many extraneous legendary and novelesque themes, a decline in the sober and dignified tone that had characterized the epic in its heyday, and a tendency toward uncritical and unrestrained glorification of epic heroes. Also during this period, the decline of the traditional epic leads to a complete breakdown of the long poems that had been popular for so long, and from them emerges a new and shorter type of traditional narrative poem, the historical ballad (i.e., *romance*).[24]

The Theory of Fragmentation and the Rise of Spanish Ballads

The demise of the long epic poems and the rise of the *romance* lead us into another but related area of scholarly research. At least since the early nineteenth century, when scholars imbued with Romantic ideas about popular poetry began serious study of traditional or folkloric texts, the question of ballad origins has occupied the attention of innumerable investigators all over the world. As a result of many scholars working with different ballad traditions, a great many theories have evolved—it seems at times that there are almost as many theories as there are cultures studied—and it would be foolish to expect, as some scholars did in an earlier day, that the origins of different ballad traditions in all parts of the world could be explained in identical or similar terms. Yet no treatment of the Spanish epic would be complete without consideration of the rise of the Spanish romance as a lineal descendant of the old epic poems, and no discussion of general ballad theory can fail to take into account the monumental studies that Hispanists, particularly Menéndez Pidal, have made of the Spanish romance. What makes their studies so intriguing is the fact that in Spain as in few other cultural areas, the tie between the ballad tradition of the fourteenth to the twentieth centuries and the old epic poems of the twelfth to the fourteenth centuries can be clearly established. This has given rise to a theory substantiated by convincing proof that the "fragmentation" of the long epic poems of medieval tradition produced the Spanish romances. Before discussing these subjects in detail, however, a look at one other aspect of the remote origins of the old long epics is called for.

In the early years of the nineteenth century, before the rise of either "individualist" or "traditionalist" theories of epic origins, such scholars as Ferdinand Wolf, Agustín Durán, and Gaston Paris theorized that juglares had created long poems like the *Cantar de mío Cid* by linking together numerous shorter and older poems about legendary heroes. The supposition was that the epic-lyric romances about such themes as the Cid, the Infantes de Lara, and the siege of Zamora, which were still very much alive in nineteenth-century oral tradition, were probably remnants or vestiges of very old short songs (they were referred to as *cantilenae*) that had been grouped together to create long epics like the poems about Charlemagne in France or *Mío Cid* in Spain.[25] By the mid-1800s the great Catalán scholar, Manuel Milá y Fontanals, who earlier had accepted the *cantilena* theory, was offering conclusive evidence that the long poems must have antedated the romances and that the latter, far from being of extreme antiquity, actually were of relatively recent date and were in many cases fragments of the long cantares.[26] Other scholars like Marcelino Menéndez y Pelayo accepted Milá's findings and even elaborated upon them in a significant manner, but it remained for Menéndez Pidal, beginning late in the century, to develop the theory of "fragmentation" with a mass of hard documentary evidence. He was able to show that some of the earliest of the old historical ballads, like the songs about the Infantes de Lara, did indeed evolve directly from the epics during the period when the old epic tradition entered its period of decline in the fourteenth and fifteenth centuries.

Briefly stated, Menéndez Pidal's theory of "fragmentation" posits that as the old epic fell upon hard times, juglares found that their audiences displayed an affinity for hearing certain favorite parts of the old cantares, usually brief narrative episodes or dramatic exchanges of dialogue that marked moments of high tension in the traditional epic songs, and that these sections lifted from the longer poems came to be sung independently.[27] Everyone was thoroughly familiar with the substance of the tales and legends about the principal epic heroes, so listeners could mentally place the isolated episodes in their proper historical or legendary context. With the passage of time, so the theory goes, many of the fragments, presumably the best ones, came to have an independent existence of their own. Sung not only by juglares but by non-professionals as well—a singer of folksongs did not have to have the memory of a professional performer to remember a song of a few dozen or even a few hundred lines—these earliest romances passed into general oral tradition and sparked a new kind of development that has flourished in the Hispanic world ever since.

The evidence that Menéndez Pidal offers in support of his theory of fragmentation is most impressive. Some of the earliest of the old ballads (*romances viejos*) clearly come almost verbatim from several of the old epic texts so carefully reconstructed from the thirteenth- and fourteenth-century chronicles, and most scholars find it very difficult to argue against Menéndez Pidal's brilliant treatises on the genesis of *at least some of the oldest of Spanish ballads*. Yet, irresistible as his arguments are in explaining the origins of a goodly number of well-known romances, the theory of fragmentation does not explain all of the old ballads, nor does Menéndez Pidal claim this. He does maintain, however, that problems which arise from the fact that many old romances do not seem to be derived from any known epic texts should not be exaggerated inasmuch as there is no doubt that only a very few of the old poems have survived even as prose texts imbedded in historical chronicles. To other objections he gives similarly reasonable counter-arguments supported by evidence drawn from his vast store of erudition.

The Romance's Subsequent Development and Spanish Ballad Theory

With the decline of Spain's medieval epic in the fourteenth and fifteenth centuries, the history of the Hispanic epic is actually only half told because the rise of the short narrative romances represented more a change of form, style, and tone than a radical departure from the basic epic stream, and in its ballad guise the epic tradition has continued, strong and vigorous, for another five hundred years. The Cid, Bernardo del Carpio, the Infantes de Lara, and, in fact, most of the old epic heroes have remained alive and well in Hispanic song and legend, though sometimes with changes in emphasis or even radical transformation. The best example of this latter phenomenon is the Cid himself, who in ballad lore and folk legend is generally a flamboyant and reckless youth, not the mature and seasoned warrior of the *Cantar de mío Cid*. The origins of this newer Cid tradition are to be found in a late cantar, *Las mocedades de Rodrigo (The Youth of Rodrigo),* which most scholars consider to be a good example of the decadent poems that appeared around 1400 during the last period of the old epic's development.

The vigorous cultivation of the romance over some five centuries, not only in Spain but in the New World as well, is in many ways, then, simply an extension of the ancient epic into modern times, and some of the processes that must have shaped the medieval cantares, particularly those which govern the existence of narrative songs in oral tradition, have continued to work on romances to a degree not experienced by their epic progenitors. Precisely because these relatively recent songs lend themselves to more exhaustive study than the older epic, mostly because thousands of ballad texts have survived either as printed in numerous songbooks (*romanceros*) beginning in the sixteenth century or, more dynamically, as collected from oral folklore in many parts of the world, it is fitting that we take a brief look at certain aspects of ballad theory as developed by Spain's best scholars, led once again by Menéndez Pidal, in order to round out this discussion of the Hispanic epic tradition.

As was true in his interpretation of the medieval epic, so in studying Spanish romances Pidal stresses the paramount importance of *oral,* as opposed to written, transmission of traditional folk poetry. Extremely noteworthy here is the fact that the epic poems belonged primarily to a relatively few professional juglares, while the more folkloric romances are the property of anybody who cares to sing them, professional or non-professional. Under these conditions every individual singer participates in a very real sense in the process of "creating" a ballad. Within certain broad limits set by folk tastes and accepted norms, any singer feels free to do whatever he pleases with the text he has received from oral tradition: to shorten it, to lengthen it (though this is not a usual practice), to reorder lines or whole passages, to alter words or lines with an eye toward enhancing either narrative or dialogue, to change terms or phrases that for any reason seem inappropriate or unpoetic or unclear, to suppress anything that lessens dramatic tension—in short, to "improve" the ballad in any way he deems desirable. If any of his innovations strike a responsive chord among his listeners, who themselves are potential singers of the same traditional song, they may choose to repeat the ballad in the "new" manner; if others also find the innovation to their liking, the "new" variant of the romance may in time supersede the older traditional way of singing it. If, on the other hand, any given innovation encounters no favorable response among those who hear and judge it, then it disappears quickly and quietly, leaving not even a ripple in folk tradition. As a result of this kind of slow creative process repeated thousands and millions of times on countless ballads over many centuries, truly traditional narrative romances have through such honing and pruning developed certain salient characteristics that set them apart from their medieval progenitors. They are usually relatively short (most traditional texts vary from a dozen to perhaps fifty lines or so) because excess verbiage has been pared away. They are wont to begin abruptly *in medias res,* because introductions or explanations are superfluous to an audience thoroughly familiar with the subject matter treated, and frequently they leap from one dramatic scene to another with little or no narrative transition. Dialogue is usually cut back to a few sparse lines dramatizing personal conflict or deep emotion, and descriptive passages, even descriptive adjectives, are customarily used most sparingly. Like ballads everywhere, they also lean heavily on formulaic lines and phrases. Almost all of these stylistic procedures were, to be sure, widely cultivated in their cantares by medieval juglares, but the extremes to which balladeers go in such matters contrast even with the generally terse epic style and give the romances an unmistakable aura of lean but dramatic sobriety uniquely their own.

To be derived from all the evidence that Menéndez Pidal and his followers assemble in documenting such important matters as these is an understanding of the peculiarly *dynamic* quality of a ballad's existence in oral tradition; in the last analysis this aspect of Pidal's work is most important to both epic and ballad studies not only in Spain but wherever these genres of popular literature are found in oral tradition. Precisely because the existence of a folkloric romance, like the oral epics before it, cannot be treated as static or stable (Pidal's conception of "tradition" was never that of certain folklorists who were content to study "fossils" or "vestiges" or even "survivals," except insofar as survivals are living organisms), any search for the "first" text or the "best" text of either an epic or a ballad (scholars of the "individualist" school tended to equate the two) is usually of secondary or only archeological interest, as are, of course, most attempts to determine the "first" author of a ballad text. Even more than in the case of epic poems, avers Menéndez Pidal, the authors who created any given romance, through the process described above, were truly "legion." Furthermore, all this is as true of folkloric literature in the twentieth century as it was in the twelfth, and it is this dynamic conception of oral tradition as it works upon folkloric texts that makes Menéndez Pidal's work on the epic and the ballad so important not only for the understanding it affords of the Hispanic tradition immediately under investigation, but also for the important broader insights it provides of the slow, inexorable, but very vital processes that, we can assume, are at work anywhere in the world where folksongs, or indeed any other kinds of folklore, live in the minds and hearts and on the lips of the folk who nurture them.

NOTES

1. The most accessible authoritative version of the text along with notes and an excellent introduction is the "Clásicos Castellanos" edition prepared by Ramón Menéndez Pidal, *Poema de mío Cid,* 11th ed. (Madrid: Espasa-Calpe, 1966). There are other more scholarly editions, also by Menéndez Pidal: *Poema de mío Cid: Edición facsímil del Códice de Per Abat, conservado en la Biblioteca Nacional,* 2 vols. (Madrid: Dirección General de Archivos y Bibliotecas, 1961), and *Cantar de mío Cid: Texto, gramática y vocabulario,* 3rd ed., 3 vols. (Madrid: Espasa-Calpe, 1966).

The date of composition of the poem and that of the extant manuscript as established by Menéndez Pidal have occasionally been subjected to critical scrutiny. A recent article which deals with the problem is Colin Smith's "The Personages of the 'Poema de mío Cid' and the Date of the Poem," *Modern Language Review* 66 (1971): 580–98. Smith offers some very cogent reasons for questioning whether the poem was composed as early as Pidal believed, though he does not claim to have proven conclusively that Pidal was in error.

2. Edmund de Chasca, *El arte juglaresco en el "Cantar de mío Cid,"* segunda edición aumentada (Madrid: Editorial Gredos, 1972), p. 55. All translations of Spanish texts in this chapter are my own.

3. Ibid., pp. 63–124.

4. Dámaso Alonso, "Estilo y creación en el *Poema del Cid,*" in *Ensayos sobre poesía española* (Madrid: Revista de Occidente, 1944), p. 83.

5. Ferdinand Wolf, *Studien zur Geschichte der spanischen und portugiesischen Nationalliteratur* (Berlin: A. Asher, 1859), p. 30.

6. Menéndez Pidal, *Poema de mío Cid*, pp. 95–96.

7. Karl Vossler, "Carta española a Hugo von Hoffmannsthal," in *Algunos caracteres de la cultura española* (Buenos Aires: Espasa-Calpe, 1943), p. 11.

8. Edmund de Chasca, *El arte juglaresco en el "Cantar de mío Cid"* (Madrid: Editorial Gredos, 1967), pp. 61–80.

9. Leo Spitzer, "Sobre el carácter histórico del Cantar de mío Cid," *Nueva Revista de Filología Hispánica* 2 (1948): 105–17.

10. Ramón Menéndez Pidal, "Problemas de la poesía épica," in *Mis páginas preferidas: Temas literarios* (Madrid: Editorial Gredos, 1957), p. 45.

11. Gaston Paris, *La littérature française au Moyen-Age (XIe-XIVe siècles)*, 2nd ed. (Paris: Hachette et Cie, 1890).

12. Ramón Menéndez Pidal, "Orígenes de la epopeya castellana," in *La epopeya castellana a través de la literatura española* (Buenos Aires and México: Espasa-Calpe, 1945), pp. 11–40.

13. Ramón Menéndez Pidal, "Los godos y el origen de la epopeya española," in *España y su historia*, I (Madrid: Ediciones Minotauro, 1957), pp. 284–85.

14. Menéndez Pidal, "Poema de mío Cid," in *España y su historia*, I, p. 667.

15. Julián Ribera, "Poesía épica entre los musulmanes españoles," *Discurso de recepción en la Academia de la Historia* (Madrid, 1915).

16. Joseph Bédier, *Les légends épiques: Recherches sur la formation des chansons de geste*, 2nd ed., 4 vols. (Paris: H. Champion, 1914–21).

17. Ramón Menéndez Pidal, *Reliquias de la poesía épica* (Madrid: Espasa-Calpe, 1951), p. ix.

18. Menéndez Pidal develops his theories of the epic in many places. However, a complete statement of his ideas can be found in *La Chanson de Roland y el neotradicionalismo (orígenes de la épica románica)* (Madrid: Espasa-Calpe, 1959), translated as *La Chanson de Roland et la tradition épique des Francs* (Paris: Editions A. et J. Picard et Cie, 1960). The French edition is to be preferred over the original Spanish version because in preparing the French edition the author revised his work and added material in collaboration with a distinguished French scholar, René Louis.

19. Menéndez Pidal, *Reliquias*, p. xi.

20. Ibid., p. xii.

21. Madrid: Hijos de J. M. Ducazcal, 1896. There is a more recent edition: Madrid: Librería y Casa Editorial Hernando, 1934.

22. Ramón Menéndez Pidal, "Roncesvalles: Un nuevo cantar de gesta español del siglo XIII," *Revista de Filología Española* (Madrid) 4 (1917): 105–204. See also Jules Horrent, *Roncesvalles: Étude sur le fragment de gesta conservé à l'Archivo de Navarra (Pamplona)* (Liege: Bibliothèque de Philosophie et Lettres, 1951).

23. Dámaso Alonso, "La primitiva épica francesa a la luz de una nota emilianense," in *Primavera temprana de la literatura europea* (Madrid: Guadarrama, 1961), pp. 83–200.

24. Ramón Menéndez Pidal, *Poesía juglaresca y orígenes de las literaturas románicas*, 6th ed. (Madrid: Instituto de Estudios Políticos, 1957), III, pp. 240–332. This work was originally published with the title *Poesía juglaresca y juglares: Aspectos de la historia literaria y cultural de España* (Madrid: Tip. de la "Revista de Archivos," 1924).

25. Gaston Paris developed this theory in a much more scientific and objective

manner than earlier scholars in his *Histoire poétique de Charlemagne (XIᵉ-XIVᵉ siècles)* (Paris: A. Franck, 1865).

26. The most important statement of his findings about the Spanish epic and romances is his *De la poesía heroico-popular castellana* (Barcelona: Librería de A. Verdaguer, 1874; also Barcelona: Consejo Superior de Investigaciones Científicas, Instituto Miguel de Cervantes, 1959).

27. His ideas are developed in many studies, but the most complete summary of them in one place is contained in *Romancero hispánico (hispano-portugués, americano y sefardí)*, 2 vols. (Madrid: Espasa-Calpe, 1953). Almost all of the romance problems that I deal with from this point to the end of my essay are treated in one way or another at various points in this long and quite exhaustive study by Pidal. Good bibliographic leads for further study of specific topics are also provided in Pidal's footnotes, so I do not include them here.

BIBLIOGRAPHY

Editions of Original Manuscript Texts

Menéndez Pidal, Ramón. *Cantar de mío Cid: Texto, gramática y vocabulario*. 3rd ed. 3 vols. Madrid: Espasa-Calpe, 1966.

———. *Poema de mío Cid*. Madrid: "La Lectura," 1966. Clásicos castellanos, 24. The best popular and easily accessible edition of the poem in Spanish.

———. *Poema de mío Cid: Edición facsímil del Códice de Per Abat, conservado en la Biblioteca Nacional*. Madrid: Hauser y Menet, 1961.

———. *Poema de mío Cid: Facsímil de la edición paleográfica por don R. Menéndez Pidal*. Madrid: Tipografía Moderna [Valencia], 1961. This work and the facsimile edition of the *Códice de Per Abat* listed above are generally sold as a two-volume set.

———. "Roncesvalles: Un nuevo cantar de gesta español del siglo XIII." *Revista de Filología Española* 4 (1917): 105–204.

Texts in English Translations

Gibson, James Young. *The Cid Ballads and Other Poems and Translations from Spanish and German*. 2nd ed. London: Kegan Paul, Trench, Trübner & Co., 1898. Offers translations, mostly into rhymed quatrains, of many Spanish romances. Most are about the Cid, but a few are historical or Carolingian ballads.

Huntington, A. M. *The Poem of the Cid*. 3 vols. New York: The Hispanic Society of America, 1921. Vol. I gives the text in Spanish, vol. II offers Huntington's translation of the poem into unrhymed verse, and vol. III contains extensive notes.

Lockhart, John G. *Ancient Spanish Ballads: Historical and Romantic*. Revised edition. London: John Murray, 1841. There were nine editions of this famous collection before 1890, the first being in 1823. The translations are in rhymed couplets and include the most famous Cid and historical romances.

Merwin, W. S. *The Poem of the Cid*. London: J. M. Dent & Sons Ltd., 1959. A translation into unrhymed verse. There is a brief foreword.

———. *Some Spanish Ballads*. New York: Abelard Schuman, 1961. Offers unrhymed verse translations of selected romances including several from the epic cycles. Includes also a brief introduction, a short bibliography, and some notes.

Ormsby, John. *The Poem of the Cid: A Translation from the Spanish*. New York: G. E. Stechert & Co., 1915. First published in London in 1879. A translation in rhymed couplets and prose. Includes an introduction.

Rose, R. Selden, and Leonard Bacon. *The Lay of the Cid: Translated into English Verse*. Berkeley: University of California Press, 1919. Translates the poem into rhymed couplets. There is a brief introduction.

Simpson, Lesley Bird. *The Poem of the Cid*. Berkeley and Los Angeles: University of California Press, 1957. This is a prose translation with a brief introduction.

Studies in English

Clissold, S. *In Search of the Cid*. London: Hodder and Stoughton, 1965. A good treatment of the Cid and his times intended for the general reader.

Deyermond, A. D. *Epic Poetry and the Clergy: Studies on the "Mocedades de Rodrigo."* London: Tamesis Books Limited, 1969. Studies many aspects of the late epic entitled *Las mocedades de Rodrigo* and places it in epic tradition. Deyermond holds that it is the work of a learned poet, not of a decadent juglar, as most scholars have believed.

Entwistle, W. J. *European Balladry*. Oxford: Oxford University Press, 1939. An excellent standard work on European balladry in general, it includes a chapter on Hispanic ballads (pp. 152-94). A distinguished Hispanist himself, Entwistle takes issue with some of Menéndez Pidal's ideas on balladry and expresses his own doubts about certain aspects of the "fragmentation" theory.

Foster, David William. *The Early Spanish Ballad*. New York: Twayne Publishers, Inc., 1971. A book of basic information about ballads studied primarily from a literary perspective. Includes many ballad texts, footnotes, and a good bibliography.

Menéndez Pidal, Ramón. *The Cid and His Spain*. Translated by Harold Sunderland. London: F. Cass, 1971. A partial translation of *La España del Cid*. Offers a historico-literary study of the Spanish hero, his times, and epic poems and ballads about him.

Smith, C. Colin. *Poema de mío Cid*. Oxford: Clarendon Press, 1972. A very fine edition of the text in Spanish accompanied by excellent notes. Very important is Smith's informative introduction in English, which treats practically all aspects of the poem and takes issue with some of Menéndez Pidal's conclusions. Students interested in going beyond generally accepted views of the poem, which I have attempted to summarize in my own essay, would do well to study this book's introduction, its appendices, and its very useful bibliography.

————. *Spanish Ballads*. New York: Pergamon Press, 1964. An anthology of ballad texts in Spanish with helpful notes, this work contains a very good introduction in English (pp. 1-50) that includes a great deal of basic information about romances and scholarship in the field.

12   Russian Byliny

Felix J. Oinas

The heroic epic is found among the Orthodox Slavs—Russians, Serbs, Bulgarians, and Macedonians—and, in a later form, among the Ukrainians. The Roman Catholic Croats also know it, though in a somewhat modernized form which is demythologized, historicized, and psychologized. All these peoples have undergone prolonged domination by foreign invaders, especially by non-Christians. It can be assumed that they came to look upon the period preceding foreign domination as a heroic age that was glorified in heroic songs.[1]

When we speak of the Russian heroic epic, we think of the *bylina,* though not all *byliny* are heroic. The *bylina* has been defined as "a special type of epic folk song, often loosely connected with some historical movement or event and embellished with much fantasy or hyperbole."[2] The term "bylina" was first applied by I. P. Saxarov in the 1830s. Saxarov misunderstood the word *bylina* (an event of the past) in the opening passage of the *Igor' Tale,* interpreting it as "an ancient poem." Subsequent usage perpetuated his error, and bylina became a purely scholarly term. The folk themselves call these songs *stariny* or *starinki* (stories of long ago). The byliny are epic songs varying in length from fewer than 100 lines to 1,000 or more. There has been no Homer or Lönnrot among the Russians to create a single long Russian epic, though attempts have been made at concatenating existing byliny.

Collection

Byliny have been recorded in Russia since the seventeenth century. The earliest records were prose paraphrases made for the purpose of providing interesting reading material. Among the early collections, there is one of great significance: the collection compiled by the Cossack Kirša Danilov in the Ural region during the middle of the eighteenth century. This collection, which contains about seventy songs from western Siberia, was evidently prepared for the mill owner P. A. Demidov. The texts are rather faithful recordings of byliny and historical songs, although they contain some traces of the collector's emendation. In the first half of the nineteenth century, byliny were recorded in various parts of Russia and were sent to the collector and folklore expert P. V. Kireevskij, who included them in his large collection of folksongs.

Byliny, believed to be on the verge of extinction, were rediscovered by P. N. Rybnikov in the former Olonec province as a genre still very much alive. Rybnikov was an official in the Russian civil service who, for political reasons, had been sent to serve in Petrozavodsk on Lake Onega. He has left us a picturesque account of his first experiences during his search for byliny. He writes that he had heard of people in Olonec who sang byliny, but had not succeeded in getting to know them, since the peasants had a traditional distrust of officials. One day in 1860, he was overtaken by a storm while crossing Lake Onega and had to take refuge on an island. At night he lay down on the shore outside an overcrowded barn. He was awakened by the strange sounds of a song of a kind he had never heard before. The song was "vivacious, fantastic, and gay; now it grew quicker, now it slowed down, and recalled by its tune something from very long ago, forgotten by his generation." It was the bylina "Sadko." Several peasants were sitting around the fire listening to the singer, an old man with a bushy white beard and bright eyes. Needless to say, Rybnikov was on his feet in a moment. He asked the old man to repeat the song and wrote it down from his lips. The man sang several byliny for him and later helped him to contact other bylina singers.[3] Rybnikov collected 224 texts of byliny which were published in four volumes in 1861–67. The discovery of a still flourishing bylina tradition in Olonec so surprised and astounded the educated world that the collection was received at first with some skepticism, like Macpherson's *Ossian Songs* in England.

Some ten years later, Russian philologist and historian A. F. Gil'ferding set out for the same region in order to supplement Rybnikov's work. He interviewed several of the same singers Rybnikov had heard and, going further to the north, found much new material. His collection of 318 texts was published posthumously in 1873. This collection, in which the songs were arranged by singer rather than by subject, became a model for subsequent publications of Russian folklore.

The work of Rybnikov and Gil'ferding initiated a systematic search for byliny everywhere in northern Russia, a search that has continued to the present time. The results have been most gratifying. Byliny were found to have survived not only in Olonec (in Zaonež'e and to the east of Lake Onega), but also on the shores of the White Sea (Pomor'e, the Tersk Coast, and the Zimnij Coast) and of the rivers flowing to the north (Pinega, Kuloj, Mezen', and Pečora). In none of these areas, however, was the bylina tradition as strong as in Olonec.

Origin and Dissemination

Though preserved best in the northern regions of European Russia, byliny could not have originated there. Byliny frequently mention southern Russian

cities (Černigov, Kiev, Smolensk) and personages (the Kievan Prince Vladimir), indicating that byliny must stem from the south. There are a number of
details in them that refer specifically to Kiev, such as the Počajna River (given
as "Pučaj River" or "Pučajnaja" in byliny), located on the outskirts of Kiev.
In some byliny the "Relics of Boris" are mentioned as the designation for a
ford at Vyšgorod, a suburb of Kiev. Boris was one of Prince Vladimir's two
sons, who were murdered by order of their half-brother in 1015. Boris' relics
were placed in a church in Vyšgorod. During the Tatar invasion in 1240, this
suburb was destroyed and the relics were lost.[4]

The majority of Russian folklorists concur that byliny as a genre arose in
the so-called Kievan period, during the tenth and eleventh centuries. Some
scholars (such as the late V. Ja. Propp and B. N. Putilov) are inclined to shift
the origin to a considerably earlier time. It is plausible that mythological songs
of the East Slavs were the predecessors of the byliny, but the sweeping
historical events of the Kievan period must have caused a thorough change or
a mutation in these songs. These events began with the Christianization of
Russia in the tenth century and skirmishes with waves of Asian intruders, such
as the Polovetsians and Pechenegs. They culminated with the arrival of the
Tatars in Russia in the thirteenth century, the devastation of the land, the
destruction of the Old East Slavic civilization, and the domination of the
people by the Tatars.

In byliny, historical events are alluded to only vaguely and often allegori-
cally. The Russian conversion to Christianity is echoed in byliny as the battle
with the dragon. The Polovetsian Tugor Khan has become the dragon Tugarin, and Šaragan (or Šarakan) appears as Šark the Giant. A number of byliny
have as their subject the Tatar invasion and the Russians' struggle against the
Tatars. The first encounter between the Russians and Tatars in 1224 at the
Kalka River may be reflected in the bylina "Kamsk Battle," which ends with
the demise of the Russian epic heroes. Contrary to historical truth, most of the
byliny about the battles against the Tatars give victory to the Russians. Similarly, great liberties are taken in the byliny whose theme is the payment of
tribute to the princes of the Golden Horde. In these byliny, instead of paying
tribute, the Russian *bogatyrs* collect it from the rulers of the Horde. Later
events in Russian history, beginning with Ivan the Terrible in the sixteenth
century, are the subject not of byliny, but of another genre, the historical
song. Historical songs are shorter, less fantastic, and closer to historical
truth.[5]

According to the main representative of the so-called historical school of
Russian folkloristics, Vsevolod Miller, byliny originated in the upper classes
among the singers of the princes' retinue. Later they were taken over by the
skomoroxi, the wandering minstrels, singers, and buffoons of the lower
classes (comparable to the French *jongleurs* and German *Spielmänner*). In the
hands of the skomoroxi, byliny received their final form, with special stylistic
peculiarities, formulas, and other embellishments. The minstrels performed

historical and religious songs, tales, and legends in addition to byliny, thereby enriching the subject matter of the byliny with motifs from a great variety of sources. Since their profession involved constant travel, the skomoroxi were crucial to the dissemination of byliny and other folklore. Subject to constant attacks by the clergy ever since the Christianization of Kievan Russia, the skomoroxi were greatly persecuted during the seventeenth century, particularly during the reign of Tsar Aleksej Mixajlovič. Although called a meek tsar, Aleksej Mixajlovič used extremely cruel methods for the persecution of these wandering minstrels. By order of the Tsar, the musical instruments used by the skomoroxi were confiscated and burned, and the skomoroxi themselves were subject to severe penalties. First and second offenders were whipped, while those caught for the third or fourth time were exiled to the border regions.[6] The skomoroxi took byliny to the North, and through their mediation, the bylina tradition was handed over to the peasants and fishermen there.

The view that the skomoroxi played a significant role in the dissemination of byliny to the North is generally shared by folklorists. On the other hand, the role of colonization has also been stressed as a reason for the spread of byliny. Recently some Soviet scholars (notably A. N. Nasonov and M. V. Vitov) have endeavored to correlate the different bylina areas in the Russian North with the difference in their colonization patterns. Thus they suggest that the eastern part of the northern bylina area (from the Zimnij Coast and Kuloj to Pečora), in which the heroic byliny predominate, were peopled with Slavs from the lower reaches of the Dvina earlier (after the eleventh-twelfth centuries) than were other regions in the North. The epic tradition of the western part of the bylina area (the Pinega, the Tersk and the Pomor'e Coasts), which has a considerable portion of ballad-like byliny, received several colonization waves of Novgorodians and a stream of settlers from Moscow after the defeat of Novgorod the Great in the fifteenth century. The area of Olonec around Lake Onega, which has a strong tradition of novella-type byliny, is supposed to reflect a later stage in the history of colonization in the North, since the local Finnish-Karelians defending their lands "did not let Novgorodians establish peaceful settlements in the Transonega region and east of Lake Onega. Such settlements became possible there only late in the fourteenth and early in the fifteenth centuries."[7]

In the North, the byliny were cherished and preserved longer than anywhere else, partly because of the backwardness of these areas and their isolation from cultural centers. This isolation became almost complete after the conquest of the Baltic region by Peter the Great at the beginning of the eighteenth century, when ports in Estonia and Latvia were opened for commerce and the northern trade route to the west via Olonec was abandoned. Thus the life line that connected northern Russia with the outside world was cut off. This secluded and godforsaken area proved to be a fertile garden for folklore; here byliny found favorable conditions for preservation.

Furthermore, the northern way of life and the northern climate provided an atmosphere conducive to relating and listening to long, tranquil tales of antiquity. The fishermen sometimes had to wait for days or weeks for a storm to pass; the woodcutters had to spend long fall and winter nights in huts in the depths of the forests. Such intervals were filled with songs and stories. The North provided tellers and singers with the eager and grateful audiences that are indispensable to folklore tradition.[8]

In the South, the birthplace of byliny, hardly any traces of this genre have been found. N. I. Kostomarov explained that the absence of byliny in the Ukraine was due to extraordinary historical events during the so-called Cossack era (sixteenth-seventeenth centuries) that shook the consciousness of the Ukrainian people, causing them to look to the present and the future rather than to the past. The people began singing of the feats of contemporary heroes who came from their own ranks and embodied their struggle to remain independent and free. Thus the songs about the old heroes gave place to *dumy* (from *duma*, originally meaning "thought"), a new tradition similar to the Russian historical songs.[9]

Bylina Cycles

Numerous attempts at a classification of byliny have been made, but no complete agreement has been reached. The protagonists of the mythological school distinguished between the byliny about the so-called older and younger heroes. In the first group were the heroes having mythological features; in the second, the heroes who resembled real human beings. Scholars of the historical school classified byliny according to the principalities in which the action took place: Kievan, Novgorodian, Galician-Volhynian, etc. Attempts have also been made by various scholars to group the byliny by content: heroic, fairy tale type, novella type, ballad-byliny, and so on. However, the classification of byliny by principality is accepted most widely, and we will follow it in our discussion. Byliny exhibiting some mythological features do not lend themselves to classification by a definite principality and are usually discussed as a separate group.

MYTHOLOGICAL BYLINY

The mythological byliny, probably the most ancient category, have Volx, Svjatogor, and Mikula as their heroes. The bylina of Volx (from Russian *volxv* "magician") Vseslav'evič has some shamanistic overtones. By changing himself into a gray wolf, an aurochs, and a falcon, Volx hunts all kinds of animals. In the shape of a bird, he penetrates into the Indian realm where he overhears the plans of the emperor and empress. After he destroys the emperor's weapons, he with his retinue attacks and smashes him, and thus saves his country from the peril. It is possible that the bylina of Volx reflects the miraculous life of Prince Vseslav of Polock (d. 1101).[10]

Svjatogor is a giant, so powerful that Mother Earth cannot carry him, and so he has to live in the mountains. He is, however, destined to perish, and his eventual death is reported in different ways. In one bylina, he boasts that he could lift the whole world if only he could find the point of support. He finds a shoulder bag sent by God and tries to lift it, but cannot do so and dies. In another bylina, Svjatogor and Il'ja come across a coffin. When Svjatogor lies down in the coffin, he cannot get out of it and is doomed to die there.

Mikula Seljaninovič is a miraculous plowman who works so fast that Prince Vol'ga (probably from Oleg, one of the historical princes) can overtake him only in three days. Vol'ga persuades Mikula to follow him as his companion on a mission. Vol'ga is put to shame when he and his retinue cannot remove a plow from the ground, whereas the plowman himself lifts it with one hand and throws it into the bush. This bylina, as well as those of Svjatogor, are based on international migratory themes.[11]

KIEVAN CYCLE

The byliny of the largest cycle, the Kievan, center around Vladimir, Grand Prince of Kiev (usually referred to as Vladimir "the Fair Sun," *krasnoe solnyško*) in the same way that the legends of the knights of the Round Table center around King Arthur. The figure of Prince Vladimir may incorporate various princes of Old Russia, primarily Vladimir I (d. 1015) and Vladimir II Monomax (d. 1125). During the reigns of both, there was strife between southern Russian principalities and the nomads of the steppe, who came from Asia. Vladimir I fought against the Pechenegs and Vladimir II against the Polovetsians. In byliny, all the hostile nomad armies against whom the Russians fight are collectively called Tatars, since it was the Tatar rule under which the Russians suffered hardest and longest (from the thirteenth to the sixteenth centuries). The term "Tatar" is applied also to Polish and Lithuanian troops in later byliny.

In byliny, Prince Vladimir arranges big feasts in his palace, gives various tasks to the heroes (who form his entourage), and rewards and punishes them according to their acts. However, he himself never functions as a principal figure. The byliny sing of the exploits of his *bogatyri* (epic heroes), whose primary duty while stationed either in Kiev or at Russian bogatyr outposts is to protect the Kievan state against foreign invaders: heathen tsars, hostile heroes, and formidable monsters. They also fight against internal enemies, such as robbers and brigands. Occasionally they settle accounts between themselves or even quarrel with Prince Vladimir. Their leisure is spent in hunting game and having amorous adventures.

The most prominent heroes of the Kievan byliny are Il'ja Muromec, Dobrynja Nikitič, and Aleša Popovič. Among them, Il'ja Muromec has the leading position. Il'ja is adorned with the ideal features of the bogatyr. A brave, unselfish servant of his country, he protects it against numerous enemies and defends its orphans, widows, and poor. He himself says:

I am going to serve for the Christian faith,
And for the Russian land,
And for the City of Kiev,
And for the widows, orphans, and the poor.[12]

Il'ja appears as a peasant's son in several byliny. He was paralyzed for thirty-three years before being healed by Jesus and two apostles or by several saints, who bestowed exceptional strength upon him. He was told that he was not destined to die in battle. Il'ja applied his strength first to clear the land of his parents' farm, then he went to Kiev to Prince Vladimir. On his way he conquered monstrous Solovej Razbojnik (Nightingale the Robber), who controlled the highway between Černigov and Kiev. He took Solovej Razbojnik to Prince Vladimir and killed him there.

Il'ja's further feats include his victory over another monster, Idolišče (Monstrous Idol), whom he approaches in pilgrim's garb. When Idolišče attacks him, Il'ja grabs him by the legs and, using him as a weapon, destroys Idolišče's Tatar army.

Il'ja even has to fight his own son. This is an international theme which is found in a number of works, including the German *Thidreks saga,* in which Hildebrand fights Hadubrand, and the Iranian national epic by Ferdowsi (Firdausi) in which Rustam and Sohrab fight.[13] Il'ja's son, Sokol'nik (Falconer), comes as an intruder to the Kievan borders guarded by the Russian heroes. The long fight between Il'ja and Sokol'nik, during which the father and the son recognize each other, ends with the death of the young, relentless hero.

Il'ja's hardest fight is with Kalin Tsar, who demands from Prince Vladimir the surrender of Kiev. The Prince, who had imprisoned Il'ja, frees him and, together with a group of heroes, Il'ja goes against Kalin Tsar. However, he falls into a pit dug by the Tatars and is captured by them. When he is being taken to the place of execution, he prays fervently to God. His prayer is heard, and through divine intervention he finds himself freed from his fetters. He then destroys Kalin Tsar and his army. After several more exploits, including the destruction of a camp of brigands who wanted to rob him, Il'ja finds a hidden treasure, gives it away, and goes into the Kievan crypts, where he is petrified.

The byliny about Il'ja can be used to exemplify the evolution of the byliny—their creation and transformation over a long period of time. Il'ja's development into a powerful hero is manifestly connected with Kiev's rise to prominence. When the power of the Kievan princes increased, Il'ja became a symbol of the self-consciousness of the people. Some mythological songs and legends already in existence, such as those about the liberation of the areas from highwaymen and monsters, were reinterpreted and attached to Il'ja ("Il'ja and Solovej Razbojnik" and "Il'ja and Idolišče"), in the same manner as Theseus was developed into the national hero of Athens. The following period of Tatar rule left its imprint on the byliny about Il'ja: the enemies against whom he fought were called Tatars (Il'ja's fight with Kalin Tsar and others); Idolišče became the leader of the Tatar army; and Solovej Razbojnik received a Tatar patronymic, "Odixmant'ev" or "Raxmatovič." In the seventeenth century Il'ja acquired different attributes from the circles in which byliny about his deeds were sung. In the North the peasants considered him one of themselves and attached the attribute "peasant's son" to him. In the South the Cossacks in their turn proudly associated him with themselves and called him the "Old Cossack." During the peasant revolts of the seventeenth century (such as the uprising of Stenka Razin), the byliny about Il'ja the Rebel were created (e.g., Il'ja's quarrel with Prince Vladimir and Il'ja's association with the poor people of the tavern). One of the most recent byliny (created in the 1930s) is about Il'ja's marriage. Since Il'ja was known to have a son, then logically he must have had a wedding.[14]

Dobrynja Nikitič is an ideal knightly diplomat. He has good manners, clever speech, and he enjoys great respect from the Prince and the heroes. Many-sided and talented, he plays well at dice, cards, and checkers, shoots excellently, swims expertly, and plays and sings like a real skomorox.

The bylina "Dobrynja's Fight with the Dragon" graphically displays Dobrynja's heroic qualities. When Dobrynja, against the advice of his mother, goes swimming in Pučaj River, he is attacked by a dragon. Their fight ends temporarily with a nonaggression pact between Dobrynja and the dragon, but when the dragon later violates this agreement, Dobrynja attacks and kills him.

Dobrynja is given the most complicated and delicate assignments, which require not only strength and boldness, but also diplomatic abilities and tact.[15] When Djuk Stepanovič arrives and begins boasting of his riches, Dobrynja is assigned to head the embassy sent to Djuk's mother to verify the correctness of her son's assertions. When Il'ja, who has not been invited to the Prince's feast, goes berserk and begins raging and smashing up churches in Kiev, it is Dobrynja whom the Prince sends to pacify him. The bylina "Dobrynja the Matchmaker" relates how Dobrynja, helped by Dunaj, forces the Lithuanian king's daughter to come to Prince Vladimir to be his bride. Another tells how Dobrynja, together with Vasilij Kazimirov, goes to the Polovetsian tsar to arrange the payment of taxes that have been overdue for twelve years. Defeating the Polovetsian tsar at dice, cards, and shooting with the bow and arrow, then successfully attacking his troops, Dobrynja makes the Polovetsian tsar Prince Vladimir's debtor and, with his companion, brings the tribute from the tsar to Prince Vladimir.

"Dobrynja and Marinka" shows the hero in the hands of an amorous witch, whom he finally succeeds in outwitting and killing. The witch here may be an echo of Marinka Mniszek, the Polish wife of the False Dmitrij, who was greatly despised by the Russians. The False Dmitrij, evidently a former monk, ascended the Russian throne in 1605 and ruled Russia for about one year.

Aleša Popovič appears in several byliny as Il'ja's and Dobrynja's companion and comrade-in-arms. Aleša is distinguished by agility, prowess, and bravery, as well as by cheerfulness, craftiness, and cheekiness.[16] After he kills Tugarin Zmeevič (Dragon's Son), he becomes a much-admired hero in Kiev. Accompanied by Ekim Ivanovič, Aleša learns from a pilgrim (*kalika*) that a terrible monster is nearby. By exchanging clothes with the pilgrim and pretending to be hard of hearing, Aleša gets close to Tugarin and kills him. A comical final effect is achieved in the story (a detail probably added by the skomoroxi) when Ekim mistakes Aleša for Tugarin and attacks him violently.

The heroic features in Aleša's character are combined with negative ones. Thus he can be jealous, arrogant, and boastful. Negative features may be attributed to him because of his supposed priestly descent (Popovič means "priest's son").[17] In the bylina "Dobrynja and Aleša," Aleša deceives even his sworn brother Dobrynja. Dobrynja rides off into the open plain and advises his wife that, if he does not return in six years, she may marry whomever she wants—except Aleša. Aleša, however, brings home false tidings that Dobrynja is dead and begins to besiege the young "widow" with marriage proposals. Dobrynja's wife, under pressure from Prince Vladimir and the Princess, finally agrees to marry Aleša. Dobrynja arrives home during the wedding celebration, attends the wedding party disguised as a skomorox, and claims his wife. He teaches Aleša and the Prince and Princess a good lesson. This bylina, the most popular among the Russian byliny, is modeled on the international theme "The husband at the wedding of his wife" (AT 974), which also appears in Boccaccio's *Decameron,* in a German folksong about the noble Möringer, and in the Turkic story about Ashik Garip.

It is somewhat surprising that bylina heroes must sometimes rely on various tricks or a *deus ex machina* to secure their victories. Such actions do not seem at all honest or heroic. Thus Il'ja and Aleša use disguises: they don the clothes of wandering pilgrims to put their unsuspecting enemies off guard. Or Aleša pretends to be deaf, so as to get close to the monster. In one bylina, Tugarin in the shape of a dragon flies high in the air and is out of reach of the hero. Then Aleša asks God to send rain. Rain comes, soaks the dragon's paper wings, and the dragon falls to the ground. In another bylina, Il'ja's prayer saves him from certain death.

These episodes show that the bylina singers did not make any distinction between exploits based on the personal excellence of the hero and those due to cunning, miraculous intervention, or outside help. The same is true of other epics. In the *Iliad,* although Achilles conquers Hector with the cunning assistance of the goddess Athena, her help does not tarnish the victor's crown. Victory is victory, by whatever means it is won.[18]

Among the major bylina heroes, Dobrynja and Aleša are evidently historical. Dobrynja's prototype is supposed to be Prince Vladimir's maternal uncle, who is also called Dobrynja. Chronicles characterize Dobrynja as a significant historical figure, first as the protector and supporter of the Prince, and later as his collaborator. Possibly Aleša Popovič was originally a retainer (*xrabr*) of the Prince of Rostov. The local legends and fourteenth and fifteenth century byliny about him became a part of the all-Russian tradition, and he anachronistically became a hero of Prince Vladimir. Through byliny Aleša was introduced into the chronicle accounts about the battle at the Kalka River (1224).[19]

There is as yet no unanimity about Il'ja Muromec's origin. Some Western scholars see in his appellative "Muromec" a corruption of "Norman" (Old Norse Norðmaðr) and think that Il'ja was originally a Scandinavian (Varangian) leader active in Russia. Soviet scholars, who are antagonistic to the "Norman theory," connect the bylina hero Muromec with the ancient Russian principality of Murom. They contend that the byliny about Il'ja Muromec could have been based on Muron-Rjazan' local legends, which were later included in the Kievan cycle.

Il'ja appears in Germanic sources earlier than in Russian sources. Thirteenth century Germanic sagas mention Ilias von Riuzen (Ilias from Russia) and Ilias, Jarl of Greka (Ilias, Prince of Greece). This does not prove the existence of epic songs about Il'ja among the Germanic peoples, but only their familiarity with the Russian hero. In Russian historical sources, Il'ja's name is first mentioned in 1574, transferred from the byliny and legends about him.[20]

In the Kievan cycle there appear numerous other heroes, both romantic lovers and chivalrous, brave fighters. Here belong, for example, Čurilo Plenkovič, Solovej (Nightingale) Budimirovič, Mixajlo Potyk, and Suxman, to mention just a few. The handsome Čurilo Plenkovič, who comes to Kiev from the southern frontier areas of Prince Vladimir's possessions, becomes a ladies' man at the court. When even the Prince's wife cannot turn her eyes from him and wants him to be her chamberlain, the Prince has no other choice but to send him back home. Čurilo is finally killed by an outraged husband, who surprises him in bed with his wife.

Solovej Budimirovič, a merchant and a singer, comes to Kiev with many ships, builds a palace there during one night and—contrary to the established custom—receives a marriage proposal from Prince Vladimir's niece, Zabava Putjatična. The girl's proposal to the man is not at all surprising if we interpret the building of the palace as a marriage trial. Scholars have sought to connect the bylina of Solovej Budimirovič with an historical wedding between a Norwegian Viking and the daughter of a Kievan prince.

Mixajlo Potyk's love for the White Swan is so strong that, when she dies, he has himself buried with her. But when she is resuscitated, she turns out to be an unfaithful witch, and Mixajlo kills her.

The fate of the brave hero Suxman is tragic. Going out to find a live bird for Prince Vladimir, he chances upon a Tatar army. He kills all the Tatars, but is himself wounded. When the Prince, distrusting his honesty and patriotism, humiliates him by incarceration, Suxman commits suicide.

NOVGOROD CYCLE

The Novgorod cycle of byliny differs in basic character from the Kievan cycle. Novgorod was a rich commercial city connected by Hanseatic ties to

Western Europe. The daily life of Novgorod, with its marked antagonism between different social classes, which occasionally flared into real clashes and fights, serves as the theme of the Novgorod byliny. These byliny, devoid of any heroism, are close in spirit to the medieval ballads.

The main protagonists of the Novgorod cycle are Sadko and Vasilij Buslaev. Sadko is a poor *gusli* player who, with the help of the Tsar of Lake Il'men, becomes a rich merchant. When he sails out to sea with his fleet of thirty ships, the sea is becalmed because taxes have not been paid to the sea king, and Sadko's ships cannot proceed. Despite all his ruses, Sadko himself has to be sacrificed to the sea king to get the ships moving. However, he fares quite well in the kingdom of the sea ruler and eventually returns to his native Novgorod. The bylina reiterates the Jonah motif (Jon. 1:4 ff.), which is based on the age-old sailor's belief that if there is an evildoer on board a ship, the whole crew must suffer.[21]

While the byliny about Sadko abound in fairy tale elements, those about Vasilij Buslaev are rather realistic. They display the negative side of city life in this rich trading republic. In the byliny about Vasilij Buslaev, the son of a middle-class family, we hear first of his childhood pranks and then of his and his retinue's fight against the men of Novgorod, whom Vasilij has provoked. Vasilij's group would have slain all the men of Novgorod had not Vasilij's mother wrapped him in her sable cloak and carried him off to her palace. Vasilij's career ends with his pilgrimage to the Holy Land, evidently undertaken for the atonement of his former sins; he perishes on the return journey. Attempts have been made to identify both Sadko and Vasilij Buslaev with certain historical figures mentioned in the old Novgorod chronicles, but the question has not yet been decided.

GALICIAN-VOLHYNIAN CYCLE

The byliny of the Galician-Volhynian cycle reflect the economic flowering of this principality which—unlike Kiev—had been spared devastation by the Tatars. Its best-known hero, Djuk Stepanovič, arrives in Kiev as a visiting foreigner and attracts attention by his sneering mockery of the poverty of the city and the court. He wins a wager with Čurilo Plenkovič by parading in innumerable new suits and by jumping on horseback across the Dnieper River. Djuk's possessions and wealth are so fantastic that the inventory takers sent by Prince Vladimir must ask the Prince to sell his cities in order to purchase sufficient writing paper, pens, and ink.

The byliny of Prince Roman reflect the hostilities between the western principalities and their neighbors further west. Prince Roman can hardly be identified with any historical prince by this name (thirteenth-fourteenth centuries), but he can be viewed as the generalized figure of the defenders of these areas. In one bylina, he conquers the Livik brothers, "the king's nephews" (obviously from Lithuania), who had invaded Russia and had burned villages and destroyed churches. In another, Roman plays a more passive role. The bylina tells the story of his faithful wife Mar'ja, who is kidnapped by a prince from the west, but who escapes from captivity and returns home.

Structure and Form

The structure of byliny consists of three basic parts: the introduction, the narrative portion, and the epilogue. In addition, some byliny have an introductory verse whose purpose is to favorably dispose the audience to listening to the long epic narrative. The prevailing type of introduction to Kievan byliny describes a feast at Prince Vladimir's palace in Kiev. At the feast the heroes boast and are given certain tasks to fulfill. This serves as the starting point of the action. Some byliny begin with a description of how one or more heroes set out on a mission.

The basic narrative portion of a bylina relates an extraordinary adventure. A bylina is concerned with one hero and his foe; all other persons merely form a "resonant background." As A. P. Skaftymov showed in a detailed study, the structure of the bylina is based on an effort to elicit surprise and astonishment from the audience.[22] This striving for strong effects leads to the abundant use of contrasts in the depiction of the hero and his opponent. At first the hero is minimized and the enemy is hyperbolized. The hero may appear as sick and helpless. Il'ja Muromec in the bylina about his healing is crippled and not even able to give water to the holy men who ask him for it. Or the hero is too young or too plain, and his burst of bravado does not inspire any trust. He is cautioned, held back, warned of inevitable ruin. When young Mixajlo Danilovič volunteers to go alone against a hostile army after his father has retired to a monastery, Prince Vladimir says to him:

> Don't flit about, fledgling, while you are so young;
> there are those stronger than you and more powerful.

In contrast to the insignificant main hero, his enemy is shown as having invincible strength and power. People are afraid of him and overwhelmed by his violence. Solovej Razbojnik, a kind of mythical creature, does not let anyone pass; his whistling, like a storm, causes great destruction in nature: the forests bow to the earth, the herbage and grass wither up, the flowers wilt, and every mortal falls dead. The heathen Idolišče is two certified fathoms tall; he eats three cows and a hundred pounds of bread and keeps a king as his cook. Tugarin Zmeevič is likewise gluttonous and haughty. He is carried to Vladimir's table with thirty bogatyrs at each end. He swallows a whole swan, tucks a whole loaf into his cheek, and drinks by the pailful. The steed under him is terrifying; from its jaws pour searing flames, from its ears issues a column of smoke. There is no doubt that it is a hippomorphous dragon.

One might suspect that the enormously powerful enemy could crush the hero like a toy. But this is not the case; instead, the hero playfully conquers him with amazing ease. There is no element of struggle in the battle description. If the hero needs more time for the fight (sometimes even as much as three days), then the hostile armies are described as so big that merely butchering them takes days.

After the exploit is completed, the narration usually ends. The epilogue is either a hint to the host for a reward or treat, or a reference to the sea:

> And they tell the bylina about Dobrynja,
> to calm down the blue sea,
> and for you all to hear, good people.[23]

This latter type of epilogue may reflect the magical function of the singing or rhythmic recitation of byliny to calm down the stormy sea or lake. People in northern Russia used to pacify the raging waters by presenting byliny.[24]

Attempts at creating longer epic cycles have been made in Russia, but without lasting success. Two epic songs were recorded in Olonec in the 1920s and 30s, one composed of eight byliny and the other of six; these presented the complete biography of Il'ja Muromec. Both of them had a fairy tale character and were told, not sung. They were not created from the genuine byliny known locally, but were based on summaries in cheap printed booklets or on concatenated texts of byliny which had been widely distributed for commercial purposes.[25]

A more ambitious attempt at creating an epic for Russian youth was undertaken by V. P. Avenarius. His *Book of the Kievan Heroes* is interesting in that it shows one of the ways in which an epic can be compiled.[26] Avenarius intended to restore the ancient epic through a complete unification of the Kievan and Novgorodian cycles of byliny. For this purpose he compared all the known variants of the byliny line by line and selected the best verses. "By removing or softening everything that was too harsh and by polishing the roughness of versification that hindered the smooth flow of the verses" he created the composite texts of twenty-four byliny. After that he arranged the texts chronologically and united them "into as consistent a chronicle as possible."[27] This description shows that Avenarius' *Book of the Kievan Heroes* was based on genuine folklore, but modified by the author. The resulting composite texts were arranged into a miniature epic considered suitable for use by Russian youth.

As does folklore in general, byliny rely heavily on the use of commonplaces (*loci communes*).[28] Commonplaces are formulaic, stereotypic descriptions of recurring situations, such as the banquet at Prince Vladimir's, the hero's entrance into the halls, the jumping of the horse, and the slaughter of the enemy. The formulas often begin the bylina or appear in transitional places that connect two episodes of the action. For instance, a typical banquet is described in Russian byliny as follows:

> In the glorious city of Kiev,
> it happened that gracious Prince Vladimir
> made a banquet, an honourable feast,
> for his company of princes and boyars,

for all the merchants invited and received,
invited and received, and come from afar.
All had eaten their fill at the honourable feast,
all had drunk their fill at the honourable feast,
all at the feast began to boast of this and that.[29]

Whenever the singer has to describe a banquet, he uses the same basic description with only slight modifications. This gives him an opportunity to relax and simultaneously to plan ahead.

The geographical distribution of commonplaces varies greatly. Those mentioned above are found wherever the byliny are recited and obviously are the oldest. Some commonplaces are known in a single region (e.g., the saddling of the horse in the North), some are restricted to narrators of a single district or a single school (e.g., the fleeting passage of time in the Onega area), and some are used only by individual singers. The study of commonplaces can be used for a variety of practical purposes, such as determining the singer and his teacher, pinpointing the area of origin for certain variants, and discovering falsifications of texts.[30]

There is a tendency in byliny to use fixed epithets, that is, to qualify a certain noun with a certain epithet. The horse, for instance, in about ninety-five percent of the cases is "good," the field is "open," the birch tree, the day, the swan, and the tent are "white," the table and gate are "high," the sun and gold are "red," the wolf and goose are "gray," and the steppe, road, and yard are "broad." According to P. D. Uxov, fixed epithets function as means of generalization and typification, pointing to the more characteristic, permanent, typical features of certain objects and phenomena.[31] The expression "fair maid" connotes that this is a peasant girl, moderately pretty (but not beautiful) and moderately plain (but not ugly); she is of average height, has a nice figure, and is neither rich nor poor. In other words, a "fair maid" does not stand out from the other peasant girls in any way. If, however, an individualized, non-typical characterization is desired, then the fixed epithets yield to specifying and particularizing epithets. When Prince Vladimir wants to marry and asks his heroes for suitable candidates, one of them describes to him the virtues of the daughter of the Prince of Polock:

The eldest daughter is not young in age,
and her mind is very sensible,
the girl has been taught to read and write,
and her face is white as winter snow,
she is endowed with a falcon's eyes,
and she possesses a sable's brows,
she walks about like a little swan,
and when she glances, it's the bright, bright day.[32]

The use of fixed epithets has become automatic: whenever a certain noun is used, it appears with its epithet. The Tatar Kalin Tsar even calls his own subjects by the derogatory epithet "heathen Tatars." The epithet for Kalin Tsar is "dog," thus he is normally referred to as "the dog Kalin Tsar" (*sobaka Kalin tsar'*). Even the Tatar, who has to relay a message from Kalin Tsar, addresses his emperor by this epithet. "The dog Kalin Tsar" in byliny corresponds to the historical Khan Nogai. The Khan's name *Nogai,* meaning "dog," was translated into Russian, where it became a derogatory epithet; the derogatory epithet applied to him, *Kalyn,* meaning "fat" or "stout," was left untranslated and became his personal name.[33]

The byliny have several types of meters, but the most common of them has three stresses per line and a varying number (one to three) of unstressed syllables between stresses. Usually the ending is dactylic and may receive a secondary stress on the last syllable. For example:

Pó sadu, sádu po zelénomu,
xodíla-guljála molodá knjažná,
molodá knjažna Márfa Vvesláv'evna.
Ona s kámenju skočíla na ljutá zmeja,
na ljútogo na zméja na Gorýniča.

> Through the garden, garden green
> walked-meandered the young princess,
> the young princess, Marfa Vseslav'evna.
> She leaped off a stone on a serpent fierce,
> on the fierce serpent Gorynič.[34]

The singers do not learn long epic songs by heart, but compose them while singing. As Parry and Lord have shown, the basis of the technique of composition is the formula.[35] The singer either repeats the formulas exactly or replaces the key words in them by others. Studies have proven that Russian singers use the formulaic technique in their presentations of byliny.[36]

In former times musical instruments were generally used to accompany bylina singing. The oldest instrument used for this purpose was the *gusli*—a low, irregular four-sided box with the strings stretched over the cover (originally having five to twelve strings, later eighteen to thirty-two). The term "gusli" denotes an old Slavic string instrument (cf. Serbocroatian *gusle*). However, the instrument itself is not Slavic in its origin. It was demonstrated recently that the Russians in the Old Novgorod area took over the Balto-Finnic and Baltic psaltry-type musical instrument and gave it their own name after some of these tribes were assimilated by the Russians.[37] A few centuries later, when the gusli came to be used primarily for the accompaniment of dancing, a "blade" was added to the instrument for accentuating the rhythm. The gusli's place as accompaniment to bylina singing was taken eventually by the balalaika, a triangular instrument played by plucking the strings. In some areas, the balalaika was used up to recent times, in others (like Olonec), it went out of use some time ago.

When the Bolsheviks came to power, the byliny were at first looked down upon. Considered to be the creation of singers of the higher, princely class, byliny did not fit into the reality of a communist state. In 1936 the Soviet government came out with a well-calculated plan, devised to reverse the ideas regarding the aristocratic origin of the byliny. The Soviet poet Dem'jan Bednyj had written the libretto for a comic opera, *The Epic Heroes (Bogatyri),* which was being presented in the Kamernyj Theater in Moscow. The epic heroes were shown in the opera as representatives of the feudal aristocracy with all possible defects and vices, whereas the villains whom they fought were glorified as the "revolutionary element." In November 1936 this opera, on an order from a government committee, was removed from the theater for misinterpreting Russian history and epic heroes. A series of articles appeared simultaneously in the leading newspapers, accusing the theater and especially the folklorists of falsifying the Russian historical past. Curiously enough, the accusatory articles were written by nonfolklorists—scholars of literature, historians, theoreticians of Marxism–Leninism, and others. Folklorists were condemned for their tendency to deny the creative abilities of the working people.

Folklorists, taken aback by these accusations, were silent for some time. When they did respond, it turned out that they had changed their views about the origin of byliny and had adopted those of their critics. In 1937 the leading Russian folklorist, Jurij Sokolov, for instance, modified the former theory by allotting the working people an essential part in the creation of byliny. He stressed that "the majority of byliny came from the masses of the working people." This view, adopted by all Soviet folklorists and nonfolklorists alike in their public pronouncements, has since then become one of the cornerstones of Soviet folkloristics. However, the study of the structure of byliny speaks against this theory.[38] Numerous old byliny contain two basic themes, hunting and fighting: the heroes undertake a hunting trip before engaging in combat. Both hunting and fighting were the main activities of Old Russian princes, as the chronicle reports of Vladimir Monomax and others testify. This fact supports Vsevolod Miller's conclusion that the byliny, which express princely pursuits and ideals, were created within princely circles, evidently by some talented singers in the princes' retinues, just as the West European heroic epic was created and nurtured in the court and aristocratic circles. Since the military retinue consisted not only of princes and boyars, but also of boyars' servants and peasants, the creators of byliny came from various social strata. Only in the sixteenth and seventeenth centuries did byliny become the exclusive property of peasants and workers.

Noviny

In the mid-1930s a new type of heroic song made its appearance in Russia; it was called "the new song" (*novina*). It imitated the bylina by making use of motifs and poetical devices, but the subject-matter was contemporary life. Protagonists were no longer the ancient epic heroes, but—according to the narrators themselves—"the new Soviet hero-innovators and defenders of the socialist fatherland, the *kolkhoz* [collective farm] heroes and factory heroes." Most often, Soviet government and military leaders, such as Lenin, Stalin, Čapaev (a leader of Red partisan units), Budennyj (a commander of Red cavalry forces), and others, functioned as the heroes. The creation of *noviny* and other genres of Soviet folklore (tales, legends, laments) was encouraged by the government. Master singers attended special seminars and lectures given for their edification; tutors from among the writers and folklorists were assigned to help them with facts and ideology.

Stalin's death (1953) and de-Stalinization (1956) brought about the reevaluation of the *noviny*. Highly regarded during Stalin's lifetime, the *noviny* were now subjected to harsh criticism. Aspects of *noviny* that were especially criticized included the discrepancy between their modern contents and archaic form, the creative help rendered to singers by writers and folklorists, and the fact that this new folklore had remained on paper and had not entered oral tradition. The songs created to extol Stalin and his cohorts were labeled "pseudo-folklore," and were no longer created or studied.[39] Interest now reverted to the byliny; but, alas, this interest was evinced more by folklore scholars than by the people.

Among the people, the byliny had outlived their time. Whereas in patriarchal Russia they captivated and thrilled people of all walks of life until the nineteenth century, they did not satisfy the cultural needs of the present technological age. People felt byliny to be uninteresting and boring compared to radio, television, theater, movies, newspapers, and novels.

Under these circumstances, the number of bylina singers and tellers has, in recent years, diminished drastically.[40] The range of bylina themes has become smaller and the texts corrupt and fragmentary. Even the principal episodes of byliny have become distorted and schematic, and the so-called epic ceremonialism (commonplaces, repetitions, fixed epithets, and so on) is being discarded. The introduction of new vocabulary, bookish terms, and trivial details of contemporary life is undermining the former monumental nature of the byliny. Thus, the bylina genre is like a neglected field that is gradually being covered by weeds and will soon be completely overgrown.

NOTES

1. William E. Harkins, *Bibliography of Slavic Folk Literature* (New York: King's Crown Press, 1953), p. 5.

2. William E. Harkins, *Dictionary of Russian Literature* (Paterson, N. J.: Littlefield, Adams, and Co., 1959), p. 35.

3. N. Kershaw Chadwick, *Russian Heroic Poetry* (New York: Russell and Russell, 1964), pp. 4–5, following P. N. Rybnikov.

4. M. M. Pliseckij, "Geographic Names in the Byliny," in *The Study of Russian*

Folklore, ed. Felix J. Oinas and Stephen Soudakoff, Slavistic Printings and Reprintings, Textbook Series, 4 (The Hague: Mouton and Co., 1975), pp. 49 ff.

5. For historical songs, see Carl Stief, *Studies in the Russian Historical Song* (Copenhagen: Rosenkilde and Bagger, 1953).

6. Russell Zguta, *"Skomorokhi:* The Russian Minstrel-Entertainers," *Slavic Review* 31 (1972): 306.

7. Their views are summarized by S. I. Dmitrieva in a mimeographed paper, "Methods in the Study of Russian Epics," given at the 9th International Congress of Anthropological and Ethnological Sciences in Chicago, August-September 1973.

8. Y. M. Sokolov, *Russian Folklore* (Hatboro, Pa.: Folklore Associates, 1966), pp. 296–99.

9. Russell Zguta, "Kievan *Byliny:* Their Enigmatic Disappearance from Kievan Territory," *Journal of the Folklore Institute* 9 (1972): 188–89.

10. Roman Jakobson and Mark Szeftel, "The Vseslav Epos," in Roman Jakobson, *Selected Writings,* IV: *Slavic Epic Studies* (The Hague and Paris: Mouton and Co., 1966), pp. 301 ff.

11. A. Mazon, "Mikula, le prodigieux laboureur," *Revue des Études Slaves* 11 (1931): 149–70; A. Mazon, "Svjatogor ou Saint-Mont le Géant," *Revue des Études Slaves* 12 (1932): 160–201.

12. A. M. Astaxova, ed., *Il'ja Muromec* (Moscow and Leningrad: Akademija nauk SSSR, 1958), p. 395.

13. Reinhold Trautmann, *Die Volksdichtung der Grossrussen,* I: *Das Heldenlied (Die Byline)* (Heidelberg: Carl Winter, 1935), pp. 304–308.

14. Astaxova, pp. 410–18.

15. Ju. I. Smirnov and V. G. Smolickij, eds., *Dobrynja Nikitič i Aleša Popovič* (Moscow: Nauka, 1974), pp. 343–44.

16. Ibid., p. 344.

17. Ibid., p. 350.

18. A. P. Skaftymov, "The Structure of the *Byliny,*" in Oinas and Soudakoff, p. 151.

19. D. S. Lixačev, "Letopisnye izvestija ob Aleksandre Popoviče," *Trudy otdela drevnerusskoj literatury* 7 (1949): 17–51.

20. Astaxova, pp. 408–409.

21. Lutz Röhrich, "Die Volksballade von 'Herrn Peters Seefahrt' und die Menschenopfer-Sagen," *Märchen, Mythos, Dichtung: Festschrift zum 90. Geburtstag Friedrich von der Leyens* (Munich: C. H. Beck, 1963), pp. 187 ff.

22. Skaftymov, pp. 218 ff.

23. [P. N. Rybnikov,] *Pesni sobrannye P. N. Rybnikovym,* I (Moscow: Tipografija A. Semena, 1861), p. 139.

24. È. V. Pomeranceva, "Narodnye verovanija i utnoe poètičeskoe tvorčestvo," in *Fol'klor i ètnografija,* ed. Kollektiv avtorov (Leningrad: Nauka, 1970), pp. 161–62.

25. A. M. Astaxova, *Russkij bylinnyj èpos na severe* (Petrozavodsk: Gosudarstvennoe izdatel'stvo Karelo-Finskoj SSR, 1948), pp. 104–105.

26. *Kniga o kievskix bogatyrjax* (St. Petersburg: Tip. M. Stasjuleviča, 1876).

27. Astaxova, *Russkij bylinnyj èpos na severe,* p. 300.

28. P. D. Uxov, "Commonplaces (*loci communes*) as Means of Documenting *Byliny,*" in Oinas and Soudakoff, pp. 207 ff.; P. D. Uxov, *Atribucii russkix bylin* (Moscow: Moskovskij universitet, 1970).

29. Chadwick, p. 124.

30. Uxov, *Atribucii russkix bylin,* pp. 139–70, 186–87.

31. P. D. Uxov, "Fixed Epithets in the *Byliny* as Means of Creating and Typifying Images," in Oinas and Soudakoff, pp. 219 ff. Here Uxov elaborates the ideas suggested previously by A. M. Astaxova (*Russkoe narodnoe poètičeskoe tvorčestvo,* II/1 [Moscow and Leningrad: Akademija nauk SSSR, 1955], p. 190), without referring to her.

32. Uxov, "Fixed Epithets in the *Byliny,*" p. 228.

33. Roman Jakobson, "Sobaka Kalin tsar'," *Selected Writings,* IV, p. 70.

34. Jakobson and Szeftel, "The Vseslav Epos," pp. 308, 363.

35. Albert B. Lord, *The Singer of Tales* (Cambridge, Mass.: Harvard University Press, 1960), pp. 30–67.

36. Patricia Arant, "Formulaic Style and the Russian *Bylina,*" *Indiana Slavic Studies,* 4 (Bloomington: Indiana University Press, 1967), pp. 7–51; Vil'jam Xarkins (William E. Harkins), "O metričeskoj roli slovesnyx formul v serbo-xorvatskom i russkom narodnom èpose," in *American Contributions to the Fifth International Congress of Slavists,* II, Sofia, September 1963 (The Hague: Mouton and Co., 1963), pp. 147–65.

37. I. Tõnurist, "Kannel Vepsamaast Setumaani" (with a Russian résumé), in E. Rüütel, ed., *Soome-ugri rahvaste muusika pärandist* (Tallinn: Eesti Raamat, 1977), pp. 149–78.

38. Felix J. Oinas, "The Problem of the Aristocratic Origin of Russian *Byliny,*" *Slavic Review* 30 (1971): 514 ff.; Felix J. Oinas, "The Political Uses and Themes of Folklore in the Soviet Union," *Journal of the Folklore Institute* 12 (1975): 166–69.

39. Felix J. Oinas, "Folklore and Politics in the Soviet Union," *Slavic Review* 32 (1973): 49–52, 55–56.

40. È. V. Pomeranceva, "The State of the *Bylina* in the Post-War Years," in Oinas and Soudakoff, pp. 291 ff.

BIBLIOGRAPHY

Collections and Anthologies

Astaxova, A. M. *Byliny severa* [Byliny of the North]. 2 vols. Moscow and Leningrad: Akademija nauk SSSR, 1938–51. Contains byliny, collected in the area of Mezen', Pečora, Prionež'e, Pinega, and Pomor'e in the 1920s and the early 30s. Introduction about the bylina tradition in northern Russia; detailed notes. Includes music.

———, ed. *Il'ja Muromec.* Moscow and Leningrad: Akademija nauk SSSR, 1958. Collection of the byliny, Cossack songs, and tales of Il'ja Muromec, with excellent commentaries.

———, V. V. Mitrofanova, and M. O. Skripil', eds. *Byliny v zapisjax i pereskazax XVII–XVIII vekov* [Byliny in Recordings and Retellings from the 17th to 18th Centuries]. Moscow and Leningrad: Akademija nauk SSSR, 1960. Byliny and their retellings found in the manuscripts from the seventeenth to the beginning of the nineteenth century and in bylina publications of the eighteenth century (except for the Kirša Danilov collection), with commentaries.

[Danilov, Kirša.] *Drevnie rossijskie stixotvorenija, sobrannye Kiršeju Danilovym* [Ancient Russian Poems, Collected by Kirša Danilov]. Edited by A. P. Evgen'eva and B. N. Putilov. Moscow and Leningrad: Akademija nauk SSSR, 1958. The first

Russian bylina collection, from the middle of the seventeenth century, first published (only partially) in 1804.

[Gil'ferding, A. F.] *Onežskie byliny, zapisannye A. F. Gil'ferdingom letom 1871 goda* [Onega Byliny, Recorded by A. F. Gil'ferding in the Summer of 1871]. 3 vols. 4th ed. by A. I. Nikiforov and G. S. Vinogradov. Moscow and Leningrad: Akademija nauk SSR, 1949–51. The second collection of Olonec byliny, arranged by singer. Important introduction. First ed. in 1 vol., St. Petersburg, 1873.

Grigor'ev, A. D. *Arxangel'skie byliny i istoričeskie pesni* [Arxangel'sk Byliny and Historical Songs]. Vol. I, Moscow: Imp. Akademija nauk, 1904. Vol. III, St. Petersburg: Imp. Akademija nauk, 1910. A large collection of byliny and historical songs recorded by Grigor'ev in the Arxangel'sk province during the summers of 1889–1901. Vol. I contains the texts from Pomor'e and Pinega, vol. III those from Mezen'. Has comments and musical notes. Vol. II has not been published.

Markov, A. V. *Belomorskie byliny* [White Sea Byliny]. Moscow: T-vo skoropeč. A. A. Levensona, 1901. Collection of byliny from the White Sea region. Preface by V. F. Miller.

Ončukov, N. E. *Pečorskie byliny* [Pečora Byliny]. St. Petersburg: Imp. Russkoe geografičeskoe obščestvo, 1904. Byliny collected by Ončukov on the lower reaches of the Pečora River in 1901 and 1902, with a survey of the local bylina tradition.

Propp, V. Ja., and B. N. Putilov, eds. *Byliny*. 2 vols. Moscow: Gosudarstvennoe izdatel'stvo xudožestvennoj literatury, 1958. An anthology of Russian byliny. Vol. I is arranged according to bylina heroes, vol. II according to genres. Has a good introduction and commentaries.

[Rybnikov, P. N.] *Pesni, sobrannye P. N. Rybnikovym* [Songs, Collected by P. N. Rybnikov]. 3 vols. 2nd ed. by A. E. Gruzinskij. Moscow: Sotrudnik škol, 1909–10. The first collection of byliny from the Olonec region, the most important bylina area in Russia. "The Collector's Note" gives information about the singers. First ed. in 4 vols.; Moscow, 1861–67.

Smirnov, Ju. I., and V. G. Smolickij, eds. *Dobrynja Nikitič i Aleša Popovič* [Dobrynja Nikitič and Aleša Popovič]. Moscow: Nauka, 1974. A collection of the byliny about Dobrynja Nikitič and Aleša Popovič. Detailed commentaries.

Sokolov, Ju. M., ed. *Onežskie byliny* [Onega Byliny]. Letopisi, 13. Moscow: Gosudarstvennyj literaturnyj muzej, 1948. Byliny collected by the expedition organized by the brothers Sokolov to the Onega Lake region in 1926–28. Comments and an important survey by Čičerov of Onega and Kargopol' bylina singers.

Translations

Chadwick, Nora K. *Russian Heroic Poetry*. New York: Russell and Russell, 1964. A collection of Russian byliny and historical songs in English translation. First published in 1932. The introduction and headnotes are outdated.

Trautmann, Reinhold. (See Studies.)

Studies

Alexander, Alex E. *Bylina and Fairy Tale: The Origins of Russian Heroic Poetry*. Slavistic Printings and Reprintings, 281. The Hague: Mouton and Co., 1973. Discussion of the possible evolution of byliny from fairy tales.

Astaxova, A. M. *Byliny: Itogi i problemy izučenija* [Byliny: The Results and the Problems of their Study]. Moscow and Leningrad: Nauka, 1966. A critical discussion of studies on byliny published primarily in the Soviet Union.

———. *Russkij bylinnyj èpos na severe* [The Russian Bylina Epic in the North]. Petrozavodsk: Gosudarstvennoe izdatel'stvo Karelo-Finskoj SSR, 1948. A comprehensive study of the byliny in northern Russia. Unlike the leading prerevolutionary folklorists, Astaxova studies the byliny not as archaic, stagnant phenomena, but as living processes. Analyzing the bylina tradition of the last one hundred-fifty years, she establishes basic laws pertaining to the creative process of the folk epic and considers the significance of the environment and the influence of written literature on the byliny.

Chettéoui, Wilfrid. *Un rapsode russe: Rjabinin le Père. La byline au XIXᵉ siècle.* Paris: Librairie Ancienne Honoré Champion, 1942. A survey of the famous bylina singer from the Olonec province, Trofim Rjabinin—his life, bylina repertoire, and his art. Contains also a detailed analysis of the poetics of Russian byliny.

Hartmann, Karl. *Volksepik am Weissen Meer: A. M. Krjukova—Eine Sängermonographie.* Munich: Wilhelm Fink, 1974. A monograph about Agrafena Krjukova, a celebrated bylina singer from the White Sea region: her life, personality, repertoire, and art, presented against the background of the Russian tradition.

Oinas, Felix J., and Stephen Soudakoff, eds. *The Study of Russian Folklore.* Slavistic Printings and Reprintings, Textbook Series, 4, and Indiana University Folklore Monograph Series, 25. The Hague: Mouton and Co., 1975. Contains, among other items, English translations of several essays on byliny by Russian folklorists (A. M. Astaxova, M. O. Gabel', M. M. Pliseckij, È. V. Pomeranceva, A. P. Skaftymov, P. D. Uxov, and V. M. Žirmunskij).

Propp, V. Ja. *Russkij geroičeskij èpos* [The Russian Heroic Epic]. 2nd ed. Moscow: Gosudarstvennoe izdatel'stvo xudožestvennoj literatury, 1958. In this work Propp, following Belinskij, endeavors to formulate the basic idea of each bylina, contending that the idea of a bylina expresses the ideals of the corresponding epoch. Numerous assertions are disputable.

Skaftymov, A. P. *Poètika i genezis bylin: Očerki* [The Poetics and Genesis of Byliny: Essays]. Moscow and Saratov: Knigoizdatel'stvo V. Z. Jaksanova, 1924. A formalistic study that emphasizes the significance of the investigation of bylina structure over that of ideology. The central portion was republished in Skaftymov's *Stat'i o russkoj literature* [Essays on Russian Literature], pp. 3–76. Saratov: Saratovskoe knižnoe izdatel'stvo, 1958.

Sokolov, Y. M. "Byliny." In his *Russian Folklore,* pp. 291–370. Hatboro, Pa.: Folklore Associates, 1966. A general survey of byliny with useful bibliography.

Trautmann, Reinhold. *Die Volksdichtung der Grossrussen,* I: *Das Heldenlied (Die Byline).* Heidelberg: Carl Winter, 1935. A comprehensive, though somewhat outdated, survey of Russian byliny. While the first part deals with bylina genre in general, the second gives German translations (slightly abbreviated) and comments on individual byliny. Trautmann tends to assign a later origin to a number of byliny than do the majority of bylina scholars.

Žirmunskij, V. "Èpos slavjanskix narodov v sravnitel'no–istoričeskom osveščenii" [The Epic of the Slavic Peoples in a Comparative-Historical Interpretation]. In his *Narodnyi geroičeskij èpos* [The Popular Heroic Epic], pp. 75–194. Moscow and Leningrad: Gosudarstvennoe izdatel'stvo xudožestvennoj literatury, 1962. A stimulating comparative discussion of epic songs. Similarities between numerous Slavic and other epic songs of the feudal period are shown as being typological rather than genetic. The work is available also in German translation: Viktor Schirmunski, *Vergleichende Epenforschung,* I. Berlin: Akademie-Verlag, 1961.

12   Serbocroatian Heroic Songs

Mary P. Coote

The Tradition

The folk poetry of the South Slavs is unusually rich in narrative songs on heroic subjects. Among speakers of Serbocroatian (the principal language of Yugoslavia), the tradition of singing narrative poetry, which probably dates at least to the Common Slavic period before the seventh century A.D., has survived through numerous sea-changes to the present day. Heroic songs occupy a place of honor in Serbocroatian traditional lore because of their long association with the ideals and aspirations of the peoples of Yugoslavia. Outside Yugoslavia they have also become known among scholars of literature and folklore as a model of a living oral tradition.

Serbocroatian heroic songs belong to an oral tradition. The oral tradition, however, has existed side by side with a written literature since the ninth and tenth centuries, when literacy was introduced to the South Slavs with their conversion to Christianity. The two traditions, literate and non-literate, have been in constant contact and have exercised significant influence upon each other. The non-literate has contributed to the literate an abundance of story material, characters, poetic forms, and language, as well as its veneration for the lore of the past. Conversely it has received from the literate culture not only song texts and historical data, but also the literate culture's idea of historical fact and the sanctity of the fixed written word.

The core of South Slavic heroic song was located among the Orthodox Christians in the southeastern part of the Balkan peninsula (Serbia, Macedonia, western Bulgaria), from which it spread through migration of peoples and cultural contact to the north and west among Roman Catholics and Slavs who later converted to Islam. Singing is presumed to have flourished in the Middle Ages in the courts of the Serbian aristocracy as it did in medieval Europe,[1] although evidence for this period is mostly conjectural. The milieu which fostered singing as we know it from the nineteenth century on was the long era of Turkish rule in the Balkans from the late fourteenth to the early twentieth centuries. While the Turks moved up the peninsula from the southeast, taking Bulgaria, Macedonia, Serbia, and a large part of Croatia and Hungary, the Hapsburg Empire in the north and northwest and the Venetians on the Adriatic coast expanded to meet them. The people of what is now Yugoslavia were divided by religious faith and political and cultural orientation into many mutually hostile groups. Constant conflict over the boundaries of these groups created a prolonged "Heroic Age" during which the deeds and qualities of heroes were essential to the survival of society. Heroism was the business of every grown male, and a necessary concomitant of heroism were the songs that celebrated it and made it immortal. The withdrawal of the Turks, completed only in 1913, brought this age to a close, although it did not put an end to warfare and foreign domination for the South Slavs. The preservation of the singing tradition in new circumstances depended upon its continuing to function as a means of edification and entertainment. Eventually, as values changed and occasions both for traditional heroism and for singing heroic songs became less frequent, singing also changed its style and subject. Today the performance of heroic songs is still valued as part of the national heritage, but conditions for the continued creation of new songs in the oral heroic tradition hardly exist.

Evidence for the existence of a singing tradition predates all extant records of what was sung in early times. For example, the Byzantine historian Procopius in the sixth century mentioned that the Slav warriors who pushed through the Balkans to the walls of Thessalonica were known to sing songs. Similar allusions to singers or singing were made by other historians and travelers through the succeeding centuries. We cannot be sure, however, that the South Slavs of these times were singing heroic songs as we know them. The earliest reference to what must be heroic song comes from Benedict Kuripešič, a Slovene who traveled through Bosnia as a member of an embassy from the Hapsburg court to the Turkish sultan and noted in his account of the journey (1531) that he heard songs about figures such as Miloš Obilić, the Serbian hero of the battle of Kosovo (1389).

The songs themselves seem to indicate a long history which is more extensive than the meager written records show. Since they are fluid like all products of oral tradition, it is difficult to reconstruct that history on the basis of textual evidence. Elements of traditional stories that allude to identifiable places, personages, or events are presumed to have originated in those times and places. The age of a song, however, is not the same as the age of its motifs, as individual songs are concatenations of motifs which can be dated only to the time they are recorded and acquire a fixed form in written transmission. The presence of archaic motifs in a song may be evidence of the antiquity of the singing tradition as a whole, but not of the given song.

The traditional singers themselves, unaware of the fluidity of their songs and having no esteem for innovation or originality, believe that they preserve and hand on songs unchanged, since change would violate the truth of the song. A song is supposed to arise in response to an event and preserve that event as it "really" happened through all its retellings. Accomplished singers do compose songs on contemporary events they have witnessed, but it is not necessary to assume that all stories, even those with clearly historical motifs, can be traced to originals composed about real and current events.

The earliest records of song texts were made by literary men who embedded folksongs in their own works for esthetic or didactic purposes. The first published heroic songs appeared in *Fishing* (*Ribanje*, 1556), an eclogue by Peter Hektorović of Hvar, in which the author included the words and music of two songs sung to him by his boatmen "in the Serbian manner." Besides providing direct evidence of singing, these texts represent early examples of the long *bugarštica* line in narrative song and the earliest recorded story about the popular hero Marko Kraljević.

The most significant publication before the nineteenth century was Andrija Kačić-Miošić's *Pleasant Relation of the Slavic People* (*Razgovor ugodni naroda slovinskoga,* 1756, 1759). A Franciscan monk who traveled and taught in Dalmatia, Bosnia, and Hercegovina, Kačić decided to write a history of all the South Slavs that might edify and inspire his people. In order to reach simple folk he drew on folk tradition for the form and, to some extent, for the content of his work, presenting his history in a series of poems celebrating heroes and events of the past. The poems in the *Pleasant Relation* are in the ten-syllable line, the predominant meter of heroic song. Only two or three of the songs are of folk or oral origin. Kačić's book, however, became so popular, especially among the Roman Catholic Croats, that a number of his creations later entered oral tradition. Literate culture thus began to have its effect upon non-literate culture, most significantly by fostering among the folk, as well as among observers of the tradition, the persistent notion that heroic songs constitute history in the sense that people with written records understand history. With his popularization of heroic songs, Kačić stimulated interest in collecting folksongs in other South Slavic areas and also provided the source for some of the first translations of Serbocroatian folk poetry into European languages.[2]

The singing tradition of the late seventeenth and eighteenth centuries is known to us in a number of manuscript collections which were discovered and published only in the nineteenth and twentieth centuries. Several of these were compiled in the coastal area of Dubrovnik and the Gulf of Kotor. They contain texts in both the *bugarštica* line and the ten-syllable line.[3] Another collection including heroic songs in ten-syllable lines is attributed to an anonymous German-speaking collector who worked in the Military border of Croatia during the early eighteenth century.[4] Like most efforts to record songs for preservation from Hektorović's time on, these manuscripts were written in areas on the periphery of the heroic song region by people raised in the literate culture.

Systematic collecting and printing of heroic songs began in the nineteenth century with the publications of Vuk Stefanović Karadžić, the remarkable Serbian ethnographer who combined in his own person both the literate and non-literate cultures.[5] From the folk, among whom he grew up absorbing the tradition at first hand, he learned that the heroic songs were ancient, venerable, and true, while from his literate mentors outside Serbia he learned that they represented the history and spirit of his people. His aim in recording Serbian oral traditions was two-fold: to display to the rest of the world the beauties of Serbian folk poetry, just when the vogue for popular poetry was at its height in the Romantic era, and to preserve this peculiar heritage for the Serbs themselves.[6] In addition to texts of songs, tales, and proverbs, Vuk published observations on the life and customs, including singing, in Serbian traditional society. Thanks to the acclaim they received both in Europe (especially Germany) and at home, Vuk's song texts have become canonical for singers and scholars alike. His views on the age and historicity, as well as on the nature and the quality of the songs, came to dominate generations of scholarship.

Vuk's example and encouragement inspired further collecting activity throughout the Balkans. Not to be outdone by the collectors at work in Serbia, Montenegro, Bosnia, and Hercegovina, later in the century the Croatian learned society, Matica hrvatska, began a collecting and publishing program that resulted in ten volumes of narrative and lyric songs, covering a wide area of northern and western Yugoslavia (1896–1941).[7] The two volumes of Moslem heroic songs in the series have particular interest because, along with Kosta Hörmann's two volumes, they give thorough coverage to an area and a tradition that were poorly represented in Vuk's *Serbian Folk Songs*.[8] In the twentieth century with the introduction of sound recording equipment, collecting has increased in extent and accuracy. A number of institutes of folklore and ethnography in Yugoslavia are continuing the work of recording and preserving oral tradition. Also in the twentieth century, a resurgence of attention to Serbocroatian folksongs as a model of traditional poetry has prompted non-Yugoslav scholars to undertake collection in the Balkans. One of the most notable results of these endeavors is the Milman Parry Collection of Oral Literature at Harvard University, which has grown out of Parry's expeditions to Yugoslavia in 1933 and 1934–35.[9]

Classification

In most general terms, Serbocroatian heroic songs deal with the deeds of heroes: slaying monsters, winning brides, rescuing captives, and restoring order from chaos. The underlying story patterns are mythic, expressive of the persistent concerns of mankind. Narrators in various eras and regions have shaped these patterns in different ways to celebrate figures and events that have particular meaning for their audiences. While in some cultures such stories are told in cosmic terms and set in mythical time, in the Serbocroatian tradition the heroic song became a medium for relating the activity of heroic men in historical times and places. Thus the heroes' struggles are located in actual geography and often connected with historical events; monsters assume the guise of national or religious foes such as the Turk, the black Arab (i.e., the Moor), or the outlaw; heroes use human strength and wit, albeit of epic proportions, rather than supernatural means to attain their ends. The involvement of heroic songs with daily life gives them the air of realism and historicity that distinguishes the Serbocroatian from other traditions, even from close relatives like the Macedonian and Bulgarian traditions.

Overtly supernatural phenomena play a minor role in Serbocroatian heroic songs, although the prevalence of so-called archaic and mythical motifs in west Bulgarian and Macedonian songs gives grounds for supposing that the supernatural figured in early Common South Slavic singing.[10] Serbocroatian singers have rationalized the supernatural so that it appears only in vestigial forms, for example in the dragon-like features of some villains: one has three heads and breathes fire, another has three hearts, each with a snake dwelling in it.[11] The only purely supernatural creatures present in the heroic songs are the *vilas,* female spirits of the mountains, forests, and lakes. Often the vilas serve merely as devices for communicating information to the human heroes, rather than as agents in the plot. Their mythical quality is evident in songs in which they act as adversaries of the hero, as does the vila toll-taker, the guardian of a mountain lake who rides a stag harnessed with snakes and exacts from every man who disturbs the waters the two forelegs of his horse and his own two eyes.

Following the example of Vuk Karadžić, scholars customarily divide the heroic songs into groups according to the historical era from which their principal characters and events are drawn. Nine or more cycles have been defined on this basis: (1) Non-historical songs, (2) songs of medieval Serbia, (3) songs related to the battle of Kosovo (1389) and its heroes, (4) songs about the leaders of the South Slavs in Turkish times, (5) songs about Marko Kraljević, (6) songs about outlaws and pirates (*hajduci* and *uskoci*), (7) songs of the Slavs of the Moslem faith, (8) songs about the wars of liberation from the Turks in Montenegro and Hercegovina, and (9) songs about the liberation of Serbia. These nine cover the songs recorded during the classic period of collecting in the nineteenth century, that is, chiefly those represented in Vuk's books. As the tradition continued to produce songs on current events right through World War II and the civil war in Yugoslavia, new cycles have been recognized in the literature.

NON-HISTORICAL CYCLE

The songs in the non-historical cycle are not properly heroic. Many are saints' legends and apocryphal tales cast in the heroic song form; others, such as "The Serpent Bridegroom" (AT 433B; Vuk II, 11), deal with wondrous events and creatures more at home in the folktale than in the epic.[12] In Yugoslav scholarship they are often termed mythological, myth being understood as opposed to history and associated with Christian or pre-Christian religious beliefs. The songs on Christian subjects reflect the influence of the church on the popular tradition and illustrate how Christian teaching was adapted by the people to traditional ways of thinking.[13] For example, in "The Saints Divide the Treasure" (Vuk II, 1), when the saints in heaven are distressed by the sins of folk on earth, the sins enumerated are all violations of traditional Serbian family and ritual relationships. After the saints divide their treasure, assigning to each his customary attributes and thus establishing order in heaven, they obtain God's permission to disrupt the cycle of the seasons on earth until the sinners repent and order can be restored there as well.

SONGS OF MEDIEVAL SERBIA

The earliest historical cycle contains songs about the noble families of medieval Serbia, the Nemanjići, Mrnjavčevići, and others, and includes some of the best known stories in the tradition. These songs represent the closest approach in Serbian to the medieval European model in which knightly deeds were celebrated by singers maintained at the courts of aristocratic patrons. They provide material for the proponents of the theory of the aristocratic origin of heroic songs[14] and also for comparative studies drawing parallels between the Serbian and the Romance traditions.[15] If these songs, relatively few in number, are an indication that singing flourished in the Serbian empire, very little of the tradition of that time survived in later singing. It is argued that the defeat of Serbia and her allies at the battle of Kosovo, leading to the eventual conquest of the Balkans, was an event of such cataclysmic import that it caused a break in the tradition.[16] Songs about the old and splendid life before the Turks came were neglected as singers took up the new and compelling theme of the struggle between Moslems and Christians, the theme that nurtured most of the tradition as it has been preserved in records.

Many of the songs in this cycle cast historical figures in internationally known tale plots. For example, "The Building of Skadar" (Vuk II, 25) is based on the motif of a blood sacrifice being required to make a building stand. When the three brothers Mrnjavčević undertake to build a fortress, they are hindered in their work by a vila until finally the youngest brother's wife, a nursing mother, is walled into the foundations. "The Wedding of Emperor Dušan" (Vuk II, 28) tells of overcoming numerous obstacles to win a bride from a foreign and hostile land. The bridegroom, the Serbian emperor, is represented in the contests for the hand of the daughter of the Latin king by an uninvited member of his retinue, who is his young nephew Miloš Vojinović in disguise. Miloš performs the feats of skill required by the Latins and then lingers behind the wedding party to slay the monstrous knight sent out by the bride's family to recover her. The historical Dušan ruled the Serbian empire at its height (1331–55) and married a Bulgarian princess. The story told about his wedding is one that recurs in the tradition attached to other heroes as well and has little connection with fact.[17]

KOSOVO CYCLE

The central event in Serbian tradition is the battle of Kosovo, which took place on St. Vitus' Day, June 15 (*o.s.*), 1389. On that occasion the Serbs and their allies under Prince Lazar were defeated by the Turks, and both Lazar and the Turkish sultan Murad were killed on the field. Although Turkish conquest of the Balkans was gradual, Kosovo was a decisive battle that came to epitomize the loss of Serbia's independence and grandeur. In time, legends filled out the scanty historical record, creating a gallery of characters whose destinies were linked with Serbia's at Kosovo. Prince Lazar and Miloš Obilić, who assassinated the sultan, became the heroes of the legend, the one a martyr king who preferred the heavenly kingdom to an earthly kingdom, the other a perfect knight who sacrificed his life to save his honor and to display Serbian heroism. Legend also required a villain, and so made a traitor of Vuk Branković, even though the historical Vuk seems to have been loyal to Lazar, and the Branković family ruled the remnant of Serbia after Kosovo. Blame for the disaster was laid upon disunity among the Serbs: a quarrel arose between Lazar's daughters, the wives of Vuk and Miloš, which set the two sons-in-law at odds and caused Vuk to slander Miloš as a traitor before Lazar at their last supper together on the eve of battle, thus provoking Miloš to his daring act. The story says that Miloš gained access to the sultan by claiming to be a defector, and that it was Vuk who did defect and betray his country by withdrawing his troops from the field and causing the battle to turn against Serbia.

The essential elements of the Kosovo legend had been put together at least by 1601, when Mavro Orbini published an account of the battle in his history of the Slavs.[18] We do not have evidence, however, that the legend immediately took the form of heroic song. Recorded songs of Kosovo are of relatively late origin and in most cases deal with events peripheral to the main battle, often in balladic or elegaic, rather than heroic, style. The earliest known song on Kosovo is a bugarštica accompanied by a page reference to Orbini's history, which is copied in the oldest part of the Dubrovnik manuscript dating from 1690–1700. It tells how Miloš Dragilović or Obilović was wounded and died at Kosovo and gives the last words and testament of the dying hero. There is scant record of songs on the events of Kosovo before Vuk Karadžić, little even in Vuk's early publications. The bulk of the Kosovo cycle appears in Vuk's later collections as the result of deliberate search and solicitation of songs on a subject Vuk and his contemporaries were convinced must exist in heroic song. It is noteworthy that the Kosovo songs were not collected in the Kosovo region, but only in the free areas across the Danube from old Serbia or in Dalmatia. The singing of heroic songs about Kosovo, if any existed, may have been suppressed by Turkish rulers in occupied Serbia.[19]

Songs about Kosovo depict the preparation and departure of heroes for battle ("Musić Stefan," Vuk II, 46) and the forebodings of their womenfolk at parting ("Prince Lazar and Princess Milica," Vuk II, 44). Events on the battlefield are told in the aftermath rather than as they occur. A maiden searches the field for her promised husband and groomsmen ("The Kosovo Maiden," Vuk II, 50); she encounters a hero late to arrive and tells him of the bloodshed ("Musić Stefan"); a messenger recounts the outcome to Lazar's wife ("Milica and General Vladeta," Vuk II, 48); ravens bring the news to the mother of nine sons that all of them have fallen ("The Death of the Mother of the Jugovići," Vuk II, 47). The action is told in dialogue form from the point of view of the survivors, often women, after the manner of ballads or laments. Despite the significance of Miloš Obilić's heroic deed in the Kosovo tradition, Vuk did not publish any songs that told his story directly, although a song on this subject has been found in a manuscript collection dating from 1778–81.[20] The lack of a song about Miloš Obilić was subsequently filled; today, for example, a "Death of Sultan Murat," evidently not of oral traditional origin, is current.

After Kosovo the remnant of the Serbian state maintained its independence in the northwest, in the Danube River region bordering on Hungary. Many Serbs fled there, as well as to the mountain stronghold of Montenegro, and took the singing tradition with them. Members of the surviving ruling families, such as the Brankovići in Smederevo and the Crnojevići in Montenegro, joined the medieval rulers as the subjects of hero tales. For instance, the last despot of Serbia (1471–85) appears in the tradition as Zmaj-despot Vuk, or Zmaj Ognjeni Vuk (Vuk (or Wolf) the Fire-Drake), a character who figures in songs as a werewolf hero and dragon slayer.[21]

SONGS ABOUT MARKO KRALJEVIĆ

Besides the Kosovo legend, Serbian tradition created another great legend out of the subjection to Turkey, the figure of Marko Kraljević, "the king's son."[22] In contrast to the elegaic and fragmentary Kosovo cycle, the Marko cycle contains countless songs, most of them properly heroic. Marko's name is historically attested: it belonged to a minor prince in Macedonia who became a Turkish vassal even before the battle of Kosovo and died in Romania fighting with the Turks against his fellow Christians. Inspired by national feeling, tradition has made Marko into an invincible warrior, a defender of the poor and oppressed, and a champion of Serbdom against all enemies. Yet traditional songs also portray him as the sultan's foster son, fighting for the Turkish cause, and a character not without faults or above the use of trickery and deceit. Marko is a composite of the historical, the traditional, and the patriotic. His name is attached to a certain type of hero that may have been known in narratives in the Balkans long before Kosovo. In Turkish times he came to embody the experience of the subject peoples as a hero who continued to play his role even as a vassal of the sultan. His exploits provided themes more congenial to heroic song than the tragic tales of Kosovo and more acceptable and even entertaining to the Turkish rulers than the deeds of the sultan's murderer, Miloš Obilić.

Marko's most prominent role is that of the slayer of monsters. Among these are Musa the Highwayman (Vuk II, 66), an Albanian who blocks commerce on the sultan's highways, and Djemo the Mountaineer (Vuk II, 67), Musa's brother, who captures the unarmed Marko as Marko is going in quest of fish to serve his guests, but is dissuaded from hanging his captive because the local people believe that Marko's murder on their land would cause the harvests to fail. Marko also defeats a black Arab who threatens to rape the sultan's daughter (Vuk II, 65) and another black Arab who imposes an exorbitant wedding tax on all the youth of Kosovo Plain (Vuk II, 68). He struggles with hostile vilas, the vila toll-taker (Matica hrvatska II, 2) and vila Ravijojla, who in jealousy of the fine singing of Marko's companion Miloš shoots Miloš through the throat (Vuk II, 37). All these antagonists are withholders of the prosperity and happiness that Marko restores to society with his victories. They have a fantastic and supernatural aura about them and cannot be over-powered simply by human physical strength. Often when the struggle goes against him, Marko resorts to wit and trickery or to the aid of his companions, not warriors like himself, but vilas or tavern-maids, his sworn sisters, or his heroic piebald horse Šarac.

Marko also figures in stories about troubled family relationships. Tradition pictures him without progeny to carry on his line, and a number of tales are told about the loss or near loss of his siblings or wife. For example, in Hektorović's song he kills his brother Andrijaš in a quarrel over booty. In other songs Marko himself is killed by his long lost brother, who does not recognize him. Most stories involving brothers and sisters come either from Croatia or from Bulgaria and Macedonia (where Marko is equally as popular as in Serbia); in Serbian tradition, Marko usually has only a wise old mother at home. Marko's unsuccessful attempts at wooing are told in stories such as "Captain Leka's Sister" (Vuk II, 39), in which he kills the girl for mocking him and his companions, and "A Maiden Outwits Marko" (Vuk II, 40), in which the girl thwarts Marko's threatening advances by claiming him as a godfather, a ritual relationship that precludes a sexual relationship. Fear of the strange and mighty Amazon maiden who seeks Marko as a husband drives Marko to use a trick to kill her (Matica hrvatska II, 49). Likewise, he deceit-fully promises to marry an Arab princess in return for her rescuing him from prison, and then kills her because he dislikes her swarthy complexion. Several stories are told of his difficulties in keeping a wife once won. "The Marriage of Marko Kraljević" (Vuk II, 55) tells how he nearly lost his Bulgarian bride through the treachery of his bridal godfather, the doge of Venice (Venetians were ever untrustworthy in this tradition); the artful maiden herself prevents this dishonor. In a number of instances the wife is wooed or abducted by a rival, sometimes with her connivance, sometimes against her will. For example, in "Marko and Mina of Kostur" (Vuk II, 61), Marko's wife is stolen by Mina during Marko's absence at the sultan's wars with the Arabs, and Marko returns in disguise just in time to avert her remarriage.[23]

Marko's appeal as a national hero derives in part from his reckless disregard for the precepts and boundaries that restrict ordinary folk. Only he can move freely in both Christian and Turkish society, indulging his desire for drink and pleasure and giving free reign to his hasty temper. In "Marko Drinks Wine in Ramazan" (Vuk II, 70) he breaks Moslem law with impunity, while in other stories such as those about the vila toll-taker and the vila Ravijojla he defies the prohibitions of supernatural creatures in an unreal setting. His defiant spirit is expressed also in songs in which he outbluffs the arrogant Turks who come unbidden to his feast (Vuk II, 71) and intimidates the sultan into rewarding him richly for his indispensable services as a warrior (Vuk II, 69). In a humorous tale, he responds to his mother's request that he find a peaceful profession by using a plow to waylay and rob a Turkish caravan (Vuk II, 72).

Many songs give Marko more serious knightly qualities as an upholder of custom and justice and a defender of the weak, especially the Christian peasants. He displays such chivalry in "Marko Abolishes the Wedding Tax" (Vuk II, 68), and in "Uroš and the Mrljavčevići (Mrnjavčevići)" (Vuk II, 33), in which Marko rules on the succession to the Serbian throne against the claims of his own father. In "Marko and Bey Kostadin" (Vuk II, 59) and "Marko and Alil-aga" (Vuk II, 60), Marko's righteousness and generosity are contrasted to the injustice and rapacity of the Turks. The songs and legends of Marko's death (Vuk II, 73 and others) recorded by Vuk give him his apotheosis as the Serbian hero who never dies but lies slumbering to awaken in the hour of his people's greatest need.

OUTLAW (*HAJDUK* AND *USKOK*) SONGS

Songs of what Vuk called "intermediate times," that is, the period between the fourteenth century, the classic age of Kosovo and Marko, and Vuk's own era, show how particular groups involved in the conflict between Christians and Moslems carried on the singing tradition and produced heroes from among their own kind.[24] The most famous among these are the *hajduks,* or outlaws, who took to the woods in rebellion against all authority, whether Turkish or other, and lived mainly by plunder. Among a population obliged to resign itself to foreign occupation, the hajduks were admired for their desperate courage, the only kind of heroic resistance the weak could put up against the strong. They emerged as military leaders in the Serbian uprising of Vuk's time and were celebrated in the folk and art literature of the nineteenth century as national heroes. The hajduks' way of life provided both subjects and occasions for singing heroic songs, the subjects being the outlaws' adventures and the occasions being the nights spent lying low in hideouts in the woods or in friendly villages, especially during the long idle winter. Several of their heroes became legendary and widely known in the tradition: for example, Starina (Old Man) Novak and his company who roam the greenwood on Mt. Romanija between Serbia and Bosnia (Novak may be a historical figure of the late sixteenth century, but the songs place him with the Brankovići in the fifteenth), and Captain Mijat Tomić and Bajo Pivljanin of Hercegovina, both dated to the seventeenth century. Similarly the *uskoks* (renegades), refugees from Turkish-held lands who crossed into Austrian and Venetian territory and raided mostly by sea, cultivated a branch of the heroic tradition celebrating such heroes as Stojan Janković of Kotari near Zadar, a military leader of the seventeenth century.

Among the patriarchal tribes and clans of Montenegro, the cult of heroism and heroic song was highly developed. Montenegrins are pictured as constantly engaged in warfare, not only in conflict with Turks and Moslem Slavs, but also in blood feuds that served them as a system of administering justice. Their songs are characterized by elementary plots and factual narration of everyday incidents of sheep stealing, combat, and killing.[25] Since the Montenegrin tradition continued to be productive until recent times, it has provided a model of how the heroic song form can be used to chronicle actual events.

In Vuk's time it seemed clear that the function of heroic song was precisely to serve as a chronicle of events, in particular those of the last days of the four centuries of Turkish rule. After the collapse of the first Serbian uprising (1804–13) Vuk found talented singers among the refugees from reoccupied Serbia who composed songs about the crucial battles of the rising, such as "The Battle on the Mišar" (Vuk IV, 30). The most famous of these songs, "The Beginning of the Rebellion against the Dahis" (Vuk IV, 24) by Filip Višnjić, recounts the Serbian resistance under Karageorge to the cruelties of the *dahis* (Turkish governors), who were themselves in rebellion against the sultan. Similarly the eighteenth- and nineteenth-century wars of liberation in Montenegro and Hercegovina provided subjects for singing. Serbs who served in the Austrian armies also used the heroic song form to memorialize their deeds in the Turkish and European wars of the late seventeenth to the nineteenth centuries.[26]

KRAJINA SONGS

The Slavs in Bosnia and Hercegovina who converted to Islam (and in their loyalty to the Ottoman Empire called themselves Turks) maintained the tradition of oral narrative song while adapting the story material to the Turkish point of view. Moslem songs from Hercegovina resemble Christian songs of the same area in everything but the names of the protagonists. Singers in

Bosnia, however, created a distinctive type of heroic song, differing from the
Vukovian type in style and content. These "songs of the Krajina" (i.e., of the
northwestern border of the Ottoman Empire) moved to the Southeast, in
contrast to the northwestern migration of Serbian songs, and are to be found
also among the Moslems of the Novi Pazar area and Albania.[27]

In the Krajina songs, Bosnian devotion to the sultan is embodied in the
character of Djerzelez Alija, whose customary role is to rescue the sultan from
difficulties created by incompetent or disloyal advisers and commanders close
to the throne in Istanbul. He is the only champion who can be found to stand
up to the challenges of the most formidable Christian heroes (Matica hrvatska
III, 1); he is the only one who can take Bagdad after twenty years of unsuccessful siege (in one version his betrothed in disguise as a warrior makes the
conquest by capturing the Queen of Bagdad; Parry I, 1). Other heroes in
Moslem songs are involved in struggles on the Balkan frontiers with the
Latins (Roman Catholics under Venetian sovereignty) on the coast and the
Hungarians to the north. Mustajbeg of the Lika, identified with a commander
of the Lika in the seventeenth century, is traditionally the supreme commander of the Bosnian forces. He is supported by the two brothers Hrnjičić or
Hrnjica of Kladuša. Sirdar Mujo, the elder, is a mighty but guileless warrior;
Halil is a ladies' man and more adept at disguise and strategem than his
brother. Expeditions are rarely undertaken without Tale the Fool, a curious
hero whose attributes include miserliness, greed, and buffoonery used for
comic effect, as well as extraordinary wisdom and strength. As singers explain his character, Tale's rags and clowning are only a cover for his special,
almost supernatural powers. He usually is responsible for directing military
operations, dividing the spoils of battle, and executing judgment on the van-
quished.[28]

The Krajina songs tell of conflicts on a grander scale than the Christian
songs do, dealing with sieges of cities and battles between huge armies in far
away places like Crete, Bagdad, and Budapest. They also dwell on romantic
episodes concerning the wooing, abduction, or rescue of beautiful women,
usually from the possession of an infidel. Such episodes commonly provide
the pretext for single combats and major battles between Turks and Christians,
as in, for example, "Bojičić Alija Rescues the Children of Alibey" (Parry I,
26). A romantic intrigue may run parallel to a military conflict. Thus "The
Wedding of Smailagić Meho" (Parry III), one of the longest songs recorded
in Serbocroatian, combines two plots: one tells of the journey of young Meho
to be invested with the rank of commander-in-chief, succeeding his father,
and to win a bride; the other is a tale of the treason of the vizier of Buda and
his overthrow by the zealous Bosnian forces. Few of the Krajina songs end
without including both a heroic combat and a wedding.

Heroic song in Serbocroatian continues to show vitality even though songs
on subjects of recent date are not ranked with the best of the old tradition. The

heroic age is considered to have closed, last of all in Montenegro, in the late nineteenth or early twentieth century. Collectors from outside Yugoslavia, such as Matthias Murko or Milman Parry and Albert Lord, speak of the art of singing as in a state of decline, thanks to changes in the economic and educational condition of the people. New ways of composing and singing have replaced the old with the spread of literacy and contact with other forms of musical entertainment. Nevertheless, the heroic song is still regarded as the appropriate form for celebrating contemporary deeds of military prowess, as well as for preserving treasured legends of the past. Heroic singing has been officially encouraged both in pre-war and in post-war Yugoslavia, and songs have been created there and in emigre communities about the battles of two world wars, the Yugoslav civil war and revolution, and other events of the present time.

Performance and Composition

Heroic songs of the type Vuk published are usually taken as the norm for the Serbocroatian tradition. Vuk defined this type in terms of the manner of its performance:

> All our folksongs are divided into heroic songs on the one hand, which men sing to the gusle, and women's songs on the other, which are sung not only by women and girls, but also by men, especially young men, mostly two singing in unison. Women's songs are sung by one or two people simply for their own enjoyment, while heroic songs are sung chiefly for others to listen to. . . .[29]

Songs conforming to Vuk's model predominate among the collected and published songs and occur widely in the central region of Yugoslavia. Their closeness to the Romantic ideal of what an epic folksong should be—a record of history and an expression of national feeling—further enhanced their reputation, as did Vuk's own prestige later on. There are many variations from this norm, however, in the peripheral areas where songs have developed in a local tradition.

The core of the recorded song tradition lies in the Dinaric mountain range which runs from northwest to southeast through the middle of Yugoslavia. Vuk found songs abundant in Bosnia, Hercegovina, Montenegro, and southern Serbia, where he said there was a *gusle* in every home, and to a lesser extent among the Serbs who had settled to the north, where there was at least one gusle in every village.[30] Outside this area, especially in the hinterland of the Dalmatian coast and in Slavonia, heroic songs were also to be heard, but not always in the Vukovian style. They were sung to different instruments, by different kinds of performers, or in different settings. Since the Dalmatian songs share a number of features with the other main branch of the South Slavic tradition, the Bulgarian-Macedonian tradition, the spread of the Serbian type seems to have driven a wedge through another type and dispersed it to the fringes of the heroic song area.

We know very little about the singers of heroic songs before Vuk's time. Were there professional minstrels in medieval Serbia, or did early songs come from non-professionals among the folk? What singers created new songs, and did some simply perform well-known songs composed by others? What regions did singers come from and where did they perform? The answers to such questions about the creators of the songs would tell us much about the early Serbocroatian tradition. In the absence of direct evidence, the indications we have are often interpreted to support various literary or political theories as to the social, ethnic, and geographical origin of the songs.[31]

Vuk noted in his observations that singers were generally men and that songs were performed chiefly by two groups, hajduks and blind beggars.[32] Of his two best informants, one, Tešan Podrugović, was a hajduk and the other, Filip Višnjić, was a blind man who lived by singing. Among the hajduks, as well as in the villages of Serbia and Montenegro, singing was not done by professionals. Any man in the community with talent might sing for the entertainment of his household and friends. For the blind, however, singing was one of the few means of livelihood available. Blind singers formed a sort of craft guild with its own jargon, through which new performers could be recruited and trained and songs could be shared. These singers gravitated toward the monasteries north of the Sava River, where they would receive alms and ply their trade at church festivals as well as at fairs in nearby market towns. Most likely it is through their connection with the Orthodox Church that religious and national feeling came to infuse heroic songs, especially songs in the non-historical, medieval, Kosovo, and Marko cycles. In their wandering about through occupied and free Serbia and beyond, the blind beggars helped to circulate song subjects throughout the South Slavic area.

Other collections present a slightly different picture of the singers. While in Vuk's model it was exceptional for women to sing heroic songs, the Matica hrvatska volumes, for example, include many heroic songs of considerable length performed by women, particularly in Dalmatia. The distinction between heroic and women's songs was less sharply drawn in this area. Women singers also performed both ballads and heroic songs on older subjects in Slavonia. When the Slavist Matthias Murko made surveys of epic singing in Bosnia and Hercegovina in 1913–14, and more extensively in Yugoslavia in 1930–32,[33] he too found women singers outside of the patriarchal region. He also concluded, as did Parry and Lord,[34] that blind singers were not prominent bearers of the tradition. Despite the brilliant examples of Višnjić and the Moslem Ćor Huso, the blind seem to have been the rhapsodes rather than the bards of the tradition in modern times.

Collectors who worked among the Moslems of northwest Bosnia discovered in that region a kind of professionalism among singers.[35] In Bosnia in Turkish times there was an upper class of landowning beys and agas capable of patronizing singers, a class which died out after World War I. Older singers interviewed by Parry in 1934–35 recalled singing in aristocratic houses, though in the 1930s they sang mainly to fellow villagers and tradesmen in coffeehouses. They were paid for their performances, often by being treated to coffee and cigarettes, but had other occupations as their regular means of support. The legendary Ćor Huso of Kolašin seems to have been an exceptional case: he was said to have lived by singing and to have traveled widely, even to the court of Franz Joseph in Vienna, to give performances. Parry's prize singer, Avdo Medjedović of Bijelo Polje, who kept a butcher shop and worked a small farm, is a more typical example.[36] Even in the Moslem situation, the chief requirement for becoming a singer was talent, rather than economic need; true professionalism existed only among beggars and was not necessarily associated with superior ability.

Occasions for singing to an audience with the leisure and inclination to listen to long performances of heroic songs were frequent in the traditional village way of life in Yugoslavia. Any time men could gather in a home or coffeehouse or tavern, on religious holidays, or for the festival of a family's patron saint, weddings, working gatherings, or simply social gatherings, the gusle might be brought out and a singer induced to perform. Men in military service might listen in the evenings in camps or barracks. In Bosnia the Moslem nobles would summon singers when they were entertaining guests in their homes. The best opportunity for hearing Moslem songs was during the month of Ramazan when, according to Islamic law, everyone fasts all day long and the men spend most of the night in coffeehouses enjoying refreshment and conversation. The owners of coffeehouses would compete to engage the best singers, whether Christian or Moslem, to entertain their patrons; it would be a singer's boast that he knew thirty songs, one for each night of the month, and each long enough to last through the night.[37]

Heroic songs in Serbocroatian are customarily sung to the accompaniment of the *gusle*. The gusle is a string instrument, apparently of eastern origin, played with an arc-shaped bow and having one or two horse hair strings, a rounded body, a long neck with no frets, and a carved head, often depicting an animal such as a wild goat or a deer. The instrument is related to other Balkan string instruments, such as the Adriatic *lijerica,* the Bulgarian *gudulka,* and the Albanian *lahuta,* while its name is cognate with the Russian *gusli* (an instrument of a different type).[38] In the Serbian tradition the gusle is used exclusively with heroic songs; only in regions where heroic singing is not practiced is it used for other purposes, such as dance music. Through its association with heroic songs it has become the symbol of heroism and of Serbian nationality. Playing the gusle is still encouraged as an act of patriotism, and outstanding performers are recognized as folk or national gusle players (*narodni guslari;* although in the folk terminology they are more often called "singers," rather than "guslars").

In the peripheral areas the mode of performance may vary from the norm of solo performances accompanied by the gusle. The Moslem singers in north-west Bosnia use the *tambura,* a two-stringed, plucked instrument with metal strings, also of eastern origin, which came into Balkan music later than the gusle. The tambura and even bagpipes may accompany the songs in Slavonia. Women as a rule do not play musical instruments, at least not in public; when they perform heroic songs they sing unaccompanied or recite their texts. Songs sung outdoors while traveling, doing farm work, or fishing also have no accompaniment. Narrative songs are sung on occasion by groups of people during round dances (*uz kolo*), in which case the rhythm of the verse is adapted to the music of the dance.[39]

Most Serbocroatian heroic songs are composed in lines of ten syllables without rhyme or other strophic organization. The line has a predominantly trochaic rhythm, due to the nature of Serbocroatian accentuation, and regularly has a word boundary after the fourth syllable and a long vowel in the ninth.

$$-\cup-\cup \quad -\cup-\cup-\cup$$

Podiže se   Crnojević Ivo
  Crnojević Ivo arose

According to Roman Jakobson, the Serbocroatian ten-syllable line represents a Common Slavic verse form of Indo-European origin and is cognate to the north Russian ten-syllable *bylina* line.[40] Its use is not restricted to the heroic song; especially in areas where the heroic song flourishes, the line is widely used in folksongs of other types, such as ballads and laments, and even in such prosaic genres as political speeches and school compositions.

The oldest recorded songs use a different line, the *bugarštica,* or long line. The bugarštica line consists of fifteen or sixteen syllables, divided into seven plus eight, or eight plus eight syllables, usually with a refrain after every line or a group of two or more lines:

Ali poče Vuk despot   Barbari odgovarati
Muči, ljubi Barbaro   radi Boga velikoga
                                    Nebgo ljubovce

  But Vuk despot began to reply to Barbara
  Be silent, wife Barbara, for God's sake
                                    Poor wife

The name of the line "bugarštica," points to an origin in the southeast, in Bulgaria. The structure resembles that of the modern Greek *politikos* line (fifteen syllables divided eight plus seven) and also has been linked with the Slavic eight-syllable line used in Bulgarian heroic songs on historical subjects and in Serbocroatian lyrics.

The discovery of songs in the bugarštica line in the nineteenth century provoked a continuing debate concerning the origins and relative age of the bugarštica and the ten-syllable line.[41] If indeed the ten-syllable line is traceable to Common Slavic, there is no record of what its uses were until it was written down in the eighteenth century. Was it being used for heroic songs all along, or was it newly adopted for the purpose in place of the bugarštica? As for the bugarštica, why were these songs on Serbian subjects found only in Croatia and Dalmatia, and why did the form die out? The bugarštica may have been the vehicle for aristocratic heroic songs in the Middle Ages. Studies of the language and style indicate that bugarštica songs reflect the tastes of a literate upper class, such as frequented the Serbian noble courts. Alois Schmaus, for example, has shown that the long line permits the use of double epithets, of which the second one is regularly an attribute of the object or person per se and the first pertains to the social rank of the thing or its possessor; the singers of the ten-syllable poetry had no sense of this distinction and used epithets singly, indifferent to the social values they might imply.[42] The subjects of the bugarštica songs suggest that they were sung in Dušan's and Marko's times in the southeast and carried by refugees after Kosovo to the lower Danube, where new ones were created about Serbian and Hungarian heroes of the fifteenth century. If the songs originated in Old Serbia and in the Danube region, another wave of migration after the fall of the Serbian rulers in the north in the early sixteenth century must have brought them to the Dalmatian coast, to the ears of people like Hektorović who were curious enough to record them.[43] A few of them were also written down in Croatia and Slavonia. The process of replacement of the bugarštica line in the eighteenth century is illustrated by the Perast manuscript from the Gulf of Kotor, which has parallel versions of eight songs, the bugarštica texts being dated to 1700 and the ten-syllable texts to 1775. Thus the ten-syllable line superseded the bugarštica, possibly because its singers or its subjects were more truly popular, and became the productive medium of heroic song.

Serbocroatian songs range in length from one hundred or so lines to several thousand lines. Songs in the Christian tradition are generally shorter, averaging about two hundred lines, while the Moslem Krajina songs run to greater length. Luka Marjanović, the editor of the Matica hrvatska collection, calculated the average for Krajina songs as 873 lines.[44] The two longest songs on record, both performed for Milman Parry by Avdo Medjedović, are 12,323 and 13,331 lines long.

The length and complexity of the Krajina songs have given them a special significance in the study of the oral traditional epic. Milman Parry, whose interest in the Yugoslav songs was aroused by his investigation of the language of Homer, found in the performance of the Krajina songs the closest living parallels to the Homeric songs and the most fruitful occasions to observe singers at work. He therefore concentrated on Moslem singers in making his collection and in analyzing their technique of composition. Alois

Schmaus devoted a monograph to the structure of the Krajina songs and concluded from his study of the Matica hrvatska and Hörmann collections that they represented a development of a more archaic song type in the direction of a true epic.[45] In his view the evolution from song to epic was cut short by the collapse of the Bosnian social order in the early twentieth century, which destroyed the conditions fostering the tradition.

The Krajina songs are distinguished from the Christian and Moslem songs of the Vukovian type by the elaboration of their plots. While in the Vukovian type the action is compressed into a single plot line, often a single episode, dominated by a small number of protagonists, the Krajina songs are more expansive. They regularly contain two major episodes, each consisting of a revelation of a need for action, preparation and excursion to a foreign land, battle, rescue or capture, return, and wedding. The second may be linked to the first by a failure to complete the mission of the first (for example, the hero of the first is captured or killed or unable to fulfill his task without reinforcements) or by conditions created in the resolution of the first (for example, a captive hero is released on parole to go home in the first and returns in the second to pay his ransom and to rescue a fellow captive). The two episodes are sometimes joined in sequence and sometimes interwoven, with one embedded in the other as a story told by one of the characters.

Schmaus has pointed out another feature of the plots which he called "two-sidedness" (*dvostranost*).[46] Krajina songs dwell on events in the enemy camp as well as on the protagonists, thus dramatizing motivations for action which in the Vukovian type are only implied or briefly stated. Consequently, intermediary figures, such as messengers, spies, and eavesdroppers, who move between the two realms, play large roles in the songs. Singers handle more complicated plots with more changes of scene and larger casts of characters in the Moslem tradition than in the Christian tradition.

Moslem singers are also known for their skill in ornamenting their narrative. They lavish attention on descriptions of the heroes' arms and accoutrements, horses' trappings, and prize girls' beauty, as well as on catalogues of warriors and large-scale battle scenes. Moslem audiences evidently delighted in this kind of embellishment, no matter how much it retarded the unfolding of the plot, although sometimes it exceeds what collectors' and readers' tastes can tolerate.[47]

How can songs of such length be created, retained, and transmitted without the aid of writing? An answer to this question was proposed by Parry and further expounded by Albert Lord in *The Singer of Tales*.[48] The Parry-Lord theory holds that the songs are recomposed orally in performance, not memorized as fixed texts. A singer is able to tell a story in a rapid sequence of ten-syllable lines of sung verse (ten to twenty per minute),[49] at the same time playing an instrument, because the tradition, created by all the singers who have faced the same problems, provides the means of fulfilling the conditions imposed by the narrative form. The singer is repeating a story he has heard and perhaps even sung before, but he is not required to reproduce his story "word for word," as the literate mind understands repetition, from a model. No two oral compositions are exactly the same; every performance is a unique variation on traditional material.

When learning to tell stories in the heroic song form the singer acquires a special language that is part of his normal language but governed by extra sets of rules which limit the discourse in that language to sung ten-syllable verse. Listening to other singers, he picks up not only the vocabulary of this language, the words of songs, but also the patterns of the phrases that fit the ten-syllable line. At the same time he learns to sing and play his instrument and absorbs the musical patterns of the voice melody and accompaniment. The music is an essential component of the language: many singers have difficulty producing poems if they cannot play and sing as they narrate.[50]

The text of the heroic song displays patterns of various kinds: metrical, acoustic, syntactic, and semantic. The most inflexible of these is the metrical requirement that each line have ten syllables divided into four plus six. As Parry and Lord showed, in order to produce metrically correct lines, the singer relies on repeated semantic and syntactic patterns. The semantic patterns, or exact repetitions of a certain set of words, are called formulas.[51] Recurrent basic ideas in the text tend to be expressed in formulas. When the singer wishes to express a non-recurrent idea, he creates a line or half line that varies from other lines and half lines by the substitution of key words in a syntactic pattern. For example, to express the idea of mounting a horse he has numerous ways to vary the pattern of verb plus object, "mount + horse," in the six syllables of the second half line:[52]

zasedem (I will mount)	hajvana (beast)
zasede (he mounts)	djogata (white horse)
zasednu (he mounted)	dorata (chestnut)
zasedi (Mount!)	vranina (black horse)
zaseo (he has mounted)	menzila (post horse)
	maljina (roan horse)

Further variation could substitute some other concept such as "coach" (*kočiju*) for "horse" or change the verb to "dismount" or "spur," and so on. Acoustic patterns of alliteration, assonance, and rhyme further help restrict the singer's choice of words in a given context. Formulas are often marked by euphonic devices:

Sultan Selim, od svijeta sunce!	Sultan Selim, light of the world!
Nit' mu vara nadje od duvara	Nor any break in the walls

Formulaic variation may take place within a framework of phonetic repetition:

Jenjičara, sužnja nevoljnoga	Of janissaries, involuntary captives
Jenjičara, sina njegovoga	Of janissaries, his sons

In an analysis of a sample fifteen lines of a Serbocroatian heroic song, Lord found that all the lines were exact or slightly varied repetitions of lines occurring elsewhere in a corpus of 12,000 lines all from one singer.[53] Such density of repetition is a distinctive feature of orally composed verse as opposed to verse composed in writing. The singer in oral tradition does not simply repeat scattered commonplaces as a convention of his style; his texts are permeated with repetition because he relies on repetition and variation to compose every line. Some of his formulas will be part of the common property of many singers, while others will be his own solutions to problems of expression.

Besides having conspicuous repetition on the semantic level, orally composed texts are characterized by repetition of patterns in the structure of the narrative. The tradition supplies the elements of the narrative in the form of themes (type-scenes) such as assembly, arming, summoning warriors to a campaign, battle, discovery of a girl. Each singer develops sets of formulas for themes he uses frequently. He adapts the themes to the particular story he is telling by supplying the names of the characters and the places and fitting the action to the plot. Yet the themes remain partly independent of the given plot and derive some of their meaning from their associations with all the contexts in which they appear in the tradition. Sometimes these associations may lead to incongruity in the development of a particular plot.[54]

The tradition also provides underlying patterns of events in narrative, the plots that govern the organization of themes. An example of a traditional story pattern is the return-rescue pattern, in which Parry and Lord took a particular interest because of its parallels to the *Odyssey*.[55] Return and rescue songs deal with a hero detained away from home by an enemy: in the return story he bargains with his captor for release and returns unrecognized to his home in time to remedy the disorder caused by his absence; in the rescue story the absent hero is sought by his family or sends to them and is rescued by an expedition to the enemy's country. Both types are concerned with the crossing of dangerous borders and incorporation into society on the other side. The basic elements of a return story, disguise, deceptive story, recognition, contests, and wedding, therefore may occur also in a rescue story, even though it takes place in enemy country rather than at home, and in other types of story not ostensibly about a returning hero. The patterns are held together by traditional associations and easily merge into one another. For example, the capture of a bride in a wedding song and the capture of a city have affinities with the rescue of a prisoner and may attract elements of the rescue story.

The singer does not mechanically reproduce plots or their constituent themes in the same way every time he uses them. He adapts them to specific stories; he embellishes them to suit the taste and leisure of himself and his audience. He may include new elements by association with other stories; he may inadvertently omit elements that both he and the audience know belong in the traditional pattern and do not necessarily miss when they are not articulated. The structure of the narrative is as flexible and variable as are the lines of the poetry. Unlike the formula, themes and story patterns are not peculiar to orally composed narrative, but they are as essential as the formula to the technique of oral composition.

The impact of the theory of oral composition on comparative studies in literature and folklore has spread the fame of Serbocroatian heroic songs. Until recently the Serbocroatian tradition has been the only model of oral composition that has been thoroughly documented and investigated. It is used as an analogy to argue for the oral provenience of traditional works of unknown origin and to describe the workings of other living oral traditions.[56] The prestige the heroic songs have always enjoyed in Yugoslavia is being matched, as it was in Vuk's day, by interest among scholars from abroad.

NOTES

1. The general tendency in Yugoslav scholarship is to interpret the evidence in favor of the antiquity of the songs. See, for example, Vuk St.Karadžić, "Preface to the Leipzig edition, 1823–33," in *Srpske narodne pjesme* (Belgrade: Prosveta, 1964), I, pp. xxx–xxxi; Vatroslav Jagić, "Južnoslavenska narodna epika u prošlosti," trans.

from the German by Mihovil Kombol, in Vatroslav Jagić, *Rasprave, članci i sjećanja,* Pet stoljeća hrvatske književnosti, 43 (Zagreb: Matica hrvatska, 1963), pp. 255–301, originally published in *Archiv für slavische Philologie* 4 (Berlin, 1880). A contrary opinion was expressed by Tomo Maretić (*Naša narodna epika* [Belgrade: Nolit, 1966], 1st pub. 1909), who maintained that heroic songs could not be dated to a time prior to their being recorded and so fixed the point of origin around 1500. This view has been vigorously disputed in numerous essays, e.g., in Svetozar Matić, "Otkad počinje naše epsko pevanje," in *Naš narodni ep i naš stih* (Novi Sad: Matica srpska, 1964), pp. 227–45.

2. Alberto Fortis published three of Kačić's songs in Italian translation in his *Saggio d' osservazioni sopra l' isola di Cherso ed Ossero* (Venice, 1771), and in his *Viaggio in Dalmazia,* 2 vols. (Venice, 1774), printed from an original not published until the nineteenth century, the text and translation of "The Wife of Hasanaga," a ballad that became the most famous song in Serbocroatian traditional literature. Fortis' books were the source of the first translations into German, which popularized Serbocroatian folksong throughout Europe.

3. Bugarštice were first published by F. Miklošič in *Beiträge zur slavischen Volks-poesie,* I: *Die Volksepik der Kroaten,* Denkschriften der Kaiserl. Akademie der Wissenschaften, Phil.-hist. Kl., 19 (Vienna, 1870). The most complete publication is Valtazar Bogišić, *Narodne pjesme iz starijih, najviše primorskih zapisa,* Glasnik srpskog učenog društva, II odeljenje, 10 (Belgrade, 1878).

4. Gerhard Gesemann, *Erlangenski rukopis starih srpsko-hrvatskih narodnih pesama,* Srpska kraljevska akademija, Zbornik za istoriju, jezik i književnost srpskoga naroda, I odeljenje, 12 (Sremski Karlovci, 1925).

5. Vuk's first publication of songs was the *Mala prostonarodna slaveno-serbska pesnarica,* published in Vienna in 1814, followed by a second book in 1815. More extensive editions were published in Leipzig, 1823–33, and in Vienna, 1841–66, and a nine-volume edition was brought out posthumously by the state in 1887–1902.

6. See Duncan Wilson, *The Life and Times of Vuk St. Karadžić, 1787–1864* (Oxford: Clarendon Press, 1970).

7. [Matica hrvatska] *Hrvatske narodne pjesme* (Zagreb: Matica hrvatska, 1896–1941), esp. vol. II, *Junačke pjesme,* and vols. III and IV, *Junačke pjesme (muhamedovske).*

8. Kosta Hörmann, *Narodne pjesme Muslimana u Bosni i Hercegovini,* 2nd ed. (Sarajevo: Kurtović and Kušan, 1933).

9. Milman Parry and Albert B. Lord, *Serbocroatian Heroic Songs,* 4 vols. (Cambridge, Mass.: Harvard University Press, 1953–74).

10. Concerning the existence of an archaic and mythological stratum in South Slavic heroic song see Alois Schmaus, "Die balkanische Volksepik: Typologie und Kontinuitätsproblem," *Zeitschrift für Balkanologie* 1 (1962): 133–52, and Dagmar Burkhart, *Untersuchungen zur Stratigraphie und Chronologie der südslavischen Volksepik,* Slavistische Beiträge, 33 (Munich, 1968), esp. pp. 35–58.

11. Albert B. Lord, "Some Common Themes in Balkan Slavic Epic: Dragons" (Paper given at the First International Congress of Balkanologists, Sofija, 1966).

12. All citations of songs in Vuk Karadžić's collection are from the four-volume edition of *Srpske narodne pjesme* (hereafter *SNP*) (Belgrade: Prosveta, 1964). Many of

the songs cited have been recorded and published in other versions as well; Vuk's versions, however, are generally the most familiar and accessible.

13. Jovan Brkić, *Moral Concepts in Traditional Serbian Epic Poetry* (The Hague: Mouton & Co., 1961).

14. The theory of aristocratic origin is most fully presented by N. I. Kravcov in *Serbskij èpos* (Moscow and Leningrad: Academia, 1933), in which the author gives an orthodox Marxist interpretation of the feudal era in Serbia. Kravcov later allowed his support of the theory to lapse. In an article "Serbskij èpos i istorija," *Sovetskaja ètnografija* 3 (1948): 90–107, he adhered to the prevailing Soviet theory, which also is the most widespread in Yugoslav scholarship, that of the popular and democratic origin of heroic songs. On the theory of aristocratic origin, see Felix J. Oinas, "The Problem of the Aristocratic Origin of Russian *Byliny,*" *Slavic Review* 30 (1971): 513–22.

15. N. Banašević, in "Le cycle de Kosovo et les chansons de gestes," *Revue des Études slaves* 6 (1926): 222–44, and *Ciklus Marka Kraljevića i odjeci francusko-talijanske viteške književnosti,* Knjige skopskog naučnog društva, 3 (Skopje, 1935), uses material chiefly from three cycles, the medieval, Kosovo, and Marko cycles, to argue that elements from Romance traditions brought by *jongleurs* to the Balkans during the Crusades were assimilated in the South Slavic tradition because of the similarity in social structure and historical experience of Europe and Serbia in the Middle Ages. On the possible influence of *chansons de gestes* on Serbocroatian heroic songs, see also André Vaillant, "Les chants épiques des Slaves du Sud," *Revue des Cours et Conférences* 33 (1932): 635–47.

16. The argument was first made by Vuk Karadžić in his preface to the Leipzig edition (*SNP,* pp. xxx–xxxi), later by Jagić, St. Novaković, and others. One of the points frequently made is that it is unlikely that a heroic song tradition would be created new in the aftermath of the fall of Serbia; the medium must have existed prior to the events that form the subjects of recorded songs.

17. The motif of the human sacrifice in the foundations of a building is found in the Balkans in Greek and Romanian ballads as well. It has been made famous in Yugoslav literature by its appearance in Ivo Andrić's novel *The Bridge on the Drina,* which draws on another version of the same motif. Stories similar to that of Dušan's wedding are told of Sibinjanin Janko in one of Kačić's genuine folksongs (*Djela Andrije Kačića-Miošića, I,* Stari pisci hrvatski, 27 [Zagreb, 1964], pp. 332–34), and of Djuro of Smederevo in Vuk II, 78. On the motif of the wedding with obstacles in South Slavic tradition, see Burkhart, pp. 94–109 and 302–31.

18. Mavro Orbini of Dubrovnik published his history, *Il Regno degli Slavi,* in Pesaro, Italy, in 1601.

19. The foremost, and practically sole, exponent of the theory of recent origin for Vuk's Kosovo songs is Svetozar Matić. He argues, in "Poreklo kosoviskih pesama kratkoga stiha," *Naš narodni ep,* pp. 95–125, and in "Odbrana teze o kosovskim pesama," ibid., pp. 126–51, that the Kosovo songs were created in the eighteenth and nineteenth centuries in Srem among Serbs who had fled from Turkish Serbia. This was a time of rising national feeling, when the leaders of Serbian cultural and religious life deliberately fostered the cult of Kosovo, Lazar (who was regarded as a saint), and Miloš. Most scholars treat the Kosovo tradition as continuous from the fourteenth century. See, for example, André Vaillant, "Les chants épiques," pp. 641–47; N. Banašević, "Le cycle de Kosovo," passim.

20. Vladan Nedić, "Epske narodne pesme u zborniku Avrama Miletića," *Zbornik Matice srpske za književnost i jezik* 12 (1964): 61–74.

21. Roman Jakobson and Gojko Ružičić, "The Serbian Zmaj Ognjeni Vuk and the Russian Vseslav Epos," in Jakobson, *Selected Writings*, IV (The Hague: Mouton & Co., 1966), pp. 369–79.

22. A classic work comparing Marko with heroes of Russian and other epics is M. E. Xalanskij, "Južnoslavjanskie skazanija o Kraleviče Marke v svajzi s proizvedenijami russkogo bylevogo èposa," *Russkij filologičeskij vestnik* 27–34 (Warsaw, 1892–95). See also N. Banašević, *Ciklus Marka Kraljevića.* Vojislav Djurić, in "Prince Marko in Epic Poetry," *Journal of the Folklore Institute* 3 (1966): 315–30, summarizes the prevailing view of the figure of Marko. S. Matić, in "Markova legenda," *Novi ogledi o našem narodnom epu* (Novi Sad: Matica srpska, 1972), pp. 194–234, develops the idea, mentioned also by Vaillant in "Les chants épiques," p. 638, that Marko's character is to be explained by the nature of the coexistence between Serbs and Turks. For an English translation of much of the "Marko cycle," see D. H. Low, *The Ballads of Marko Kraljević* (Cambridge: The University Press, 1922).

23. The motif of "The husband at his wife's wedding" recurs in Serbocroatian songs, for example, in "The Captivity of Janković Stojan" (Vuk III, 25) and "The Return of Djulić Ibrahim" (Parry I, 4). The parallels between the Serbocroatian and the Homeric traditions offered by such songs have been the subject of several studies, among them: Radoslav Medenica, "Muž na svadbi svoje žene," *Prilozi proučavanju narodne poezije* 1 (1934): 33–61; Stjepan Banović, "Motivi iz Odiseje u hrvatskoj narodnoj pjesmi iz Makarskog Primorja," *Zbornik za narodni život i običaje južnih slavena* 35 (1951): 139–244; Miloš N. Djurić, "Veze Homerove poezije s našem narodnom i umetničkom poezijom," *Zbornik radova SAN*, 10 (1951): 165–216.

24. See Vuk, *Srpske narodne pjesme*, III (Belgrade: Prosveta, 1964). Salko Nazečić, in *Iz naše narodne epike* (Sarajevo: Svjetlost, 1959), compares the songs with the historical evidence for the activity of the hajduks, especially in their relations with the Republic of Dubrovnik.

25. See Vuk, *Srpske narodne pjesme*, IV, for songs on the conflicts in Montenegro and on the Serbian rising.

26. Miodrag Maticki, *Srpskohrvatska graničarska epika* (Belgrade: Institut za književnost i umetnost, 1974). Vuk and his followers concentrated on singing of the type found in Hercegovina and tended to neglect the types from the peripheral areas such as the Austrian Military Border (Krajina).

27. See Matica hrvatska, *Hrvatske narodne pjesme*, III and IV; Kosta Hörmann, *Narodne pjesme Muslimana;* Milman Parry and Albert B. Lord, *Serbocroatian Heroic Songs*. On connections with the Albanian tradition, Stavro Skendi, *Albanian and South Slavic Oral Epic Poetry*, Memoirs of the American Folklore Society, 44 (Philadelphia, 1954).

28. On Djerzelez Alija, see D. Marjanović, "Problem Djerzelez Alije," *Prilozi proučavanju narodne poezije* 3 (1936): 90–101. A. Olesnicki, "Tko je zapravo bio Djerzelez Alija?" *Zbornik za narodni život i običaje* 29/1 (1933): 18–37; and "Još o ličnosti Djerzelez Alije," *Zbornik za narodni život i običaje* 29/2 (1934): 20–55. On Mujo and Halil, see Skendi, *Albanian and South Slavic Oral Epic Poetry*. On Tale, see Parry and Lord, *Serbocroatian Heroic Songs*, I, p. 336; and III, pp. 30–32.

29. Vuk, "Preface to the Leipzig Edition," *SNP*, p. xvi. A translation of most of

this important treatise is given in Duncan Wilson, *The Life and Times of Vuk St. Karadžić*, Appendix E, pp. 395–400.

30. Alois Schmaus discusses the division of the South Slavic tradition into regions where narrative, or epic, style predominates and regions where lyric style predominates in "Gattung und Stil in der Volksdichtung," *Rad kongresa folklorista* 4 (1957): 169–73. Vuk's observations are in the "Preface to the Leipzig Edition," *SNP*, pp. xvi–xvii.

31. Some studies of the question: Vido Latković, "O pevačima srpskohrvatskih narodnih epskih pesama," *Prilozi za književnost, jezik, istoriju i folklor* 12 (1954): 184–202; S. Matić, "Tvorci narodnog epa," *Naš narodni ep*, pp. 289–308; Alois Schmaus, "Neki oblici epskog pevanja u prošlosti," *Prilozi proučavanju narodne poezije* 1 (1934): 15–25.

32. Vuk, "Preface," *SNP*, p. xxviii.

33. Matthias Murko, *Tragom srpskohrvatske narodne epike*, 2 vols., Djela JAZU, 42 (Zagreb, 1951).

34. Murko, *Tragom*, I, pp. 206–17; Albert B. Lord, *The Singer of Tales* (New York: Atheneum, 1965), pp. 19–20.

35. Murko, *Tragom*, I, pp. 61-62, 362–68; Alois Schmaus, *Studije o krajinskoj epici*, Rad JAZU, 297 (Zagreb, 1953), pp. 99–103; Lord, *Singer*, p. 16.

36. "The Singer's Life and Times," in Parry and Lord, *Serbocroatian Heroic Songs*, III, pp. 37–52.

37. Lord, *Singer*, p. 15.

38. Walter Wunsch, "Geschichte und Namen der volkstümlichen Streichinstrumente des Balkans," *Zeitschrift für Balkanologie* 2 (1964): 190–97; Murko, *Tragom*, pp. 322–39.

39. On modes of performance differing from Vuk's model: Murko, *Tragom*, passim; Vladan Nedić, "Srpskohrvatska osmeračka epika," *Prilozi za književnost, jezik, istoriju i folklor* 36 (1970): 196–213; Mira Sertić, *Forma i funkcija narodne balade*, Rad JAZU, 338 (Zagreb, 1970), pp. 196–213.

40. Roman Jakobson, "Slavic Epic Verse: Studies in Comparative Metrics," in *Selected Writings*, IV (The Hague: Mouton & Co., 1966), pp. 414–63. In this paper Jakobson revises the view he had expressed in "Über den Versbau der serbokroatischen Volksepen," in *Selected Writings*, IV, pp. 51–61 (1st pub. 1933) that the origin of the ten-syllable line should not be placed too early. Vladan Nedić, in "Srpskohrvatska osmeračka usmena epika," suggests that the ten-syllable line is based on the eight-syllable line. André Vaillant ("Les chants épiques," p. 445) traces the ten-syllable line to old Slavic religious poetry and ultimately to a Greek twelve-syllable line.

41. See the introduction to V. Bogišić, *Narodne pjesme;* Alois Schmaus, "Die balkanische Volksepik: Typologie und Kontinuitätsproblem," *Zeitschrift für Balkanologie* 1 (1962): 133–52; Franjo Švelec, "O dosegu najstarijih vijesti o bugaršticama," *Prilozi za književnost, jezik, istoriju i folklor* 37 (1971): 240–54; André Vaillant, "Les chants épiques," pp. 441–47; Tvrtko Čubelić, Introduction to *Lirske narodne pjesme: Antologija* (Zagreb: Školska knjiga, 1963).

42. Alois Schmaus, "Stilanalyse und Chronologie (Bugarštica und Zehnsilberepik)," *Rad kongresa folklorista* 4 (1959): 111–15.

43. Svetozar Matić, "O glavnim pitanjima bugarštica," *Novi ogledi*, pp. 217–34,

summarizing and defending the views of Asmus Soerensen in "Beitrag zur Geschichte der Entwicklung der serbischen Heldendichtung," *Archiv für slavische Philologie* 14–20 (Berlin, 1892–98), against the criticism directed at Soerensen by Jagić and other scholars.

44. Matica hrvatska, *Hrvatske narodne pjesme*, III, p. xi.

45. Alois Schmaus, *Studije o krajinskoj epici*, Rad JAZU, 297 (Zagreb, 1953), pp. 89–247.

46. See Schmaus, *Studije*, pp. 126–32.

47. Luka Marjanović comments on the verbosity of some of the singers recorded by the Matica hrvatska in his introduction to vol. III, *Hrvatske narodne pjesme*, pp. xxiii and xxxiii.

48. Lord, *Singer*.

49. Ibid., p. 17.

50. Ibid., p. 99; Parry and Lord, *Serbocroatian Heroic Songs*, I, p. 8.

51. The formula is "a group of words which is regularly employed under the same metrical conditions to express a given essential idea." Lord, *Singer*, p. 30.

52. Taken from Lord, *Singer*, p. 48.

53. Ibid., p. 46.

54. Ibid., pp. 94 and 113.

55. Lord discusses the return-rescue pattern in *Singer*, pp. 121–23, and Appendixes III and IV, pp. 242–65. He also treats the parallels between the *Odyssey* and the Serbocroatian songs in "Homeric Echoes in Bihać," *Zbornik za narodni život i običaje* 40 (1962): 313–20, and in the introduction to Parry and Lord, *Serbocroatian Heroic Songs*, III: *The Wedding of Smailagić Meho* [by] *Avdo Medjedović* (Cambridge, Mass.: Harvard University Press, 1974). See also David E. Bynum, "Themes of the Young Hero in Serbocroatian Oral Epic Tradition," *PMLA* 83 (1968): 1296–1303.

56. Edward R. Haymes, *A Bibliography of Studies Relating to Parry's and Lord's Oral Theory* (Cambridge, Mass.: Publications of the Milman Parry Collection, 1973).

BIBLIOGRAPHY

Collections and Anthologies

Bogišić, Valtazar. *Narodne pjesme iz starijih, najviše primorskih zapisa* [Folksongs from Older Manuscripts Chiefly from the Adriatic Coast]. Glasnik srpskog učenog društva, II odeljenje, 10. Belgrade: 1878. A publication of the principal manuscripts containing poems in the bugarštica line, with detailed introduction.

Čubelić, Tvrtko. *Epske narodne pjesme* [Epic Folksongs]. Usmena narodna književnost, 3. Zagreb: 1970. An anthology of texts selected from the major cycles, with commentaries. Introduction discusses the style and history of heroic songs and reviews the scholarship.

Djurić, Vojislav. *Antologija narodnih junačkih pesama* [Anthology of Heroic Folksongs]. Belgrade: Srpska književna zadruga, 1954. 5th expanded ed., 1969. Selected songs grouped according to Vuk's historical divisions, concentrating on songs of the older and middle periods, with notes to the texts. General introduction emphasizes that songs are an expression of the revolutionary spirit of the masses.

Gesemann, Gerhard. *Erlangenski rukopis starih srpskohrvatskih narodnih pesama* [The Erlangen Manuscript of Old Serbocroatian Folksongs]. Srpska kraljevska akademija, Zbornik za istoriju, jezik i književnost srpskoga naroda, I odeljenje, 12. Sremski Karlovci, 1925. Publication of an important manuscript dating from the early eighteenth century, with thorough discussion of provenience and contents.

Hörmann, Kosta. *Narodne pjesme Muslimana u Bosni i Hercegovini* [Folksongs of the Moslems in Bosnia and Hercegovina]. 2 vols. 2nd ed. Sarajevo: Kurtović and Kušan, 1933. Collected and first published in 1888–89. Supplemented by *Narodne pjesme Muslimana u Bosni i Hercegovini iz rukopisne ostavštine Koste Hörmanna* [Folksongs of the Moslems in Bosnia and Hercegovina from the manuscripts left by Kosta Hörmann], edited by Djenana Buturović. Sarajevo: Zemaljski muzej Bosne i Hercegovine, 1966.

Karadžić, Vuk St. *Srpske narodne pjesme* [Serbian Folksongs]. 4 vols. Belgrade Prosveta, 1964. The classic collection of Serbian folksongs. This publication is based on Vuk's Vienna edition of 1841, supplemented by material from earlier editions, including Vuk's important discussion of heroic songs in the introduction to his 1824 volume. Notes by modern editors. Supplemented by *Srpske narodne pjesme iz neobjavljenih rukopisa Vuka St. Karadžića* [Serbian Folksongs from the Unpublished Manuscripts of Vuk St. Karadžić], edited by Živomir Mladenović and Vladan Nedić. 5 vols. Belgrade: SANU, 1973–75. Lengthy introduction by Mladenović in vol. I on Vuk's collecting and editing work.

[Matica hrvatska.] *Hrvatske narodne pjesme* [Croatian Folksongs]. 10 vols. Zagreb: Matica hrvatska, 1896–1941. Vol. II (1897), edited by Stjepan Bosanac, contains songs of Marko Kraljević from the Croatian tradition. Vols. III and IV (1898–99), edited by Luka Marjanović, are an extensive collection of Moslem Krajina songs with a valuable description of the singers in the introduction.

Parry, Milman, and Albert B. Lord. *Serbocroatian Heroic Songs*. Cambridge, Mass.: Harvard University Press, 1953–74. 4 vols. Part of a projected series of publications of the Parry Collection. Vol. I contains annotated prose translations by Albert Lord of songs from the Novi Pazar area, interviews with the singers, a survey of Parry's collecting activity, and transcriptions by Béla Bartok of some of the music of the singing. Vol. II has the Serbocroatian texts of the Novi Pazar songs. Vol. III includes Lord's translation of the 1935 performance of "The Wedding of Smailagić Meho," by Avdo Medjedović, and David Bynum's translation of "The Singer's Life and Times," copious notes, and summaries of other versions and variants of the song. Vol. IV is the Serbocroatian text.

Translations

Ćurčija-Prodanović, Nada. *Heroes of Serbia*. London: Oxford University Press, 1963. Lively prose retellings of selected songs from Vuk.

Goleniščev-Kutuzov, I. N. *Èpos serbskogo naroda* [The Epic of the Serbian People]. Moscow: Akademija nauk SSSR, 1963. Translations into Russian poetry, some by prominent poets such as Anna Axmatova.

Low, David Halyburton. *The Ballads of Marko Kraljević*. Cambridge: The University Press, 1922. Reprinted New York: Greenwood Press, 1968. Line by line translations from Vuk.

Noyes, George Rapall, and Leonard Bacon. *Heroic Ballads of Servia*. Boston: Sherman, French & Co., 1913. Translated, not altogether successfully, into rhymed couplets in English ballad meter.

Studies

Braun, Maximilian. *Das serbokroatische Heldenlied*. Göttingen: Vandenhoeck &

Ruprecht, 1961. A useful survey. Part I gives an introduction to the genre in its cultural setting, Part II a discussion of the structure and themes of the songs.

Burkhart, Dagmar. *Untersuchungen zur Stratigraphie und Chronologie der südslavischen Volksepik.* Munich: Slavistische Beiträge 33, 1968. Includes useful summaries of the content and history of collected songs, but the material is poorly organized. Aims to differentiate an archaic and mythological level from an historical level in West Bulgarian and Macedonian songs through study of two types of story, stories of dragon slaying and of bride winning, throughout the South Slavic tradition.

Chadwick, Hector M., and Nora K. Chadwick. "Yugoslav Oral Poetry." In their *The Growth of Literature.* 3 vols., II/2, pp. 299–456. Cambridge: Cambridge University Press, 1932–40. A thorough survey, though outdated in some respects, describing songs from a comparative point of view as products of an "Heroic Age."

Gesemann, Gerhard. *Studien zur südslavischen Volksepik.* Reichenberg: Gebr. Stiepel, 1926. An introduction to structural devices and motifs in the songs. Discusses the process of stylization as an historical or autobiographical event is cast into heroic song.

Koljević, Svetozar. *Naš junački ep* [Our Heroic Epic]. Belgrade: Nolit, 1974. A synthetic view concentrating on "Vuk's epic" as the culmination of a long poetic tradition and taking account of the theory of oral composition.

Kravcov, N. I. *Serbskij èpos* [The Serbian Epic]. Moscow and Leningrad: Academia, 1933. Texts translated into Russian, with lengthy introduction presenting the theory, now generally rejected, that the songs are the creation of the military aristocracy.

Lord, Albert B. *The Singer of Tales.* Cambridge, Mass.: Harvard University Press, 1960. Reprinted New York: Atheneum, 1965. Exposition of the Parry-Lord theory of oral composition in Serbocroatian songs, with applications to the Homeric and medieval traditions.

Maretić, Tomo. *Naša narodna epika* [Our Folk Epic]. Edited by Vladan Nedić. Belgrade: Nolit, 1966. First published, 1909. Comments on the historical origins of songs and song characters and on international motifs. Argues for dating the origin of the songs in the sixteenth century.

Matić, Svetozar. *Naš narodni ep i naš stih* [Our Folk Epic and Our Versification]. Novi Sad: Matica srpska, 1964. A collection of essays reprinted from various journals, presenting Matić's often controversial views on Vuk's work, the history of the singing tradition, and other topics.

Murko, Matthias. *La poésie populaire épique en Yougoslavie au début du XXᵉ siècle.* Travaux publiés par l'Institut d'études slaves, 10. Paris: 1929. A brief survey of Murko's first researches in the field.

Murko, Matthias. *Tragom srpsko-hrvatske narodne epike* [Tracing the Serbocroatian Folk Epic]. 2 vols. Djela JAZU, 42. Zagreb: 1951. An account of Murko's expedition in 1930–32, describing the singers and the state of the singing tradition. Also includes extensive description of the genre and surveys of the collections and scholarship. Vol. II contains photographs and catalogues of singers.

Putilov, B. N. *Russkij i južnoslavjanskij geroičeskij èpos* [Russian and South Slavic Heroic Epic]. Moscow: Nauka, 1971. Draws typological parallels between songs and motifs in the two traditions.

Schmaus, Alois. *Studije o krajinskoj epici* [Studies of the Krajina Epic]. Rad JAZU, 297. Zagreb: 1953. Pp. 89–247. An important monograph on the special style and structure of the Moslem Krajina songs.

Skendi, Stavro, *Albanian and South Slavic Oral Epic Poetry.* Memoirs of the American Folklore Society, 44. Philadelphia: 1954. Describes Serbocroatian and Albanian songs in their cultural and historical setting and the influence of the Serbocroatian on the Albanian, especially the adoption of Moslem Krajina songs into Albanian.

Subotić, Dragutin. *Yugoslav Popular Ballads*. Cambridge: The University Press, 1932. Presents Serbocroatian songs for European readers, comparing them with English and Scottish popular ballads. Generally outdated, but has useful bibliography of older translations.

Vaillant, André. "Les chants épiques des Slaves du Sud." *Revue des Cours et Conférences* 33 (1932): 309–26, 431–46, 635–47. Brief and comprehensive survey with special attention to the Kosovo and Marko Kraljević cycles. Views on the origin of the verse and foreign influences on the songs are debatable. First published in *Byzantinoslavica* 4 (1932).

13   The Balto-Finnic Epics

Felix J. Oinas

Among the Balto-Finnic peoples, who live to the east of the Baltic Sea (the Finns, Estonians, Karelians, Vepsians, Votes, and Lives), only the Finns and the Estonians have their heroic epics. Both works were compiled during the first half and the middle of the last century and were inspired by the Romantic national movement, which rolled, like a powerful wave, over Western Europe.

The Kalevala

The *Kalevala* is the epic of both the Finns and their close kin, the Karelians, since the materials for it were collected from both of them. The Karelians' contribution to the final edition of the epic (1894) is especially prominent.

The compiler of the *Kalevala*, Elias Lönnrot (1802–84), developed a deep interest in Finnish folklore and epic heroes during his study at Turku University.[1] His master's thesis, "On Väinämöinen, the Divinity of the Ancient Finns" (1827, in Latin), explored the time and place of origin of the main hero of the Finnish epic songs. When the University closed after the 1827 fire that destroyed the city of Turku, Lönnrot set out to collect folklore. His trip took him from western Finland as far east as Finnish Karelia, where his findings were unexpectedly rich. After settling in Helsinki in 1828 to study medicine at the University, he published four fascicles of folksongs under the title *Harp* (*Kantele*).[2] His idea of uniting folksongs into larger units resulted first in the compilation of songs about the hero Lemminkäinen. After Lönnrot's trip to East Karelia where he found folksongs flourishing, he compiled the miniature epics "Väinämöinen" and "The Songs of the Wedding Party," which—like the small epic "Lemminkäinen"—remained in manuscript form.

In 1833 Lönnrot became a medical officer in the city of Kajaani in northern Finland. Since the people rarely turned to a doctor for help, Lönnrot had sufficient time during that year to complete a preliminary version of the epic referred to as the *Proto-Kalevala (Alku Kalevala)*, which contained 5,052 lines, divided into 16 songs. He requested that the printing of this work be postponed until he had once more visited East Karelia. The new journey, during which he met the greatest folk singers of Karelia, yielded a rich harvest that was incorporated into the first version of the *Kalevala*,[3] the so-called *Old Kalevala (Vanha Kalevala)*, which was published in 1835–36 and consisted of 36 songs comprising 12,078 lines. From extensive additional folksong material which was recorded partly by Lönnrot himself, but mostly by others (especially by D. E. D. Europaeus) in East Karelia and eastern Finland, Lönnrot prepared a greatly expanded and changed version of the *Kalevala*. This was published in 1849; it comprised 22,795 lines and was divided into 50 songs. When referring to the Finnish epic, we mean this *New Kalevala;* the *Old Kalevala* is primarily of historical interest.

Synopsis of the Kalevala

I. The Introduction (songs 1–2).[4] The creation of the universe from eggs laid by a goldeneye and Väinämöinen's birth by the mother of water are described. Sämpsä, Spirit of Arable, and Väinämöinen cooperate in securing the growth of trees and grain.

II. Aino's Ruin (songs 3–5). After Väinämöinen's fame spreads, Joukahainen challenges him to a duel. Väinämöinen becomes irritated and sings Joukahainen into a fern. In order to escape, Joukahainen promises his sister Aino to Väinämöinen. Aino, who does not want to marry the terribly old man, strays onto a strange seashore and drowns. Väinämöinen catches her (now changed into a fish) on his hook, but does not recognize her and loses her forever.

III. The Forging of the Sampo (songs 6–10). Following the advice of his deceased mother, Väinämöinen sets out on a horse of straw to woo the maiden of Pohjola (North, North Farm). Joukahainen, who bears a grudge against him, shoots at Väinämöinen, but hits the horse instead. Väinämöinen falls into the water and is carried by a strong wind toward Pohjola. There Louhi, the mistress of Pohjola, takes good care of him and promises to send him back home and give him her daughter if he will forge a Sampo for her. Väinämöinen promises to send the smith Ilmarinen to do the job. On his journey home, Väinämöinen sees the charming maid of Pohjola, who agrees to marry the love-sick old man if he will perform a series of wooing tasks. During his final task—the building of a boat—Väinämöinen wounds himself seriously on the knee and has to seek an old man's help to cure it. Back at home he urges Ilmarinen to go to Pohjola to forge the Sampo. When Ilmarinen is reluctant to go, Väinämöinen raises a storm and sends him there. In Pohjola, Ilmarinen forges the Sampo, but does not get the maiden as his reward.

IV. The Myth of Lemminkäinen (songs 11–15). Lemminkäinen sets out to woo the high-born maid of the Island. He manages to break the resistance of

Kyllikki, whom he abducts, by promising never to set out to war. Kyllikki in turn promises never to gad about, but later breaks the promise. Thereupon Lemminkäinen, despite his mother's warnings, decides to go to Pohjola to woo the maiden of Pohjola. In Pohjola, he bewitches everyone except a loathsome cattle herder. Louhi, the mistress of Pohjola, assigns him three tasks. When he arrives at the River of Death's Domain to accomplish the last of them, the cattle herder kills him and throws his body into Death's Rapids. His mother, suspecting his fate, hurries to Pohjola, rakes the pieces of his body together, and resuscitates him.

V. Väinämöinen's Adventures (songs 16–17). Väinämöinen is making a boat by singing charms. He lacks three charms and decides to go to Death's Domain for them. Not only does he not get any charms there, but he barely manages to return. He finally receives the charms from the belly of a famous shaman, Antero Vipunen, whom he awakens from his long sleep underground.

VI. The Competition in Wooing (songs 18–20). With the boat finished, Väinämöinen sets sail to woo the maid of Pohjola. Ilmarinen, getting word of Väinämöinen's destination, hurries on his horse to Pohjola. When the two suitors arrive, the maiden vows to marry Ilmarinen, forger of the Sampo. Ilmarinen successfully completes the wooing tasks, and the maiden is betrothed to him.

VII. The Wedding of Pohjola (songs 21–25). In Pohjola a huge steer is slaughtered for the wedding; beer is brewed and food prepared. With the exception of Lemminkäinen, all the people are invited and they are fed and given drink in profusion. The bride wails and is comforted and counseled. The bridegroom is advised about how to treat the bride; then Ilmarinen snatches his bride into the sled and leaves. At his home the young couple and the escorts are received and entertained. Väinämöinen, who has sung during the whole wedding, has an accident on his way home; his sled is broken and must be repaired.

VIII. Lemminkäinen's Second Journey to Pohjola (songs 26–30). Lemminkäinen, angered for not being invited to the wedding, nevertheless decides to go to Pohjola. By virtue of his knowledge, he gets through all the mortally dangerous places on the way. At Pohjola, Lemminkäinen has a quarrel with the master of Pohjola. In the ensuing duel, he strikes the master's head off. After fleeing home, he decides to follow the advice of his mother and go into hiding on an island. Since he lives recklessly with women, he finally has to flee from men's rage. After a shipwreck, he swims to shore and finds that the people of Pohjola have burned down his house. Together with his former comrade-in-arms, Tiera, Lemminkäinen sets out to wage war against Pohjola, but a severe cold spell sent by Louhi forces them to turn back.

IX. The Serf Kullervo's Tragedy (songs 31–36). A feud between two brothers, Untamo and Kalervo, ends with the former massacring Kalervo and his family. Only one pregnant woman survives; she later gives birth to a son,

Kullervo. Fearing his revenge, Untamo unsuccessfully tries to kill the boy. When Kullervo grows bigger, he is sold to Ilmarinen as a slave. Ilmarinen's wife, the former maiden of Pohjola, sets Kullervo to herding and roguishly bakes a stone into his luncheon loaf. While cutting the loaf, Kullervo breaks his knife and, in revenge, he drives home a pack of wolves and bears, in the form of cattle, which tear the mistress to pieces. An accidental meeting with his sister results in Kullervo's seduction of her. When their relation to one another is discovered, she jumps into a river. Finally, Kullervo destroys Untamo's family and ends his life with a sword.

X. Ilmarinen Seeks Consolation (songs 37–38). Ilmarinen, after losing his wife, forges himself a new wife of gold and silver. But since she is cold, he casts her away and goes to Pohjola to woo the younger sister of his former wife. When he is received in a hostile manner, Ilmarinen abducts the girl and, on the return journey, sings her into a sea gull.

XI. The Theft of the Sampo (songs 39–42). When Väinämöinen hears of Pohjola's carefree life thanks to the Sampo, he and Ilmarinen decide to steal the Sampo for themselves. Lemminkäinen joins them as the third man. On the way, Väinämöinen makes a harp from the jawbone of a big pike and plays it, to the delight of all living creatures. At Pohjola, Väinämöinen puts the people to sleep with his harp; they bring the Sampo to the boat and leave for home.

XII. The Flight (songs 43–44). Louhi awakens, prepares a warship and sets out to pursue the abductors of the Sampo. When the ship goes aground, she changes herself into an eagle and takes the warriors under her wings. In the ensuing fight the Kalevala (Kaleva District) men gain the victory, but the Sampo falls into the sea and is broken. Louhi retreats dejectedly. On the shore, Väinämöinen gathers up the fragments of the Sampo, gets them to grow, and hopes for good fortune for all time. Since his harp was lost during the storm at sea, he makes a new birchwood harp.

XIII. The Last Fights (songs 45–49). Louhi, angered by the news of prosperity in Kalevala, prepares unusual diseases for them, conjures up a bear to destroy their cattle, hides the sun and moon inside a hill, and steals the fire. However, Väinämöinen manages to overcome all these calamities.

XIV. Väinämöinen's Departure (song 50). The virgin Marjatta gives birth to a boy. In the controversy about the boy's baptism, Väinämöinen, acting as the judge, decides that he has to be put to death, but the infant, who receives the faculty of speech, upbraids Väinämöinen for his own sins. The boy is baptized as King of Karelia, and Väinämöinen, utterly frustrated, departs in a copper boat for "between heaven and earth."

The Technique of Compilation

Lönnrot's contemporaries, as is typical of the romanticists in general, were of the opinion that Lönnrot had "found the epic in the forest," i.e., had restored the original form of the epic. That is, of course, only an illusion. In reality, in its structure the Kalevala was entirely Lönnrot's compilation. This compilation was based on the best and most complete variants of the songs that he had at his disposal, with the addition of verses from other variants and even from other songs. Research has revealed that Lönnrot did not take more than three or four consecutive lines from the same variant. Therefore, the majority of sequences of lines (verses) in the *Kalevala* never appeared this way in the oral tradition. This technique of compilation is unique in world literature. It has been pointed out half jokingly that Lönnrot, who in his youth worked for his father as a tailor's apprentice, made use of his tailoring skill while compiling the *Kalevala*.

The *Kalevala* reflects Lönnrot's ideas of the epic, his worldview, and his taste. Working with a definite artistic goal in mind, he chose from the vast material he had at his disposal the portions suitable for the epic and discarded those that were contradictory or violated the style. If it was necessary for the epic as a whole, he developed some seemingly insignificant details into important components of the work.[5] His editorial practices betray his tendency to reduce the Christian and legendary features, while strengthening both the heathen and the historical-realistic elements. He normalized the language, corrected the metrical defects, occasionally changed the names of persons and places, and created linking verses wherever necessary. The few hundred linking verses added by the compiler form less than five per cent of the epic, and even these are adaptations of verses used in folksongs.

The most important building materials for the creation of the *Kalevala* were the epic songs. Lönnrot had in his possession about thirty different epic songs, each of them in numerous variants. In addition, he used lyric songs, charms (incantations), wedding songs, laments, and proverbs. The charms were employed generously; about one-fifth of the whole epic is made up of charms. There are sections in the *Kalevala* which look more like collections of charms than parts of an epic, such as the curing of Väinämöinen's knee wound, the driving out of the cattle by Ilmarinen's wife, and Väinämöinen's trip to Antero Vipunen. Because of its richness in charms, the Italian scholar Domenico Comparetti called the *Kalevala* "the epic of charms."

The Sampo Epic

Finnish and Karelian epic songs are rather short—from 50 to 400 lines. Seldom containing more than one episode, they endeavor to achieve a strong effect by telling the story briefly and dramatically. Some songs with an identical central theme have been combined by singers into a single cycle. The most noteworthy of them is the Sampo cycle, a miniature epic created in the far-distant past.[6] This epic, which does not exceed 400 lines, is about the forging and theft of the Sampo, a miraculous object that brings riches and happiness to its owner. The Sampo epic was used by Lönnrot as the nucleus for the *Kalevala* (cycles III, XI, XII).

The Sampo epic as sung by the Karelian singers is close to the version presented by Lönnrot in the *Kalevala*. In this epic, a nameless Lapp bears a grudge against Väinämöinen and shoots the horse from under him. Väinämöinen drifts on the sea to Pohjola, where he is forced to promise a Sampo to the mistress of Pohjola. Back at home, Väinämöinen sends Ilmarinen to Pohjola, sometimes using a trick. There Ilmarinen forges the Sampo and receives the girl as his reward. News of a carefree life in Pohjola causes Väinämöinen to contrive to steal the Sampo. He goes to Pohjola with his companions, puts the people to sleep with magic needles, and takes the Sampo to the boat. When the mistress of Pohjola wakes up, she goes in pursuit of the thieves. During the fight, the Sampo falls into the sea.

It has been shown that the oldest episode of the Sampo epic is the theft of the Sampo. The warlike spirit of this song reflects the restlessness of the Middle Iron Age (A.D. 400–800) or the beginning of the Viking Age (A.D. 800–1050). The song about the theft of the Sampo was created, as Nils Lid showed, under the influence of the Norwegian *troll* songs, which drew their materials from the Nordic *fornaldar* (legendary) sagas.[7] The troll songs and fornaldar sagas contain descriptions of journeys to a mythical land in the north (*Trollebotn, Nordbotn*), where there lives a great-nosed witch *gygr* (cf. Louhi "with a nose like a hook"). The journey to the north is usually undertaken by two heroes for the purpose of rescuing a maiden or, as in the *Bósa saga,* for obtaining the egg of the *gamr* bird. In the last-mentioned saga, the hero called Smiðr strikes his opponent, who changes into a flying dragon, to the ground with his magic sword; this incident can be compared with the fight over the Sampo and Louhi's transformation into an eagle.

Once the song about the theft of the Sampo had arisen, other songs of this cycle were added as a necessary introduction in order to explain the circumstances that led to this daring enterprise.

But what is this mystical object, the Sampo? According to the prevailing view originally advanced by Uno Harva, the Sampo is the pillar (Finnish *sammas*) of the world, the world axis, around which the vault of the sky unceasingly rotates. (The word for the Sampo used in parallelism is *kirjokansi*, "the decorated lid," i.e., the starred sky.) In Europe the representations of the world pillar were erected for cult purposes by the Saxons and the Lapps. The Saxon *Irminsûl* (the great pillar) was a wooden post erected in the town of Eresburg under the free sky; this was destroyed by Charlemagne in 772. The Lapp *Maylmen stytte* (the world pillar), likewise of wood, was worshipped with blood sacrifices in order to avoid the collapse of the world. Replicas of the world axis have been widely employed among the Finno-Ugric and Altaic peoples in Asia.[8]

The concept of the universe revolving around the world pillar or axis evokes the idea of a gigantic mill. This interpretation is actually reflected in the description of the Sampo as a miraculous mill:

He [Väinämöinen] made the Sampo ready,
on one side he made a grain mill,

on the second side a salt mill,
on the third a money mill.[9]

Thus the Sampo can be compared to the Old Scandinavian *Grotte,* a gigantic hand-driven mill, which was supposed to produce anything wanted by its owner.

The Sampo has also been described as having the characteristics of a tree. When Ilmarinen finishes forging the Sampo, Louhi takes it to the hill of rock. "There it struck root to the depth of nine fathoms."[10] In some verses that have become disassociated from this song (but reinstated in the *Kalevala*), one root of the Sampo is said to have struck into Mother Earth, the second into the sky, and the third into the water's edge.[11]

The tree-shaped Sampo is identical with the Tree of Life, widely known in Eurasian folklore. According to the Old Iranians, the Tree of Life grows on the summit of the mountain of iron, and beneath it springs the Water of Life.[12] Similar ideas exist among the peoples of Central Asia, the Yakuts, Indians, Egyptians, Old Scandinavians (in the *Edda*), and others. The concept of the Tree of Life is related to that of the world pillar and has obviously developed from it. The fact that the Sampo represents both the world pillar and the Tree of Life indicates that the Finns and Karelians were also familiar with these ideas.

Lönnrot, when using the Sampo cycle as the basis for the plot of the epic *Kalevala*,[13] elaborated the themes of Väinämöinen's accidental arrival in Pohjola, Ilmarinen's forced creation of the Sampo, and the theft of the Sampo, which in the Sampo cycle were told in a nutshell. He furthermore interspersed the individual episodes of the Sampo cycle with accounts about Lemminkäinen's adventures and about Kullervo's unfortunate fate. All this diversity of persons and events was reduced to a kind of cosmic unity by beginning the epic with the description of the mythical creation of the world and ending it with the departure of Väinämöinen in a copper boat "toward the upper reaches of the world, to the lower reaches of the heavens."

The *Kalevala* was developed by Lönnrot into a broad panorama of the life of two tribes—the Kalevala and the Pohjola. The relations between them are shown both under peace-time conditions and in times of hostilities. The people of Pohjola are represented by the ruling family headed by Louhi. The heroes of Kalevala are not members of the same family, but they have close relations. Väinämöinen often calls Ilmarinen his brother, and he undertakes voyages together with him and Lemminkäinen. Kullervo is Ilmarinen's serf.

Only a few episodes in the *Kalevala* can be termed heroic. All of these reflect the Viking Age, when the heroic ideal of men was to surpass all others in strength and courage and win fame for posterity. This spirit appears in the fierce struggle of Väinämöinen and his companions with the forces of Pohjola in order to obtain the Sampo. We also find it in some folksongs about Lemminkäinen which were originally associated with other heroes. The last phase of Lemminkäinen's duel with the master of Pohjola in the *Kalevala* is modelled after the song of Kaukomieli (or Kauko or Kaukomoinen). Kaukomieli, during a drinking bout, kills Veitikkä (rascal) because he spilled beer on his mantle. This garment was the symbol of his stature as a warrior, since it had been gained "by blood." Following the feudal notion of honor, its soiling could be compensated for only with blood.

Lemminkäinen's abandonment of his young wife Kyllikki on the Island in the *Kalevala* is based on the "Ahti and Kyllikki Song," and is in the same spirit. For Ahti Saarelainen ("Ahti of the Island") the passion for sea adventures and battles is so strong that he hears even his boat complaining for not going to war. When Ahti's wife breaks her promise, he decides to leave her and set out to sea. His young companion Teuri (Tiera), who like Ahti has just married, cannot contain his craving for battle and hastens along with him.

Kalevala *as a Shamanistic Epic*

Except for these episodes, the *Kalevala* is not a heroic epic in the usual sense of this term, but can best be termed a shamanistic epic in which great deeds are accomplished, not by feats of arms, but by magical means—by the power of words and incantations. Thus it belongs to the peculiar arctic culture extending from Lapland to eastern Siberia and across the Bering Strait as far as Greenland. Its heroes are shamans and sorcerers who transcend the limits of the real world. Some of them are even demigods and culture heroes who participated in the creation or rendered great services to the people.

In Väinämöinen the Finns have the figure of an eternal sage, a great shaman, who in his capacity as the spiritual leader of his tribe possesses the deepest knowledge.[14] He undertakes a journey to the other world in search of knowledge and encounters deadly dangers on his way, as do the shamans of the arctic peoples in their "soul travels." For the same purpose he pays a visit to the dead shaman Antero Vipunen, whose body, during its long separation from the soul, has so badly rotted that the soul cannot return to it anymore. In the singing competition with Joukahainen, Väinämöinen sings his magic song so powerfully that his opponent sinks into the swamp and his horse and harness are transformed into different beings and things. In the song about his mastery at kantele playing, Väinämöinen reaches the stature of the ancient Orpheus: he enchants all the animals and birds of the forest, the fish of the sea, and the nature spirits. His music makes all those present, including the musician himself, shed tears. He builds a boat from a bit of distaff and creates a reef from pieces of flint and tinder-fungus on which Louhi's warship goes aground. Martti Haavio assumes that some of the songs of Väinämöinen may have been created at the latest in the ninth century in the coastal areas of western Finland, on the basis of legends about a great shaman who lived in Finland and enjoyed high esteem among the members of his tribe.

In his attempt to abolish darkness, Väinämöinen (together with his companion Ilmarinen) brings fire to the people and thereby acquires the dimensions of a demigod, a culture hero. By rescuing some pieces of the broken Sampo from Louhi, he secures the abundance of fish in the sea and the fertility of the land. As culture heroes finally vanish, so Väinämöinen—after his young successor, the "King of Karelia," has emerged—disappears (according to numerous variants) into the mouth of the Maelstrom.[15] However, traces of him still appear in the elements where he once toiled, traces such as "Väinämöinen's scythe" (Orion) and "Väinämöinen's route" (a calm streak on the surface of rippling water) on the waters.[16]

Ilmarinen is also known in Finnish mythology as a culture hero, as the great smith who created the vault of the sky and furnished it with stars. A northern relative of Hephaestus, he succeeded in obtaining iron from crude ore in order to forge the Sampo. With Väinämöinen he obtained the first spark of fire which had fallen from the sky and entered the belly of a blue trout. Originally he may have been the ruler of the weather. The popularity enjoyed by Ilmarinen among the people caused him to be extended into numerous secondary roles.[17]

Lemminkäinen's figure in Finnish folklore is very complex and has caused widely differing interpretations. His shamanistic nature appears in a journey to the festivities in Päivölä (in the *Kalevala*: Pohjola), during which he overcomes three deadly perils, and also in his slithering unnoticed into the house in the shape of a snake. The singing competition between Lemminkäinen and the master of the house can be compared to that of Väinämöinen and Joukahainen. Both are contests of magic between two sorcerers in which the local sorcerer triumphs. As Martti Haavio recently demonstrated, the song of Lemminkäinen's journey evidently was created under the influence of the Russian bylina "Vavilo and the Troubadours," which in turn goes back to an ancient Egyptian story.[18]

Lemminkäinen's chivalric features, as mentioned above, are carried over from other figures. Due to a similarity between Lemminkäinen and Kaukomieli, Karelian singers had attributed some of Kaukomieli's adventures to Lemminkäinen and vice versa. Lönnrot, however, went still further in the *Kalevala*: he transferred the events connected with another Viking Age figure, Ahti Saarelainen, to Lemminkäinen and added the names of Ahti and Kauko or Kaukomieli as secondary names of Lemminkäinen.

Kullervo, Ilmarinen's vengeful serf-boy, applies witchcraft to turn wolves into cows and bears into cattle; these kill Ilmarinen's wife (the former maiden of Pohjola). Louhi, the mistress of Pohjola, is the personification of the powers of witchcraft, although in the use of magic she ultimately proves inferior to the Kalevala heroes.

The Share of West Finland and Karelia in the Kalevala Songs

The ancient Finnish songs (the so-called Kalevala songs) were best preserved in the east—in Russian and Finnish Karelia. About a dozen of these songs are known also in Estonia; they either originated in the Estonian-Finnish common period, or were brought by later emigrants from Estonia to Finland or from Finland to Estonia. Since only some relics of ancient western Finnish folksongs have been preserved, and since the Estonian and Ingrian songs have undergone great changes during a long period of serfdom, modern comparative research is not in a position to pinpoint the area of origin of these Estonian-Finnish songs.[19]

A group of the ancient songs shows clear signs of having arisen in and migrated from the west, the area of Turku. This has been demonstrated, for example, in songs, with the use of loan words from Swedish (e.g., *luote* "charm") which are, in the Finnish language, restricted to the west, where the Swedish influence has been the strongest. Some songs also mention artifacts that have their closest correspondents in Scandinavia. In a description of a spear it is said that

The wolf spoke at the socket,
the bear roared on the nail . . .[20]

In Scandinavia two spears from the seventh century have been found on which the rivets that fasten the socket to the shaft are decorated with a sculptured bear. In one song it is said that the handle of the steering oar of the ship was bent or crooked. Such steering oars were used in Gotland and Denmark during the fifth century.[21]

The ancient folksongs, for the most part, had disappeared in western Finland before the recording of folklore began. In the east (i.e., in Karelia), where the songs had migrated, they were preserved well into the last century, and a few of them survived into the present time. The reason for this is that in western Finland, Roman Catholicism and Lutheranism waged an intensive campaign against the ancient beliefs and against the songs which contained rudiments of heathen beliefs. Russian Orthodoxy in Karelia was much more tolerant of old customs and practices, old beliefs, and old songs. It should also be remembered that West European culture spread first to western Finland, whereas in Karelia, which was a great distance from the cultural centers, life continued in ancient ways for centuries.

As Martti Haavio has demonstrated, the songs about Väinämöinen reflect the typical West Finnish milieu with its maritime setting and fisherman's sphere of interest.[22] Their creators must have been fishermen who were well acquainted with all facets of sea life. The creation song tells of the origin of the world on the sea. The competition between Väinämöinen and Joukahainen in singing contains numerous metamorphoses related to the sea: Väinämöinen sang Joukahainen's horse into leaping like a seal, Joukahainen's whip into a reed, and Joukahainen's saddle into a duck on the sea. When Väinämöinen made his journey to Pohjola, he rode on a horse of straw on the surface of the sea. Väinämöinen's wooing trip to Pohjola, when competing with Ilmarinen, was made again by sea. Likewise, the theft of the Sampo was undertaken by sea. This milieu of the high seas easily adjusted itself to the wildernesses in Karelia with their great lakes rich in fish and fowl.

Ancient Finnish-Karelian songs had a mythical basis; they existed in association with cult practices and ritual ceremonies. In former times, singing them was not a leisurely pastime or art for art's sake, but an act of magical significance. These songs contained the most sacred and powerful knowledge that could be used to influence man's life. The song of Väinämöinen's kantele music was used as a kind of incantation, now for fishing, now for hunting. Chr. Ganander wrote in 1789: "Fowlers, hunters, and woodsmen asked Väinämöinen to play his harp, so that its sweet music would call forth all the game...."[23] To increase the fertility of the fields, the spring and autumn sowing were accompanied by the singing of Sämpsä Pellervoinen's song, which reiterated the primeval sowing. The sowing incantation, followed by the song of the forging and stealing of the Sampo and the pursuit of the mistress of Pohjola, was sung at the spring and autumn plowing. Some statements made by the singers attribute the riches of the sea to the Sampo's falling into the sea and point to the ritualistic use of the Sampo sequence, not only in agriculture, but also in fishing. The latter ritual is no doubt more ancient.[24]

Composition and Form

The plot of the *Kalevala,* as devised by Lönnrot, centers around the fight over the maiden of Pohjola and possession of the Sampo. Väinämöinen, initially guided by his own personal interests, woos Aino; then, after losing her and still endeavoring to secure his personal happiness, he pursues the maiden of Pohjola. His egotism results in the loss of the Sampo to Pohjola. In the second part of the epic, after the old Väinämöinen has been rejected, he begins to act for the benefit of his tribe, for the happiness of his land and his people.

The *Kalevala* as a work of art is well balanced and symmetrical, as August Annist has demonstrated.[25] It can be divided in the middle, after the twenty-fifth song, into two parts. The epic begins with an introduction and ends with closing words. Väinämöinen's birth at the beginning and his departure at the end are also symmetrical. The drama of Aino, who drowns herself to avoid becoming the wife of an old man, and the tragedy of the virgin Marjatta (based on the apocryphal legend of the Virgin Mary) likewise constitute parallels.

The central part of the epic is made up of four larger cycles which deal with the relations between Kalevala and Pohjola: the forging of the Sampo (cycle III), the wooing of the maiden of Pohjola and the wedding celebration (V–VII), the theft of the Sampo (XI, XII), and the revenge of the mistress of Pohjola (XIII). The first two relate friendly, peaceful visits, while the last two describe hostility and fighting. Between these four main cycles there are three secondary ones which deal with Lemminkäinen (IV, VIII) and Kullervo (IX). These secondary cycles have little significance from the point of view of the main plot. Lemminkäinen kills the master of Pohjola, and Kullervo has the former maiden of Pohjola (Ilmarinen's wife) killed by wild beasts. These events contribute to the worsening of relations between the two tribes, but they do not lead to fights over possession of the Sampo.

Very common in the Kalevala songs is the use of parallelism—the repetition of the idea of a line (verse) in the following line or lines in different words. The lines that are parallel are also close grammatically, e.g.:

Tuo venettä, Tuonen tytti,	Bring me a boat, you daughter of Tuoni,
lauttoa, Manalan lapsi.[26]	a ferry, daughter of Manala.

Primarily on the basis of the syntactic types of parallelism, Matti Kuusi has set up certain stylistic criteria for establishing the chronology of individual songs.[27] At the earliest period—which coincides roughly with the Proto-Finnic era (ca. 500 B.C. to A.D. 500)—each verse of the so-called Pre-Finnic poetry contained only a short independent clause, e.g.:

Kuuluvi mereltä itku,	Weeping from the sea is to be heard,
juorotanta lainehilta;	lamentation from the billows,
ei ole itku lapsen itku	the weeping is no child's weeping,
eikä itku vaimon itku,	it is no woman's weeping,
itku on partasuun urohon,	it is the weeping of a bearded man,
jouhileuan juorotanta.[28]	the lamentation of someone with a beard.

The second period, the so-called Early Kalevala poetry, is characterized by the appearance of the correlative parallelism in which independent and dependent clauses alternate, e.g.:

Mi munan alainen puoli,	What was the lower half of the egg,
alaiseksi maaemäksi;	became the earth beneath;
mi munan yläinen puoli,	what was the top half of the egg,
yläiseksi taivahaksi.[29]	became the heavens above.

During the third period, the "Mid-Kalevala poetry," more complicated sentence types appeared, e.g.:

Ei sitä metsässä ollut	In the woods there was not one
kahden siiven lentävätä,	whirring on two wings,
jalan neljän juoksevata,	running on four feet,
joka ei tullut kuulemahan	that did not come to listen
soitellessa Väinämöisen	to Väinämöinen's playing
kalanluista kanteletta.[30]	of the fish-bone *kantele*.

In the following period, the Viking Age, the syntax and diction of the Kalevala poetry becomes still freer and more complex. The gradual change of the Kalevala poetry manifested itself not only in the syntax, but simultaneously in themes, images, and heroes. The development proceeded from the originally mythical and etiological songs that depicted various aspects of creation toward greater humanization: the culture heroes of gigantic strength, hewn as if out of rock, were replaced in the course of time by human beings with their extraordinary adventures and passions. In the Viking Age, love was finally deemed worthy of being included in epic songs, but it was sung of as a human reality—completely sinless, just like any earthly sensual joy. Examples of it are to be seen in Kaukamoinen's adventures with the maidens of the Island, the episode of Ahti's and Kyllikki's first night, and Ilmarinen's return from Pohjola with his young wife. In the latter song, Ilmarinen had "one hand in a mottled glove, the other on the woman's breasts, one leg on the side of the sled, the other on the woman's thigh."[31]

The *Kalevala* frequently uses three-fold repetition and gradation. The maiden of Pohjola is being wooed and courtship tasks are being performed by Väinämöinen, Ilmarinen, and Lemminkäinen—and then by both Väinämöinen and Ilmarinen at the same time. The courtship tasks themselves have been grouped in such a way that the most difficult one comes last. Thus Väinämöinen has to cleave a swan, knot an egg, and finally make a boat out of the fragments of a distaff. The last task causes him almost insurmountable difficulty. Lemminkäinen has to catch the Demon's elk, bridle the Demon's fire-breathing gelding, and shoot the swan of Death's Domain. He is killed while attempting to shoot the swan. Ilmarinen first plows a snake-infested field, then gets Death's bear and the wolf of the Abode of the Dead, and finally catches the gigantic pike in the River of Death's Domain. The successful completion of the last task secures him his goal of obtaining the maiden of Pohjola for his wife.

The losses of Pohjola are presented in three groups: first, the loss of three members of their family—the maiden and the master of Pohjola are both killed and the second maiden of Pohjola is transformed into a sea gull; second, the theft of the Sampo; and third, the failure of three attacks against Kalevala undertaken by Pohjola.

The gradation appears not only in individual episodes, but in the structure of the epic as a whole. The initially peaceful and friendly relations between Kalevala and Pohjola become increasingly strained. The antagonism deepens until it flares into open war and finally assumes the magnitude of an all-out struggle for life and death. Pohjola, by sending the sicknesses and the bear and by stealing the sun and the moon, strives for the complete annihilation of its adversary, Kalevala. That it does not succeed is due to Väinämöinen, the great sage of Kalevala.[32] This gradual intensification of the antagonism between Kalevala and Pohjola is primarily Lönnrot's own invention, used for the purpose of building up dramatic tension.

The *Kalevala* as a work of art cannot escape criticism.[33] The action is thin in comparison with the great bulk of the epic, and some digressions that delay or interrupt the main course of events are rather tedious. In the eighth song, Väinämöinen wounds himself in the knee while building a boat. When we meet him again in the sixteenth song, he is still busy building it. The epic also suffers from repetitions. Väinämöinen goes to the realm of death twice, and he enchants people and animals twice with his kantele playing. Kullervo's demonstration of tremendous strength is also described twice. Väinämöinen and Lemminkäinen get into similar troubles at sea, and so forth.

The *Kalevala* is both a wooing and a war epic. However, there is much more wooing than fighting in it. There are seven or eight wooing stories, but only three or four descriptions of combat; the latter include the death of the master of Pohjola, the theft of the Sampo, the destruction of Untamo's farm, and Väinämöinen's last fights with Pohjola. The combats are described very briefly. For instance, the theft of the Sampo and the fights following it are discussed in two songs, but the preparations for these fights (looking for a horse, catching a big pike, and Väinämöinen's kantele playing) are told in three songs. Also characteristic is Kullervo's retaliation against Untamo: the preparations for it (including the news about the death of the members of the family and Kullervo's reaction) take 250 lines, but the destruction of Untola only 8 lines. Väinämöinen's second campaign against Pohjola is also presented laconically. It is obvious that Lönnrot wanted to depict his heroes, not so much fighting, as leading everyday lives with their pleasures and sorrows.[34] It is for this reason that the *Kalevala* is a national epic.

The so-called Kalevala meter is the eight-syllable trochaic line ($-\cup|-\cup|-\cup|-\cup$) in which a long first syllable of a word (always stressed) can appear only at the beginning of a foot with a short syllable at the end of a foot.[35] Thus, only the length of the first syllable has significance for the Kalevala meter, because in Proto-Finnic—and for a long time afterwards—the long vowels were to be found solely in the first syllable of a word. It was necessary that word pairs like *tuulen* (of wind)–*tulen* (of fire), *piian* (of the maiden)–*pian* (soon), etc., having the distinction of length in the first syllable not be confused. Since there is a tendency to stretch syllables under ictus (metrical stress) in singing, the short vowels, if they had occurred in the ictus position, would have been lengthened and would thus have coincided with the long vowels. This was avoided by using them only in the non-ictus position.

There are two types of verse in the Kalevala songs: (a) the normal verse, with ceasura after the second foot:

$-\cup-\cup\|-\cup-\quad\cup$ metrical stress (marked by —)

/   /   /   (/)   word stress
va-ka van-ha Väi-nä-möi-nen
1 2 3 4   5 6   7 8

(the old steadfast Väinämöinen)

and (b) the so-called broken verse, in which the metrical stress and the word stress do not coincide:

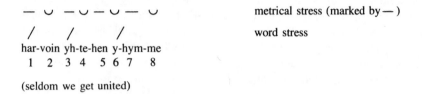

— ∪ — ∪ — ∪ — ∪   metrical stress (marked by —)

/   /   /   word stress
har-voin yh-te-hen y-hym-me
1 2 3 4 5 6 7   8

(seldom we get united)

In the latter example there is a discrepancy between the metrical stress and the word stress in syllables 5 (an unstressed syllable in the ictus position), 6 (a stressed syllable in the non-ictus position), and 7 (the same as 5). The use of the normal and broken verses in consecutive lines keeps the verses from becoming stereotypic and monotonous.

The Kalevala songs make abundant use of alliteration—the repetition of initial identical consonant sounds or vowel sounds in successive or closely associated words. The following is an example of alliteration occurring in verse pairs:

lauloi Joukamon hevosen	he sang Joukamo's horse
hylkeheksi hyppimähän,	to leap like a seal,
lauloi Joukamon satulan	sang Joukamo's saddle
sorsaksi sarajahasen,	into a duck on the sea,
lauloi lääpän Joukamoisen	sang Joukamo's collar-tree
lähtehesen läikkymähän,	into a splashing spring,
lauloi ruoskan Joukamoisen	sang Joukamo's whip
ruovikkohon roiskimahan.[36]	into a swaying reed.

The Kalevala songs were sung by two men while a third man accompanied them on the kantele. The singers sat either side by side or opposite each other with one hand joined, swaying their bodies and sipping from their beer tankards. One of them, the fore-singer, sang a line which was repeated by the after-singer; the fore-singer then sang the next line, and so on. The specific position taken by the singers and their cooperation could be a vestige of shaman activity. The fore-singer corresponded to the shaman and the after-singer to the shaman's helper. This is highly plausible since the singing in ancient times was an act of magic significance.

Curiously enough, in the last century a "myth" developed in Finland about the manner of presenting songs, which did not at all correspond to the traditional practice. Two singers sitting opposite each other had to have both of their hands clasped while swaying their bodies to the beat of the song. This "myth" about the singing of ancient songs had its origin in the incorrect description given by two foreigners in their travelogues, which became well-known in Finland. When performances were arranged in schools and at festivals, the singers were placed in this unnatural position. Under the influence of advisers and vociferous promoters of popular culture, the singers themselves began to adopt this position. The origins of this false image, which had so suggestively influenced the entire national culture, were revealed only in the 1940s.[37]

The Finns have no other work whose influence would have been as all-encompassing as that of the *Kalevala*. The *Kalevala* has enriched all areas of Finnish art, most notably in the paintings of Akseli Gallén-Kallela and sculpture of Väino Aaltonen, in Jean Sibelius' symphony *Kullervo,* and in musical compositions of Aarre Merikanto and Uuno Klami. In literature, numerous classical works owe their existence to the *Kalevala,* from Aleksis Kivi's drama *Kullervo* to Eino Leino's *Helkavirsiä*. A complete change in the literary language was effected by the *Kalevala:* under its influence, the awkward Finnish language gradually developed into a vehicle capable of expressing all the nuances of human thoughts and moods. Most importantly, however, the *Kalevala* awakened national ideas, interests, and aspirations. In the hard times of Finnish history at the turn of the century and during the 1930s and 40s, the *Kalevala* was an essential source of strength from which the people drew their faith for the future.[38]

The Kalevipoeg

The *Kalevipoeg* (The Son of Kalev), the Estonian national epic based on folklore, followed on the heels of the Finnish *Kalevala.*[39] The preparations for its compilation, begun in the 1830s by Friedrich Robert Faehlmann, a medical doctor, were instigated by the mood of Herderian romantic nationalism as well as by the publication of the *Kalevala*. The work was completed by Friedrich Reinhold Kreutzwald (1803–82), who was also a doctor and a poet. The epic appeared in a scholarly publication with the German translation in 1857–61 and as a popular edition in 1862. It contains twenty songs with 19,033 verses in all.

The *Kalevipoeg* consists of a series of adventures experienced by its main protagonist, Kalevipoeg, the posthumous son of Kalev, the king of Estonia. When his mother has been carried away by a Finnish sorcerer, Kalevipoeg goes to Finland to search for her. On this trip, he burdens himself with two crimes. He causes the death of a girl he seduces on an island (she turns out to be his own sister) and he kills the son of a Finnish blacksmith. To retaliate, the smith, who is the master of Kalevipoeg's sword, conjures the sword. Upon his return home, Kalevipoeg becomes king of Estonia, builds towns, and tills the land. He later undertakes a trip to the end of the world and visits hell. His several fights with the devil culminate in the chaining of the prince of darkness to the wall of hell. After being defeated by foreign invaders while defending his country, Kalevipoeg, in melancholy, retires to the forest. There he steps into a river, and his sword, which was lying on the bottom, cuts off his legs, in fulfillment of the Finnish blacksmith's curse. Gods send him on horseback to the gates of hell, where he is to keep watch over the devil and his hosts until the day of redemption dawns.

The epic *Kalevipoeg* is based on numerous prose legends and tales that were versified by Kreutzwald, one of the best poets of his time and also a collector of folksongs. He applied the Estonian folksong meter (the four-syllable trochaic line) and the embellishments of folksongs—the alliteration, assonance, and parallelism—to the *Kalevipoeg*. About 12 percent of the verses were carried over directly from the folksongs.

The legends and tales included in the *Kalevipoeg* belong to the following categories: etiological and local legends, the so-called proportion fantasies, and fairy tales. The oldest legends about Kalevipoeg derive from the first millennium of our era; but the bulk of them come from the period 800–1200, and some are of later origin.[40]

The most ancient group of legends shows Kalevipoeg as a titanic giant, who left traces of his existence in the Estonian terrain.[41] Big boulders are said to have been thrown or carried by him or his wife, marks of his hands and feet are still evident in rocks, and places where he slept show resulting depressions and valleys. As a prodigious plowman, Kalevipoeg changed the shape of the terrain. All these legends are obviously based on ancient European tradition preserved in East Estonia, where the ice age carved out furrowlike hills and valleys that give the impression of having been formed by a superhuman being.[42]

In another group of legends, Kalevipoeg appears as an evil giant who is severely punished.[43] Said to be Jesus' godson, he was good at first, but later became wanton: he plowed the fields so that grass could no longer grow and he chased women. In response to this behavior, Jesus grabbed him by his genitals, threw him into a swamp or a river, and changed him into an otter. According to another legend, to punish Kalevipoeg for boasting of his strength in heaving rocks, God got his hands stuck under a rock.

Legends about Kalevipoeg's trip to hell on the back of the devil-turned-into-a-horse are widely known in Estonia.[44] On God's order, he strikes against the gate, but as he does so, either his hand gets stuck or he is chained to the gate of hell. The devil and his helpers, in an effort to get rid of Kalevipoeg, burn his fetters with splinters lit at both ends. By Christmas, the chains are as thin as horsehair, but the hallelujahs in the church or the blows of the smiths on the bare anvil make them thick again.[45]

The legend of Kalevipoeg's tragedy reached Estonia from the east. It goes back to the Caucasian myth about Amirani, and has also been applied to such titans and monsters as the Devil, Prometheus, Loki, Dukljanin (Diocletianus), and others. The myth of the return of the hero has been attached to Kalevipoeg just as it has to numerous historical and mythical beings (Charlemagne, Friedrich Barbarossa, King Arthur, etc.).[46]

These legends about Kalevipoeg depict him with a great many diverse, often contradictory, features. When Faehlmann and later Kreutzwald began compiling the Estonian epic, they had to create a rather unified hero from these conflicting traditions. The legends had to be partly reinterpreted, so that the national hero, the king of the Estonians during the time of ancient independence, would emerge. Kalevipoeg in the epic was depicted as a typical peasant king, who tilled the land and cared for his people. From being the prisoner in hell, Kalevipoeg was made the guard of the devil. Whereas originally the burning of the splinters had been feared, lest Kalevipoeg escape from hell, it now became a wish–dream about the liberation of Kalevipoeg:

> But once the time will come,
> When all the splinters will
> Flare up at both ends;
> Then the flame will cut
> The hero's hand loose from the rock.

The *Kalevipoeg* had a great national significance. Even before the epic was created, this significance was emphasized by a leading member of the Estonian Literary Society, who asked, "How must our Society further most successfully the enlightenment and the spiritual renascence of the people liberated from serfdom?" And he answered, "I think, by two things: let us give them the epic and the history, and everything is won."[47]

Kreutzwald himself was convinced that through the epic the Estonian people acquired much glory: "The name of the Estonian people, trampled underfoot and abused in several ways so far, has, due to the *Kalevipoeg,* become at once the name of honor."[48] Kreutzwald advised Estonian youth to learn from the epic how their forefathers had sung, and he admonished them to love their fatherland more than they had before.[49]

Like the *Kalevala* in Finland, the *Kalevipoeg* became the most cherished work of Estonian literature. Poets, writers, artists, sculptors, and musicians used its themes for their creations. During the dark times of foreign oppression, the people have drawn from the epic national spirit and the hope for freedom and a better future.

NOTES

1. A convenient source for the basic data of Lönnrot's life and work on the *Kalevala* is Elias Lönnrot, "Materials for the Study of the *Kalevala,*" in *The Kalevala or Poems of the Kaleva District,* trans. Francis P. Magoun, Jr. (Cambridge, Mass.: Harvard University Press, 1963), pp. 341–61. For more detailed information, see Jouko

Hautala, *Finnish Folklore Research 1828–1918* (Helsinki: Societas Scientiarum Fennica, n.d.), pp. 21 ff.

2. The name of the Finnish musical instrument, *kantele,* is usually translated into English as "harp," and we are following this usage here. Actually, the Finnish kantele and its relatives in Estonia, Latvia, and Lithuania are closest to the stringed instrument *psaltery.* (See Stephan Reynolds, "The Baltic Psaltery: Bibliographical Problems and Desiderata," *The Second Conference on Baltic Studies in Scandinavia,* II [Stockholm: Baltiska Institutet, 1973], pp. 7–30.) This ancient Balto-Finnic and Baltic musical instrument was adopted in Old Russia, where a genuine Slavic name, *gusli,* was assigned to it. (See I. Tõnurist, "Kannel Vepsamaast Setumaani," in *Soome-ugri rahvaste muusika pärandist,* ed. E. Rüütel [Tallinn: Eesti Raamat, 1977], pp. 149–78.)

3. The title of the epic was *Kalewala taikka wanhoja Karjalan runoja Suomen kansan muinaisista ajoista* [The Kalevala, or Old Karelian Songs from the Ancient Times of the Finnish People].

4. The synopsis of the *Kalevala* is based partly on F. P. Magoun's translation of Lönnrot's summaries of individual songs, published as a headnote to each song (see note 1).

5. Vjajne [Väinö] Kaukonen, "Sozdanie èposa 'Kalevaly,'" in *Učenye zapiski Leningradskogo universiteta,* 314: *Finno-ugorskaja filologija* (Leningrad, 1962), p. 113.

6. Matti Kuusi, *Sampo-eepos: Typologinen analyysi,* Mémoires de la Société Finno-ougrienne, 96 (Helsinki: Suomalais-ugrilainen Seura, 1949).

7. Nils Lid, "Kalevalan Pohjola," *Kalevalaseuren vuosikirja* 29 (1949): 104–20. Matti Kuusi has shown that the theft of the Sampo aroused strong interest among the ancient Karelian singers and their audiences because of the identification of the *Sampo* with *sampi* (sturgeon). According to Finnish-Karelian-Estonian beliefs, luck in fishing was secured by setting up pictures of fish on the shore. If a picture was stolen, the fishing luck was transferred to the area where the picture was taken. When the fish picture was brought back, luck in fishing was restored. Kuusi points out that *sampi* (sturgeon) may have been associated with the ideas (widespread in Eurasia) of a gigantic fish as the supporter of the earth (*sampi* is related to *sammas* "pole," i.e., the world pole). See Matti Kuusi, "Kaloista vanhin," *Kalevalaseuran Vuosikirja* 56 (1976): 318 ff.

8. Uno Holmberg (Harva), "Lisiä Sammon selityksiin," *Virittäjä* 22 (1918): 136; Uno Holmberg [Harva], *Finno-Ugric, Siberian* [*Mythology*], in *The Mythology of All Races,* ed. C. J. A. MacCulloch (New York: Cooper Square Publishers, 1964; reprint), pp. 333 ff.

9. *Suomen kansan vanhat runot,* I: *Vienan läänin runot,* I, ed. A. R. Niemi (Helsinki: Suomalaisen Kirjallisuuden Seura, 1908), no. 34, p. 56.

10. Ibid., no. 79a, p. 132.

11. Ibid., no. 412, p. 527.

12. Holmberg [Harva], pp. 349 ff., especially 358.

13. The term "Kalevala" appears in folk poetry as a geographical designation. Lönnrot knew it only from one ballad, which was not connected with any of the heroes of the epic; it occurred in the expression *Kalevalan kankahilla* (on the heaths of Kalevala). Lönnrot applied the term "Kalevala," in counterbalance to "Pohjola," as

the designation of the home of a group of heroes. After long deliberation and hesitation, he finally decided to use this term as the name of the national epic (Kaukonen, p. 113).

14. Martti Haavio, *Väinämöinen: Eternal Sage,* Folklore Fellows Communications, no. 144 (Helsinki: Suomalainen Tiedeakatemia, 1952).

15. E. M. Meletinskij, *Proisxoždenie geroičeskogo èposa* (Moscow: Izdatel'stvo vostočnoj literatury, 1963), p. 137.

16. Haavio, pp. 20 ff.

17. Lauri Honko, "Finnische Mythologie," in *Wörterbuch der Mythologie,* II: *Das alte Europa,* ed. H. W. Haussig (Stuttgart: E. Klett, n.d.), pp. 309–11.

18. Martti Haavio, *Suomalainen mytologia* (Porvoo and Helsinki: Werner Söderström, 1967), pp. 238 ff.

19. Matti Kuusi, "Kalevalainen kertomarunous," *Oma maa* 4 (1958): 254.

20. Martti Haavio, *Kirjokansi: Suomen kansan kertomarunoutta* (Porvoo and Helsinki: Werner Söderström, 1952), p. 85.

21. Björn Collinder, "The Kalevala and its Background," *ARV: Journal of Scandinavian Folklore* 20 (1964): 77–78.

22. Haavio, *Väinämöinen,* pp. 63, 80–81, et passim.

23. Ibid., p. 171.

24. Matti Kuusi, "Kalevalainen kertomarunous," p. 250; Matti Kuusi, *Suomen kirjallisuus,* I (Helsinki: Suomalaisen Kirjallisuuden Seura and Otava, 1963), pp. 73, 227; Kuusi, "Kaloista vanhin," p. 326; Haavio, *Väinämöinen,* pp. 171–73.

25. August Annist, *"Kalevala" kui kunstiteos* (Tallinn: Eesti Raamat, 1969), pp. 180–89.

26. *Kalevala,* 16: 163–164.

27. Kuusi, "Kalevalainen kertomarunous," pp. 247 ff.; Kuusi, *Suomen kirjallisuus,* I, pp. 147 ff., 165–66, 219 ff., 230 ff., et passim.

28. Kuusi, "Kalevalainen kertomarunous," p. 247.

29. Ibid., p. 248.

30. Kuusi, *Suomen kirjallisuus,* I, p. 232.

31. Kuusi, "Kalevalainen kertomarunous," p. 252.

32. On repetitions and the gradation in the *Kalevala,* see Annist, *"Kalevala" kui kunstitieos,* pp. 184–87.

33. For a summary of these criticisms, see Collinder, "The Kalevala and its Background," pp. 32–34.

34. Annist, *"Kalevala" kui kunstiteos,* pp. 187–89.

35. This rule does not apply to the first foot, the structure of which permits greater freedom.

36. Kuusi, "Kalevalainen kertomarunous," p. 246. On alliteration in Finnish, see the detailed study by Pentti Leino, *Strukturaalinen alkusointu suomessa* (Helsinki: Suomalaisen Kirjallisuuden Seura, 1970), with an English résumé: "Structural alliteration in Finnish."

37. Elsa Enäjärvi-Haavio, "On the Performance of the Finnish Folk Runes," *Folk-Liv* 14–15 (1951): 130–66. On singing in Karelia, see also Leea Virtanen, *Kalevalainen laulutapa Karjalassa,* Suomi, 113/1 (Helsinki: Suomalaisen Kirjallisuuden Seura, 1968).

38. Martti Haavio, "Das Kalevala—ein nationales Symbol," in *Finnland: Ge-*

schichte und Gegenwart (Porvoo and Helsinki: Werner Söderström, 1961), pp. 234–35.

39. A. Ja. Annist, "Èstonskaja èpičeskaja tradicija i èpos 'Kalevipoeg,'" *Sovetskaja ètnografija* 1 (1965): 58.

40. Annist, pp. 52 ff.; Felix Oinas, " 'Kalevipoeg' ja selle kodumaine ning rahvusvaheline tagapõhi," *Mana* 40 (1973): 5–10.

41. Aug. Anni(st), *F. R. Kreutzwaldi "Kalevipoeg,"* I, E. V. Tartu Ülikooli Toimetused, B, 32 (Tartu, 1934), pp. 31–78.

42. Oinas, pp. 6–7.

43. Annist, pp. 122–23.

44. Annist, pp. 117–48.

45. Annist, ibid.: Felix J. Oinas, "The Tragedy of Kalevipoeg and of the South Slavic Heroes," *Tractata Altaica: Denis Sinor sexagenario optime de rebus altaicis merito dedicata,* ed. Walther Heissig, et al. (Wiesbaden: Otto Harrassowitz, 1976), pp. 452 ff.

46. Martti Haavio, "Tyrannisoiva myytti," reprint of the *Finnish Society for the Study of Comparative Religion,* 9 (Helsinki, 1967); Oinas, "The Tragedy of Kalevipoeg," pp. 454–55, 457–58.

47. Aug. Annist, *F. R. Kreutzwaldi "Kalevipoeg,"* II, E. V. Tartu Ülikooli Toimetused, B, 33 (Tartu, 1936), p. 59, fn. 82.

48. Annist, p. 208.

49. Annist, p. 207.

BIBLIOGRAPHY
The Kalevala

Text and Translations

Lönnrot, Elias. *Kalevala.* 24th ed. Helsinki: Suomalaisen Kirjallisuuden Seura, 1964 (or other editions).

————. *Kalevala: The Land of the Heroes.* 2 vols. Translated from the original Finnish by W. F. Kirby. New York: E. P. Dutton and Co., 1961. A verse translation of the *Kalevala.* Originally published in London in 1907.

————. *Kalevala.* A prose translation from the Finnish by Aili Kolehmainen Johnson. Hancock, Mich.: Book Concern, 1950. A non-literal prose translation of the *Kalevala.*

————. *The Kalevala or Poems of the Kaleva District.* A prose translation with foreword and appendices by Francis P. Magoun, Jr. Cambridge, Mass.: Harvard University Press, 1963. Among the translations into English, closest to the Finnish original. Also contains much useful material on Lönnrot.

————. *Kalevala.* Translated from the original Finnish text by Lore Fromm and Hans

Fromm. Munich: Carl Hanser, 1967. The best of the *Kalevala* translations in German available.

Studies

Annist, August. *"Kalevala" kui kunstiteos* [The *Kalevala* as a Work of Art]. Tallinn: Eesti Raamat, 1969. A comprehensive up-to-date survey of the *Kalevala* in Estonian, dealing with all aspects of the epic, but especially with its thematic structure.

Collinder, Björn. "The Kalevala and Its Background." *ARV: Journal of Scandinavian Folklore* 20 (1964): 5–111. A general survey of the *Kalevala*—its origin, composition, influence, poetic form, singers, and the geographical, historical, and mythical background.

Comparetti, Domenico. *The Traditional Poetry of the Finns.* London, New York, and Bombay: Longmans, Green, and Co., 1898. The English translation of a work published in Italian in 1891. Following Aug. Ahlqvist, Comparetti attributes the origin of the Finnish-Karelian Kalevala songs to Scandinavian influence. Strongly antiquated.

Fromm, Hans. *Kalevala Kommentar.* Munich: Carl Hanser, 1967. An extensive commentary on the *Kalevala,* organized by songs in the following order: a characterization of the song, bibliography and notes on and explanations of individual verses or words.

Haavio, Martti. *Kirjokansi: Suomen kansan kertomarunoutta* [The Patterned Cover: Epic Poetry of the Finnish People]. Porvoo and Helsinki: Werner Söderström, 1952. An anthology of Finnish epic songs for the general public. The song texts are slightly modified to comply with the normal structural pattern as established by the editor. Though the selection has primarily esthetic goals, the comments attached contain results of scholarly research on each song.

―――. *Väinämöinen: Eternal Sage.* Folklore Fellows Communications, no. 144. Helsinki: Suomalainen Tiedeakatemia, 1952. A detailed study of the central figure of the old songs of the Finnish people. Analyzing the more important songs of Väinämöinen and the milieu reflected in them and making use of extensive comparative material from all over the world, Haavio modifies considerably the concept of Väinämöinen that had prevailed.

Hautala, Jouko. *Finnish Folklore Research 1828–1918.* Helsinki: Finnish Society of Sciences, 1968. An abbreviated version of the central portion of Hautala's detailed *Suomalaisen kansanrunouden tutkimus* [The Study of Finnish Folklore] (Helsinki: Suomalaisen Kirjallisuuden Seura, 1954). Finnish folklore research before 1928 is summarized briefly, whereas the present-day study of folklore has been omitted. The *Kalevala* is the center of the discussion.

Kaukonen, Väinö. *Elias Lönnrotin Kalevalan toinen painos* [The Second Edition of Lönnrot's *Kalevala*]. Helsinki: Suomalaisen Kirjallisuuden Seura, 1956. A detailed study of the second edition of Lönnrot's *Kalevala:* the history of each line of the text, survey of the compilation of the epic, and the complete vocabulary.

Kolehmainen, John I. *Epic of the North: The Story of Finland's Kalevala.* New York Mills, Minn.: The Northwestern Publishing Company, 1973. A broad popular survey of the *Kalevala* dealing with the history of the compilation of the epic, the singers, the ancient rites and customs, and the influence of the *Kalevala* on Finnish culture.

Krohn, Kaarle. *Kalevalastudien.* 4 vols. Folklore Fellows Communications, nos. 53, 67, 71, 72, 75, 76. Helsinki: Suomalainen Tiedeakatemia, 1924–28. Contains the sum total of Kaarle Krohn's studies on ancient Finnish folk poetry. Although Krohn's underlying theory of the historicity of the Kalevala songs has been refuted by later scholars, the work has still preserved its value as the most detailed over-all study on the Finnish epic.

Kuusi, Matti. *Sampo-eepos: Typologinen analyysi* [The Sampo Epic: A Typological Analysis]. Mémoires de la Société Finno-ougrienne, no. 96. Helsinki: Suomalais-ugrilainen Seura, 1949. A meticulous typological study of five songs, the so-called *Sampo* epic, that constitute the epic kernel of the *Kalevala*. Applying primarily an analysis of style and using data on the history of colonization, the author establishes the mutual relations between these songs and their chronology.

———. *Suomen kirjallisuus, 1: Kirjoittamaton kirjallisuus* [Finnish Literature, 1, Unwritten Literature]. Helsinki: Suomalaisen Kirjallisuuden Seura and Otava, 1963. A broad survey of Finnish folklore, including the epic songs, presented against the Finno-Ugric and Baltic background.

———, Keith Bosley, and Michael Branch, eds. and trans. *Finnish Folk Poetry: Epic: An Anthology in Finnish and English*. Helsinki: Finnish Literature Society, 1977. Contains a large selection of Finnish and Karelian epic songs, many of them used by Lönnrot for the compilation of the *Kalevala*. Has a lengthy introduction and an extensive commentary. A work of prime importance.

Lönnrot, Elias. *The Old Kalevala and Certain Antecedents*. Prose translations with foreword and appendices by Francis Peabody Magoun, Jr. Cambridge, Mass.: Harvard University Press, 1969. Contains the prose translations of Elias Lönnrot's *Old Kalevala* (1835–36) and the "Proto-Kalevala" (1833), Reinhold von Becker's essay "On Väinämöinen" (1820), and Lönnrot's dissertation on Väinämöinen (1827), with commentaries.

Turunen, Aimo. *Kalevalan sanakirja* [Kalevala Dictionary]. Helsinki: Suomalaisen Kirjallisuuden Seura, 1949. A broadly devised dictionary of words and notions appearing in the *Kalevala*, which helps to understand the ancient way of life, beliefs, and customs as reflected in the epic. The work is being translated into English.

The Kalevipoeg

Text and Translations

Kreutzwald, Fr. R. (See Studies.)

Kirby, W. F. *The Hero of Esthonia and Other Studies in the Romantic Literature of That Country*. 2 vols. London: J. C. Nimmo, 1895. Vol. I contains the prose retelling of the *Kalevipoeg*, with fragments of the translations in verses.

Kalewipoeg. Aus dem Estnischen übertragen von F. Löwe. Edited by W. Reiman. Reval: F. Kluge, 1900. The best, though somewhat archaic, translation of the *Kalevipoeg* in German.

Studies

Anni(st), Aug. *F. R. Kreutzwaldi "Kalevipoeg"* [F. R. Kreutzwald's "Kalevipoeg"]. 3 vols. (E. V.) Tartu Ülikooli Toimetused, B, 32, 33, and 50. Tartu, 1934–44. A thorough study of all aspects of the *Kalevipoeg* by the great Estonian folklorist. Vol. I examines Kalevipoeg in Estonian folklore, vol. II, the compilation of the *Kalevipoeg*, and vol. III, the epic as a work of art.

Kreutzwald, Fr. R. *Kalevipoeg*. 2 vols. Tallinn: Eesti Riiklik Kirjastus, 1961–63. Vol. I contains the text critical edition of the *Kalevipoeg*, and vol. II, the detailed commentaries.

Laugaste, E., and E. Normann, eds. *Muistendid Kalevipojast* [Legends about Kalevipoeg]. Tallinn: Eesti Raamat, 1959. The complete collection of legends about Kalevipoeg, with commentaries.

Oinas, Felix J. "The Tragedy of Kalevipoeg and of the South Slavic Heroes." *Tractata Altaica: Denis Sinor sexagenario optime de rebus altaicis merito dedicata.* Edited by Walther Heissig et al., pp. 447–62. Wiesbaden: Otto Harrassowitz, 1976. Examines the similarities between Kalevipoeg's and the Yugoslav epic heroes' tragic falls, their causes and consequences.

14   The Epic Tradition among Turkic Peoples

Ilhan Başgöz

The studies and collections of the folklore of Turkic-speaking peoples done since 1840, when M. A. Castrén and V. Titov (a Finnish and a Russian philologist) wrote down the first specimens of the Turkish heroic poems, have unearthed the greatest epic tradition of the world.[1] Two million verses of the Kirghiz epic *Manas,* 65 Uzbek popular epics, 20,000 verses of a single Karakalpak epic, 34 episodes of the *Köroglu* epic collected in Turkey, Azerbaijan and Uzbekistan, and the great romantic epic repertoire which contains 100 plots in Turkey alone, are but a part of this gigantic tradition. The tradition is not unaffected by the rapid social and cultural changes of the twentieth century, which are everywhere putting an end to orally transmitted literature. Even among the Turks the era of the great epic singers seems to be ending. Saghimbai Orozbakov, from whom 250,000 verses of *Manas* were recorded, died in 1930. Another famous Kirghiz bard, Saiakbai Karalaev, was a very old man in 1963. Uzbek epic singer Ergash Jumanbulbul-ogli, whose great repertoire was recorded in the 1920s, may not be alive any more. The Karakalpak bard, the singer of the 20,000 verse *Kirk Kiz,* died in 1957, and the great *Köroglu* teller of Turkey, Sabit Müdami, passed away in 1968. The apprentices of the great singers, though not as accomplished as their masters, will of course keep the declining tradition alive for a while.

Žirmunskij points out the importance of studies of this living epic tradition: "From the theoretic point of view, we have here a key to the problem of the epic in general, since the ancient, medieval European, Indian and Iranian epopees have come down to us as reflected in written literary forms and adaptations, which can be understood from the point of view of their creation and propagation only through comparison with the living epic created and performed in the present, before our very eyes."[2]

From the anthropological point of view, we may add, the opportunity offered by this epic tradition is even greater. The Turkic–speaking peoples live in a vast geographic area which stretches from China to Romania and is under many forms of government.[3] They represent every level of social and economic development, including small clans, nomadic and semi-nomadic tribes, peasants, and all kinds of urban dwellers. Although the great majority of the Turks are Muslims, Christianity and even shamanism are also practiced by a very small percentage of the people. Interacting for at least a span of thirteen centuries with the major civilizations of Asia and the Middle East on this large cultural mosaic, the Turkic-speaking peoples evolved an epic tradition that has developed and survived to this day.

It is exciting both to folklorists and to cultural anthropologists to find, for example, the return episode of Odysseus in a small Altaic tribe of Central Asia as a heroic folktale, to follow its development into a full epic among the Uzbeks, to observe its incorporation into the *Grandfather Qorqut* epic (*Kitabi Dede Korkut*) in Anatolia, and then to see its transformation into a folktale again by non-professional narrators in Turkey.[4]

The extensive use and great love of improvised poetry in the social and private life of the Turks, the continuous state of fighting necessitated by the nomadic social pattern, and the existence of a heroic age have been proposed as reasons for the great Turkic epic tradition.[5] None of these hypotheses will satisfy us completely. We will perhaps never know why the same social and cultural conditions produce an epic poetry among some peoples but not among others. One of the significant elements, however, in the development of the epic tradition among the Turks seems to be the very early existence of the custom of singing eulogies in praise of an individual both during his life and after his death. A very important account of the usage of the laudatory songs, directly connected with the actual fighting, is given by several travelers and scholars: "Among the Turkmen it is the custom to sing war songs when entering into battle or when setting out on a foray ... when the two hostile armies are going to meet, before they engage in battle, they animate each other, and scoff at their opponents."[6]

It is interesting to note that the texts mentioned as early examples of the epic tradition among Turkic peoples (the Orkhon inscriptions and the poetry in *Divan-i Lugat-it Türk*) can also be considered as laments and eulogies. The idealization of an individual in panegyric and funeral songs plays an important part in the characterization of the hero in epic poetry. This feature of the poetry of the *Grandfather Qorqut* epic will be discussed below.

The observations of a Roman ambassador at a feast of the Huns (A.D. 453) about two singers who narrated the heroic fights of their chief Attila are presented by some scholars as the earliest evidence of the epic tradition among the Turkic peoples.[7] The evidence should be taken cautiously, because the Turkic origin of the Huns is still in doubt, although some Turkic tribes may have been part of the Hun federation.

The Orkhon inscriptions (eighth century A.D.), the earliest source of the Turkic languages, include some passages in rhythmical prose. These parts, which relate the battle scenes of Bilge Khan, are similar to the rhythmical prose of the Turkic epic tradition. Some scholars have used this similarity as the main argument for considering the Orkhon inscriptions as an early example of the epic tradition. Certain of the characteristics of the prose in that source, for example syntactical parallelism of sentences, alliterations, and some elements of traditional poetic imagery, are similar to the epic poetry of the Turks. However, the historical character of the Orkhon monument, which records an address of a khan to his people, prevents us from seeing the inscriptions as examples of an epic genre, although some stylistic features of epic narration are evident.

Divan-i Lugat-it Türk, written in 1073 by Mahmut al Kashgari, gives us the first examples of heroic poems, undoubtedly taken from oral sources. This dictionary of the Turkish language includes several independent stanzas of four lines. By grouping together several stanzas, scholars reconstructed longer songs that contain remarks on the history of the Oghuz Turks from the eighth to the eleventh centuries. The stanzas mention the names of epic heroes also known from other sources and describe their battles. Not the theme alone, but the formal nature of the poetry is very similar to the epic tradition of the Turkic peoples. We have, however, no evidence to substantiate the opinion that these songs were fragments of a large, true heroic epic.

Information obtained from remarks by historians and from short legends found in twelfth- and thirteenth-century sources supports the existence of a heroic epic tradition among the Turkic peoples.[8] Still, not a single complete text of an epic has come down to us from this era. Not until the fifteenth century do we find such an epic.

The Book of My Grandfather Qorqut

The oldest complete record of a heroic epic tradition of the Turkic-speaking peoples (the Oghuz Turks) is preserved and has come down to us in two manuscripts found in the Dresden and Vatican libraries.[9] The title of the Dresden manuscript is "The Book of My Grandfather Qorqut" (*Kitab-i Dedem Qorqut*). The Vatican manuscript has a slightly different title: "The Story of Oguzname—the Oghuz Epic—of Kazan Beg and the Others" (*Hikayet-i Oguzname-i Kazan Beg ve Gayri*). Both manuscripts were probably copied from the original which was composed and written in the second half of the fifteenth century by an unknown artist, perhaps an epic singer himself.[10] The epic stories given in the *Book of Grandfather Qorqut* apparently lived in the oral tradition and circulated in this form among the people long before the fifteenth century. In fact, starting from the thirteenth century, in the historical sources of Persians, Arabs, and Turks, references are made to some plots of the *Grandfather Qorqut* epic.[11] A great artist unknown to us must have collected, edited, and written down these oral versions, using his artistic talent and individual creativity to give them a new form. Thus the original manuscript of *Grandfather Qorqut* is composed in the same way as other great epics of the world. The Dresden manuscript contains twelve epic stories, eight of which are found verbatim in the Vatican version.

Grandfather Qorqut is presented at the end of the epic stories as a bard, an epic singer-teller or *ozan,* who composes the epic and sings and narrates it with the accompaniment of his *kopuz,* a stringed instrument, in the presence of Oghuz khans and beys. He is also the wise man and the sorcerer-magician of the Oghuz people, and functions in these capacities in other public rituals, such as in the giving of a name to a boy and in the preparation of marriages. Sources other than the manuscript reveal that Grandfather Qorqut is known by other Turkic-speaking peoples and has a more complex image. He combines in his personality the characteristics of a mythical ancestor (the eponym of the Turks), of a shaman-sorcerer of the pre-Islamic era, of a political counselor of the rulers, and of a Muslim saint. Thus the bard-sorcerer of the *Grandfather Qorqut* epic embodies the traces of several layers of the social and cultural background of the Turkic peoples from the pagan era to the Islamic period of the fifteenth century.

Of the twelve epic stories in the manuscript, eight are the narration of the heroic deeds of the Muslim Oghuz Turks in their fights against the Christians (unbelievers in the epic) of the Byzantine state of Trebizond, the Georgians, and the Kipchak. Although the struggle is between Muslims and unbelievers, the actual fights are never religiously motivated. They are undertaken in order to rescue one of the khans of the Oghuz tribes or a member of his family who has been taken prisoner. Bugach Khan fights with the enemy to save his father (story no. 1). Salur Kazan goes to battle with the unbelievers to rescue his mother, wife, and son (story no. 2). The mother saves the life of her husband and her son following a heroic fight (story no. 4). A small boy grows, fights with the unbelievers and rescues his father who has spent sixteen years in a dungeon (story no. 7). The plots of "The Story of Emrem" (no. 9) and "The Story of the Captivity of Salur Kazan" (no. 11) are the same, except that the lengths of the fathers' captivities vary.

This characteristic of the heroic fight waged to save a member of a tribal ruling family supplies further evidence for the theory of the creation of the epic proposed by W. Wünsch: "An element necessary for the creation and development of true epics is the uniting of a group with close blood ties for common defense; the enemy may be the nobility, a foreign conqueror or some supernatural being."[12]

The remaining epic stories of *Grandfather Qorqut* contain different themes, although heroic action is still the dominant feature of the plots. The fight of the young Oghuz warrior Kan Turali with a bull, a camel, and a lion to win the hand of a Christian girl is the theme of "The Story of Kan Turali." "The Story of Basat Who Kills the One-Eyed Giant" relates a legend similar to the story of the Cyclops in the Homeric epic. The Oghuz bey Basat, who is reared on the milk of a lion, kills the one-eyed giant Depegöz, who was born from the union of a shepherd and a fairy girl. In *Bamsi Beyrek,* the mixture of a romance and heroic story, a Christian girl falls in love with the Oghuz bey Bamsi Beyrek and rescues him from her father's prison. The fight between the Angel of Death Azrail and the young Oghuz warrior Deli Dumrul is related in

"The Story of Deli Dumrul." The last story of the manuscript describes an internal struggle between two factions of the Oghuz tribes, Ich-oghuz and Tish-oghuz, during which Bamsi Beyrek is killed.

The epic stories of *Grandfather Qorqut* are in prose and narrated in the third person. The prose contains various characteristics of oral epics, such as the traditional formulas, syntactical parallelism of the sentences, repeated images and symbols in each story, and formulaic narration throughout the epic lays, with the repeated formulas especially in the beginning and at the end of each story. The extensive usage of formulas in a prose epic makes it quite necessary to reevaluate the oral formula theory, which considers metrics and music as indivisible parts of formula pattern. Each story begins with a conventional formula that consists either of the characterization of a khan of khans by an extended epithet or of the description of his solemn feast by formulaic expressions. "The Story of the Sack of the House of Salur Kazan," for example, begins with the following epithet: "One day the son of Ulash, the young of the feathering bird, the hope of the poor, the lion of Emet stream, the tiger of Karachuk mountain, the owner of the chestnut-brown horse, the father of Khan Uruz, the son-in-law of Bayindir Khan, the pride of . . . the Oghuz people, the support of young warriors in distress, Salur Kazan roused himself."[13] Such extended epithets, also found in other Turkic epics, have various functions. They characterize the hero, repeat the account of his heroic adventure in micro-form, help the narrator remember the story, and also express the community's concept of heroism.

The epic narration usually ends with the intervention of Grandfather Qorqut. The ending of "The Story of Kan Turali" is typical: "Kan Turali entered his nuptial tent and had his wish fulfilled. Grandfather Qorqut came, played the tune of happiness on his *kopuz*, sang a eulogy, composed the epic story and narrated the adventures of Muslim warriors." After reciting a short poem, he ends with the following prayer which is found in each story: "When death comes, may you not be without your faith. May Allah never make you beholden to the mean. May you never lose the hope given you by Allah. . . . May he save you and forgive your sins, my khan."

When the emotion runs high, the dominant prose narrative of the epic shifts to a rudimentary poetry that can hardly be differentiated from rhythmic prose. Such parts are incorporated into the prose by the formula "Let us see what *soylama* he sang here." The word *soylama*, which is used for song, means to sing a eulogy in praise of an ancestor or of the hero himself. The accompaniment with a kopuz is also mentioned before beginning the song and helps us to recognize the verse part.

The verse section is not stanzaic and has no final rhyme. However, it uses an equal number of syllables in each line, mainly 8, 11, and 9, divided with a caesura as $4 + 4$; $4 + 4 + 3$; or $4 + 1 + 4$. Thematically these poetic sections are almost all panegyrics and laments. The hero sings them in the first person in praise of the father, mother, wife, husband, and son. Self-praise before meeting an enemy, or praise of a horse, a musical instrument, or various scenes from nature also occur. The verses are often formulaic and are repeated in several stories by different characters.

Two strata of historical events can be recognized in the background of the *Grandfather Qorqut* epic. The first stems from the eighth to the tenth centuries, when the Oghuz Turks lived in their original homeland on the banks of Syr-Darya River in Central Asia, and consists of the narration of their struggle with the Kipchaks and the Pechenegs. The memories of the social life of the Oghuz of that period were brought to Anatolia when the Oghuz moved westward (beginning in the tenth century). These were clustered around the name of Kazan Khan of the Salur tribe.

The second layer contains the life and struggle of the Oghuz tribes in their new land and includes their fights with Georgians, the Kipchaks, and especially with the Greeks of the Trebizond Byzantine state. The characteristics of the heroic actions, the names of some heroes, and the geographical background of the epic can be attributed especially to the thirteenth century, when Oghuz tribes were united under the Akkoyunlu dynasty and formed a mighty state. The Akkoyunlu empire occupied Eastern Anatolia, southern Caucasia, and the west and southwest of Iran. Many of the geographical names mentioned in the *Grandfather Qorqut* epic are to be found in this area. V. Žirmunskij is of the opinion that "The Story of the Sack of the House of Salur Kazan," "The Story of Basat Who Killed Depegöz," and "The Story of Bamsi Beyrek" are connected with the first historical stratum. "The Story of Deli Dumrul" and "The Story of Kan Turali" belong to the second historical layer.[14] In fact, the name of Kan Turali was mentioned in Byzantine sources as one of the Akkoyunlu Turkmen emirs who attacked Trebizond in 1384.[15]

The *Grandfather Qorqut* epic includes the Turkic themes and motifs that reflect the social life, the ethical and religious concepts of the Oghuz Turks, their social and economic institutions, and struggles with their neighbors. On the other hand, this epic also makes use of the international folklore stock. Thus, the theme of Bamsi Beyrek is that of the return of Odysseus, the story of Basat reiterates the killing of Cyclops, and the story of Deli Dumrul is based on the theme of a fight with the Angel of Death, a theme found in the Byzantine epic poem *Digenis Akritas,* and in the work of Euripides, *Alcestis.*[16]

Köroglu (The Blindman's Son) Epic

In 1580 an imperial decree was issued in Istanbul by the Ottoman Sultan which ordered the governor of Bolu to arrest a bandit called Köroglu Rushen, who had kidnapped a boy.[17] There was also an *ashik* named Köroglu (in the seventeenth century) who left us some poems. The artist and bandit Köroglu may or may not be the same person. Nevertheless, around the name of this rather unimportant local bandit-minstrel one of the largest epic cycles of the Turkic-speaking peoples was created.[18] The *Köroglu* epic cycle is known among the Anatolian Turks, the Azeri, the Turkmen, the Uzbeks, the Kazakhs, and the Karakalpaks. It is also told among non-Turkic peoples such as the Tajiks, the Kurds, the Armenians, and the Arabs of Central Asia.

In the Anatolian versions and in the majority of the Azeri narrations, Köroglu, the hero of the epic, is depicted as a social bandit and a benevolent outlaw. Like Robin Hood, he revolts against the injustice of society. He lives in the mountain forest Chamlibel under his own law. His father, a horseman of the Shah of Iran, is blinded by the Shah, and Köroglu becomes an outlaw to revenge this act of tyranny.

Köroglu and his 365 brave men, who live in a primitive republic of ideal justice, are not the typical epic heroes of noble origins. They come from the modest families of farmers, blacksmiths, butchers, and coppersmiths. They fight against the representatives of the Ottoman states, the pashas, the beys, the governors, and the wealthy members of society, the merchants and the caravan owners. They, however, respect the sultan.

The general character of their fights was the same as the character of the so-called Jelali revolt in Ottoman history. For two hundred years, starting from the sixteenth century, Jelali bandits attacked the cities and plundered the wealth of the Ottoman aristocracy, posing from time to time a serious threat to the state due to the sympathetic support of the poor and the desperate masses. Köroglu and some of his brave men whose names are mentioned in the epic were historical figures who participated in Jelali revolts. Their participation in such an internal upheaval caused them to be looked upon as enforcers of social justice and protectors of the poor.

In his fight with the mighty, the epic hero Köroglu gets the greatest support from his horse Kyrat (Gray Horse). Born of a sea giant and made immortal by drinking the water of life, Kyrat can speak, never failing to advise the right course of action when Köroglu is in trouble, and can fly, covering great distances in a few seconds. "Köroglu's horse Kyrat, even more than its master, is the true hero of the cycle, coveted as it is by potentates and loved and admired by all. Köroglu hardly seems to have an existence apart from his horse, whom he loves as his own soul."[19] This legendary horse is a typical example of the extraordinary horses in the epics of the Turkic-speaking peoples. White Colt of the *Ai Margan* epic poem, Bozat (Gray Horse) of Bamsi Beyrek in *The Book of Grandfather Qorqut*, the horse Teke-Sarqil of the *Er Töshtük* epic, and Akkula (White Horse) of *Manas* all have similar superequine qualities and play the same important roles in the epic.

The *Köroglu* cycle assumes the characteristics of a true epic in Central Asia, especially among the Uzbeks and the Turkmen. There Köroglu is not a bandit anymore; he is the ruler of a Turkmen tribe, of noble descent and legendary birth. Born in the grave of a woman buried pregnant, he is called Guroglu (the son of the grave). He is the heroic defender of his kingdom and his people against the attacks of outside enemies, especially the Arabs. The childless bandit of Anatolian versions acquires a son and even a grandson in this new social milieu, and their adventures form a separate epic cycle. We find the heroic actions of the trilogy of the father, son, and grandson also in the epic cycle of *Manas*.

As a chief of a tribe and defender of the people, Köroglu reflects a different historical background in the Central Asiatic version. This background comprises the endless tribal strife between the Turkmen tribes and their revolts against the authority of the states. Pertev Boratav also sees in this version the seeds of a religious struggle, the Alevi-Sunni struggle between Turks and Iranians.[20]

The Köroglu epic is told as several independent plots called *kol* (arm) in Turkey and *dastan* (epic lay) in Central Asia. The number of kols, which have been recorded among the Turkic peoples, is thirty-four, some of which may be reconstructions of the same adventures attributed to different heroes.[21] Each of these kols relates the campaigns of Köroglu or one of his men. Though independent in action, the plots have some common elements. The action usually starts and ends in Chamlibel, the forest where Köroglu and his friend have set up their headquarters. Köroglu organizes the campaigns, selects the right men for their success and, in many kols, he himself goes to help his men when they are in real trouble.

The *Köroglu* epic is in prose interspersed with poetry. Prose is dominant in the Anatolian, Azeri, and Turkmen versions. However, in some Kazakh and Turkmen versions verse predominates. It is only among the Tajiks that the *Köroglu* epic is narrated entirely in verse form. An *ashik,* a professional teller-singer, narrates the epic while walking around among the audience, and sings the songs with the accompaniment of a stringed instrument—the *saz* in Turkey, the *dutar* and the *chungur* in Azerbaijan, and the *kopuz* among Turkmen.

The verse form is used when the emotion of the hero is high and cannot be described in prose. In such passages the teller gets the help of music and poetry, and the hero speaks in the first person through the mouth of the teller. The songs do not advance the narration of the events, but praise the girls, the heroes, and the horse, and express the love, joy, and desperation of the hero. Heroism is one of the dominant themes of the song of the *Köroglu* epic.

The poetry here is no longer the rudimentary poetry of the *Grandfather Qorqut* epic, but represents a later development of Turkic folk poetry created by the ashiks, the itinerant minstrels, after the fifteenth century. The main form of this poetry is called *koshma* in Turkey and usually consists of three, five, or seven stanzas of four lines with end rhymes *abcb, dddb,* and *eeeb.* It uses the typical metric system of Turkic folk poetry, which is based on the usage of an equal number of syllables in each line. The line consists usually of eight or eleven syllables with a caesura (4 + 4 or 6 + 5).

The songs in the *Köroglu* cycle change from teller to teller, from people to people. In new geographical and ethnic environments, new and different songs are incorporated into the epic. There are, however, a few songs that have been recorded from different Turkic peoples which have preserved the form of the Anatolian versions. Although various tale motifs and legendary and epic elements of ancient origin are incorporated into the *Köroglu* cycle, the epic as a whole originated not earlier than the sixteenth century. Historical sources tell us that the ashiks already narrated the *Köroglu* stories in the seventeenth century.

In all plots of the epic, Köroglu is presented not only as a hero or bandit-hero, but also as a bandit-minstrel who improvises and sings poems and plays a musical instrument. His artistic talent originates from a magical froth he drinks. The magical origin of his inspiration as a poet links the Köroglu tradition with the Turkish romances whose hero becomes an ashik by drinking a love potion in a dream. Because of this characteristic of his personality, hundreds of poems were attributed to Köroglu, and thus a great collection of poetry outside of the epic came into existence and was preserved both in manuscripts and in oral tradition. Several musical tunes are named after him and are still used by the minstrels as Köroglu tunes. A group of folk dances in Anatolia and Azerbaijan, some of them symbolizing Köroglu's heroic fights, are called today "Köroglu dances."[22]

The Manas Epic

The *Manas* epic of the Kirghiz takes its name from the central figure, Manas, the mighty general, the defender and the uniter of the Kirghiz tribes and the conqueror of the neighboring lands of the enemy. But he who combines the image of a great fighter and a wise sovereign is a legendary hero and has no historical counterpart.[23]

Č. Valixanov, a pioneer of the *Manas* studies, who collected some parts of the epic in 1856, gave the following description of it: "The Manas epic may be called the encyclopedia of the Kirghiz people who live among the inaccessible mountains of Central Asia. It is an encyclopedia which contains the tales, the mythology, the way of life of the Kirghiz and the history of their relations with neighbors, and expresses them clustered around the name of a single hero, Manas. It is the *Iliad* of the Kirghiz."[24] And W. Radloff, to whom we owe the most extensive recordings of the *Manas,* wrote: "The Manas epic not only embodies all forms of Kirghiz poetry including the lyric poems, but also encompasses all prose narratives of the Kirghiz people."[25]

The *Manas* epic, of which two million verses have been collected, dominates the folklore of the Kirghiz people. Even though a bard also sings and narrates other folklore forms, he is called *Manasci,* the *Manas* singer. Two kinds of *Manasci* are known: the *Chon Manasci,* the great creative artist, and *Chala Manasci,* the ordinary singer with a small repertoire. The Chon Manasci is the active tradition bearer and can sing the whole trilogy, i.e., the *Manas* cycle, the cycle of his son Semetey and his grandson Seytek. His narration may last for six months. The Chon Manascis are few in number; they improvise and create new plots within the traditional frame. The adventures of the great-grandsons of Manas, which are incorporated into the *Manas* cycle, and the new versions of the epic relating the heroes of the Soviet period evidently originate from such creative singers.[26]

Popular imagination makes great singers legendary heroes themselves by attributing magical origins to their talent and extraordinary power to their singing. For example, when the Chon Manasci Keldibek (born probably in 1750) sang the epic, the listeners could hear the hoof beats of a galloping horse and could feel the tent shake; the shepherd would leave his flock to listen, but the wolf would not touch the animals.[27] The great *Manas* singers receive their vocation in a dream in which they usually see Manas call upon them to take up the profession. The dream, similar to that of the ashiks, is reminiscent of and connected with the initiatory dreams of the Turkish shaman.[28] Because of the origin of their profession, the *Manas* singers are considered magicians, healers, and sometimes shamans. For this reason they are called to sing the *Manas* epic to avoid a natural disaster, to heal animals, and even to cure human illnesses.

The Manasci may or may not accompany his singing with a musical instrument. If he does, he uses a kopuz or *kiyak,* a stringed instrument. According to Radloff, "the minstrel invariably employs two melodies, one executed in quick tempo, for the course of the action, the other in slow tempo and as a solemn recitative for the speeches."[29] If he does not use a musical instrument, he achieves a dramatic representation in his performance by the extensive use of gestures and mimicry.

Although a few lines of explanatory prose may be used here and there, as in the presentation of the genealogy and the birth of Manas in one version,[30] the entire epic is in verse. Three- or four-line stanzas are occasionally found in the epic. The poetry as a whole, however, is not stanzaic. The meter is based on the number of syllables, seven or eight, in a line with a caesura (4 + 3 or 4 + 4). End rhyme is not obligatory, though it is often encountered. Internal and initial rhyme, syntactic parallelism, and alliteration are the important elements of the prosody.

Even in a very condensed form, the plots of this grandiose epic cycle, which consists of the heroic exploits of three generations, are impossible to summarize within the limits of an essay. I will give an idea of the most important plots of the *Manas* cycle, skipping entirely the adventures of Semetey and Seytek.

Some plots of the epic take Manas' biography as their subject and deal with his birth, marriage, and death. Manas is born from the marriage of Jakub Khan and Chyrysy when they are over forty, after fourteen childless years of marriage. Following the prayer of the father and the dream of the mother, in which she eats a magical apple, Manas is conceived. He is born with a clot of blood in his hand, the symbol of "the ruthless quest of power,"[31] and with an erection, the symbol of virility. He is very strong and fearless because his mother ate the heart of a tiger when she was pregnant. He speaks as soon as he is born, declares his campaigns, and attacks the Kalmuks when he is nine years old. With the victory over, the Kalmuks start the great campaigns of Manas.

His father finds Kanikey, the daughter of Temir Khan of Tajik, suitable for his son to marry and gets her father's agreement by paying a high bride price. However, the opposition of the Khan's vizier, the blue-bearded Mendibay, introduces intrigue and paves the way for conflict and fighting. Following the death and the resurrection of the hero, in Radloff's version, Kanikey becomes Manas' wife. She represents the image of an affectionate mother, of a wise spouse who advises her husband on important matters, and of a great fighter who rules and defends the kingdom in the absence of her husband.[32]

Manas is an invincible hero. His invulnerability partially derives from his armor, his sword, his spear, and, in some variants, his rifle. The blow which causes his death is inflicted upon him at the time when Manas has taken off his armor to perform a *namaz,* a Muslim ritual. This takes place at the end of the Great Campaign, Manas' attack on Bechin or Pechin (China). Konurbay, the chief enemy of Manas, ambushes him with a poisoned weapon. A grave in the Talas Valley, which is accepted as the burial place of Manas, is still a center of veneration by the people.

Life in peace time, various entertainments, contests and festivals of birth, marriage, and death constitute the social background for some plots of the *Manas* epic. Although such activities take place at the beginning or end of several episodes, one of them, "The Funeral of Koketey," becomes an independent plot. All Kirghiz and federated Turkic tribes, as well as the Kalmuks and the Chinese, are invited to the funeral. The victory of the Kirghiz in all contests causes the vengeful attacks of the Kalmuks and the Chinese, and great fighting erupts. Žirmunskij is of the opinion that this marks the beginning of the political expansion and the internal conflicts which are the topics of other campaigns of Manas.[33]

A typical example of the internal conflict with relatives and with vassal khans is given in the episode about Kos Koman. He is Manas' uncle, who had been captured by the Kalmuks as a child, grew up among them, got married, and accepted their way of life. Following the advice of Manas' friend Al-mambet, he returns to his land together with his four sons, who have also become Kalmuks. During the Great Campaign, he and his sons participate in a plot against Manas' life. After the death of Manas, the eldest son of Kos Koman rules Manas' family and wants to marry Kanikey.

The campaigns of Manas against the Kalmuks, the Chinese, and some other tribes are the contents of some long plots in the epic. The Great Campaign alone contains 28,000 verses. These campaigns are launched to obtain the independence of the Kirghiz tribes, to unite them in a strong tribal federation, and to recapture Issyk-kul, the homeland of the Kirghiz. The religious motivation in some campaigns is also apparent; however, this must be a recent incorporation into the epic.[34]

The Great Campaign against Bechin, undertaken against Kalmuks who are imagined as living in China, is a plot typical of this more recent development. It relates the conversion of Almambet, the son of a Kalmuk khan, to Islam and his travel to the land of Er Kökchö to find refuge. Following the intrigues of the jealous commanders of Er Kökchö, who accuse Almambet of having relations with Er Kökchö's wife, he joins Manas, receives a very warm welcome, and becomes one of the most trusted men of the Manas' camp.

The analysis of the historical background of the epic *Manas* poses the same difficulties as that of other epics. The remnants and the memories of almost thirteen centuries of Kirghiz history overlap and form a complex of events that is difficult to separate into its component parts. A. N. Bernston's early theory, which identifies Manas as the Kirghiz commander who died in 847 during a battle against the Uighur, and sees in the Great Campaign the traces of the Uighur-Kirghiz war of the ninth century, is refuted by Žirmunskij in a careful analysis. Žirmunskij poses the following opinion: "We have every reason to believe that the ninth to tenth century struggle of the Kirghiz against the Chinese and the Uighur is transformed into the epopee. Yet the following centuries of struggle of the Kirghiz people erased from the epic tradition almost all memory of this most ancient period of Kirghiz history. As a result of changes in the historical situation, the Kalmuks appear as the enemy of the Kirghiz in *Manas*."[35]

The Oirat Kalmuks formed a powerful state following the collapse of the Mongol Empire of Genghis Khan and occupied Issyk-kul and Tyanshan, the land of the Kirghiz. This heathen Kalmuk state, which existed for 300 years from the fifteenth to the eighteenth centuries, when it was destroyed by the Chinese in 1758, was considered the most dangerous enemy of the Kirghiz and other Muslim Turkic tribes. The Kirghiz, who were subject to Kalmuk rule, revolted against them from time to time and gained control of Western Turkestan in 1514 and Eastern Turkestan in 1558. The Kazakh and Nogai tribes were the allies of the Kirghiz and, as a part of the tribal union controlled by them, participated in several battles against the Kalmuks.

These Kirghiz-Kalmuk struggles form the historical background of the *Manas* epic. The names of some heroes in the epic are found among the historical figures of the Kirghiz, the Kazakh and the Nogai tribal chiefs of that era. The main hero of the epic, Manas, was one of the Sari Nogai (Yellow Nogai) tribal chiefs.[36] The historical and imaginary figures in the epic are supplemented by legendary and mythical characters. They originated from the heroic tales and mythology of the Turkic-speaking peoples. Manas himself with his superhuman features, the gigantic Joloy, who is Manas' Kalmuk enemy, and the one-eyed giant represent such figures in the epic.

Several important elements of the *Manas* epic are found among the epics of the other Turkic peoples, and are also connected with the common epic repertoire of the Central Asiatic peoples, Turks, and others. "Such common features of the heroic epic include the role of the *bogatyr* [hero] as the

defender of his homeland against foreign aggressors, the miraculous birth of
the hero, his gigantic stature and early feats, the plot of heroic matchmaking,
the image of the warrior-maiden, the role of the bogatyr's horse, the magic
invulnerability of the hero, typical scenes of duels between bogatyrs and of
mass battles, and the depiction of hostile bogatyr-giants."[37]

Other Epics

The epic repertoire of the Turkic peoples contains, besides the great traditions mentioned above, a considerable number of lesser known and smaller
epics. I will limit myself to the presentation of a representative selection of
them.

The *Er Töshtük* epic is considered a part of the *Manas* cycle, because "Er
Töshtuk" is mentioned in *Manas* as one of the commanders. However, in the
Er Töshtük epic no reference is made to Manas, and it has all the characteristics of an independent heroic poetry tradition. The Kirghiz version of the *Er
Töshtük* epic contains 12,316 verses, mainly of seven syllables (4 + 3),
recorded from Saiakbai Karalaev. The shorter Kazakh and Tatar versions are
in prose.[38]

The main plot of the *Er Töshtük* epic relates the hero's journey to the
underworld, which includes battles with several giants (among them the one-
eyed giant Yelmoguz), and his return to the upper world with the help of a
gigantic bird, Black Eagle. This international tale type (AT 301A, B) is
transformed into an epic by the incorporation of a realistic background from
the life of the Kirghiz and by the inclusion of a stratum which contains various
elements of Kirghiz oral literature.[39]

The epic *Alpamysh* (Alyp Bamysh) "is to be found over the entire territory
inhabited by the Turkic peoples—from the Altai across Central Asia to the
Volga and the Ural Mountains on the one hand, and to Transcaucasia and Asia
Minor on the other. At the same time, it is one of the oldest, perhaps even the
oldest, of the great epic tales of these peoples."[40] Variants of the epic have
been recorded in prose, in verse, and in a mixture of both from various Turkic
peoples.

The most ancient forms of the epic, which consist of a heroic tale with
dominant magical and mythological elements, have been collected from small
Altaic tribes. They go back to the seventh and eighth centuries. The massive
Turkish invasion of the Middle East and Asia Minor, which started in the
tenth century, carried the tradition to the west. It was included in the Oghuz
epic, *Grandfather Qorqut,* under the title "The Story of Bamsi Beyrek." The
most complete form, the Uzbek version, which contains 14,000 verses, must
have developed later, following the Uzbek-Kalmuk wars (from the sixteenth
to eighteenth centuries). This version consists of the epic narration of a love
theme. Alpamysh and Borchin, the children of two brothers, are betrothed in
the cradle. Following a quarrel between the parents, they are separated from
each other. The young boy Alpamysh has to win a hard contest (horse race,
archery, and wrestling) to marry Borchin. During a war with the Kalmuks

after the marriage, Alpamysh is taken prisoner and spends seven years in a dungeon. The daughter of the Kalmuk shah, who falls in love with him, rescues the hero. Alpamysh returns to his land when his wife is about to marry his rival.[41] The short versions of the epic that have become folktales were recorded in Turkey between 1930 and 1950.[42]

The epic *Edige*, recorded among Kazakhs, Karakalpaks, Nogais, Uzbeks, Crimean Tatars, and the Turkic tribes of Siberia, is a typical example of the epic tradition developed around the name of a well-known historical person. The last emir of the Golden Horde, the Emir Edige (d. 1419), participated in the historical events which involved Tokthamysh (d. 1406) and Tamerlane (1336–1405). The epic relates the supernatural birth of Edige and his childhood and early life as a poor shepherd. He meets one of the khans of Tokthamysh, secures his protection because of his great wisdom, and is accepted into his palace.

The epic tradition of historical figures also includes the epic of Tamerlane and the epic of Genghis Khan (1167–1227), the ruler of the Mongols, both transmitted in written form. The epic of *Chara Batyr*, which narrates the conquest of Kazan' in 1552 by the Russians, and the epic of *Adil Sultan*, the biographical story of Adil Giray Khan (1666–71) of Crimea, and some others, such as the epics of *Ayman Sholpan, Urak Batyr, Er Targyn, Ali Khan, Er Sayin,* and *Koblandy Batyr*, should also be mentioned as parts of the historical epic tradition.

The epic *Ai Margan and Ai Dolai*, the earliest epic chant, was recorded by western scholars from the isolated Altaic tribes which remained pagan.[43] This verse epic tells of the adventure of the aged ruler Altin Khan and the boy Ai Margan. Kuday Alp (celestial God), Kutay (the giant of the underworld), the magical White Colt, and the Swan Maiden are among the characters of the epic. It typifies the earliest stage of the epic tradition among the Turks in which the heroes possess supernatural qualities. For example, Ai Margan remains chained to a rock for seven years; his fight continues on the sea of fire and under seventeen layers of the earth. White Colt can transform himself into a girl, a fish, and a duck. Thirty girls may become a single individual.

In this early magical stage should be included some other epic poems in which the mythological and magical elements play an equally important role. Such are *Ak Kobok*,[44] *Kadysh Margan*, and *Kara Kokol*, all of which have been recorded from small Siberian Turkic tribes.

The epic *Forty Maidens (Kirg Kiz)*, discovered among Karakalpaks during World War II, comprises 20,000 verses. Gul-Aim and her thirty-nine friends are all warrior-maidens who fight to liberate their land from the occupation of the Kalmuk khan and of Nadir Shah (1736–47), the ruler of Iran.

Tradition of Muslim Epic Among Turks

The Arab-Byzantine war of the eighth century, which was fought against Christians and thus received the character of a "holy war," produced a series of legends around the name of an Arab commander, Abd-Allah al-Battal, who probably died in 740 on the battlefield. After the ninth century, the legends became an epic-novel called *Delhamma* among Arabs.

The Turkish *Battalname,* the epic book of Battal, must have originated from the legends which arose around the name of this Arab commander, and which have circulated in Turkey since the thirteenth century. The earliest version of the Turkish Battal epic-novel is in prose, but it was versified later several times. *Battalname* bears no similarity to the Turkish epic tradition as exemplified in the *Book of My Grandfather Qorqut.* The dominant religious theme and the hero who achieves heroic feats by means of magic as well as by his physical and mental capabilities are the basic features which distinguish it from the Turkic tradition, if formal characteristics are not considered. The Turkish *Battalname* relates fights between the Christians and the Muslims in the twelfth century around Miletene (Malatya), a central Anatolian city. The same fights and epic tradition about them constitute the basis of another epic-novel, *Danishmendname,* created in Turkey by the Turks around the name of Emir Danishmend (d. 1104), the founder of Danishmend Emirate. Both epic-novels emerged and survived in written form. They were not narrated by a bard, but were read to a religiously oriented audience.[45]

Romance Tradition *(Hikaye)*

The transformation of tribal society into a feudal state brought about important changes in the life and literary tastes of the tribal aristocracy. With the sedentarization of nomads, the Turkish khans, who lived in tents and spent much time on horseback, started to enjoy the material comfort of palaces and courts. The cultural tradition of the court, unknown to the Turks, was imported from Iran. The images of superhuman fighters and of maiden-warriors did not fit the lofty atmosphere of palaces. They were replaced, starting in the fifteenth century, by the figures of cupbearers and romantic lovers who appear in Iranian literary forms.

The first Turkish literary romances *(masnawi)* emerged to satisfy the literary demand of this social milieu. Ali Shir Nevai (1441–1501) firmly established the tradition by writing *Hamse* (Five Romances) in verse. His model was the work of the great Iranian poet Nizami (1152–1205?). The following generations of Ottoman poets continued to develop the romance genre, and Fuzuli (sixteenth century) and Seyh Galip (eighteenth century) created the most lyrical poetry of romance in Ottoman classical literature.

The influence of the literary romance tradition and the impact of court poetry were soon accepted by the oral poets as the highest literary models of their time. The expansion of Islam through education and the popularity of mystical poetry facilitated the contact of the masses with the court literature. The bard who was the epic singer, the magician, and the wise man of the tribal society felt the changing mood of the social environment and responded by assuming the new name, ashik (lover). He combined his oral tradition with the new literary movement and thus achieved a new synthesis. He replaced his kopuz with a more developed musical instrument and began to sing different songs. The poetry created by the ashik on the one hand, which is very different from epic poetry, and the hikaye on the other, are products of this synthesis. It is the ashik, the professional minstrel, who composed, developed, and transmitted the hikaye, probably starting from the end of the sixteenth century.

The form of the hikaye as popular romance is a mixture of prose and poetry. In contrast to the epic, the poetry never becomes dominant in the hikaye, but is interspersed here and there without contributing to the development of the plot. The prose contains the basic characteristics of oral narration with the conventional formulas in the beginning and at the end of the hikaye. Such narrative devices are also used to indicate the shift to poetry, to describe the beauty of women, battle scenes, nature, the onset of dawn and dusk, and long journeys. They do not function, as in heroic poetry, to facilitate oral composition. The formulas function as stylistic devices for the purpose of "decorating" the prose with previously tested and socially accepted and appreciated literary and conventional devices. The teller uses them also to encourage interaction with the audience and to project his own opinions and feelings into the performance. During his career, each ashik may create his own repertoire of formulas or just repeat what he has learned from the tradition. However, we find formulas which are used by a school of artists and some which occur cross-culturally in the Middle East. Some of the formulas may have a long history. In the 1940s we recorded formulas from oral tradition in Turkey that were used in the *Grandfather Qorqut* epic of the sixteenth century.

The poetry of the hikaye is the typical poetry of the ashik, known under the name koshma (see above). In a few hikaye borrowed from classical repertoire, like *Ferhad and Shirin* and *Tahir and Zühre*, however, a different form, *mâni*, is used instead of koshma. It consists of an independent stanza of four lines of seven or eight syllables (4 + 3 or 4 + 4) with the end rhyme *aaba*.

Generally the poems are sung by the same ashik who narrates the hikaye, while walking around in the middle of his audience. He carries a musical instrument hanging on his neck and uses it when the prose narration shifts to poetry. We recorded hikaye in Eastern Anatolia, however, from a teller who could not play the saz. In such cases, he gets help from an instrumentalist who accompanies his songs, or takes a stick in his hand, pretends to play the saz, and sings without the accompaniment of the instrument. In Iranian Azerbaijan, the teller is joined by a band of three musicians who stay next to him during his narration and provide music when he starts singing. Although the poetry is sung by a single ashik, it may take the form of a dialogue or sometimes trio through the participation of one or more persons from the audience. In such instances, the ashik plays the music, sings the first stanza, and the others sing the following stanzas, alternating with the ashik.

The dominant theme of the hikaye is passionate, romantic love. The love originates from a dream, in which the hero sees a girl, falls in love with her and drinks a love potion—*ashk badesi* or *dolusu*—from the hand of a holy person. The dream, in which some mystical elements are found, reminds us of the initiation ceremony of the Turkish shaman and marks not only the beginning of love but also the beginning of the vocation as an artist, singer, and poet. The hero will spend his entire life searching for the beauty he has fallen in love with in his dream. The hikaye ends with the marriage of the lover and the beloved. A tragic ending is rare.

The poetry in the hikaye is the direct speech of the hero (in first person) and is used to express moving emotion. Although the theme of this poetry is primarily love, it can also be the sorrow of separation, the joy of union, or the praise of nature or the horse. Heroism is a favorite theme of the poems of fighting heroes, and panegyric and lament are also often employed.

The composition or creation of a hikaye is done in two ways: (a) An ashik writes the poetry and composes the prose section of the hikaye. He is in this case the author-composer of the whole romance. Ashik Shenlik (d. 1913), for example, is the individual creator of three hikaye: *Salman Bey, Sevdakâr,* and *Latif Shah,* which deal with imaginary figures created by him. (b) An ashik can develop his own biography into a hikaye by interspersing it with his own poetry. We were able to investigate this process in the lives of Ashik Ali Izzet and Ashik Talibi. Although these works have not yet assumed a complete traditional form, they are useful for demonstrating how the stories about the lives of ashiks came into being.

In either case, when the teller-singers begin to narrate the individual creation of an ashik, both the prose and poetry sections undergo changes due to oral transmission. The poems may be replaced by different ones; some of them may be dropped or others may be added. Thus their number may increase or decrease. New motifs, themes, and episodes may likewise be added or dropped. It may be told in greater or lesser detail, depending upon the wishes of the audience.[46]

In the creation of a hikaye, the ashik uses several sources of inspiration. The plot of the hikaye of *Gül and Ali Shir* composed by Ashik Sabit Müdami in 1944 is an episode from the life of Ali Shir Nevai, a poet and statesman of the fifteenth century. A folktale may be transformed into a hikaye by the incorporation of poetry. A simple marriage festival in the small Eastern Anatolian village of Karalar, which ended with the killing of the groom, was the basis of the hikaye called *Ummani* composed by Ashik Mehmet of Sosgert. Similar plots of the Köroglu kols are used in the creation of a series of hikaye such as *Celali Bey and Mehmet Bey, Kirmanshah, Eshef Bey* and some others. Heroic themes are dominant in such hikaye. The popularization of classical masnawi like *Tahir and Zühre, Asuman and Zeycan,* and *Ferhad and Shirin* are also included in the hikaye repertoire.

The social background of the hikaye and its main characters are often drawn from feudal society. The society in the hikaye includes various social classes—the rulers, the merchants, the clergy, and the poor. The conflict is not between the hero and an outside or supernatural common enemy, but between characters of a humble or poor origin and the aristocracy of the feudal society, the beys, the pashas, rich merchants, and powerful hodjas.

A typical example of this conflict is given in the hikaye of *Ashik Garip and Shah Sanem*. Resul, the young son of a rich merchant in Tabriz, loses his father and wastes his great wealth. The family becomes poor, and Resul tries to find a job. However, as a spoiled boy of a rich family he does not have success in any of the trades he enters. Finally, on a holy evening, he prays to God in despair and hopelessness and asks for his help in finding a profession. In a dream that night, he sees Shah Sanem, the daughter of a rich merchant in Tiflis, and drinks a love potion (*ashk badesi*) from the hand of a *pir* (a holy figure of mystical orders). The next morning he gets up as a new person, a lover and a God-inspired ashik (*Hak Ashigi*) who can compose beautiful poems and sing them on his saz. He adopts a pseudonym, Ashik Garip.

He searches for the girl, and after having overcome several difficulties, finds her in Tiflis. But the father of the girl refuses the demand of marriage to a poor ashik, who cannot pay a large amount for the bride. Ashik Garip leaves Tiflis and stays in Aleppo for seven years, singing in a coffeehouse first, and then in the palace of the pasha of Aleppo as his court poet. He earns enough money and decides to return to Tiflis because his beloved is about to marry someone else. Following another version of the return of Odysseus theme, Ashik Garip arrives at Tiflis on the wedding night and is recognized by Shah Sanem from the way he sings and plays. The story ends with their marriage.

Except for the supernatural help of Hizir, who carries Ashik Garip from Aleppo to Tiflis in a few seconds, the whole adventure contains the realistic traits of a novel and includes eighteen poems interspersed with the prose narration. There is reason to believe that Ashik Garip was a real ashik who lived at the end of the sixteenth century in the geographical locations described in the hikaye.

The hikaye tradition of the Turkic-speaking peoples is as extensive as that of the epic. The collection made only in Turkey exceeds 100 plots which are preserved in various official and individual archives.[47] The repertoire includes the following biographical hikaye of ashiks: *Ashik Garip and Shah Sanem, Ashik Kerem and Asli, Ashik Abbas of Tufargan, Ashik Kurbani and Perizat, Ashik Summani and Gülperi, Ashik Minhaci, Ashik Emrah and Selvihan,* and *Karaca Oglan*. Most of these romances are known in Azerbaijan in Iran and in Soviet Azerbaijan.

The hikaye taken from classical repertoire and known in Turkey, Azerbaijan, Turkmenistan, and Uzbekistan are the following: *Asuman and Zeycan, Tahir and Zuhre, Yusuf and Zuleiha, Leyla and Mejnun, Gül and Sitemkar,* and some others. Some examples of hikaye that have heroic-romantic plots are *Kuntogmysh, Shirin and Sheker, Rustam Khan* in Uzbekistan, and *Shah*

Ismail, Salman Bey, Latif Shah, Yarali Mahmut, Hurshit Bey, Cihan and Abdullah, Ahmet Khan, Mustafa Bey, and *Jelali Bey and Mehmet Bey* in Turkey.

Among Kazakhs, Uzbeks, and Turkmen the following hikaye (Uzbeks and Turkmen call them *dastar*) are part of the tradition: *Gul and Bilbil, Sayrat and Hamra, Sanauber, Muradhan, Arzigul, Kozi Korpos, Hurlugga and Hamra,* and *Yadgar.*[48]

The hikaye of the oral tradition have also been preserved in manuscript form. These are just short versions of the oral narrations written for a literate audience or used as an aid by the ashik in remembering at least the cadre of the hikaye. They were published in lithograph until the turn of the nineteenth century and as peddlers' books since then. The oral tradition, of course, loses its charm and attractiveness in books, though some devices from the oral sources have still been preserved. The published hikaye exert influence on the standing oral tradition or even become the source of a new oral narration. There are ashiks who have learned their hikaye, not from a master singer, but from a book. In this way the interrelation between the oral and written tradition of the hikaye is becoming more complex.

The hikaye tradition is still alive in Turkey, Azerbaijan, Iran, and Soviet Uzbekistan and Turkmenistan.[49] Although this tradition does not produce great storytellers anymore, and the oral performances do not attract sizable crowds, the popularity of the hikaye continues in Turkey and in Iranian Azerbaijan in cheap book form. A new generation of peasants, at least in Turkey, who learned to read and write following the adoption of the Latin alphabet, is the main market for such popular books. Hundreds of peddlers, traveling in remote villages, always add a bag of hikaye books to the loads of their donkeys and sell them for payment in kind, accepting almost anything—eggs, cheese, butter, wheat, and chicken.

The great circulation of these peddlers' books has made the Turkish government interested in the modernization of such books in order to propagate the principles of the Republic among peasants. A contest was held among writers to propagate the ideology of the regime through traditional hikaye. A few works were submitted, and the government published and distributed them in villages in 1928. The peasants, however, did not find these modern hikaye to their tastes and have continued to read the peddlers' versions.

NOTES

1. M. A. Castrén, *Versuch einer koibalischen und karagassischen Sprachlehre* (St. Petersburg: Buchdr. der Kaiserlichen Akademie der Wissenschaften, 1857), pp. 169–208.

2. V. M. Zhirmunsky, "On the Comparative Study of the Heroic Epic of the

Peoples of Central Asia," *Proceedings of the XXV International Congress of Orientalists*, III (Moscow: Izd. vostočnoj literatury, 1963), pp. 241–52.

3. Under "Turkic-speaking peoples" we include the Chinese Uigurs living in northwestern China, the Kazakhs, Kirghiz, Turkmen, Azeri, Uzbeks, Karakalpaks, Tatars, and other smaller ethnic groups living in Soviet Central Asia, the Azeri living in Iran, and the Turkmen living in Iraq in the Kerkuk region. We do not include the small Turkish minorities living in the Balkan countries, because the epic tradition did not survive among them.

4. For this development see V. Zhirmunsky, "The Epic of Alpamysh and the Return of Odysseus," *Proceedings of the British Academy* 53 (1966): 267–86.

5. See Nora K. Chadwick and V. Zhirmunsky, *Oral Epics of Central Asia* (Cambridge: Cambridge University Press, 1969), p. 27, and A. Vámbery, *Travels in Central Asia* (New York: Harper and Brothers, 1865), pp. 317–19.

6. Chadwick and Zhirmunsky, p. 74.

7. V. M. Žirmunskij and T. Zarifov, *Uzbekskij narodnyj geroičeskij èpos* (Moscow: Gos. izdatel'stvo xudožestvennoj literatury, 1947), p. 8.

8. For these sources see: W. Bang and Rahmeti Arat, *Oguz Kagan Destani* (Istanbul: Türkiyat Enstitüsü, 1936); Z. V. Togan, *Umumi Türk Tarihine Giriş* (Istanbul: Akgün Matbaasi, 1946), p. 210; and Pertev Boratav, "Dede Korkut Destanindaki Tarihi Olaylar," *Türkiyat Mecmuasi* 13 (1958): 31–62.

9. For the Dresden manuscript see H. L. Flesisher, *Catalogue Codicum Manuscriptorium Orientalum Bibliothecae Reigae Dresdenis* (Leipzig, 1931), 86; for the Vatican manuscript see Ettore Rossi, *Il "Kitab-i Dede Korkut": Racconti epic-cavalereschi dei Turchi Oguz* (The Vatican: Biblioteca Apostolica Vaticana, 1952).

10. See the Introduction of *The Book of Dede Korkut*, trans. Geoffrey Lewis (Harmondsworth, Middlesex, England: Penguin Books, 1974).

11. These sources can be found in the preface of *Dede Korkut Kitabi*, I, by Muharrem Ergin (Ankara: Türk Dil Kurumu Publication no. 169, 1958).

12. Quoted from W. Wünsch, *Heldensagen in Südost Europa*, p. 11, by Wolfram Eberhard, in *Minstrel Tales from Southeastern Turkey* (Berkeley and Los Angeles: University of California Press, 1955), p. 3.

13. *The Book of Dede Korkut*, trans. and ed. Faruk Sümer, Ahmet E. Uysal, and Warren S. Walker (Austin, Texas: University of Texas Press, 1972), p. 23.

14. V. M. Zhirmunsky, "Kitabi-i Dede Korkut je Oguz Destani Gelenegi," *T. T. K. Belleten* 25 (1961): 609–29.

15. E. Rossi, p. 32; A. Erzi, "Akkoyunlu ve Karakoyunlu Tarihi Hakkinda Araştirmalar," *T. T. K. Belleten* 18 (1954): 179–221.

16. For the latter parallel see Zhirmunsky, "Kitab-i Dede Korkut," p. 616.

17. Pertev Boratav, "Köroglu'nun Tarihi Shahsiyeti," *Türk Tarih Kongresi*, III (Ankara: Türk Tarih Kurumu publ., 1948), pp. 124–30.

18. Pertev Boratav sees the pre-existence of a blind man's son legend in Anatolia as the main reason for transforming the Köroglu bandit into the hero of an epic. Pertev Boratav, "Köroglu," *Islam Ansiklopedisi*, VI (Istanbul, 1951).

19. Chadwick and Zhirmunsky, p. 60.

20. Boratav, "Köroglu."

21. Ibid.

22. Ibid.

23. His name is derived from Alp Manash, the name of a Turkmen ruler found in the genealogy of Turkmen written by Ebulgazi Bahadur Khan. Žirmunskij attributes its origin to the sixth-eighth centuries A.D. See V. Žirmunskij, "Vvedenie v izučenie èposa 'Manas'," in *Kirgizskij geroičeskij èpos*, ed. M. I. Bogdanov, V. M. Žirmunskij, and A. A. Petrosjan (Moscow: Akademija nauk, 1961), pp. 85–196.

24. Č. Valixanov, *Sočinenija*, 29 (St. Petersburg, 1904), pp. 70–74.

25. W. Radloff [V. V. Radlov], *Proben der Volkslitteratur der türkischen Stämme*, V (St. Petersburg: Kaiserliche Akademie der Wissenschaften, 1885).

26. The contribution of each teller to the structure of the thirteen versions of the *Manas* epic is analyzed by B. Yunusaliev. See the introduction of *Manas*, bk. 1 (Frunze, 1958), p. xvi.

27. A. Inan, "Manas Destani Üzerine Notlar," *Türk Dili Araştirma Yilliği Belleten* (Ankara, 1959), p. 131.

28. For the origin and distribution of this dream see V. M. Žirmunskij, "Legenda o prizvanii pevca," in *Issledovanija po kul'ture narodov vostoka*, ed. V. V. Struve (Moscow: Akademija nauk, 1960), pp. 185–95; Ilhan Başgöz, "Dream Motif and Shamanistic Initiation," *Asian Folklore Studies* 1 (1967): 1–18.

29. Chadwick and Zhirmunsky, p. 221.

30. A. T. Hatto, "The Birth of Manas," *Asia Minor* 2 (1969): 219.

31. Ibid., p. 236.

32. In other versions of the epic, Manas has two and even four wives, the limit of Islamic law.

33. Žirmunskij, "Vvedenie v izučenie èposa 'Manas'," p. 112.

34. The appearance of Jehangir Hodja, who attacked Chinese Turkestan in 1822–28, is seen in one of the *Manas* versions. Ibid., p. 134.

35. Ibid., p. 143.

36. Sari Nogai was a close union of Kirghiz and Nogai tribes formed for the purpose of fighting against their common enemy, the Kalmuks.

37. Žirmunskij, "Vvedenie v izučenie èposa 'Manas'," p. 120.

38. An excellent French translation of *Er Toshtük* by Pertev N. Boratav, published in 1967, represents the only Kirghiz epic available in western languages in the full text.

39. For the analysis of this transformation, see Pertev Boratav, "L'épopée d'Er-Töštük et le conte populaire," in *Volksepen der uralischen und altaischen Völker*, ed. Wolfgang Veenker, Vorträge des Hamburger Symposions von 16.–17. Dez. 1965 (Wiesbaden: Otto Harrassowitz, 1968), pp. 75–86.

40. Chadwick and Zhirmunsky, p. 292.

41. For a comparative analysis of the return episode, see Zhirmunsky, "The Epic of Alpamysh and the Return of Odysseus."

42. Pertev Boratav, *Bey Böyrek Hikaysine ait Metinler* (Ankara, 1939), pp. 14–17.

43. Castrén, pp. 169–208; partial English translation by Norman Cohn, *The Gold Khan* (London: Secker and Warburg, 1946).

44. For a French summary of the epic poem, see Pertev Boratav, "L'Épopée et la Hikaye," *Philologiae Turcicae Fundamenta*, II (Wiesbaden, 1965), p. 19.

45. For further information see: Pertev Boratav, "Battal," *Islam Ansiklopedisi*, II; Irene Melikoff, *La Geste de Melik Danishmend* (Paris: Franz Steiner, Librarie D'Amerique et D'Orient, 1960), pp. 41–52.

46. For an analysis of this change see Ilhan Başgöz, "The Teller and His Audi-

ence," in *Folklore, Communication and Performance*, ed. Dan Ben-Amos and Kenneth Goldstein (The Hague: Mouton and Co., 1975), pp. 143–203.

47. They are located in the National Library of Ankara, collected by Ilhan Başgöz; in Pertev Boratav's private library, collected by him and his students; in the Institute of Literature of the Ankara University, collected by Muhan Bali; and in the Folklore Archives of the Turkic Peoples at Indiana University, Uralic and Altaic Studies Department, collected by Ilhan Başgöz. The romances collected from the Turks living in the Soviet Union are preserved in the archives of the Academy of Sciences of the Turkic Republics.

48. For the names of the hikaye collected or known in Turkey, refer to Boratav, *Halk Hikayeleri ve Halk Hikayeciligi* (Ankara: Milli Egitim Basimevi, 1946); in Azerbaijan Iran, Başgöz, "Turkish Hikaye Telling Tradition in Azerbaijan Iran," *Journal of American Folklore* 83 (1970): 390–415; in the Turkish republics of the USSR, Chadwick and Zhirmunsky, pp. 282–90.

49. In 1967 there was one coffeehouse in Kars and one in Erzurum, two eastern Anatolian cities in Turkey, in which the hikaye was being told on long winter evenings. Wolfram Eberhard made recordings of the hikaye from southeastern Anatolia in 1952 (*Minstrel Tales*). I attended hikaye narrations in two coffeehouses in Tabriz, one in Rezaiyeh, and one in Hoy in Azerbaijan Iran in 1967 ("Turkish Hikaye").

BIBLIOGRAPHY

General

Boratav, P. Naili. "L'Épopée et la Hikaye." In *Philologiae Turcicae Fundamenta*, II, pp. 11–44. Wiesbaden: F. Steiner, 1965. The article is part of an important contribution to Turkish folklore, entitled "La Littérature Oral" (pp. 1–146 in the same volume). It surveys all genres of Turkish folklore and includes the most complete bibliography of it.

Bowra, C. M. *Heroic Poetry*. London: Macmillan and Company, 1952. This classical work on heroic epics contains valuable analyses of various aspects of the heroic epics of the Turkic-speaking peoples.

Chadwick, Nora K., and Victor Zhirmunsky [Žirmunskij]. *Oral Epics of Central Asia*. Cambridge: Cambridge University Press, 1969. The most important study in English. The first ten chapters are written by N. Chadwick and are reprinted from her survey of Tatar epics, in *The Growth of Literature*, III (Cambridge: Cambridge University Press, 1940). Žirmunskij contributes the remaining three chapters. The bibliography is the best available, especially rich in publications from the USSR.

Čičerov, V. *Voprosy izučenija èposa narodov SSSR* [Questions on the Study of the Epics of the Peoples of the USSR]. Moscow: Sovetskij pisatel', 1958. A very informative study of the epics of the Turkic-speaking peoples, especially Uzbeks and Azerbaijanis, which includes contributions by V. M. Žirmunskij, A. K. Borovkov, T. Zarifov and M. Toxmasib.

Hatto, A. T. "Hamasa." In *The Encyclopedia of Islam*, III. Leiden: E. J. Brill, 1971. Short survey of the epics of the Turkic peoples in Central Asia, with a rich bibliography.

Radloff, W. [Radlov, V. V.]. *Proben der Volkslitteratur der türkischen Stämme*. 10 vols. St. Petersburg: Kaiserliche Akademie der Wissenschaften, 1866–1904. The earliest and most extensive collection of the folklore of the Turkic-speaking peoples. Vols. I–VI were translated into German by Radlov. Vol. VIII contains the material collected by I. Kunos, vol. IX by N. F. Katanov, and vol. X by V. Muškov.

Žirmunskij, V. M., and T. Zarifov. *Uzbekskij narodnyi geroičeskij èpos* [The Uzbek Heroic Folk Epic]. Moscow: Gosudarstvennoe izdatel'stvo xudožestvennoj literatury, 1947. A leading study of Uzbek epics which investigates epic repertoire, epics of historical content, romantic epics, the Köroglu cycle, epics of literary origin, and general characteristics of Uzbek epics.

Zhirmunsky [Žirmunskij], V. "On the Comparative Study of the Heroic Epic of the Peoples of Central Asia." In *Proceedings of the XXV International Congress of Orientalists*, III, pp. 241–52. Moscow: Izd. vostočnoj literatury, 1963.

Dede Qorqut Epic

Bartol'd [Barthold], V. V. *Kniga moego deda Korkuta* [The Book of My Grandfather Qorqut]. Moscow-Leningrad: Akademija nauk SSSR, 1962. A leading study which includes the Russian translation of the twelve Dede Qorqut stories and contributions by several Soviet scholars (V. V. Bartol'd, A. Jakubovskij, V. M. Žirmunskij).

The Book of Dede Korkut. Translated and with an introduction by Geoffrey Lewis. London: Penguin Books, 1974.

Boratav, P. Naili. "Ak-Köbök, Salur Kazan et Sosurga, un motif de l'épopée Oghuz et son rayonnement en Anatolie au Caucase et en Asie Centrale." *L'Homme* 3 (1963): 86–105. A comparative study of a short epic poem about Ak Köbök (White Froth) and its geographical distribution among Turkic and Caucasian peoples.

———. "Dede Korkut Hikayelerindeki Tarihi Olaylar ve Kitabyn Te'lif Tarihi" [The Historical Background of Dede Qorqut Epic and Its Time of Composition]. *Türkiyat Mecmuasi* 13 (1958): 32–62. The most comprehensive analysis of the historical background of *Dede Qorqut* epic.

———. "Korkut." *Islam Ansiklopedisi*, VI. Istanbul: Tevlet Basimevi, 1951. A brief up-to-date analysis of the legendary personality of Dede Qorqut.

Ergin, Muharrem. *Dede Korkut Kitabi: Giris, Metin, Faksimile* [The Book of Dede Qorqut: Introduction, Text, Facsimile]. 2 vols. Türk Dil Kurumu, 169. Ankara: Türk Tarih Kurumu Basimevi, 1968. Includes the facsimilies of the two manuscripts, Dresden and Vatican, and their transliteration into the modern Turkish alphabet. A bibliography and survey of previous work are given in the introduction. The second volume consists of the index and grammar of the language of the *Dede Qorqut* epic.

Gökyay, Orhan Saik. *Dede Korkut*. Istanbul: Arkadaş Matbaasi, 1938. The first publication of the Dresden manuscript in the modern Turkish alphabet. The introduction summarizes the previous studies on the epic and contains a useful bibliography.

Mundy, C. S. "Polyphemus and Tepegöz." *Bulletin of the School of Oriental and African Studies* 18 (1956): 279–302. A comparative study of Polyphemus of the Greek epic and the one-eyed giant, Tepegöz, of the *Book of Dede Qorqut*.

Rossi, Ettore. *Il Kitabi-i Dede Qorqut: Racconti epiccavalereschi dei Turchi Oguz*. The Vatican: Biblioteca Apostolica Vaticana, 1952. The facsimile and Italian translation of the eight epic stories of the Vatican manuscript, with a large introduction devoted to the discussion of the various problems of *Dede Qorqut*.

Ruben, Walter, "Zwölf Erzählungen des Dede Korkut." *Ozean der Märchenströme*, I: *Die zwölf Erzählungen des Dämons*. Folklore Fellows Communications, 133. Helsinki, 1964. An important cross-cultural comparative study of the themes and

motifs of *Dede Qorqut*, using especially Middle Eastern, Asian, and Hindu sources.
Sümer, Faruk, E. Ahmet Uysal, and S. Warren Walker. *The Book of Dede Korkut: A Turkish Epic*. Austin, Texas: University of Texas Press, 1972. The English translation of the *Kitab-i Dedem Qorqut* (the twelve epic stories of the Dresden manuscript).

Köroglu Epic

Alizada, H. *Köroglu*. Baku, 1941. Nine Koroglu episodes collected from Azerbaijan of the USSR between 1929 and 1940.
Ashyrov, N. *Gorogly*. Ashkhabad: Turmen Dovlet Neshir, 1958. Twelve Köroglu episodes collected among Turkmen.
Boratav, P. Naili. *Köroglu Destani* [The Köroglu Epic]. Istanbul: Evkaf Matbaasi, 1931. The earliest study of the *Köroglu* epic in Turkey which discusses the epic among the Turkic-speaking peoples and gives summaries of the main variants.
————. "Köroglu." In *Islam Ansiklopedisi*, VI. Istanbul: Devlet Matbaasi, 1951. Concise and up-to-date analysis of various Köroglu episodes and their historical background.
————. "Köroglu'nun Tarihi Şohsiyeti" [The Historical Personality of Köroglu]. In *Türk Tarih Kongresi*, pp. 124–30. Ankara: Türk Tarih Kurumu Basimevi, 1948. Discussion of the historical personality of Köroglu and the texts of the imperial firman, which order the arrest of Köroglu and his Jelali friends.
Chodzko, A. Borejko, intr. and transl. *Specimens of the Popular Poetry of Persia as Found in the Adventures and Improvisations of Kurroghlu*. London: Wh. Allen Co., 1842. The oldest text of the *Köroglu* epic, collected in Azerbaijan Iran in 1834. The prose section is in Persian, songs in Turkish.
Huluflu, V. *Köroglu*. Baku, 1927. Texts of seven Köroglu episodes, collected in Azerbaijan of the USSR.
Karryev, B. A. *Ker-ogly: Èpičeskie skazanija tjurko-jazyčnyx narodov* [Köroglu: Epic Legends among Turkic-Speaking Peoples]. Moscow: Izd. vostočnoj literatury, 1968. A very important contribution to the study of the *Köroglu* epic, containing a discussion of its origin and development and of its versions among various Turkic-speaking peoples.
Takhmasib, M. *Köroglu*. Baku, 1949. The texts of twelve Köroglu episodes.

Manas Epic

Bogdanov, M. I., V. M. Žirmunskij, and A. A. Petrosjan. *Kirgizskij geroičeskij èpos* [The Kirghiz Heroic Epic]. Moscow: Akademija nauk SSSR, 1961. The most important source for Manas studies which contains contributions by leading Manas scholars (A. A. Petrosjan, M. Auezov, V. M. Žirmunskij, M. Bogdanova, P. N. Berkov, A. Tokombaev, T. Sydykbekov, B. Junusaliev, E. K. Sagidova).
Hatto, A. T. "Almambet, Er Kökcho and Ak Erkech." *Central Asiatic Journal* 13 (1969): 161–98.
————. "The Birth of Manas." *Asia Major* 14 (1969): 217–41.
————. "Köz Kaman." *Central Asiatic Journal* 15 (1970): 81–101.
————. "'Kukotay and Box Murun', a Comparison of Two Related Heroic Epic Poems of the Kirgiz," I–II. *Bulletin of the School of Oriental and African Studies* 32 (1969): 344–78, 541–71.
Manas. 3 vols. Introduction by B. M. Junusaliev. Frunze: Akademija nauk, 1958–59. The most complete *Manas* text.
Manas: Èpizody iz kirgizskogo narodnogo èposa [Manas: Episodes from the Kirghiz

Folk Epic]. Translated by S. Lipkin and L. Pen'kovskij. Moscow: Akademija nauk SSSR, 1960. Contains episodes from the first of the *Manas* trilogy, translated from a composite text. No indication from which versions the composite was made.

Musaev, S. *Manas: Geroičeskij èpos kirgizskogo naroda* [Manas: The Heroic Epic of the Kirghiz People]. Frunze: Akademija nauk, 1968. Contains contributions by S. Musaev, V. V. Radlov, Č. Č. Valixanov, G. Almašy, P. Falev, E. D. Polivanov, K. A. Raxmatullin, A. N. Bernštam, P. N. Berkov, S. M. Abramson, B. M. Junusaliev.

Er-Töshtük Epic

Boratav, P. Naili. *Er-Töshtük*. Collection UNESCO d'oeuvres représentatives série Kirghize. Paris: Gallimard, 1965. The translation of Saiakbai Karalaev's version of the *Er-Töshtük* epic (13,000 verses), with introduction and notes by Boratav. An important contribution to the *Er-Töshtük* studies.

Boratav, P. Naili. "L'épopée d'Er-Töštük et le conte populaire." In *Volksepen der uralischen und altaischen Völker: Vorträge des Hamburger Symposions vom 16.-17. Dezember 1965,* edited by Wolfgang Veenker, pp. 75–86. Wiesbaden: Otto Harrassowitz, 1968. A structural analysis of the epic with special emphasis on the relations between the folktale and the epic.

Alpamysh Epic

Zhirmunskij, V. "The Epic of Alpamysh and the Return of Odysseus." In *Proceedings of the British Academy,* pp. 267–86. London: Oxford University Press, 1967. A comprehensive account of the Alpamysh version among the Turkic peoples, and a comparative study of Odysseus and Alpamysh with special reference to the return episode. See also *General:* Chadwick, Nora K., and Victor Zhirmunsky.

Edige Epic

Chagatay, Saadet. "Die Ädigä Sage." *Ural-altaische Jahrbücher* 25 (1953): 243 ff. See also *General:* Chadwick, Nora K., and Victor Zhirmunsky.

The Epic of Forty Maidens

See *General:* Chadwick, Nora K., and Victor Zhirmunsky, pp. 282–83.

The Epic of Ai Margan and Ai Doloy

Cohn, Norman. *Gold Khan.* London: Secker and Warburg, 1946. English translation of *Ai Margan and Ai Doloy* from M. A. Castrén, *Versuch einer koibalischen und karagassischen Sprachlehre.* St. Petersburg: Kaiserliche Akademie der Wissenschaften, 1857.

See also *General:* Boratav, P. Naili; and *Dede Qorqut Epic:* Boratav, P. Naili. "Ak-Köbök."

Romances (Hikaye)

Başgöz, Ilhan. "Dream Motif and Shamanistic Initiation." *Asian Folklore Studies* 1 (1967): 1–18.

―――――. "The Structure of Turkish Romances." In *Folklore Today: A Festschrift for Richard M. Dorson,* edited by Linda Dégh, Henry Glassie, and Felix J. Oinas, pp. 11–23. Bloomington, Ind.: Research Center for Language and Semiotic Studies, 1976.

―――――. "The Tale-Singer and his Audience." In *Folklore, Performance and Communication,* edited by Dan Ben-Amos and Kenneth Goldstein, pp. 143–203. The Hague: Mouton and Co., 1975.

———. "Turkish Folk-Stories About the Lives of Minstrels." *Journal of American Folklore* 65 (1952): 331-39.

———. "Turkish Hikaye Telling Tradition in Azerbaijan Iran." *Journal of American Folklore* 83 (1970): 390-405.

Boratav, P. Naili. *Türk Halk Hikayeleri ve Halk Hikayeciligi* [The Hikaye and Hikaye Tradition in Turkey]. Ankara: Milli Egitim Basimevi, 1946. Leading study on romances in Turkish. Contains discussion and analysis of the process and composition, old and new themes, form and style, the relation of epic, novel, tale, and hikaye, historical background, transmission, and change. The book includes the texts of the hikaye of Gül and Alishir, parts of two Köroglu *kols* (episodes), and Celali Bey and Mahmet Bey.

———. "L'État actuel des études des récits populaires (hikaye) Turks." In *Actas do Congresso Internationale de Etnografia,* pp. 1-6. Lisbon, 1965. An account of the research done and the collections made in Turkey on the hikaye.

Eberhard, Wolfram. *Minstrel Tales from Southeastern Turkey.* Berkeley and Los Angeles: University of California Press, 1955. A sociological analysis of the continuity and change in hikaye transmission. Includes texts of Gündeshli Oglu hikaye, synopses of some Köroglu versions collected by him in Southeastern Turkey. Zirmunskij, V. "Legenda o prizvanii pevca" [The Legend about a Singer's Calling]. In *Issledovanija po istorii kul'tury narodov vostoka,* edited by V. V. Struve, pp. 185-95. Moscow: Akademija nauk SSSR, 1960. A cross-cultural analysis of the dream through which a singer receives the talent of singing and composing poetry, with special emphasis on the similarities of calling among shamans, ashiks, and Manas singers.

15　　　　　The African Heroic Epic

Daniel P. Biebuyck

Documentation

Detailed syntheses of African heroic epics are not yet available.[1] In her
pioneering study on African oral literature, Ruth Finnegan pays almost no
attention to the African epic. She dismisses the epic with the assertion that
"all in all, epic poetry does not seem to be a typical African form."[2] Surely,
in contrast to the wide-ranging information that we possess about other literary genres, our published documentation on the African heroic epic is very
limited and sometimes sketchy. This fact is not entirely astonishing. Epics are
long, orally transmitted poetic narratives presented in an episodic manner and
intermittently. They occur in many versions and are built around central
thematic cores and plans by many, frequently unrelated, and independently
working bards. These individuals, and the "schools" or "systems of tradition" that they represent, perform, create, and recreate the specific epic
tradition in their own manner. Performance and content may vary according to
the occasion or the particular audience. Epic narratives are formulated in a
rich, highly poetic, difficult African language. They are also sung, which
makes the performance even more complex. Parts of the epic themes, characters, episodes, and events are sometimes known, in a more or less fragmentary manner, to common storytellers who construct short tales around such
fragments. In the light of these and other facts it is easy to understand why
such long and difficult texts may escape the attention of the foreign researcher
or surpass his linguistic and ethnographic capabilities. It is also easy to understand how such texts are sometimes abstracted and summarized by the out-
sider, or only more or less coherent fragments may be recorded. Epics *per se*
are not secret in the ethnic groups where they occur; many are publicly sung
before a large and diverse audience, and the themes are known to the general
public. Yet, it is my experience that such huge texts, which contain an

extraordinary amount of information about institutions, values, modes of thinking, behavior, and history, are not easily given away to foreign researchers. It is also possible that the lack of information for large parts of Africa is partially due to the fact that heroic epics are less widely distributed than one might be inclined to think.

Distribution

The present evidence points to a strong occurrence of heroic epics in two major areas: the Mande-speakers (Mandeka, Bambara, Soninke) and groups closely interrelated with them (Fulani) in West Africa; several Bantu-speaking ethnic groups ranging from the Gabon Republic (Fang) to the Zaïre Republic (Mongo, Lega, Nyanga, Mbole and Tetela clusters). But outside this general area of concentration, epics were also recorded among the Bantu-speaking Sotho of South Africa, the Swahili of East Africa, the Benamukuni of Zambia, among the Ijaw of Southern Nigeria, and Adangme of Ghana. Beyond this immediate evidence, it is difficult to assess from published sources the degree to which texts known to us as myths or tales might be fragments of larger unrecorded epic wholes.[3]

The presently known heroic epics occur in societies that exhibit a wide range of social structures, political and religious systems, and historical backgrounds. Although no easy explanations for the phenomena can be found, nor any fully significant correlations can as yet be constructed, it is worth stressing the following points. The two major traditions of heroic epics seem to occur, respectively, among Mande-speaking peoples in West Africa and some Bantu-speaking groups of Central Africa. In both areas of occurrence a common epic patrimony exists at the transtribal level among a number of more or less related ethnic groups. The heroic epics are found among peoples like the Bambara, the Fang, the Mongo, the Lega, and the Nyanga, where hunting traditions are ideologically and sociologically very significant. In several of these areas the cultural impact of Pygmies is explicit and deep. Except for the Nyanga, who represent a unique case, all epic-producing ethnic groups have elaborate traditions of migration, expansion, and cultural assimilation, or well-established traditions of conquest and warfare. Some of these societies are politically integrated into kingdoms and chiefdoms, some belong to ancient traditions of political systems of great amplitude, but others have, as far as ethnohistory can be retraced, never had any centralized political structure with kings, chiefs, or rulers of great power. Two other points are worth remembering. Among most of the ethnic groups involved there exist extremely elaborate initiation systems connected with puberty ceremonies and membership in voluntary associations. Such ethnic groups as Bambara, Fang, and Lega have some of the most outstanding artistic traditions of the African continent. Of these observations, the most fascinating is probably that great heroic epic traditions do also occur among people who have no traditions of conquest or a centralized political system. The Lega of the Zaïre Republic are probably the best example of such a social context.

Scope of the Study

In the following pages, I present a short summary of the contents of some of the better known heroic epics. In this brief survey I am not concerned with the vast amount of praises and heroic poems that have been aptly analyzed for several East and South African populations in a number of recent works.[4] These heroic poems have a particularly strong distribution among various clusters of Bantu-speaking peoples of South Africa. The panegyrics celebrate persons (chiefs, warriors, common people) as well as animals, plants, natural features, and objects. Some are very short; others include hundreds of verse stanzas or "paragraphs."[5] Similar praises addressed to divinities or chiefs, or evoking the names of social groups and the deeds of persons, form part of the oral literature of many other ethnic groups. The heroic war poetry of Rwanda, the *ijala* salutes of the Oyo Yoruba, the heroic hunters' songs of the Mande, the *kasala* songs of the Luba-Kasai are cases in point.[6] The abundant animal epic cycles, of which we possess many more or less comprehensive examples for various parts of Africa, also fall outside the scope of this study.[7]

Epic-like narratives and recitations centered around ancestors, kings, genealogies, migrations, places, battles, group histories, are not covered in this survey. Prominent examples of these narratives are the royal *nshoong atoot* recitations of the Kuba (Zaïre Republic), the dispersal of the Kusa of the Soninke (Mali Republic), the story of Wagadu of the Soninke, and the story of Wamara and his descendants among the Haya (Tanzania).[8] Finally, I exclude from consideration the written epics of the Swahili of East Africa, and some other epics more recently written by African creative writers.[9]

In this study, I limit myself to the discussion of a number of well-established, adequately documented, and orally transmitted heroic epics, mostly from Mande-speaking peoples in West Africa and from Bantu-speakers in Central Africa. The major focus is on the Sunjata, Monzon, and Silamaka epic traditions from the Mandeka, Bambara, and Fulani in West Africa; on the *mvet* traditions of the Fang in Cameroun; on the Mubila, Mwindo, Lianja, Lofokefoke, and Kudukese epics from the Lega, Nyanga, Mongo, Hamba, and Mbole in the Zaïre Republic. Some other epic traditions from Nigeria, Ghana, and East and South Africa are briefly mentioned as well.

Epics from West Africa

The Monzon Cycle of the Bambara

The Monzon epic cycle of the Bambara (Mali Republic) centers around Monzon and his son, Da Monzon, two historically known kings who ruled over Ségu (Mali Republic) from 1787 to 1827. Three fairly long episodes of this cycle have been published.[10] Scores of similar episodes are known to the bards, and many different versions of the epic are sung.[11] No complete text or advanced analysis is available. Thus the relationships between episodes, their place in the total epic, and the full content of the epic are as yet undocumented.

In the episode of *Monzon and Duga,* the bard evokes the causes of the conflict between Monzon and Duga, the king of Kore; the role played by Monzon's son in the subsequent battles; the death of both Monzon and Duga; and the enthronement of Da, the son of Monzon.[12] The principal events narrated in this passage are as follows. The son of one of Monzon's greatest bards visits Duga and decides to remain with him. Monzon, deeply affected by this insult, asks his son, Tiéfolo, to capture Duga. He refuses and is, therefore, killed. But Monzon's other son, Da, accepts the challenge and musters a large army. Soon Da sets up camp around the city of Kore, but the beleaguered Duga refuses to take the matter seriously. He invites Da for a hydromel party. Duga's first wife has heard many things about Da; out of love for him, she manages during the night to join Da, who has gone back to his troops. Da asks for her help and promises to marry her after Duga's defeat. So Duga's wife secretly overhears a divination ceremony between her husband and the great interpreter and sacrificer of the caiman god. She secretly transmits all instructions and details to Da. Duga is defeated and captured. Transforming himself into an eagle, then into a lion by means of powerful amulets, Duga warns about the imminent death of Monzon, Da's father. Duga kills himself with a gunshot. Da's intentions to marry Duga's wife are opposed by his father's counselors, and they secretly kill her. Soon after, Monzon dies as predicted from a sudden sickness. Da is installed as the new king.

The episode *Da Monzon of Ségu* is a panegyric for the king, Da Monzon, who ruled for about forty years over the kingdom of Ségu.[13] The praises center around Ségu, its king and his powerful magical devices, his sages and seers, his warriors, his subjects. The king is glorified as "he who does not share power with anybody," and "the most glorious master on earth."

The passage *Da Monzon and Karta Thiéma* celebrates one of the many conflicts in which Da Monzon was involved against his vassals.[14] Thiéma, the ruler of Karta (a province depending on the kingdom of Ségu), tired of being a subordinate, revolts against Da Monzon, and explains his intentions during a splendid feast, the circumstances and discussions of which are evoked in detail by the bard. A female master-singer warns him against Ségu, but he rejects her advice. An old woman, known for her impudence, helps Thiéma invent a way to send a major insult to Da Monzon. The bard describes in great detail the preparations, the arrival of the messengers, the actual insults, and subsequent dialogues and speeches. For three months Da Monzon and his people are involved in preparations. Outside the walls of Karta, several encounters between horsemen take place. In each battle Thiéma's warriors are easily decimated. Thiéma himself takes up the fight. He is equipped with various magical devices and is invulnerable (because his body is washed with twenty-two different concoctions). In various individual engagements against some of Da Monzon's finest warriors, Thiéma is completely successful. The battle scene climaxes with an encounter between Thiéma and the Fulani Chief, Hambodédio Paté. Hambodédio is the stronger. Karta is set afire, and Thiéma is captured and taken back to Ségu. People await in vain his public punishment. But no one ever found out exactly what happened to him. Only the Niger River, it is said, knows the full story. Hambodédio, on the other hand, becomes Da Monzon's son-in-law.

The poetic verse or lines, in which these published fragments of the Da Monzon Cycle are formulated, abound with beautiful passages. There are long, lofty speeches interspersed with succinct aphoristic statements; lively dialogues; descriptions of scenes of festivity, of battle, of divination; praises and imprecations; evocations of great deeds and suggestions of extraordinary magical possessions; secret councils and public statements.

The Silamaka Epic of the Fulani

A long and magnificent passage of this epic was narrated by the Fulani bard, Marabal Samburu, in the Macina area (Mali Republic).[15] The epic is also known in other regions inhabited by the Fulani.[16] Silamaka, the central hero of the epic, is a historical figure. As a leader (*ardo*) of the Fulani, he lived under the previously mentioned Da Monzon, the King of Ségu, and rebelled against him. The epic narrates the following events. Hammadi, a leader of the Fulani and a vassal of Da Monzon, has a son, Silamaka. Silamaka's closest friend and companion is Puluru, the son of Hammadi's house slave, Baba. Forty days after his birth, Silamaka gives signs of his exceptional qualities. While Da Monzon's messengers are collecting tribute in his father's homestead, Silamaka, seated on a mat, is not even bothered by a horsefly sucking blood from his forehead. The messengers take the extraordinary news back to Da Monzon. Seers and sages are consulted. They announce the birth of "a terrible child" that can be killed only by powerful magic. But no magic can destroy Silamaka and his friend, Puluru. Silamaka and Puluru grow up. A young woman, courted by many men, challenges Silamaka to give proof of his much lauded bravery against Da Monzon. Silamaka consults a geomancer. To become invulnerable he must capture alive the sacred serpent of the *gala-mani* woods, mark it with signs, cover it with leather, and wear it as a belt. Hundreds of his warriors fail to achieve this deed, but riding his white horse, Soperekagne, the hero himself captures the serpent and makes it into a belt. There follows a long passage in which three bards from the West arrive consecutively in the villages of the four foremost Fulani leaders. Everywhere Silamaka is quoted as the bravest of them all. The next passage celebrates a conflict between the two heroes, Silamaka and Hambodédio, because of an insult made by the latter against Silamaka's friend. Silamaka, on the winning side, shows mercy for Hambodédio, who asks for forgiveness.

The following year we are back in Silamaka's village where Da Monzon's messengers have come to collect tribute. But Silamaka hides the gold and insults Da Monzon. There follow a number of unsuccessful attempts by Da Monzon's messengers and horsemen to capture Silamaka. He defeats successive waves of attackers, but in a battle that opposes him to a Fularadio, he must flee back to his village. He is helped by his sister and consoled by his friend, Puluru. In a renewed battle against Fularadio and five hundred horsemen, Silamaka kills Fularadio. Larger and larger waves of horsemen sent out by Da Monzon in vain attack Silamaka, his friend, and a small number of horsemen. Silamaka, in doubt about the death of so many people and the consequences of his acts, consults a diviner, and his coming glorious death is predicted.

In the meantime Da Monzon, with the help of many sages and seers, has prepared a powerful magical device that will destroy Silamaka. Before embarking on his last battle, Silamaka sends his friend, Puluru, off with a secret message for Hambodédio. In it he announces his coming death and the supreme leadership of Hambodédio. During the ensuing battle, Silamaka is killed by an uncircumcised young albino with an arrow dipped in the pounded bones of a black steer. The horse of the dying hero carries him back to the village where the returning Puluru can only weep for his friend's death. Da Monzon sends many horsemen against Silamaka's village, but Puluru flees on horseback with his and Silamaka's sons. Carrying Silamaka's enchanted spear, he splits the attacking horsemen into two groups: one group which he pursues, one group by which he is pursued. Night falls, all disappear. Nobody knows where they really went, but legend has it that they all went to heaven. Hambodédio finally obtains from Da Monzon the concession that the Macina area, over which Silamaka ruled, will not be reduced to the state of captivity.

In the beautiful poetic verse or lines of this epic, the bard harmoniously intermingles the narrative of events and deeds with praises, aphoristic expressions, conversations, and challenges.

The Sunjata Epic of the Mandeka

The epic of this thirteenth-century king of the Mali Empire is well-known through various sources.[17] It is still widely sung in many areas that at one time formed part of the Mali Empire.[18] It is part of a common, central tradition that links many Mande-speaking peoples across several West African countries, such as Guinea, Mali, Senegal, the Gambie, Ivory Coast, Upper Volta, and Ghana. The thematic material of the epic obviously varies from performer to performer, from performance to performance, and probably also from region to region. Charles Bird, however, has clearly delineated the central core of the epic which, in the various known versions, centers around a triple set of data: the events leading to the birth of Sunjata, his youth and exile from the Mande, his return to reconquer the Mande from the impostor, Sumanguru.[19] The thematic outline is as follows. Faraku Magan Cenyi, father of the future hero,

Sunjata, receives the prophecy that he will beget a son who will become a great king. For the prophecy to come true, Magan must marry a woman brought to him by a hunter. The story then shifts to two hunters traveling through the bush in pursuit of an enormous buffalo, which has decimated many subjects of a local king. They meet with an old woman, whom they befriend, and who is none other than the buffalo (the woman, in other words, has the power of metamorphosis). She explains to the hunters the secrets for killing the buffalo on the condition that the hunters ask the local king for the ugliest woman as a prize for their efforts.

Having achieved their task, the hunters claim and receive the ugliest woman, called Sogolon. The senior of the two hunters does not want to take her as a wife because, as is stated in one of the versions, he saw rising from her body a column of light. The hunters arrive in Magan's village and present him with Sogolon. Magan's first wife, Sasuma Berete, and his second wife, Sogolon, become pregnant the same day. The same day they give birth to two sons, respectively called Dankarantuma and Sunjata. Magan proclaims Sunjata as his heir, but the jealous Sasuma places a curse on him. For seven (or nine) years Sunjata is unable to walk. When he finally stands up, leaning on a gigantic iron staff, it is to revenge the honor of his mother. Growing up as a youth in his village, Sunjata accumulates extraordinary hunting and magical skills, and establishes alliances with the spirits of the bush. An intense conflict develops between him and his half-brother, Dankarantuma. Feeling the existence of his mother, brother, and sister threatened, Sunjata takes his mother and brother into exile to Mema, in Mossi country. Here he lives by hunting. His skills are much appreciated by the local king and he stays for many years.

In the meantime, Dankarantuma is chased from his kingdom by Sumanguru, the blacksmith-king of Sosso. Terror reigns everywhere and all the oracles point to Sunjata as the possible savior of his people. Messengers sent out to find him convince Sunjata to return. His mother, Sogolon, dies on the way home. Sunjata sets up alliances with various kings and builds an army to reconquer Mande from Sumanguru. Sumanguru has an immense power; in one version it is said that he has sixty-nine ways of metamorphosis. In the first two encounters, Sunjata is defeated. Finally, with the help of his sister and of Fakoli, Sumanguru's nephew, Sunjata learns about Sumanguru's secrets. He achieves a complete victory on the Niger plain at Kirina. Samanguru, fleeing northward, is trapped but manages to transform himself into stone. The open-ended epic glorifies the further expansion and stabilization of the empire up to Sunjata's death. In one version Sunjata, having broken an ancestral pact with the Fulani, drowns and is changed into a hippopotamus. Some versions may include an account of Sunjata's descendants and the history of the empire up to the present day.

Other Epics from West Africa

The Ozidi epic of the Ijaw of Southern Nigeria is only partially known to me.[20] In the city-state of Orua there are many warlords, but Ozidi is the most prominent of them all. King after king dies and finally Temugedege, Ozidi's idiotic brother, is made king. Ozidi, angered over his brother's behavior, abuses the town. Several warlords conspire against him and kill him in ambush. Ozidi's wife and her mother fly back to their home town, and there the wife becomes posthumously pregnant. After a normal pregnancy, she delivers a son, the younger Ozidi, at the end of a seven-day-long labor coinciding with a great storm. The remaining part of the epic deals with the extraordinary events of his youth, his apprenticeships with his grandmother, the great witch Oreami. The hero goes through many battles and adventures to regain the lost glory of his lineage. In the words of Clark: "In this process, he oversteps the natural bounds set to his quest, and it is not until he has received divine visitation from the Small-Pox King that he emerges purged and vindicated."[21]

Various sources mention other epics from West Africa, such as Klama of the Adangme (Ghana) and Gassire of the Soninke.[22] The published documentation, however, does not allow further discussion of them.

Epics of the Bantu-Speaking Peoples

The Mwindo Cycle of the Banyanga

I have recorded four epics and several epic fragments among the Nyanga (Zaïre Republic). The epics center around the hero, Mwindo, also called in some versions Mwindo Mboru and Kaboru ka Mwindo.[23] In one published version of the Mwindo epic from the Banyanga (Zaïre Republic) the central hero, Mwindo, is the miraculously born son of Chief Shemwindo and his preferred wife.[24] Rejected by his father, who did not want any of his wives to bear sons, the newly born Mwindo successfully escapes his father's attempts to kill him. Locked up in a drum by his father's counselors, he travels in a river in search of his father's sister, who is married to Water-Serpent. Liberated from the drum by his paternal aunt, Iyangura, he returns with her to his village in search of his father.

Mwindo could walk and talk from birth. He had the gift of premonition and was born with a magical scepter and shoulderbag. Thus, on the journey home he performs extraordinary deeds until he reaches his village from which his father has escaped. He destroys the village and sets out, in subterranean travels, in search of his father. In the realm of subterranean beings and divinities he successfully performs many Herculean tasks, until his father is turned over to him. He carries his father home, revivifying on his way the many enemies whom he had overcome. A great council is convened in which all parties express opinions. The kingdom is divided into two parts, one ruled by the hero, one ruled by his father. But the troubles are not finished. Mwindo's Pygmies, on a hunting party, are swallowed by the dragon, Kirimu. Mwindo himself goes to defeat the dragon and to liberate his Pygmies. But the destruction of the dragon disturbs Lightning, a friend and ally of both Mwindo and dragon. Lightning comes to seize the hero, and rambles with him in the celestial realms of Moon, Sun, Star, and others for one full year. Here the powerless hero undergoes, in pure passivity, his final purification. He is returned to earth with plenty of warnings and prescriptions. Mwindo now rules as a glorious chief, prescribing for his people a set of rules for harmonious interrelationships.

The Lianja Epic Cycle of the Mongo

Several versions of the Lianja epic of the Mongo (Zaïre Republic) have been published by E. Boelaert and his collaborators.[25] The thematic core of these epics has been synthesized by A. De Rop.[26] I present his synthesis in summary. The different versions generally begin with a longer or shorter introduction in which the creation of the world or the ancestors of the hero (beginning with his great-grandfather) are depicted. The world of Lianja's ancestors is already filled with extraordinary events. Mbombe, the mother of the hero to be born, eats only a rare *losau* fruit during her pregnancy. Her husband, Ilele, compelled to search for it, has initial successes, but finally dies in his many battles with animals and birds around the mysterious tree. When the news of her husband's death reaches the village, Mbombe begins to give birth to various animals and humans. Finally her twin children, Lianja and his sister, Nsongo, are born. According to some versions, the birth is miraculous. Lianja comes out of his mother's tibia with all the weapons and insignia of his father. Nsongo, carrying various objects, is born fully adult and beautiful. Right after birth, Lianja sets out to revenge his father. In one version he is accompanied by an army that includes Pygmoids, members of different Mongo tribes, and insects (ants, bees, wasps). Having destroyed his father's murderer, Lianja now leads his people to a promised land near the river. He conquers several forest tribes and, at the request of his sister, incorporates them into his army. He also fights with ogres. As they progress towards the river, various groups stay behind and settle the land. Arriving near the river, Lianja establishes his people, then assembles them around a tall palm tree. Carrying his sister on the hip, his senior brother on the knees, his mother on the shoulders, he disappears into the sky. One version deals with the descendants of Lianja, his son and his grandson who continue their battles against enemy tribes, and his daughter, who gives birth to the ancestors of the Whites.

The Mubila Epic of the Balega (Zaïre Republic)

This is one of a cycle of epics that revolve around various heroes.[27] The epic begins with the circumstances that lead to the hero's birth. His father, Yombi, has forty-one wives. Thirty-nine sons and one daughter are born of his first forty wives in rapid succession. Thereafter, his most junior and beloved wife gives birth to the hero, Mubila. Before and after birth, Mubila has many properties and characteristics. He speaks in the womb, uses magical formulas, and selects his own name. The hero is born holding a spear, a knife, a shield, a belt, and a necklace. Mubila has a shoulderbag in which he can hide all his followers, and he possesses a love whistle. He has very long nails and eyebrows like an elephant tail. He has in him an immaterial substance which he consults and which advises him in all difficulties. Mubila has the gift of prophecy and great physical strength. He can fly through the air. He is vulnerable, but possesses the power of resuscitation. Right after birth, Mubila is ready for exceptional action which he himself elicits. The hero acts as the senior of all the brothers. He decides to build his own village, leaves his father behind with one of his brothers, and settles with the others in the new village. Soon after, he hears the news of his father's death. He accuses his brother, Youthful-Greatness, of his father's death, compelling him to flee to a remote village.

This event gives rise to a first set of episodes. Mubila, in search of his brother, is faced with events that rapidly develop in a consecutive chain of difficulties, confrontations, and successes. For example, he seduces and marries his first wife, Kabungulu, who becomes his most powerful ally. He enters into conflict with several diviners. He seduces and marries his second wife and pursues those who eloped with his sister. He has encounters with the Maiden-with-the-half-closed-eyes, with Fish and Water-Serpent, with Snail-shell-collector, and so on. One event leads to another, each apparently re-solved conflict develops into a new one. And, particularly, Mubila is in-cessantly faced by new dilemmas at the Junction-of-the-one-hundred-forty-trails. In one of his violent encounters, Mubila is speared and apparently dies. In the meantime, his newborn son, Ashes, sets out to recover his father's body. Faced by his son and wife, Mubila's body revivifies.

A new set of episodes develop while Mubila is in search of Shrieking-Song, who had killed him, and of Bungoe, who had given hospitality to Shrieking-Song. In the course of this action Mubila, with the help of his wives and brothers, engages in many battles and other activities. He fights with heroes and personified animals. He marries his third wife. He is involved in hunting, honey gathering, felling trees, trapping, dice and ball games. He is partially initiated into the *bwami* association and undergoes a second circumcision. He dies and is resuscitated again. An endless series of events and feats build up around each action. The constant flow of these extraordinary situations is regularly interrupted by the hero's return to his village and by his return to the Junction-of-one-hundred-forty-trails, where new dilemmas pose themselves. The long epic ends, rather abruptly, *in medias res,* in Mubila's home village, which he has cleared from an intruder, and where people engage in drumming and dancing.

The Kudukese and Lofokefoke Epics

Shorter epics from the Mongo-related Mbole and Hamba (Zaïre Republic) have been published by John Jacobs.[28] The heroes in these epics (Kudukese, among the Hamba, and Lofokefoke, among the Mbole) are different from the central characters in the previously discussed epics in that they combine both human and animal traits. *The Kudukese epic* opens with the history of two beings, Mbodyetonga and Ehanjola, and the magical tricks they play on each other. This leads to a wonderful forest world and the fantastic hunting adventures of Cetakolo and Ngengu (two personified animals). Attracted by the voices of women, these two hunters travel for hundreds of miles through the forest to find a giant tree loaded with young women. The hunters, and many other animals, try in vain to reach the women. Kudukese finally emerges, dressed as a great initiate and carrying his divination calabash. With the help of magical means he reaches the women, takes one for himself and distributes the others among the animals. Kudukese now travels through the land, destroying his many enemies who try to seize his wife. In these encounters he dies and is resuscitated two times. His third death, however, is fatal. Ofunga, a sorcerer who killed Kudukese, seizes the latter's wife. Kudukese is buried, and soon thereafter his wife is expecting a child. Ofunga is killed by Kudukese's followers, and when she hears about his death, his wife gives birth to various things: rivers, a giant spider, and to the hero, Okangate.

Okangate is miraculously born. He speaks in the womb. He is fully adult from birth on and extremely tall. His mother dies after his birth. Okangate performs many wonderful deeds, but children scorn him as an orphan. Therefore, he brings his mother back to life, and engages in a series of feats to find out where and by whom his father was killed. From each of these expeditions he returns without his father, but loaded with many things for his mother (baskets, sheep, pigs, elephants, blacksmiths, even the sun and the moon). In each crisis his major help comes from the giant spider. The open-ended epic finishes abruptly. The narrator simply states that Okangate, his mother, and the giant spider died of hunger, and that Okangate was buried in a cave.

In *The Lofokefoke epic* of the Mbole (Bambuli), the central hero, Lofokefoke, presents himself in a semi-animal (rodent) and semi-human form. A hunter encounters a large tree filled with women. He and some of his people, however, are unable to get at them, so they send for Bakese Bonyonga, who lives in a remote area, past the region of the spirits of the dead. Bakese succeeds in his efforts. With his wife, whom he has taught a magical incantation and given a powerful amulet, Bakese successfully defeats many animal foes. He arrives in the village of Bosunga. After a good reception, the conflicts begin. Bakese (standing on the roofs of the houses and intercepting spears thrown at him) kills Bosunga's people, but finally Bosunga kills him and takes his wife. Soon thereafter the woman is pregnant. She desires to eat only certain fruits which Bosunga must collect. Bosunga is killed by the spirits of the dead.

For a full year the woman continues to weep for her deceased first husband. As she goes on, all persons killed by Bakese come to life. She gives birth to seven children, the last of whom is Lofokefoke. The miraculously born Lofokefoke immediately inquires about the place where his father has died.

Relentlessly, he performs many amazing deeds that prove his invulnerability. For seven years Lofokefoke and his brothers pursue an elephant, which he has killed before and which has magically escaped him. The elephant is finally found dead in his village. Lofokefoke plays ball with the elephants, batting with a whole tree and throwing the ball as high as the sun. He captures the discouraged elephant and returns home. On his homebound journey, he decimates the people of many villages with his knives, Longombo and Lolakanga. He crosses the Lomami River, whose waters separate for him. He then arrives in the villages of several brothers, always in a destructive mood, but he does not succeed in killing them. After his return, he fights for seven years against his senior brother, Basele, without result. He kills his sister Mangana, and he resumes the fight against Basele without success. He engages in many other fights, hunts, killings, and extraordinary feats. The epic ends with a number of exploits, which Lofokefoke performs to convince his son of his force. During his last effort to kill all the hippopotami of the Lomami River, Lofokefoke is killed. All his children are killed trying to destroy the hippopotami.

The Akoma Mba Cycle

Among the Fang and some other groups in a wide area of the Gabon, the Cameroun Republic, and the Rio Muni, an elaborate epic cycle centers around the hero, Akoma Mba, a ruler of Engong.[29] Akoma Mba, conceived out of incestuous relationships between a brother and a sister, is miraculously born after his mother has carried him for one hundred and fifty years. He terrorizes his entourage and is, therefore, given to a certain Mba of the Ekang tribe who marries his mother. His father calls him "Wrinkle of Elephant, son of Mba," but since he becomes fiercer and fiercer, people call him Akoma Mba, the Creator of Mba (as if he had brought forth his own father). During his entire youth, Akoma Mba engages in many extraordinary exploits to become the ruler of all the Ekang. Having taken power, he goes to establish himself with his people, the Ekang, at Engong. Akoma Mba rules as absolute monarch among a strong people, for all Ekang are invulnerable, invincible, and immortal.[30]

One long text celebrates the conflict between Akoma Mba and Abo Mama. Dissatisfied with the choice of a certain Otungu Mba as territorial chief, Abo Mama removes Otungu Mba far into the forest away from his people. In the meantime, two cousins are born the same day that they were conceived. Their mission it is to find and to revenge Otungu Mba. Before embarking on his task, however, one of the cousins, Mengana Mba, crosses the universe in search of "that to which nothing can be compared." After many peripeties, he finally arrives in the land of King Mfim Ekie and is transformed into a woman. Akoma Mba gets the news; he assembles his people, and engages in a war against Mfim. Akoma Mba locks the entire country of Mfim up in a rock which he transports home. Mfin becomes Akoma Mba's subject; he and his people must do all the agricultural work for the Ekang. In a following passage Akoma Mba is involved in a war against Abo Mama, which he finally wins after many initial difficulties.[31]

The Mvet of Zwe Nguema

The action in this epic centers around the humans of the land of Oku who try to steal immortality from the immortal beings of Engong Country.[32] The prologue of the epic gives an elaborate introduction to the immortal beings of Engong (their origins, their genealogy, their leaders, the events in which they were involved) and how the people of Oku separated from them. Soon a conflict develops between the two groups. Zong Midzi, of the land of Oku, sends a challenge to the land of Engong, because a certain Angone Endong over there does not let him breathe freely. Informed about the arrival of messengers, the people of Engong, under the command of Akoma Mba, assemble to hear the announcement of the coming battle. On the point of leaving to confront Zong Midzi alone, Angone Endong deposits his weapons at the request of Nkudang. She is a girl who had remained indifferent before thousands of suitors and who now desires Zong Midzi, whom she has never seen but whose name she likes. Unable to find messengers, she convinces her mother to accompany her to her maternal uncle's in the land of Oku. During the journey she learns that for Zong Midzi nobody counts more than his wife, the beautiful Esone Abeng. Arriving at her maternal uncle's, Nkudang asks him to go and fetch Zong Midzi. In the meantime, many suitors visit her, but only Nsure Afane, the incomparable boy, enjoys her favors. Zong Midzi receives the message of her arrival. Irritated and intrigued, he arms himself and goes, accompanied by his wife Esone Abeng. They spend the night on the road. That night, Nsure Afane feels that disaster is coming. He alerts the village and returns with Nkudang and her mother to the land of Engong. Zong Midzi and his wife pursue them and meet with them at the crossroads of eight trails. Soon a conflict develops. Zong Midzi beheads Nkudang. Nsure Afane beheads Zong Midzi's wife and flies on a magic ball back to Engong, carrying the two heads. The ill fate is already known in Engong, for Akoma Mba has seen all events in his mirror. It is decided that Nsure Afane must die, but he manages to escape on the magic ball. Zong Midzi is now ravaging the village of Nsure.

Meanwhile the best warriors of Engong, flying with iron wings, are in pursuit of him. Nsure Afane, having returned to his village, engages in a fantastic combat with Zong Midzi. The battle continues when one of the Engong warriors takes over. Zong Midzi is immobilized for a moment, but manages to disappear under the ground where his ancestors protect him. He returns after four days, equipped with magic weapons. The warriors of Engong get seriously hurt. They use new devices, however, and blind Zong Midzi with a tuft of feathers. One Engong warrior captures him, and flies back with him to Engong, while the others continue to ravage the land of Oku.

Badly guarded in the place of the secret council, Zong Midzi escapes and returns to his ancestors in Oku. They decide to make him immortal like the people of Engong, but their work is interrupted by Scorpion, who was sent out by the Engong people to track him.

Akoma Mba and his magician in Engong see at a distance everything that happens. Foreseeing the dangers involved in Zong Midzi's immortality, they request the ancestors of Engong to halt the transformation of Zong Midzi. He returns to his normal state, but receives from his ancestors a magical gun whose bullets follow their aim wherever he goes. Entrenched in his cavern, Zong Midzi must come out of it to avoid being asphyxiated by the warriors of Engong. The bullets work relentlessly, but one of the Engong warriors manages to stick a magnetized shield to Zong Midzi's back and propel him to Engong by means of a magic ball. Zong Midzi is now back in Engong in the place of the Secret Council. His charms are removed. Akoma Mba makes his belly explode and Zong Midzi dies.

Kapepe

Among the Benamukuni (Lenje) of Zambia, an epic text that shows many similarities with the Nyanga epics glorifies Kapepe.[33] Born against his father's will, but aided by his mother, some cousins and an old woman, Kapepe must marry the daughter of the supreme god, Lesa. On his journey, the hero receives from an old woman a magical feather which counsels him in all circumstances. Many obstacles notwithstanding (elephants, buffaloes, serpents, lions, large rivers, mountains) the hero arrives in the city of God. Here he overcomes all tricks and successfully passes through all the ordeals that are imposed upon him. Having received God's daughter, he clears all the new obstacles and dilemmas that confront him on the home journey. Soon, however, the divine wife, bored with terrestrial life, returns home, followed by Kapepe, who also decides to remain in God's realm.[34]

General Survey of the African Epics

The Bards

The various bards who actually sang, recited, and narrated the epic texts discussed in this study are obviously known by name.[35] Many interesting data are available about the general social background and position of these bards and their methods of performance. More work, however, is to be done on their personalities, their methods of learning, and their individual creative talents.

Among the Mande-speaking populations, these bards, called *griot* in the literature, constitute distinctive groups of specialists in a caste-like structure. Among the Bambara, the epic-singing bards (*jeli*) form one of several artisan castes. They hold the exclusive patrimony of the great epics, such as Sunjata and Da Monzon. The female bards of this caste specialize in praise songs.[36]

The bards in this culture are many things: musicians; arbiters and negotiators; counselors of headmen, chiefs, and kings; historians. Of course, not everybody in such a caste is a musician or bard. Young individuals are carefully selected because of their talents. They specialize in the playing of different musical instruments. An apprenticeship lasts from five to ten years, and combines manual and intellectual work. The *mvet* performers of the Gabon and Cameroun area fall into two categories: those who sing and play the *mvet* instrument, and those who sing and are accompanied by another musician. A good performer always has several apprentices, sometimes from different villages. When an apprentice is well instructed, he passes through a formal initiation that may last several days. During the secret part of the initiation, he receives the magic objects that will stimulate his imagination and instruct him in the various prescriptions linked with his function. During the public part of the initiation, he drinks and eats prescribed concoctions, undergoes a test of cleverness, and gives a night performance.[37]

The bards of the Nyanga do not belong to any kind of specialized or exclusive lineages or clans. However, the epic-singing bards of the Nyanga, whom I have studied, have close connections through their ascendancy, or in the line of bards whose traditions they perpetuate, with the Pygmies. From many points of view, their social position is not different from that of other narrators or musicians; only their fame is greater.

The published literature does not yet allow us to fully assess the degree to which, and the manner in which, the individual creative art of each bard is reflected in his performance, and how this individual creativity may be at work from performance to performance. The element of individual variability is undoubtedly strong, because the bard is, as Albert Lord has pointed out for other epic traditions, not just a performing, but also a creative artist. He creates while he performs. He selects, adjusts, and modifies episodes, sometimes in response to the actual composition of his audience or in response to the social position of his hosts and sponsors. On the other hand, he acts and performs in an ethnic world where principles of conformity and tradition are very strong. Moreover, he consciously represents and follows certain "schools" of tradition, since he is a member of a certain family of bards or a certain lineage, and since he learned his art from particular masters. Among the Fang, for example, the great bards give genealogies of the specific narrators (as many as eleven in some cases) whose traditions they perpetuate. Among the Nyanga, each bard clearly indicates a line of three to four narrators whose tradition he represents.

In other words, in judging individual creativity we must realize that there exist within any given ethnic group many parallel traditions developing within the overall stylistic and thematic tradition. A comparison of four epics of the Mwindo cycle indicates considerable differences in actual wording, poetic imagery, number and arrangement of episodes, elaboration of heroic themes and characters, and value emphasis. But all this is worked into a stable core of epic themes, structure, and plan. Nobody knows exactly how many epic texts (full texts, independent episodes, and fragments) a single bard may know, and how extensive his knowledge of the other genres is. Among the Bambara, a single griot may know as many as twelve episodes of ten thousand verses each.[38] A narrator like Sherungu among the Nyanga knows only one fairly complete, but short, epic, but his knowledge of songs, proverbs, riddles, prayers, formulas, and tales includes several hundreds of texts. There are definitely great differences from narrator to narrator. In some areas, like Nyanga or Hamba, the number of bards knowing more or less complete versions of an epic had dwindled to a few individuals during the fifties and sixties. Elsewhere, as among the Bambara or Mongo, their numbers are much larger.

The Performances

The performances of the epics are highly complex events which must be viewed as total social and artistic phenomena. Besides the actual bard and his aides (eventually including the apprentices), there is a diverse, and sometimes large, actively participating audience. There is a constant interplay among these three categories of participants. The actual presentation of the epic narrative is enhanced with musical performance (one or more musical instruments, eventually of different type); appropriate costumes and adornments; singing, chanting, praising, dialoguing; dancing, gesticulation, handclapping; dramatic re-enactments; and gift exchanges.

In most areas, the bards are specially dressed or adorned for the performance. The paraphernalia are minimal among the Nyanga; the bard holds in his hands a calabash rattle and a small scepter (made of a roughly carved wooden handle that is adorned with some feathers). The Mongo bards, wearing feather hats, adorn their bodies and faces with various geometrical designs. They carry a ceremonial knife or spear. Among the Fang, the bards wear a feather hat, a mane-like coiffure, a fiber skirt, a multitude of wild animal skins that hang from their arms and waist, and anklet bells.[39] Some of these simple paraphernalia seem to have very special meanings. For one, the bards strongly identify with the principal hero of the epic; they may suggest his physical presence by means of some of the objects and accoutrements. The scepter carried by the Nyanga bard, Rureke, suggests the magical *conga-*scepter of the hero, Mwindo. The spear or knife held by the Mongo bards evokes the same objects with which the hero, Lianja, was born. Mongo bards assert that they could not sing and recite the epic without having these objects, which they receive from their teachers as a sign of their full-fledged status as bards.

During the narration the bards can be seated, but they also engage in acting, miming, gesticulating, and dancing. The Nyanga bard interrupts the narration to enact certain activities or events in which the hero is involved. This acting is also the reason that some bards among the Fang prefer to leave the handling of musical instruments to their aides.

Musical instruments, played by the bard and/or his aides, are an essential part of the performance. In some areas the type and number of musical instruments used are strictly determined. Among the Nyanga, the bard accompanies himself with a calabash-rattle, while three aides do the percussion on a dry housebeam or bamboo. The Mongo bard is accompanied by a small *lokole*-drum which may be replaced by two blocks of wood, each beaten in a different rhythm by a percussionist. The Fang bard can accompany himself with an elaborate chordophone called *mvet*. One or two of these instruments can be played by his helpers, while other aides do the percussion on a dry bamboo, a piece of banana stipe, or on a rolled-up hide. Other Fang bards may be accompanied by slit-drums and membranophones. In the Mande area of West Africa, the twenty-one string lute-harp (*Kora*) is mostly used, but other instruments, such as xylophones, drums, or a four-stringed banjo-like instrument, may be preferred.[40] The audience itself invariably responds to the songs, and among the Hamba one of the listeners provides the rhythm by beating two sticks together. The aides, only male in some areas, both male and female in other areas, may include apprentices and kinsfolk. Among the Fang, one such group comprises the wives and children of the bard.[41]

In several regions the entire epic is sung or chanted. Among the Mongo and related groups, certain portions of the epic are sung and others are narrated. The Nyanga bards sing the entire text, short episode after episode. After each sung episode, they pause and re-narrate the text with appropriate acting.

Each performance has its own flavor of originality. The bard is not bound by a rigid text that he must follow with precision. He can introduce into the narrative certain episodes or characters, and leave others out. He inserts personal reflections, proverbs, statements. He digresses to speak about himself, his ancestors, his experiences, his clan or caste, his artistry, his musical instrument, his teachers and predecessors, or about certain members of the audience. The narrative may be interspersed with longer pauses, to eat or drink, for dance performances, for dramatic action, for musical interludes, for praises.

On the whole, the performances are not linked with specific, narrowly defined ceremonies, rites, or periods of time. Bards perform at their own initiative, or at the request of a patron or host. For their rewards they largely depend on the generosity of the audience and the hosts. Most epics belong, so to speak, to the entire community, to all the people. A large, mixed, nonexclusive audience listens to and participates in the performance. The audience responds with dialogue and praises, refrain singing and dances, handclapping and percussion. The epic performance is an outstanding example of collective rejoicing and of entertainment that enriches and enlightens.

Performances take place in the open air, in the setting of a village or a compound. The bard and his aides may also sit under a shed or in a communal house, as is the case among the Fang. In most instances no specific time is prescribed, but bards, like other narrators, seem generally to prefer the evening and the night. The actual length of the performance is variable. This is understandable; the performance can easily be restricted to one or more self-contained episodes, and there is also the factor of fatigue. Episodes narrated among the Hamba lasted about two and one-half hours. The *Mvet* of Zwe Nguema among the Fang was performed in one nightly session and without interruption for ten hours. Mongo bards also prefer one long continuous performance of the entire epic. The Nyanga and Lega performances that I attended unrolled episode after episode for several hours a day, and for several days.

Content and Structure

It is clear from the foregoing summaries that the contents of these epics vary widely from ethnic group to ethnic group. It is also certain that within any of the epic-producing ethnic groups there exist a great number of parallel epic traditions, clustering about different, related or unrelated, central heroic figures. There exist also within the ethnic group numerous parallel traditions of the same epic, because of the occurrence of independently working bards of different families, lineages, and clans, trained in different "schools" of tradition. Individual variability and creativity are at work, marking off one performer from another, and one performance from another. On the other hand, similar epic traditions may be distributed at the multi-ethnic level among closely and more remotely related peoples. The Lianja epic, for example, is found among such Mongo-speaking, closely related tribes as Nkundo, Boyela, Ekota, Ekonda, and Mongo of Basankusu. Epics very closely akin in themes and structure to Lianja occur among more remotely related groups as Hamba, Mbole (Bambuli), Langa, Basiamba.[42] The epic traditions are pretty much open-ended. One performer may start with a great number of preludes and introductions, tracing the origins of the heroes and the antecedents of the events and actions, and introducing elaborate genealogies and cosmologies. Another performer may begin, so to speak, *in medias res,* with a vital event or activity that leads right into the main action, without bothering about preliminaries and other explanatory materials. One performer may focus in great detail on certain episodes and heroes, omitting or barely suggesting other events and characters. Another performer may indulge in numerous digressions of all sorts, praising his hosts or himself, alluding to personal experiences, and introducing anecdotes, explanations, philosophical and moral reflections. Some bards delight in detailed descriptions of councils, divination and healing scenes, speeches, conversations, and verbal challenges. Others pass rapidly over such points, to ensure a steady flow of action. Some bards finish the epic with the death or glorification of the main hero, others pursue the story of his heroic descendants.

Regardless of these many differences, however, for each epic tradition there seems to be a central core. In the various known versions of the Sunjata epic, Bird perceives a clear-cut central core of thematic material. It includes events leading to the birth of the hero, the hero's youth and exile from the Mande, and the hero's return to reconquer the Mande from Sumanguru. Each major set includes a recurring number of episodes.[43] De Rop has also shown the recurrence, in the various versions of the Lianja epic, of a central core constructed around the ancestors of the hero, the hero's parents and his father's death, the extraordinary birth of the hero, the hero's revenge of his father's death, the exodus to the promised land.[44] In a forthcoming work on the different versions of the Mwindo epic from the Nyanga, I have also analyzed the core materials. More importantly perhaps, I have shown how these Nyanga epics explicitly and implicitly follow a common spatial plan, in which the main hero acts in the four cosmic spheres and their subdivisions as the Nyanga recognize them.[45] Such a common thematic plan may even underlie epics from different, but related and/or contiguous, ethnic groups. Jacobs has indicated how epics collected by him among the Hamba, Mbole, Langa, Nkutshu, Kuni, Jonga, and Basiamba are constituted around the following essential parts: the discovery of a tree with women, the pregnancy of the hero's mother and her desire for a certain type of fruit, death of the hero's father, miraculous birth of the hero, the hero's adventures and journeys in search of revenge for his father's death, the death of the hero (often presented as three consecutive deaths of the same hero).[46]

Underlying the various epics are, of course, many of the quasi-universal epic patterns, with many variations from culture to culture and within the same culture. To give a few examples, the epics illustrate many different cases of a miraculous conception and birth. One hero is born the same day that he was conceived, another is born after the one hundred-fifty year long pregnancy of his mother, still another is born through parthenogenesis. Some of the heroes are active and can talk while they are still in their mother's womb. They leave and reenter the womb freely and also decide autonomously the manner and moment of birth. One is born from the palm of his mother's hand, another through his mother's medius, another one by ripping her belly open. The heroes are born possessing certain gifts (the capacity to walk and talk, the foreknowledge of events, and invulnerability) and holding certain objects (knives, scepters, spears, shoulderbags). Most heroes are ready for great action right after birth, but Sunjata is weak and cannot walk for many years after his birth. There are numerous other common patterns: Herculean deeds; extraterrestrial journeys; fierce individual battles with heroes, with divinities, with animals, dragons, and monsters; possession of extraordinary magical devices; tests of strength and intelligence; games. Some of the heroes are quasi-invulnerable and invincible; others have the capacity to resuscitate themselves and to revivify others, to make themselves invisible, and so on. Whereas most of the main heroes are fierce warriors and ruthless fighters possessing superhuman strength, there are exceptions to this pattern.

Mwindo, the hero of the Nyanga, is a small being; he is not a great killer or fighter; he pays great attention to revivifying his defeated enemies, and becomes, through purification in the celestial sphere, a poised, peace-minded, and balanced leader of his people.[47]

Whatever the character of the heroes and the development and elaboration of the epic patterns may be, all epics obviously provide rich, unsolicited information on the cultures and societies in which they occur. References to customs, institutions, patterns of behavior, techniques, beliefs, and values, particularly at certain stages through catalogues, genealogies, and descriptions, appear throughout the narrative. The ways in which and the extent to which the cultural patterns are directly or indirectly reflected, distorted, or omitted from these epics, need further detailed study. The analysis of the Mwindo epics from the Nyanga shows, on the one hand, an immense amount of accurate detail on various aspects of culture, and on the other hand, a lack of such precision, a more or less deliberate distortion, and a conscious omission of other cultural features. This is not the result of the relative knowledge of individual narrators, nor a random situation, but a reflection of deep values and thought patterns in Nyanga.[48] The West African epics of Sunjata, Monzon, and Silamaka offer considerable insight into the history of the Mandeka, Bambara, and Fulani peoples. The central heroes of these epics are known historical figures. But even here, there is obviously much manipulation of objective history for purposes of glorification, extravagance, factionalism, and regionalism.[49] The extent to which history is reflected in the epics of the Fang, the Mongo, the Nyanga or the Lega is difficult to perceive. The central heroes are not immediately known historical figures. These epics more or less explicitly refer to historical migrations, conflicts, feuds, and wars in which such large, politically uncentralized ethnic groups as the Fang and Mongo have been involved. The Mubila epic of the Lega largely bears on an early historical period when the Lega, divided by internecine war, had not yet found the unifying bond of the *bwami* association.[50] The Mwindo epics of the Nyanga, on the other hand, provide very little historical evidence—so little that even in casual statements, in vocabulary and description, extremely few indications occur that the Nyanga migrated into the forest regions from East Africa, and are in contact with other African peoples and also with Europeans.

African epics present extremely significant testimonies about the value systems and patterns of thought of African peoples. Several authors have pointed out that in the Sunjata epic the main hero is depicted as a good leader whose destiny it is to make immortal the name of the Mali Empire. He is a good leader because by going into exile he avoids bringing to a climax the intense rivalry between himself and his father's son. He returns only after the throne has been left vacant and has been usurped by a foreigner.[51] Bird sees a political charter underlying the Sunjata epic: it instructs the king in how to deal with people, and the people about their rights and their duties towards the king. The king can be harsh and severe, but not unjust; he must respect the forces of love, trust, allegiance, that keep society together. In a certain sense the hero, Sunjata, is a spiritual more than a physical force. The Mwindo epic of the Nyanga explicitly stresses the values of hospitality, generosity, kinship, clemency, reconciliation, filial piety, and so forth. The character of the hero, however, is for a major portion of the epic in flagrant contradiction with the value code of the Nyanga. Through much of the epic, Mwindo is arrogant, boisterous, aggressive, verbose, irascible, quarrelsome, and pugnacious. These traits make him somewhat funny and unlikely for the Nyanga. Ultimately, in a totally passive manner, he goes through a complete catharsis and transformation at the hands of the celestial elements. He returns to earth to rule in glory as a poised, peace-loving, reflective chief. Mubila, the ruthless, militant, pompous hero of one of the Lega epics, is throughout the epic in flagrant opposition to the value code of moderation and temperance that prevails in the *bwami* association that dominates Lega social and moral life. He illustrates, so to speak, an earlier, archaic, unacceptable type of leader. In the Lianja epic the values of perseverance, tenacity of purpose, courage, and honor are prominently emphasized. The hero, in his pursuit of glory, must avoid all actions that are blameworthy and shameful.[52]

Age, Origin, and Authorship of the Epics

The questions of age and origin of the orally transmitted African epics—so important for the scientific study of the epic traditions of other world literatures—are of relatively little relevance in this study. For one, it does not seem to be possible to ever find reasonable answers to these questions. Let us look at the Nyanga. This small, forest-dwelling population, which possesses an extremely complex and diversified culture, has very limited historical interests. The Nyanga are conscious of having immigrated from Uganda (East Africa) into the deep rain forest where they now live and where they encountered and assimilated Pygmies and other archaic groups. The actual processes, stages, and time periods at which all this happened are largely irrelevant to them. The Nyanga bards, who otherwise know so many things, have only a shallow recollection of the predecessors whose traditions they follow. The few indications that they provide point to the possibility that the epics, or at least the materials of which epics are made, were already known to the Pygmies before the Nyanga encountered them. Furthermore, our present knowledge of the distribution of epics among Bantu-speaking peoples points to areas where, as among the Fang, the Mongo, the Mbole, the Nyanga, and the Lega, Pygmy influences are very old and very significant. Is this, at the same time, an indication of the great age of these epic materials? Yet all this offers only a relative time indication. The Sunjata epic celebrates a ruler of the thirteenth century. It is possible that the core materials of the epic texts are as old as Sunjata, or even older. For there are also in these areas hunters' epics. which may be much older than Sunjata and which have probably served as models for it.

It is also difficult, at this stage, to establish clear connections between the epics of different ethnic groups. Let us take the epic-producing forest-dwelling populations of Central Africa. The Mbole, Hamba, Basiamba, and others have remote historical, linguistic, and cultural connections with the Mongo. Therefore, it is not surprising that certain common details in pattern, structure, heroic characters, and events occur. The Nyanga and Lega have certain rather remote cultural and historical connections, and they are territorially close to each other. There is, however, a radical difference between the epic traditions of both groups, and an even greater difference between any one of them and the Mongo.

Finally, the individual creators or bards who first developed or synthesized particular epic traditions are not known by name.[53] As already explained, the living bards may only recall a few predecessors and teachers in their own line of tradition. They do not bother about the original version or archetype, or about the first compiler-creator of the epics.

Style

All African epics seem to be sung, in their entirety or partially. Shorter passages may be chanted or recited, but even these portions are performed against a background of music. The musical accompaniment is frequently made, in the first place, by the bard himself, but close aides can take over this role. There are always several other musicians who contribute to the musical background. And, of course, members of the audience, with or without musical instruments, intervene in the recitation—as a choir to sing refrains, to engage in dialogue, and to praise. The bards of the Bambara are musicians as well as singers.[54] There is an inseparable bond between the singer, his musical instrument, his text; this is reflected among the Fang in the generic term *mvett* or *mver,* which bears on all three.[55] Bambara epics have their characteristic air, and each hero has his musical theme.[56] Musical interludes, formal songs with refrains, musical dialogues between the bard and his aides and/or audience are of essence in the performance of epics. Much further research is, therefore, needed on the relationships between music and epic style. Some of the African epics are quite obviously formulated in verse form or ''lines.'' Others seem to consist of an alteration between rhythmic prose and poetic songs. But even the so-called rhythmic prose abounds with poetic formulas that range from aphorisms to epithets. Bird has concluded that the Sunjata epic consists of ''lines,'' the rhythmic constituents of which are defined not by accents or the number of syllables, but by the musical rhythm. He finds a high correspondence between the poetic line and the measure of four accented beats.[57]

The bards have at their disposal a vast repertoire of literary genres, and esthetic, stylistic, and linguistic devices which they harmoniously blend in their epic narratives.[58] The epic style is riddled with aphorisms and other terse statements, formulas, incantations, songs, conversations, dialogues, speeches, succinct references to tales, prayers, praises, improvised reflections, and remarks. These features contribute to the enhancement of a vivid, poetic, and florid style. The bards are masters of the verb. They have an extraordinary grasp of the vocabulary and its metaphorical properties, and of the grammar and its flexibilities. They are masters in the poetic usage of various stylistic and esthetic devices: repetition; reduplication of cores, radicals and cores; onomatopoeia and other numerous effects; exclamations; enjambments. The formulas are particularly abundant and varied: epithets; patronymics; titles; stereotyped phrases; praises; aphorisms; riddles; incantations; standard place, time, and action references; and repetitions of words and ideas. Some Nyanga bards show a particular preference for the indirect discourse, sometimes mixed in the same statement with direct discourse.[59] The art of praise, glorification, amplification, and embellishment is vigorously practised by the bards in the characterization of the heroes, their manner of speaking, their manner of interpreting events. The vivacity of the performance, its color and intensity, are also greatly enhanced by the nonverbal and nonmusical elements of the presentation. It must be kept in mind that the bard acts, gesticulates, mimics, and dances.[60] No written, or even taped, analysis of the living epic can ever capture this atmosphere of action and reaction by the singer, the musicians, and the audience.[61] The total action in which the epic evolves lends particular vigor and poetry to the performance and its content.

NOTES

1. Good general information is available in: Amadou H. Ba and Lilyan Resteloot, "Les épopées de l'ouest africain," *Abbia* 14–15 (1966): 165–205; Daniel Biebuyck, "The Epic as a Genre in Congo Oral Literature," in *African Folklore*, ed. Richard M. Dorson, pp. 257–73; Robert Cornevin, "Les poèmes épiques africains et la notion d'épopée vivante," *Présence Africaine*, n.s. 60 (1966): 140–45; John Jacobs, "Vergelijkende studie van enkele Afrikaanse heldenepen," *Bulletin des Séances ARSOM*, n.s. 18 (1972): 486–91; Jan Knappert, "The Epic in Africa," pp. 171–90.

2. Ruth Finnegan, *Oral Literature in Africa* (Oxford: The Clarendon Press, 1970), pp. 108–109, is unnecessarily sceptical about the existence of African epics, and the unity of such great texts as the Lianja epic of the Mongo.

3. These various epics, and the relevant bibliographical references, are mentioned below. Many texts presented as unconnected tales or myths may be part of larger structured wholes that have escaped superficial observation.

4. See, for example, Trevor Cope, *Izibongo: Zulu Praise-Poems* (Oxford: The Clarendon Press, 1968); Daniel P. Kunene, *Heroic Poetry of the Basotho* (Oxford: The Clarendon Press, 1971); H. F. Morris, *The Heroic Recitations of the Bahima of Ankole* (Oxford: The Clarendon Press, 1964); I. Schapera, *Praise-Poems of Tswana Chiefs* (Oxford: The Clarendon Press, 1965). Jan Knappert, "The Epic in Africa," *Journal of the Folklore Institute* 4 (1967): 171–90, provides useful information on these and other heroic and epic-like genres.

5. Kunene, *Heroic Poetry,* pp. 53–67.

6. For discussions of these genres, see A. Coupez and Th. Kamanzi, *Récits historiques Rwanda* (Tervuren: Musée royal de l'Afrique Centrale, 1962); A. Coupez and Th. Kamanzi, *Littérature de cour au Rwanda* (Oxford: The Clarendon Press, 1970); Alexis Kagame, *La poésie dynastique au Rwanda* (Brussels: Institut Royal Colonial Belge, 1951); S. A. Babalola, *The Content and Form of Yoruba Ijala* (Oxford: The Clarendon Press, 1966); Charles Bird, "Heroic Songs of the Mande Hunters," in *African Folklore,* ed. Richard M. Dorson (Garden City: Doubleday and Company, 1972), pp. 275–93; Patrice Mufuta, *Le chant kasala des Luba* (Paris: Julliard, 1969); Pierre-Francis Lacroix, *Poésie peule de l'Adamawa,* 2 vols. (Paris: Julliard, 1965).

7. For a discussion of the animal tales, see Finnegan, *Oral Literature in Africa,* pp. 343–54, and passim. Particularly interesting examples of specific animal cycles are found in the following collections of tales: W. H. I. Bleek, *Reynard the Fox in South Africa* (London: Trübner, 1864) [weasel]; H. Callaway, *Nursery Tales, Traditions and Histories of the Zulus* (London: Trübner and Co., 1868) [weasel]; E. E. Evans-Pritchard, *The Zande Trickster* (Oxford: The Clarendon Press, 1967) [spider]; G. Hulstaert, *Contes mongo* (Brussels: Académie royale des Sciences d'Outre-Mer, 1965) [turtle]; John Jacobs, *Tetela-Teksten* (Tervuren: Musée royal de l'Afrique Centrale, 1959) [dwarf antelope]; H. A. Junod, *Les chants et les contes des Baronga de la Baie de Delagoa* (Lausanne: George Bridel, 1897) [toad]; H. A. Junod, *The Life of a South African Tribe,* 2 vols. (London, 1927) [hare]; Gerhard Lindblom, *Kamba Folklore,* I: *Tales of Animals* (Uppsala: Appelbergs Bocktryckeri Aktiebolag, 1928) [hare]; R. S. Rattray, *Akan-Ashanti Folktales* (Oxford: The Clarendon Press, 1930) [spider]; Leo Stappers, *Textes luba: Contes d'animaux* (Tervuren: Musée royal de l'Afrique Centrale, 1962) [dwarf antelope]; R. Van Caeneghem, *Kabundi sprookjes* (Brussels: Vromant, 1938) [a mixture of squirrel and marten].

8. John Jacobs and Jan Vansina, "Nsong Atoot: Het koninklijk epos der Bushong," *Kongo-Overzee* 22 (1956): 1–39; Claude Meillassoux, Lassana Doucouré, and Diaowé Simagha, *Légende de la dispersion des Kusa: Epopée Soninké* (Dakar: IFAN, 1957); Vincent Monteil, "La légende de Wagadou: Texte Soninke de Malamine Tandyan," *Bulletin de l'IFAN* 29, sér. B (1967): 134–49; P. Césard, "Comment les Bahaya interprètent leurs origines," *Anthropos* 22 (1927): 441–65; P. Césard, "Histoire des rois du Kyamtwara d'après l'ensemble des traditions des familles régnantes," *Anthropos* 26 (1931): 533–43. A large number of texts center around founding ancestors, early kings, and leaders; these texts contain the materials of which epics are made. I place in this category, for example, the stories about Faran Maka Bote, the ancestor of the Sorko fishermen (J. Rouch); Aura Poku, the legendary queen of the Baule (H. Himmelheber); Maso-mandala and his sons among the Duala (Fr. Ebding); Nyikang, the ancestor-culture-hero of the Shilluk (D. Westermann); Sudika-mbambi and his brother among the Mbundu (H. Chatelain); Kintu, the "great ancestor of very long ago" among the Ganda (John Roscoe), and so many others.

9. Knappert, "The Epic in Africa," pp. 182–85, gives a succinct discussion of these epics. The texts of some Swahili epics can be found in Lyndon Harries, *Swahili Poetry* (Oxford: The Clarendon Press, 1962), pp. 24–171; Jan Knappert, *Traditional Swahili Poetry: An Investigation into the Concepts of East African Islam as Reflected in the Utenzi Literature* (Leiden: E. J. Brill, 1967); Edward Steere, *Swahili Tales as Told by Natives of Zanzibar* (London: Bell and Daldy, 1870). Among the epics constructed by African creative writers, the following may be mentioned: Alexis Kagame, *La Divine Pastorale* (Brussels, 1952), and *La Naissance de l'Univers* (Brussels,

1955); Thomas Mofolo, *Chaka: An Historical Romance* (London: Oxford University Press, 1931).

10. The French translations of these texts are published in Amadou H. Ba, "Monzon et le roi de Koré," *Présence Africaine* 58 (1966): 99–127, and Amadou H. Ba and Lilyan Kesteloot, "Les épopées de l'ouest africain," *Abbia* 14–15 (1966): 165–205. A shorter fragment, which I have not seen, is also available in Amadou Doucouré, "Défi, de Déissé-Koro, roi du Kaarta à Da Monzon, roi de Ségou," *France-Eurafrique* 171 (1966): 43–45.

11. Lilyan Kesteloot, "Les épopées de l'ouest africain," *Présence Africaine* 58 (1966): 206, indicates that the published fragments are but a fraction of a vast epic cycle, and that many different versions are still sung today. The figure of Da Monzon also occurs among the Fulani. (See further under the Silamaka epic of the Fulani.) Ba and Kesteloot, "Les épopées de l'ouest africain," p. 167, state that in the Mali Republic alone, twenty epics have been registered. Other central heroes mentioned are Sunjata, Sumanguru, Ferobe, Irlaybe, the forty kings of Gana, Deforabe, Biton of Segu, El Hadj Omar, the Nabas of the Mossi.

12. Ba, "Monzon et le roi de Koré," pp. 99–127. The original is not provided. The translation is by Ba. No information is given about the bard or the circumstances of the narration.

13. Ba and Kesteloot, "Les épopées de l'ouest africain," pp. 171–78. The original text, which is not reproduced, is translated from Bambara by Mamadou Konaté.

14. Ba and Kesteloot, "Les épopées de l'ouest africain," pp. 179–209. The original is not published. The long text in verse-lines is translated by the two authors of the study. According to the authors, more than ten of such episodes are known, in which Da Monzon is involved in conflicts with his vassals.

15. The text of this epic episode, collected around 1957 by Amadou Hampaté Ba and Lilyan Kesteloot, was published as "Une épopée peule: Silamaka," *L'Homme* 8 (1968): 5–36.

16. According to Ba and Kesteloot, "Silamaka," p. 5, several other versions were recorded among different Fulani groups in the Niger Republic. This episode is also sung by Bambara bards.

17. The name, Sunjata, is variously written as Sundiata, Soundjata, Sonjata. I follow the spelling proposed by Bird. One classic version of this epic was published in French translation by Djibril T. Niane, *Soundjata ou l'épopée manolingue* (Paris: Présence Africaine, 1960). An English translation of this text was made by G. D. Pickett, *Sundiata: An Epic of Old Mali* (London: Longsmans, Green and Co., 1965). Various recorded and transcribed versions of the epic made by Charles Bird and his collaborators are available at the Indiana University Archives of Traditional Music. Numerous studies on this epic by Bird, Humblot, Niane, Shelton, Sidibé, and Paguard are listed in the bibliography.

18. Charles Bird, "Some Remarks on the Sunjata Epic." (Unpublished manuscript, 1974). I am indebted to Dr. Bird for allowing me to use this extremely well-documented manuscript.

19. Bird, "Sunjata Epic," pp. 8–11.

20. J. P. Clark, "The Ozidi Saga," *Black Orpheus* 2/2 (1968): 18–24, gives in translation the opening of the prologue to this extraordinary text, and a short summary. The entire text to be published in two volumes was narrated with music, dance, and mime in seven nights by Okabu of Sama Town.

21. The so-called Ogboingba myth of the Ijaw has also many epic elements, and might as well be an episode of a much longer text. See Gabriel Okaro, "Ogboingba: The Ijaw Creation Myth," *Black Orpheus* 1 (1957): 9–17.

22. D. A. Puplampu, "The National Epic of the Adangme," *African Affairs* 50 (1951): 236–41, gives short fragments of the Klama epic, which is said to consist of more than six thousand stanzas. Leo Frobenius, *Spielmannsgeschichten der Sahel* (Jena, 1921) provides a summary of the Gassire text.

23. The manuscript by Daniel Biebuyck, *The Mwindo Epic: New Versions,* is now in its last stages of preparation for publication by the University of California Press.

24. Daniel Biebuyck and Kahombo Mateene, *The Mwindo Epic from the Banyanga (Congo Republic)* (Berkeley and Los Angeles: University of California Press, 1969). This work gives the complete Nyanga text, in the original and in translation, together with an introduction and a large number of explanatory notes.

25. The texts (original, and French or Dutch translations) are published in: E. Boelaert, "Nsong'a Lianja: Het groote epos der Nkundo-Mongo," *Congo* 1 (1932): 49–79, 198–215; E. Boelaert, *Nsong'a Lianja: L'épopée nationale des Nkundo* (Antwerp: de Sikkel, 1949); E. Boelaert, *Lianja-Verhalan, I; Ekofo-versie* (Tervuren: Musée royal du Congo Belge, 1957); E. Boelaert, *Lianja-Verhalen, II: De voorouders van Lianja* (Tervuren: Musée royal du Congo Belge, 1958). An important new work by A. de Rop, *Versions et fragments de l'épopée des Mongo,* is forthcoming.

26. A. de Rop, "L'épopée des Knundo. L'original et la copie," *Kongo-Overzee* 24 (1958): 170–78; A. de Rop, "Lianja-Verhalen," *Band* 18 (1959): 149–50; A. de Rop, *Lianja: L'épopée des Mongo* (Brussels: Académie royale des Sciences d'Outre-Mer, 1964).

27. Daniel Biebuyck, "Mubila: Een epos der Balega," *Band* 12 (1953): 68–74; Daniel Biebuyck, "The Epic as a Genre in Congo Oral Literature," in *African Folklore,* ed. Richard M. Dorson, pp. 257–73. The full text of the Mubila epic is now being prepared by Daniel Biebuyck for publication by the University of California Press. An important dissertation on another Lega epic was produced by J. B. N'sanda, *Epopée Kiguma: Essai d'étude d'un genre littéraire Lega* (Kinshasa: Lovanium University). Unfortunately, this text was not available to me at this time.

28. The translations of these shorter epic texts are available in John Jacobs, "Le récit épique de Lofokefoke, le héros des Mbole (Bambuli)," *Aequatoria* 24 (1961): 81–92; John Jacobs, "Het epos van Kudukese, de 'Culture Hero' van de Hamba," *Africa-Tervuren* 9 (1963): 33–36.

29. A vast number of epic texts centering around the hero, Akoma Mba, have already been recorded, and a few of them published. Some of these texts begin with the origin of the world and of the first humans, and deal with the birth of the heroes. Others concentrate on the deeds of the central hero, Akoma Mba, in conflict with many other heroes. A text of 2438 lines (in the original, and in French translation) can be found in Stanislas Awona, "La guerre d'Akoma Mba contre Abo Mama," *Abbia* 9–10 (1965): 180–213, and *Abbia* 12–13 (1966): 109–209. A huge text, divided into twelve songs and interludes (original and translation) is available in Herbert Pepper, *Un mvet de Zwè Nguéma: Chant épique Fang* (Paris: Armand Colin, 1972). The first part of another epic, centering around Oveng Ndumu Obame, is published in French translation by Tsira Ndoutoume Ndong, *Le Mvett* (Paris: Présence Africaine, 1970).

30. This short synthesis is given in Gaspard Towo-Atangana, "Le mvet: Genre majeur de la littérature orale des populations Pahouines," *Abbia* 9–10 (1965): 171–72.

31. Publication of this text is mentioned in Stanislas Awona, *Abbia* 12–13 (1966): 112.

32. The complete text (original and French translation) of this epic, together with summaries and notes, is found in Herbert Pepper, *Un mvet de Zwè Nguéma* (Paris: Armand Colin, 1972).

33. The text narrated and sung by Mwana Mbirika is reproduced in J. Torrend, *Specimens of Bantu Folk-lore from Northern Rhodesia* (London: Kegan Paul, 1921), pp. 98–144.

34. Other epic-like texts, or summaries of such texts, from Bantu-speaking peoples can be found, for example, in Piliwe Kisala, "Lubango Knundungulu: A Kaonde Epic," *Jewel of Africa* 2/3–4 (1970): 9–16; John Roscoe, *The Baganda: An Account of Their Native Customs and Beliefs* (London: Macmillan and Co., 1911), pp. 460–64; Harold Scheub, "A Xhosa Narrative," in *African Folklore*, ed. Richard M. Dorson, pp. 523–61.

35. I have indicated some of these names in the preceding notes. In general, little information is given about the social background and the individual artistry of the bards. Biebuyck and Mateene, *The Mwindo Epic*, pp. 15–19, provide such information for the bard Shekarisi Candi Rureke. Excellent general information on the *mvet* singers and players can be found in Towo-Atangana, pp. 163–77, Philippe Ndoutoume Ndong, "Le Mvett," *Présence Africaine* 59 (1966): 57–76, and Elie Ekogamve, "La littérature orale des Fang," *African Arts* 2 (1969): 14–19, 77–78. The bards of the Mandeka and Bambara are very well discussed in Charles Bird, "Heroic Songs of the Mande Hunters," in *African Folklore*, ed. Richard M. Dorson, pp. 278–79; Mamby Sidibé, "Les gens de caste ou nyamakala au Soudan Français," *Notes Africaines* 81 (1959): 13–17; Hugo Zemp, "La légende des griots malinké," *Cahiers d'Etudes Africaines* 6 (1966): 611–42.

36. Bird, "Some remarks on the Sunjata Epic," pp. 3–4.

37. Ekogamve, "La littérature orale des Fang," pp. 77–78.

38. Kesteloot, "Les épopées de l'ouest africain," p. 205.

39. For the Nyanga bard, see frontispiece in Biebuyck and Kahombo, *The Mwindo Epic*. For the Mongo, see Boelaert, *Nsong'a Lianja*, p. 4, and de Rop, *Lianja: L'épopée des Mongo*, p. 18. For the way in which the *mvet* players and bards among the Fang are dressed, see plates in Awona, *Abbia* 12–13 (1966): 164–65, and 190–91, and Towo-Atangana, *Abbia* 9–10 (1965): 162, 166, 170, and 174.

40. Information on the musical instruments is provided in the above-mentioned sources.

41. The epics seem to be essentially a male art, but women are, in several instances, not entirely dissociated from the epic performances. Bird, "Some Remarks on the Sunjata Epic," p. 4, indicates female bards specialize in praise-songs that are associated with the epics.

42. de Rop, "L'épopée des Nkundo," p. 170; Jacobs, "Le récit épique de Lofokefoke," p. 81. In the context of the Lianja epic of the Mongo many historically known ethnic groups, such as Ngombe, Elinga, Bafoto, Baenga, Balumbe, occur in battles led by Lianja.

43. Bird, "Some Remarks on the Sunjata Epic," pp. 8–11.

44. de Rop, *Lianja: L'épopée des Mongo*, pp. 71–88.

45. Biebuyck, *The Mwindo Epic: New Versions*. See also Biebuyck and Mateene, *The Mwindo Epic*, pp. 19–32. The spatial plan situates the hero's actions on earth, in

the underworld, in the sky, and in the air (or atmosphere). His terrestrial exploits take place in the village, in the fields, in the abandoned village, in the virgin forest, and in the water (river, pool, pond).

46. Jacobs, "Het epos van Kudukese," p. 36.

47. Biebuyck and Mateene, *The Mwindo Epic,* pp. 33–35, and 144. The theme of the revivification of slain enemies is also strongly developed in the Lianja epic.

48. Certainly ritually very important animals (such as the hornbill) or persons (such as the *kihanga* spirit-wives or circumcisors) do not occur in the various texts that I recorded among the Nyanga.

49. See, for example, A. J. Shelton, "The Problem of Griot Interpretation and the Actual Causes of War in Soundjata," *Présence Africaine,* n.s. 66 (1968): 145–52.

50. The *bwami* association, and its moral philosophy of goodness and beauty, are analyzed in Daniel Biebuyck, *Lega Culture: Art, Initiation, and Moral Philosophy among a Central African People* (Berkeley and Los Angeles: The University of California Press, 1973).

51. The avoidance of rivalry among the sons of the same father, as reflected in the Sunjata Epic, is discussed in Bird, "Some Remarks on the Sunjata Epic," pp. 11–13, and R. Pageard, "Soundiata Keita et la tradition orale," *Présence Africaine,* n.s. 36 (1961): 61.

52. de Rop, *Lianja: L'épopée des Mongo,* p. 12, and passim.

53. Various oral traditions about the origins of the *mvet* and certain epic traditions occur among the Fang-Ntumu. See Towo-Atangana, *Abbia* 9–10 (1965): 164–72.

54. Kesteloot, "Les épopées de l'ouest africain," p. 168; Zemp, p. 611. In Mongo terminology, the bards "sing" the epic, even when they recite and narrate; the bard is called a singer (*wembi*).

55. Ndong, "Le Mvett," p. 57.

56. Kesteloot, "Les épopées de l'ouest africain," p. 168. This is not very different from the mask traditions in some African ethnic groups, where each masker has his own musical theme to announce him.

57. Bird, "Some Remarks on the Sunjata Epic," pp. 5–6, has made this fundamental discovery, which may influence much future analysis.

58. Biebuyck, "The Epic as a Genre in Congo Oral Literature," pp. 266–67, stresses this point.

59. Biebuyck and Mateene, *The Mwindo Epic,* p. 37, and passim. Meillassoux, Doucouré, and Simagha, *Légende de la dispersion des Kusa,* p. 7, also emphasize this point.

60. Ekogamve, "La littérature orale des Fang," pp. 14–19; Ndong, *Le Mvett,* p. 18.

61. Ndong (*Le Mvett,* pp. 18–19), who is himself a famed *mvet* player, asks for his readers' indulgence, because a written text cannot re-create the musical rhythm, the dance movements, the reaction of the public, the general atmosphere of the village where the recitation takes place.

BIBLIOGRAPHY

Awona, Stanislas. "La guerre d'Akoma Mba contre Abo Mama (Epopée du mvet)."

Abbia 9–10 (1965): 180–213. Together with Awona, 1966, contains two thousand four hundred and thirty-eight lines in the original and in French translation of an epic text illustrating the battle between Akoma Mba and Abo Mama. There is almost no explanation of the text.

———. "La guerre d'Akoma Mba contre Abo Mama." *Abbia* 12–13 (1966): 109–209.

Ba, Amadou Hampaté. "Monzon et le roi de Koré." *Présence Africaine* 58 (1966): 99–127.

Ba, Amadou Hampaté, and Lilyan Kesteloot. "Les épopées de l'ouest africain." *Abbia* 14–15 (1966): 165–205. These two studies by Ba give in French translation three longer excerpts of the Monzon epic of the Bambara. There is a useful general introduction to the West African epics.

———. "Une épopée peule: Silamaka." *L'Homme* 8 (1968): 5–36. Provides the French translation of a Fulani epic and a useful explanation.

Babalola, S. A. *The Content and Form of Yoruba Ijala.* Oxford: The Clarendon Press, 1966.

Balandier, Georges. "Un chef: Chaka." *Présence Africaine* 8–9 (n.d.): 159–66.

Biebuyck, Daniel. "Mubila: Een epos der Balega." *Band* 12 (1953): 68–74. Gives in Dutch translation the only published fragment of the Mubila epic of the Lega, together with general remarks about the narrator and the mode of narration.

———. "The Epic as a Genre in Congo Oral Literature." In *African Folklore,* edited by Richard M. Dorson, pp. 257–73. Garden City: Doubleday and Company, 1972. A general discussion of various aspects of form, style, and content in the epics of the Lega, Mongo, Tetela, Hamba, and Nyanga of the Zaïre Republic.

———. *The Mubila Epic from the Balega.* Berkeley: University of California Press, forthcoming. Provides the complete text of a long epic from the Lega, together with a detailed discussion of cultural content, performance, style, and meaning.

———. *The Mwindo Epic: New Versions.* Berkeley: University of California Press, forthcoming. Three versions of the Mwindo epic and several epic fragments from the Nyanga, with ample discussion of form and content, narrator, mode of narration, thematic core, and spatial plan. This work complements Biebuyck and Mateene, 1969.

Biebuyck, Daniel, and Kahombo Mateene. *The Mwindo Epic from the Bayanga (Congo Republic).* Berkeley and Los Angeles: University of California Press, 1969. Paperback, 1971. Provides the complete Nyanga text and the English translation of a Nyanga epic, together with many cultural data and information on the narrator and the performance.

———. *Anthologie de la littérature orale nyanga.* Brussels: Académie royale des Sciences d'Outre-Mer, 1970. Discusses and illustrates, with appropriate texts in Nyanga and in French translation, the various literary genres recognized by the Nyanga. A short epic text is included.

Bird, Charles. "Bambara Oral Prose and Verse Narratives." In *African Folklore,* edited by Richard M. Dorson, pp. 441–77. Garden City: Doubleday and Company, 1972.

———. "Heroic Songs of the Mande Hunters." In *African Folklore,* edited by Richard M. Dorson, pp. 275–93. Garden City: Doubleday and Company, 1972.

———. "Some Remarks on the Sunjata Epic." Unpublished manuscript, 1974. This manuscript contains a significant number of new data on the Sunjata epic tradition of the Mandeka.

Bleek, W. H. I. *Reynard the Fox in South Africa, or Hottentot Fables and Tales.* London, 1864.

Boelaert, E. "Nsong'a Lianja: Het groote epos der Nkundo-Mongo." *Congo* 1 (1932): 49–79, 198–215.

———. *Nsong'a Lianja: L'épopée nationale des Nkundo.* Antwerp: de Sikkel, 1949.

Text and French translation of a composite synthesis of the Lianja epic of the Mongo (Zaïre Republic).

———. "Nog over het epos van de Mongo: Hoe hij heldenzanger werd," *Kongo-Overzee* 20 (1952): 289–92.

———. *Lianja-Verhalen, I: Ekofo-versis.* Tervuren: Musée royal du Congo Belge, 1957. Text and Dutch translation of a very detailed and complete version of the Lianja epic.

———. *Lianja-Verhalen, II: De voorouders van Lianja.* Tervuren: Musée royal du Congo Belge, 1958. Text and Dutch translation of one version of the Lianja epic that illustrates the deeds of Lianja's ancestors.

———. "Lianja: Het nationaal epos der Mongo." *Verhandelingen K. V. H. U.* (1960): 3–58.

———. "La procession de Lianja." *Aequatoria* 25 (1962): 1–9.

Callaway, H. *Nursery Tales, Traditions, and Histories of the Zulus.* London: Trübner and Co., 1868.

Césard, P. "Comment les Bahaya interprètent leurs origines." *Anthropos* 22 (1927): 441–65.

———. "Histoire des rois du Kyamtwara d'après l'ensemble des traditions des familles régnantes." *Anthropos* 26 (1931): 533–43.

Chatelain, Heli. *Folk-Tales of Angola.* Boston and New York: Houghton, Mifflin and Co., 1894.

Clark, J. P. "The Ozidi Saga." *Black Orpheus* 2/2 (1968): 18–24.

Cope, Trevor. *Izibongo: Zulu Praise-Poems.* Oxford: The Clarendon Press, 1968.

Cornevin, Robert. "Les poèmes épiques africains et la notion d'épopée vivante." *Présence Africaine,* n.s. 60 (1966): 140–45.

Coupez, A., and Th. Kamanzi. *Récits historiques Rwanda.* Tervuren: Musée royal de l'Afrique Centrale, 1962.

———. *Littérature de cour au Rwanda.* Oxford: The Clarendon Press, 1970.

de Rop, A. "L'épopée des Nkundo. L'original et la copie." *Kongo-Overzee* 24 (1958): 170–78.

———. "Lianja-Verhalen." *Band* 18 (1959): 149–50.

———. *Lianja: L'épopée des Mongo.* Brussels: Académie royale des Sciences d'Outre-Mer, 1964. Interesting comparative study of various versions of the Lianja epic, with a detailed discussion of thematic core.

Dorson, Richard M., ed. *African Folklore.* Garden City: Doubleday and Company, 1972.

Doucouré, Amadou. "Défi, de Déissé-Koro, roi du Kaarta à Da Monzon, roi de Ségou." *France-Eurafrique* 171 (1966): 43–45.

Ebding, Friedrich. *Duala Märchen.* Gesammelt und übersetzt von Friedrich Ebding. Berlin: W. De Gruyter, 1938.

Ekogamve, Elie. "La Littérature orale des Fang. The Oral Literature of the Fang." *African Arts* 2 (1969): 14–19, 77–78.

Evans-Pritchard, E. E. *The Zande Trickster.* Oxford: The Clarendon Press, 1967.

Finnegan, Ruth. *Oral Literature in Africa.* Oxford: The Clarendon Press, 1970.

Frobenius, Leo. *Spielmannsgeschichten der Sahel.* Atlantis, 6. Jena, 1921.

Goody, Jack. *The Myth of the Bagre.* Oxford: The Clarendon Press, 1972.

Görög, Veronika. "Littérature orale africaine: Bibliographie analytique." *Cahiers d'Etudes Africaines* 8 (1968): 453–501; 9 (1969): 641–66; 10 (1970): 583–627; 12 (1972): 174–92.

Harries, Lyndon. *Swahili Poetry.* Oxford: The Clarendon Press, 1962.

Himmelheber, Hans. *Aura Poku: Mythen, Tiergeschichten und Sagen, Sprichwörter, Fabeln und Rätsel.* 2nd ed. Eisenach: Erich Röth, 1951.

Hulstaert, G. *Contes Mongo.* Brussels: Académie royale des Sciences d'Outre-Mer, 1965.

Humblot, P. "Episodes de la légende de Soundiata." *Notes Africaines* 52 (1951): 111–13.

Jacobs, John. *Tetela-Teksten*. Tervuren: Musée royal de l'Afrique Centrale, 1959.

————. "Le récit épique de Lofokefoke, le héros des Mbole (Bambuli)." *Acquatoria* 24 (1961): 81–92. French translation of an epic text from the Mbole (Bambuli) of the Zaïre Republic.

————. "Het epos van Kudukese, de 'Culture Hero' van de Hamba (Kongo)." *Africa-Tervuren* 9 (1963): 33–36. Dutch summary of an epic from the Hamba (Zaïre Republic) and interesting comparative data on the distribution of epics among a number of smaller ethnic groups related to the Mongo.

————. "Voorstelling van een Werk van E. P. A. de Rop: Versions et fragments de l'épopée des Mongo." *Bulletin des Séances ARSOM*, n.s. 17 (1971): 206–208.

————. "Vergelijkende studie van enkele Afrikaanse heldenepen." *Bulletin des Séances ARSOM*, n.s. 18 (1972): 486–91. Brief discussion of different epic genres (called mythical, historical, and cyclic).

Jacobs, John, and Jan Vansina. "Nsong Atoot: Het koninklijk epos der Bushong." *Kongo-Overzee* 22 (1956): 1–39.

Junod, H. A. *Les chants et les contes des Baronga de la Baie de Delagoa*. Lausanne: George Bridel, 1897.

————. *The Life of a South African Tribe*. 2 vols. London: Macmillan, 1927.

Kagame, Alexis. *La poésie dynastique au Rwanda*. Brussels: Institut Royal Colonial Belge, 1951.

Kesteloot, Lilyan. "Les épopées de l'ouest africain." *Présence Africaine* 58 (1966): 204–209.

Kisala, Piliwe. "Lubango Nkundungulu: A Kaonde Epic, ed. and intro. Han F. W. Bantje." *Jewel of Africa* 2/3–4 (1970): 9–16.

Knappert, Jan. "The Epic in Africa." *Journal of the Folklore Institute* 4 (1967): 171–90. A general overview of various types of epic literature (orally transmitted or written) including heroic epics, animal epic cycles, praise poems, and Islamic epics.

————. *Traditional Swahili Poetry: An Investigation into the Concepts of East African Islam as Reflected in the Utenzi Literature*. Leiden: E. J. Brill, 1967.

————. *Myths and Legends of the Congo*. London: Heinemann, 1971.

Kunene, Daniel P. *Heroic Poetry of the Basotho*. Oxford: The Clarendon Press, 1971.

Lacroix, Pierre-Francis. *Poésie peule de l'Adamawa*. 2 vols. Paris: Julliard, 1965.

Lindblom, Gerhard. *Kamba Folklore, I: Tales of Animals*. Uppsala: Appelbergs Bocktryckeri Aktiebolag, 1928.

Mboui, J., and P. Nguijol. "Les chants d'hilun: Ngog bilon (poème tragique)." *Abbia* 17–18 (1967): 135–80.

Meillassoux, Claude, Lassana Doucouré, and Diaowé Simagha. *Légende de la dispersion des Kusa (Epopée soninké)*. Dakar: IFAN, 1967.

Mofolo, Thomas. *Chaka: An Historical Romance*. Translated from the original Sesuto by F. H. Dutton. London: Oxford University Press, 1931.

Monteil, Vincent. "La légende de Wagadou: Texte Soninke de Malamine Tandyan, retranscrit, traduit et annoté par Abdoulaye Bathily, d'après Charles Monteil." *Bulletin de l'IFAN* 29, sér. B (1967): 134–49.

Morris, H. F. *The Heroic Recitations of the Bahima of Ankole*. Oxford: The Clarendon Press, 1964.

Mufuta, Patrice. *Le chant kasala des Luba*. Paris: Hilliard, 1969.

Ndong Ndoutoume, Philippe. *Le Mvett*. Paris: Présence Africaine, 1970. French translation by a bard from Cameroun of the epic of Oveng Ndumu Obame from the Fang.

Nguijol, P. "Les Basa." *Abbia* 17–18 (1967): 181–86.

Niane, Djibril T. "Le problème de Soundjata." *Notes Africaines* 88 (1960): 123–26.

————. *Soundjata ou l'épopée mandingue*. Paris: Présence Africaine, 1960. Translated by G. D. Pickett as *Sundiata: An Epic of Old Mali*. London: Longmans, Green and Co., 1965. French translation of one version of the Sunjata epic.

N'sanda, J. B. "*Epopée* Kiguma: Essai d'étude d'un genre littéraire Lega." Ph.D. dissertation, Lovanium University, 1970.

Okaro, Gabriel. "Ogboingba: The Ijaw Creation Myth." *Black Orpheus* 1 (1957): 9–17.

Pageard, R. "Soundiata Keita et la tradition orale," *Présence Africaine*, n.s. 36 (1961): 51–70.

Pepper, Herbert, *Un mvet de Zwè Nguéma: Chant épique Fang*. Recueilli par Herbert Pepper, Edité par Paul et Paule de Wolf. Paris: Armand Colin, 1972. An important text in Fang and French translation, with introduction, summaries, and notes of explanation.

Puplampu, D. A. "The National Epic of the Adangme." *African Affairs* 1 (1951): 236–41.

Rattray, R. S. *Akan-Ashanti Folktales*. Oxford: The Clarendon Press, 1930.

Roscoe, John. *The Baganda: An Account of Their Native Customs and Beliefs*. London: Macmillan and Co., 1911.

Rouch, Jean. *La religion et la magie Songhay*. Paris: Presses Universitaires de France, 1960.

Schapera, L. *Praise-Poems of Tswana Chiefs*. Oxford: The Clarendon Press, 1965.

Scheub, Harold. "The Art of Nongenile Mazithatu Zenani, A Gcaleka Ntsomi Performer." In *African Folklore*, edited by Richard M. Dorson, pp. 115–42. Garden City: Doubleday and Company, 1972.

————. "A Xhosa Narrative." In *African Folklore*, edited by Richard M. Dorson, pp. 523–66. Garden City: Doubleday and Company, 1972.

Shelton, A. J. "The Problem of Griot Interpretation and the Actual Causes of War in Soundjata." *Présence Africaine*, n.s. 66 (1968): 145–52.

Sidibé, Mamby. "Les gens de caste ou nyamakala au Soudan Français." *Notes Africaines* 81 (1959): 13–17.

————. "Soundiata Keita: Héros historique et légendaire, Empereur du Manding." *Notes Africaines* 82 (1959): 41–51.

Stappers, Leo. *Textes luba: Contes d'animaux*. Tervuren: Musée royal de l'Afrique Centrale, 1962.

Steere, Edward. *Swahili Tales as told by Natives of Zanzibar*. London: Bell and Daldy, 1870.

Torrend, J. *Specimens of Bantu Folk-lore from Northern Rhodesia*. London: Kegan Paul, 1921. Pp. 98–144.

Towo-Atangana, Gaspard. "Le mvet: Genre majeur de la littérature orale des populations Pahouines (Bulu, Beti, Fang-Ntumu)." *Abbia* 9–10 (1965): 163–79. Significant information on the *mvet* as a musical instrument and as a literary genre.

Van Caeneghem, R. *Kabundi sprookjes*. Brussels: Vroment, 1938.

Westermann, Dietrich. *The Shilluk People: Their Language and Folklore*. Berlin: Reimer, 1912.

Zemp, Hugo. "La Légende des griots malinké." *Cahiers d'Etudes Africaines* 6 (1966): 611–42.

Index

Heroes and Main Characters

Abo Mama, 347
Abraham, 198
Achilles, 4–5, 7–8, 19, 23, 244
Aegisthus, 8
Aeneas, 8–9
Aesir, 133, 138–40
Afrāsiyāb, 82–83, 85, 87
Agamemnon, 7–8, 10, 12, 21
Agga, 33
Ahti Saarelainen, 293–94, 298
Ai Margan, 323
Ailill, 173–74, 184, 186–87
Aino, 287
Ajax, 19
Akoma Mba, 347–49
Alberich, 121, 127
Alboin, 133
Alda, 197, 206
Aleša Popovič, 241, 243–45
Alfonso VI, King of Castile, 217–18
Ali, 93
Almabet, 320–31
Alpamysh, 322–23
Altin Khan, 323
Ami, 205
Amile, 205
Andrijaš, 265
Antero Vipunen, 290, 293
Anzu-bird, 30–31, 34
Arjuna, 4, 52–56
Ashik Garip, 244, 327

Ashkabus, 83–84
Aśvins, 96
Athena, 7, 18, 20–21
Atli, 123, 131–33
Azrail, 313

Baldr, 134
Baligant, 197–98
Balmung, 121
Basat, 313, 315
Basmi Beyrek, 313–16
Battal, 324
Baudouin, 205
Beowulf, 5, 102–4, 106–15
Bernardo del Campio, 230
Berte, 206
Bharata, 57–58, 60
Bhīma, 52–56
Bhīshma, 52–54
Bizhan, 85
Blund-Ketill, 152–57
Borchin, 322
Bramimonde, 199
Bricriu, 185–87
Brunhild, 121, 123, 126, 128, 134–36

Caílte mac Rónáin, 188
Cet mac Mágach, 187
Charlemagne, 186–97, 199–202, 204–6
Cid, the, 217–22, 230
Clytemnestra, 8

369

Conall Cernach, 185–87
Conchobar, 185–88
Cormac mac Airt, 188
Cú Chulainn, 5, 183–86
Cú Roí, 186
Čurilo Plenkovič, 245–46
Cyclops, the, 313, 315

Da Monzon, 338–41
Dagda, 182
Dancwart, 121, 123
Dankarantuma, 342
Deirdre, 185
Deli Dumrul, 313, 315
Depegöz, 313
Dhṛṣṭadyumna, 52, 70–71
Dhṛtarāṣṭra, 53–56
Dietrich, 122–23
Djerzelez Alija, 268
Djuk Stepanovič, 243, 246
Dobrynja Nikitič, 241, 243–44
Don Rodrigo, 227
Doña Elvira, 217
Doña Sol, 217
Donn Cuailnge, 184
Draupadī, 54–56
Droṇa, 52, 54, 70–71
Duga, 339
Duḥśāsana, 52–53, 55
Dukljanin (Diocletianus), 303
Dunaj, 243
Duryodhana, 53–54
Dušan, 262

Eanna, 41
Eldige, 323
Emperor Dušan. See Dušan
Enki, 29
Enkidu, 33–36, 39–40, 42–43
Enmerkar, 27–32
Eormanric, 102, 105
Er Töshtuk, 322
Esfandiyār, 85
Étaín, 182
Etzel (Attila), 120, 122–23, 125, 128–31, 138
Eumaeus, 21

Fafnir, 140
Faraku Magan Cenyi, 341
Fenrir, 133
Fergus mac Roich, 184
Feridun, 81
Fernán González, 227
Finn, 99, 102, 105
Finnbennach, 184
Fionn, 188
Fitela, 102, 105, 107
Freawaru, 103–4
Freyja, 139
Freyr, 134, 138
Fuamnach, 182

Gāndhārī, 53, 56
Ganelon, 196–97, 200–1
Garm, 133
Genghis Khan, 323
Gernot, 120, 122
Gibech, 131
Gilgamesh, 4–5, 27–28, 33–40, 42
Giselher, 120, 122, 129, 131
Gizurr þorvaldsson, 158–59
Glámr, 161
Goshtāsp, 96
Grandfather Qorqut, 313–14
Grendel, 5, 102–4, 107, 109–11, 113, 115
Grettir, 158, 161
Gudrun, 131, 133
Guibourc, 203
Gul-Aim, 323
Gunnar, 132
Gunther, 120–21, 123, 126, 128–29, 131–33, 138
Guroglu, 316
Guthorm, 131

Hadubrand, 124, 242
Haethcyn, 103–4
Hagen, 114, 121–34, 139
Hama, 102, 105
Hambodédio, 340–41
Hammadi, 340
Hanuman, 58–60
Heardred, 104

Hector, 7, 244
Helche, 122
Helen, 7, 20, 23
Helgi, 152, 156
Heremod, 5, 102–5
Hermod, 138
Hersteinn, 154–55
Hildebrand, 123, 242
Hnaef, 99, 102, 105
Hœnsa þórir, 152–58
Hogni, 132
Ḥoseyn, 93
Hrolf. *See* Hrothulf
Hrómundr Gripsson, 161–62
Hrothgar, 5, 102–4, 106, 108–11, 113, 115
Hrothulf, 115
Hugo, 202
Humbaba, 33, 35, 42
Hygelac, 102–4
Hymir, 138

Idolišče (Monstrous Idol), 242–43, 247
Il'ja Muromec, 241–45, 247–48
Ilmarinen, 287–89, 291–92, 294, 296–98
Inanna, 28, 30–31
Indra, 53, 57, 60–61, 68
Infantes de Lara, 227, 230
Ingeld, 99, 103–5, 112

Joloy, 321
Jormunrekk, 124
Joukahainen, 287, 295

Kalev, 302
Kalevipoeg, 302–3
Kalin Tsar, 242–43, 249
Kan Turali, 313–15
Kanikey, 320
Kapepe, 349
Karṇa, 54
Kaukomieli (Kauko, Kaukomoinen), 293–94
Kauravas, 51
Kāva, 81
Key Khosrow, 83, 85, 87
King Alfonso VI. *See* Alfonso VI

Konurbay, 320
Köroglu, 315–18
Kos Koman, 320
Kriemhild, 120–23, 126, 128–29, 131, 133–34
Kṛṣṇa, 54–56
Kudukese, 345–46
Kullervo, 289, 292, 294, 297, 299
Kuntī. *See* Lady Kuntī
Kurus, 51, 53–55
Kyllikki, 288, 293, 298
Kyrat, 316

Lady Kuntī, 53–54
Lakṣmaṇa, 57–63, 72
Lazar, 263
Lemminkäinen, 287–89, 292–94, 297–99
Lianja, 344
Liudegast, 121
Liudeger, 121
Lóegaire Buadach, 185
Lofokefoke, 345–47
Lohrāsp, 96
Loki, 133
Lord of Aratta, 28–30
Louhi, 287–89, 291–92, 294
Lugalbanda, 27–28, 30–32, 38, 40, 44

Mac Da Tho, 186–87
Macha, 184
Mādrī, 53
Máel Fhothartaig, 188
Magan, 342
Manas, 5, 319–22
Manizha, 85
Manuchehr, 81–82
Marjatta, 296
Marko Kraljević, 5, 259, 264–66
Marsile, 196–98, 201
Medb, 173–74, 184, 186–87
Mendibay, 320
Menelaus, 7, 19–21
Midir, 182
Mikula Seljaninovič, 240–41
Miloš Obilić, 258, 263–64
Miloš Vojinović, 262
Mixajlo Potyk, 245

Mohammad, 93
Mokhtār, 93
Monzon, 338–39
Mubila, 5, 344–45, 356
Musa the Highwayman, 265
Mwindo, 343–45, 356

Nakula, 53, 55–56
Nestor, 20–22
Nibelung(s), 121–22, 125–26
Njall, 154

Oddr, 153
Odin, 133–34, 138, 140
Odoacer, 99
Odysseus, 5, 8, 11, 15, 17, 20–21, 23,
    311, 315, 327
Offa, 99
Oisín, 188
Okangate, 346
Olaf (Saint), 145–46
Olaf Tryggvason, 145–46
Olafr liðmannakonungr, 161–62
Oliver, 197–98, 201, 205–6
Ongentheow, 104–5
Orn, 152
Ortlieb, 122–23
Othello, 126
Ozidi, 342–43

Pāṇḍavas, 51, 53–56
Pāṇḍu(s), 51, 53–54
Paris, 7–8, 23
Patroclus, 7, 19
Penelope, 8
Pepin, 206
Prince Roman, 246
Prince Vladimir, 241–45, 247–49
Puluru, 340

Qorqut. See Grandfather Qorqut
Queen Wealhtheow. See Wealhtheow

Rainouart, 203
Rakhsh, 90
Rāma, 55, 57–63, 68, 72
Raoul, 204

Rāvaṇa, 58–62, 68, 72
Renaud, 205
Resul, 327
Rodrigo Diaz de Vivar (the Cid), 217
Rohhām, 83–84
Roland, 4–5, 195–98, 200–1, 205–6, 219
Roman. See Prince Roman
Rónán, 188
Rosemund, 133–34
Rostam, 4–5, 79–80, 82–86, 89–90, 92,
    95, 242
Rudāba, 81
Rüdiger, 122–23, 129–30, 134
Rustam. See Rostam

Sadko, 246
Sahadeva, 53, 55–56
Salur Kazan, 313–14
Sām, 81
Śatrughna, 57
Scyld Scefing, 102, 107, 114
Seilbung, 121
Semetey, 319
Seytek, 319
Shah Sanem, 327
Shamash, 42
Shirin, 86
Siegfried, 120–28, 133–36, 140
Sieglind, 121
Siegmund, 121
Sigemund, 102, 105, 107
Sigurd, 134, 140
Śikhaṇḍin, 52
Silamaka, 340–41
Simorgh, 81, 85
Sītā, 55, 57–62, 68, 72
Siyāvush, 83
Skirner, 138
Sohrāb, 82–83, 242
Sokol'nik (Falconer), 242
Solovej (Nightingale) Budimirovič, 245
Solovej Razbojnik (Nightingale the Rob-
    ber), 242–43, 247
Starina Novak, 267
Sugrīva, 57–58, 60
Sumanguru, 341–42, 354
Sunjata, 342

Suxman, 245
Svanhit, 162
Svjatogor, 240–41

Tahmina, 82
Tale the Fool, 268
Tamerlane, 323
Telemachus, 15, 20–21
Theoclymenus, 21–22
Thiéma, 339–40
Thor, 133–34, 137–40
Thrym, 138–39
Tugarin Zmeevič (Dragon's Son), 244, 247
Tungu-Oddr, 152–54

Unferth, 102–3, 108, 124
Utnapishtim, 36
Utu, 44

Vafthrudnir, 138
Väinämöinen, 287–96, 298–99
Vasilij Buslaev, 246
Viṣṇu, 55, 60
Viśvāmitra, 57
Vivien, 203
Vladimir. See Prince Vladimir

Volx Vseslav'evič, 240
Vuk Branković, 263
Vyāsa, 53–54

Walter of Visigothic Aquitaine, 99
Walther, 124
Wealhtheow, 102, 111–12
Weland, 102, 105
White Div, 82
Wiglaf, 103, 106
William of Orange, 203–4
Wolfhart, 124

Ximena, 217–18

Yudhiṣṭhira, 53–56

Zaḥḥāk, 81
Zāl, 80–81, 95
Zeus, 7, 18–20
Zmaj Ognjeni Vuk, 264
Zmaj-despot Vuk, 264
Zong Midzi, 347–49

þorkell, 153
þórðr gellir, 153